Photographer's Guide to the Leica C-Lux

Photographer's Guide to the Leica C-Lux

Getting the Most from Leica's Compact Digital Camera

Alexander S. White

WHITE KNIGHT PRESS
HENRICO, VIRGINIA

Published by
White Knight Press
9704 Old Club Trace
Henrico, Virginia 23238
www.whiteknightpress.com
contact@whiteknightpress.com

ISBN: 978-1-937986-76-6 (paperback)
978-1-937986-77-3 (ebook)

Printed in the United States of America

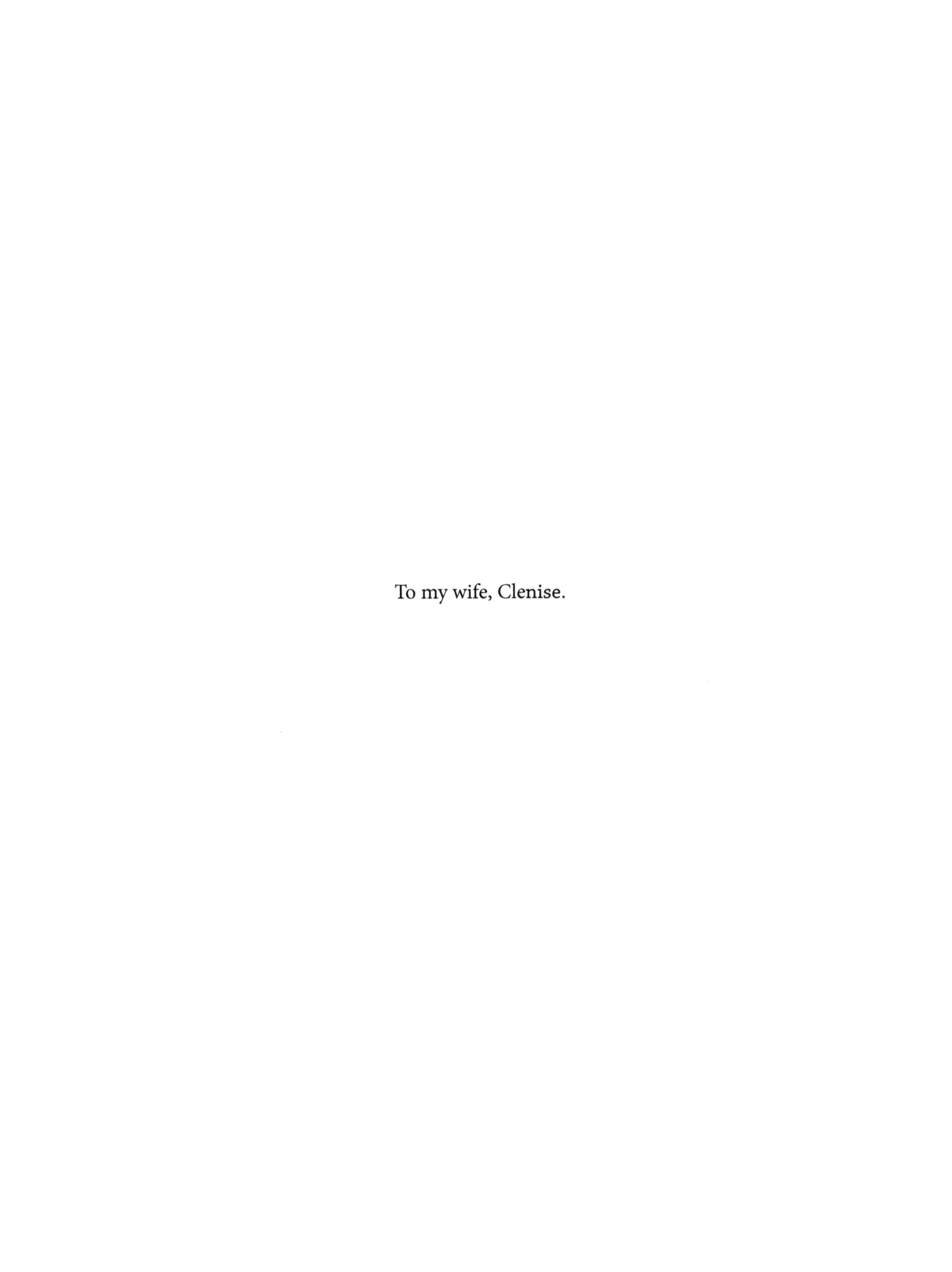

To my wife, Clenise.

Contents

Chapter 5: Physical Controls 91

Chapter 6: Playback 123

Chapter 7: Custom Menu, Setup Menu, and My Menu 137

Introduction

This book is a guide to the operation, features, and capabilities of the Leica C-Lux, one of the most capable and versatile "point-and-shoot" digital compact cameras available today. I chose this camera to write about partly because of my experience with other Leica compact models, including the D-Lux 4, D-Lux 5, D-Lux 6, and D-Lux (Typ 109), but also because this camera has excellent features in a small package.

To begin with, the C-Lux uses a "one-inch-type" image sensor, the same size sensor used in several other advanced compact models, such as the Sony DSC-RX100 and its five (as of this writing) successor models. This sensor is larger than those of many compact cameras, and it lets the C-Lux provide great image quality with good performance in low light.

The camera also has an excellent optical zoom range of 24mm to 360mm and advanced features such as Raw image quality, manual control of exposure and focus, and excellent burst capability for continuous shooting. The C-Lux also provides very good video features, centered around its capability to capture 4K (ultra-HD) video. In addition, the camera has a large, 3-inch (7.5 cm) diagonal and very sharp (1.2 million pixels) LCD monitor with touch-screen features; a high-quality Leica lens with a wide 24mm equivalent focal length, and a built-in electronic viewfinder with more than two million pixels of resolution. It has a strong set of Wi-Fi and Bluetooth features, enabling remote control from a smartphone and transfer of images from the camera to other devices over a wireless network.

Many photographers will welcome the inclusion of physical switches and dials on the C-Lux to control many functions, so they don't have to navigate through menus to adjust exposure compensation, white balance, drive mode, and other settings. Several of these controls are programmable to operate any one of numerous functions, and the camera also has five "virtual" function buttons included with its touch screen capabilities.

Also, the C-Lux includes a self-timer, macro (closeup shooting) focus mode, a wide range of shutter speeds (1/16000 second to 60 seconds as well as longer time exposures), many different "filter effect" settings (such as miniature effect, soft focus, sepia, and monochrome, among others), and several features for capturing images with broad dynamic range, including a built-in HDR (high dynamic range) option.

Is anything lacking in the C-Lux? Some people would like the camera to be smaller, so it could fit more easily into a pocket. It also would be nice if the LCD screen could swivel and tilt. The camera could use better audio recording features, such as a jack for an external microphone, to support its excellent video capability. It also lacks the ability to connect to a smartphone or tablet using the NFC (near field communication) protocol, though it can connect using standard procedures through menus and apps, and it has no accessory shoe for a larger flash or other accessories.

But given that no camera can meet every possible need, the C-Lux is an outstanding compact camera. My goal is to provide a useful introduction to the C-Lux's controls and operation along with tips and advice as to when and how to use various features. This book does not provide advanced technical information. If you already understand how to use every feature of the camera and when to use it and are looking for new insights, I have included some references in the Appendices that can provide further information. This book is geared to the beginning to intermediate user who is not satisfied with the documentation provided with the camera, and who is looking for a reference guide that offers additional help in mastering the camera's features.

It is worth noting that the C-Lux is closely related to the Panasonic Lumix DC-ZS200 (known as the TZ200 and other labels in some areas). I published a guide book for that camera in June 2018, and it was an easy decision to do a separate book for the C-Lux camera. I have revised the book where necessary to discuss features that are different on the C-Lux. Where the shooting, playback, and menu screens on the C-Lux have different appearances from the corresponding screens on the ZS200, I have created new images. Where the screens have no significant differences, I have used images created with the ZS200 camera where appropriate.

If a reader has any suggestions for improving this book or sees anything that needs correcting, please contact me through my website, whiteknightpress.com.

Chapter 1: Preliminary Setup

When you first receive your C-Lux, the box should contain the camera itself, battery, battery charger, USB cable, hand strap, brief instruction pamphlet, and warranty pamphlet. There is no software disc in the box, but Leica provides a free 90-day subscription to the Adobe Creative Cloud photography plan. To receive that benefit, you have to register the camera at http://owners.leica-camera.com and enter the camera's serial number and TAN number, both of which are found on the last page of the warranty pamphlet. With that plan, you receive access to Photoshop and Lightroom software, that lets you process and edit Raw and JPEG files.

Charging and Inserting the Battery

The C-Lux ships with a single rechargeable lithium-ion battery, model number BP-DC15-U (in the United States). This battery is designed to be charged inside the camera, but it also can be charged in an optional external charger. I will discuss various options for powering the camera and recharging batteries in Appendix A.

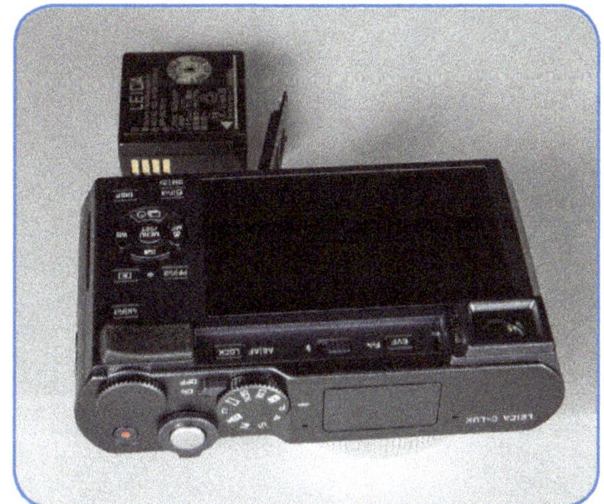

Figure 1-1. Battery Lined Up to Go Into Camera

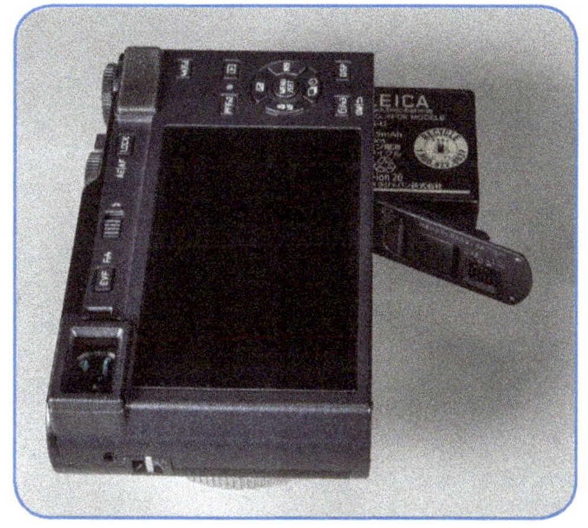

Figure 1-2. Battery Going into Camera

To charge the battery in the camera, slide the latch on the camera's bottom and open the battery compartment door. You can only insert the battery into the camera one way; look for the set of four goldish-colored metal contact strips on the battery, then look for the corresponding set of contacts inside the camera, and insert the battery so the two sets of contacts will meet, as shown in Figures 1-1 and 1-2.

Slide the battery all the way in so it is firmly seated in the camera with the latch clicked into place above the battery, as shown in Figure 1-3, and close and latch the battery compartment door.

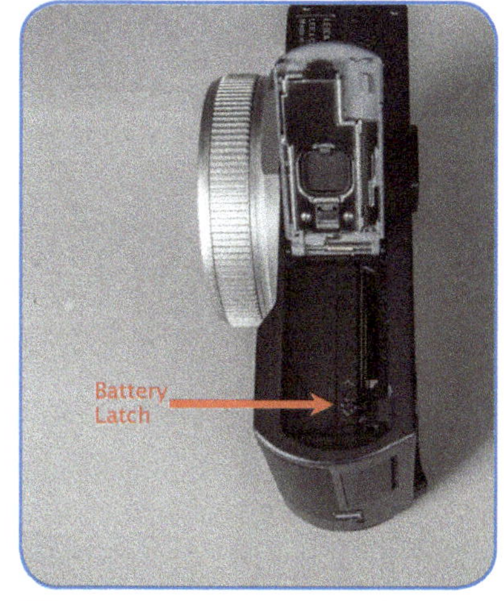

Figure 1-3. Battery Secured by Latch

With the battery inserted, plug the small end of the camera's USB cable into the USB charging port, which is the lower port located inside a small flap on the right side of the camera, as shown in Figure 1-4.

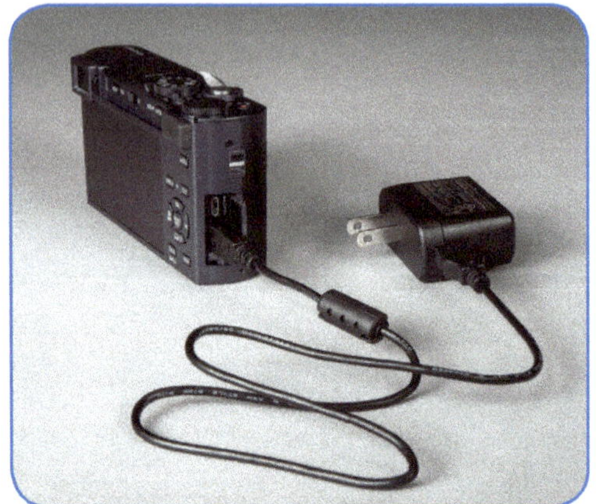

Figure 1-4. Battery Charger Plugged into Camera

Plug the larger end of the cable into the AC adapter, and plug the adapter into an electrical outlet. A red light on the back of the camera, between the Fn2 button and the Playback button, will glow while charging is in progress, and will turn off when charging is complete. It should take about 190 minutes to charge the battery fully.

Inserting the Memory Card

The C-Lux does not ship with a memory card. If you turn the camera on with no card inserted, you will see the message "No memory card" in the center of the screen. If you ignore this message and press the shutter button to take a picture, don't be fooled into thinking that the camera is somehow storing it in internal memory. Some camera models have a small amount of built-in memory so you can take and store a few pictures even without a card, but the C-Lux does not have that safety net.

To avoid the frustration of having a great camera that can't save images, you need to use a memory card. The C-Lux uses three varieties of card: Secure Digital (SD), Secure Digital High-Capacity (SDHC), and Secure Digital Extended Capacity (SDXC), representative samples of which are shown in Figure 1-5. All three types of SD card are the same size, about the size of a postage stamp. The standard card, SD, comes in capacities from 8 MB (megabytes) to 2 GB (gigabytes). The higher-capacity card, SDHC, comes in sizes from 4 GB to 32 GB.

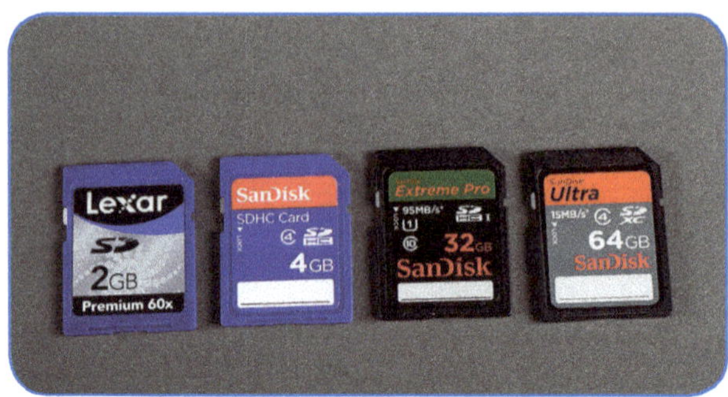

Figure 1-5. Various Sizes of Memory Card

The newest type, SDXC, at this writing is available in a 48 GB, 64 GB, 128 GB, 256 GB, or 512 GB size, though its maximum capacity theoretically is 2 terabytes, or about 2,000 GB. Currently 512 GB cards are selling for between $150.00 and $300.00, so they may be impractical for many photographers.

A 128 GB card, though, can be a good option, which I have used successfully in the C-Lux. I also have used a 256 GB card with no problems, and I have used a SanDisk Extreme Pro 512 GB SDXC card in the C-Lux with excellent results.

When choosing a memory card, there is one important point to bear in mind: If you want to use the excellent 4K video, 4K Photo, Post Focus, or high speed video recording capability of the C-Lux, Leica states that you have to use a card rated in UHS Speed Class 3, for ultra-high speed class 3. An example of that type of card is shown in Figure 1-6. The numeral 3 inside the U shape on the label indicates this speed class.

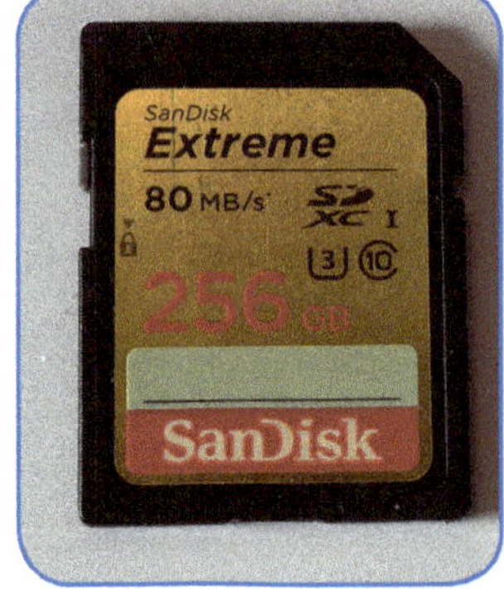

Figure 1-6. Memory Card in Speed Class UHS-3

When I tried to record 4K video using a card rated only in Speed Class 4, the camera did record for several seconds, but then the recording stopped and the camera displayed a message saying the recording stopped because of the memory card's insufficient speed. So, the camera may not warn you about using an inadequate card until it is too late. Apparently, it records a small amount of video into its internal buffer, but, when it needs to write data to the card, the recording halts.

Even if you don't plan to record 4K video or use the 4K Photo or Post Focus feature, I recommend you purchase a card rated in UHS Speed Class 3, because it will help with burst shooting as well as with 4K video.

If you're not planning to use the camera's 4K video and other advanced features listed above, you still should get a large-sized, high-speed card if possible. If you're planning to record a good deal of high-definition (HD) video or many Raw photos, you need a card with a fairly large capacity. There are several variables to take into account in computing how many images or videos you can store on a particular size of card, such as the aspect ratio you're using (1:1, 3:2, 4:3, or 16:9), picture size, and quality.

I installed a 64 GB SDXC card and formatted it in the camera to see how many images could be stored using various settings. I set the aspect ratio to 3:2 for all options. Table 1-1 shows the results.

Table 1-1. Number of Still Images That Can be Stored on 64 GB Card at Large Size

Raw + Fine	1785
Raw	2616
Fine	5632
Standard	9999+

For video, using the same 64 GB card, you can store just one hour and 25 minutes using the highest quality 4K format; with the lowest quality of video, you can store more than twelve hours.

Note, though, that there is an important caveat for video recording lengths with the C-Lux, as with most compact cameras designed primarily for still photography. There are built-in limitations on the length of continuous video recording. In most cases, you can record only about 30 minutes of video in any one scene; you then have to stop and re-start your recording. With 4K video, the limit for continuous recording is 15 minutes. Also, as you may expect, some video formats consume memory very rapidly, so some smaller SD cards cannot record for the full amount of time that the camera would permit. There are some other considerations to be discussed with regard to recording limits; I will discuss video recording in more detail in Chapter 8.

I often use a 64 GB SanDisk Extreme Pro card, rated at a transfer level of 95 MB/second. That speed is more than enough to get good results for recording still images and HD video with this camera. As noted above, if you are planning to record 4K video or use 4K Photo, Post Focus, or high speed video recording, you need to use a card with a speed designation of UHS Speed Class 3. (If the card has a UHS-I or UHS-II designation, that label has to do with a certain type of transport system the card uses, not the speed. You need to make sure the UHS Speed Class is 3.)

Whatever type of SD card you get, once you have the card, open the same door on the bottom of the camera that covers the battery compartment and slide the card in until it catches. The card goes in with its label facing the front of the camera, as shown in Figure 1-7.

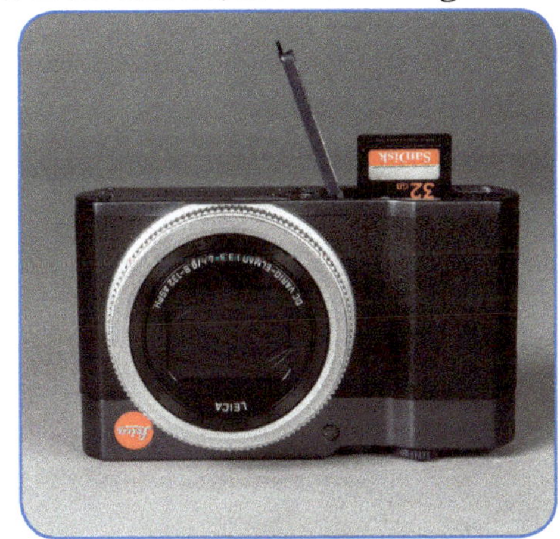

Figure 1-7. Memory Card Going into Camera

Once the card has been pushed down until it catches, close the compartment door and push the latch back to the locking position. To remove the card, push down on it until it releases and springs up so you can grab it.

When the C-Lux is recording images or videos to an SD card, a red icon appears on the left side of the screen showing an arrow pointing to the right inside a little box representing the SD card, as shown in Figure 1-8.

When that indicator is visible on the display, it's important not to turn off the camera or otherwise interrupt its functioning, such as by taking out the battery or disconnecting an AC power adapter. You need to let the card complete its recording process.

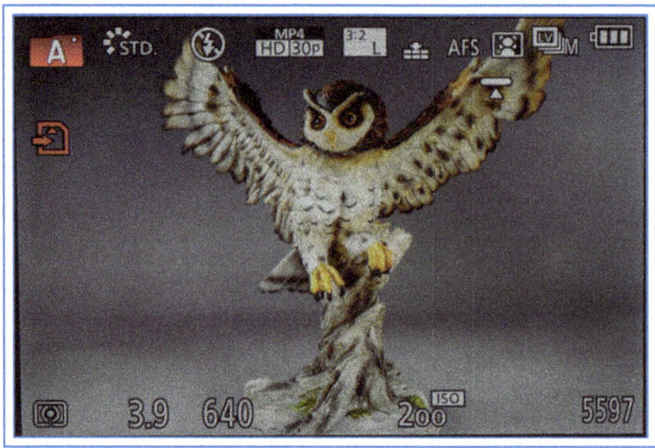

Figure 1-8. Red Icon When Data Being Written to Card

Introduction to Main Controls

Before I discuss options for setting up the camera using the menu system and controls, I will introduce the main controls so you'll have a better idea of which button or dial is which. I won't discuss all of the controls here; they will be covered in some detail in Chapter 5. For now, I'm including a series of images that show the major items. You may want to refer back to these images for a reminder about each control.

Top of Camera

On top of the camera are some of the more important controls, as shown in Figure 1-9.

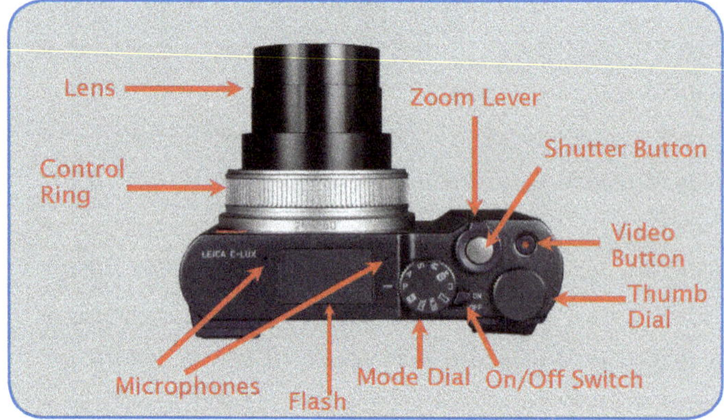

Figure 1-9. Controls on Top of Camera

The on/off switch turns the camera on and off. If you hold down the Playback button while turning on this switch, the camera will start up in playback mode. You press the shutter button all the way down to take a picture; press it halfway to cause the camera to evaluate focus and exposure. The mode dial sets the camera to a shooting mode for still images or movies. The zoom lever, surrounding the shutter button, zooms the lens from the wide-angle (W) setting to the telephoto (T) setting. The flash is stored inside the top of the camera; you pop it up with the flash release lever on the camera's back. The two microphone openings receive sounds to be recorded with videos. The control ring is used for focus and other operations, depending on current settings. The red video button starts and stops the recording of a movie sequence. The ridged thumb dial acts as a rotary wheel for changing settings, moving through menu items and options on various screens of settings, as well as for other purposes, such as moving through recorded images and videos. You can program it to handle one particular function, if you want.

Back of Camera

Figure 1-10 shows the controls on the camera's back.

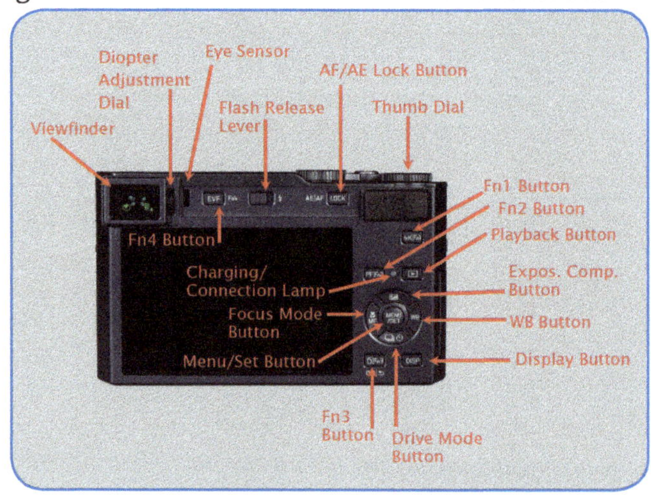

Figure 1-10. Controls on Back of Camera

The viewfinder window is where you look through the camera's electronic viewfinder (EVF). The slit to its right is the eye sensor, which senses the presence of your head and switches between the EVF and the LCD screen display. The diopter adjustment wheel lets you adjust the view in the EVF for your vision. The flash release lever is used to release the camera's built-in flash unit so it will pop up, ready for use.

The AF/AE Lock button is used to lock exposure and/or focus, depending on settings you make through the menu system. The Playback button puts the camera into playback mode so you can review your recorded images and videos. The four cursor buttons (called the Up, Down, Left, and Right buttons in this book) control the settings of exposure compensation, drive mode, focus mode, and white balance. The Menu/Set button, in the center of the dial, is used to get access to the menu system and to select or confirm various menu options.

The four function buttons are initially assigned to particular operations, but they all can be assigned to other purposes through the menu system. The Fn1 button is initially assigned as the 4K button, to give you access to the camera's 4K photo shooting ability. The Fn2 button is initially set as the Post Focus button, which lets you shoot images whose focus point can be set after shooting. The Fn3 button is initially assigned as the Q.Menu button, which activates the Quick Menu system that gives instant access to various menu settings. The Fn4 button is initially set as the EVF button, which lets you set the live viewfinder so it is automatically switched by the eye sensor, or so either the EVF or the LCD screen is active.

The Display button is used to switch among the various displays of information in the EVF and on the LCD screen in both shooting and playback modes. When a menu screen is displayed, you can press this button to display a brief explanation of the highlighted item. The LCD monitor displays the live view, control settings, menu screens, and other information when you are not using the viewfinder. It also displays recorded images and videos when the camera is in playback mode.

The LCD screen also has useful touch capabilities, letting you control many of the camera's features by touching icons or other areas on the screen. The charging/connection lamp, located between the Fn2 and Playback buttons, lights up red when the battery is being charged inside the camera or blue when the camera's Wi-Fi or Bluetooth capability is active.

Front of Camera

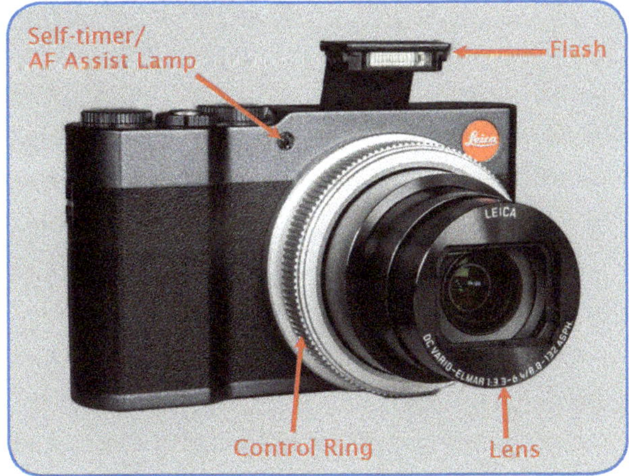

Figure 1-11. Items on Front of Camera

There are only a few items to point out on the camera's front, shown in Figure 1-11. The Self-timer/AF Assist lamp lights up to indicate the operation of the self-timer and also turns on in dim light to assist the camera's autofocus system, unless you disable it for that purpose through the menu system. The lens is a high-quality zoom lens with a maximum aperture of f/3.3 at the wide-angle setting, changing to a maximum of f/6.4 at the telephoto end of its range.

The focal length of the lens varies from 8.8mm at the wide-angle range to 132mm at the telephoto setting. Ordinarily, these focal lengths are stated using "35mm-equivalent" figures, meaning the values that these figures would correspond to for a camera using a full-frame, 35mm image sensor. Therefore, the focal length range of the lens is ordinarily stated as from 24mm to 360mm.

Right Side of Camera

Inside the door on the right side of the camera are the HDMI port and the USB port, as seen in Figures 1-12 and 1-13.

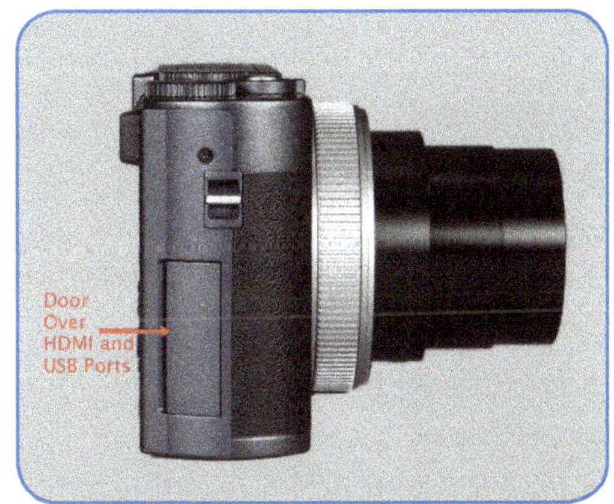

Figure 1-12. Right Side of Camera - Port Door Closed

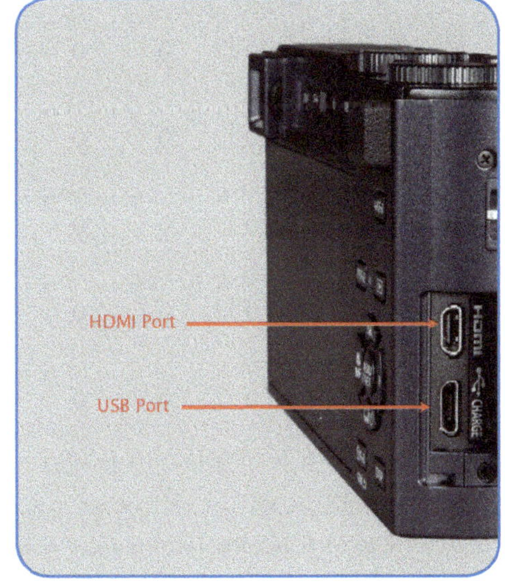

Figure 1-13. Right Side of Camera - Port Door Open

The HDMI port is where you plug in an optional micro-HDMI cable to display images and videos from the camera on an HDTV set. The USB port is where you plug in the camera's USB cable to charge the battery or to transfer images and videos to a computer. And, you can use this port to connect to a PictBridge-compliant printer to print images directly from the camera.

Bottom of Camera

Finally, as shown in Figure 1-14, on the bottom of the camera are the speaker, the tripod socket, the door for the battery and memory card compartment, and the small flap that is used to accommodate the cord for the AC adapter when it is connected to the camera, as discussed in Appendix A.

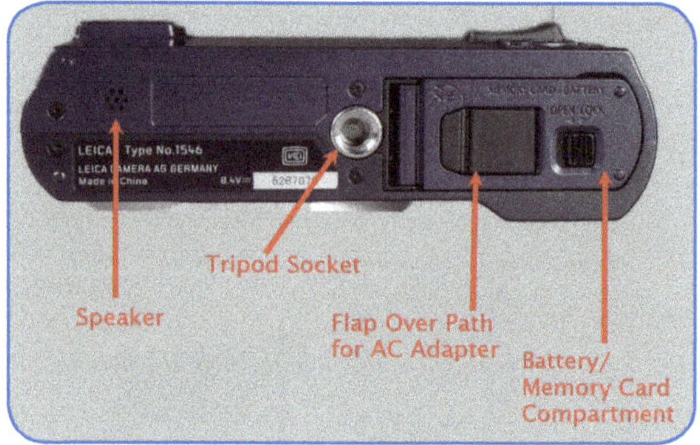

Figure 1-14. Items on Bottom of Camera

The Menu Systems

Although the C-Lux's physical controls are important for controlling the camera, for many settings and operations you also need to use the camera's system of menus, from which you can select options for how the exposure, focus, video recording, audio, and other features work, and how the camera's own systems, such as the LCD screen and viewfinder, function. I will discuss the individual menu options in detail in later chapters. For now, I will give a brief overview of the various menus available with the C-Lux.

One point that can be confusing is that the contents of the menu systems change somewhat according to what shooting mode is currently set on the camera's mode dial. For example, if the dial is set at the P position for Program mode, you can get access to many of the options on the various menus. However, if it is set to the A on a light background, for Snapshot mode, you can get access to a smaller selection of options. For the present discussion, I will assume that the dial is set to the Snapshot mode position.

With the mode dial at the Snapshot position, press the Menu/Set button, located in the center of the camera's back. You should see a display similar to that in Figure 1-15. The large area on the right side of the display is a screen of the currently selected menu system, and the icons in a vertical line at the left side of the display represent the various menu systems that are available. If you don't see the red line that divides the line of icons from the menu screen, press the Left button (marked with a flower icon and MF) to make the red line appear. Then, if necessary, press the Up button (marked with a black and white square) until the top icon, showing a camera shape with the letter A inside it, is highlighted.

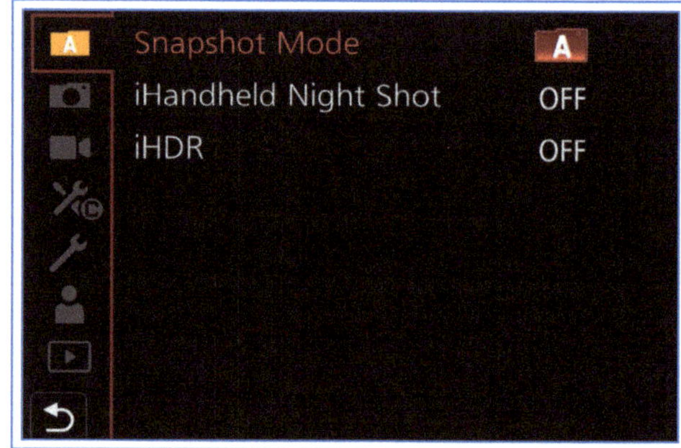

Figure 1-15. Menu Icons at Left Side of Display Screen

In Figure 1-15, the icons at the left side of the screen represent the multiple menu systems currently available, starting at the top: Snapshot Mode; Recording; Motion Picture; Custom; Setup; My Menu; and Playback. The backward-curving arrow at the bottom of the line of icons indicates that you can press the Fn3 button, at the bottom left of the physical controls on the back of the camera, to exit from a menu screen to a previous screen and eventually to shooting mode or playback mode.

To move from one menu system to another, with the red line displayed at the left, press the Down button (marked with icons for multiple frames and a timer) to highlight the icon for the menu you want to use, such as Recording or Setup. When that icon is highlighted, press the Right button (marked with WB) to move the highlight into the currently displayed screen for that menu. For example, Figure 1-16 shows the display after I pressed the Right button to move the highlight into the single screen of the Snapshot Mode menu.

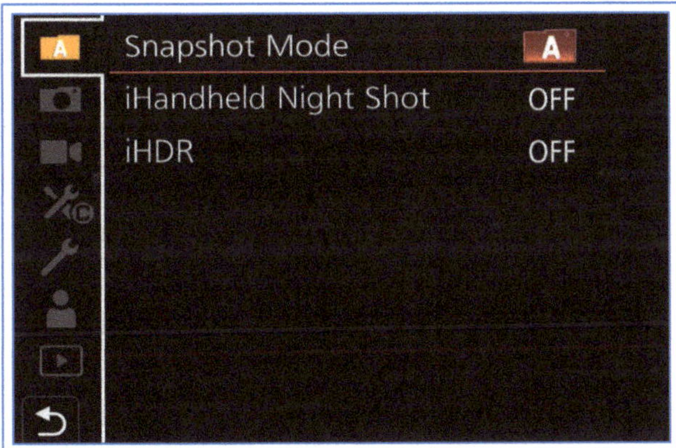

Figure 1-16. Single Screen of Snapshot Mode Menu

To move to an item on the Setup menu, press the Left button to move the highlight to the left column of menu icons, then the Down button to move it to the solitary wrench icon, which indicates the Setup menu, as shown in Figure 1-17, and then back to the right, into one of the four screens of that menu system, as shown in Figure 1-18.

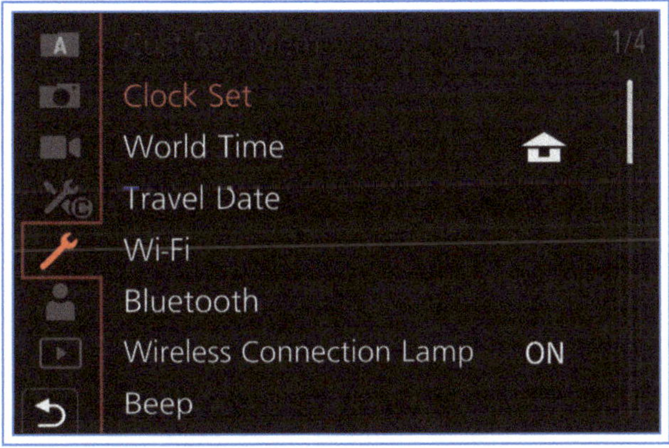

Figure 1-17. Wrench Icon for Setup Menu Highlighted

Once the highlight bar and red line are displayed, as in Figure 1-18, press the Up and Down buttons as needed to move to the item you want to use, such as Clock Set, Wi-Fi, Bluetooth, or another, on this menu screen.

To move immediately from the current menu screen to the next screen, turn the thumb dial at the top of the camera or press the zoom lever. You also can touch the LCD screen to move among menu options, assuming the touch screen features are turned on.

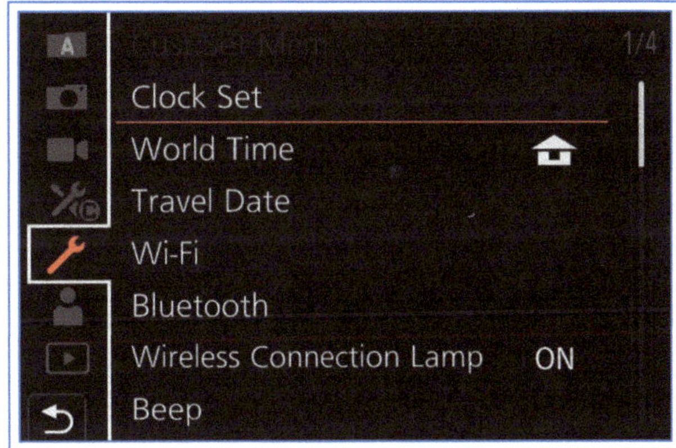

Figure 1-18. Red Line and Highlight Bar in List of Setup Menu Items

Setting the Date, Time, and Language

It's important to set the date and time correctly before you start taking pictures, because the camera records that information invisibly with each image and displays it later if you want. Someday you may be very glad to have the date (and even the time of day) correctly recorded with your archives of digital images.

To get these items set, move the On/Off switch, on top of the camera, to the On position. Then press the Menu/Set button to enter the menu system, and press the Left button to move the selection into the column for choosing the menu type. Press the Down button to highlight the solitary wrench icon (not the tools icon with the letter C), as shown in Figure 1-17. Then press the Right button to place the selection bar in the list of Setup menu items, as shown in Figure 1-18.

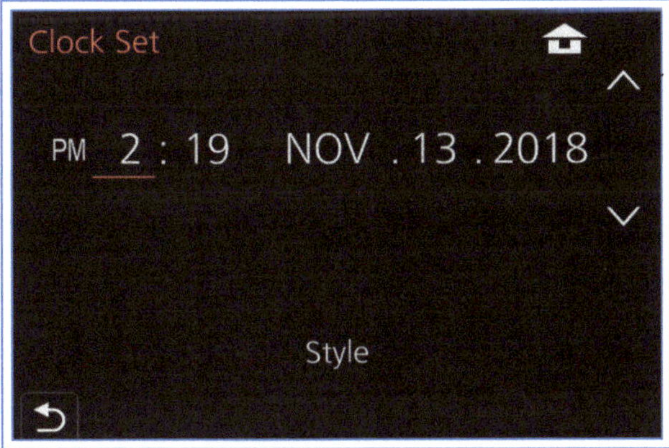

Figure 1-19. Screen for Setting Date and Time

By pressing the Up and Down buttons, move the red line until Clock Set is highlighted on the first Setup menu screen. Then press the Right button to get access to the time and date settings, as shown in Figure 1-19.

Navigate through the settings for time, month, date, and year by pressing the Left and Right buttons or by turning the thumb dial, and select the value for each setting with the Up and Down buttons. When you're done, press the Right button enough times to highlight the Set icon in the lower right corner of the screen, and press the Menu/Set button to save the settings. (The Set icon appears only if some change has been made to the date and time.) Then, using a similar procedure, navigate to the Language option on the third screen of the Setup menu, if necessary, and change the language the camera uses for menus and messages.

Chapter 2: Basic Operations

Taking Pictures

Once the camera has the correct time and date set and has a fully charged battery inserted along with a memory card, it is ready for picture-taking. For now, I won't get into discussions of the various options and why you might choose one over another. I'll just describe a set of actions for recording a good image on your memory card.

Fully Automatic: Snapshot Mode

Here's a set of steps to follow to set the camera to its most automatic mode and let it make most of the decisions for you. This is a good setup if you need to grab a quick shot without fiddling with settings, or if you want to get good results without having to provide much input by making numerous decisions.

1. Move the On/Off switch on the camera's top to the On position. The camera makes a whirring sound, the lens extends outward to its open position, and the LCD screen lights up.

2. Turn the mode dial on top of the camera to select the A on a light background, which selects the Snapshot mode of shooting. You should see a red camera icon with A and possibly a white plus sign in the upper left corner of the display, as shown in Figure 2-1. (If you don't see this icon, press the Display button at the lower right of the camera's back one or more times until the icon appears.)

3. Press the Left button (marked with a flower and MF). The camera will display the focus mode menu, as shown in Figure 2-2.

4. Use the cursor buttons (or the touch screen) to select AF, the left-most option, if it is not already selected. That sets the camera to use autofocus instead of manual focus. Press the Menu button to return to the shooting screen.

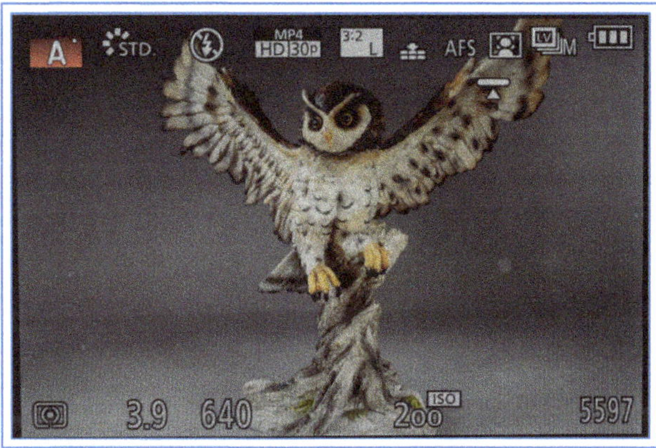

Figure 2-1. Snapshot Mode Icon on Shooting Screen

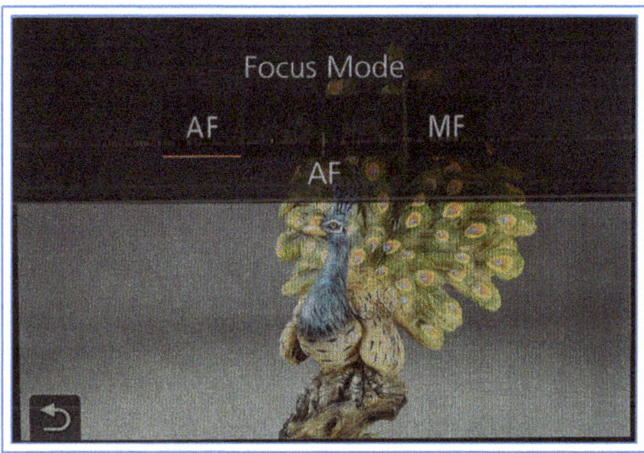

Figure 2-2. Focus Mode Menu

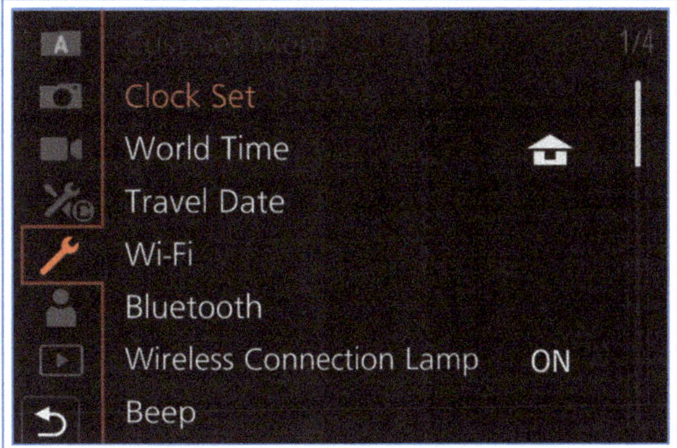

Figure 2-3. Menu Icons Highlighted at Left

5. Press the Menu/Set button in the center of the cursor buttons on the back of the camera to display

the menu system. Press the Left button if necessary to highlight the line of icons at the far left of the screen; when they are highlighted, you will see a red line, as in Figure 2-3.

6. Use the Up and Down buttons as necessary to highlight the A icon at the top of the line of icons, as shown in Figure 2-4. Then press the Right button to move to the screen shown in Figure 2-5. Make sure the Red highlight bar is under the top line, Snapshot Mode. If that line includes the A+ icon, for Snapshot Plus mode, press the Menu/Set button to move to the screen shown in Figure 2-6, showing the A icon and the A+ icon. Use the buttons as necessary to make sure the A icon is highlighted, as shown in Figure 2-7. Press Menu/Set to confirm that selection. (You can press menu items and icons on the touch screen to make selections if you prefer.)

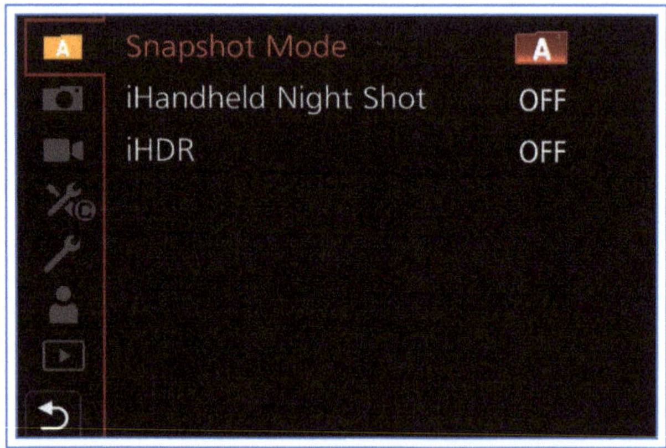

Figure 2-4. Snapshot Mode Icon Highlighted at Top of Menu Icons

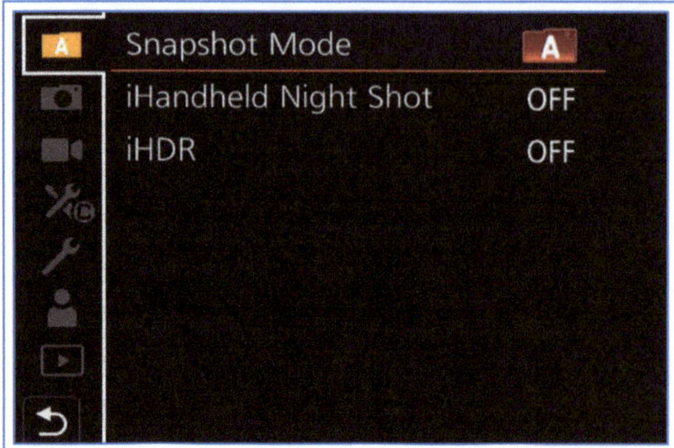

Figure 2-5. Selection Bar on Snapshot Mode Menu Option

7. Move down to the next two settings on the menu screen, iHandheld Night Shot and iHDR, and leave them set to Off, as shown in Figure 2-5.

8. Navigate to the red camera icon for the Recording menu in the column to the left of the menu screen, then press the Right button to move the highlight into the menu screen. Using the procedure discussed above, make the settings in Table 2-1 for the other items on the Recording menu. (If you prefer to use the touch screen to make these settings, just touch the appropriate menu options and icons to select them.)

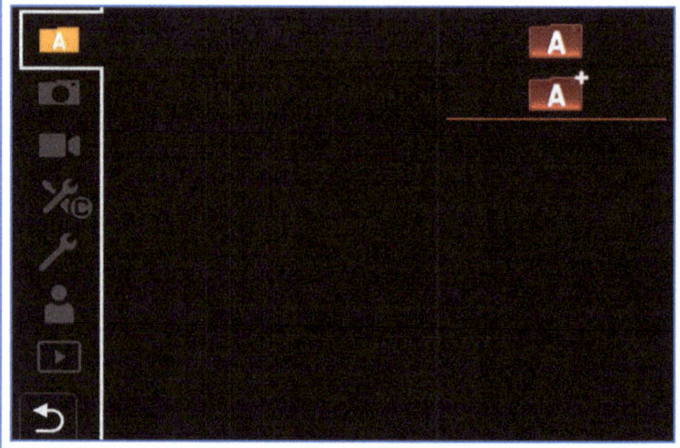

Figure 2-6. Screen to Select A or A+ Mode

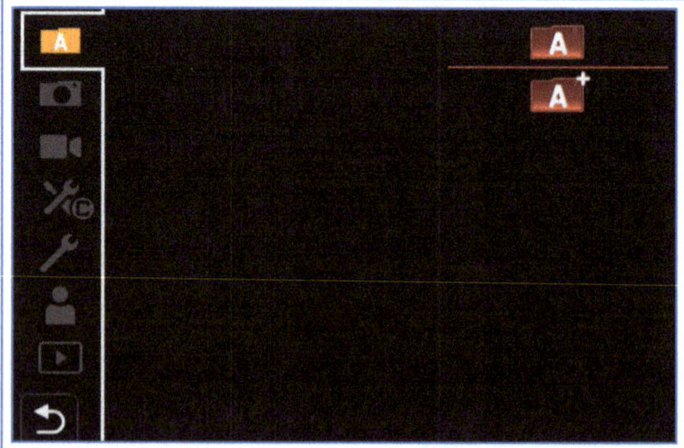

Figure 2-7. A Icon Highlighted on Menu Screen

Table 2-1. Recommended Settings for General Shooting in Snapshot Mode

Menu Option	Setting
Aspect Ratio	3:2
Picture Size	L
AFS/AFF/AFC	AFS
AF Mode	Face/Eye Detection
Burst Rate	H
4K Photo	4K Burst
Self Timer	Any setting
Time Lapse Shot	No setting needed
Stop Motion Animation	No setting needed
Silent Mode	Off

9. If you're taking a picture indoors, or it's dark enough that you think you might need the camera's flash, find the flash release lever at the top center of the camera's back and slide it to the right to pop up the built-in flash. If the camera determines that flash is needed, the flash will fire automatically; you cannot change the flash mode setting in this shooting mode. (When you're done with the flash, press it gently back down into the top of the camera.)
10. Aim the camera at the subject and look at the screen (or into the viewfinder window) to compose the picture as you want it. Locate the zoom lever on the ring that surrounds the shutter button on the top right of the camera. Push that lever to the left to get a wider-angle shot (including more of the scene in the picture), or to the right to get a telephoto, zoomed-in shot.
11. Once the picture looks good on the display, press the shutter button halfway down. You should hear a beep and see a steady (not blinking) green dot in the upper right corner of the screen, indicating that the picture will be in focus, as shown in Figure 2-8.

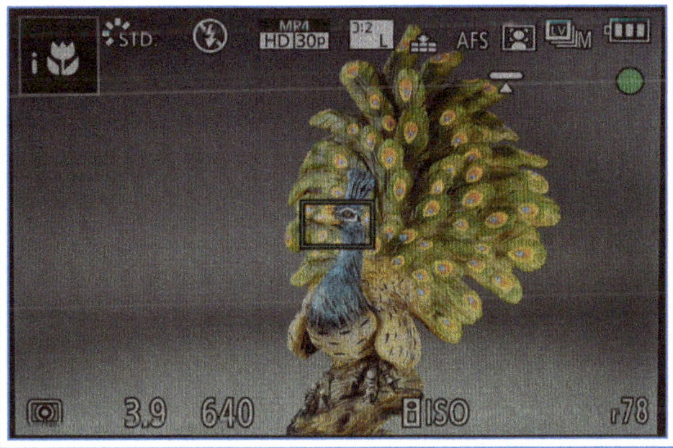

Figure 2-8. Green Dot and Frame Indicating Sharp Focus

12. You also may see some green focus frames. (If you hear a series of four quick beeps and see a blinking green dot, that means the camera was unable to focus. Try moving to a slightly different angle and then test the focus again by pressing the shutter button halfway down.) Then press the shutter button all the way down to take the picture.

Variations from Fully Automatic

Although the C-Lux takes care of several settings for you when it's set to Snapshot mode, the camera still lets you make a few adjustments to fine-tune the shooting process. I will discuss some of these options next. For this discussion I am assuming the default settings are in effect. If some options, such as MF Assist and peaking, do not work as described below, go to the Setup menu (wrench icon) and select the Reset option on screen 3 to reset the settings to their factory configuration.

Focus

In Snapshot mode, the C-Lux has limited options for focus settings. If you want to use some of the more sophisticated autofocus settings, you have to switch to an advanced shooting mode, such as Program or Aperture Priority. In Snapshot mode, though, you can adjust some aspects of how the camera uses autofocus and you can choose manual focus.

First, when the camera is set to autofocus mode, you can choose between Face/Eye Detection and Tracking Focus. As discussed earlier, enter the menu system by pressing the Menu/Set button, then press the Left button to move to the list of menu icons; make sure the red camera icon, for the Recording menu, is highlighted. Then press the Right button to put the red selection line into the list of menu items. Highlight the AF Mode item on the first screen of the menu, as shown in Figure 2-9, and press the Menu/Set button to bring up a menu with AF Mode options.

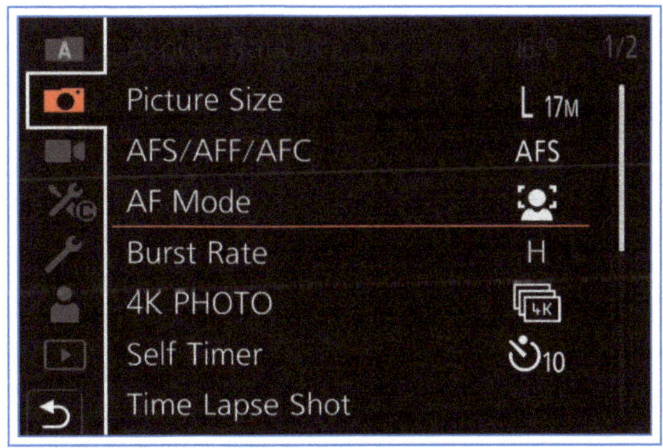

Figure 2-9. AF Mode Option Highlighted on Menu

In Table 2-1, I recommended that you choose the first option on the left for this menu item—Face/Eye Detection. With that setting, the camera uses its face detection focusing system. It will display a yellow focus frame if it detects a human face. This system works well for portraits and other shots including people, especially if they are not moving. If you are photographing moving subjects, whether people or objects, you may prefer to use tracking focus.

To change to tracking focus, select the second option for AF Mode, whose icon looks like a series of small frames, as shown in Figure 2-10.

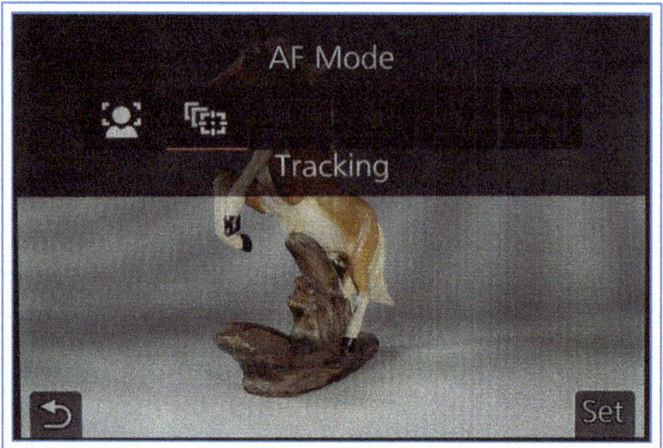

Figure 2-10. Tracking AF Option Highlighted for AF Mode

With this setting, when you first aim at the subject you should see on the shooting screen a white focus frame with small lines protruding in horizontal and vertical directions, as shown in Figure 2-11.

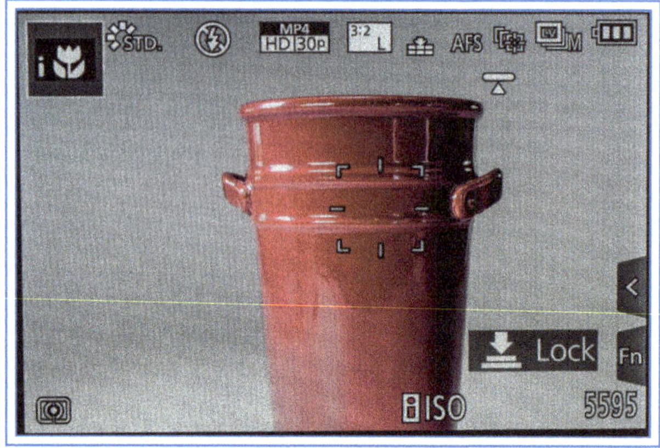

Figure 2-11. Tracking AF Frame in Use

Aim the white focus-tracking frame at your subject and press the shutter button halfway. If the camera can lock on the subject, the frame will turn yellow and then green as focus is locked. Release the shutter button, and the yellow frame will follow a moving subject to maintain focus as the distance changes.

When you are ready, press the shutter button halfway down to lock focus, and all the way down to take the picture. To release the frame so you can start focusing again, press the Menu/Set button.

When the camera is in Snapshot mode, there is also another way to change from Face/Eye Detection focus to Tracking Focus. Just aim the camera at a subject and touch the subject on the touch screen with your finger, and the camera will switch to tracking focus and begin tracking that subject.

Another autofocus option you can control in this shooting mode is the AFS/AFF/AFC setting. To make this choice, navigate to that setting on the first screen of the Recording menu, and press the Right button or Menu/Set to move to the list of three options for this setting, as shown in Figure 2-12.

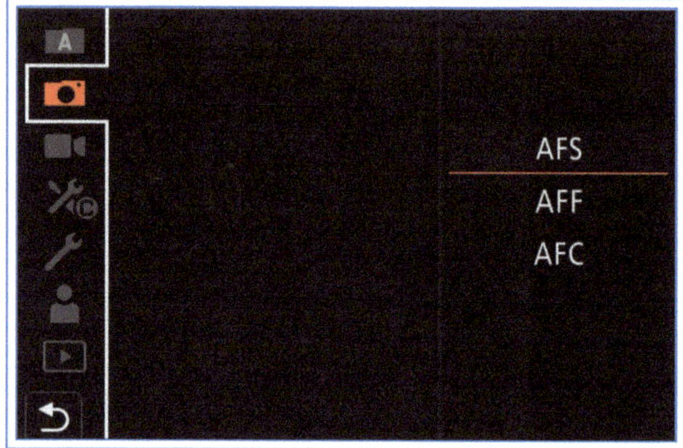

Figure 2-12. AFS/AFF/AFC Menu Options Screen

The three available choices control how the camera uses its autofocus process. If you select AFS, for autofocus single, the camera will focus on the subject when you press the shutter button halfway and it will keep the focus locked while you hold the button in that position.

If you choose AFF, for autofocus flexible, the camera will focus on the subject as with AFS, but, if the subject then moves, the camera will adjust its focus as needed. With the final option, AFC, for autofocus continuous, the camera will continuously adjust the focus, even if the subject is not moving. This option uses more battery power than the other two.

If you are taking photographs of subjects in motion, such as pets or children at play, using the AFC setting will keep the focus approximately correct as the subjects move, and it should result in more accurate focusing when you press the shutter button to take the picture. If you are photographing stationary subjects, stick with the AFS setting to save battery power. I rarely use AFF, though you may find situations in which it is useful.

Manual Focus

The other major option for focusing is manual focus, which requires you to adjust focus yourself. Many photographers like the control that comes from setting the focus exactly how they want it. In some situations, such as shooting in dark areas or areas behind glass, where there are objects at various distances from the camera, or when you're shooting a small object at a very close distance, and only a narrow range of the subject can be in sharp focus, it may be useful to control exactly where the point of sharpest focus lies.

To use manual focus, press the Left cursor button to display the focus mode menu, as shown earlier in Figure 2-2. In the Snapshot shooting mode, the only choices that can be selected are AF or MF, for autofocus or manual focus. Using the cursor buttons, the thumb dial, or the touch screen, select MF, and the letters MF will appear in the upper right corner of the screen. Now, instead of relying on the camera to focus automatically, you now need to use the control ring (the large, ridged ring around the lens) to adjust focus manually.

When you start turning the ring, the camera will enlarge the display to assist you in deciding when focus is sharp, as shown in Figure 2-13.

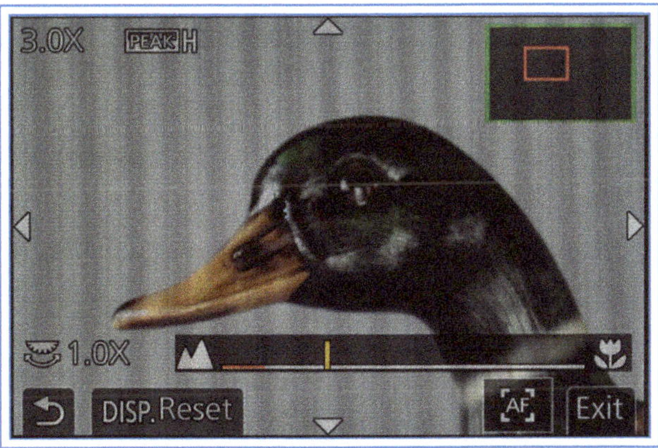

Figure 2-13. Enlarged Screen for Manual Focus

(In recording modes other than Snapshot, including Snapshot Plus, you need to use the MF Assist option on screen 3 of the Custom menu to activate this enlargement feature. See Chapter 7 for details about the MF Assist menu option.)

You can use the four direction buttons or scroll the touch screen with your finger to select the area that is enlarged, and you can turn the thumb dial (on the right side of the camera's top), or pinch and pull the screen with your fingers, to change the enlargement factor. To reset the enlarged area to the center of the scene, press the Display button. To return to the normal-sized display, press the Menu/Set button. Continue turning the control ring until the part of the scene that needs to be in focus looks sharp and clear.

The camera may add colored pixels to the display to outline areas that are in sharp focus, using a feature known as peaking. When an area of colored pixels appears at its strongest, the image should be in focus at that point. The peaking feature is turned on or off through screen 4 of the Custom menu. You cannot get access to that menu option in Snapshot mode, but peaking will operate in Snapshot mode if it has been turned on while the camera was in another shooting mode.

Drive Mode

In Snapshot mode, you can control several options for burst shooting and the self-timer using the drive mode menu. I will discuss the basics of these features here; further details are in Chapter 5, where I discuss the physical controls.

The self-timer causes the camera to delay for a few seconds after you press the shutter button, before it actually takes a picture. To use this feature, press the Down button, which is labeled with icons for a stack of frames and a timer dial. The camera will display the drive mode menu, as shown in Figure 2-14.

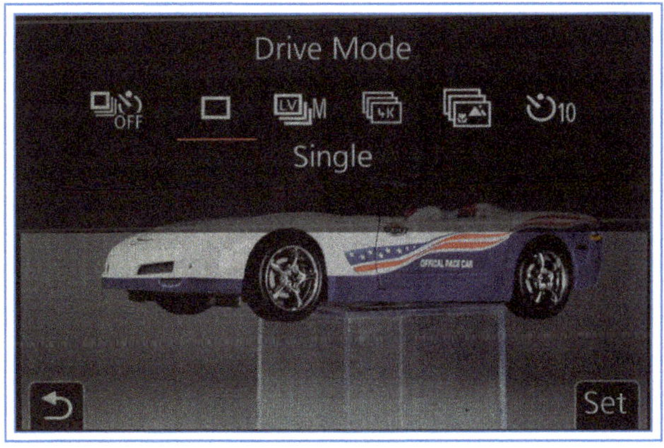

Figure 2-14. Drive Mode Menu

Using the cursor buttons, the thumb dial, or the touch screen, navigate to the dial icon at the far right. When it is highlighted, press the Up button or the More Settings icon on the screen to move to the self-timer settings screen, as shown in Figure 2-15.

From the left, the choices are ten-second delay; ten-second delay with multiple shots; and two-second delay. With the middle option, the camera will take three shots after the delay instead of just one. Highlight your choice and press the Menu/Set button to confirm it and return to the shooting screen.

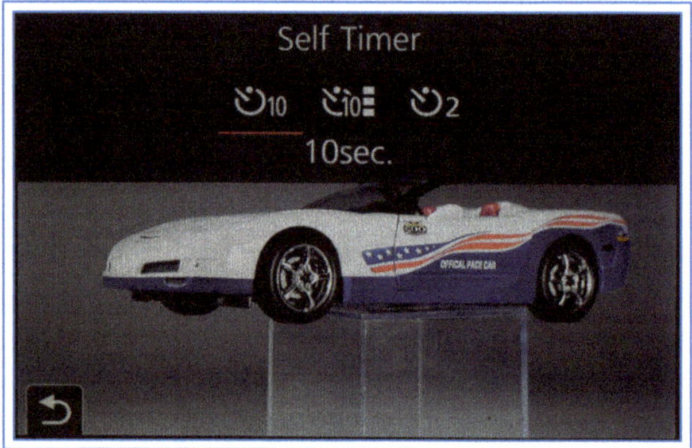

Figure 2-15. Self-timer More Settings Screen

Choose the ten-second delay when you need to leave the camera on a tripod and join a group picture. The two-second setting is useful when the camera is on a tripod and you want to make sure the camera is not moved when you press the shutter button to take a picture. This setting is especially important when you are taking a closeup shot or a shot using a long telephoto setting, when any motion of the camera is likely to blur the image. The setting with three shots is good when taking a group photo, to make it more likely that the camera will capture at least one image with everybody smiling and with open eyes.

You also can use the drive mode menu to select either standard burst shooting or 4K burst shooting. With these settings, the camera will capture a rapid burst of shots while you hold down the shutter button. I will discuss these features in more detail in Chapter 5. For now, if you encounter a situation where burst shooting would be useful, such as a sporting event, select the Burst option, choose H for Burst Rate from the More Settings screen, and hold down the shutter button to capture a group of images.

To turn off all drive mode settings and return to normal shooting, select either of the two left-most icons on the drive mode menu.

Snapshot Plus Mode

There is another important setting available when the camera's mode dial is set to the Snapshot position. That setting lets you choose between two different varieties of Snapshot mode: basic Snapshot and Snapshot Plus. In this chapter, I have been discussing the use of basic Snapshot mode, in which the camera controls most settings and leaves few menu options that you can change. If you choose Snapshot Plus instead, the camera opens up numerous other options for adjustment.

To make this setting, with the mode dial at Snapshot, press the Menu/Set button, then press the Left button to highlight the column of menu icons at the far left. Using the Up and Down buttons, navigate to and highlight the A icon at the top of the column. Press the Right button to move the red selection bar into the screen with three menu options. Highlight the Snapshot Mode option at the top, and press the Menu/Set button to select it. The camera will display a small menu with choices of the A icon or the A+ icon. Highlight the A+ icon and select it, then press the Fn3 button or press the shutter button halfway to return to the shooting screen. You should now see the A+ icon in the top left corner of the screen. (You may instead see an icon showing what kind of scene the camera has detected, such as macro or portrait.)

For a quicker way to switch between Snapshot and Snapshot Plus modes, if the touch screen is turned on, just touch the A or A+ icon in the upper left corner of the display, and the camera will display a screen for selecting one of those two modes. On that screen, touch the icon for the mode you want and then touch the Set icon in the lower right corner of the display to confirm the setting.

When Snapshot Plus mode is in effect, two differences from the standard Snapshot mode are that you can adjust brightness and use the defocus control option. To adjust brightness, press the Up button and you will see a screen with an exposure compensation scale at the bottom, as shown in Figure 2-16.

To adjust the exposure, use the Left and Right buttons, the thumb dial, or the touch screen to make a brightness adjustment on the camera's display, to compensate for a subject that is excessively bright or dark. I will discuss that process further in Chapter 5, where I discuss the physical controls.

The other feature that is available after pressing the Up button in this mode is defocus control. That option lets you set a wider aperture, which may result in a pleasantly blurred background. As I will discuss in Chapter 3, in Aperture Priority mode you can control the aperture setting more directly. The wider the aperture (the lower the aperture number, such as f/3.3), the more likely it is that the background will be blurred, while the foreground remains sharp.

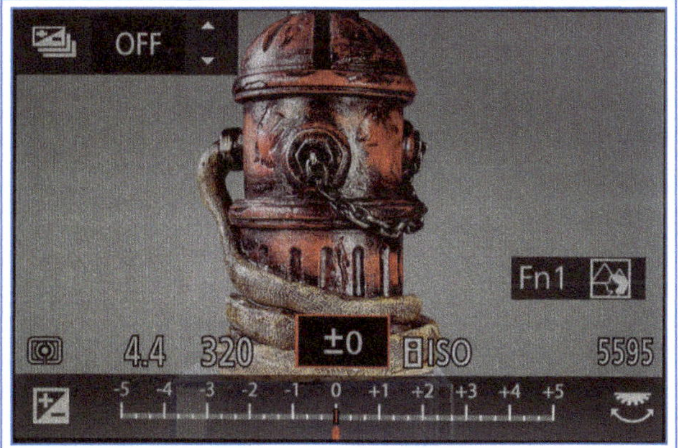

Figure 2-16. Exposure Compensation Scale on Shooting Screen

In Snapshot Plus mode, the camera selects the aperture initially, based on its automatic exposure reading. However, when you activate defocus control, you can change that setting. To do this, after pressing the Up button to bring up the screen for adjusting brightness, press the Fn1 button, as indicated by the icon for that button on the shooting screen. (The Fn1 icon disappears after a few seconds, but you can still activate defocus control by pressing that button, even after the icon has disappeared.)

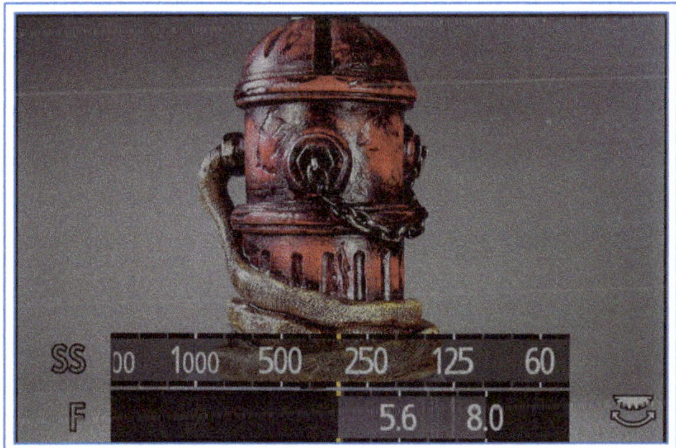

Figure 2-17. Defocus Control Screen

When you press the Fn1 button, the camera displays graphic displays with values, as shown in Figure 2-17. The top line of values shows the shutter speed, and the bottom one shows the aperture. If you turn the thumb dial or press the Left and Right buttons (or touch the scale with your finger), these settings will change. The lower the aperture number you can set, the better the chance there will be of having a blurred background.

When defocus control is in use, the camera sets the autofocus mode to 1-Area, which I will discuss in Chapter 4. With that setting, the camera uses a single autofocus frame, which you can move around the screen with your finger.

In Snapshot Plus mode, you also can press the Right button to bring up a screen to add a color tone to the image, as discussed in Chapter 3.

In addition, with Snapshot Plus selected, the camera lets you choose more options from the Recording, Motion Picture, and Custom menus than in Snapshot mode. For example, you can select Quality, Photo Style, Color Space, Stabilizer, and Shutter Type from the Recording menu. You can select Continuous AF, AF Mode, Photo Style, and others from the Motion Picture menu, as well as Half Press Release, Focus/Release Priority, MF Assist, and others from the Custom menu.

There still are some important settings you cannot make in Snapshot Plus mode, such as ISO (Sensitivity), Metering Mode, Highlight Shadow, i.Dynamic, Flash, HDR, and Multiple Exposure. For those settings, you need to select an advanced shooting mode such as Program, Aperture Priority, Shutter Priority, or Manual. However, you may sometimes want to select Snapshot Plus mode so you can make some settings that are unavailable in Snapshot mode, while still getting the benefit of the camera's automation.

Motion Picture Recording

Next, I'll discuss steps for recording a motion picture sequence with the C-Lux. Later, I'll discuss other options for movie recording, but for now I'll stick to the basics.

1. With the camera set to Snapshot mode, press the Menu/Set button to enter the menu system, and then press the Left button followed by the Up or Down button, to highlight the Motion Picture menu, symbolized by the icon of a movie camera, as shown in Figure 2-18.

2. Press the Right button to go to the list of menu options. Highlight Recording Quality, the first option, and press the Right button, giving the choices of 4K/100M/30p; 4K/100M/24p; FHD/28M/60p; FHD/20M/30p; and HD/10M/30p, as shown in Figure 2-19.

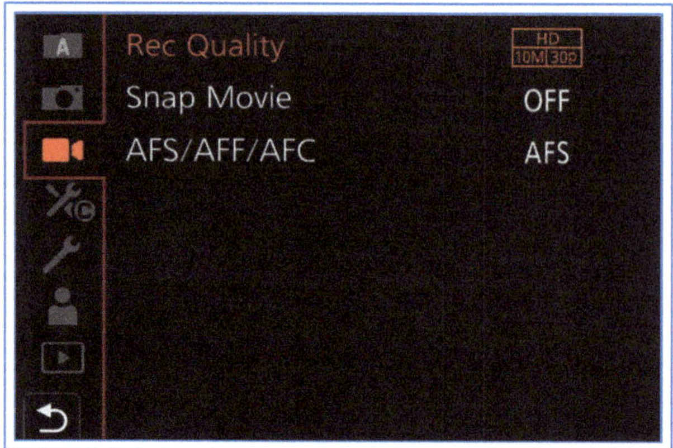

Figure 2-18. Motion Picture Menu Icon Highlighted

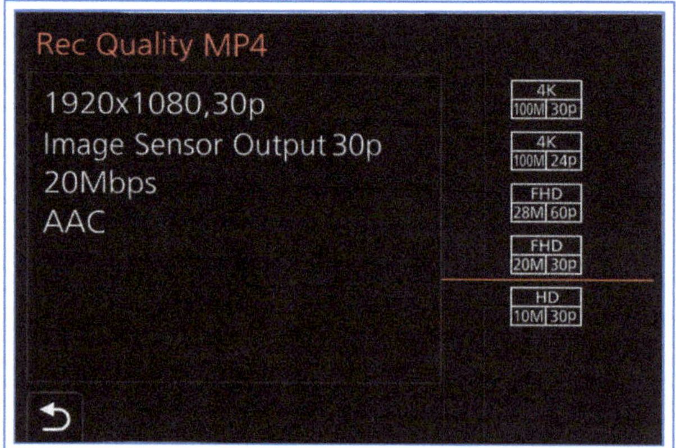

Figure 2-19. Recording Quality Menu Options Screen

3. Highlight FHD/20M/30p, for High Definition, the fourth option down, as shown in Figure 2-19, and press Menu/Set to select it. Then press the Fn3/Q. Menu button to return to the shooting screen.
4. Be sure the focus mode is set to AF. If it is not, press the Left button to select the focus mode menu and select AF.
5. Compose the shot the way you want it, and when you're ready, press the red video button on top of the camera, to the right of the shutter button. Don't hold the button down; just press and release it. The LCD screen will show a blinking red dot as a recording indicator along with a countdown of recording time remaining in the lower right corner and a counter of elapsed time in the upper left corner, as seen in Figure 2-20. The camera will keep recording until it runs out of storage space or reaches a recording limit, or until you press the video button again to stop the recording.

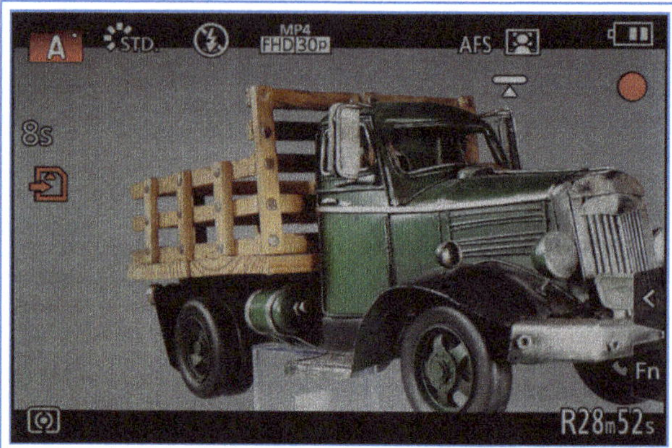

Figure 2-20. Video Recording Screen

6. The C-Lux will adjust focus and exposure automatically as necessary, and you are free to zoom in and out as the movie is recording. (The sound of the zooming mechanism may be audible on the sound track, though, so you may want to keep zooming to a minimum.)

There are many other options for motion picture recording, which I will discuss in Chapter 8.

Basic Playback

Playback of images or videos is activated by pressing the Playback button, located near the top right on the back of the camera with a triangle icon. When you press that button, if there are pictures or videos on the memory card, you will see whatever image or video was last displayed; the camera remembers which item was most recently viewed even after being turned off and back on.

To move to the next picture or video, press the Right button; to move back one item, press the Left button. You can hold either of those buttons down to move quickly through the images and videos. If you prefer, you can move through the items with left or right turns of the thumb dial or by scrolling the touch screen with your finger. The display on the screen will tell you the number of the picture being displayed. (If it doesn't, press the Display button until it does.) This number will have a three-digit prefix, followed by a dash and then a sequence number. For example, the card in my camera right now is showing picture number 100-0450; the next one is 100-0451.

To see an index view of multiple pictures, use the zoom lever on the top of the camera. Move it to the left one time, and the display changes to show 12 images in three rows of four, as shown in Figure 2-21.

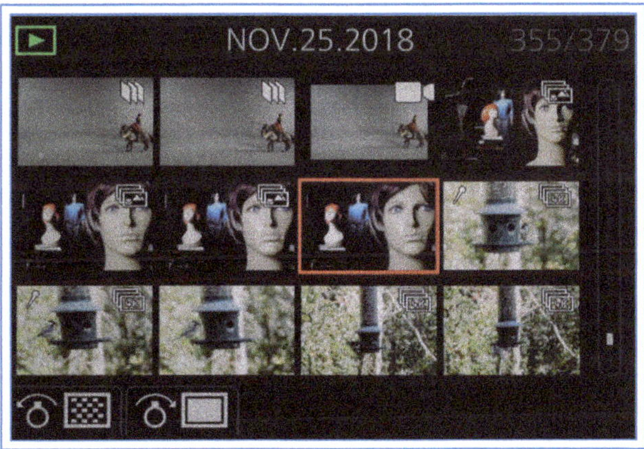

Figure 2-21. Playback Index Screen with 12 Images

Move it to the left one more time, and it shows 30 pictures at a time, as shown in Figure 2-22.

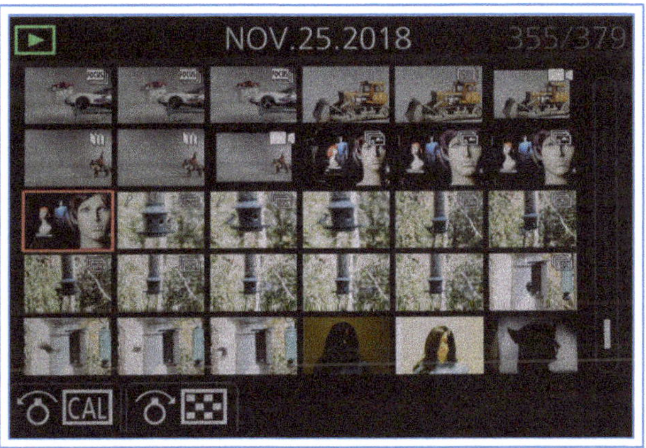

Figure 2-22. Playback Index Screen with 30 Images

Give it one final leftward push and the screen shows a calendar from which you can select a date to view all images taken on that date, as shown in Figure 2-23.

You can also move the zoom lever to the right to retrace your steps through the options for multi-image viewing and back to viewing single images.

For now, move the zoom lever once to the left to see the 12-picture screen. Note that the Right and Left buttons now move through the pictures on this screen one at a time, while the Up and Down buttons move you up and down through the rows. If you move to the last row or the last image, the proper button will move you to the next screen of images. Once you've moved the selector to the image you want to view, press the Menu/Set button, and that image is chosen for individual viewing.

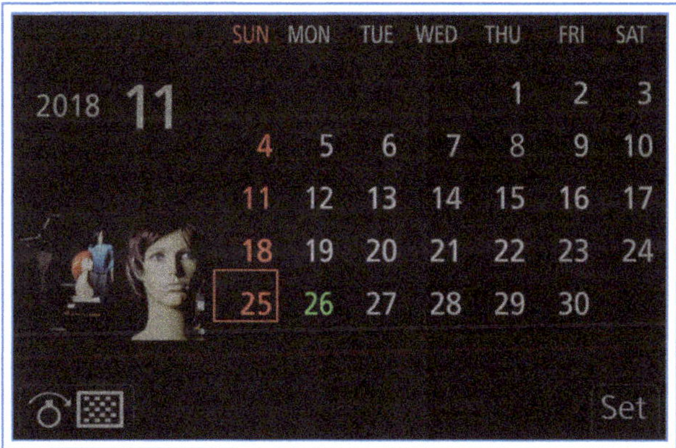

Figure 2-23. Playback Calendar Index Screen

Once you have the single image you want displayed on the screen, you have more options. Press the zoom lever once to the right to zoom the image to twice its normal size, as shown in Figure 2-24. You also can tap twice on the screen to enlarge an image; tap twice again to reduce it to normal size.

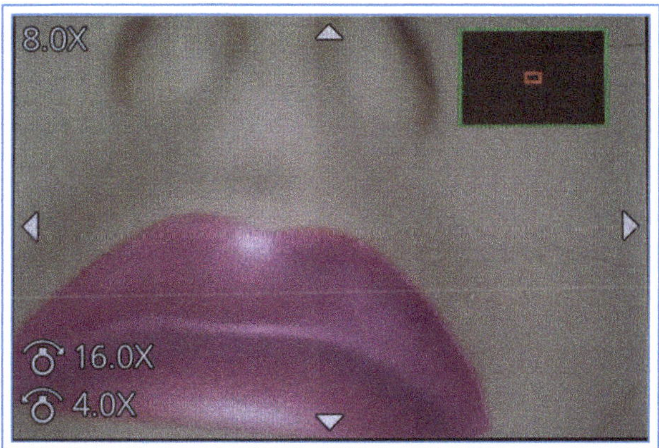

Figure 2-24. Image Enlarged in Playback Mode

Press the lever repeatedly to zoom up to 16 times normal size. Press the zoom lever to the left to reduce the enlargement in the same increments. Or, you can press the Menu/Set button to return the image immediately to normal size. You can pinch and pull on the touch screen with your fingers to change the enlargement of the image, also.

While the zoomed picture is displayed, you can scroll it in any direction with the direction buttons or with a finger on the screen. You can review other images at the same zoom level by turning the thumb dial to navigate to the next or prior image, while the image is still zoomed.

Playing Movies

To play movies, navigate through the images by the methods described above until you find one that has a movie-camera icon with an upward-pointing triangle at the upper left and a playback triangle icon in the center, as in Figure 2-25. (If you don't see these icons, press the Display button until the screen that shows them appears.)

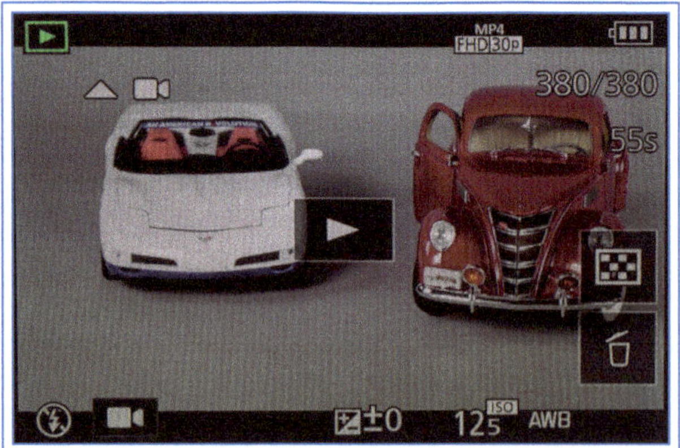

Figure 2-25. Movie Ready to Play in Camera

The upward-pointing triangle icon indicates that you press the Up button to start the movie playing. With the first frame of the motion picture displayed on the screen, press the Up button to start playback.

After the movie starts to play, you can use the four direction buttons as a set of DVR controls; the camera will briefly display icons that show the arrangement of those controls, as seen in Figure 2-26. The Up button is Play/Pause; the Right button is Fast Forward (or frame advance when paused); the Down button is Stop; the Left button is Rewind (or frame reverse when paused).

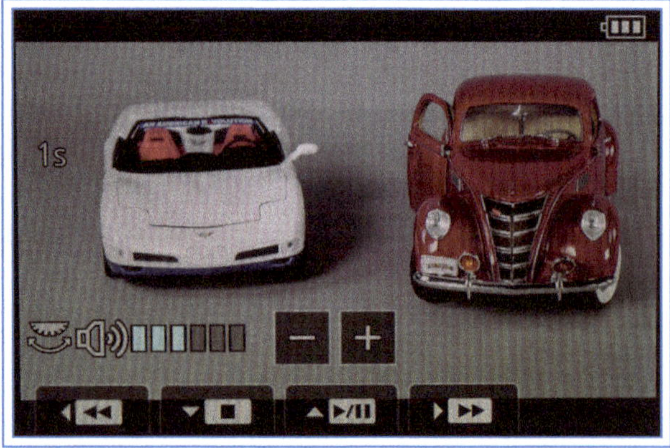

Figure 2-26. Movie Playback Icons on Screen

You can raise or lower the volume of the audio by turning the thumb dial to the right or left. You will see a volume display when you activate this control, as shown in Figure 2-26. (This volume control will not appear when the camera is connected to a TV set, because the volume is adjusted by the TV's controls in that situation.)

If you want to play your movies on a computer or edit them with video-editing software, they will import nicely into software such as iMovie for the Macintosh, or into any other Mac or Windows program that can deal with video files with the extension .mp4. This is a file extension used by Apple Computer's QuickTime video software; QuickTime itself can be downloaded from Apple's website. You can edit these files on a Windows-based computer using Easy Movie Maker, Adobe Premiere Elements, or any one of a number of other programs.

To save a frame from a movie as a single image, play the movie to the approximate location of the image you want, then press the Up button, which acts as the Play/Pause button in this context. Then press the Left and Right buttons to maneuver to the exact frame you want to save. While you are viewing this frame, press the Menu/Set button to select it, then, when prompted, on the screen shown in Figure 2-27, highlight Yes and press Menu/Set to confirm, and you will have a new still image at the end of the current group of recorded images.

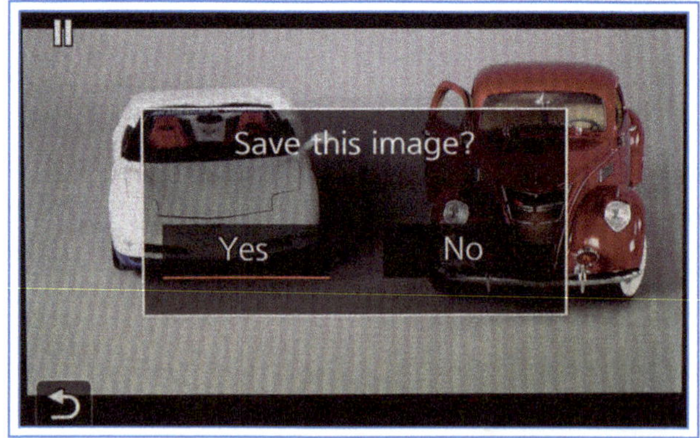

Figure 2-27. Confirmation Screen to Save Frame from Movie

Press the Down button (Stop) to exit the motion picture playback mode. Any still images saved from Full HD or HD video will be a JPEG with Quality set to Fine and will be no larger than 2 MP in size. If you need to save higher-resolution still images from movie files, save them from 4K videos or use the 4K Photo option, discussed in Chapter 5.

Chapter 3: The Recording Modes

Until now I have discussed basic settings for quick shots, relying heavily on Snapshot mode, in which settings are controlled mostly by the camera's automation. Like other sophisticated cameras, though, the C-Lux has many options for setting up the camera to take pictures. One of the goals of this book is to explain those options clearly. To do this, I need to cover several areas, including recording modes, menu items, and physical controls. In this chapter, I will discuss the camera's recording modes and how the selection of one of these modes affects your images.

Choosing a Recording Mode

Whenever you set out to capture still images or videos, an important first step is to select a recording mode, sometimes called a shooting mode. This "mode" controls the camera's behavior for adjusting exposure and other options. As with most advanced cameras, the C-Lux provides a standard set of modes: Snapshot, Program AE (also known as Program), Aperture Priority, Shutter Priority, and Manual exposure. These last four are often known as the PASM modes, for the first letter of each mode. This camera also offers some more specialized modes: Creative Video, Custom, Panorama, Scene, and Creative Control.

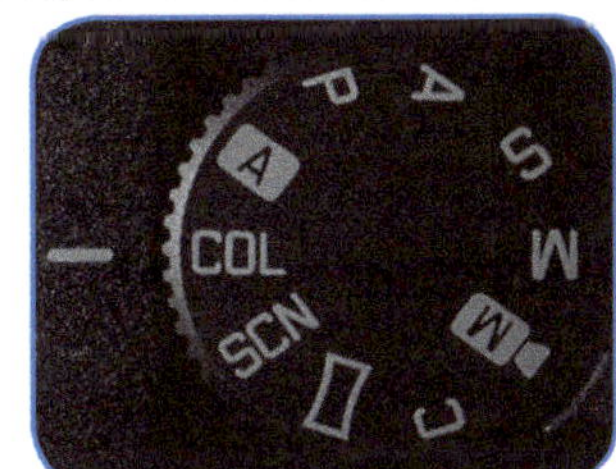

Figure 3-1. Mode Dial at Creative Control

Each of the C-Lux's ten shooting modes is assigned a slot on the mode dial; you select the mode by turning the dial so the mode's icon is next to the white selector mark. For example, Figure 3-1 shows the dial when Creative Control mode is selected.

With that introduction to the recording modes, I will provide more detailed explanations of the modes in this chapter.

Snapshot Mode

This is the mode to choose if you need to have the camera ready for a quick shot in an environment with fast-paced events when you won't have time to fuss with settings. It's also handy if you need to hand the camera to a stranger to take a picture of your group. Figure 3-2 is an image I captured using this mode for a shot of a drink booth at a local arts and crafts fair.

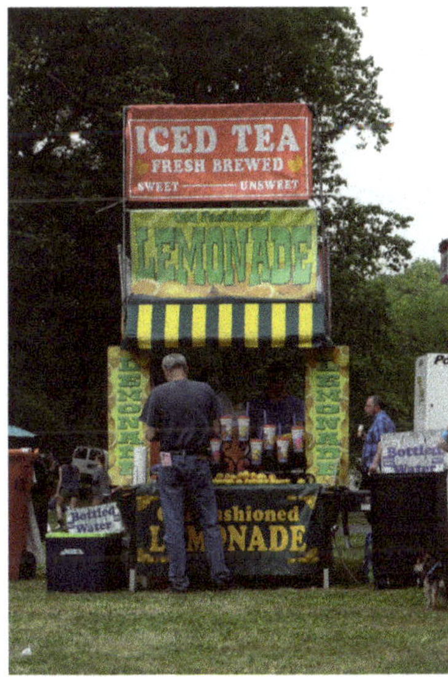

Figure 3-2. Snapshot Example

To make this setting, turn the mode dial on top of the camera so the A icon inside a light-colored rectangle is next to the white indicator mark, as shown in Figure 3-3. You then should see a red camera icon with a white letter A in the upper left corner of the screen, as shown in Figure 3-4. If the icon has a white plus sign at the right, as shown in Figure 3-5, the camera is set to Snapshot Plus mode.

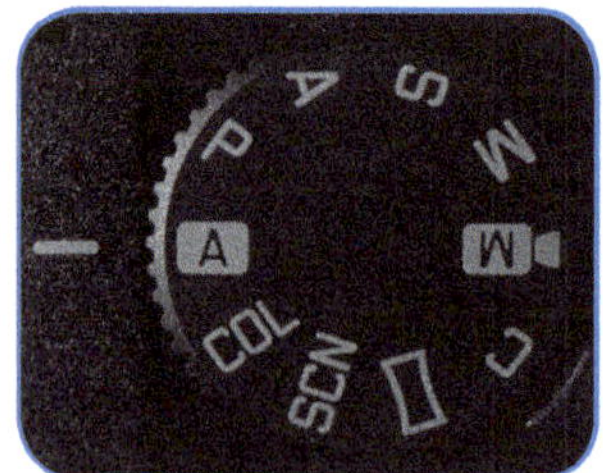

Figure 3-3. Mode Dial at Snapshot

To change it back to the standard Snapshot mode, press the Menu/Set button to enter the menu system, and navigate to the A icon at the top of the column of icons at the far left of the screen. Then press the Right button to move the highlight to the right side of the menu screen and, with the red highlight bar on the Snapshot Mode item, press the Menu/Set button to open a menu with choices for A or A+ mode, as shown in Figure 3-6. Highlight the top icon for A mode and press the Menu/Set button to select it. Then press the Fn3 button to return to the shooting screen. (I will discuss the differences between the two Snapshot modes later in this section; for now, it will be simpler to leave the camera in basic Snapshot mode.)

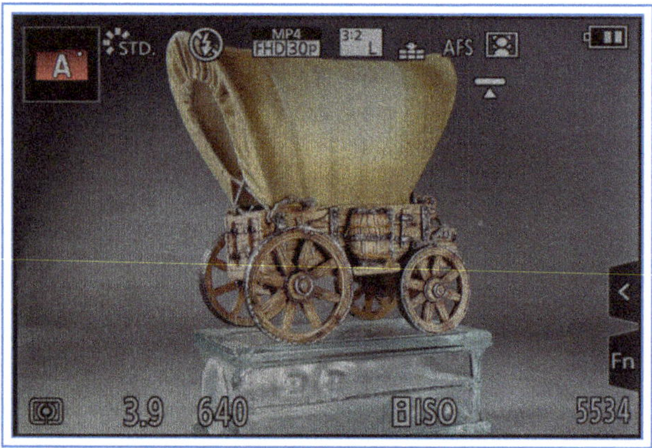

Figure 3-4. A Icon on Shooting Screen

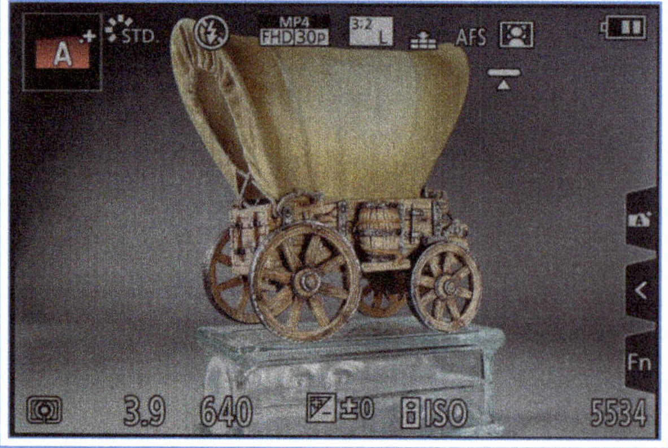

Figure 3-5. A+ Icon on Shooting Screen

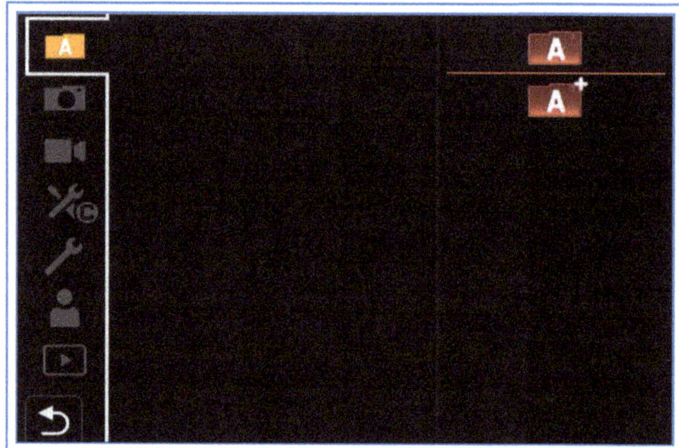

Figure 3-6. Selection Screen for A or A+ Mode

Or, if you prefer, you can just touch the A+ icon on the camera's shooting screen to bring up a screen for changing to A mode.

In the basic Snapshot mode, the camera limits the settings you can make, in order to simplify things. For example, you cannot adjust items such as exposure compensation, white balance, ISO, Photo Style, Metering Mode, Filter Settings, most settings for AF Mode (setting the area for autofocus) and several others. You can select manual focus, though.

The camera turns on several settings, including Auto White Balance, scene detection, image stabilization, and backlight compensation, all of which are useful settings that will not unduly limit your options in most cases. I'll discuss those items in Chapter 4 in connection with Recording menu settings, except scene detection and backlight compensation, which I will discuss here, because they are not menu options; the camera uses them automatically in Snapshot mode.

With scene detection, the camera attempts to figure out if a particular scene type should be used for the current situation. The camera uses its programming to detect certain subjects or environments. For example, it looks for people; babies (if you have registered them using the Face Recognition menu option); night scenes; close-ups; sunsets; food; and portraits. It will identify scenes calling for the iHandheld Night Shot setting if that option is turned on through the menu system, as discussed later in this section. If the camera detects one of these factors, it displays an icon for that type of scene and adjusts its settings accordingly. Otherwise, it displays the standard A icon.

For example, in Figure 3-7, the camera detected the mannequins' faces and displayed the icon for portrait scene detection.

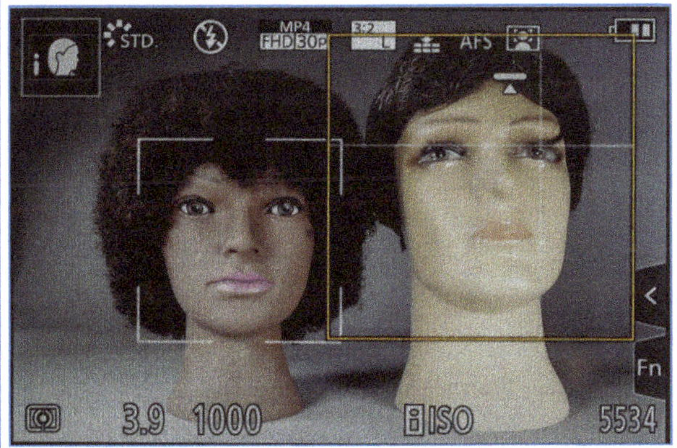

Figure 3-7. Portrait Scene Detection Icon

In Figure 3-8, the camera detected a closeup situation when I aimed the camera at a small bell, and it displayed the flower icon that indicates a macro shot.

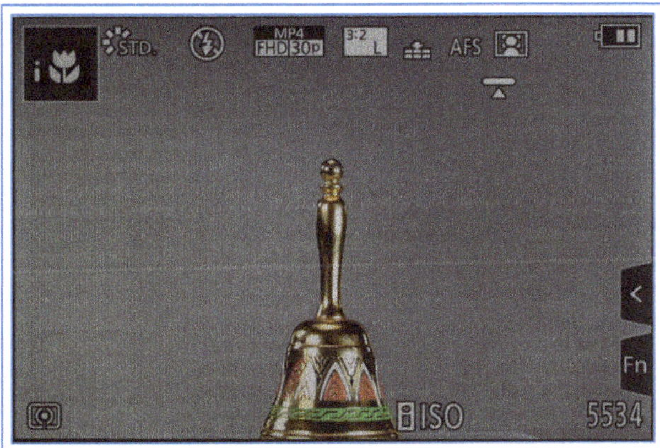

Figure 3-8. Macro Scene Detection Icon

When shooting motion pictures or using the 4K Photo or Post Focus features, the camera detects fewer scene types: only portraits, scenery, low light, and macro shots.

With backlight compensation, the camera will try to detect situations in which the subject of the photograph is lighted from behind. This sort of lighting can "fool" the camera's metering system into making the exposure too dark, because of the light shining toward the lens. The result would be a subject that is too dark, without backlight compensation. With this setting, the camera automatically adjusts its exposure to be brighter, to overcome the effects of the backlighting.

Even though the C-Lux makes several automatic settings in Snapshot mode, there are still some options you can adjust using the menu system and, to some extent, the physical control buttons.

Options on Special Menu for Snapshot Mode

First, you can use the special menu for Snapshot mode to turn on two settings that can improve your photographs in challenging lighting conditions. As shown in Figure 3-9, when the camera is in Snapshot or Snapshot Plus mode, the top icon in the column of menu system icons is the A (or A+) icon.

If you highlight that icon and press the Right button, the red highlight bar will be in the single screen for these special menu options. There are three choices: Snapshot Mode, iHandheld Night Shot, and iHDR. Earlier in this chapter, I discussed the first option, which lets you choose the basic Snapshot mode or Snapshot Plus mode. The other two options are discussed next.

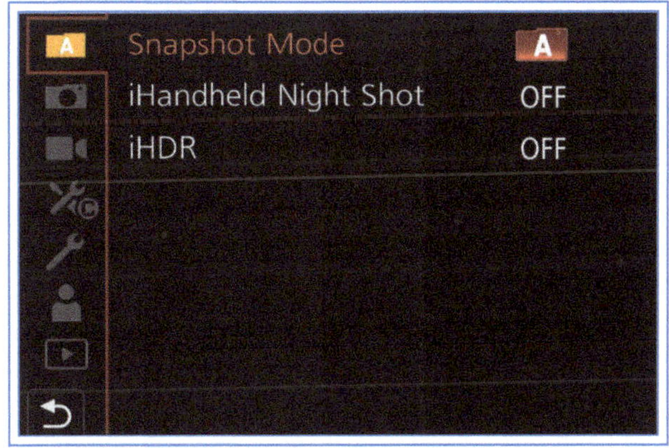

Figure 3-9. Icon for Special Snapshot Mode Menu

The iHandheld Night Shot option is designed to minimize the motion blur that can result from taking a handheld shot at the slow shutter speed that is likely to be needed to get a sufficient exposure at night. When iHandheld Night Shot is turned on, if the camera detects darkness and senses that it is handheld, the camera will raise its ISO setting in order to permit the use of a faster than normal shutter speed. Also, because using a higher ISO can increase the visual "noise" or grainy look in an image, the camera will take a burst of several shots and combine them internally into a final image. By blending the contents of several images together, the camera can reduce the noise in the final, composite result. This setting is useful when shooting in low-light conditions without flash or a tripod.

You cannot decide when to capture an image with this feature yourself—all you can do is turn it on and see if the camera determines that conditions call for it to be used.

The other choice on this special menu screen, iHDR, also will be activated only when the camera determines that its use is called for. If the iHDR option is turned on through the menu, it is triggered when the camera detects a scene with strong contrast between the dark and light areas. When the camera makes that determination, the C-Lux will take a burst of shots and combine them internally to create a final result. In this situation, the camera will place on the screen a message saying HDR Shutters 3 to let you know that the shutter will fire three times. You should try to hold the camera steady while it takes the burst of shots.

I will discuss high dynamic range, or HDR photography, further in Chapter 4. Essentially, with HDR, the camera combines the most normally exposed parts of multiple images in order to achieve a final result that appears to be properly exposed throughout most or all of its various areas. This setting can be useful when you are taking photographs in highly contrasty conditions.

Options on Other Menus

Second, in Snapshot mode you can use the Recording menu (designated in the menu system by the camera icon) to select certain settings, although the choices are sharply limited compared to the many options that are available in other still-shooting modes. In those other modes (including Snapshot Plus), there are four screens of options available on the Recording menu; in basic Snapshot mode, there are only two screens of options. I will discuss those options in Chapter 4. I included a table of recommended settings for general picture-taking in this mode in Chapter 2.

Third, when the shooting screen is displayed, you can press the Left button to bring up the focus mode menu and select either AF for autofocus or MF for manual focus. I discussed the general use of those settings in Chapter 2 and I will provide more details in Chapter 5.

Fourth, you can press the Down button from the shooting screen to call up the drive mode menu, which I mentioned briefly in Chapter 2. In Snapshot mode, you can select burst shooting, 4K Photo, Post Focus, or the self-timer from the drive mode menu. I will provide further information in Chapter 5.

You also can use other controls for their intended purposes in this mode, such as the 4K button to get access to the 4K settings and the Q.Menu button to get access to the Quick Menu. You can pop up the flash with the flash release button, but the camera will decide whether to use it; there are no flash mode settings you can make in this shooting mode. I will discuss various options for the use of these and other physical controls in Chapter 5.

In summary, although the Snapshot shooting mode lets the camera make most of the technical decisions, you still can have a fair amount of involvement in making settings for photographs (and movies). Especially when you're just starting out to use the C-Lux, the basic Snapshot mode provides a good start for exploring the camera's features. The automation in this mode is sophisticated and will often produce excellent results; the drawback is that you don't have as much creative control as you might like. But for ordinary picture-taking opportunities, vacation photos, and quick shots when you don't have much time to decide on particular settings, Snapshot is a useful tool to have at your fingertips.

Snapshot Plus Mode

If you want the camera to make its own decisions for several options but you want to be able to make more settings from the menus and physical controls, you can select Snapshot Plus mode. As I discussed earlier, to set this mode, navigate to the A icon at the top of the line of menu icons at the far left of the menu system, then move back to the right side and select the Snapshot Mode option, and choose the A icon with a plus sign, as shown in Figure 3-10.

In this mode, the camera gives you access to the same special menu for Snapshot Mode options as it does in the basic Snapshot mode, as discussed above, including iHandheld Night Shot and iHDR. In addition, the camera displays four screens of the Recording menu, instead of only two screens, as in the basic Snapshot mode.

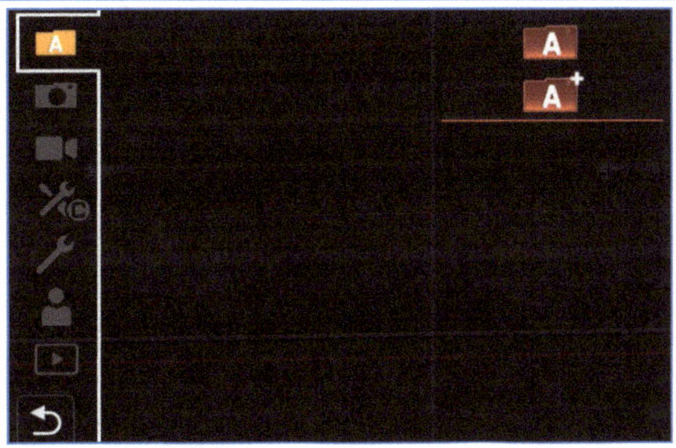

Figure 3-10. Icon for Snapshot Plus Mode Highlighted

However, some of the menu items, such as Sensitivity, Filter Settings, Metering Mode, Highlight Shadow, and several others, are dimmed and unavailable for selection because the camera chooses those settings automatically in this mode. The C-Lux also gives you access to many more options on the Custom menu than are available in basic Snapshot mode, including items such as Half Press Release, Focus/Release Priority, MF Assist, and others. Those features are discussed in Chapter 7.

Using the Up Button: Exposure Compensation, Bracketing, and Defocus Control

In addition, with Snapshot Plus mode in effect, you can press the Up button to get access to the exposure compensation function, as well as to the defocus control option.

To use exposure compensation, when the shooting screen is displayed, press the Up button one or more times until the adjustment scale shown in Figure 3-11 appears.

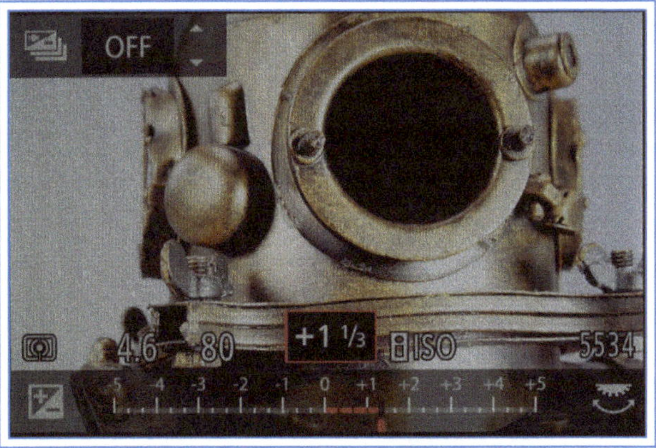

Figure 3-11. Exposure Compensation Scale

With that scale on the display, use the thumb dial, the Left and Right buttons, or the touch screen to select a value for positive or negative exposure compensation, up to 5 EV (exposure value) units in either direction. The screen will grow brighter or darker to indicate the effect of the setting.

Press the Menu/Set button or press the shutter button halfway, to accept the setting and return to the normal shooting screen. A scale at the bottom center of the screen will show the degree of exposure compensation that is in effect, as seen in Figure 3-12, which shows +1⅓ EV (exposure value). I will discuss an example of the use of exposure compensation in Chapter 5.

While the exposure compensation scale is displayed, if you press the Up or Down button, the camera will turn on the setting for exposure bracketing, which is represented by an icon and numbers in the upper left corner of the display. When exposure bracketing is activated, the camera will take multiple shots with one press of the shutter button, each shot at a different exposure setting, so you will have several images to select from.

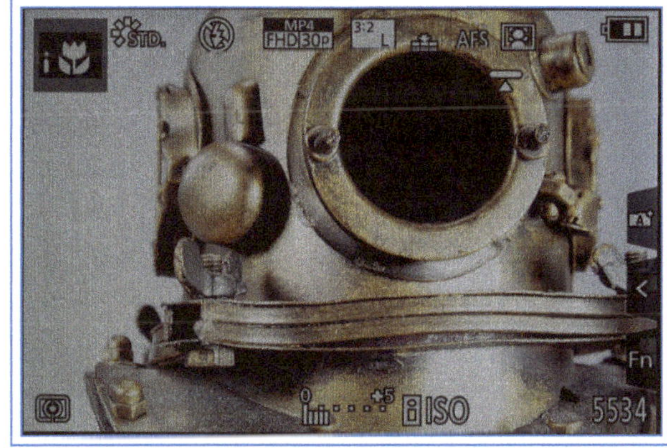

Figure 3-12. Exposure Compensation Adjustment Shown on Shooting Screen

The bracketing display indicates how many shots will be taken and at what exposure interval. For example, in Figure 3-13, where the display shows 5•1/3, the camera is set to take five shots at intervals of 1/3 EV between them. The red markers at the bottom of the exposure compensation scale also show graphically the number of shots and the exposure interval. You can keep pressing the Up or Down button to cycle through the various options for number and interval. I will discuss bracketing further in Chapter 4.

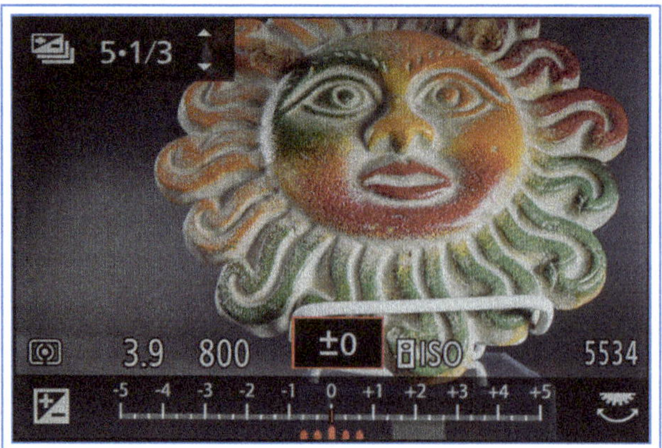

Figure 3-13. Screen Showing Exposure Bracketing Settings

If you press the Fn1 button while the exposure compensation scale is displayed in this shooting mode, the camera will display the settings scales for the defocus control option, as shown in Figure 3-14.

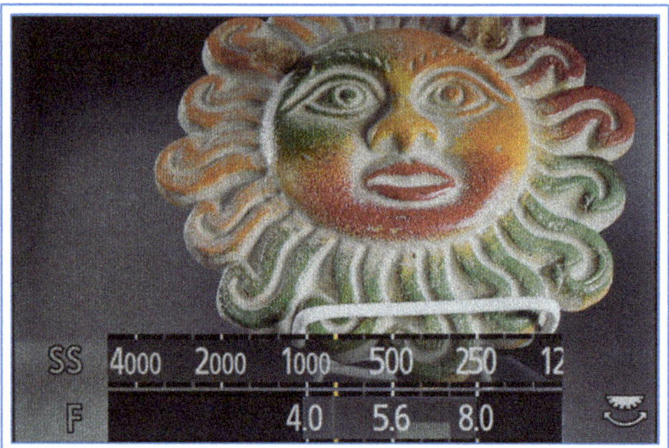

Figure 3-14. Screen for Adjusting Defocus Control

As discussed in Chapter 2, you can then use the thumb dial, the Left and Right buttons, or the touch screen to set the aperture to a wider value (lower number), in order to help blur the background. To dismiss the adjustment scales, press the Fn1 button again.

Using the Right Button: Color Tone Control

When the camera is in Snapshot Plus mode, if you press the Right button, the camera will display a screen for adjusting color tone, as shown in Figure 3-15.

If you then turn the thumb dial to the right or press the Right button, colors will be adjusted to the bluish, or "cooler" side; if you make an adjustment to the left, colors will be adjusted to the reddish, or "warmer" side. You also can use the touch screen for adjustments. If any adjustment is made, a small color block will appear in the lower right corner of the shooting screen after the adjustment scale is dismissed, as shown in Figure 3-16.

You also can activate exposure compensation, defocus control, and color control using the A+ touch icon at the right of the display, as shown in Figure 3-16.

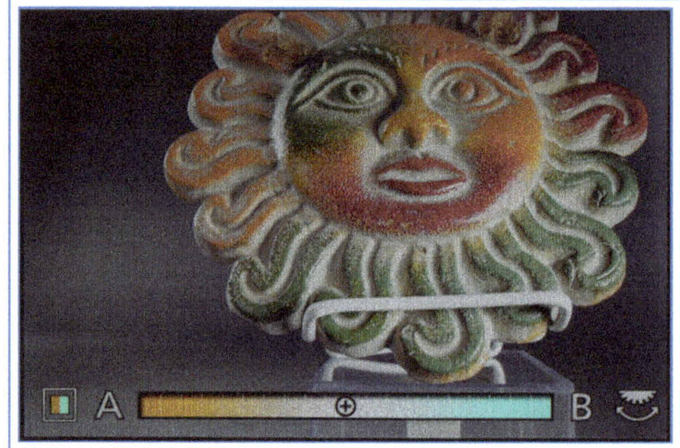

Figure 3-15. Screen for Adjusting Color Tone

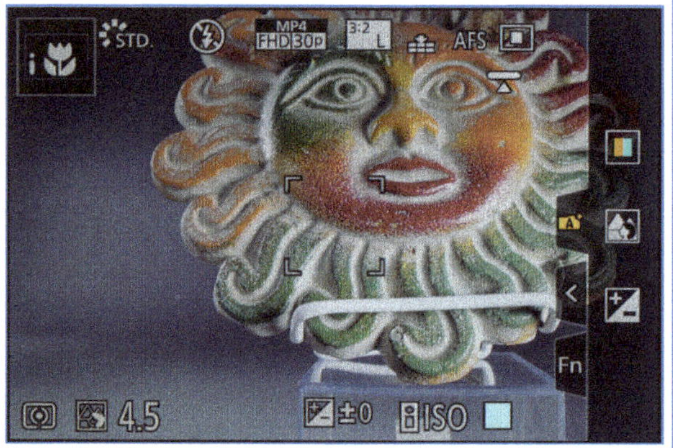

Figure 3-16. Color Tone Adjustment Icon on Shooting Screen

In Snapshot Plus mode, as in basic Snapshot mode, you can pop up the camera's built-in flash unit, but you have no control over whether the camera will cause it to fire; that process will be handled automatically by the camera. If you don't want the flash to fire, leave it retracted inside the camera.

Program Mode

Program mode, with the mode dial set as shown in Figure 3-17, is the most automatic of the four advanced (PASM) recording modes.

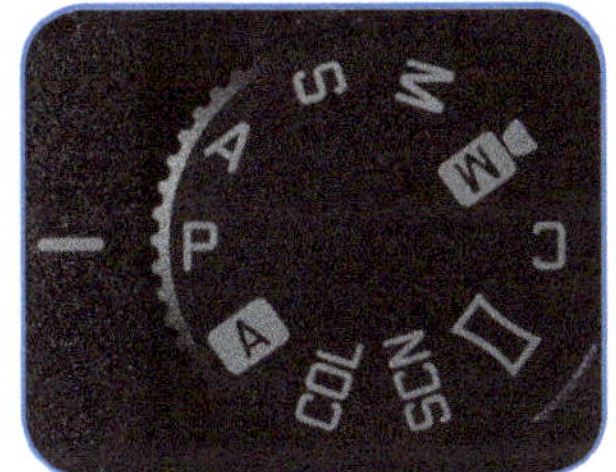

Figure 3-17. Mode Dial at Program

In this mode, the camera displays a P icon in the upper left corner of the display, as shown in Figure 3-18.

When you aim the camera at your subject, the exposure metering system will evaluate the light and choose both the shutter speed and aperture, which will be displayed in the lower left corner of the display when you press the shutter button halfway.

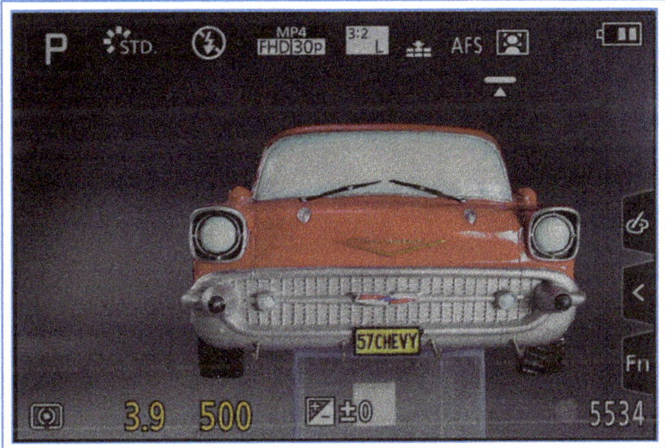

Figure 3-18. Program Mode Icon on Shooting Screen

If those two values flash in red, that means the camera is unable to find settings that will yield a proper exposure. In that case, you may need to adjust the ISO setting or change the lighting conditions by using flash or taking other steps. In this mode, the camera can use its full range of aperture settings, from f/3.3 to f/8.0, and shutter speeds from 1/2000 second to 60 seconds if the mechanical shutter is in use, or from 1/16000 second to one second if the electronic shutter is in use.

If you want to alter the camera's settings by selecting a different shutter speed or aperture while keeping the same overall exposure, you can do that (if conditions permit) by using a feature called Program Shift. After you press the shutter button halfway to evaluate exposure, you can turn the thumb dial (on back of the camera) or the control ring (around the lens) within the next 10 seconds, and the camera will try to select another combination of shutter speed and aperture settings that will result in a normal exposure.

For example, if the camera initially selects settings of f/4.5 and 1/125 second, when you turn the control ring or the thumb dial, the camera may change the settings to f/5.0 and 1/100 second, or f/5.6 and 1/80 second. If you turn the ring or dial in the other direction, the camera may change the settings to f/4.0 and 1/160 second, or f/3.5 and 1/200 second.

However, if ISO is set to Auto ISO instead of a specific numerical value, the camera may shift the aperture value and ISO value, but not the shutter speed. If ISO is set to Intelligent ISO, Program Shift is not available. (ISO settings are discussed in Chapter 4.)

Program Shift can be useful if you want to have the camera make the initial choice of settings, but you want to tweak them to use a slightly higher shutter speed to stop action, or a wider aperture to blur the background, for example. When Program Shift is in effect, the camera displays the P icon with a double-ended arrow in the lower left corner of the screen, as shown in Figure 3-19.

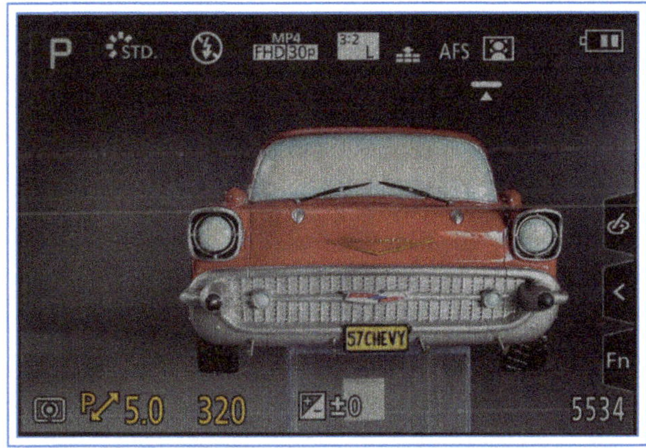

Figure 3-19. Program Shift Icon on Shooting Screen

In addition, if the Exposure Meter option is turned on through screen 5 of the Custom menu, the camera will show the shutter speed and aperture settings in two moving strips, as seen in Figure 3-20.

Program Shift is not available when recording motion pictures or 4K photos, when using the Post Focus feature, or when using flash.

With Program mode, as with Snapshot mode, the camera will select both the shutter speed and the aperture. However, unlike Snapshot mode, with Program mode you can control many settings besides shutter speed and aperture. You don't have to make a lot of decisions if you don't want to, however, because the camera will make reasonable choices for you as defaults.

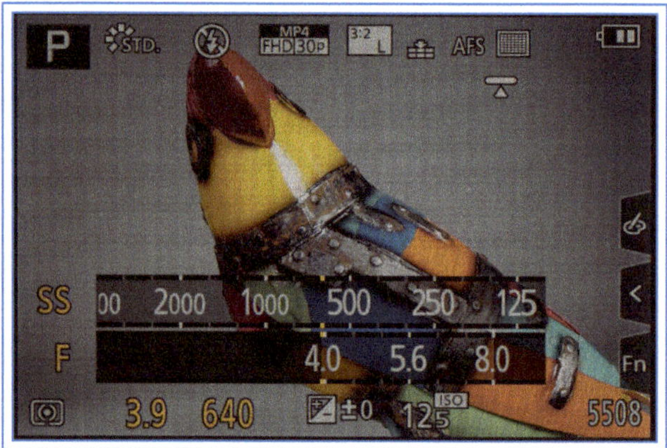

Figure 3-20. Exposure Meter Display for Program Shift

Program mode greatly expands the choices available through the Recording menu. You will be able to make choices involving white balance, image stabilization, ISO sensitivity, filter effects, metering method, autofocus area, and others. If you want to explore that topic, see the discussion of the Recording menu in Chapter 4.

Besides unlocking many options in the Recording menu, choosing Program mode provides you with access to settings on the Custom menu that are not available in Snapshot Mode, such as various focus-related settings and options for setting the operation of the camera's controls, including the AF/AE Lock button. I will discuss those options in Chapter 7.

Using Program mode does involve some tradeoffs. The most obvious issue is that you don't have complete control over the camera's settings. You can set many options, such as Photo Style, Quality, Picture Size, and ISO, but you can't directly control the aperture or shutter speed, which are set according to the camera's programming. You can exercise a good deal of control through exposure compensation, exposure bracketing, and Program Shift, but that's not the same as selecting a particular aperture or shutter speed at the outset. If you want that degree of control, you'll need to select Aperture Priority, Shutter Priority, or Manual exposure for your recording mode.

Aperture Priority Mode

This mode is similar to Program mode in the functions available for you to control, but, as the name implies, it gives you more control over the camera's aperture.

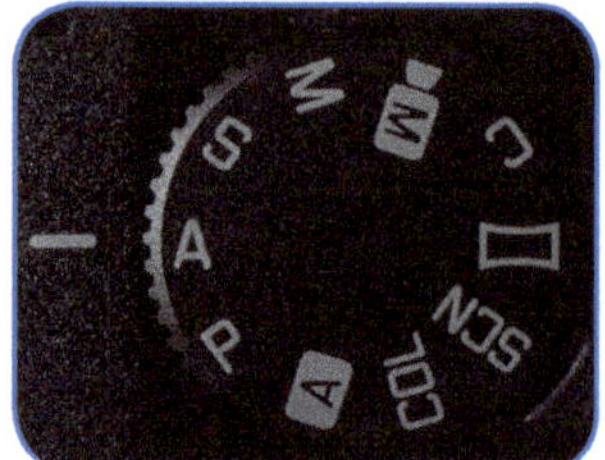

Figure 3-21. Mode Dial at Aperture Priority

In this mode, set by turning the mode dial to A, as shown in Figure 3-21, you select the aperture setting and the camera will select a shutter speed that will result in normal exposure, if possible. The camera will choose a shutter speed anywhere from 60 seconds to 1/2000 second when the mechanical shutter is in use. (The range is one second to 1/16000 second when the electronic shutter is in use; the Shutter Type menu settings are discussed in Chapter 4.) If none of these values can produce a normal exposure, both the shutter speed and aperture values will turn red and flash. In that case, you may need to adjust the aperture or the ISO setting, or change the lighting conditions.

The main reason to choose this mode is so you can select an aperture to achieve a broad depth of field, with objects in focus at different distances from the lens, or a shallow depth of field, with only one subject in sharp focus and other parts of the image blurred to reduce distractions. With a narrow aperture (higher f-stop number) such as f/8.0, the depth of field will be relatively broad; with a wider aperture such as f/3.3, it will be shallower, resulting in the possibility of a blurred background.

Because the range between the widest and narrowest aperture settings available on the C-Lux is not very great, this camera does not readily produce dramatically blurred backgrounds just from changing the aperture. However, there can be a noticeable difference from this setting. For example, in Figures 3-22 and 3-23, I made the same shot with two different aperture settings. I focused on the lantern in the foreground in each case.

For Figure 3-22, I set the aperture of the C-Lux to f/3.3, the widest possible. With this setting, because the depth of field at this aperture was relatively shallow, the items in the background are blurry. I took Figure 3-23 with the camera's aperture set to f/8.0, the narrowest possible setting, resulting in a broader depth of field, and bringing the background into sharper focus.

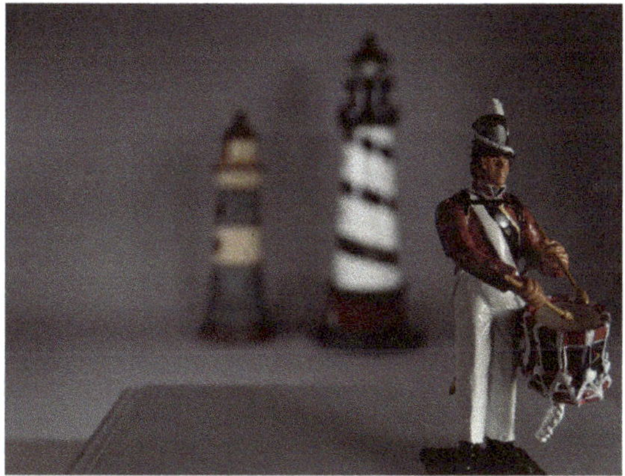

Figure 3-22. Aperture Set to f/3.3

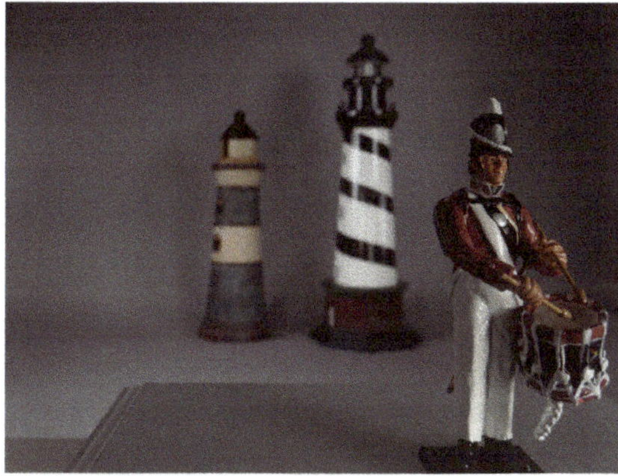

Figure 3-23. Aperture Set to f/8.0

These two photos show the effects of varying the aperture by setting it wide (low numbers) to blur the background or narrow (high numbers) to achieve a broad depth of field and keep subjects at varying distances in sharp focus. There are two other ways to achieve a blurred background. First, you can zoom the lens in to a telephoto setting, which reduces the depth of field and renders the background blurry, if the foreground subject is not too distant from the lens. Second, if you focus on a subject at a very close distance, the depth of field will be minimal, and the background will be blurry.

Of course, with either of those techniques, you have to accept the other effects of the setting—either a telephoto shot or a closeup shot, which may not be practical for the image you are making. For example, with a portrait, you may find that the best option for blurring the background is to choose the widest possible aperture.

To set the aperture, turn either the thumb dial or the control ring, and the number of the f-stop will appear in the lower left corner of the screen, as shown in Figure 3-24, where the value is f/3.9.

The shutter speed will be displayed also, but not until you have pressed the shutter button halfway down to let the camera evaluate the exposure.

If you turn on the Exposure Meter option on screen 5 of the Custom menu, the camera will display two strips of values showing the shutter speed and the aperture, as seen in Figure 3-25.

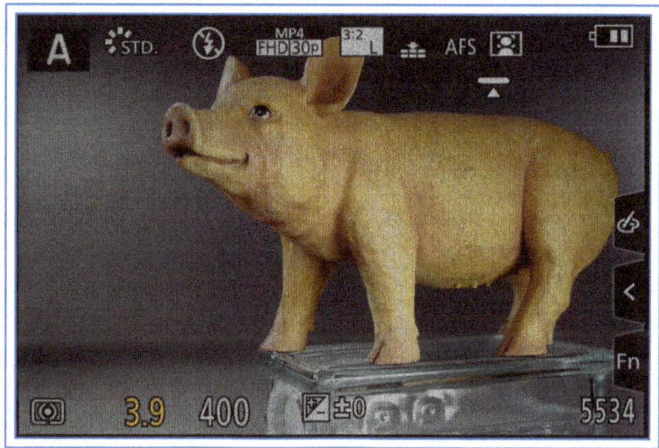

Figure 3-24. Aperture Value on Shooting Screen

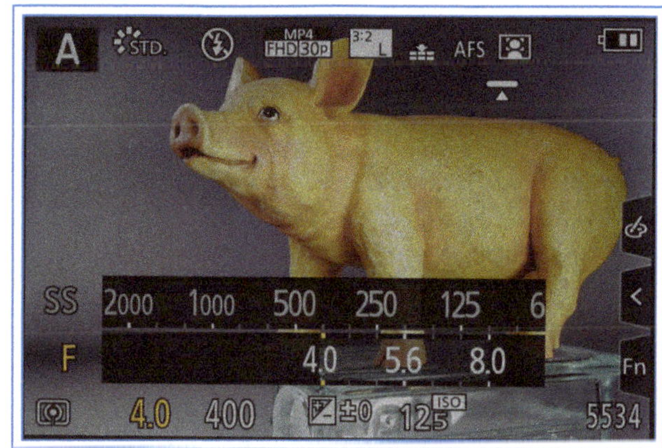

Figure 3-25. Exposure Meter Display for Aperture and Shutter Speed

Note that not all apertures are available at all times. In particular, the widest-open aperture, f/3.3, is available only when the lens is zoomed out to its wide-angle setting. At higher zoom levels, the widest aperture available changes steadily, until, when the lens is zoomed in to about the 280mm level or beyond, the widest aperture available is f/6.4.

To see an illustration of this point, here is a quick test. Zoom the lens out by moving the zoom lever all the way to the left. Then select Aperture Priority mode and set the aperture to f/3.3 by turning the thumb dial or the control ring all the way to the f/3.3 setting. Now zoom the lens in by moving the zoom lever to the right. After the zoom is complete, the aperture will have changed to f/6.4, because that is the widest the aperture can be at the maximum zoom level. (The aperture will change back to f/3.3 if you move the zoom back to the wide-angle setting; so you need to check your aperture after zooming out as well as after zooming in, to make sure you will not be surprised by an unexpected aperture setting.)

Shutter Priority Mode

The next shooting mode is a complement to Aperture Priority mode. In Shutter Priority mode, with the mode dial at the S position as shown in Figure 3-26, you choose the shutter speed and the camera will set the corresponding aperture in order to achieve a proper exposure of the image.

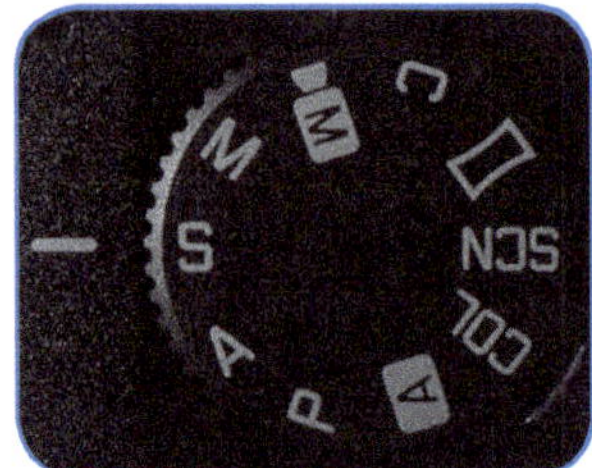

Figure 3-26. Mode Dial at Shutter Priority

In this mode, you can set the shutter for a variety of intervals ranging from 60 full seconds to 1/2000 of a second when using the mechanical shutter. With the electronic shutter, the range is from one second to 1/16000 second. I will discuss the Shutter Type menu option in Chapter 4. (The available shutter speed settings are different for motion pictures.) The camera will select an aperture from its full range of f/3.3 to f/8.0, unless the lens is zoomed in. In that case, as discussed in connection with Aperture Priority mode, the widest aperture becomes more narrow as the focal length increases, until the widest setting available is f/6.4 when the lens is zoomed to the 280mm point.

If the camera cannot set an aperture to result in a normal exposure, the shutter speed and aperture values will flash red. If you are photographing fast action, such as a baseball swing or a hurdles event at a track meet, and you want to stop the action with a minimum of blur, you should select a fast shutter speed, such as 1/500 of a second. You can use a slow shutter speed, such as 1/8 second or slower, to cause motion blur for effect, such as to smooth out the appearance of flowing water.

In Figures 3-27 and 3-28 I photographed the same action using different shutter speeds to illustrate the different effects. In both cases, I took a picture as I was pouring colorful beads into a bowl. In Figure 3-27, using a shutter speed of 1/1000 second, the camera froze the beads in mid-air, letting you see the beads individually. In Figure 3-28, using a shutter speed of 1/30 second, the beads appear to flow in a stream of color, because that shutter speed was not fast enough to stop the action.

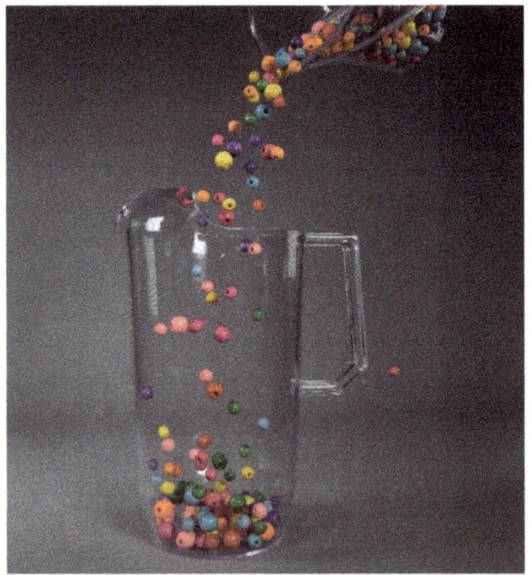

Figure 3-27. Shutter Speed Set to 1/1000 Second

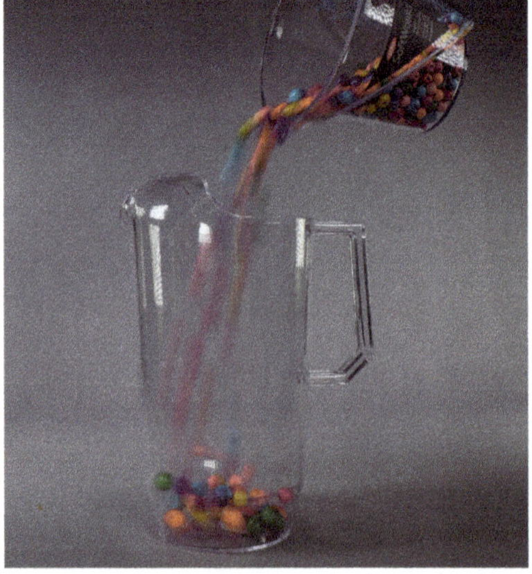

Figure 3-28. Shutter Speed Set to 1/30 Second

You select the shutter speed by turning the thumb dial or the control ring. For example, to set a value of 1/500 second, turn the dial or the ring so the 500 indication appears. Values faster than 1/2000 second are available only if the Shutter Type option on screen 4 of the Recording menu is set to Auto or Electronic, shown as ESHTR on the menu.

On the shutter speed display, be sure to distinguish between the fractions of a second and the times that are one second or longer. The longer times are displayed with what looks like double quotation marks to the right, as in Figure 3-29, which shows a shutter speed setting of four seconds.

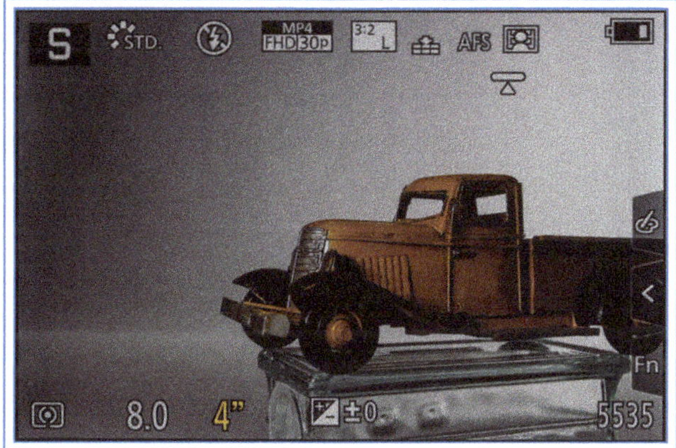

Figure 3-29. Shutter Speed of 4 Seconds Shown on Display

One aspect of the camera's display that can be confusing is that some times are a combination of fractions and decimals, such as 1/2.5 and 1/3.2. I find these numbers hard to translate mentally into a time I can understand. Here is a table that translates these numbers into a more understandable form:

Table 3-1. **Shutter Speed Equivalents**

3.2	1/3.2 = 0.31 or 5/16 second
2.5	1/2.5 = 0.4 = 2/5 second
1.6	1/1.6 = 0.625 = 5/8 second
1.3	1/1.3 = 0.77 = 10/13 second (0.8 sec)

When Shutter Priority mode is in effect, you cannot use the Intelligent ISO setting. If it was set, the camera will reset it to Auto ISO.

Manual Exposure Mode

Manual exposure mode, set by turning the mode dial to M, as shown in Figure 3-30, helps you take full control over exposure decisions.

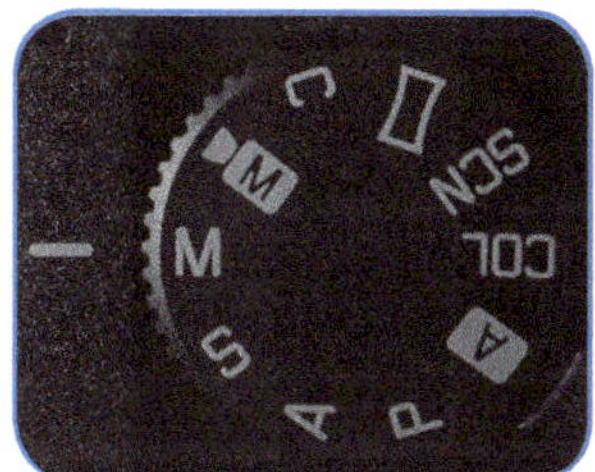

Figure 3-30. Mode Dial at Manual Exposure

For example, you may want to underexpose or overexpose an image to convey a feeling or to produce an effect, such as a silhouette. Or, if your subject is deeply shadowed you may prefer to use manual settings of aperture and shutter speed rather than relying on exposure compensation or settings such as i.Dynamic to expose the subject properly.

Manual exposure mode is useful for taking shots to be combined in software to create HDR (high dynamic range) composite images. HDR, which I will discuss further in Chapter 4, often is used when the scene is partly in darkness and partly in bright light. To even out the contrast, you can take a series of shots, some underexposed and others overexposed. You combine the shots in software that blends portions from several shots, resulting in a composite image that is well exposed through a wide range of lighting values.

Figure 3-31 is an example using Manual exposure mode to create a silhouette of a bust of Cleopatra.

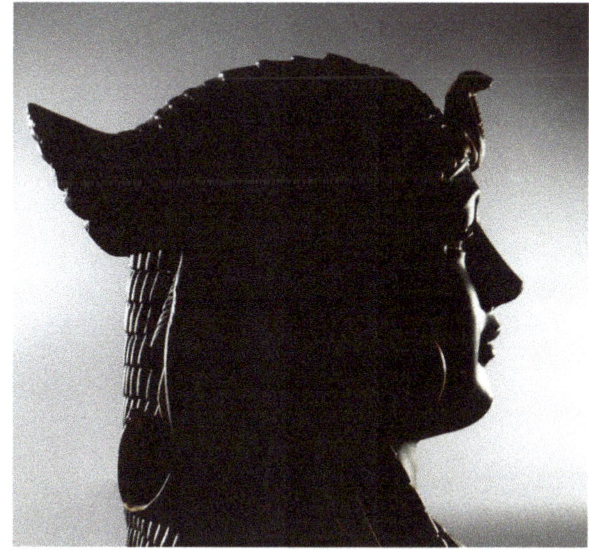

Figure 3-31. Manual Exposure Mode Example

The technique for using Manual exposure mode is not far removed from that for Aperture Priority and Shutter Priority modes. Set the shutter speed by turning the thumb dial and set the aperture by turning the control ring. (If you press the Up button, the roles of those controls will reverse, and the thumb dial will set the aperture while the control ring will adjust the shutter speed.)

The camera displays the aperture and shutter speed in the lower left corner, as shown in Figure 3-32. You also will see at the bottom center of the display either an exposure compensation icon, as shown in Figure 3-32, or a small exposure scale that can range from –3 EV to +3 EV (exposure value), as shown in Figure 3-33. As you change the exposure settings, the camera will display tick marks along the scale if the exposure as metered is too bright or too dark. For example, in Figure 3-33, there are tick marks to the right, indicating that the exposure as metered is too bright.

If no tick marks appear, the exposure compensation icon is displayed with the plus-or-minus zero symbol, meaning that the exposure is normal according to the camera's metering system. Of course, you do not have to be concerned with the indication on this on-screen scale, because you can make any settings you want; you may want a darker-than-normal image to create a silhouette, for example. But the EV scale is useful to help you decide what settings to make.

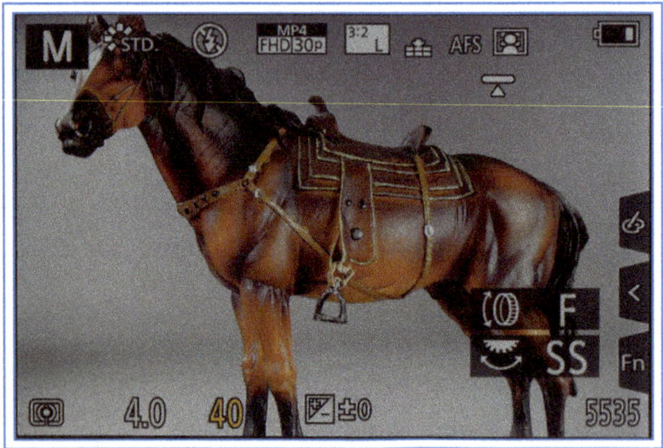

Figure 3-32. Manual Exposure Mode Screen with Exposure Compensation Icon

The camera's display will not show the effects of your settings unless you set it to do so. That is, with normal menu options, even if you set the aperture and shutter speed to values that would produce a very dark image, the image on the display will appear normal, provided there is enough ambient light to produce a normal view. If you want to see the effects of your exposure settings, go to screen 4 of the Custom menu and turn on the Constant Preview option. Then the display will become darker or brighter as the settings change. (This feature works only with Manual exposure mode, not with Aperture Priority, Shutter Priority, or Program.)

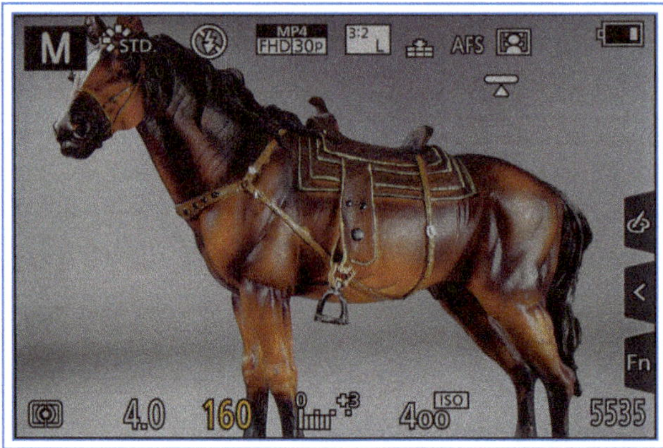

Figure 3-33. Manual Exposure Mode Screen with Tick Marks to the Right

An important feature of Manual exposure mode is that you can set ISO to Auto ISO. If you do that, then, even though the camera cannot change the aperture or the shutter speed you have set, it can vary the ISO setting within the range permitted by the ISO Auto Upper Limit option (discussed in Chapter 4). Therefore, the camera may be able to achieve a normal exposure by varying the ISO level. This is a powerful feature, which amounts in effect to giving you a new recording mode, which might be called "Aperture and Shutter Priority" mode.

For example, you might use Manual exposure mode with Auto ISO when you are taking pictures of a person working with tools in a dimly lighted workshop. You might need to use a narrow aperture such as f/8.0 in order to keep the work in focus, and a fairly fast shutter speed such as 1/250 second to avoid motion blur. You can make both of those settings and be assured that they will not vary. The camera will automatically adjust the ISO setting to achieve the best exposure possible, given the lighting conditions.

In other situations, such as when you purposely want to underexpose or overexpose an image, just set ISO to a specific numerical value and adjust the shutter speed and aperture to achieve the exposure you need. You cannot use Intelligent ISO in Manual exposure mode.

You can use exposure compensation with Manual exposure mode, but only when ISO is set to Auto ISO. You cannot use the Up button to adjust it, because that button is used to switch the functions of the thumb dial and control ring in this mode. You have to use the Quick Menu (discussed in Chapter 4) or assign exposure compensation to the control ring.

Another distinguishing feature of Manual exposure mode is that it provides you with an additional option for setting the shutter speed. With Shutter Priority mode, you can set the shutter speed anywhere from 60 seconds to 1/2000 second (when using the mechanical shutter). With Manual mode, you have the additional option of setting the shutter speed dial to the T setting, for Time exposure.

With the T setting, when you press the shutter button the shutter opens up and does not close again to end the exposure until you press it again, up to a limit of about 120 seconds. You can use this feature to take extra-long exposures of trails of cars' headlights, for fireworks, for star trails, or to turn night scenes into unusual daylight vistas. Of course, it is advisable to use a solid tripod and to trigger the camera remotely from a smartphone (as discussed in Chapter 9) when taking an exposure of this length. The time exposure feature is not available if you are using the electronic shutter, which is discussed in Chapter 4.

If you have the camera connected to a smartphone with Bluetooth, you will also have the option of using the T setting for shutter speed, which lets the shutter stay open while you keep the remote shutter button activated, for up to about 120 seconds. I will discuss this feature in Chapter 9.

Panorama Mode

This shooting mode is designed for a very specific purpose—the shooting of panoramic images. If you follow the fairly simple steps involved, the camera will stitch together a series of images internally and produce a high-quality final result that sets forth a dramatic, wide (or tall) view of a scenic view or other subject that lends itself to panoramic depiction.

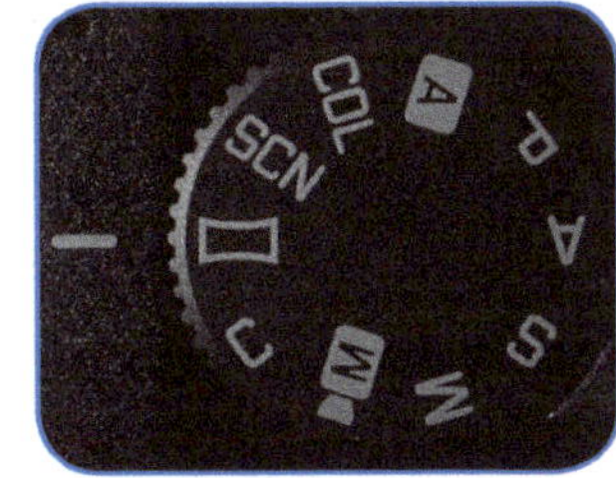

Figure 3-34. Mode Dial at Panorama

Once you turn the mode dial to the Panorama position, as seen in Figure 3-34, you will briefly see a screen showing the direction that is currently set for taking the panorama and advising you to press the shutter button and move the camera in that direction.

When that screen disappears, you will see a display like that shown in Figure 3-35, which provides a guide line for keeping your panorama level.

When you are ready, press the shutter button all the way down and release it, while moving the camera steadily in the direction selected. You will hear a continuous clicking sound as the camera takes multiple images. You should try to keep the camera steady in a single horizontal (or vertical) plane and move it at a steady rate, so that you would complete a full circle in about eight seconds. You can keep moving the camera until the panorama ends of its own accord, or you can press the shutter button down again to stop the recording at any time.

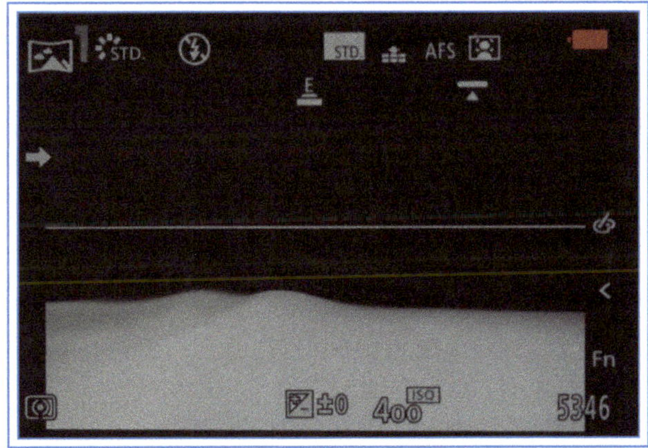

Figure 3-35. Panorama Shooting Screen

When the camera is set to Panorama mode, an icon for a new menu system appears at the top of the line of icons at the left of the menu screen. When you highlight that icon, as shown in Figure 3-36, you will see the two menu options that are available on that special Panorama mode menu: Direction and Picture Size.

The Direction item determines the direction (right, left, up, or down) that you move the camera in while shooting the panorama. The Picture Size setting lets you choose Standard or Wide for the size of the panorama. With the Standard setting, a horizontal panorama has a width of 8176 pixels and a height of 1920 pixels. A vertical panorama has a width of 2560 and a height of 7680. With the Wide setting, a horizontal panorama has a width of 8176 and a height of 960, but it covers a wider area than a Standard panorama. If you want the highest quality, choose Standard; choose Wide if you need to include a very wide view in the image.

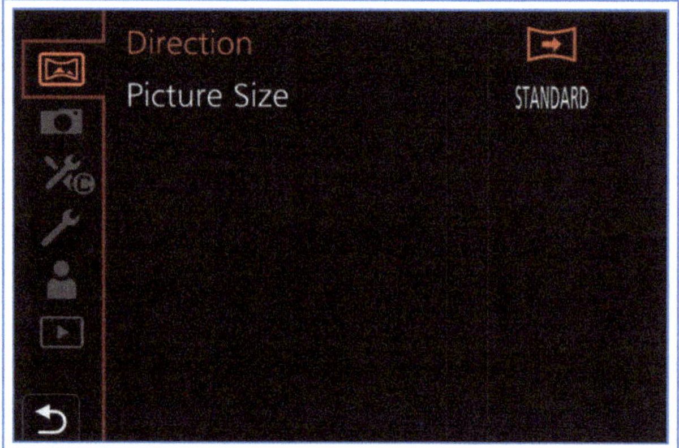

Figure 3-36. Options on Special Panorama Mode Menu

Because of the different sizes of panoramas taken with the horizontal and vertical orientations, you can use the direction settings with different orientations of the camera to achieve different results than usual. For example, if you set the direction to Down and then hold the camera sideways while you sweep it to the right, you will create a horizontal panorama that has 2560 pixels in its vertical dimension rather than the standard 1920.

I tend to shoot my panoramas moving the camera from left to right, but you may have a different preference. If you move the camera either too quickly or too slowly, the panorama will not succeed; if that happens, just try again. Generally speaking, panoramas work best when the scene does not contain moving objects such as cars or pedestrians, because, when items are in motion, the multiple shots are likely to pick up the same object more than once, in different positions.

It is advisable to use a tripod if possible, so you can keep the camera steady in a single plane as it moves. Note that focus, exposure, and white balance are fixed as soon as the first image is taken for the panorama.

To shoot a panorama with one of the filter effects settings in place (such as Expressive, Retro, Old Days, and the like), you can use the Filter Settings menu, or just turn the control ring or thumb dial. (A few effects are not available: Toy, Toy Pop, Miniature, and Sunshine.) Those controls are both set by default to select that setting in this shooting mode. (If the controls do not carry out this function, check the settings of the Ring/Dial Set option on screen 3 of the Custom menu.)

When a panoramic shot is ready to be played back in the camera, the camera prompts you to press the Up cursor button (or the on-screen icon) to start it playing back; the panorama then scrolls across the screen so it can be viewed using the full area of the screen, rather than being squeezed to fit its full extent within the screen.

Figure 3-37 is a sample panorama, shot hand-held and using the Standard setting for panorama size.

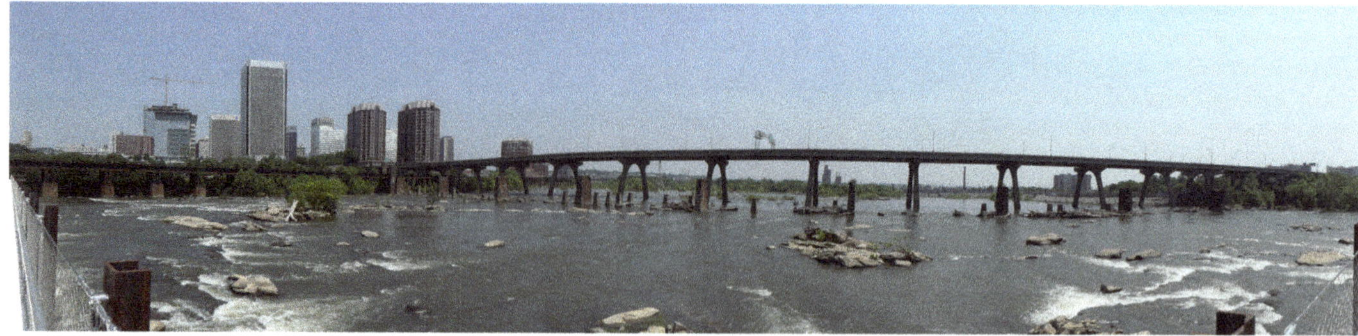

Figure 3-37. Sample Panorama: James River, Richmond, Virginia

Scene Mode

Scene mode, also called Scene Guide mode, does not have a single defining feature, such as permitting control over one or more aspects of exposure. Instead, when you select Scene mode and then choose a particular scene type within that mode, you are in effect telling the camera what sort of environment the picture is being taken in as well as what kind of image you are looking for, and you're letting the camera make a group of decisions as to what settings to use to produce that result.

Turning the mode dial to the SCN indicator, as shown in Figure 3-38, places the camera in Scene mode, but unless you want to settle for whatever scene setting is already in place, you now need to make another choice, and pick one from the fairly impressive list of possibilities.

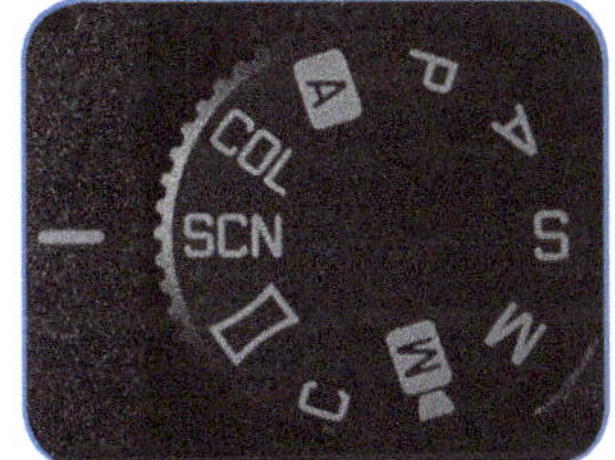

Figure 3-38. Mode Dial at Scene

To make this further choice, you can use the menu system. When you select Scene mode, the menu system itself changes. When the camera is set to Scene mode, there is a new branch of the menu system named Scene Guide, as shown in Figure 3-39.

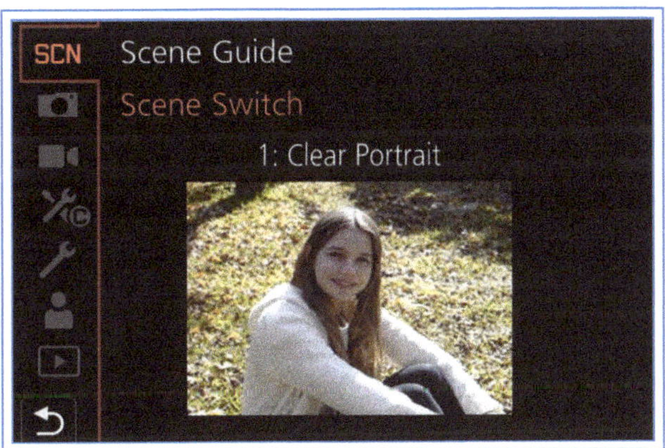

Figure 3-39. Special Menu for Scene Mode

It takes over as the first choice at the top of the menu system once you have pressed the Menu/Set button. The Scene menu also appears automatically when you select SCN on the mode dial, if the Menu Guide option is turned on through screen 6 of the Custom menu.

To change scene types, press the Menu/Set button and navigate to the SCN icon at the top of the left side of the screen. Next, press the right button, and select the Scene Switch option, as shown in Figure 3-40.

The camera then displays a series of images that will rotate as you touch them with your finger, as shown in Figure 3-41. You also can move through these images using the Left and Right buttons or the thumb dial.

If you press the Display button, the display changes to an arrangement that includes a text description of each setting, as shown in Figure 3-42. You can move through those screens using the Left and Right buttons, and scroll through hints for each setting with the Up and Down buttons or the thumb dial. If you press the Display button again, you will see an array of 12 images on the screen, as shown in Figure 3-43. You can scroll through those images using the touch screen, the cursor buttons, or the thumb dial. Using any of the three systems of display, scroll through the 24 options and select the scene type you want.

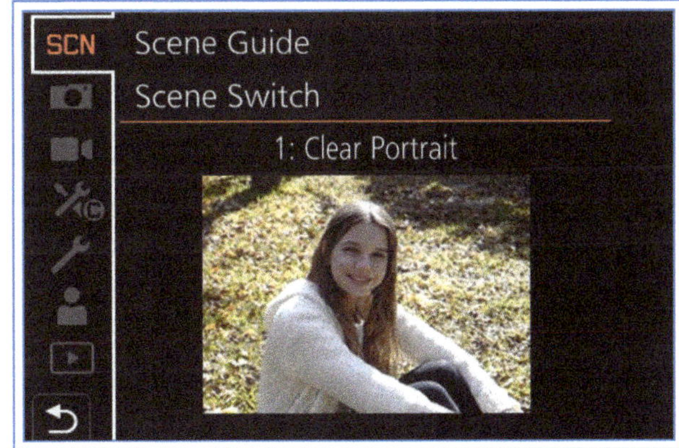

Figure 3-40. Scene Switch Option Highlighted

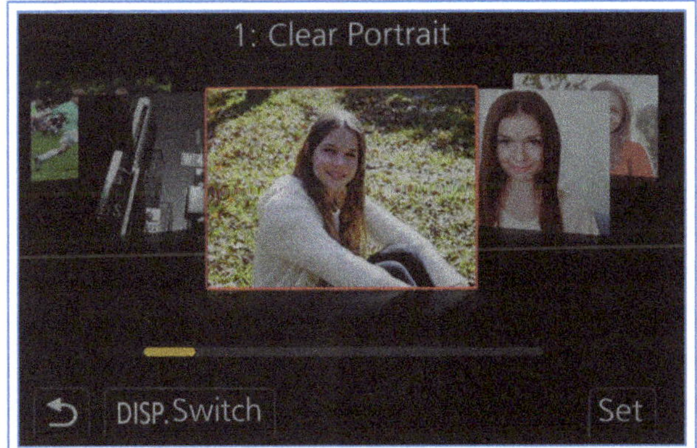

Figure 3-41. Rotating Display of Scene Type Icons

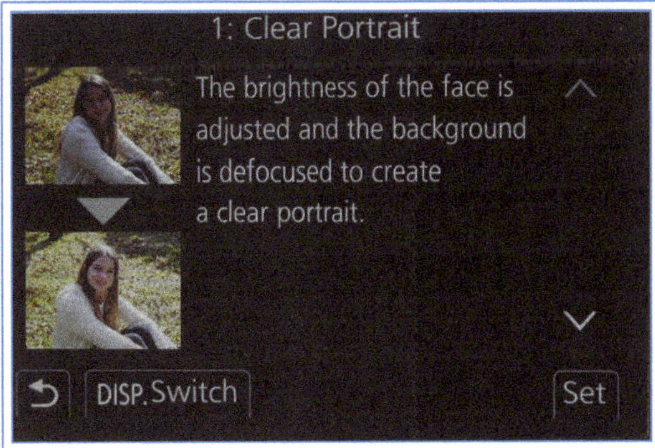

Figure 3-42. Scene Types Display with Text Descriptions

Another way to select one of the 24 scene types is to touch the Scene mode icon on the shooting screen, as shown in Figure 3-44.

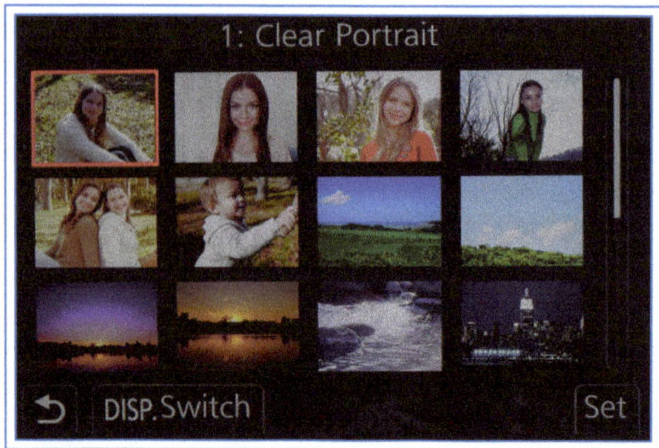

Figure 3-43. Scene Types Display with Rows of Images

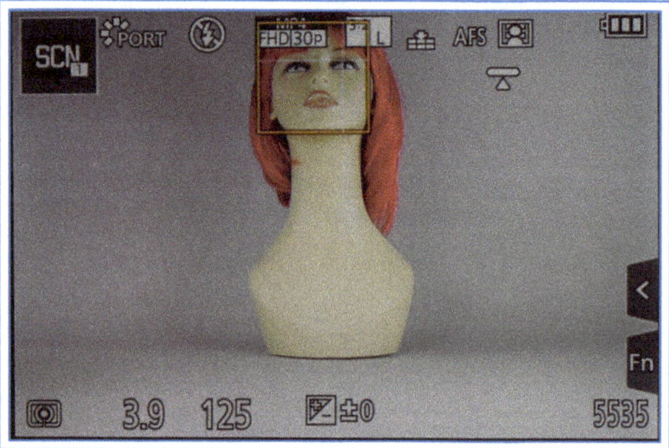

Figure 3-44. Scene Type Icon on Shooting Screen

When you touch that icon, the camera immediately displays the Scene settings menu, so you can make a selection of a scene type. Unfortunately, each icon uses the SCN designation with a small number as the only identification of the scene type, so you either have to memorize 24 scene types or press on the icon for a reminder of what scene type is currently selected.

Each scene type carries with it a variety of settings, including things like focus mode, flash status, range of shutter speeds, sensitivity to various colors, and others.

There are limitations on settings you can make in Scene mode. No matter what scene type you select, you cannot use the Sensitivity, Filter Settings, Metering Mode, Highlight Shadow, Minimum Shutter Speed, HDR, or Multiple Exposure options. For Photo Style, you cannot select a main setting, such as Portrait, Vivid, or Natural, but you can adjust contrast, sharpness, noise reduction, and saturation (including color tone or filter effect for the Monochrome option). For some settings, the camera uses Auto White Balance, but you can fine-tune white balance with color axes as discussed in Chapter 5, and you can use white balance bracketing, discussed in Chapter 4.

Except for Handheld Night Shot, with all scene settings you can set Quality to Raw. However, any special effects that are similar to the Filter Settings or Creative Control settings will not show up in the Raw images on a computer. Therefore, you should shoot using Fine, or Raw & Fine, for Quality if you use a setting of that nature. For example, with the Glistening Water setting, the Star Filter rays will not show up in a Raw file when it is opened on a computer, unless you use a program such as Irfanview, which can read the JPEG file embedded within the Raw file.

With most of the settings you can use burst shooting, and with several you can use flash. (And with some the camera asks you to use flash.) I will provide details about each of the settings, so you can make an informed choice. I will include sample images for some of the settings. Several of the settings are self-explanatory from their names, and I will not discuss them all in detail. I am including the numbers for the settings, so you can use this list as a reference when you look at the small icon on the shooting screen, which includes the number of the scene type.

1. Clear Portrait: This setting is designed to produce rich skin tones. You should get good results if you shoot close to the subject and zoom the lens in somewhat, so as to blur the background if possible. The camera sets itself to a wide aperture if it can and initially sets the autofocus mode to Face/Eye Detection. The flash mode is initially set to Forced On/Red-Eye Reduction, but you can change it to Forced On.

2. Silky Skin: This setting is similar to Portrait; it detects skin tones in faces and adds a "soft effect" to those areas, as shown in Figure 3-45. The softening increases as the image is zoomed in further. Flash mode is initially set to Forced On/Red-Eye Reduction.

3. Backlit Softness: The camera uses positive exposure compensation and disables the flash.

4. Clear in Backlight: The camera sets the flash mode to Forced On and displays a message asking you to pop up the flash, if it is not popped up. However, you can still take the picture without flash if you don't pop it up. This setting is for use when the subject is lighted from

behind and you need to use flash to make the subject show up clearly.

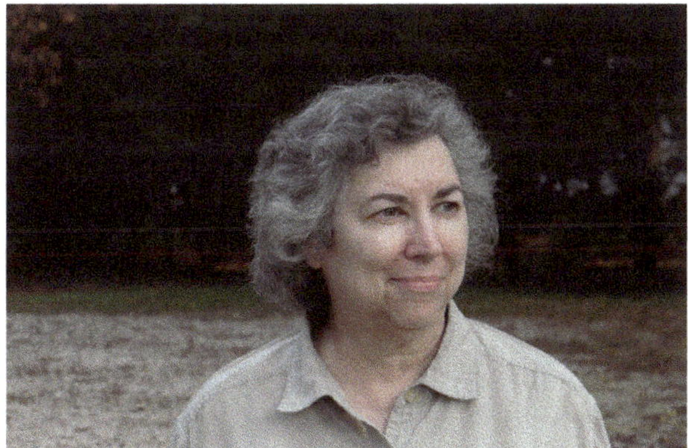

Figure 3-45. Silky Skin Example

5. Relaxing Tone: The flash is disabled and the camera uses warmer, yellowish tones to add a somewhat subdued, old-time appearance to the image.

6. Sweet Child's Face: With this setting, the flash mode is initially set to Forced On/Red-eye, but you can change it to Forced On. When you touch a face on the screen, the camera takes a picture with focus and exposure set for that face, using its setting for touch shutter. As the lens is zoomed in, a softening effect is applied increasingly.

7. Distinct Scenery: This style is intended for photographs of landscapes and subjects other than individual people. It is useful for general shots of buildings, gardens, and colorful scenery, as shown in Figure 3-46, where I took a picture of the river at a railroad bridge. The flash is disabled. You cannot select a white balance setting, presumably because you will be shooting your outdoor vistas in daylight conditions. However, you can tweak the white balance using the color axes and you can use white balance bracketing.

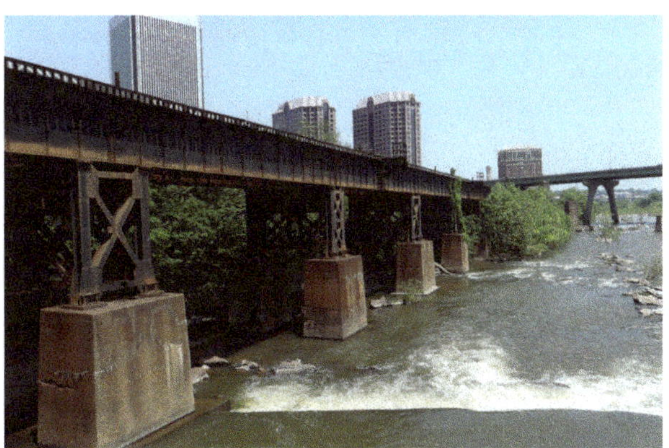

Figure 3-46. Distinct Scenery Example

8. Bright Blue Sky: The camera uses a small amount of positive exposure compensation to allow for shadows or backlighting that might be caused by the sky's brightness. You can alter that setting as you like. The flash is disabled, and white balance can be tweaked, but the basic setting cannot be changed. In Figure 3-47, I used this setting for a shot of an outdoor sculpture at the art museum on a sunny day.

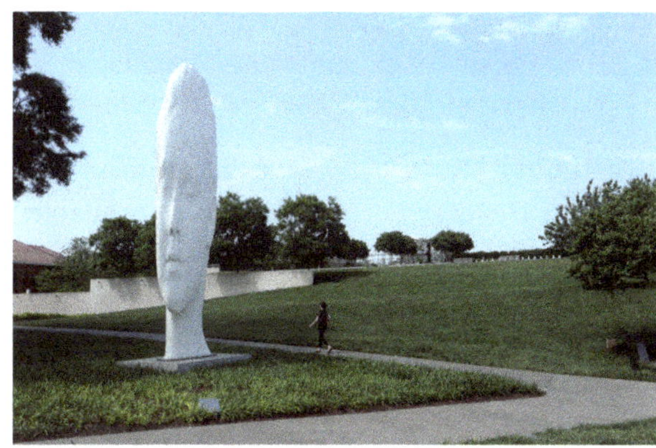

Figure 3-47. Bright Blue Sky Example

9. Romantic Sunset Glow: The camera disables the flash and adds a reddish or purplish hue to the scene to emphasize the colors of a sunrise or sunset. You can tweak white balance but not change the major setting. In Figure 3-48, I used this setting and the next one to capture the same view at the time of sunset, to show the differences in how they render colors.

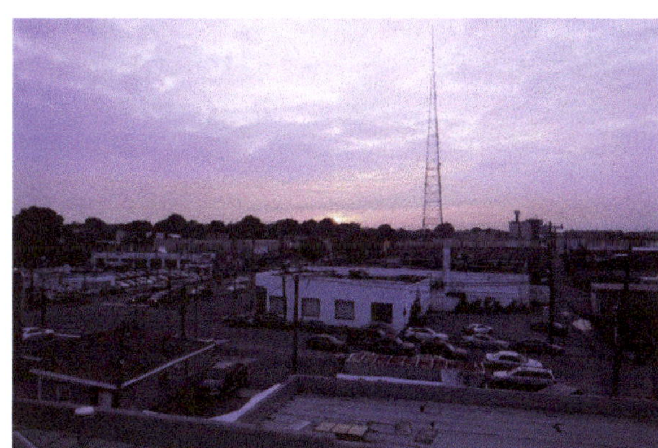

Figure 3-48. Romantic Sunset Glow Example

10. Vivid Sunset Glow: This setting is similar to the previous one, except that the camera does not add any coloration to the scene; it emphasizes the colors present in the scene naturally. In Figure 3-49, I shot the sunset at the same time and place as the previous image, to show the differences between these two settings.

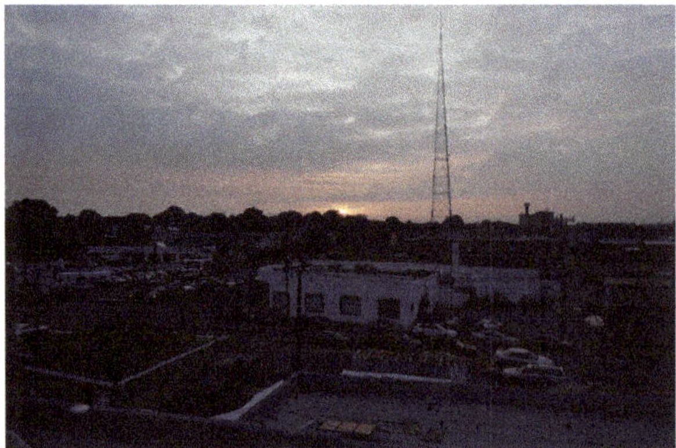

Figure 3-49. Vivid Sunset Glow Example

11. Glistening Water: The flash is disabled and the camera uses the Star Filter setting, also available with the Filter Settings option and Creative Control mode. That setting adds star-like rays to bright areas, such as the sun's reflections on water. White balance can be tweaked, but not changed to a different setting.

12. Clear Nightscape: With this setting, the flash is disabled and white balance can be tweaked but not otherwise changed. The camera is likely to use a long shutter speed to capture a natural-looking scene, such as a shot of a gas station after dark, as shown in Figure 3-50, for which the camera used a shutter speed of 0.4 second.

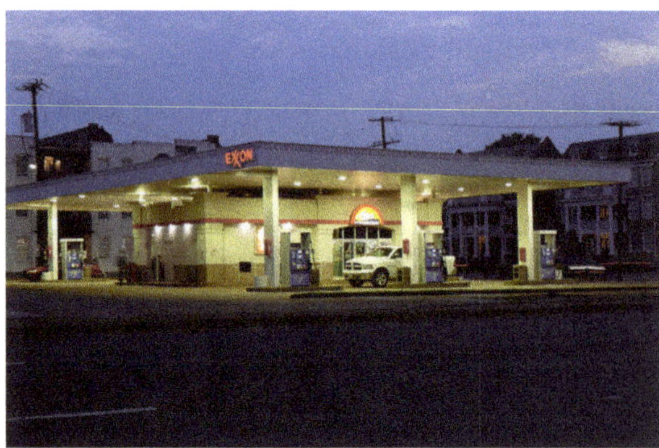

Figure 3-50. Clear Nightscape Example

It is advisable to use a tripod and to set the self-timer, so the camera will not be jiggled when you press the shutter button.

13. Cool Night Sky: This setting is similar to the previous one, except that the camera adds a bluish tone to the image, to make it look "cooler."

14. Warm Glowing Nightscape: This setting is similar to the previous two, but with this one the camera uses "warmer" reddish/yellowish tones.

15. Artistic Nightscape: This setting is also designed for night scenes, but the camera initially sets a shutter speed of 30 seconds to capture trails of cars' headlights and taillights, and similar items, to create an impressionistic view of the night scene. For good results, you should set the camera firmly on a tripod and trigger it with the self-timer or by remote control. You can change the shutter speed by turning the thumb dial or the control ring. It may take experimenting to capture an interesting mixture of lights. For Figure 3-51, I reduced the shutter speed to six seconds and used 2.66 EV of negative exposure compensation, because there were so many headlights in the view that the image would have been washed out with excessive brightness otherwise.

Figure 3-51. Artistic Nightscape Example

16. Glittering Illuminations: This setting is for capturing scenes with bright lights. The camera uses the Star Filter effect, which adds rays to the brightest areas. Here, again, it is advisable to use a tripod, though the camera is not likely to use a very long shutter speed as with the previous setting. In Figure 3-52, I used this setting to add starry rays to a shiny bowl on display under bright lighting in the art museum.

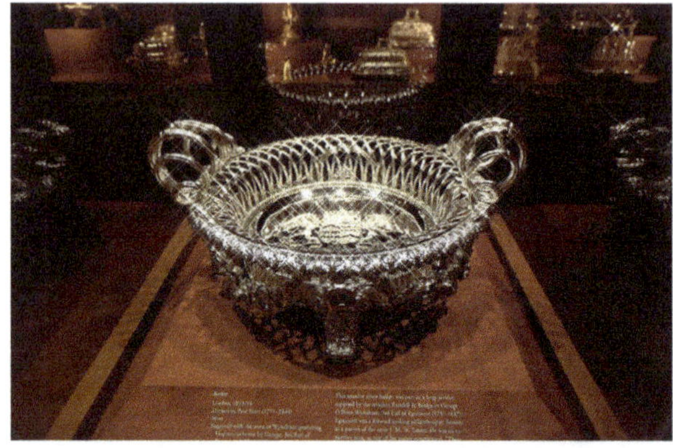

Figure 3-52. Glittering Illuminations Example

17. Handheld Night Shot: With this setting, the C-Lux uses a special process to take high-quality images in low light. The camera disables the flash and takes a rapid burst of several shots which it merges internally into a composite image. Because of this processing, the camera can use a high ISO setting, and therefore can use a fast shutter speed to minimize the blur caused by camera motion during a long exposure. Although shots with high ISO settings often have unpleasant visual noise or graininess, by combining multiple images, the camera can reduce the noise in the final result.

This setting is useful when you cannot use a tripod or flash and need to take pictures in low light. Of course, because multiple images are being taken, this setting works best for subjects that are not moving, or at least are not moving rapidly. In Figure 3-53, I used this setting for a shot of two military uniforms on display under dim lighting in a Civil War museum.

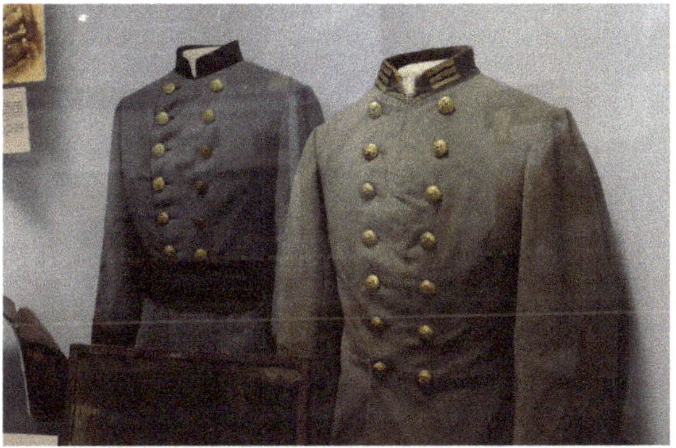

Figure 3-53. Handheld Night Shot Example

This setting is the same as the iHandheld Night Shot option, which is available only in Snapshot mode and can be selected from the special Snapshot menu, as discussed in Chapter 3.

18. Clear Night Portrait: With this setting, the camera expects you to use flash. If you pop up the flash, it will be set to Slow Sync with Red-eye Reduction. You cannot change that setting, but you can use the Flash Adjustment option under the Flash item on screen 2 of the Recording menu to make the flash output brighter or darker. If possible, the subject should be asked not to move for about a second while the image is being exposed. The purpose of the Slow Sync flash mode is to expose the main subject with the flash, but to keep the shutter open long enough to also expose the background with the ambient light.

19. Soft Image of a Flower: This setting is designed for a closeup (macro) shot of a subject such as a flower. The flash mode is initially set to Forced On, but you should avoid using the flash if the camera is very close to the subject, because the flash may overwhelm it or wash it out. It is advisable to use a tripod and the camera's self-timer. The C-Lux also applies a softening effect to the scene. In Figure 3-54, I used this setting for a picture of orchids.

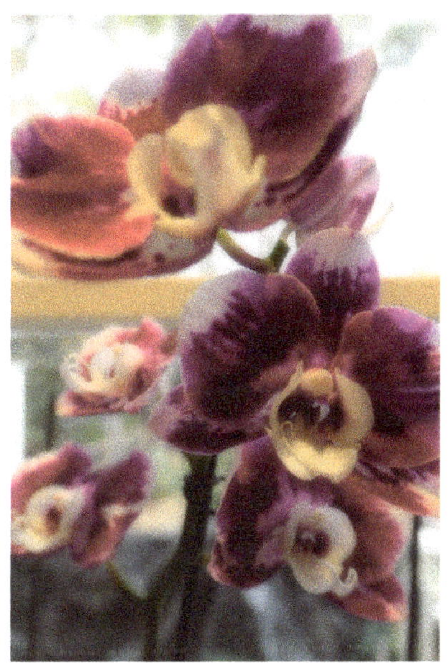

Figure 3-54. Soft Image of a Flower Example

20. Appetizing Food: This scene type is for those occasions when you're in a restaurant and are so impressed by the presentation of your meal that you want to photograph it, or for people who like to document every meal they eat. Or you could use it for taking pictures for your cookbook. In any event, the idea is to take a closeup picture without flash, though the flash will be available if you want to use it. In addition, the camera allows you to control the aperture for this setting, which usually can be done only with Aperture Priority mode and Manual exposure mode. To do that, turn either the control ring or the thumb dial to select a new aperture. You might want to do this if you want to select a wide aperture to blur the background, or a narrow aperture to achieve a broad depth of field and keep the entire scene in focus. For Figure 3-55, I used this setting to capture an image of a plate of artificial fruit.

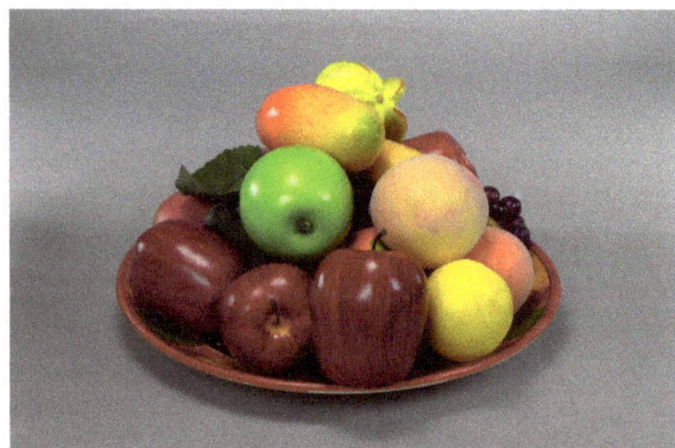
Figure 3-55. Appetizing Food Example

21. Cute Dessert: This setting is similar to the previous one, though it appears to apply somewhat more saturation and vividness to the image. However, you cannot adjust the aperture with this setting, as you can with the Appetizing Food selection.

22. Freeze Animal Motion: This setting is intended for photos of moving pets, often taken indoors. The camera uses tracking focus and turns off the AF assist lamp to avoid startling the animal, though you can turn it back on through screen 2 of the Custom menu. The camera turns on Intelligent ISO so it can use a fast shutter speed as needed. (I'll discuss ISO, or sensitivity to light, in Chapter 4. Briefly, with a higher-numbered ISO setting, the camera is more sensitive to light, and therefore can use a faster shutter speed. The tradeoff is the possibility of added "noise" or fuzziness of the image.) You can use the flash, but only with the Forced On setting. You can turn on burst shooting through the drive mode settings, as discussed in Chapter 5.

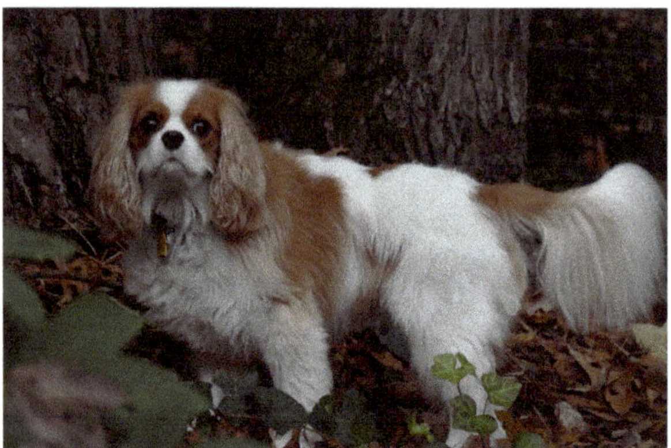
Figure 3-56. Freeze Animal Motion Example

In Figure 3-56, I used this setting to catch a shot of my family's dog enjoying a relatively quiet moment outdoors.

23. Clear Sports Shot: This style is similar to the previous one, but it is meant to stop the action of sports events in bright daylight using fast shutter speeds if necessary. The AF assist lamp is not disabled by default. For Figure 3-57, I turned an burst shooting at high speed and used this setting to capture an image of high school lacrosse players in action.

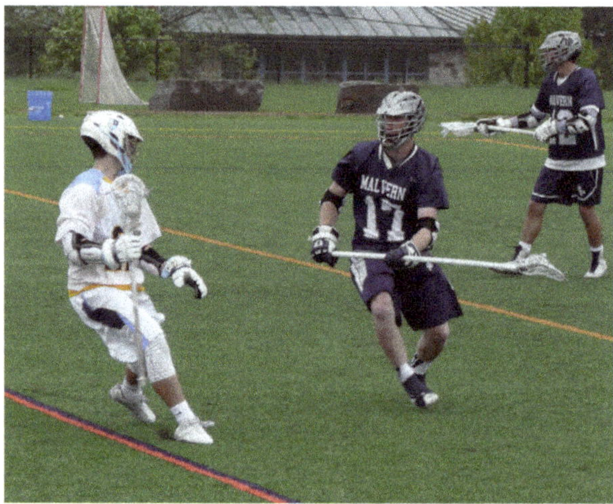

Figure 3-57. Clear Sports Shot Example

24. Monochrome: This final setting for Scene mode sets the camera to take black-and-white images. You can use any flash setting you want.

Creative Control Mode

Creative Control mode, which is similar in some ways to Scene mode, offers a range of 22 special settings for alteration of the colors and other attributes of your images. When you turn the mode dial to the artist's palette position, as shown in Figure 3-58, if the Menu Guide option on screen 6 of the Custom menu is turned on, you will immediately see a screen that lets you browse through the icons for the 22 effects. You can choose from three possible arrangements of the icons by pressing the Display button repeatedly.

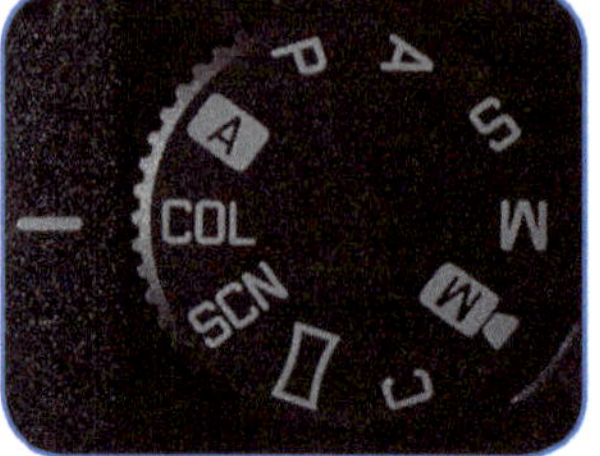

Figure 3-58. Mode Dial at Creative Control

With the Normal display, as shown in Figure 3-59, the camera displays a vertical line of icons at the right.

As you scroll up and down through that line using the Up and Down buttons or the thumb dial (or the touch screen), the camera highlights the selected icon and displays a large view at the left of the screen that applies that effect to the live view of the current scene that the camera is aimed at.

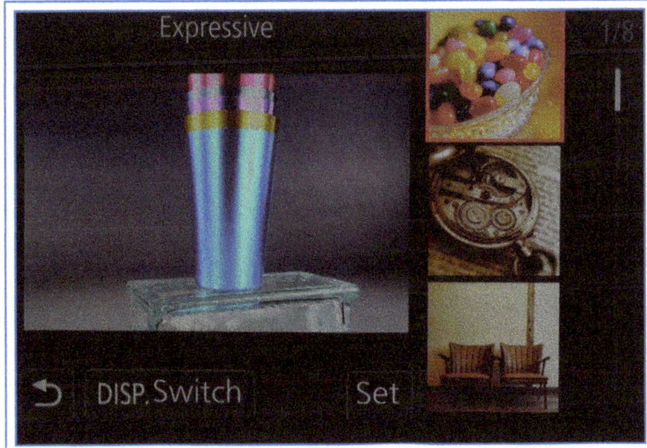

Figure 3-59. Normal Display for Creative Control Settings

With the Guide display, as shown in Figure 3-60, the setup is the same, except that, at the left of the screen, instead of displaying the appearance of the effect, the camera displays a brief description of the effect.

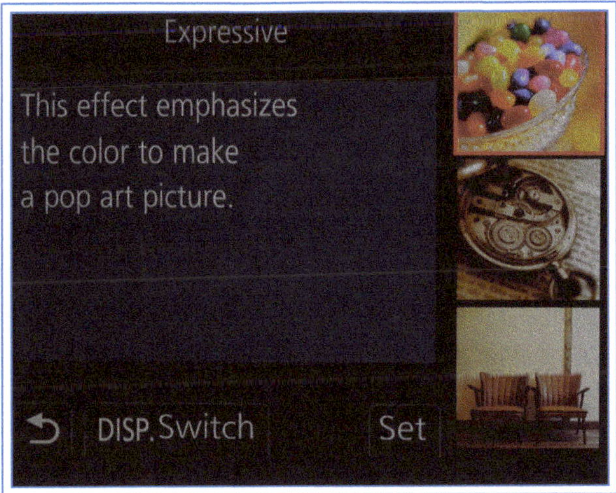

Figure 3-60. Guide Display for Creative Control Settings

With the List display, as shown in Figure 3-61, the camera displays more icons on each screen, in rows and columns. As you scroll through them, the camera displays the name of the effect at the top of the display.

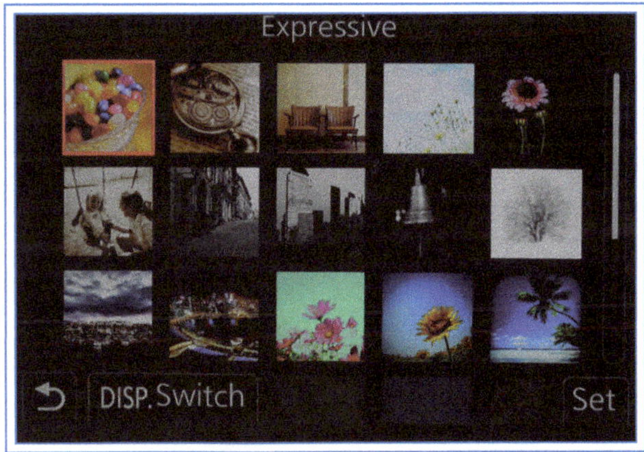

Figure 3-61. List Display for Creative Control Settings

If the Menu Guide option is not turned on, you can use the Filter Effect menu item, which appears on the special Creative Control menu, whose icon appears at the top of the line of menu icons at the left of the screen.

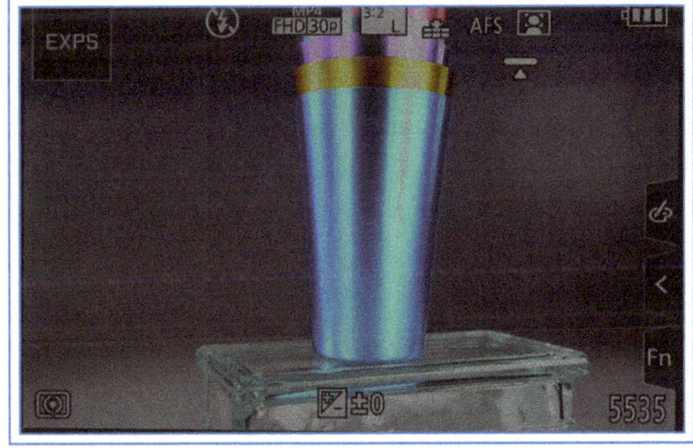

Figure 3-62. Shooting Screen with Expressive Effect Selected

When you have scrolled through the Creative Control effect icons and highlighted the one you want to use, press the Menu/Set button (or touch the Set icon on the screen) to select it and return to the recording screen. The camera's display will show the name of the effect briefly at the left, and the appearance of the scene on the display will reflect the chosen effect, as shown in Figure 3-62, where the Expressive effect is selected.

You also can select a Creative Control effect quickly by just turning the control ring or the thumb dial when the shooting screen is displayed. When you do that, the camera displays a scrolling list of effects at the bottom of the screen as shown in Figure 3-63; press the Menu/Set button to select one when it is underlined in red. (If that function does not work, make sure the control ring and thumb dial are set to their default functions through the Ring/Dial Set option on screen 3 of the Custom menu.)

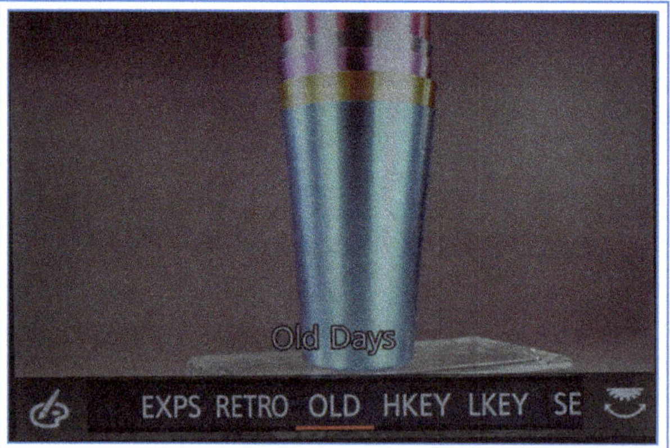

Figure 3-63. Scrolling List of Creative Control Settings

You also can change the current effect by touching the effect icon in the upper left corner of the screen, which calls up the standard menu screen for selecting an effect.

The Creative Control choices provide different "looks" for your images, in some cases producing striking alterations of the normal color, texture, and brightness. It's important to note that, because the Creative Control setting occupies its own slot on the mode dial, whatever setting you make for Creative Control is only in effect when the mode dial is set to that position. So, for example, if you switch the mode dial to Program or Aperture Priority mode, the Creative Control setting will no longer be in effect. If you later switch the dial back to Creative Control, though, whatever setting you previously made in that mode will once more take effect.

When you record a motion picture with the C-Lux, you don't need to move the mode dial; you only need to press the red video button on top of the camera. So, when you record a movie, you need to be sure the mode dial is set where you want it. For example, if you have just taken some still photos using an exotic setting from the Creative Control selections, that setting will still be in effect if you press the red button to record a movie. If you want a more ordinary look for your movie, be sure to set the mode dial back to Snapshot, Program, Creative Video, or some other standard mode, to avoid having the movie recorded using the Creative Control setting. On the other hand, being able to use Creative Control settings when shooting a movie can be an advantage when you want to add an atmospheric look to your motion pictures. I'll discuss movie settings in Chapter 8.

Another way to protect yourself against unwanted special effects in images or videos is to use the Simultaneous Record without Filter setting. That option is found on the special menu that appears at the top of the line of menu icons at the left of the menu screen, when the mode dial is set to the Creative Control position. As you can see in Figure 3-64, that menu has only two entries: Filter Effect and Simultaneous Record without Filter. As discussed earlier, if you select the Filter Effect option, the camera displays the list of Creative Control settings for you to select from.

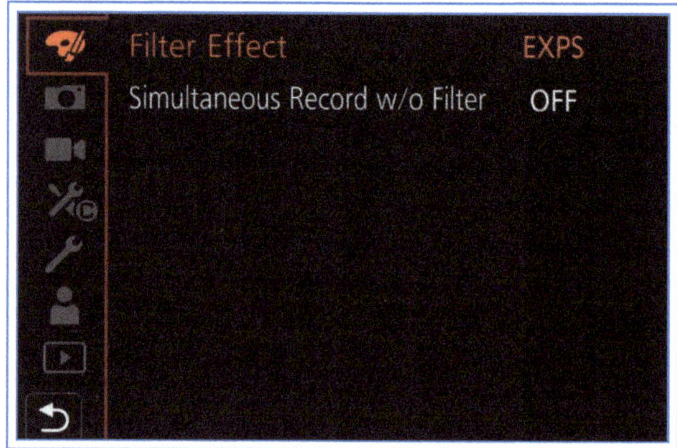

Figure 3-64. Special Menu for Creative Control Mode

The other option on the special Creative Control menu, Simultaneous Record without Filter, can be turned either off or on. If it is turned off, then, when you take an image in Creative Control mode, the camera records only the image with the selected setting. If this option is turned on, the camera records the image with the selected setting and also records an image without the special setting. In that way, if you later decide you want a normal-looking shot that is not distorted or altered by the filter setting, you will have it available. (This option is also available in some other shooting modes on screen 1 of the Recording menu, as a sub-option under the Filter Settings item.)

Once you have selected a Creative Control setting, you can still make some additional settings from the Recording menu and with the camera's physical controls. For example, you can use options such as Aspect Ratio, Picture Size, AF Mode, and Metering Mode. However, several other settings are unavailable with the Creative Control shooting mode, including white balance, ISO, Intelligent Dynamic, and Photo Style. With some of the Creative Control options you can use burst shooting or flash; I will indicate those cases as I discuss the settings individually below.

You also can use Raw for the Quality setting with the Creative Control settings. However, as with the Filter Settings menu option, discussed in Chapter 4, there is a pitfall with that capability. If you set Quality to Raw, the Creative Control effect likely will not show up in the image that opens in your Raw-processing software, such as Adobe Camera Raw. The effect may appear when you view the image in the camera or view a thumbnail in your software, but it will not be included in the image when it is opened on a computer. Instead, you should use Raw & Fine or Raw & Standard. In that way, you will have an image that includes the special effect you selected, as well as a Raw image for flexibility in processing. However, I have found one software package that can preserve the effects of Creative Control and Filter Settings effects. That program is Irfanview, a versatile, free program available from irfanview.com. That program is able to extract the 1920 x 1280-pixel preview JPEG file that is embedded in the Raw file. The extracted JPEG file includes the effects of special settings such as those of Creative Control mode.

In addition to the settings from the Recording menu and physical controls discussed above, with the Creative Control mode you can make several other adjustments, depending on which Creative Control setting is in effect. These adjustments can be made in two ways. First, you can press the Right button, which will take you to the adjustment screen for the effect that is currently selected. For example, when the Expressive effect is active, pressing the Right button takes you to the screen shown in Figure 3-65, with a sliding scale at the bottom.

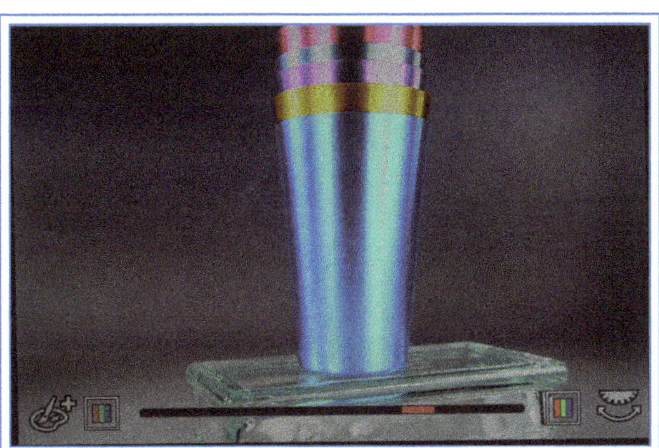

Figure 3-65. Adjustment Screen for Expressive Setting

Using the thumb dial, the Left and Right buttons, or the touch screen, you can adjust the slider along that scale to make the vividness of the effect greater or smaller. With other effects you can adjust other values, such as coloring, contrast, or graininess.

In this recording mode, you can also use exposure compensation, exposure bracketing, and defocus control in the same way as with Snapshot Plus mode. For exposure compensation, press the Up button, and then use the on-screen scale or dial to make the adjustment using the thumb dial, the Left and Right buttons, or the touch screen. From that screen, use the Up and Down buttons to set exposure bracketing, or press the Fn1 button to bring up the screen for adjusting the aperture to defocus the background.

You also can adjust all of the Creative Control mode settings using the touch screen icons. To do that, touch the small icon that looks like a painter's palette at the right edge of the screen. You will then see a vertical line of three icons at the right edge of the screen, as shown in Figure 3-66.

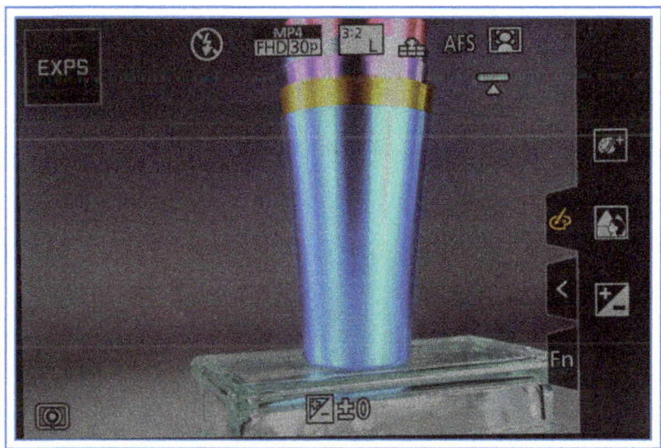

Figure 3-66. Touch Screen Icons for Creative Control Mode

Press the top icon to bring up the adjustment scale for the Creative Control effect. Press the middle icon to bring up the defocus control screen. Press the bottom icon to call up the exposure compensation screen, from which you can also adjust exposure bracketing or press Fn1 for defocus control. Press the yellow artist's palette icon to dismiss the adjustment icons.

As I discuss each Creative Control setting, I will mention what items can be controlled, if those adjustments are different from the standard ones (exposure compensation, exposure bracketing, background defocus, and intensity of the selected effect).

Following are details about each of the 22 Creative Control choices. Along with descriptions I will include a sample photograph taken using the setting being discussed, to give an idea of how the Creative Control settings affect images.

Expressive. I would call this mode something like "super-vivid"; some people call it "pop art." If you like colors with strong saturation, this style is useful. However, the Vivid setting of the Photo Style menu option can produce a similar result. The Photo Style setting is available in more advanced shooting modes such as Program, Aperture Priority, and the like, so you can use more menu and other settings in conjunction with that setting than you can with the more limiting Creative Control Expressive setting. Figure 3-67 provides an illustration, with an image that adds definition and color to a shot of an outdoor garden.

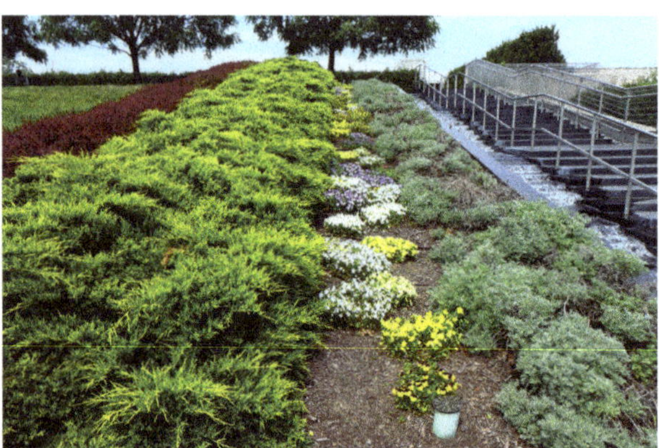

Figure 3-67. Expressive Example

Retro. This style appears to me to be the opposite of Expressive; it paints the scene with subdued, somewhat yellowish tones, de-emphasizing the glaring qualities of Expressive. It evokes a gentle feeling of past times. For this effect, adjusting the setting to the left on the scale increases yellowish tones, and adjusting it to the right increases reddish tones. In Figure 3-68, I used the Retro setting for a shot of a an antique lamp on display in the art museum.

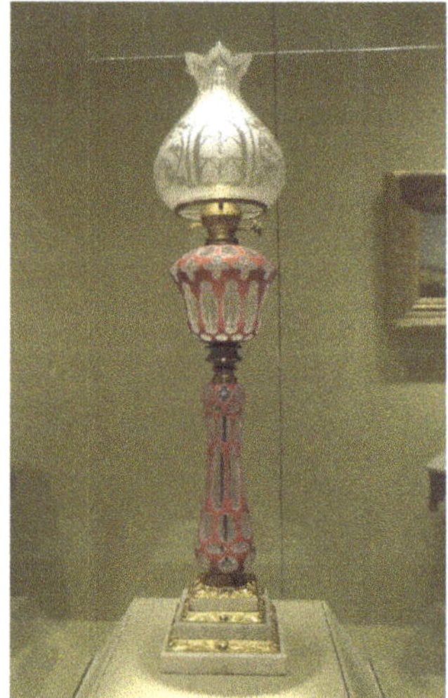

Figure 3-68. Retro Example

Old Days. This effect is intended to give a "nostalgic" look by lowering the saturation of colors and reducing contrast for an old-fashioned look. With the adjustment slider, you can vary the contrast. In Figure 3-69, I used this setting to give an aged appearance to an antique chest of drawers in the art museum.

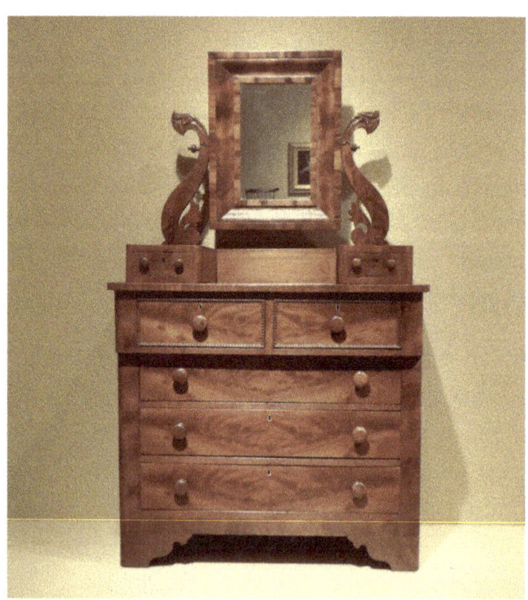

Figure 3-69. Old Days Example

High Key. "High key" is a technique that uses high-intensity lighting throughout the scene, striving for a bright look with light colors and few shadows. This technique often is used in advertising photography. With the C-Lux, this single setting cannot necessarily remake your image to look like a traditional high key shot, but the camera does boost the exposure to produce a brighter-than-normal image. Moving the slider for the effect to the left produces more pinkish tones, while setting it to the right yields bluer hues. I have found this setting useful on occasion when a scene needs general brightening Figure 3-70 provides an example, brightening an ancient statue on display in the art museum, in a setting with dim lighting.

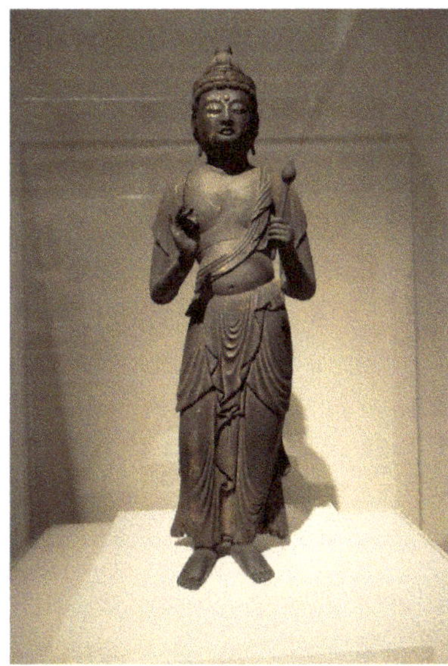

Figure 3-70. High Key Example

Low Key. "Low key" lighting, of course, is the opposite of "high key." With this approach, the photographer welcomes shadows and dark areas in the photograph. Here again, the C-Lux cannot produce a true "low key" image all by itself; what it can do is reduce the exposure and otherwise process the photograph to look more dark and shadowy than normal. Here again, as with the High Key setting, the effect's adjustment slider can be moved to the left for a redder look, or to the right for a bluer appearance. In Figure 3-71, I used this setting to lower the brightness of a shot of an outdoor fountain at the art museum on a sunny day.

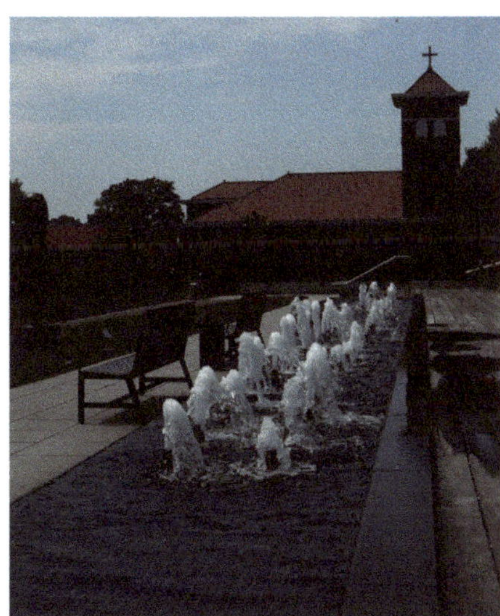

Figure 3-71. Low Key Example

Sepia. With the Sepia setting, the C-Lux produces a monochrome image with a sepia (brownish) tone and softens the contrast somewhat to give the look of an antique photograph. In this case, adjusting the setting of the adjustment slider decreases the overall contrast of the image, while moving it to the right increases the contrast, producing a somewhat harsher, darker appearance. For Figure 3-72, I used this setting for a shot of a piece of furniture in a historic house, to emphasize its antique appearance.

Monochrome. This setting gives you another way, other than the Photo Style menu option and the Scene mode option, to capture an image in traditional black and white. The adjustment slider lets you add a color tone, ranging from yellowish to bluish. For Figure 3-73, I used this setting for a shot of the main building of the art museum.

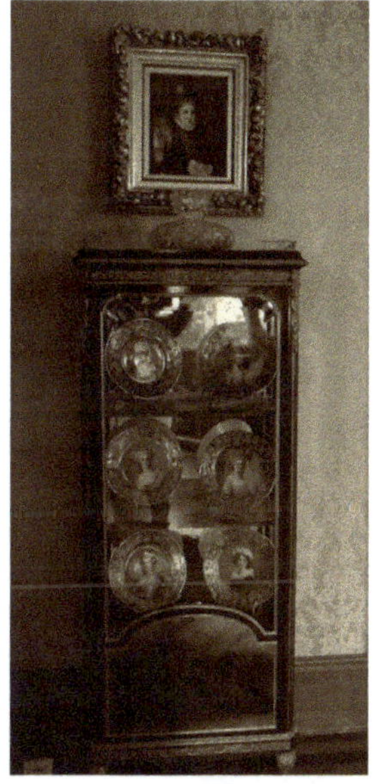

Figure 3-72. Sepia Example

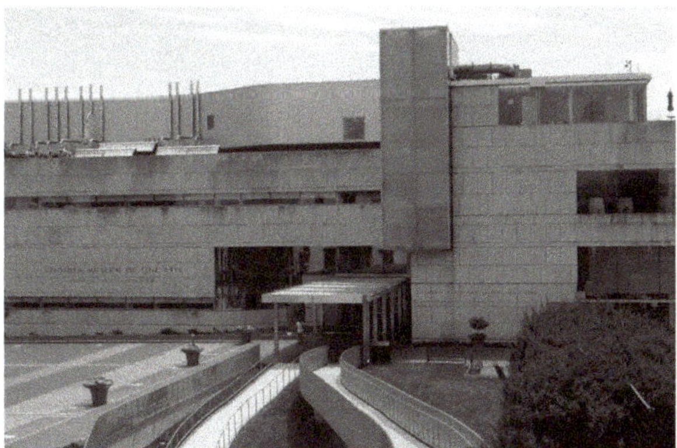

Figure 3-73. Monochrome Example

Dynamic Monochrome. This setting, illustrated in Figure 3-74, converts the image to black and white, but with heightened contrast to produce a more dramatic effect. As with Sepia, you can use the left or right adjustments to decrease or increase contrast. For Figure 3-74, I used this setting to add definition to a photo of an older house.

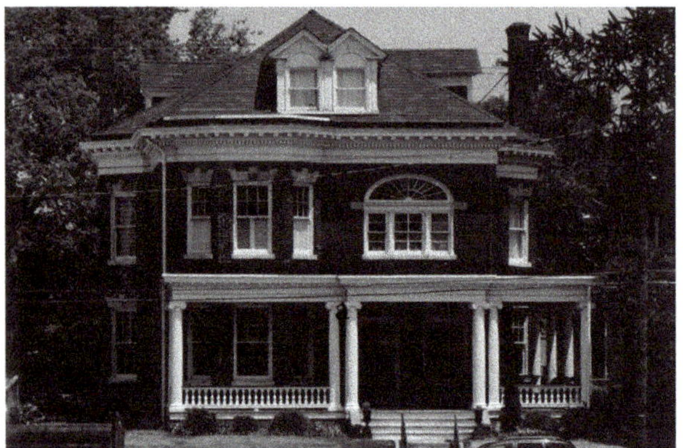

Figure 3-74. Dynamic Monochrome Example

Rough Monochrome. With this setting, the camera also records a monochrome image, but with the appearance altered to add grain by inducing visual noise, like the noise that results from using a high ISO setting. This option can be good for street photography or other situations when you want the somewhat rough look of a grainy image. The adjustment slider lets you reduce or increase the amount of graininess. You can use exposure compensation and defocus control, but not exposure bracketing. For Figure 3-75, I used this setting for a shot of the railroad bridge at the river.

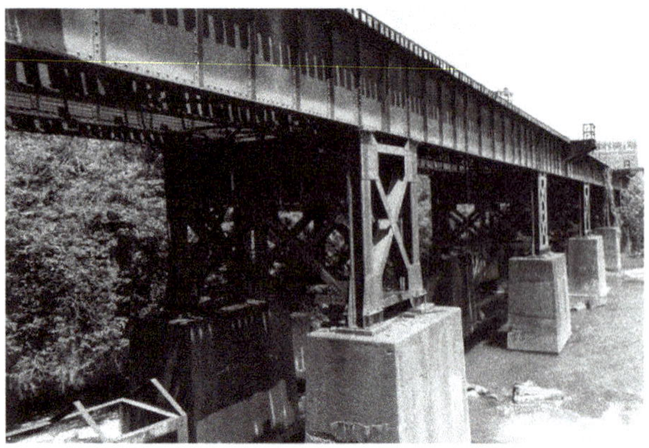

Figure 3-75. Rough Monochrome Example

Silky Monochrome. This option gives you another way to take a monochrome image. In this case, the camera puts the image slightly out of focus to add a soft or dreamlike look. With the adjustment slider, you can alter the amount of defocusing that is used. The left side of the scale provides a sharper, less defocused image. You can use exposure compensation and defocus control, but not exposure bracketing. For Figure 3-76, I used this setting for a photo of an outdoor sculpture and waterfall at the art museum.

Impressive Art. This setting has some similarities to the Expressive, Dynamic Monochrome, and High Dynamic settings. It produces images with high contrast and dramatic variations in color intensity. Using the adjustment slider, you can alter the intensity all the way to the left to produce a monochrome image, or all the way to the right to produce an oversaturated image with exploding, vibrant colors. You can achieve some fairly dramatic effects with this setting, as seen in Figure 3-77, which shows a view of the railroad bridge at the river.

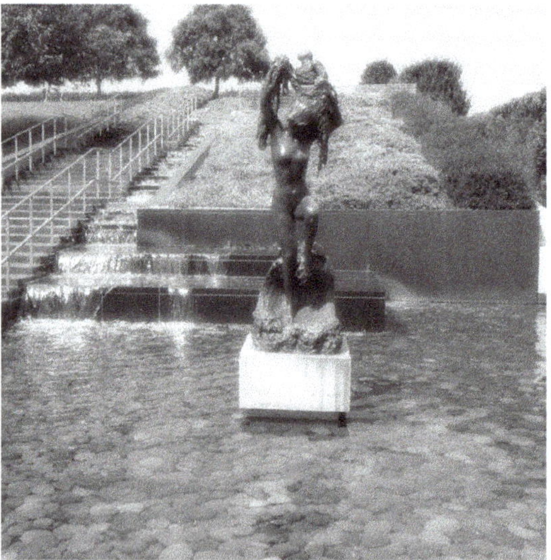

Figure 3-76. Silky Monochrome Example

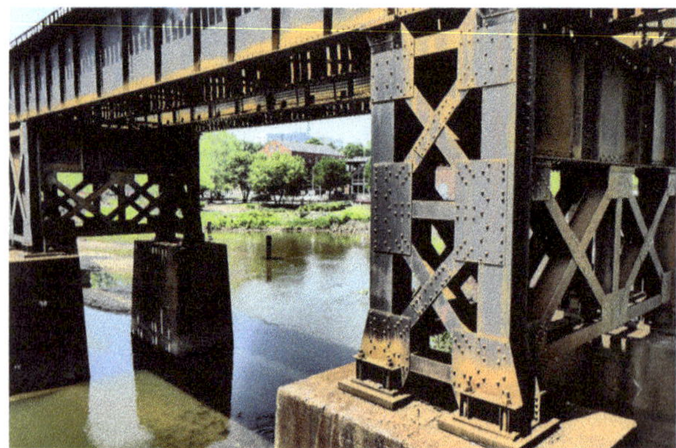

Figure 3-77. Impressive Art Example

High Dynamic. This setting is oriented less to altering the colors of the image than to leveling out the shadows and highlights. As you can see from the name, it is akin to the "high dynamic range" or HDR processing that is often done with software, and sometimes, as here, through in-camera processing. For Figure 3-78, I used this setting for a shot of a sheltered walkway at a public park, with some areas in shade and some in sunlight.

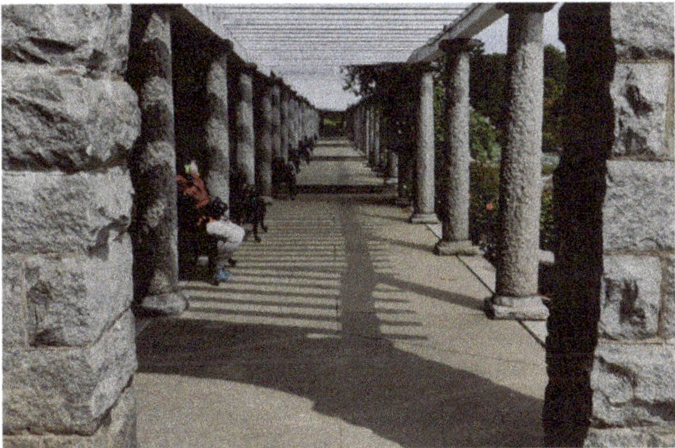

Figure 3-78. High Dynamic Example

The High Dynamic setting is useful when you're taking a picture that includes areas of both bright light and shadows. Ordinarily, a camera cannot process that sort of image and preserve the details in both areas. This setting alters the processing so more details are visible in the dark areas, and the bright areas are not so washed out and overexposed. As with the Impressive Art setting, above, the adjustment slider lets you adjust the image from monochrome at the left to oversaturated color at the right.

Cross Process. This setting gives you the ability to add a distinctive color tint to your images, in green, blue, yellow, or red. In this case, you use the adjustment screen to select one of those colors, as shown in Figure 3-79.

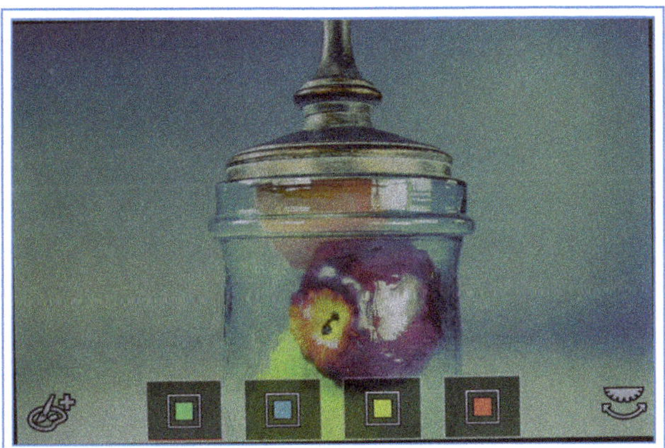

Figure 3-79. Cross Process Color Selection Screen

Once that selection has been made, your images will be tinted with the selected color. Figure 3-80 is an example of using this setting for shots of the glass jar shown in Figure 3-79. This composite image shows all four settings. Clockwise from upper left, the settings are green, blue, yellow, and red.

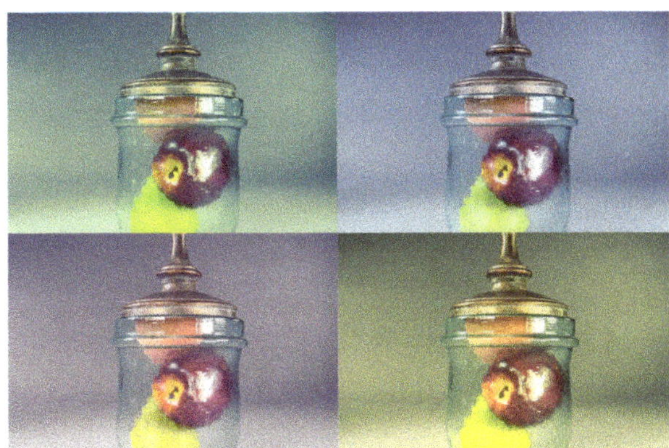

Figure 3-80. Cross Process Composite Image

Toy Effect. As with some of the other Creative Control selections, this one is not strictly an example of color processing. Rather, this setting tries to reproduce the effects that are achieved with a primitive "toy" camera. There has been a popular movement for this sort of photography in recent years, using cameras like the Holga and Diana, which are purposely constructed to lack sharpness and to suffer from vignetting at the corners. The photographs from such cameras can be quite appealing in their own way, and the Toy Effect setting lets you experiment with a good simulation of this sort of image.

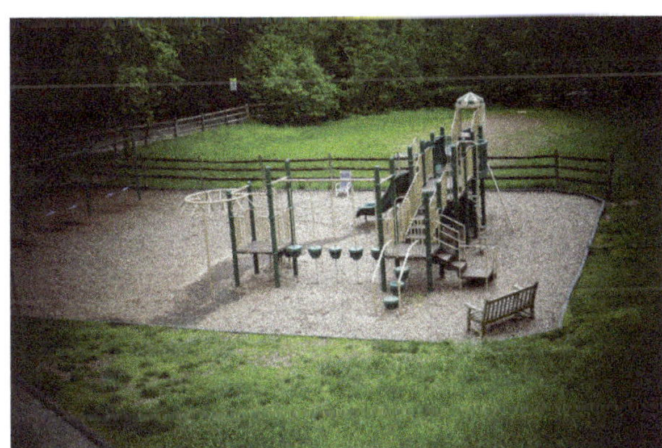

Figure 3-81. Toy Effect Example

This option can be used to highlight a single subject in the middle of the frame, as shown in Figure 3-81, which shows a play area in a botanical garden. With this setting, the adjustment screen can be used to produce more reddish or orange tones if adjusted to the left, and more bluish ones if adjusted to the right.

Toy Pop. With this setting, the camera combines the vivid, bright appearance of the Expressive setting with the vignetting of Toy Effect, discussed above. In this case, the adjustment slider controls the amount of vignetting. At the left of the scale, the vignetting is reduced so more of the image is bright; at the right, the vignetting increases to darken more of the corners. For Figure 3-82, I found that this setting was a good one to place a vignette around a small work of art displayed indoors in a spotlight at the art museum.

Bleach Bypass. This option causes images to have increased contrast and lowered color saturation, to produce a bleached, washed-out appearance. You can reduce the contrast by moving the adjustment slider to the left or increase it by moving the slider to the right. For Figure 3-83, I used this setting for a scene of a wooden bridge surrounded by arches at a botanical garden.

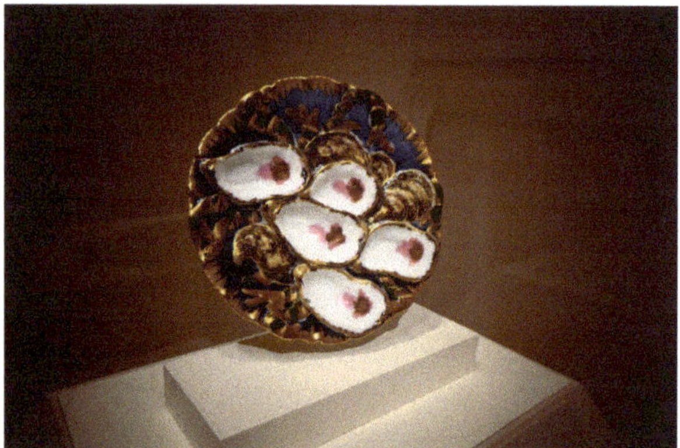

Figure 3-82. Toy Pop Example

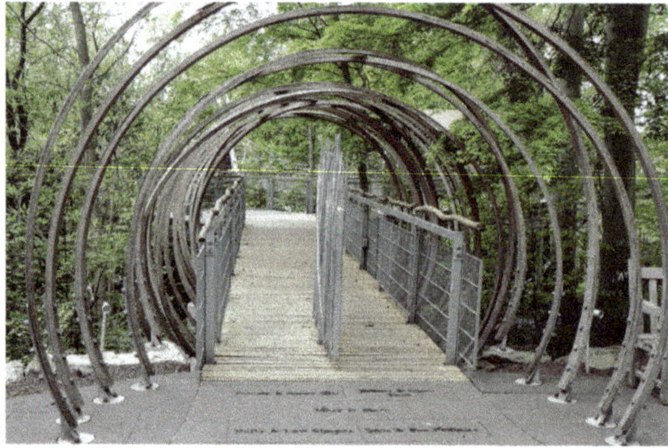

Figure 3-83. Bleach Bypass Example

Miniature. The next Creative Control setting is called the Miniature effect. When you apply this option to an image, the camera adds blurring at one or more sides of an image or at the image's top or bottom, to simulate the appearance of a photograph of a tabletop model or miniature. Such images often appear blurred in one area, either because of the narrow depth of field of these close-up photos, or because of the use of a tilt-and-shift lens, which causes blurring at the edges.

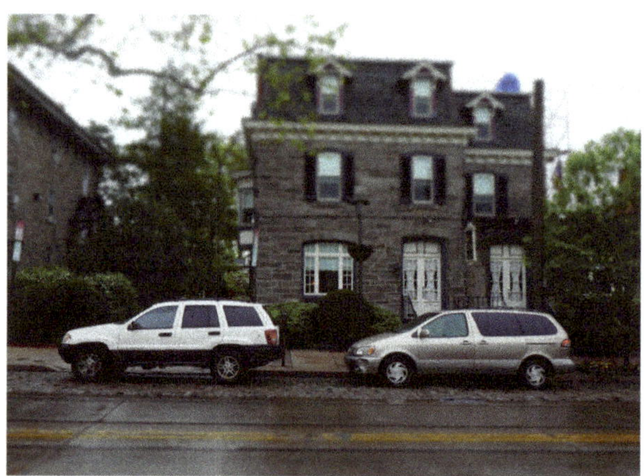

Figure 3-84. Miniature Effect Example

For this feature to work well, you need to choose an appropriate subject. I have found that the effect looks interesting when applied to something like a street scene or a house, which might actually be reproduced in a tabletop model. For example, if you are able to get a vantage point above a road intersection or across from a parking area on a street, as in Figure 3-84, you may be able to use this effect to make it look as if you had photographed a high-quality mock-up of an area with model cars and buildings.

With this setting, three icons appear at the right side of the screen when you touch the artist's-palette icon at the right side of the screen. The bottom icon adjusts brightness and the middle one adjusts the intensity of the colors. In order to adjust the settings for the miniature effect itself, you use the top icon, which looks like a rectangle with arrows pointing up and down.

When the Miniature setting has been selected, touch the artist's palette icon then touch the top (rectangle) icon, and a long red frame will appear on the screen, as shown in Figure 3-85.

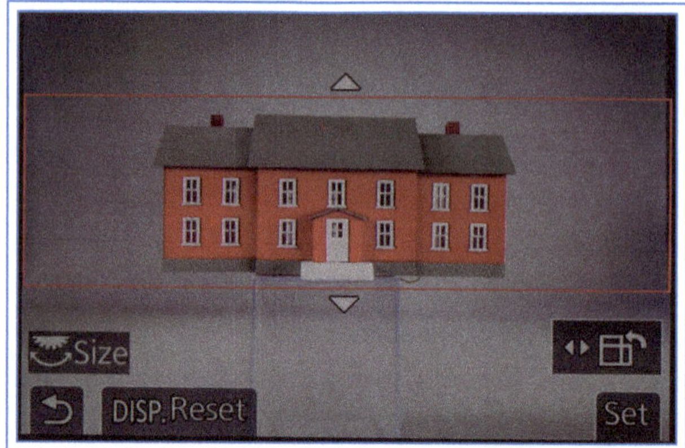

Figure 3-85. Red Frame for Miniature Effect

This frame represents the area of the image that will remain in sharp focus. The areas outside of that frame will be defocused and fuzzy, contributing to the overall effect. So, for example, if you are shooting from an overpass down toward a highway intersection, you may want to line up the red frame over the road that you want to remain in focus, leaving the areas outside the frame to be out of focus.

To move the red frame, use the four cursor buttons. When you see triangles on the frame, press the buttons corresponding to those triangles to move the frame in the direction of the triangle. Use the other two cursor buttons to flip the frame to a different orientation (horizontal or vertical). Then, turn the thumb dial to change the size of the frame. When you have the frame oriented and sized as you want it, press the Menu/Set button to return to the shooting screen and take your picture. You also can use your fingers on the touch screen to move the rectangle, to pinch it to make it larger or smaller, or to change its orientation between horizontal and vertical.

You can press the Right button to get to the adjustment slider, which adjusts color saturation. With this setting, you cannot use burst shooting or the flash, although you can use Raw image quality. You can use exposure compensation, but not bracketing or defocus control. You can use the Miniature setting when shooting movies. If you do so, no audio is recorded, and the action is speeded up to about ten times normal speed, which helps reinforce the illusion that you are filming a model scene rather than a life-sized one.

Soft Focus. With this setting, the camera defocuses the overall image to achieve a soft, hazy look, as seen in Figure 3-86. You can still use the icons at the right of the screen to control brightness, background defocus, and the overall intensity of the general defocusing effect. You cannot use burst shooting or bracketing or record movies with this setting in effect.

Fantasy. With this option, the camera alters the intensity of colors and adds a bluish color cast to the scene, resulting in a hazy, fantasy-like appearance. With the adjustment slider, you can vary the intensity of the colors. For Figure 3-87, I felt that this setting was appropriate for a shot of an historic mansion in a pubic park, to give it an aura of unreality.

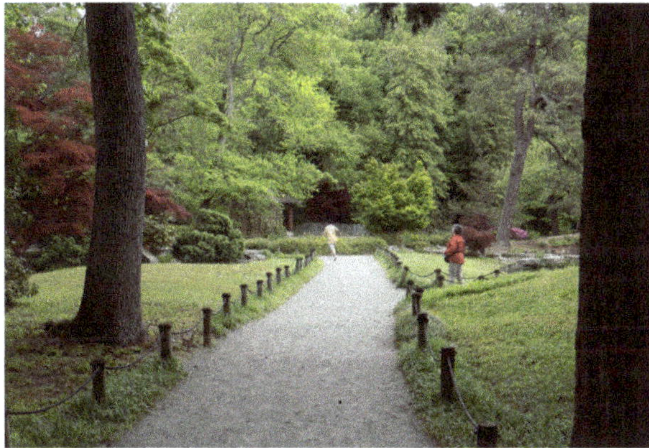

Figure 3-86. Soft Focus Example

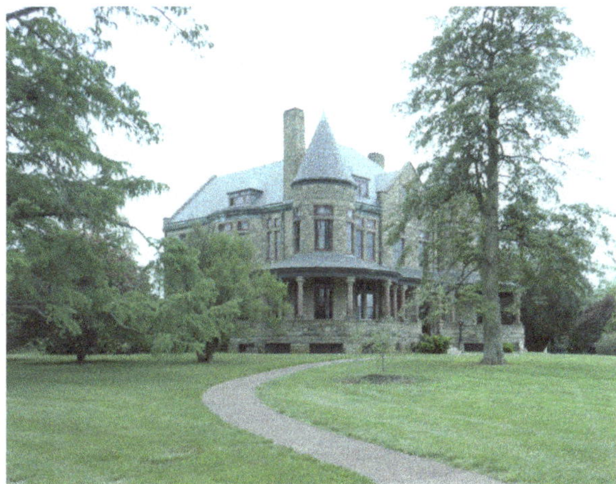

Figure 3-87. Fantasy Example

Star Filter. This setting lets you add cross-shaped "stars" of light to your images at bright points in the scene, giving a sparkling effect. This effect can be pleasing with a subject that lends itself to this look, like the silver figure photographed in the art museum in Figure 3-88.

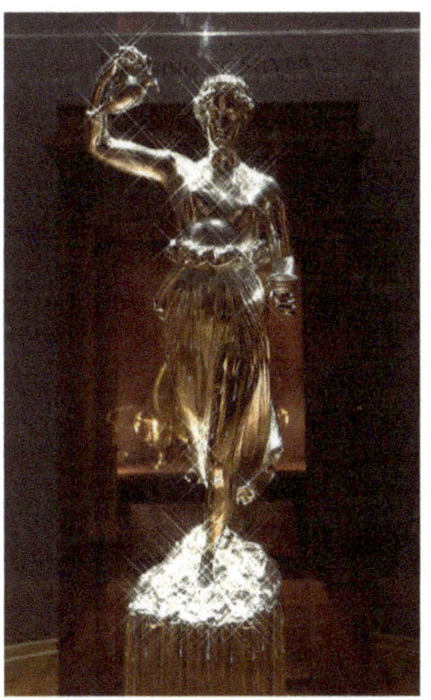

Figure 3-88. Star Filter Example

You can use exposure compensation and defocus control, but not bracketing. When you press the Right button, the camera displays three adjustment sliders, selected with the Up and Down buttons or the touch screen. The top slider controls the size of the rays of light; adjust to the left for shorter rays, and to the right for longer ones. The second one controls the number of rays, with more rays produced as you move the slider to the right. The bottom slider adjusts the angle of the rays; they rotate to the right as you adjust the slider to the right, and vice-versa. You cannot use this effect with burst shooting or when recording movies.

One Point Color. This is a setting that I enjoy quite a bit. It lets you select any one color in a scene for the camera to retain, while turning the rest of the image black and white. You can achieve a dramatic effect with this setting, by placing a clear emphasis on a small part of the scene that is in color.

To select the color that is retained, press the icon for the artist's palette at the right edge of the screen to bring up a line of four icons, as shown in Figure 3-89. Touch the top icon, which looks like an eyedropper, and a movable frame with arrows will appear in the center of the screen, as shown in Figure 3-90. Using the four direction buttons or your finger on the touch screen, place that square over the object whose color you want to retain and press the Menu/Set button (or touch the Set icon) to confirm the selection.

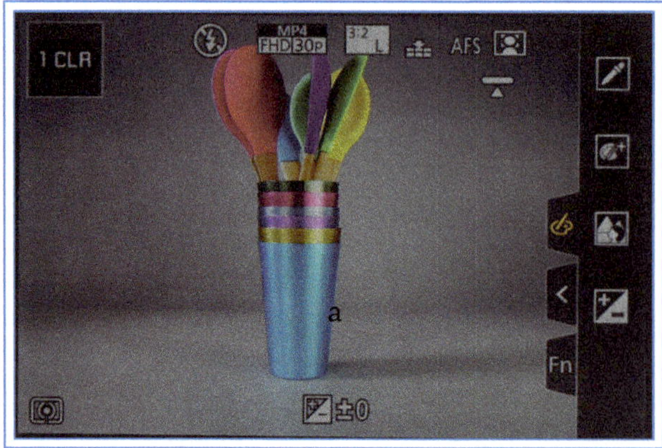

Figure 3-89. Touch Screen Icons for One Point Color Setting

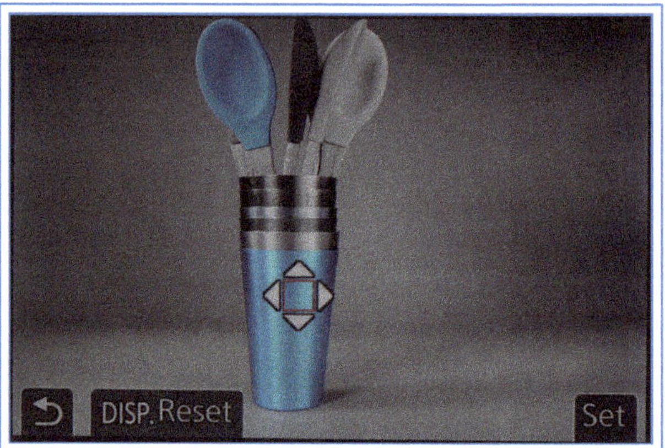

Figure 3-90. Frame to Select the Color to Be Retained

The setting's adjustment icon (which looks like a palette with a plus sign) is used to determine how closely an item must match the selected color in order to show up in color. Move the slider to the left to restrict the color selection to the minimum, and to the right to include a broader range of similar colors.

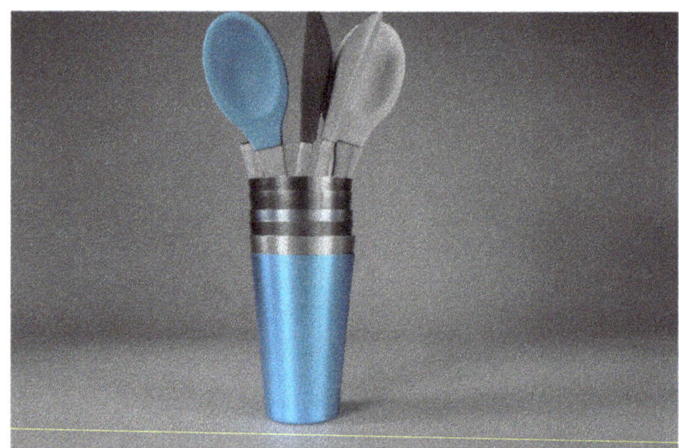

Figure 3-91. One Point Color Example

Then, as shown in Figures 3-90 and 3-91, only objects matching that color will appear in color on the shooting screen and in the final image after you take the picture. You can use burst shooting and record movies with this setting. You also can use exposure compensation and bracketing, and you can use defocus control.

Sunshine. Finally, the Sunshine option lets you add a solar flare effect to an image. After you select this option, press the artist's palette icon at the right edge of the screen, then touch the top adjustment icon, which looks like the sun, and you will see a red circle on the display. You can move that circle around the screen using the four direction buttons or your finger on the touch screen and resize it using the thumb dial or by pinching and pulling with your fingers on the screen.

When you have the solar flare sized and located as you want, press Menu/Set (or the Set icon) to lock it in. Then, press the Right button or touch the second adjustment icon (under the sun icon) and you can select yellow, red, blue, or white for the color of the flare. Press Menu/Set, and the effect will be locked in with your selections. You can move the flare outside the edges of the image to avoid having the large, bright ball in the scene.

For Figure 3-92, I used this option to add a solar flare to a King Tut bust.

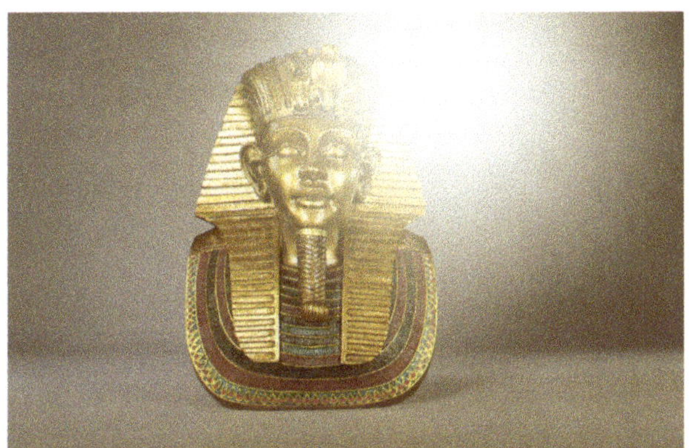

Figure 3-92. Sunshine Example

Custom Mode: C Position on Mode Dial

Finally, I will briefly discuss the C position on the mode dial, seen in Figure 3-93.

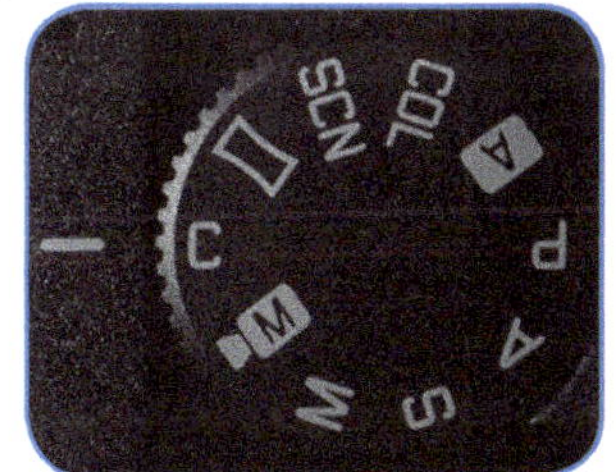

Figure 3-93. Mode Dial at Custom

(I will discuss the Creative Video mode in Chapter 8.) The C position does not represent an independent shooting mode. Instead, it is used in conjunction with the powerful Custom Set Memory menu item, which I will discuss in Chapter 7. Essentially, you can use this slot on the mode dial to recall three sets of custom values for your important menu settings and some other settings. Once you have stored the settings, just turn the mode dial to the C position to recall one of your three saved groups of settings—C1, C2, or C3. See Chapter 7 for further details.

Chapter 4: The Recording Menu and the Quick Menu

Much of the power of the C-Lux lies in the options provided in the Recording menu, which gives you control over the appearance of images and how they are captured. This menu is not the only source of creative tools for this camera; there are several important settings that can be controlled with physical buttons and dials, as I will discuss in Chapter 5, and there also is the convenient Quick Menu, which gives you ready access to several often-used options. I will discuss both the Recording menu and the Quick Menu in this chapter.

The Recording Menu

As I have discussed earlier, the main menu system of the C-Lux incudes six major menus: Recording, Motion Picture, Custom, Setup, My Menu, and Playback. I will discuss the Playback menu in Chapter 6, the Custom, Setup, and My Menu menus in Chapter 7, and the Motion Picture menu in Chapter 8. In addition, the camera includes several menus whose icons appear at the top of the line of menu icons only when the camera is set to a particular shooting mode. Those menu systems appear for the Snapshot, Creative Control, Scene, Panorama, Custom, and Creative Video modes. I discuss those systems along with each of those modes, in Chapter 3 for the still-shooting modes and Chapter 8 for Creative Video mode.

When you press the Menu/Set button, you will initially see the main menu screen, which will look generally like the screen shown in Figure 4-1 in one of the advanced shooting modes, such as Program. The actual screen that is displayed depends on the current shooting mode. In Figure 4-1, screen 3 of the Setup menu is active, with the camera set to Program mode.

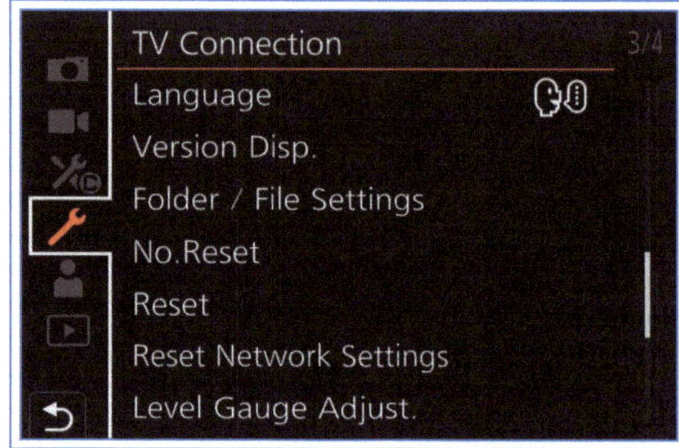

Figure 4-1. Screen 3 of Setup Menu

If, as in this example, the Recording menu screen is not displayed, press the Left button. That action will move the highlight into the left column of the menu screen, as shown in Figure 4-2, where you can navigate up and down with the direction buttons (or the touch screen) to highlight the icons for the various menu systems.

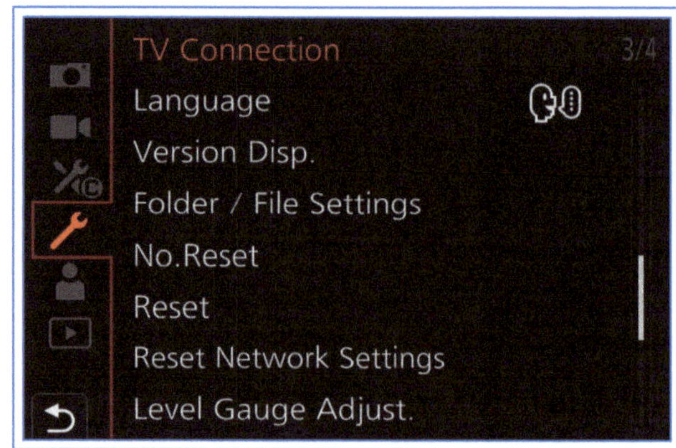

Figure 4-2. Highlight in Column with Menu Icons

If the camera is currently displaying a screen from the Custom menu, as shown in Figure 4-3, the column of icons for the main systems is not shown at the left of the screen. Instead, there is a column of icons for the five subdivisions of the Custom menu: Exposure, Focus/Release Shutter, Operation, Monitor/Display, and Lens/Others. In that case, you have to press the Left button once to get to that column of subdivisions, and then once more to reach the line of icons for the main menu systems.

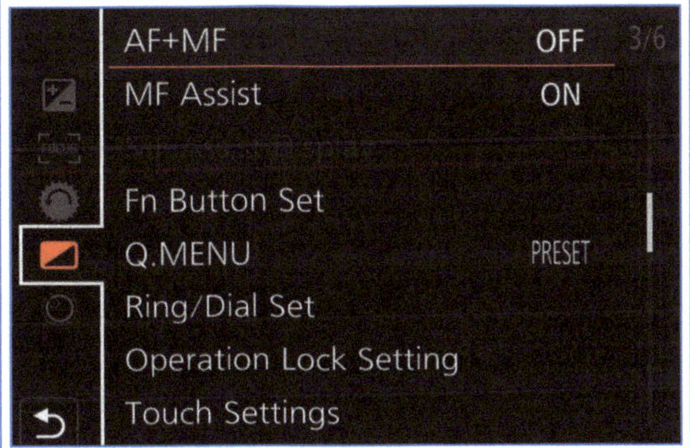

Figure 4-3. Screen 3 of Custom Menu

Once the highlight is in the column with the icons for the main menu systems, use the Up and Down buttons to highlight the red camera icon at the top of the line of icons, indicating the Recording menu, as shown in Figure 4-4. (I'm assuming the camera is in an advanced shooting mode such as Program; in other modes, such as Snapshot, Scene and Creative Control, a special icon for that menu system will be the top icon, just above the camera icon for the Recording menu.)

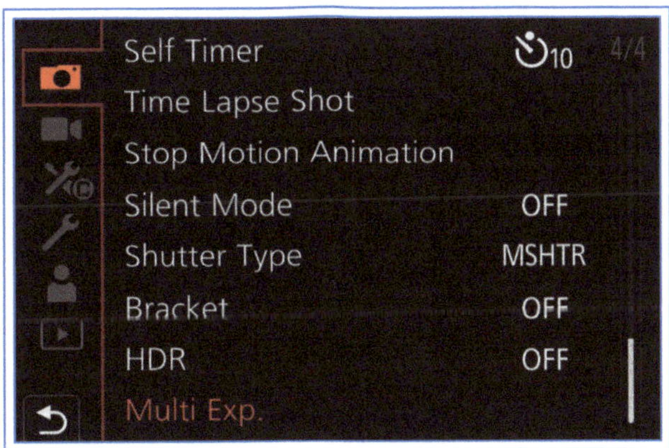

Figure 4-4. Camera Icon for Recording Menu Highlighted

Then press the Right button to move back over to the main part of the screen, with the Recording menu items. The red highlight will underline a menu item, as shown in Figure 4-5. You can then navigate through the Recording menu to find the item you want to adjust.

As I discussed earlier, the menu options will change depending on the recording mode in effect. If you're using the basic Snapshot mode, the Recording menu is limited to two screens, because that mode is for a user who wants the camera to make most of the decisions without input. For the following discussion, I'm assuming you have the camera set to one of the advanced (PASM) modes, because in those modes all four screens of the menu are available.

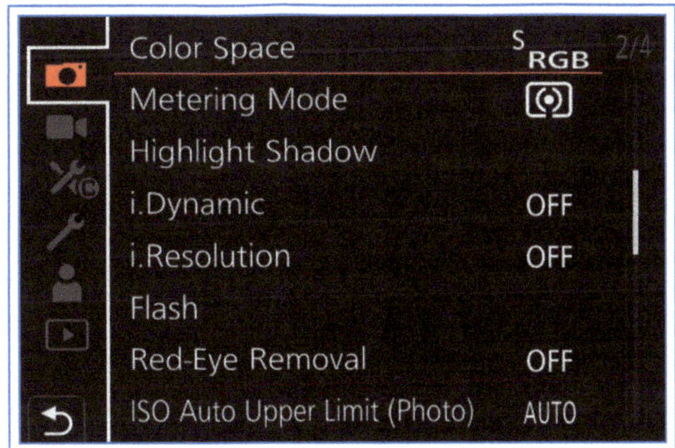

Figure 4-5. Screen 2 of Recording Menu

On the menu screens you will see a fairly long list of options, each occupying one line, with its name on the left and its current setting on the right. (In some cases, the current setting is not shown because it involves multiple options.) You have to scroll through four screens to see all of the items.

You can scroll through the items on any screen using the Up and Down buttons. If you find it tedious to scroll using that method, you can use the zoom lever to speed through the menus one full screen at a time, in either direction. Or, you can turn the thumb dial to move through menus one screen at a time. With that method, you can also move from one menu system to another (except when in the Custom menu). And, you can use the touch screen capability, by touching a desired menu option, or by touching the scroll bars at the far right of the menu screen. You can tell which numbered screen you are on by checking the numbers at the right of the screen, which show the screen numbers as 1/4, 2/4, through 4/4.

Depending on the location of a particular menu option, you may be able to reach that option more quickly by reversing direction with the direction buttons and wrapping around to reach the option you want. For example, if you're on the top line of screen 1 of the menu, at Aspect Ratio, you can scroll up to reach the bottom option on screen 4 of the menu, Multiple Exposure.

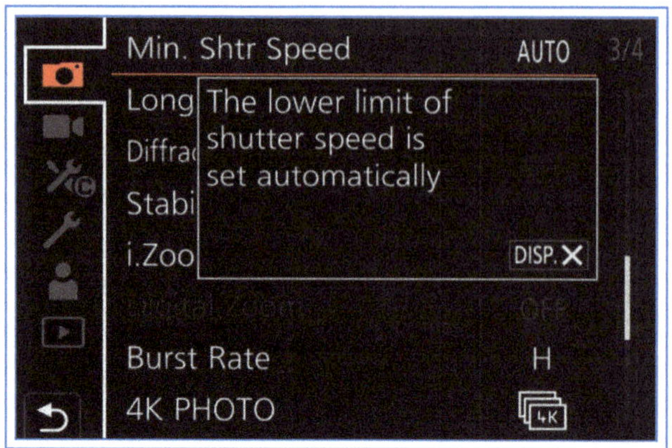

Figure 4-6. Display Button Help Text for Minimum Shutter Speed

Whenever a menu option is highlighted by the selection bar, you can press the Display button to bring up a brief explanation of the item's purpose. For example, Figure 4-6 shows the screen that was displayed when I pressed the Display button with the Minimum Shutter Speed option highlighted on screen 3 of the Recording menu. Press the Display button again to dismiss the window. In some cases, you also can press Display to see an explanation when a sub-option is highlighted. For example, if you highlight the Raw setting for Quality and press Display, the camera will pop up a brief explanation of that setting.

Some menu lines may have a dimmed, "grayed-out" appearance at times, meaning they cannot be selected under the present settings. For example, in Figure 4-7, two items are dimmed on screen 3 of the Recording menu.

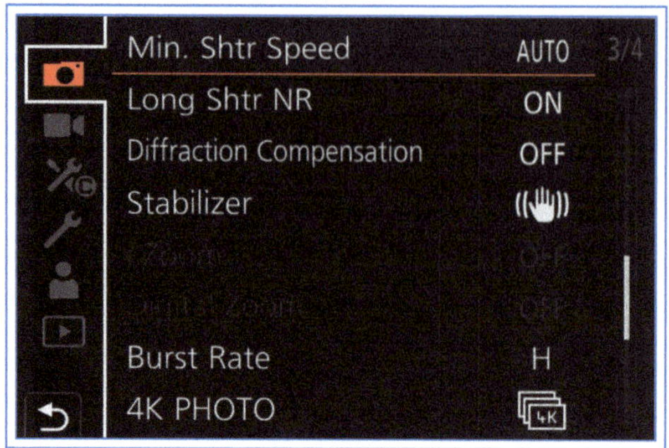

Figure 4-7. Screen 3 of Recording Menu with Items Dimmed

In this case, Quality is set to Raw and the recording mode is Program. With Quality set to Raw, you cannot select Intelligent Zoom or Digital Zoom. If you are in doubt as to why an item cannot be selected, navigate to it with the selection bar, which will be dimmed itself, and press the Menu/Set button. In many such cases, you will see a message like that in Figure 4-8, explaining why the item could not be selected.

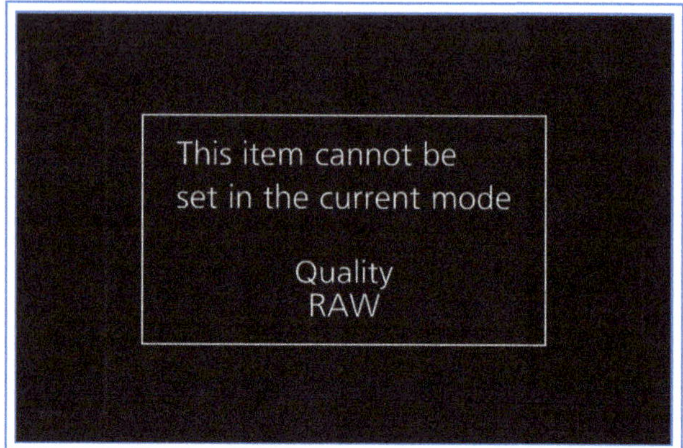

Figure 4-8. Message Explaining Inability to Select Menu Option

Because you cannot make some selections when Quality is set to Raw, if you want to follow along with the discussion of the options on the Recording menu, set Quality to Fine, which is the setting represented by the icon of an arrow pointing down onto two rows of bricks, as shown in Figure 4-9.

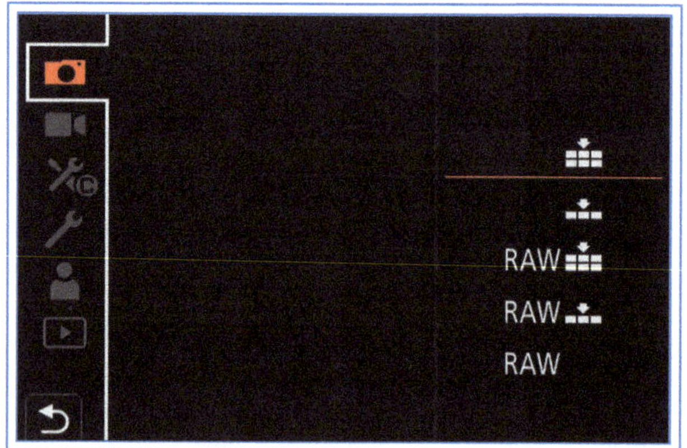

Figure 4-9. Fine Setting Highlighted for Quality

To do so, on screen 1 of the Recording menu, scroll down using the Down button until the Quality line is highlighted, then press the Right button to pop up the sub-menu. Scroll up if needed, to highlight the top icon with the six bricks, and then press the Menu/Set button to select that option.

With that setting, you will have access to most of the options on the Recording menu. I'll start at the top and discuss each option on the list. Screen 1 of this menu is shown in Figure 4-10.

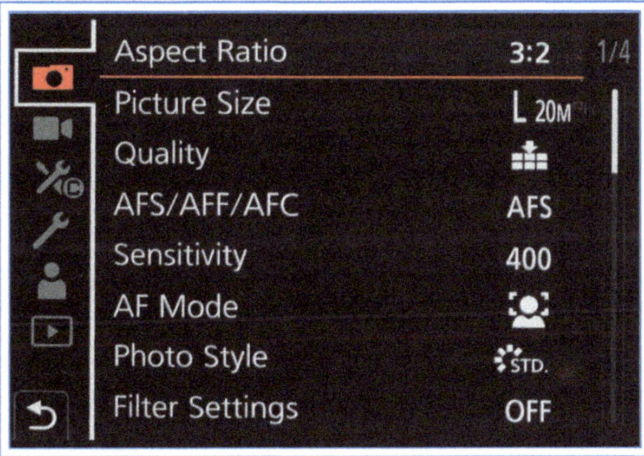

Figure 4-10. Screen 1 of Recording Menu

Aspect Ratio

This first menu option has four settings: 4:3, 3:2, 16:9, and 1:1, as shown in Figure 4-11, representing the ratio of the width of an image to its vertical height.

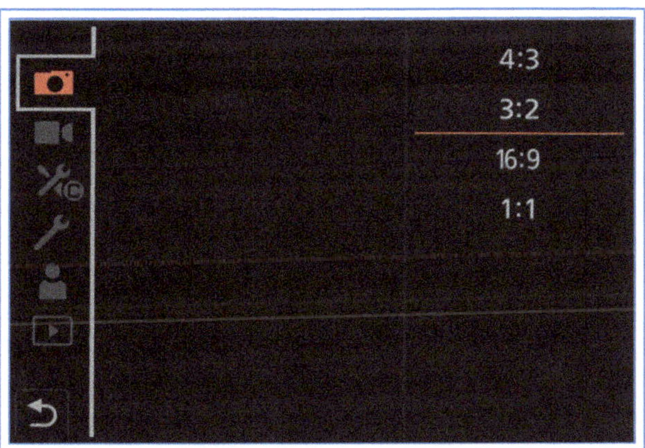

Figure 4-11. Aspect Ratio Menu Options Screen

This setting does not affect just the shape of the image; it also helps determine how many megapixels (MP or M) an image contains. When the aspect ratio is set to 3:2, the maximum resolution of 20 MP is available. When the aspect ratio is set to 4:3, the greatest possible resolution is 17.5 MP. At 16:9, the greatest possible resolution is 17 MP. At the 1:1 ratio, the largest resolution available is 13.5 MP. If you want to view the scene using the entire area of the LCD screen, choose 3:2, which is the aspect ratio of the screen. With 4:3, there will be black bars at the sides of the screen as you compose your shot; with 16:9, there will be black bars at the top and bottom of the screen; with 1:1, there will be black bars at the sides.

Figures 4-12 through 4-15 show the shapes of images taken with the C-Lux's various aspect ratio settings.

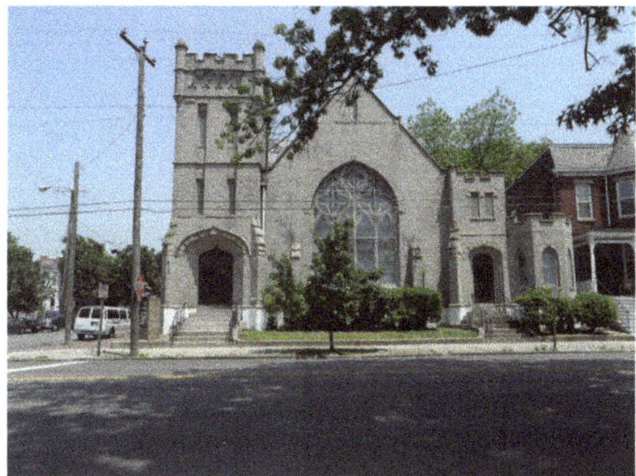

Figure 4-12. Aspect Ratio Set to 4:3

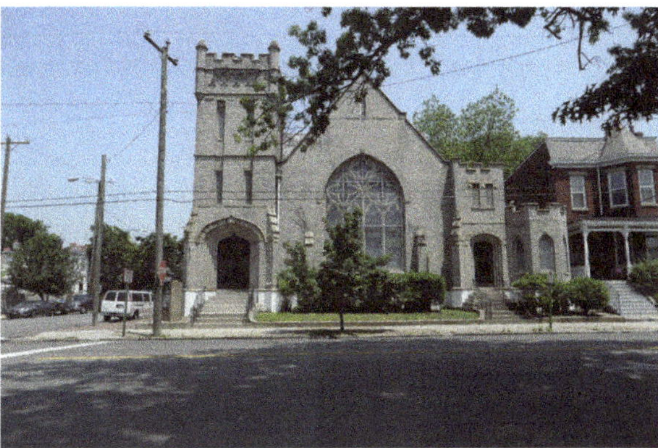

Figure 4-13. Aspect Ratio Set to 3:2

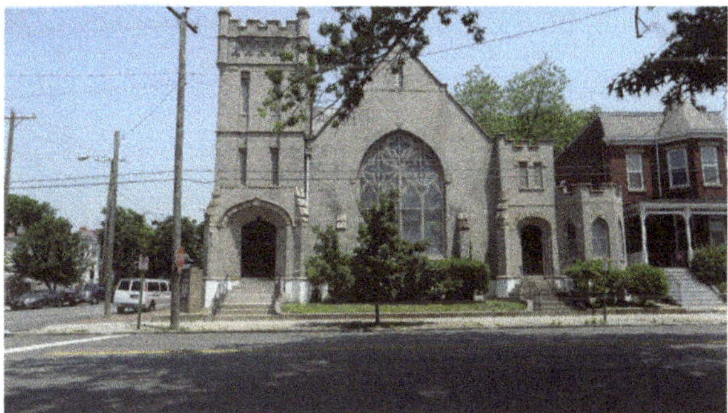

Figure 4-14. Aspect Ratio Set to 16:9

In Figure 4-12, the aspect ratio is set to 4:3. This aspect ratio crops the image slightly in the horizontal direction. Figure 4-13 is an image taken with the 3:2 setting, which uses the maximum number of available horizontal and vertical pixels. For Figure 4-14, the aspect ratio was set to the 16:9 position, which uses the maximum number of horizontal pixels, and crops the vertical pixels. Finally, the 1:1 setting was used for Figure 4-15. This setting uses the maximum number of vertical pixels but crops the pixels in the horizontal direction.

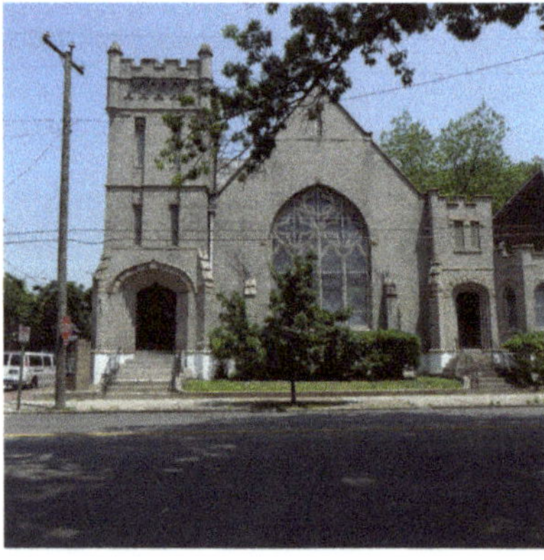

Figure 4-15. Aspect Ratio Set to 1:1

Picture Size

This next item on the Recording menu controls the number of megapixels in the images you record with the camera, up to and including its maximum of 20 MP. The maximum MP setting, using the L (for Large) setting for Picture Size, is affected by the aspect ratio that you have set using the Aspect Ratio menu item, discussed above. If you set the aspect ratio to 3:2, the maximum Picture Size setting is the full 20 MP, as shown in Figure 4-16, using the full horizontal and vertical extent of the available pixels.

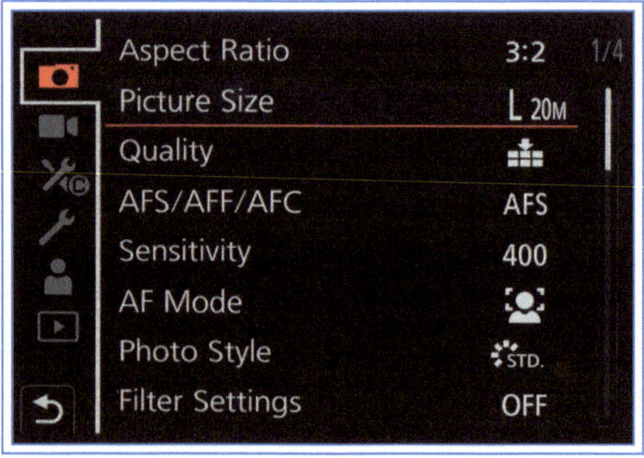

Figure 4-16. Picture Size Setting with Aspect Ratio 3:2

As noted above in connection with the aspect ratio setting, the number of megapixels decreases with other aspect ratio settings.

The higher the Picture Size setting, the better the overall quality of the image, all other factors being equal. However, you can create a fuzzy and low-quality image with a high Picture Size setting with no trouble at all; this setting does not guarantee a great image. But if all other factors are equal, a higher megapixel count should yield noticeably higher image quality. Also, when you have a large megapixel count in your image, you have some leeway for cropping it; you can select a portion of the image to enlarge to the full size of your print, and still retain acceptable image quality.

On the other hand, images with high megapixel counts eat up storage space more quickly than those with low megapixel counts. If you are running low on space on your SD card and still have a lot of images to capture, you may need to reduce your Picture Size setting so you can fit more images on the card.

As noted earlier, the Picture Size setting is dimmed and unavailable when you have selected Raw for the Quality setting. However, if you select Raw & Fine or Raw & Standard, with which the camera records both a Raw and a JPEG image, the Picture Size option is available for setting the size of the JPEG image.

Extended Optical Zoom

Another point to consider in setting Picture Size is how much zoom power you need to have available. You might not think that picture size is related to zoom, but with the C-Lux it is. The camera has a feature called Extended Optical Zoom, designated as EX on the menu screen and shooting screen. When you set the Picture Size to 5 MP (S), for example (with aspect ratio of 3:2), you will find that you can zoom in farther than you can with Picture Size set to its maximum. You will see an EX designation appear on the menu screen to the left of the Picture Size setting of S, as shown in Figure 4-17.

(You will not see the EX designation unless Quality is set to Fine or Standard, because Extended Optical Zoom is not available with Quality set to Raw. This feature also is incompatible with some other settings, such as 4K Photo, Handheld Night Shot, Multiple Exposure, HDR, and others.)

You will see that the zoom scale goes beyond the normal limit of 360mm as you move the zoom lever toward the telephoto side, as shown in Figure 4-18.

Depending on the Picture Size setting, the scale will extend to a zoom level of as much as twice normal, or about an equivalent of 720mm. (If you turn on Intelligent Zoom or Digital Zoom, discussed later in this chapter, the zoom range will extend even farther; for now, I am assuming that both of those options are turned off.)

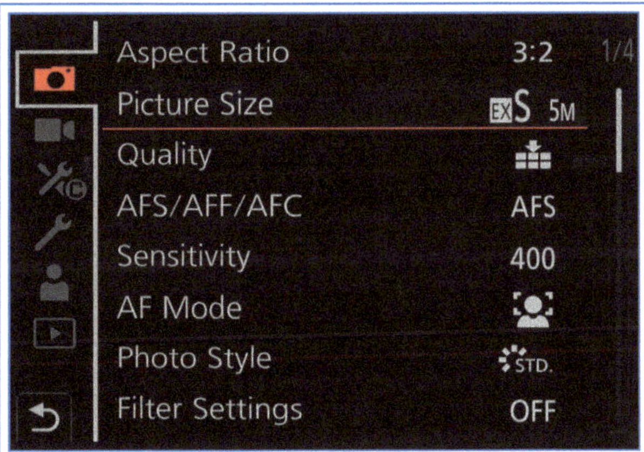

Figure 4-17. EX Designation with Picture Size Set to S

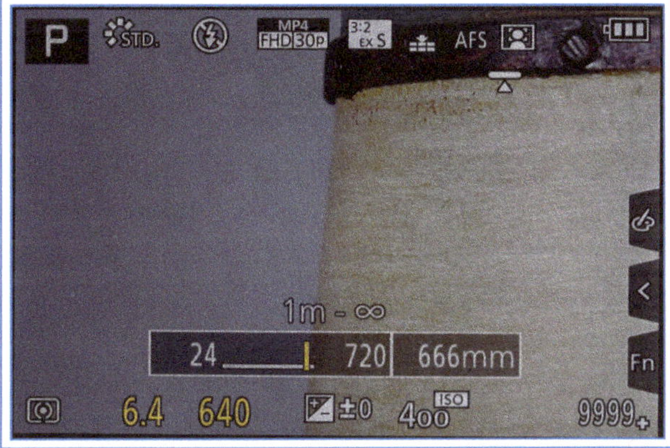

Figure 4-18. Zoom Scale Beyond Optical Zoom Limit

To summarize the situation with Extended Optical Zoom, whenever you set Picture Quality to a level below Large, you gain additional zoom power because of the reduced resolution. You could achieve the same result by taking the picture at the normal zoom range with Picture Size set to Large and then cropping the image in your computer to enlarge just the part you want. But with Extended Optical Zoom, you get the benefit of seeing a larger image on the display when you're composing the picture, and the benefit of having the camera perform its focus and exposure operations on the actual zoomed image that you want to capture, so the feature is not useless. You just need to decide whether it's of use to you in a particular situation.

I'll discuss Intelligent Zoom and Digital Zoom later, as other Recording Menu options.

Quality

The next setting on the Recording menu is Quality. It's important to distinguish the Quality setting from the Picture Size setting. Picture Size concerns the image's resolution, or the number of megapixels in the image. Quality has to do with how the image's digital information is compressed for storage on the SD card and, later, on the computer's hard drive. There are three levels of quality available in various combinations: Raw, Fine, and Standard, as shown in Figure 4-19. From the top, the five icons stand for Fine, Standard, Raw & Fine, Raw & Standard, and Raw.

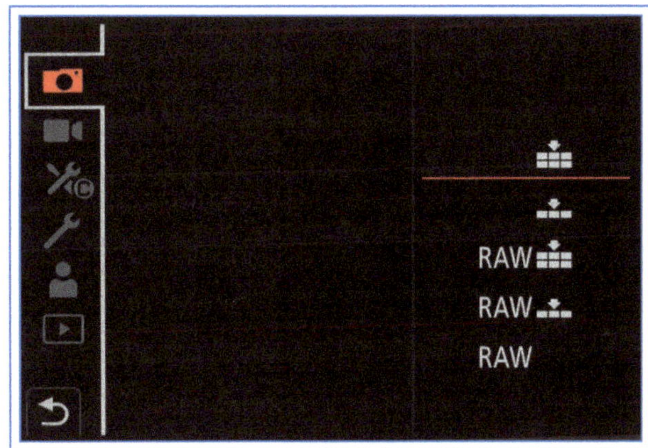

Figure 4-19. Quality Menu Options Screen

Raw is in a category by itself. There are both pros and cons to using Raw in this camera. First, the cons. A Raw file takes up a lot of space on your memory card, and, if you copy it to your computer, a lot of space on your hard drive. In addition, there are various functions of the C-Lux that don't work when you're using Raw, including panorama shooting, Intelligent Zoom, Digital Zoom, Resize, Cropping, Title Edit, Text Stamp, printing directly from the camera to a photo printer, and White Balance Bracket. You also cannot get the benefit of using the Filter Settings menu option or Creative Control mode to add picture effects to your images, though you can use those effects when shooting with Raw for Quality. (The resulting image will show the effect when displayed in the camera, but not when opened on a computer unless you use a program that can display the effect, such as Irfanview, from Irfanview.com.)

You cannot shoot in Raw quality with the Handheld Night Shot or HDR options, and burst shooting will be slowed down when shooting in Raw.

Finally, you may have problems working with Raw files on your computer because of incompatibility with editing software, though those problems can be overcome by getting updates for your program.

On the other hand, using Raw files has several advantages. The main benefit is that Raw files give you an amazing amount of control and flexibility with your images. When you open up a Raw file in a compatible photo-editing program, the software gives you the opportunity to correct problems with exposure, white balance, color tints, sharpness, and other settings. If you had the aperture of the camera too narrow when you took the picture, and it looks badly underexposed, you can make exposure adjustments in the software and recover the image to a proper brightness level. Similarly, you can adjust the white balance after the fact and remove unwanted color casts. In effect, you get a second chance at making the correct settings, rather than being stuck with an unusable image because of unfortunate settings when you pressed the shutter button.

For example, Figure 4-20 is an image I took with Quality set to Raw, but with settings purposely made to result in underexposure and incorrect white balance.

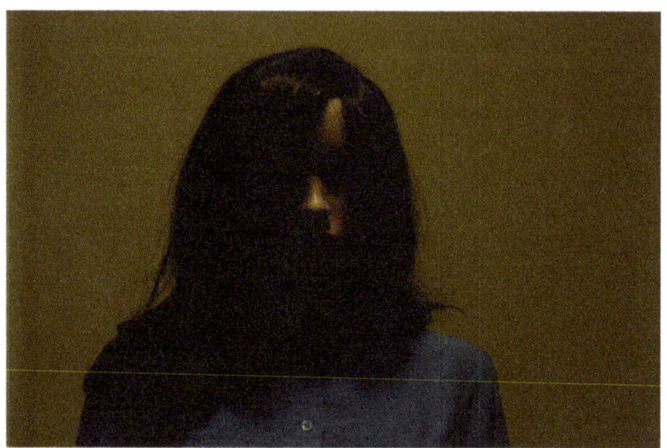

Figure 4-20. Raw Image Shot with Abnormal Settings

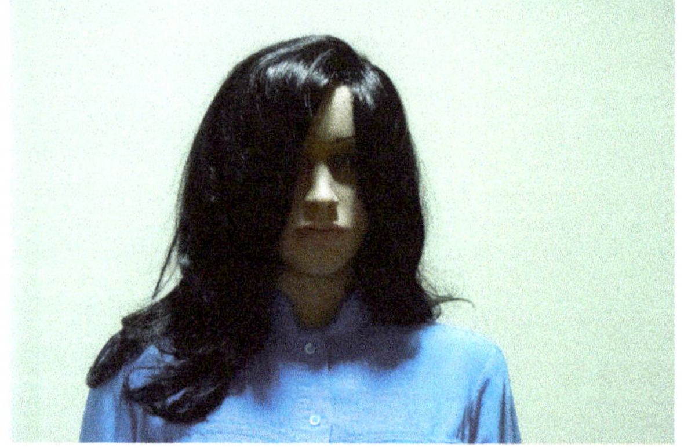

Figure 4-21. Raw Image with Settings Adjusted in Software

Figure 4-21 is the same image after I opened it using Adobe Camera Raw software and made corrections after the fact. The corrected image looks essentially as if it had been shot with proper settings to begin with.

The drawbacks to using Raw files are either not too severe or they are counterbalanced by the flexibility Raw gives you. The large size of the files may be an inconvenience, but the increasing size of hard drives and SD cards, with steadily dropping prices, makes file size much less of a concern than previously. I have had problems with Raw files not loading when I didn't have the latest Camera Raw plug-in for Adobe Photoshop or Photoshop Elements, but with a little effort, you can download an updated plug-in and the software will then process and display your Raw images.

You certainly don't have to use Raw, but you may be missing some opportunities if you avoid it.

The other two settings for Quality—Fine and Standard—are levels of compression for computer image files that use the JPEG standard. Images saved with Fine quality are subjected to less compression than those saved with Standard quality. In other words, Standard-quality images have their digital data "compressed" or "squeezed" down to a smaller size to allow more of the files to be stored on an SD card or computer drive, with a corresponding loss of image quality. The more compression an image is subjected to, the less clear detail it will contain. Unless you are running out of space on your storage medium, you probably should leave the Quality setting at Fine to ensure the best quality. (Of course, you may prefer to shoot in the Raw format for maximum quality.)

With the C-Lux, besides choosing one of the individual Quality settings (Raw, Fine, or Standard), you also have the option of setting the camera to record images in Raw plus either Fine or Standard. If you choose that option, the camera will record each image in two files—one Raw, and the other a JPEG file in either Fine or Standard quality, depending on your selection. If you then play the image back in the camera, you will see only one image, but if you copy the files to your computer, you will find two image files—one with a .jpg extension and one with an .rwl extension. The Raw file will be much larger than the JPEG one. In a few examples I just looked at on my computer, the Raw files from the C-Lux were all about 22 MB and JPEG files with Picture Size set to Large were between about 3 and 10 MB. (Note that MB stands for megabytes, a measure of file size, as distinguished from MP or M, meaning megapixels, a measure of the number of pixels in an image.)

Why would you choose the option of recording images in Raw and JPEG at the same time? If you're taking pictures of a one-time event such as a wedding or graduation, you may want to preserve them in Raw for highest quality and later processing with software, but also have them available for quick review on a computer that might not have software that reads Raw files. Or, you might want to be able to send the images to friends or post them to social media sites without translating them from Raw into a JPEG format that most people can easily view on their computers. Also, as I discussed earlier, if you are using Creative Control mode or the Filter Settings menu option to add special effects to images, those effects will not show up in Raw files when the files are opened on a computer. In order to have the benefit of the special setting as well as the benefits of a Raw file, you can use the Raw & Fine or Raw & Standard option to record images both ways.

AFS/AFF/AFC

This next menu option lets you choose how the autofocus system operates when the camera is using autofocus. With AFS, for autofocus single, when you press the shutter button halfway, the camera locks focus on the subject and keeps it locked while the button is held there, even if the subject moves. With AFF, for autofocus flexible, the camera locks focus but will adjust focus if the subject (or the camera) moves. With AFC, for autofocus continuous, the camera does not lock focus, but adjusts it continuously as the subject or camera moves.

If you are shooting images of a landscape or other stationary subject, AFS will work well. The camera will lock focus and keep it there, and the battery will not be drained by adjusting focus. If you are shooting handheld shots at a fairly close distance, though, you might want to use the AFF setting because the camera will adjust the focus if the camera moves slightly, and the focus could be thrown off by that movement, especially when the focus distance is small or the lens is zoomed in.

If you are shooting pictures of children or pets moving around unpredictably, you may want to use the AFC or AFF setting and let the camera continue to adjust focus as needed. With these settings, the camera's battery will be drained faster than with AFS, but it may be worth it to capture an action shot in sharp focus.

This setting is fixed at AFS in Panorama mode. With 4K Photo shooting, AFF is not available. Only AFS is available with the 4K Photo S/S setting.

Sensitivity (ISO)

This next setting lets you set the camera's ISO, or sensitivity to light. On the C-Lux, the available ISO settings range from 125 to 12500, though the range varies in some situations. With the lower settings, the camera produces the best image quality, but exposures require more light. With higher settings, the camera can produce good exposures in dim light, but there is likely to be an increasing amount of visual "noise" in the image as the ISO value increases.

Generally speaking, you should shoot images with the lowest ISO that will allow them to be exposed properly. (An exception is if you want the grainy look that comes with a high ISO value.) For example, if you are shooting indoors in low light, you may need to set the ISO to a high value (say, 800) so you can expose the image with a reasonably fast shutter speed. If the camera were set to a lower ISO, it would need to use a slower shutter speed to take in enough light for a proper exposure, and the resulting image would likely be blurry and possibly unusable.

The ISO setting is available only when the camera is set to one of the advanced shooting modes, including the PASM modes, Panorama, and Creative Video. To make the setting, select this menu option and a horizontal menu will appear at the bottom of the display, as shown in Figure 4-22.

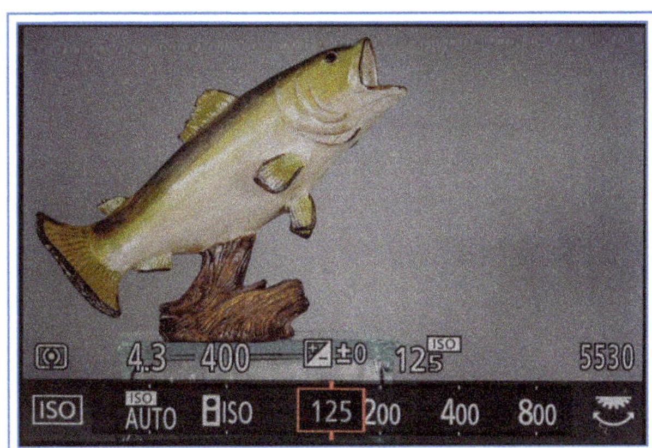

Figure 4-22. ISO Menu

You can scroll through the values on this menu by pressing the Left and Right buttons, by turning the thumb dial, or by scrolling the menu with the touch screen. The possible numerical values are 125, 200, 400, 800, 1600, 3200, 6400, and 12500, unless you change some menu settings, discussed below, to add values below 125 and above 12500, as well as intermediate values.

When you set a numerical value for ISO, the ISO Auto Upper Limit (Photo) option (discussed later in this chapter) does not apply. When you set ISO to Auto ISO, the camera automatically adjusts ISO up to the maximum value set with ISO Auto Upper Limit (Photo), based on the brightness of the scene. As discussed in Chapter 3, you can use Auto ISO with Manual exposure mode for still images, which lets you keep shutter speed and aperture fixed while the ISO varies.

When you use the Intelligent ISO setting, the camera adjusts the ISO based on the movement of the subject as well as the brightness, so the camera can set a higher shutter speed to stop the motion. Intelligent ISO is available with the Snapshot, Program, and Aperture Priority modes, but not with the Shutter Priority or Manual exposure modes, or when using the Post Focus option.

When would you want to use a numerical value for the ISO setting, rather than setting it to Auto ISO or Intelligent ISO? One example is if you want the highest quality for your image, and you aren't worried about camera movement, either because you are using a tripod so a slow shutter speed won't result in blur, or the lighting is bright enough to use a fast shutter speed. Then you could set the ISO to its lowest possible setting of 125 (or 80 if Extended ISO is turned on) to achieve high quality. On the other hand, if you definitely want a grainy, noisy look, you can set the ISO to 3200 or even higher to introduce noise into the image. You also might want a high ISO setting so you can use a fast shutter speed to stop action or in low light. In many cases, though, you can just leave the setting at Auto or Intelligent and let the camera adjust the ISO as needed.

It is important to be aware of how much a high ISO value can affect the quality of your images. Figures 4-23 and 4-24 are two images of the same subject; Figure 4-23 was taken at ISO 125 and Figure 4-24 was taken at ISO 12500. As you can see, the high-ISO image shows considerable deterioration, both in the subject itself and in the plain background. You can use this high setting when absolutely necessary to get a shot, but it's advisable to avoid the highest ISO values when possible.

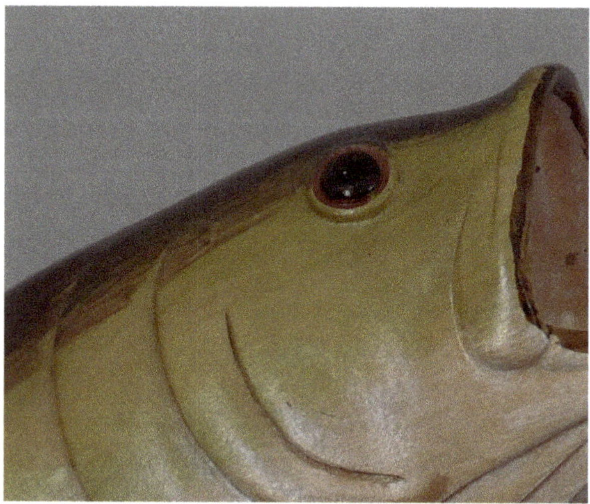

Figure 4-23. ISO Set to 125

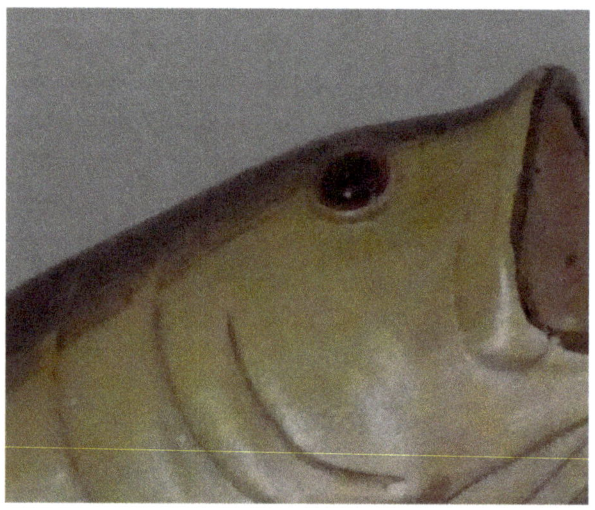

Figure 4-24. ISO Set to 12500

AF Mode

This next menu option controls what area of the scene the camera focuses on when using its autofocus capability. (You select an autofocus or manual focus mode by pressing the Left button to bring up the focus mode menu from the shooting screen.)

When you select the AF Mode menu option with the focus mode set to AF, AF Macro, or Macro Zoom, the camera displays a line of icons representing the six choices available for the AF Mode setting: Face/Eye Detection; AF Tracking; 49-Area; Custom Multi; 1-Area; and Pinpoint, as shown in Figure 4-25.

Use the thumb dial or the Left and Right buttons (or the touch screen) to highlight the choice you want. Then press the Menu/Set button or the Set icon, followed by the Fn3 button, or press the shutter button halfway, to select that setting and return to the recording screen.

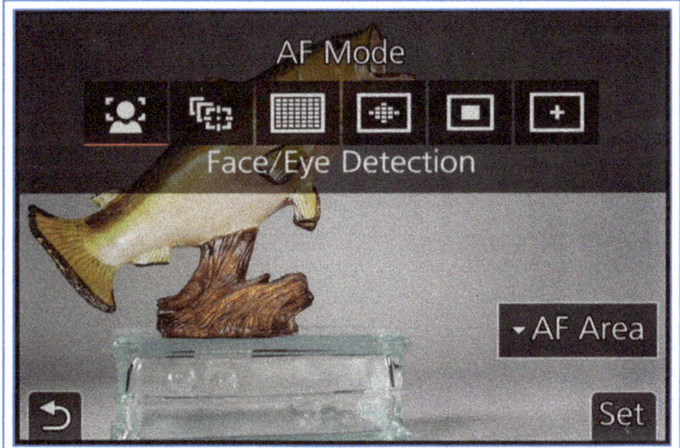

Figure 4-25. AF Mode Menu Options Screen

In Snapshot or Snapshot Plus mode, only two of these options are available: Face/Eye Detection and AF Tracking. Following are details about all six options that are available in other recording modes.

Face/Eye Detection

When you select this setting, the camera does not display any focusing brackets or rectangles until it detects a human face. If it does, it outlines the general area of the face with a yellow rectangle. Then, after you press the shutter button halfway down, the rectangle turns green when the camera has focused on the face. If the camera detects more than one face, it displays white rectangles for secondary faces, as shown in Figure 4-26.

Any faces that are the same distance away from the camera as the face within the yellow rectangle will also be in focus, but the focus will be controlled by the face in the yellow rectangle. If Metering Mode is set to Multi, the camera will also adjust its exposure for the main detected face.

With this setting, the camera also will look for human eyes. It will place a set of crosshairs across the closest eye it finds and fix focus there. If you want, you can change the eye that the camera focuses on. To do that, when the camera is displaying frames over detected faces, press the touch screen over the eye you want the camera to focus on, then press the shutter button halfway to focus. (Touching a different eye does not work in Snapshot mode; in that mode, if you touch the screen, the AF Mode setting will change to AF Tracking.)

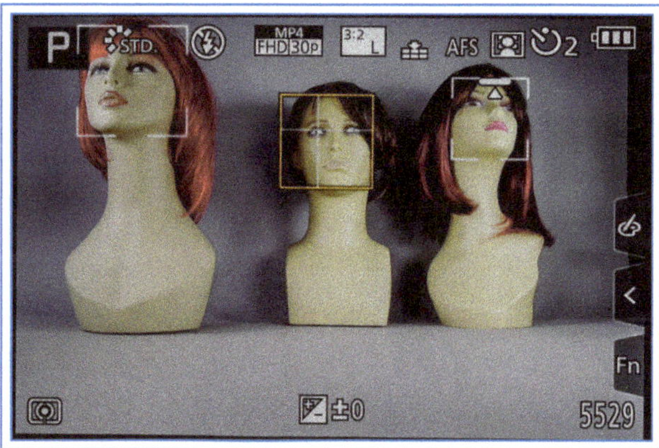

Figure 4-26. Face Detection in Use

You also can change the face that the camera focuses on. One way to do this is to touch the screen and move the focus frame with your finger. To use that system, go to the Touch Settings item on screen 3 of the Custom menu and, under Touch Settings, set Touch AF to AF. Another way to do this is to use the Direct Focus Area option. To do that, turn on the Direct Focus Area option on screen 2 of the Custom menu. Then, when the Face/Eye Detection frame is displayed on the screen, press any of the four cursor buttons to start moving the focus frame to the location where you want it. When the frame is being moved, you can also turn the thumb dial to change the frame's size.

When the focus frame is sized and located as you want, press the Menu/Set button to lock it in place. The camera will then shift its focus to the area inside that frame. You might want to use this option if you are aiming at two faces, but you want to focus on the one that is farther away from the camera. Ordinarily, the camera will focus on the closest face, but if you move the frame over the other face, the camera will direct its focus there. To reset the frame to its original position, press the Display button while the frame is movable.

AF Tracking

This next setting for AF Mode allows the camera to maintain focus on a moving subject. On the menu screen, highlight the second icon, which is a group of offset focus frames designed to look like a moving focus frame. Press the Menu/Set button or half-press the shutter button to select this option.

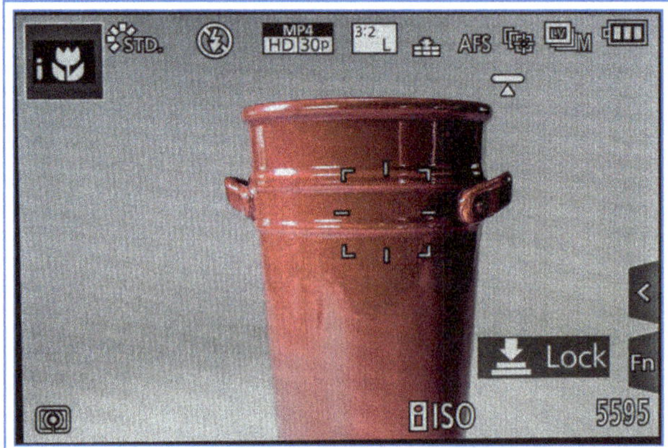

Figure 4-27. AF Tracking Focus Frame

The camera will then display a special focus frame with spokes sticking out of it, in the center of the display, as shown in Figure 4-27. Move the camera to place this focus frame over your subject and press the shutter button halfway, then release the button. If the camera can identify a subject at this location, the frame will turn yellow. The camera will then do its best to keep that target in focus, even as it (or the camera) moves. The yellow bracket should stay close to the subject on the display.

When you are ready, press the shutter button to take the picture. If you want to cancel AF Tracking, press the Menu/Set button.

If the camera is not able to maintain focus on the moving subject, the focus frame will turn red and then disappear. AF Tracking will not work when Time Lapse Shot is in use. With several Creative Control mode settings, including all of the Monochrome options; the camera will use 1-Area mode if AF Tracking is set.

To use this option with the touch screen, just touch the subject on the screen to select it, and press the AF Off icon on the screen to cancel the tracking focus.

Using AF Tracking can reduce the time to take a picture of a moving subject. If you are trying to snap a picture of a restless four-year-old child or a fidgety pet, AF Tracking can give you a head start, so the camera's focus is close to being correct and the focusing mechanism has less to do to achieve correct focus when you suddenly see the perfect moment to press the shutter button.

49-Area

This next option for AF Mode causes the camera to focus on up to 49 small focus zones within the overall autofocus area, which is the same area as that of the current aspect ratio setting. The camera then looks within the focus zones and selects however many subjects it detects that are at the same distance from the camera and can be focused on.

To make this setting, select the third icon on the AF Mode menu, which looks like a screen with multiple focus points. Then, when you push the shutter button down halfway, the camera will display green rectangles to show you which of the multiple focus areas it has selected to focus on, as shown in Figure 4-28.

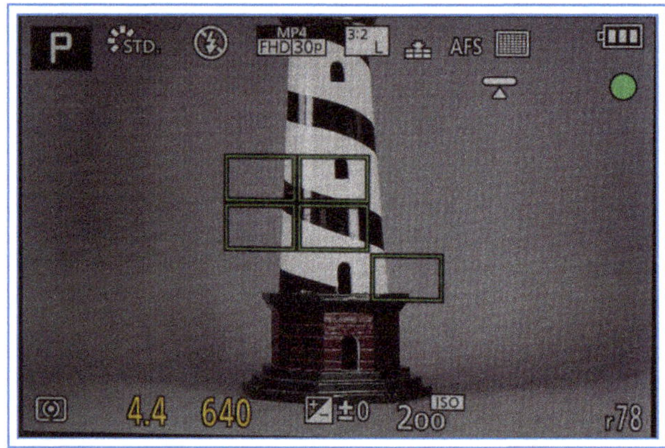

Figure 4-28. Green Focus Frames with 49-Area Setting

The name of this setting is somewhat misleading, however, because, even though the camera has 49 focus zones, it will only use a few of those zones at any one time in this mode. By default, the camera uses the nine zones in the center of the screen. With the default setting, if you focus on a scene with a prominent object at the far right, the camera will choose whatever object it can find in the center of the display to focus on, and will ignore the object at the right.

If you want the camera to direct its focus somewhere other than the center of the scene, press the Down button while the 49-Area icon is highlighted on the menu screen, and then move the block of focus zones where you want them using the cursor buttons, as shown in Figure 4-29.

If the Direct Focus Area option is enabled, you can use the cursor buttons to move the focus area around the screen when the camera is in shooting mode with the 49-Area option selected. If the Touch AF option is turned on through the Touch Settings item on screen 3 of the Custom menu, you can touch the screen in shooting mode to select the area for the focus zone.

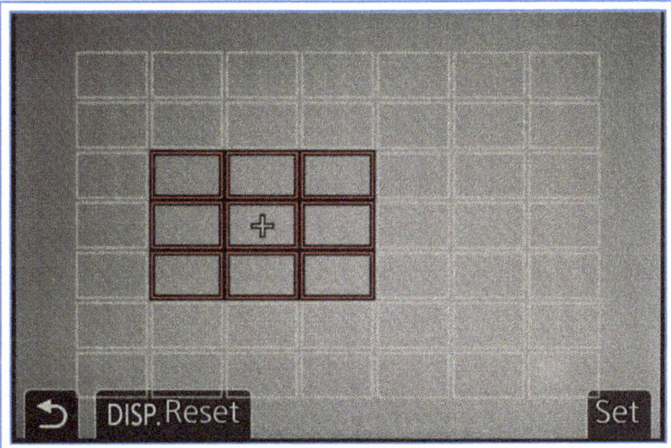

Figure 4-29. Screen for Moving Focus Blocks

When you have set the focus area using the touch screen or cursor buttons, the camera displays a small white cross on the screen to indicate the center of the block of focus zones it is currently using. (The cross will disappear if you press the Menu/Set button or the AF Off icon.)

The blocks near the center of the overall focus area have nine zones each, but the blocks near the edges of the display area have only six or four blocks.

The 49-Area method can be useful if your subject is likely to be located within a predictable area, and you want to have the option to adjust that area somewhat. It is a good mode to use when you are shooting landscapes or general scenes that do not require you to focus on faces or on any one particular object.

Custom Multi

This setting lets you create a custom-tailored focus zone out of the 49 available blocks. For example, you can create a horizontal focus area that is seven blocks across, or a vertical one of the same size. You can create a zone that has 13 blocks arranged in a pattern in the center of the screen. Or, you can create a completely free-form zone with any arrangement of blocks. Somewhat oddly, with the free-form option you can create a focus area that uses all 49 of the focus blocks, resulting in a true 49-Area focus mode, unlike the mode with that name, which can use only up to nine blocks. The process for using this option is a bit complicated, so I will lay out the steps below.

1. Go to the AF Mode item on the Recording menu and scroll to the fourth icon from the left, with the label Custom Multi below it, as shown in Figure 4-30.

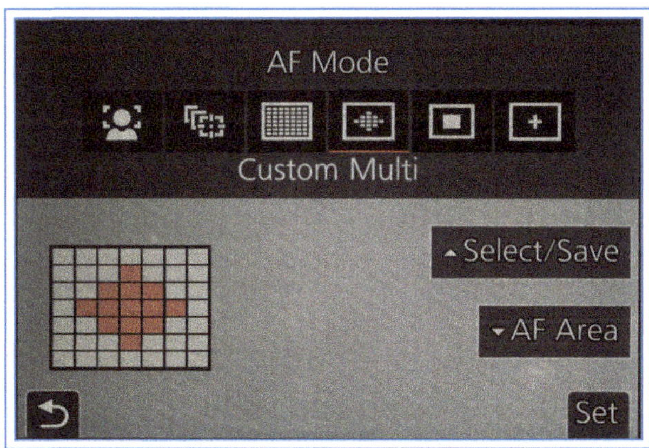

Figure 4-30. Custom Multi Option Highlighted on Menu

2. Press the Up button to move to the line of possible patterns for the focus zone, as shown in Figure 4-31.

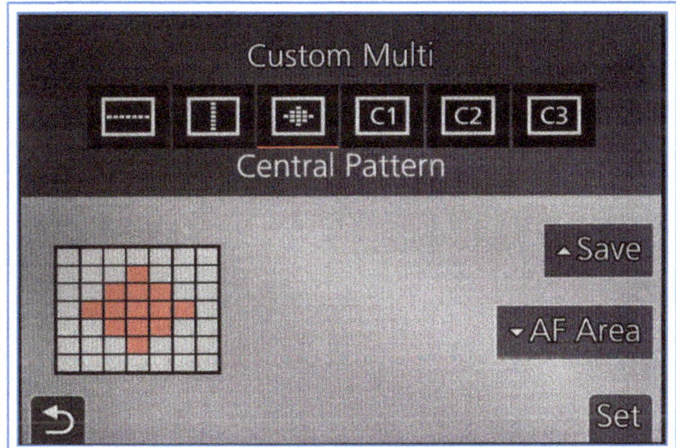

Figure 4-31. Choices for Custom Multi Pattern

3. Scroll through these icons to select the one you want. The last three—C1, C2, and C3—are for free-form custom patterns you can create and save to these numbered slots.

4. When you have selected horizontal, vertical, central, or free-form for the shape, press the Down button to move to the AF Area option. There you will see a screen with all 49 blocks, some of which will be highlighted in red for the horizontal, vertical, or central choices, but all of which will be blank for the free-form options.

5. For the horizontal, vertical, or central option, turn the thumb dial to the right to increase the size of the focus area, or turn it to the left to reduce it. You can move the line or lines across the display by pressing the appropriate direction buttons or by touching the screen. When you have the focus area positioned where you want it, press the Fn2 button, to the right of the LCD screen, to set the focus area

in place. The blocks will display for a moment and then disappear, and this focus area will be in effect.

6. For any of the three free-form options, after pressing the Up button, scroll to the icon that says C1, C2, or C3, then press the Down button to move to the AF Area screen. You will then see a display with all 49 blocks, none of which are highlighted, with a cross in the center block. Use the direction buttons to move the cross to a block you want to add to the focus pattern, and press the Menu/Set button to highlight it. You also can touch a block with your finger to highlight it. Figure 4-32 shows this screen after several blocks have been selected in this way.

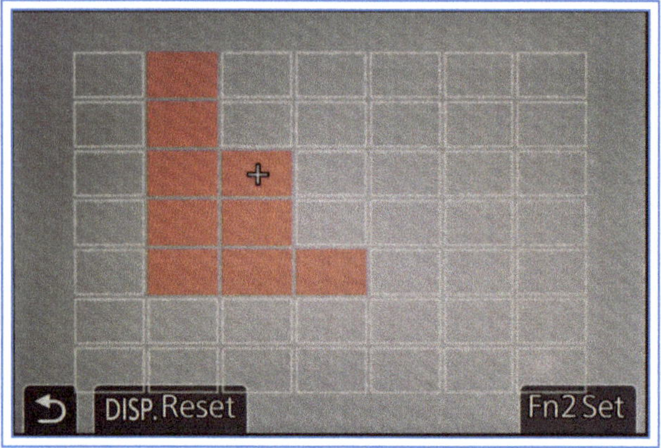

Figure 4-32. Several Focus Blocks Selected for Custom Multi

7. The blocks do not have to be contiguous; they can be in any pattern, up to and including selecting all 49 blocks. When you have finished selecting blocks, press the Fn2 button to lock in the pattern you have created.

8. To create and save a custom focus pattern, use the same procedure as in Steps 1 through 7. When you have finished, press the Menu/Set button and select the AF Mode menu option to bring the AF mode menu back on the screen. Then scroll to the Custom Multi option. Press the Up button to move to the line of options, and scroll to the focus pattern you just created, whether horizontal, vertical, central, or free-form, then press the Up button. The camera will display a screen like that in Figure 4-33, asking which Custom slot you want to save it to.

9. Highlight the one you want and press Menu/Set, then select Yes when asked if it should overwrite the existing settings. To select the saved pattern in the future, just select C1, C2, or C3, depending on what slot the pattern was saved to.

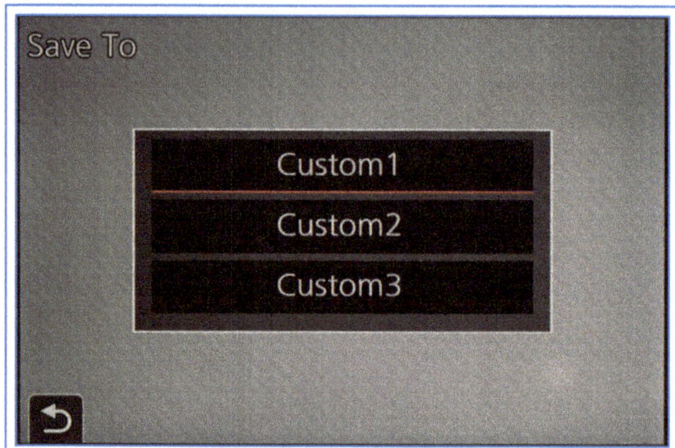

Figure 4-33. Confirmation Screen to Save Custom Multi Pattern

The Custom Multi option is useful if you have a need for specially shaped focus zones. You might want to use a horizontal zone if you are focusing on a group of artifacts that are displayed in a straight line, to make sure the camera does not accidentally focus on an object outside of that line. You also might want to create a pattern that uses all 49 focus zones, so the camera will focus on the closest object, regardless of whether it is in the center of the image, or in a particular sector of the image.

However, there is one quirk with this setting: If you don't select any blocks at all, the camera will treat the focus area as containing all 49 blocks, and will focus on any object in its view. So, to use all 49 blocks for the focus area, select Custom Multi and leave all blocks unselected. If you select one or more blocks, the camera will focus only on an object within those blocks, but if you select no blocks, the camera will use all 49 blocks.

1-Area

This AF Mode setting is selected with the next-to-last icon on the AF Mode menu, as shown in Figure 4-34. With this option, the camera uses a single focus frame, which by default is in the center of the screen. You can customize the setting by moving the frame to any position on the display and changing its size.

When you have highlighted the 1-Area icon on the AF Mode menu, press the Down button to move directly to setting the location of the autofocus frame using the direction buttons or the touch screen, as shown in Figure 4-35. You can change the size of the frame by turning the thumb dial or by pulling or pinching on the touch screen.

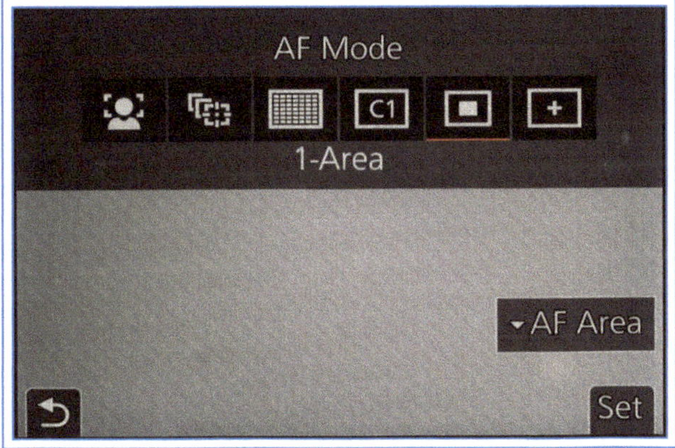

Figure 4-34. 1-Area Highlighted on AF Mode Menu

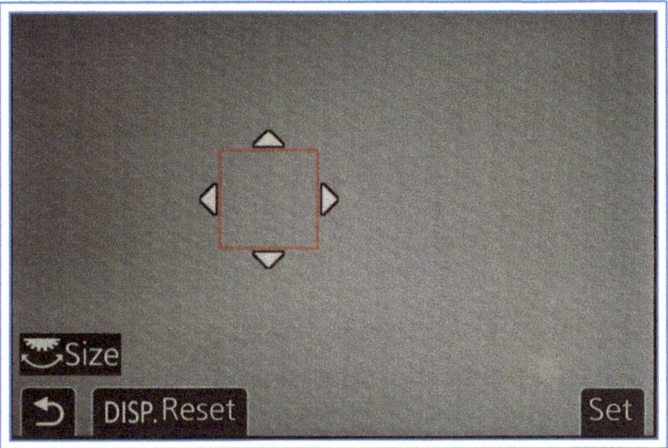

Figure 4-35. 1-Area Focus Frame Ready to be Moved

When you have finished moving and resizing the frame, press the Menu/Set button or touch the Set icon to fix the frame in place. To move the frame back to the default location in the middle of the screen or reset its size to normal, press the Display button at the bottom right of the camera's back. If the frame has been both moved and resized, you have to press Display once to reset the location and once more to reset the size.

The 1-Area method is a good setting for general shooting, because it lets you quickly position the focus area just where you want it. It is particularly helpful when you need to make sure the camera focuses on a fairly small item that is not in the center of the scene.

Pinpoint

The last icon at the right of the line of AF Mode icons, highlighted in Figure 4-36, is used to select the Pinpoint option. With this setting, you can move a single focus frame around the display and resize it, and the camera will enlarge the focus area to help you get the focus frame positioned precisely where you want it.

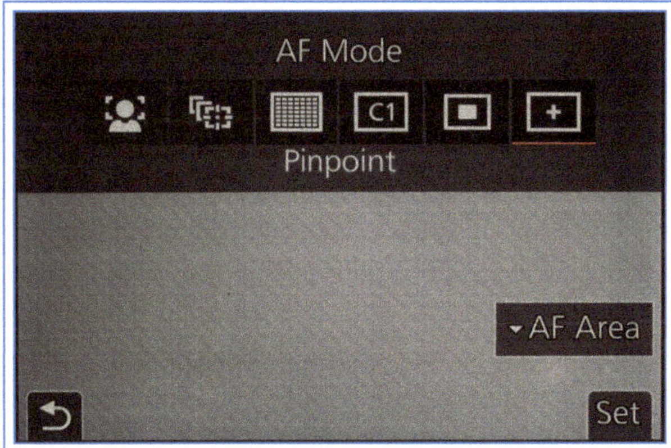

Figure 4-36. Pinpoint Highlighted on AF Mode Menu

After selecting AF Mode on the Recording menu, highlight the Pinpoint icon and press the Down button to move to the AF Area screen. Move the focus area around the display using the four direction buttons and resize it using the thumb dial, then press the Menu/Set button to set the focus area in place. You also can move and resize the focus area using the touch screen.

You can control the amount of enlargement for this display using the Pinpoint AF Display item under the Pinpoint AF Setting item on screen 2 of the Custom menu. If you select Full for that item, the image will be enlarged from three times to ten times and the enlargement will fill the display. If you select PIP, for picture-in-picture, the enlarged area will not take up the entire display, and the enlargement will only range from three times to six times. While the display is enlarged, you can vary the amount of enlargement within the specified range by turning the thumb dial or by pinching/pulling on the screen. When the focus frame is located where you want it, press the Menu/Set button to exit to the recording screen.

When you focus on an item using this setting, place the small white cross over the subject and press the shutter button halfway. The camera will enlarge the display at that area for a short time while you keep the shutter button half-pressed, to help you determine whether focus is sharp. The length of time that the display remains enlarged with this option is determined by the Pinpoint AF Time option under the Pinpoint AF Setting item on screen 2 of the Custom menu; the time can range from 0.5 second to 1.5 second. The display then returns to normal size so you can evaluate the entire scene before pressing the shutter button to take the picture.

Moving the Focus Frame or Focus Area

With all of the AF Mode options except AF Tracking, you have the ability to move the focus frame or zones. There are several ways to do this, even after you have returned the camera to the recording screen. One way to do this is to go to the AF Mode option on the Recording menu and select the current AF Mode option. Then press the Down button (or touch the AF Area icon on the screen) to go to the screen for moving the frame. Move the frame with the cursor buttons or touch screen and resize it with the thumb dial or touch screen if necessary, then press Menu/Set and you're ready to focus again with the frame in a new location.

For a faster way to move the focus frame (or broader focus area, for the 49-Area or Custom Multi setting), there are three other options. First, you can set one of the function buttons to the Focus Area Set option through the Function Button Set option on screen 3 of the Custom/Operation menu, as discussed in Chapter 5. Then, if you press that function button, the screen for moving the focus area will appear immediately. Second, you can turn on the Direct Focus Area option on screen 2 of the Custom menu. Then, from the recording screen, as soon as you press any of the four direction buttons, the focus area moving screen will appear. (A drawback of that option is that you cannot then use the direction buttons to call up options such as white balance, focus mode, and drive mode. You can use the Quick Menu to activate those items, though, or you can assign function buttons to those settings.) Third, you can use your finger to move the focus frame, if the Touch AF option is turned on through the Touch Settings item on screen 3 of the Custom menu.

Photo Style

This next item on the Recording menu gives you several options for choosing a setting that determines the overall appearance of your images. These settings yield differing results in terms of warmth, color cast, and other attributes.

To select a Photo Style setting, highlight the Photo Style line on the Recording menu and press the Right button or Menu/Set to move to the screen that displays the current setting in the upper right corner, as shown in Figure 4-37. (For all menu settings, you also can use the touch screen to make selections. I will mention that possibility from time to time, but I won't keep repeating it for every menu option.)

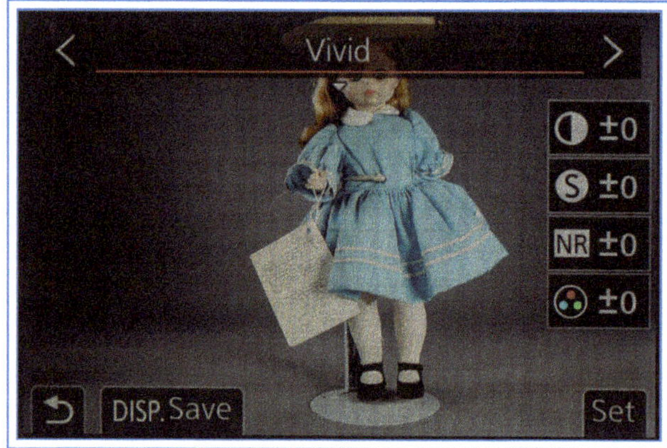

Figure 4-37. Photo Style Menu Screen

Then use the Left and Right buttons or the thumb dial to scroll through the available settings: Standard, Vivid, Natural, Monochrome, Monochrome HC, Scenery, Portrait, and Custom. When your chosen setting is highlighted at the top right of the screen, as shown in Figure 4-37, where the Vivid setting has been highlighted, press the Menu/Set button to select it, then press the Q.Menu button to exit to the shooting screen. Or, if you prefer, after highlighting the new setting, just press the shutter button halfway to select the setting and return to the shooting screen.

If you want to go further and fine-tune the setting, the C-Lux's menu system lets you adjust four parameters that are associated with the Photo Style settings: contrast, sharpness, noise reduction, and saturation. To make adjustments to those parameters, press the Down button when the main setting (such as Vivid or Natural) is highlighted with a red selection line, as in Figure 4-37. A new red highlight line will then appear in the block that contains the value for one of the four adjustable parameters, as shown in Figure 4-38.

In this case, the top line is highlighted, which means you can adjust the contrast setting; the word Contrast appears for a few seconds at the top left of the screen, indicating that that value can now be adjusted.

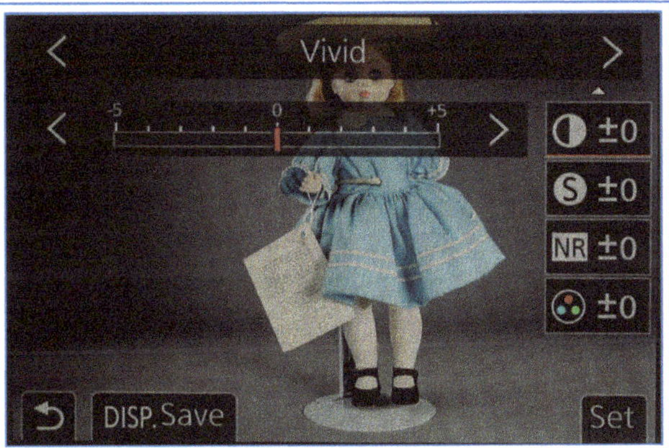

Figure 4-38. Screen to Adjust Photo Style Parameters

Once you have placed the highlight block on one of the four parameters, press the Left and Right buttons or turn the thumb dial to change the value of that parameter up to five levels, either positive or negative. A scale in the center of the screen will reflect those changes, as shown in Figure 4-39. Press Menu/Set or press the shutter button halfway to save the changes. The camera will remember those settings even when it is turned off.

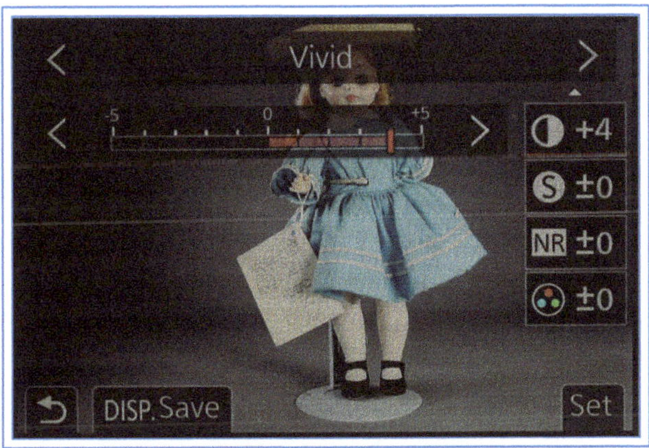

Figure 4-39. Contrast Scale with Adjustment Made

There is one additional point to make about the Monochrome and Monochrome HC settings for Photo Style. Monochrome means there is no color in the image, only shades of black, white, and gray. Therefore, the saturation adjustment does not work to increase or decrease the saturation of colors for either of the two Monochrome settings. Instead of the saturation adjustment, the camera provides two additional parameters at the bottom of the list: color tone and filter effect, as shown in Figure 4-40.

With color tone, a positive adjustment makes the monochrome effect increasingly bluish or "cooler," while a negative adjustment makes it increasingly yellowish or "warmer."

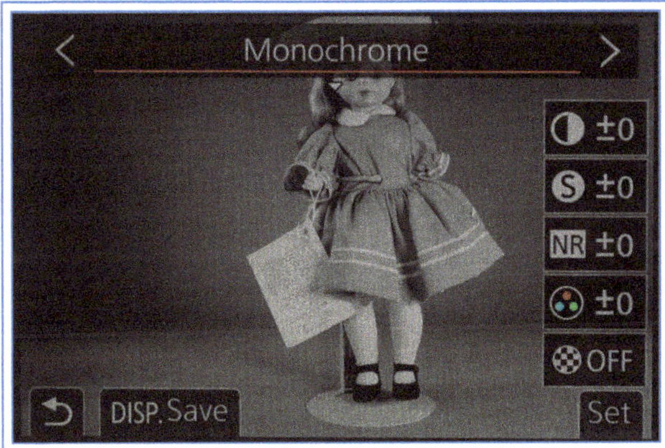

Figure 4-40. Adjustment Scales for Monochrome Setting

The filter effect adjustment lets you add a virtual filter, simulating the effect of a glass filter, which can be used on a camera's lens for black-and-white photography to enhance contrast and for other purposes. You can choose from a yellow, orange, red, or green filter, or choose the last setting, which turns the filter effect off.

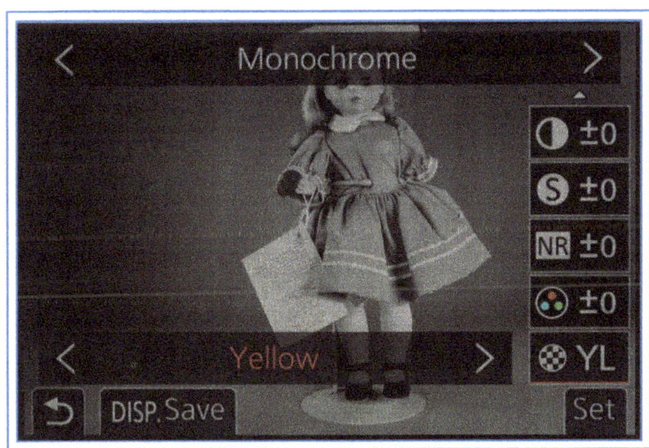

Figure 4-41. Monochrome Setting with Yellow Filter Effect

For example, Figure 4-41 shows the screen when the yellow filter effect is selected. The yellow, orange, and red effects provide increasing amounts of contrast for blue subjects and can be used to enhance the appearance of a blue sky. The green effect can be used to reduce the brightness of human skin and lips or to brighten the appearance of green foliage.

When you set Photo Style to Monochrome or Monochrome HC with Quality set to Raw, the picture you take will show up as black-and-white on the camera's LCD screen, but, when you import the image file into software that reads Raw files, the image may show up in color, depending on how the software interprets the Raw data from the sensor.

Photo Style settings are not available in the basic Snapshot mode, but they are available in all other shooting modes except Creative Control. In Snapshot Plus mode, you can select only Standard or Monochrome for Photo Style, and you cannot adjust either setting's contrast and other parameters.

In Scene mode, the camera selects a Photo Style setting according to the scene type you select, but also lets you adjust the parameters for that type. For example, if you select Clear Portrait for the scene setting, the camera selects Portrait for the Photo Style setting, but lets you adjust the contrast and other values.

The Photo Style settings also are available for recording a movie with the advanced shooting modes.

Before I provide descriptions of how the Photo Style settings affect your images, I am providing a chart in Figure 4-42 that shows the same subject photographed with each of the various settings. The last two images show the use of the Standard setting, first with its parameters all adjusted to their maximum levels, and second with all parameters at their minimum levels.

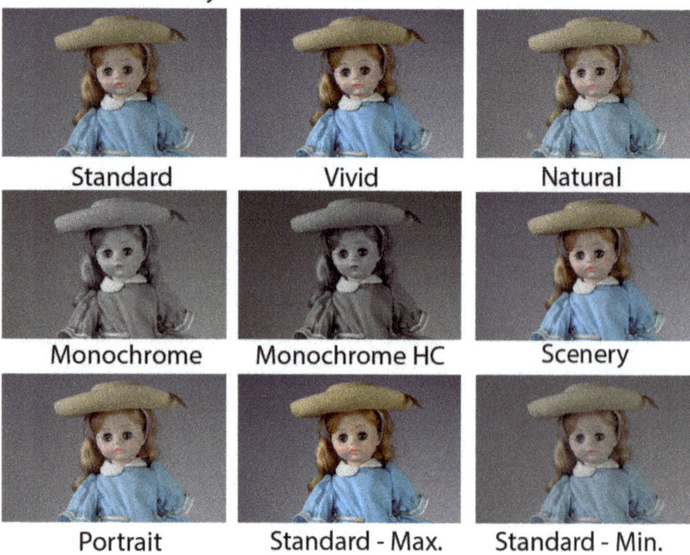

Figure 4-42. Photo Style Comparison Chart

Here are summaries of each of the Photo Style settings:

Standard: No change from the normal setting; good for general photography. The camera uses moderate sharpening and contrast to provide a clear image for everyday purposes.

Vivid: Increased saturation (intensity or vividness) and contrast of the colors in the image to make the colors "pop" out in dramatic fashion.

Natural: Reduced contrast to produce a softer, more subdued appearance.

Monochrome: Standard settings, but monochrome image, with all color removed (that is, saturation reduced to zero), unless you use the color tone adjustment to add a yellow or blue tone. You also can use the filter effect setting to add a yellow, orange, red, or green filter effect.

Monochrome HC: Similar to Monochrome but with darker, richer grays and blacks, intended to give an appearance like that of images taken with black-and-white film.

Scenery: Increased emphasis on the blues and greens of outdoor scenes, with increased saturation of those hues.

Portrait: Emphasis on flesh tones.

Custom: The Custom slot is available to store a setting that you have customized using your own settings for the parameters that can be adjusted (contrast, sharpness, saturation, and noise reduction, as well as color tone and filter effect for the Monochrome settings). To use this option, select any one of the basic Photo Style settings (Standard, Vivid, Natural, Monochrome, Monochrome HC, Scenery, or Portrait), then press the Down button and proceed to adjust any or all of the parameters for that setting as you want them. Next, press the Display button, as prompted by the DISP. Save message on the display, as shown in Figures 4-37 through 4-41.

The camera will display the message shown in Figure 4-43, asking you to confirm that you want to overwrite the current Custom setting with the settings you just made. If you highlight Yes and press Menu/Set, the settings you have made will be stored in the Custom slot of the Photo Style setting.

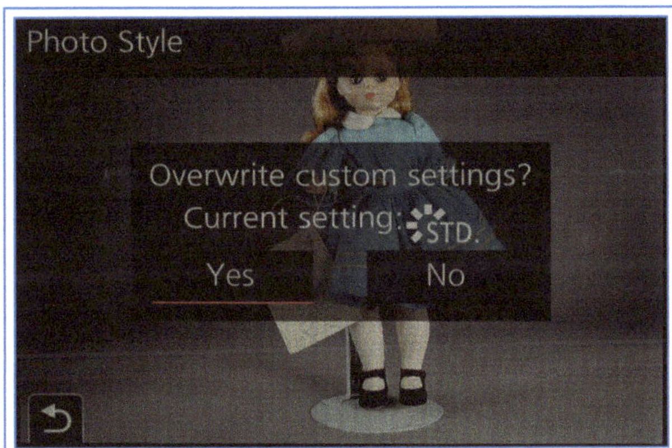

Figure 4-43. Confirmation Message to Save Custom Photo Style Setting

After you have stored the Custom setting, you can recall it at any time by selecting Custom for the Photo Style setting. You can alter the Custom setting in the future by choosing a different set of settings and storing it to the Custom slot, overwriting the previous entry.

Filter Settings

This last option on screen 1 of the Recording menu lets you apply special picture effects to your images. As I discussed in Chapter 3, the Creative Control shooting mode provides a set of 22 effects, including Expressive, Retro, Old Days, and 19 others. Each of these settings includes adjustments to things such as brightness, sharpness, focus, colors, and other factors, to achieve a special appearance for a given shot. I discussed the details of those settings in Chapter 3.

The Filter Settings menu option lets you apply any of these same effects without using that shooting mode. So, for example, while shooting in Program or Aperture Priority mode, you can select one of the 22 Filter Settings options to alter the look of an image or video. Using this option, you can have the benefit of the special setting while using one of the more advanced shooting modes. If you select one of the Filter Settings options while using Manual exposure mode, you can select the aperture and shutter speed you want, in order to have greater creative control over the image. If you use the Creative Control shooting mode, you can apply the same effects, but you have to rely on the camera's automation for the exposure.

To use this option, navigate to the Filter Settings menu item and select it. You will see a screen like that in Figure 4-44. Highlight Filter Effect and select it, and you will see a screen like that in Figure 4-45, with the choices On, Off, and Set. Select On or Off to activate or turn off the currently selected effect. Use Set to change to a different effect. When you select Set, you are taken to a screen for selecting one of the 22 available settings.

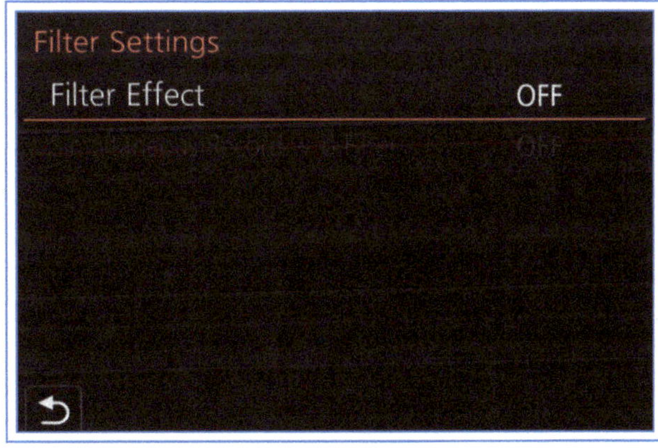

Figure 4-44. Filter Settings Menu Options Screen

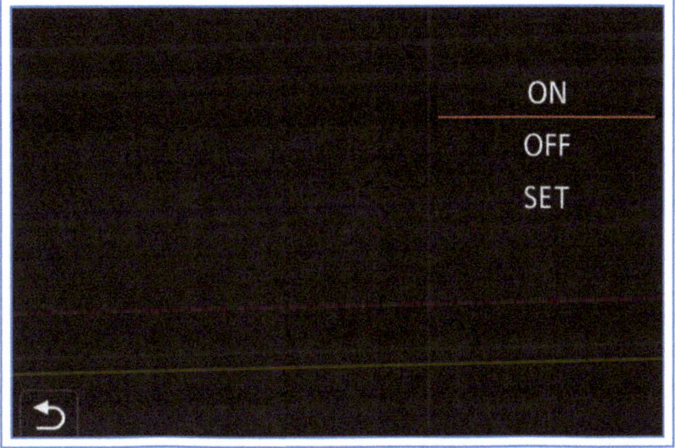

Figure 4-45. Filter Effect Menu Options Screen

The settings screen is the same as that discussed in Chapter 3 for Creative Control mode; see that chapter for details about selecting one of the settings.

If you want to protect against accidentally leaving one of the effects activated, you can go to the main options screen for Filter Settings and select Simultaneous Record Without Filter. That option can be selected only when Filter Effect is turned on through the menu.

If you turn this option on, then, when you take a picture using one of the special effects, such as Expressive, Retro, Miniature, or Soft Focus, the camera also takes an image at the same time that does not use that effect. This feature offers protection against accidentally taking a picture with the Filter Effect feature turned on, resulting in an image that is not usable for ordinary purposes because of the special coloration or other effects. I usually keep this option turned on.

You have to have one of the Filter Effects turned on and Quality set to Standard or Fine in order to turn this simultaneous recording option on. If you do that, then, when all Filter Effects are turned off, this option will be turned off. However, if you have not purposely turned this option off, it will turn itself back on automatically as soon as you activate a Filter Effect. So, I recommend that you turn on a Filter Effect, turn on this menu option, and then turn off the Filter Effect. In that way, this option will be available when needed.

As is the case with the Creative Control settings, the Filter Effects settings do not affect Raw files when those files are opened on a computer, unless you use a special program such as Irfanview. So, if you want to use one of these effects, you should shoot with Quality set to Fine or Raw & Fine.

Screen 2 of the Recording menu is shown in Figure 4-46.

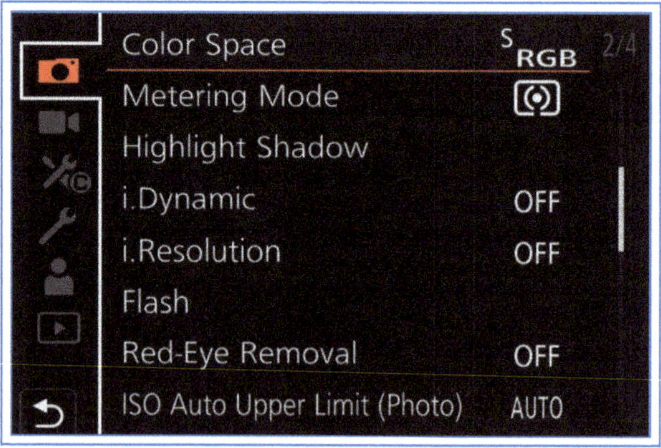

Figure 4-46. Screen 2 of Recording Menu

Color Space

With this option, you can choose to record your images using the sRGB "color space," the more common choice and the default, or the Adobe RGB color space. The sRGB color space has fewer colors than Adobe RGB; therefore, it is more suitable for producing images for the web and other forms of digital display than for printing. If your images are likely to be printed commercially in a book or magazine or it is critical that you be able to match a great many different color variations, you might want to consider using the Adobe RGB color space. I always leave the color space set to sRGB, and I recommend that you do so as well unless you have a specific need to use Adobe RGB, such as a requirement from a printing company that you are using to print your images.

If you are shooting your images with the Raw format, you don't need to worry so much about color space, because you can set it later using your Raw-processing software. This menu item is available in all shooting modes except the basic Snapshot mode, Creative Video mode, and Creative Control mode.

Metering Mode

The next option on the Recording menu lets you choose the way the camera meters the light to determine the proper exposure. The C-Lux gives you a choice of three methods: Multiple, Center-weighted, or Spot. If you choose Multiple, the camera evaluates the brightness at multiple spots in the image shown on the display and calculates an exposure that takes into account all of the various values. With Center-weighted, the camera gives greater emphasis to the brightness of the subject(s) in the center of the screen, while still taking into account the brightness of other areas in the image. With Spot, the camera evaluates only the brightness of the subject(s) in the small spot-metering area.

The Leica user's manual recommends Multiple mode for "normal usage," presumably on the theory that it produces a reasonable choice for exposure based on evaluating the overall brightness of everything in the scene. However, if you want to make sure that one particular item in the scene is properly exposed, you may want to use the Spot method, and aim the spot metering area at that object or person, then lock in the exposure. The Spot option is useful when you are photographing a performer who is lit by a spotlight on stage. For a shot with a central subject of prime importance, such as a portrait, the Center-weighted option may work best.

To make this selection, scroll to the line for Metering Mode, then press the Right button to activate the sub-menu with the three choices, as shown in Figure 4-47.

The first icon, a rectangle with a circle and a dot inside, represents Multiple mode; the second, a rectangle with a circle inside, represents Center-weighted; and the third, a rectangle with just a dot inside, represents Spot.

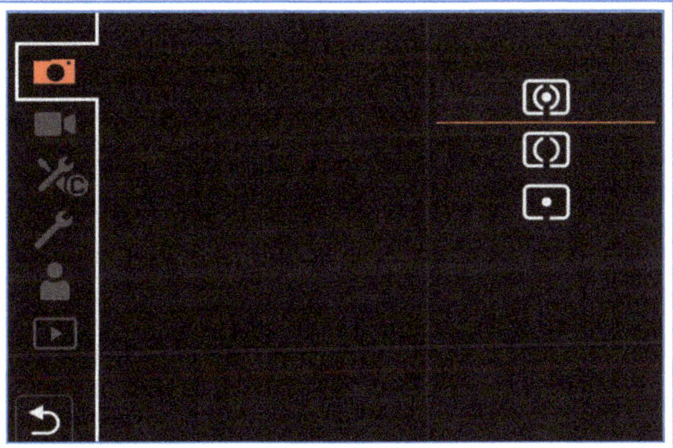

Figure 4-47. Metering Mode Menu Options Screen

With Multiple or Center-weighted, the metering process is simple: Point the camera at the subject(s) you want and let the camera compute the exposure. If you choose Spot as your metering technique, the process can be more involved. Presumably, you will have a fairly small area in mind as the most important area for having the correct exposure; perhaps it is a small object you are photographing for an online auction.

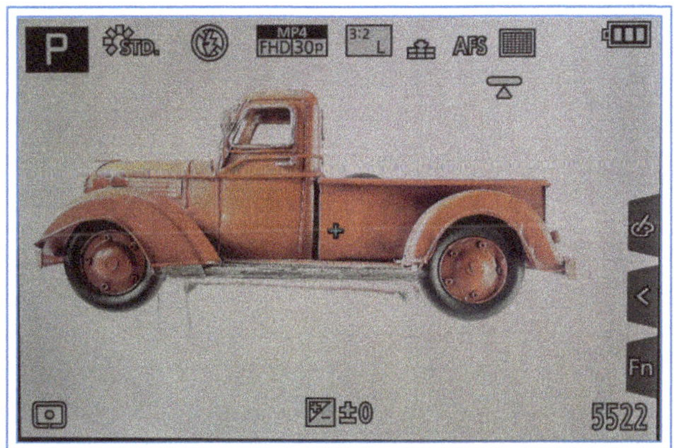

Figure 4-48. Small Blue Cross for Spot Metering Mode

The LCD screen or viewfinder will display a small blue cross in the center of the focusing brackets, as shown in Figure 4-48, and you need to be sure that the cross is over the most important object.

If your subject is not in the center of the screen, you may need to lock the exposure while the Spot-metering cross is on the subject, and then move the camera so the subject is in the proper part of the scene. To do this, press the shutter button halfway while the cross is on the subject, and hold it in that position while you move the camera back to the final position for your composition. (You also can use the AF/AE Lock button for this function, as discussed in Chapter 5.)

As another option, there is a way to move the little cross around the camera's screen so you can place it right over the area of the picture that you want properly exposed. This option is available if, in addition to using Spot metering, you are using an AF Mode setting that lets you move the autofocus frame or zones, such as 1-Area, 49-Area, or Face/Eye Detection, as discussed earlier in this chapter. In that case, whenever you move the focusing target, the Spot-metering target moves along with it, so the target serves two purposes at once. For example, Figure 4-49 shows the display when both Spot metering and 1-Area autofocus are in effect.

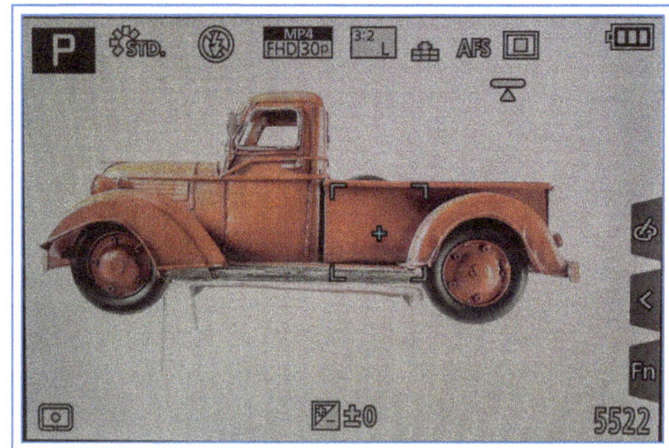

Figure 4-49. Screen with Spot Metering and 1-Area Autofocus

The Metering Mode setting is not available in Snapshot, Snapshot Plus, or Scene mode. When Multiple metering is selected and AF Mode is set to Face/Eye Detection, the camera will attempt to expose a person's face correctly, assuming a face has been detected. The current setting for Metering Mode is indicated by an icon in the lower left of the display, as shown in Figures 4-48 and 4-49.

Highlight Shadow

This menu item gives you a tool for adjusting the highlights and shadows in your images. When you select this menu option, the camera displays a screen like that shown in Figure 4-50, with seven small icons at the bottom available for selection.

(For this illustration I have scrolled to the fourth icon, so all seven icons are at least partly visible.) Each small icon represents a different curve shape for the larger graph in the center of the screen, which includes a line that represents the adjustments to highlights and shadows for your images. When the line is a straight diagonal, no adjustments are present. When the upper part of the line bulges to the left, highlights are increased. When it bulges to the right, the brightness of highlights is lowered. Similarly, the lower part of the line bulges to the left or right to increase or decrease the brightness of shadow areas.

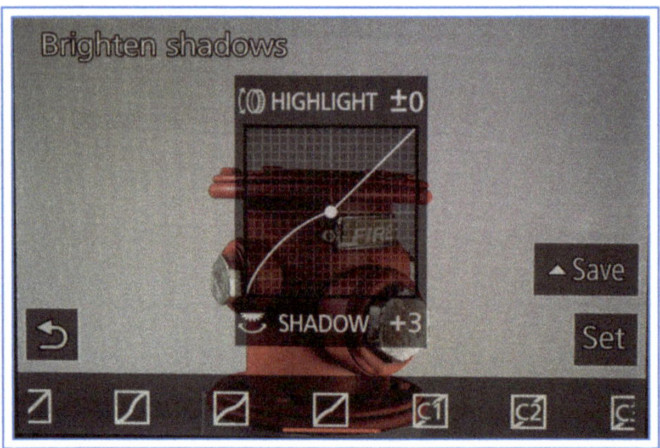

Figure 4-50. Highlight Shadow Menu Options Screen

The first four icons are presets for standard (no adjustments), higher contrast (highlights brighter and shadows darker), lower contrast (highlights darker and shadows brighter), and brighten shadows. The last three icons represent custom settings 1, 2, and 3.

If you want to use one of the four presets, just select it. If you want to make other adjustments, you can select any one of the seven icons and make adjustments to the settings. To make the highlights brighter, turn the control ring to the right; to make them darker, turn it to the left. To make the shadows brighter, turn the thumb dial to the right; to make them darker, turn it to the left. You also can adjust the curves by moving the graph lines on the touch screen. When you have adjusted the curves as you want, press the Up button to save the settings. You will then see the screen shown in Figure 4-51, prompting you to select custom 1, 2, or 3 as the slot in which to save your settings.

Highlight any one of those and press the Menu/Set button to save the settings. Then, whenever you want to recall those settings, go to the Highlight Shadow menu option and select the custom 1, 2, or 3 icon, depending on which slot you used to save your custom settings.

This option can be useful if you are often faced with situations with your subject partly in shadow and partly in bright light. It can be particularly helpful because you can see the effects of the adjustments you make on the live view, as you turn the dial and ring to adjust highlights and shadows. Of course, the C-Lux also has other options to deal with that situation, such as the HDR setting, discussed later in this chapter, and the Intelligent Dynamic setting, discussed next.

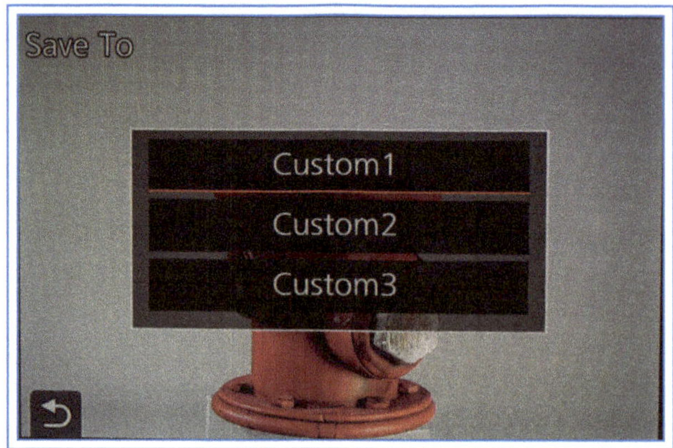

Figure 4-51. Confirmation Screen to Save Custom Highlight Shadow Setting

Intelligent Dynamic

The next option on screen 2 of the Recording menu is shown as i.Dynamic, which I will refer to here as Intelligent Dynamic. This feature gives you another way to accomplish what the Highlight Shadow option does—that is, to deal with a situation in which there is considerable contrast between the dark and bright areas of the scene. This option, unlike the previous one, does not let you make precise adjustments to the shadow and highlight curves. Instead, it adjusts contrast and exposure generally; it lets you set the intensity of the camera's adjustments to a level of Low, Standard, or High. You also can leave the option turned off, or you can set it to Auto and let the camera make the adjustments based on its analysis of the scene.

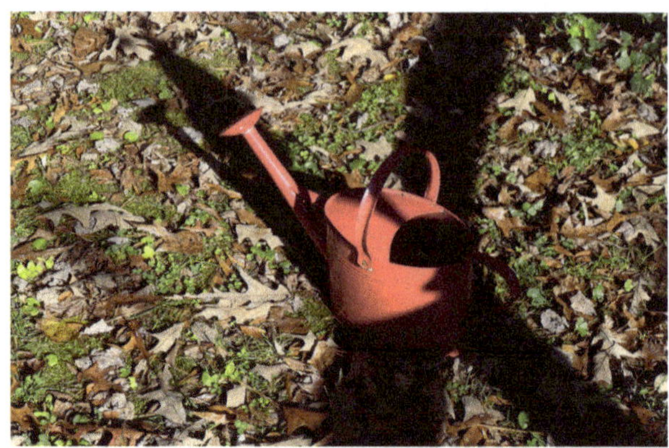
Figure 4-52. Intelligent Dynamic Turned Off

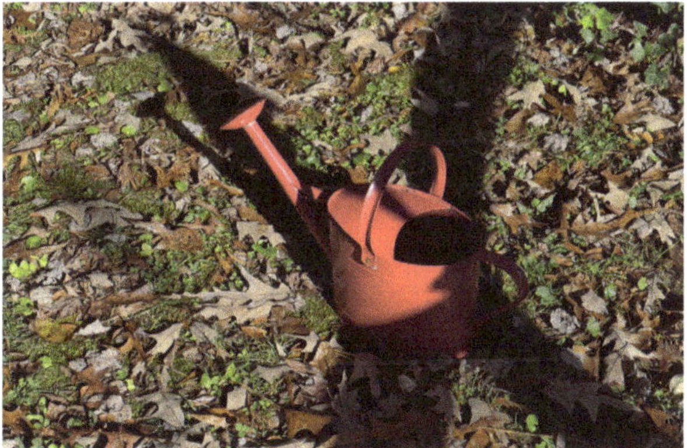

Figure 4-53. Intelligent Dynamic Set to High

Figures 4-52 and 4-53 are two views of the same outdoor scene, partly in sunlight and partly in deep shade, but taken with different settings for Intelligent Dynamic.

As you can see, in Figure 4-52, with Intelligent Dynamic turned off, the contrast is quite stark. In Figure 4-53, with Intelligent Dynamic set to High, the contrast is evened out and the shadowed areas are brightened noticeably. This is a good setting to use when you are taking photos in an area with both sunlight and shade.

Intelligent Resolution

The next option is listed on the menu as i.Resolution, which I will call Intelligent Resolution. This option can be set to Off, Low, Standard, or High, as shown in Figure 4-54.

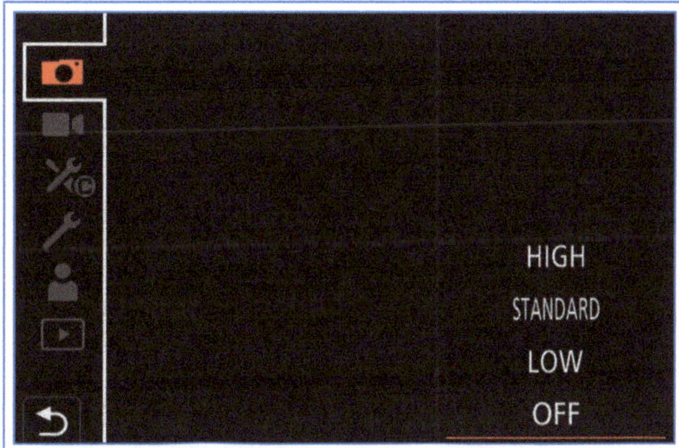

Figure 4-54. Intelligent Resolution Menu Options Screen

This setting increases the apparent resolution in images by providing additional sharpening through in-camera digital manipulation. It does seem to improve image quality somewhat in certain situations. I recommend that you try shooting with it turned on and off to see if it provides actual benefits for your shots. I do not often use it myself, because I prefer to shoot with Raw quality and add sharpening with my editing software.

Flash

The next item on the Recording menu, simply called Flash, is the gateway to several options for using the built-in flash unit. The Flash item does not appear on the menu in Snapshot mode. In that shooting mode, the camera makes flash settings based on its programming, with no input from you. In Snapshot Plus mode, the Flash item appears on the menu but is not available for selection, because the camera makes all flash decisions in that mode as well.

When you highlight Flash on the menu and press the Right button or the Menu/Set button (or press the menu item on the touch screen), the camera displays the screen shown in Figure 4-55, which has three sub-options: Flash Mode, Flash Synchro, and Flash Adjustment.

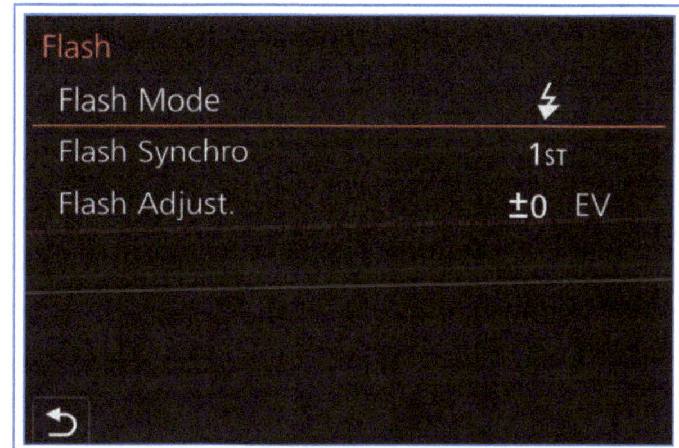

Figure 4-55. Flash Menu Options Screen

Flash Mode

This first sub-option lets you set the flash mode for your shot.

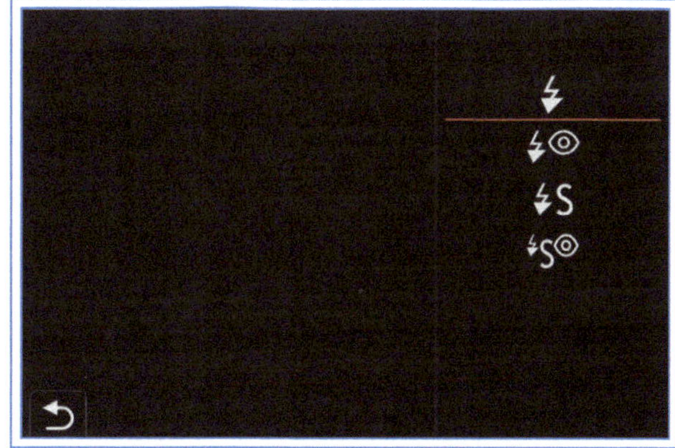

Figure 4-56. Flash Mode Menu Options Screen

There are four options for this setting, represented by the icons shown in Figure 4-56, from top to bottom: Forced On, Forced On with Red Eye, Slow Sync, and Slow Sync with Red Eye.

If you choose Forced On, sometimes referred to as fill-flash, the flash will fire every time you press the shutter button, if the flash is operating properly and no other settings interfere. This is the mode to choose when you are certain you want the flash to fire, such as when you are taking snapshots in a dimly lighted area. It also is the mode to choose when you want to use flash to soften the shadows or brighten the scene slightly when you are taking a shot, especially a portrait, outdoors. A bit of fill-flash can offset the harsh shadows and highlights from direct sunlight, and even can provide a different look for a shot taken under a cloudy sky. For example, Figure 4-57 and Figure 4-58 are two images I took outdoors near some trees on a sunny day.

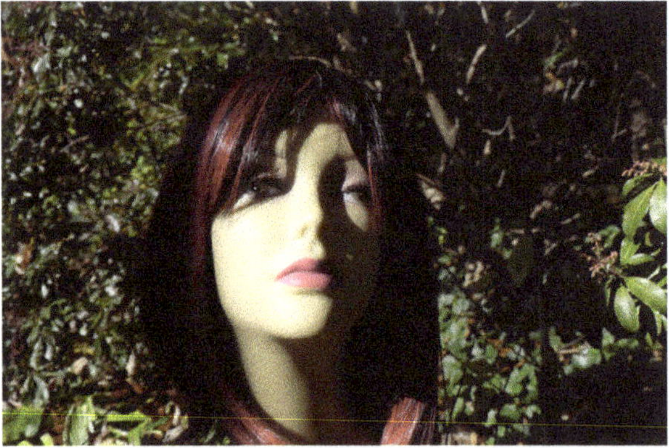

Figure 4-57. Flash Turned Off

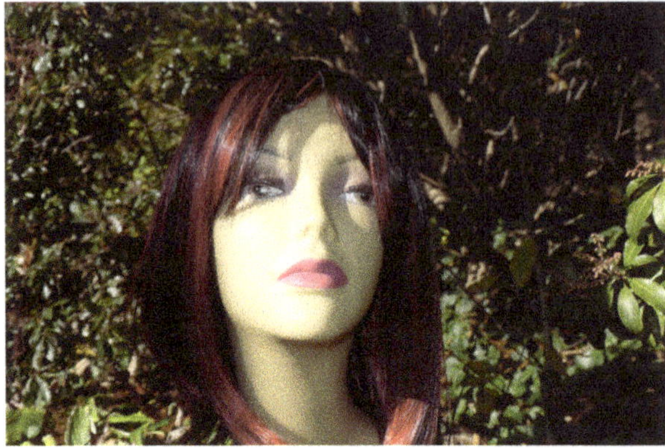

Figure 4-58. Flash Set to Forced On

For Figure 4-57, I left the flash turned off; for Figure 4-58, I used the Forced On setting. The second image has more even lighting than the first one, because the on-camera flash filled in the shadows that were cast on the subject and brightened the face.

The next option, Forced On with Red Eye, is for use when you are aiming the camera with flash directly at a person's face. In that situation, the flash can bounce off the person's retinas and light up blood vessels, resulting in the unpleasant "red eye" effect that is common in flash snapshots. With this setting, the camera will fire a pre-flash before the main flash, to narrow the subject's pupils before the image is captured and thereby reduce the risk of the red eye effect.

The next setting, Slow Sync, is for use in dark conditions when you want to give the ambient light time to illuminate the background. With a normal flash shot, the exposure may last only about 1/60 second, enough time for the flash to illuminate the subject in the foreground, but not enough time for natural lighting to reveal the background. So, you may end up with an image in which the subject is brightly lit but the background is black. With Slow Sync, the camera will use a relatively slow shutter speed so the ambient lighting will have time to register on the image.

For example, Figure 4-59 and Figure 4-60 are two images taken at the same time and in the same conditions except for the flash mode. I took Figure 4-59 with the shutter speed set at 1/60 second, in normal flash mode (Forced On). The background is quite dark, because the exposure was too short to light up the area beyond the subject. I took Figure 4-60 using Slow Sync flash mode, which caused the camera to use a shutter speed of one second, allowing time for the ambient lighting to illuminate the room behind the mannequin so the background showed up more clearly.

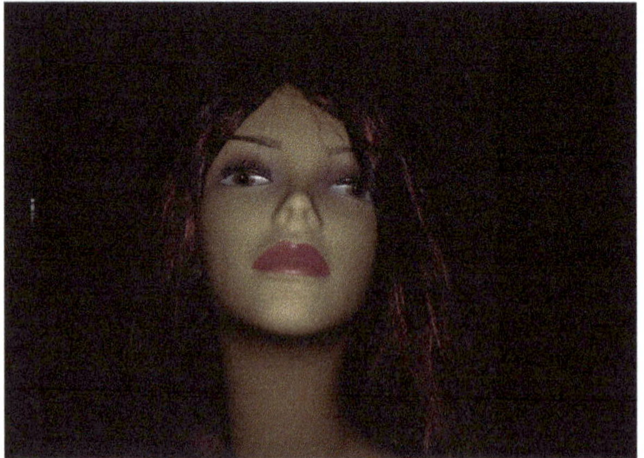

Figure 4-59. Normal Flash at 1/60 Second

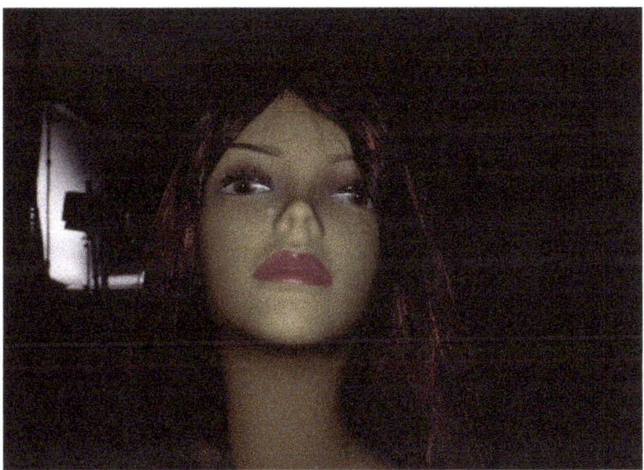

Figure 4-60. Slow Sync Flash at One Second

The Slow Sync option is not available for selection on the Recording menu when the camera is set to Shutter Priority or Manual exposure mode, because you set the shutter speed in those modes, so the camera cannot select a slow one. In the two Snapshot modes, the camera may use the Slow Sync option, but you cannot select the setting yourself in those modes.

Slow Sync with Red Eye is the same as Slow Sync, except that the camera fires a pre-flash to try to reduce the red eye effect. In Scene mode, Slow Sync with Red Eye is the only flash mode setting available when the Clear Night Portrait setting is selected. When the Monochrome scene type is selected, you can select any one of the four flash mode settings, including either of the two Slow Sync settings.

Flash Synchro

The next sub-option for the Flash menu item, Flash Synchro, is one you may not have a lot of use for unless you encounter the particular situation it is designed for.

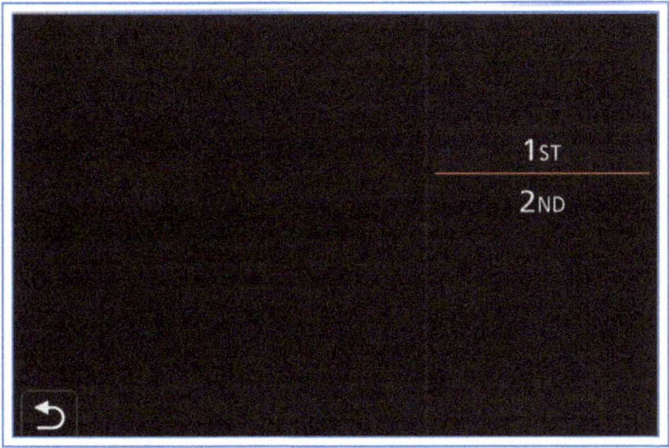

Figure 4-61. Flash Synchro Menu Options Screen

The Flash Synchro menu option, as shown in Figure 4-61, has two settings—1st and 2nd. Those terms are references to 1st-curtain sync and 2nd-curtain (also known as rear-curtain) sync. The normal setting is 1st, which causes the flash to fire early in the process when the shutter opens to expose the image. If you set it to 2nd, the flash fires later, just before the shutter closes.

The 2nd-curtain sync setting can help you avoid a strange-looking result in some situations. This issue arises when you are taking a relatively long exposure, such as 1/4 second, of a subject with taillights, such as a car or motorcycle at night, that is moving across your field of view. With 1st-curtain sync, the flash will fire early in the process, freezing the vehicle in a clear image. However, as the shutter remains open while the vehicle continues on, the camera will capture the moving taillights in a stream that seems to extend in front of the vehicle. If, instead, you use 2nd-curtain sync, the first part of the exposure will capture the lights in a trail that appears behind the vehicle, while the vehicle itself is not frozen by the flash until later in the exposure. Therefore, with 2nd-curtain sync in this particular situation, the final image is likely to look more natural than with 1st-curtain sync.

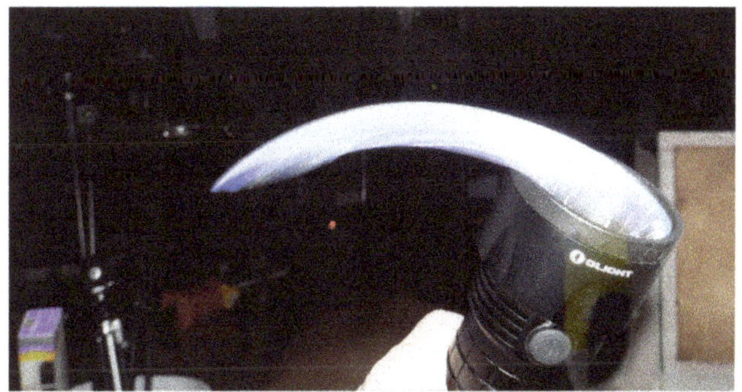

Figure 4-62. Flash Synchro Set to 1st

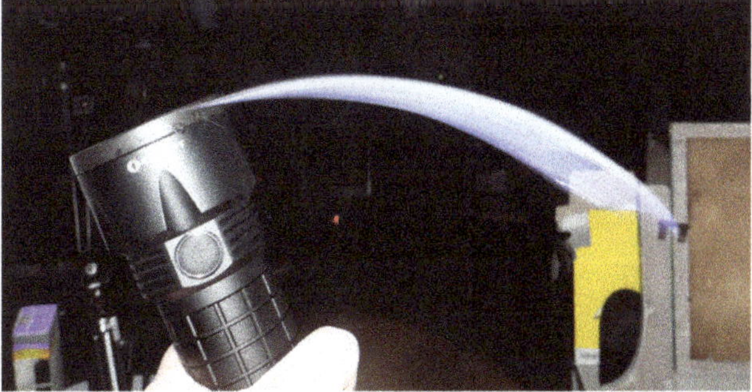

Figure 4-63. Flash Synchro Set to 2nd

Figures 4-62 and 4-63 illustrates this concept with two images, both showing a flashlight in motion from right to left. Both images were shot with the C-Lux's built-in flash, using an exposure of 1/2 second in Shutter Priority mode. In Figure 4-62, using the Forced On setting, the flash fired quickly, and the light beam continued on during the long exposure to make the streak of light appear to move in front of the flashlight's motion.

In Figure 4-63, using the 2nd setting for Flash Synchro, the flash did not fire until the flashlight had moved to the left, overtaking the place where the light had made its streak visible. If you are trying to convey a sense of natural motion, the 2nd setting for Flash Synchro is likely to give you better results than the default setting.

A good general rule is to always use the 1st setting unless you are sure you have a need for the 2nd setting. Using the 2nd setting makes it harder to compose and set up the shot, because you have to anticipate where the main subject will be when the flash finally fires late in the exposure process.

The Flash Synchro setting is available for selection only in the PASM shooting modes. When the 2d setting is turned on, you cannot use either of the Red Eye Reduction settings for flash mode.

Flash Adjustment

The Flash Adjustment sub-option lets you adjust the intensity of the flash. If the exposure with flash seems too bright or too dark, you can use this setting to adjust it downward or upward in small increments. The adjustment screen for this item is shown in Figure 4-64.

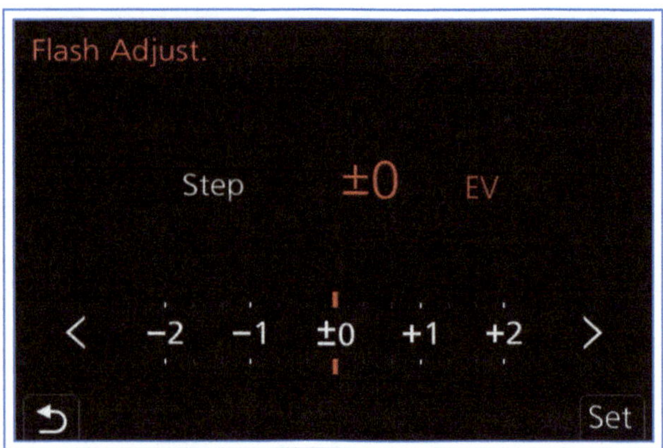

Figure 4-64. Flash Adjustment Screen

Use the thumb dial or the Left and Right buttons (or the touch screen) to dial in the amount of positive or negative EV adjustment you want. Of course, you also have the option of using regular exposure compensation, causing the camera to adjust the exposure using settings other than flash. This choice is up to you; it depends on what effect you are looking for. I rarely find a reason to increase the flash output, but I find that it can be useful to decrease the flash output to reduce the harshness of the lighting for a portrait in some cases.

Red-eye Removal

This next setting on the Recording menu is not to be confused with Red-eye Reduction, which is an aspect of how the flash fires. As I noted earlier, "red eye" is the unpleasant phenomenon that crops up when a flash picture is taken of a person, and the light illuminates his or her retinas, causing an eerie red glow to appear in the eyes. One way the C-Lux (like many cameras) deals with this problem is with the Red-eye Reduction setting for the flash mode, which causes the flash to fire twice: once to make the person's eyes contract, reducing the chance for the light to bounce off the retinas, and then a second time to take the picture.

The C-Lux has a second line of defense against red eye, called Red-eye Removal. When you select this option, which can be turned either on or off, then, whenever the flash is fired and Red-eye Reduction is activated, the camera also uses a digital red-eye correction method, to actually remove from the image the red areas that appear to be near a person's eyes. This option operates only when flash mode is set to one of the two options with Red-eye Reduction.

I do not usually use this option, because I process my images using Photoshop or other software, and it's easy to fix red eye at that stage. But I did test it, and it did a good job of removing red areas from a mannequin's eyes on which I had pasted red dots to simulate red eye.

ISO Auto Upper Limit (Photo)

This menu option, whose setting screen is shown in Figure 4-65, lets you set an upper limit for the value the camera will choose for ISO, when you have selected either Auto ISO or Intelligent ISO, as discussed earlier in this chapter. The choices for this setting are Auto, 200, 400, 800, 1600, 3200, 6400, or 12500. If you choose Auto, then the ISO limit is automatically set to 3200.

If you want to make sure the camera will use a relatively low ISO to preserve image quality, you can set this value down to 200, 400 or 800. If you are shooting in dark conditions and your priority is to make sure you can capture the image even if image quality suffers, you might want to set a high limit, such as 12500. As indicated by its name, this option does not have any effect for motion picture recording. (There is a similar setting for movies on the Motion Picture menu.)

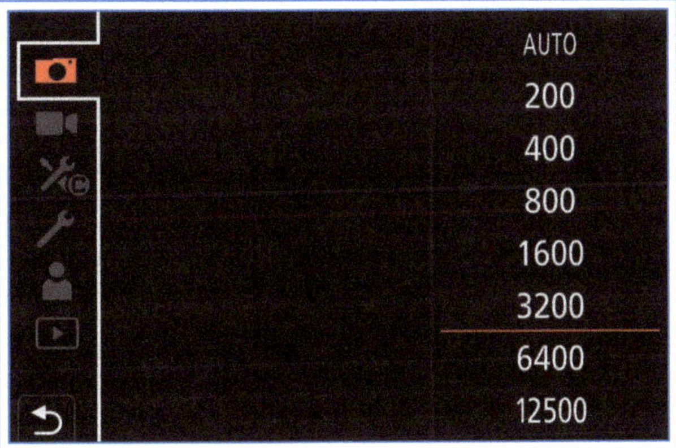

Figure 4-65. ISO Auto Upper Limit (Photo)

The settings on screen 3 of the Recording menu are shown in Figure 4-66.

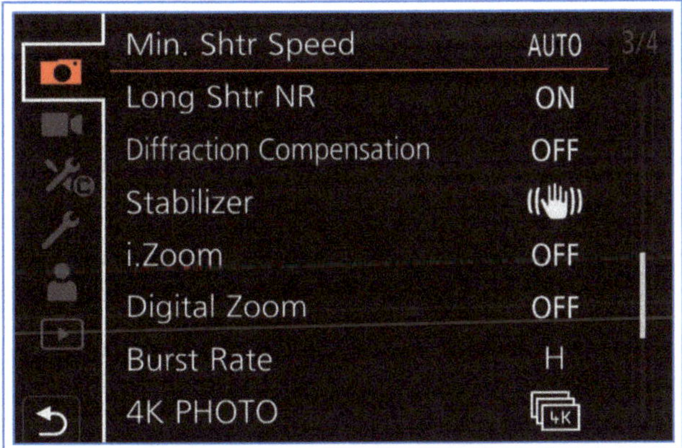

Figure 4-66. Screen 3 of Recording Menu

Minimum Shutter Speed

This first option on screen 3 of the Recording menu lets you set the minimum (slowest) shutter speed that the camera should use when Auto ISO or Intelligent ISO is in use. This option is available for use only in the Program and Aperture Priority shooting modes. The purpose of this setting is to avoid having the camera set a low ISO value that results in the use of a relatively slow shutter speed, and possible motion blur. For example, if you are photographing active children at play, you may want to set the minimum shutter speed to a value such as 1/250 second, so you will be fairly sure to freeze their actions without blurring.

This setting can be anywhere from a full second to 1/16000 of a second, or Auto; just select the desired value on the sub-menu that pops up when you select this option. If you choose Auto, the camera will select a shutter speed based on its own evaluation of the lighting conditions. Even if you choose a specific value such as 1/500 second, the camera may set a slower shutter speed if necessary to achieve a normal exposure.

Long Shutter Noise Reduction

When you take a picture using a shutter speed of several seconds, the image sensor may generate an excessive amount of visual noise because of the way its circuitry reacts to long exposures. If you turn on the Long Shutter Noise Reduction menu option, the camera will use noise-reduction processing that lasts as long as the exposure itself to reduce the noise. For example, if your exposure lasts for 12 seconds, the camera will continue processing the image for another 12 seconds after the exposure ends. This action will delay your ability to take another shot, and the processing can reduce the details in your image. If you don't want to experience this delay or if you want to deal with the possibility of noise some other way (such as using software to reduce it), turn this option off.

This option is available only in the PASM, Scene, and Creative Control shooting modes. It is not available for motion picture recording, when Post Focus is active, when recording with the 4K Photo feature, or with the electronic shutter.

Diffraction Compensation

When the camera uses a narrow aperture such as f/8.0, the diffraction effect comes into play and can cause distortion in the image. If you set the Diffraction Compensation option to Auto, the camera uses its processing to counteract that effect, when needed. If you would rather deal with that issue with your post-processing software or leave it untouched, choose Off. This option is available with all shooting modes except Snapshot and Snapshot Plus.

Stabilizer

The C-Lux is equipped with an optical image stabilization system that counteracts the effects of camera shake on the image. This system has three possible settings, as shown in Figure 4-67, from top to bottom: Normal, Panning, and Off.

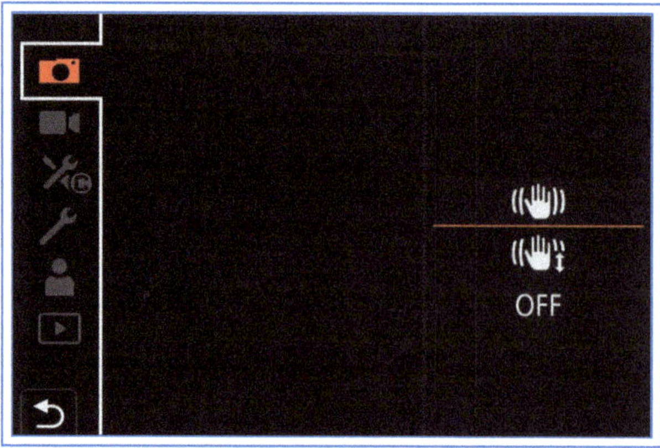

Figure 4-67. Stabilizer Menu Options Screen

With the Normal setting, the camera corrects for both horizontal and vertical motion. With the Panning setting, the camera assumes that you are moving the camera from side to side in order to pan over the scene, so it does not attempt to correct for horizontal motion, only vertical. I generally leave this setting at Normal when I am hand-holding the camera. If I have the camera on a tripod, the setting is unnecessary and possibly could cause some distortion as the camera tries to correct for camera movement that does not exist.

The Normal stabilization setting is not available when you are shooting panoramas. The Panning setting is not available when recording movies or using 4K Photo or Post Focus. The Stabilizer menu option is not available for selection in the basic Snapshot mode.

Intelligent Zoom

The Intelligent Zoom, or i.Zoom, option is related to the i.Resolution feature, discussed earlier, although you do not have to turn on i.Resolution in order to take advantage of i.Zoom. When i.Zoom is turned on, the camera automatically takes advantage of i.Resolution processing in the zoom range to improve the appearance of the image, so you can zoom to a higher level of magnification without image deterioration, using either normal optical zoom or Extended Optical Zoom. (As discussed earlier in this chapter, Extended Optical Zoom is available when Picture Size is set to Medium or Small, because extra pixels are available for enlarging the image.)

For example, without the i.Zoom setting, the limit for the optical zoom is 15x; with i.Zoom turned on, the maximum is 30x. The question of image quality in this situation is a matter of judgment; as with i.Resolution, I recommend that you try this setting to see if you are satisfied with the quality of the images. If so, you can then use an effective zoom range up to 720mm, rather than the 360mm of the optical zoom alone. (The range can be even greater if combined with Digital Zoom and Extended Optical Zoom, although the quality of the image will suffer with excessive zoom range in effect.)

The i.Zoom feature is not available in conjunction with certain types of shooting that involve special processing, including panorama shots, shots with the Raw format, Multiple Exposure, shots using the HDR or Handheld Night Shot options, or shots using the filter effects of Impressive Art, Toy, or Toy Pop. This feature is automatically turned on in Snapshot and Snapshot Plus mode.

Digital Zoom

With Digital Zoom, unlike Intelligent Zoom and Extended Optical Zoom, the camera produces what Panasonic calls "decreased" picture quality. As with many digital cameras, Digital Zoom is available on the C-Lux as a way of enlarging the pixels that are displayed so the C-Lux Appears larger; there is no additional resolution available, so the image can quickly begin to appear blocky and of low quality. Experts often recommend not using this sort of zoom feature.

As with Extended Optical Zoom and Intelligent Zoom, this option can help you in viewing a distant subject. Digital Zoom has a maximum power of four times the normal lens's magnification, or 1440mm. When you combine all of the zoom options, including Digital Zoom and using a smaller picture size for Extended Optical Zoom, there is a maximum total zoom power of eight times normal, or 2880mm.

Digital Zoom is not available in Snapshot, Snapshot Plus, or Panorama mode or with some other settings, including Raw quality, Post Focus, high speed video, Multiple Exposure, Handheld Night Shot, HDR, or with the filter effects of Impressive Art, Toy, Toy Pop, or Miniature. It also is not available when either Monitor Display Speed or EVF Display Speed, both of which are on screen 2 of the Setup menu, is set to Eco30fps. The setting of Eco30fps is the default value for Monitor Display Speed, so, when the camera is new, you may find that you cannot turn on Digital Zoom. If that is the case, change that setting to 60fps and the conflict will be resolved, unless another conflicting setting from the above list is in place.

Burst Rate

This next item on screen 3 of the Recording menu controls the rate for burst shooting. The control for selecting burst shooting from the shooting screen is the Down button, which activates the drive mode settings, including burst shooting, 4K Photo, Post Focus, and the self-timer, as discussed in Chapter 5.

When you press the Down button and activate burst shooting from the drive mode menu, you have the option to set the burst rate from that menu. However, if you want, you can set the burst rate ahead of time from this Recording menu item. In that way, you will save a step when you press the Down button to select burst shooting from the drive mode options.

The choices for burst rate are H, M, and L, for high, medium, and low. I will discuss those options in Chapter 5, in connection with the drive mode options.

4K Photo

The 4K Photo menu option, like the Burst Rate option, works together with the continuous-shooting features of the C-Lux. 4K Photo is a special type of burst shooting that involves recording a sequence using the 4K video format. It has three sub-options, for use in different types of situations.

You can activate 4K Photo from the drive mode menu by pressing the Down button from the shooting screen, or by pressing the Fn1 button, unless you have assigned that button to another function. (That button, at the upper right of the camera's back, is labeled 4K and is assigned by default to trigger 4K Photo mode.)

As with normal burst shooting, you can choose a sub-option for 4K burst shooting after you select 4K Photo using one of the above methods. However, you also can use the 4K Photo menu option to select the 4K shooting sub-option ahead of time, to save time when you press a button to activate 4K shooting. I will discuss the details of the various 4K Photo settings in Chapter 5, where I discuss the physical controls.

The options on screen 4 of the Recording menu are shown in Figure 4-68.

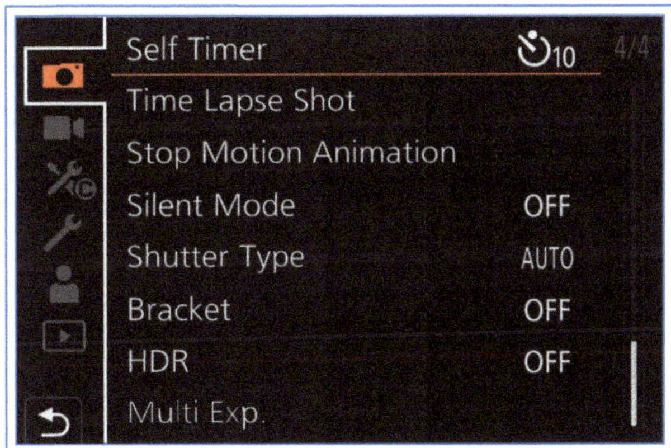

Figure 4-68. Screen 4 of Recording Menu

Self-Timer

The next menu option is another one that lets you adjust settings that are normally made through the drive mode menu after pressing the Down button from the shooting screen. With this option, you can set the self-timer to a delay of two seconds or ten seconds for a single shot, or to a delay of ten seconds with a series of three shots. In Chapter 5, I will discuss how to make these settings from the drive mode menu.

Time Lapse Shot

The Time Lapse Shot option lets you shoot a time-lapse series of photographs. You probably have seen sequences in the movies or on television in which an event that takes a fair amount of time, such as a sunset, a flower opening, clouds moving across the sky, or a parking lot filling up with cars, is shown in a speeded-up series of images, so it appears to happen in a few seconds.

The C-Lux can use its time-lapse feature with any shooting mode other than Panorama and Creative Video, including Snapshot. If you use the more advanced shooting modes, you have access to all of the major settings for your images, including Raw quality, white balance, ISO, and others.

To use this feature, highlight Time Lapse Shot on the Recording menu and press the Right button to move to the setup screen, shown in Figure 4-69.

On that screen, use the direction buttons or the thumb dial (or the touch screen) to navigate through the various options. Select a start time, the interval between shots, and the total number of shots. The interval can be set to any value from one second to 99 minutes 59 seconds. One point to bear in mind when setting the interval is that, if the lighting is very dim, the camera may need to set a long shutter speed. For example, if the camera is set to use a shutter speed of one minute, which requires a long time for in-camera processing after the exposure is made, this system will not succeed if the interval between shots is set to less than two minutes. The total number of shots can be any number up to 9,999.

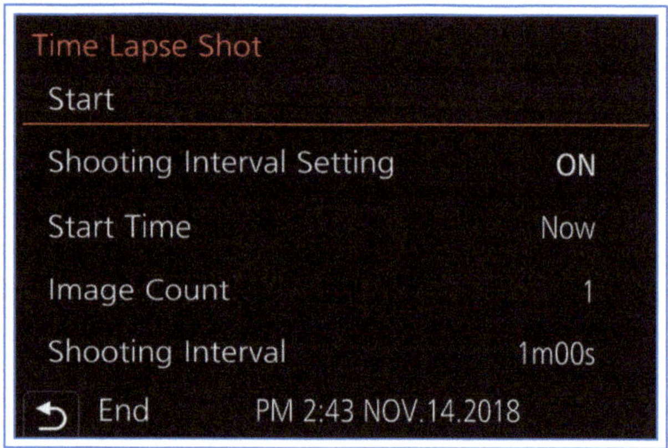

Figure 4-69. Time Lapse Shot Settings Screen

When you have made all of the settings as you want them, press the Menu/Set button, then select Start from the main options screen. The camera will display a message prompting you to press the shutter button when you're ready to start the sequence.

When you press the shutter button, the camera will take the images at the specified intervals and will repeat the process until the total number of images has been recorded. Of course, if the battery runs down or the memory card fills up, the process will end prematurely. (You can use an optional AC adapter to avoid a power issue; see Appendix A.) At any time, you can press the Fn1 button and the camera will display a screen asking if you want to continue, pause, or end the process.

When the sequence is complete, either after the full series has been taken or after an interrupted series, the camera will display a message asking if you want it to create a movie using the recorded images. If you say yes, it will take some time to process the movie, which you can then play like any movie.

If you say no to creating the movie, assuming you have a detailed display screen selected in playback mode, the first image in the series will be displayed with indications like those in Figure 4-70, showing that you can press the Up button to play back the sequence quickly, like a short movie, or the Down button for other options.

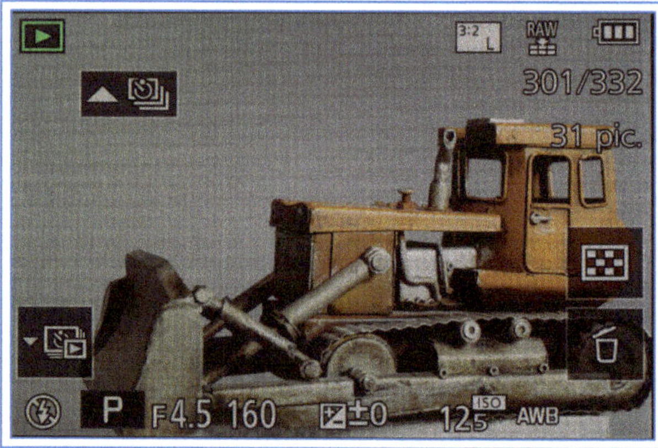

Figure 4-70. Time Lapse Shot Playback Screen

If you press the Up button, the camera will play back the images quickly, in sequence. If you press the Down button, you will see icons for two choices. If you then press the Up button, the camera will display a sub-menu with options of displaying the images sequentially starting with the first image in the sequence, or starting from the current picture. If you press the Down button, the camera will toggle between normal playback mode, in which the time-lapse images are treated as a single group, and playing the images individually.

If you don't create a movie from the shots at this point, you can do so later using the Time Lapse Video option on screen 3 of the Playback menu, as discussed in Chapter 6.

Stop Motion Animation

This next feature is similar to Time Lapse Shot, because it involves taking a series of still images, which the camera then combines into a movie. The difference is that this option is intended for use in animating objects, such as clay figures or puppets. You also can use it to make an animated movie based on drawings, as is done for cartoons and animated feature films. You need to move the figure or change the drawing very slightly for each new shot. You will need a large number of images to create a movie of any length. For example, if the final movie is to be shown at 30 frames per second, you will need to take 30 images for every second of the movie, changing the position or other aspect of the subject slightly for each successive image.

When you select this option, you will see a screen with options for Start, Auto Shooting, and Shooting

Interval. The interval option will not be available unless you first turn on Auto Shooting. If you turn on Auto Shooting, the camera will capture images on its own at the interval you specify, from one second to 60 seconds. Otherwise, you will have to trigger the camera yourself when you are ready for each shot. Because it is critical to keep the camera absolutely still throughout the image-taking process, it is advisable to use the Auto Shooting option so you will not have to touch the camera to take each shot. If you do not use Auto Shooting, you can control the camera from a smartphone or tablet by remote control, as discussed in Chapter 9.

You also may want to use an optional AC adapter, discussed in Appendix A, to make sure the camera does not lose power during the shooting. However, if the camera does turn off, you can resume the series of shots when it is turned back on. It will prompt you to do so if the series has been interrupted.

While the shooting is in progress, the camera will display an icon showing a series of frames at the right side of the display with the cumulative number of shots taken so far, as shown in Figure 4-71. It also will display an overlaid image of the previous two shots, to help you line up the next shot properly with the figure or drawing in the proper position.

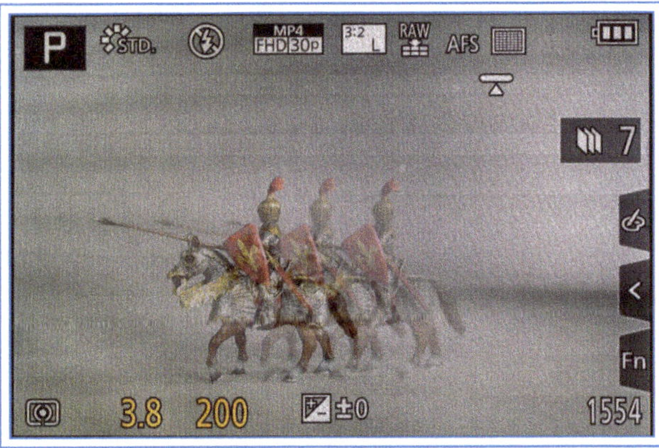

Figure 4-71. Shooting Screen During Stop Motion Animation

When you have finished your series of shots, press the Stop Motion icon, or press the Menu/Set button and go to the Stop Motion Animation menu item. Press Menu/Set when that item is highlighted, and the camera will ask whether you want to stop the shooting series. If you say yes, it will ask if you want to create the video now. If so, it will prompt you for the settings to use, including recording quality, frame rate, and whether to run the sequence forward (normal) or in reverse. For the best quality, you should select 60p for the recording quality and 60 frames per second for the frame rate (in the United States), but 30p and 30 fps will still provide a smooth flow of action. Lower settings will produce more jerky footage. Select OK when the settings are made as you want, and the camera will create the video. You can play it back in the camera by pressing the Up button.

If you don't create a movie from the shots at this point, you can do so later using the Stop Motion Video option on screen 3 of the Playback menu, as discussed in Chapter 6. As with the Time Lapse Shot option, you can view the shots in playback mode as a quick sequence using the Up button or individually from the sub-menu called up by the Down button.

Silent Mode

The Silent Mode option gives you a quick way to turn off the lights and sounds made by the camera that might distract a subject or cause a disturbance in a quiet area. When you turn this option on, the camera switches to using the electronic shutter, which is quieter than the mechanical shutter; silences all beeps and other sounds for matters such as focus and shutter operation; forces the flash off; and turns off the AF assist lamp. However, the lamp will still light up to indicate use of the self-timer, and the blue connection lamp will illuminate if you start a Wi-Fi or Bluetooth connection. If you will often use Silent Mode, you can include it as part of a group of saved settings with the Custom Set Memory option, or you can assign it to a function button.

Shutter Type

The C-Lux is equipped with two different types of shutter—electronic and mechanical. With this menu option, you can set the camera to choose the shutter type automatically, or you can select one or the other shutter type for use. The three options for this setting are Auto, MSHTR, and ESHTR. With Auto, the camera will choose the shutter type based on the current settings and conditions. With MSHTR or ESHTR, it will use only the mechanical or electronic shutter, depending on your selection.

For most purposes, the mechanical shutter is the better option. With that choice, the camera operates a physical iris with leaves that open and close to allow light to pass through to the sensor. With the electronic shutter, the circuitry in the camera starts and stops the exposure, with no mechanical parts involved. Therefore, the electronic shutter can produce faster shutter speeds than the mechanical one. Also, because of the lack of moving parts, the camera can remain silent when the electronic shutter is activated. However, using the electronic shutter can result in a "rolling" effect that distorts images or videos, especially if the camera or subject is moving horizontally.

If you select Auto or ESHTR, the shutter speed can be set as fast as 1/16000 second; with MSHTR, the fastest speed available is 1/2000 second.

I almost always leave this setting at Auto so the camera will use the electronic shutter when needed, but will use the mechanical shutter in most cases. One reason to turn on the ESHTR option would be if you want the camera to remain completely silent for a particular shooting session. Another way to make the camera silent is to select the Silent Mode menu option, discussed directly above. In that case, the camera will automatically activate the electronic shutter, even if the MSHTR option had been selected on the Recording menu.

Bracket

The Bracket menu option gives you access to several ways to take a series of images with one press of the shutter button, using a different value for a particular setting for each of those images. In this way, you will have several images to choose from, increasing your chance of having one that suits your needs for that setting. The settings that can be varied are exposure, aperture, focus, and white balance.

After highlighting the Bracket menu option, select it to move to the next screen, shown in Figure 4-72.

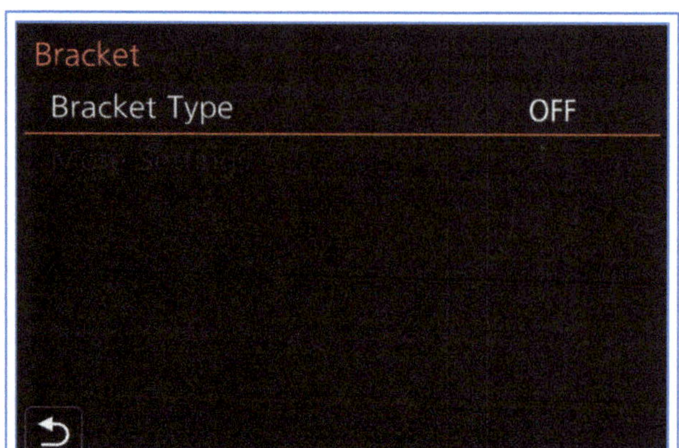

Figure 4-72. Bracket Menu Options Screen

On that screen, select Bracket Type, and the camera will display the menu shown in Figure 4-73, with a vertical line of five icons.

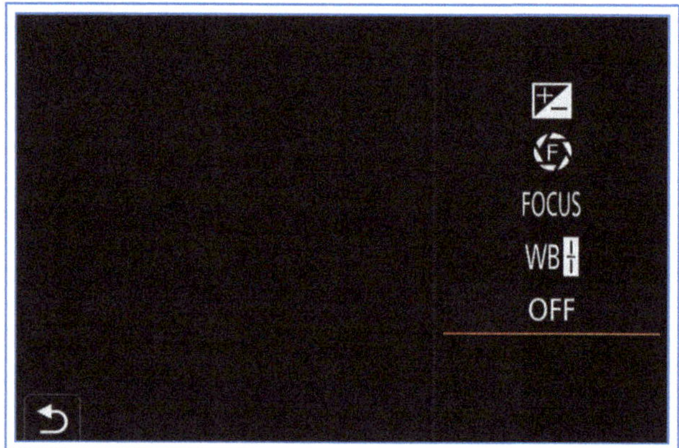

Figure 4-73. Bracket Type Menu Options Screen

From the top, the first four icons represent exposure bracket, aperture bracket, focus bracket, and white balance bracket. I will discuss each of these in turn below.

Exposure Bracket

When you select this first bracket option, the camera varies the exposure within a range you select so you will have several differently exposed images to choose from. This option gives you an added chance of getting an optimal exposure. If you're shooting with Raw quality, exposure is not so much of an issue, because you can adjust it later with software, but it's always a good idea to start with an exposure that's as accurate as possible.

Also, you can use this feature to take several differently exposed shots that you can merge into a single HDR (high dynamic range) image, to cover a wider range of lights and darks than any single image could. This merging can be accomplished with software such as Photoshop (use the command File-Automate-Merge to HDR Pro) or a specialized program such as PhotoAcute or Photomatix Pro. For HDR shooting, I suggest you set the interval between exposures to the largest available, which is 1 EV (exposure value). If possible, you should use a tripod so all images will include the same area of the scene and can be easily merged in the software.

Once you have selected this option from the Bracket menu, the More Settings menu option becomes available for selection. Select it, and the camera displays the screen shown in Figure 4-74, with options for Step, Sequence, and Single Shot Setting. First, select Step, which lets you choose the interval for the exposure difference among the multiple shots the camera will take. When you press the Menu/Set button with that option highlighted, the camera displays the screen shown in Figure 4-75, which lets you set the number of exposures and the EV interval.

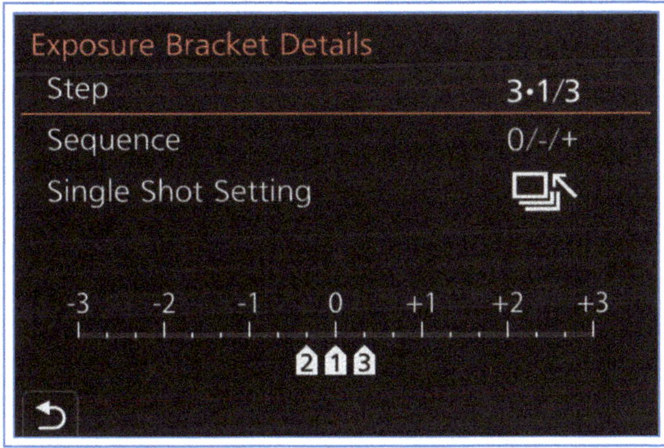

Figure 4-74. Exposure Bracket Details Screen

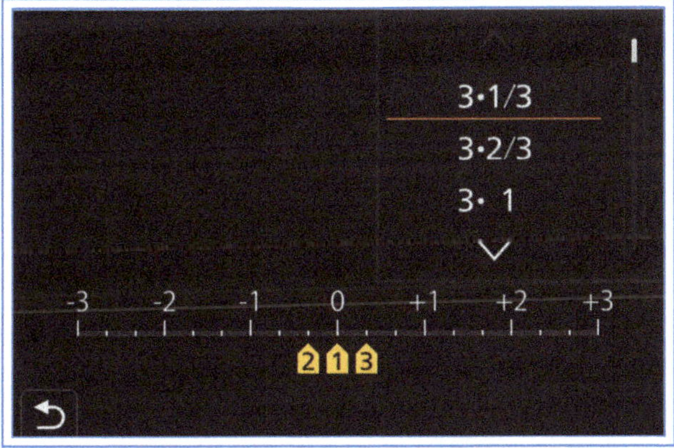

Figure 4-75. Screen to Set Exposure Bracket Interval and Shots

Then turn the thumb dial, press the Up and Down buttons, or touch the screen icons to scroll through the nine possible options. These options let you choose three, five, or seven images, taken at EV intervals of 1/3, 2/3, or one. For example, if you select the 5•2/3 option, the camera will take five images with an interval of 2/3 stop between them. Press the Menu/Set button when your chosen option is highlighted, to confirm it.

After setting the Step option, select Sequence on the Exposure Bracket Details screen. The camera will display two options at the right side of the screen: 0/-/+ and -/0/+, as shown in Figure 4-76. With the first option (the default), the exposures will be in order of normal exposure, followed by lower and then higher. With the second option, the exposures will be in order of lowest to highest. As you can see in Figures 4-74 through 4-77, the camera will display markers at the bottom of the screen indicating the order in which the images will be taken, using your chosen settings.

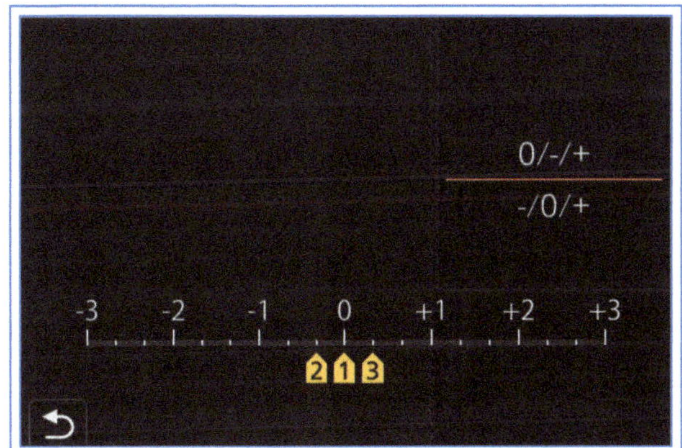

Figure 4-76. Sequence Menu Options Screen

Next, proceed to the Single Shot Setting option and select it. The camera will display the two options shown in Figure 4-77.

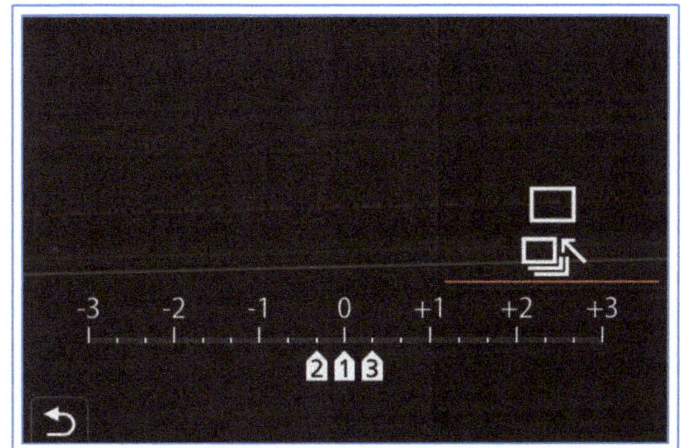

Figure 4-77. Single Shot Setting Menu Options Screen

With the top option, the camera will take the multiple (three, five, or seven) shots individually; with the bottom option, the camera will take all of the shots in a continuous burst and you will hear multiple shutter sounds as the exposures are recorded. You may want to use the individual-shots option if you need to pause after each exposure so you can evaluate the scene, adjust costumes or props, and the like. With that setting, you have to press the shutter button to take each shot in the series.

When exposure bracketing is turned on, the camera displays a BKT icon above the EV scale in the bottom center of the display, as shown in Figure 4-78.

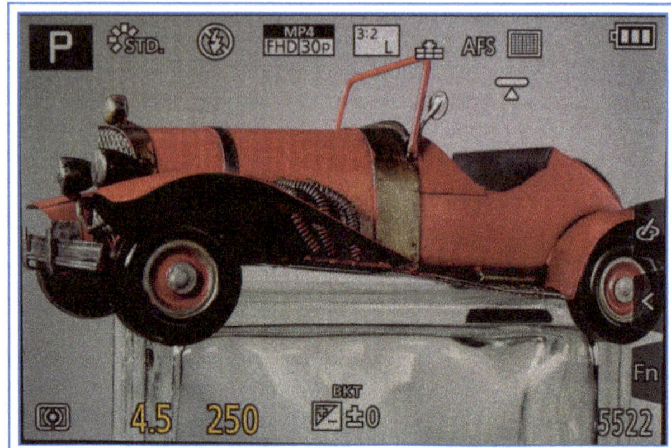

Figure 4-78. BKT Icon at Bottom of Shooting Screen

As I discussed in Chapter 2, you also can get access to exposure bracketing from the exposure compensation screen. After pressing the Up button to display the exposure compensation scale, press the Up button again to select an option for exposure bracketing.

Aperture Bracket

This option, which is available only in Aperture Priority or Manual exposure mode, sets the camera to take a series of images using different aperture settings, so you can test various approaches in order to increase the depth of field or blur the background. After you select the F icon on the Bracket Type menu that represents the f-stop (aperture), select the More Settings menu option and you will see the screen shown in Figure 4-79.

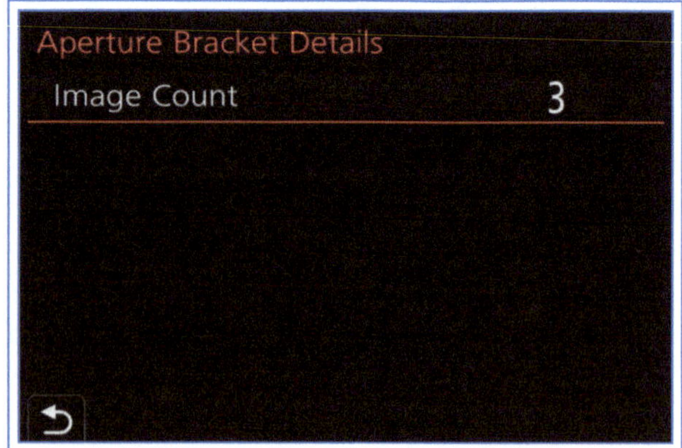

Figure 4-79. Aperture Bracket Details Screen

Select Image Count, and you will see a screen with choices of 3 or All, to select the number of different aperture settings the camera will use in its aperture bracket set.

Press the shutter button halfway or press the Fn3 button multiple times to return to the shooting screen. The camera will display a small BKT icon above the number of the f-stop that is currently selected. You can still change the initial aperture setting for the bracket; turn the thumb dial or the control ring to do so.

When you are ready, press the shutter button and the camera will take the specified series of images in a burst, starting with the aperture that is currently set. The order of the images is determined by the initial aperture and that aperture's position on the aperture scale. For example, if the initial aperture is f/3.3 and three images are selected for Image Count, the resulting images will be at f/3.3, f/4.0, and f/5.6.

If the initial aperture is f/8.0, the three images will be at f/8.0, f/5.6. and f/4.0. If Image Count is set to All and the initial aperture is f/5.6, the order of the images taken will be f/5.6, f/4.0, f/8.0, f/3.0, and f/3.3, because it would not be possible for the images to proceed in ascending or descending order through the whole group of apertures. Of course, if the lens is zoomed in to about 280mm or beyond, the widest aperture that can be included in the series will be f/6.4, because that is the widest aperture available at those focal lengths.

As noted above, the Aperture Bracket option is available only with the two shooting modes in which it is possible for the user to change the aperture: Aperture Priority and Manual exposure. However, with Manual exposure, Aperture Bracket is available only when Auto ISO is in effect.

Focus Bracket

This next option for bracketing sets the camera to take a series of images with different focus settings, so you can decide later which image has the focus point in the best location for your needs. This is a very useful option, because it helps you avoid the frustration of finding out after the fact that the camera focused on the wrong subject, or that the focus was slightly off of the subject you wanted to concentrate on. You can cause the camera to produce a large number of alternative shots and choose the one(s) with the best focus at your leisure.

After you select Focus on the Bracket Type menu, select the More Settings menu item, and the camera will display the screen shown in Figure 4-80, with options for Step, Image Count, and Sequence. You can set Step to any value from 1 to 10, which determines how much the camera will alter focus from one image to the next. Image Count can be set to any number from 1 to 999. If

Sequence is set to 0/-/+, the camera varies the focus to points both closer and farther from the lens than the original focus point. If Sequence is set to 0/+, then the camera varies the focus only to points farther from the lens than the original focus point.

You can use Focus Bracket with either autofocus or manual focus. When it is in effect, the camera displays a BKT icon above the focus mode icon in the upper right corner of the display.

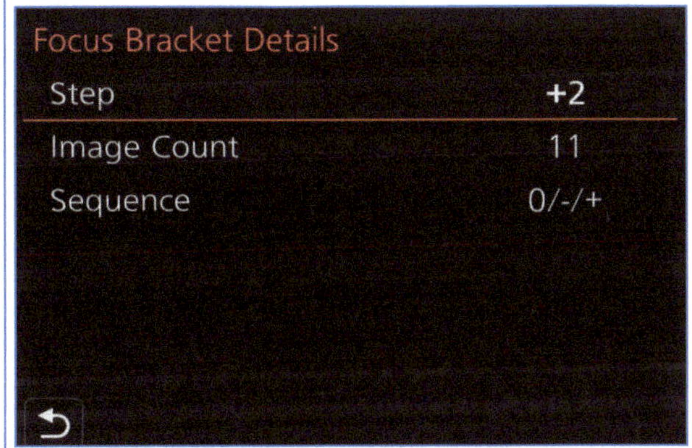

Figure 4-80. Focus Bracket Details Screen

With the Focus Bracket option, the resulting images are treated by the camera as a burst of shots. That means that, in order to view them in the camera, you need to use the playback controls for bursts. As shown in Figure 4-81, for a burst of Focus Bracket images in playback mode, the camera displays an icon at the lower left of the screen that says Focus, with a down-pointing arrow. This means that, in order to view the images within the burst, you have to press the Down button.

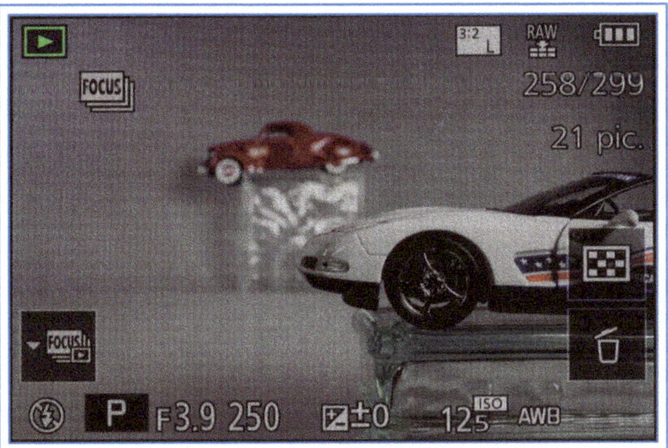

Figure 4-81. Focus Bracket Playback Screen

After you do that, the icons on the screen change, as shown in Figure 4-82, indicating that you can now view the individual images in the Focus Bracket series by scrolling through them with the normal playback controls. You can then use the Right and Left buttons, the thumb dial, or the touch screen to scroll through the images to find the ones with the best focus.

The numbers in the upper right corner, 7/11 in this example, indicate that the current image is the seventh in a series of eleven images. You will not be able to view any images outside of that set of images unless you press the Down button again to return to the normal playback mode, in which the Focus Bracket burst is displayed as a single image. You also can press the Up button, which takes you to a screen for choosing whether to view the sequence from the first image or from the current image.

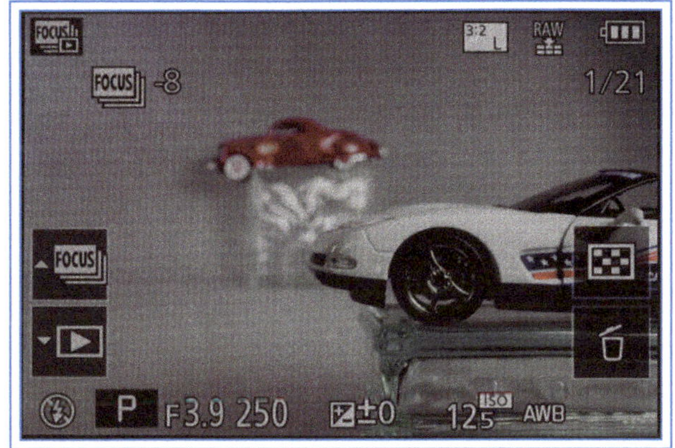

Figure 4-82. Focus Bracket Sequence After Pressing Down Button

Of course, you also can use the Post Focus option, which uses the camera's 4K video recording capability to record a burst of images from which you can select those with the best focus, but Focus Bracket lets you use more of the advanced Shooting menu options, without the constraints imposed by using 4K video-oriented settings.

White Balance Bracket

Before selecting White Balance Bracket, make sure you have the white balance setting selected as you want it; as I will discuss in Chapter 5, that setting is made by pressing the Right button and then selecting a setting such as Auto White Balance, Daylight, Cloudy, Shade, and the like. Once that setting has been made, go to the Bracket menu option and select WB for the Bracket Type option, then select the More Settings menu item. The camera will display the white balance color axes screen, as shown in Figure 4-83. This screen includes a color chart with two axes, labeled G-M for green-magenta and A-B for amber-blue.

When this screen is displayed, you need to decide on which axis to set the bracketing: the amber-blue axis, or the magenta-green axis. If you want to use the amber-blue axis, turn the thumb dial to the right; if you want to use the magenta-green axis, turn that dial to the left. As you turn the dial in either direction, you will see small circles appear on the chosen axis. The circles will spread apart as you continue to turn the dial. You also can adjust the circles using the touch screen icons on either side of the BKT and dial icons on this screen.

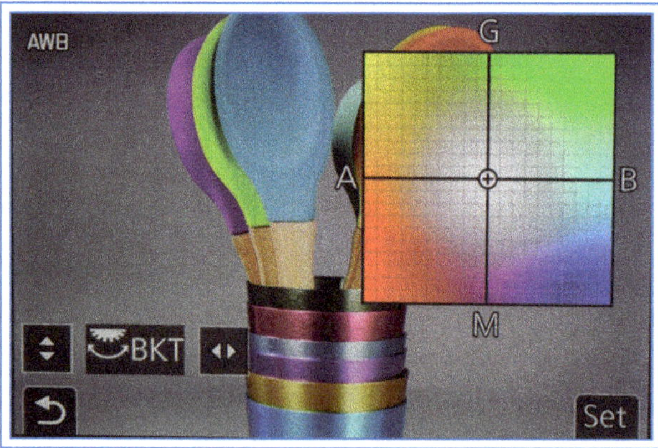

Figure 4-83. White Balance Bracket Screen

The final positions of the circles on one of the color axes indicate the differences among the three shots that the camera will take. If you have also made an adjustment to the overall white balance setting using the adjustment screen (as discussed in Chapter 5), the white balance bracketing will take the adjustment into account and bracket the exposures with the adjustment factored in.

For example, Figure 4-84 shows white balance bracketing set up to take its three shots with the greatest possible differences along the amber-blue axis.

Once the circles are set up as illustrated here, press the Fn3 button until the shooting screen is restored, or press the shutter button halfway to return to that screen.

The display will then show the BKT icon just above the icon for the white balance setting, in the lower right corner of the display. Now, when you press the shutter button, the camera will take three pictures with different white balance adjustments, from more amber to more blue. You will only hear the sound of the shutter once, though; the camera alters the white balance settings electronically. To cancel the bracketing, return to the menu and set Bracketing Type to Off.

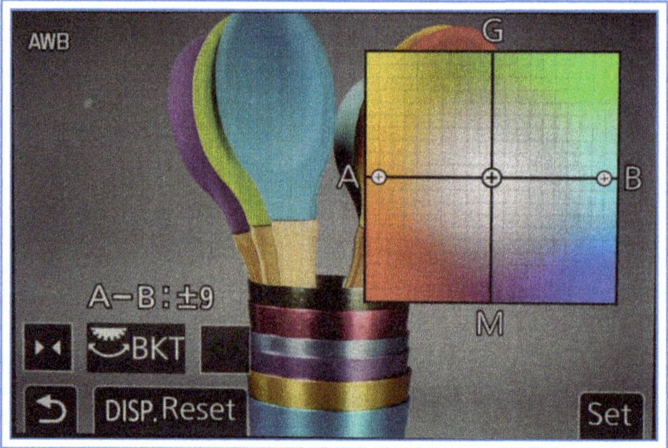

Figure 4-84. White Balance Bracket Setting in Place

This function does not work with Snapshot mode, Panorama mode, Creative Control mode, Raw images, or with certain other settings, including HDR, 4K Photo, Post Focus, burst shooting, Time Lapse Shot, and some settings of Scene mode, such as Glittering Illuminations, Handheld Night Shot, Glistening Water, and Soft Image of a Flower.

You also can turn on White Balance Bracket without using this menu option. After pressing the Right button to get to the white balance menu, press the Down button to get to the adjustment screen, then turn the thumb dial to set the bracketing as you want it. When using this method to set bracketing, you can cancel it by pressing the Display button to reset the circles.

None of the bracketing options are available with the basic Snapshot mode, Panorama mode, or when shooting movies, nor with several other settings, including some Scene mode and Creative Control mode options. The flash can be used with White Balance Bracket, but not with the other Bracket settings. Bracket options are not canceled when the camera is turned off, so be sure to cancel any bracket setting when you have finished using the feature.

HDR

The HDR option lets you set the camera to take several images in a single burst and combine them internally to form an HDR (high dynamic range) composite image, rather than using the conventional techniques of HDR photography. Those techniques were developed because cameras, whether using film or digital sensors, cannot record images that retain clear details when the scene includes wide variations in brightness. If part of the scene is in dark shadows and another part is brightly lighted, the scene has a "dynamic range" that may exceed the ability of the camera to expose both the dark and the bright areas in a way that looks good to the human eye.

A few years ago, the primary way to deal with this issue was to take multiple shots of the scene using different exposure settings, so the photographer has a range of shots, some exposed to favor dark areas, and some for bright areas. The photographer merges the images using Photoshop or special HDR software to blend differently exposed portions from all of the shots. The end result is a composite HDR image that can exhibit clear details in all parts of the image.

More recently, camera makers have incorporated HDR processing in their cameras to help even out areas of excessive brightness and darkness to preserve details, without the need to use software to merge multiple shots. With the C-Lux, Leica provides several settings for processing shots with wide dynamic range. I discussed earlier the Highlight Shadow, Intelligent Dynamic, and iHDR menu options, as well as the High Dynamic setting of Creative Control mode. The HDR option is the most direct approach to using traditional HDR techniques. It lets you take a burst of shots at different exposure levels, and the camera combines the images internally to create a composite image that attempts to even out the areas of heaviest contrast.

To use this option, highlight the HDR menu item and press the Right button or the Menu/Set button (or the menu option on the touch screen) to pop up the menu with sub-options, as shown in Figure 4-85.

Select the Set item from that sub-menu, and you will see a menu with choices of Dynamic Range and Auto Align. Highlight Dynamic Range, press the Menu/Set button, and you will see the screen shown in Figure 4-86, letting you choose the exposure interval among the three shots the camera will take.

You can choose Auto, which causes the camera to choose an interval, or you can choose a specific EV interval of one, two or three stops. Use the higher settings for scenes involving relatively large degrees of contrast, such as a view including a shaded area next to an area in bright sunshine.

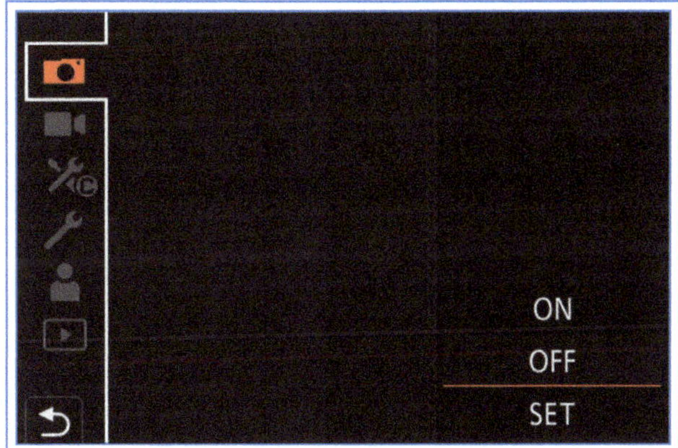

Figure 4-85. HDR Menu Options Screen

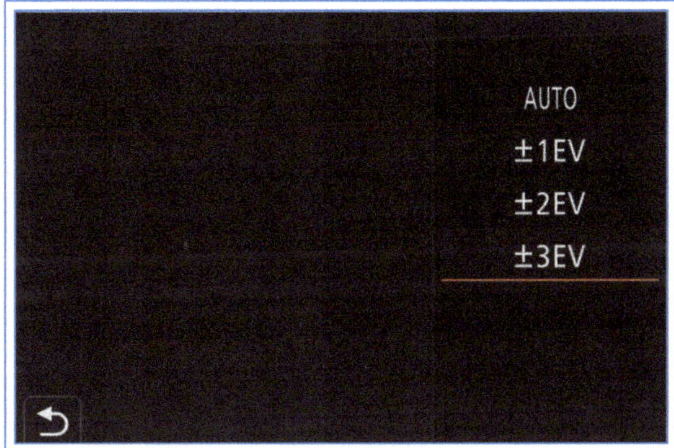

Figure 4-86. Screen to Select HDR Interval

When you have set the interval, go back to the Auto Align option on the menu and set it either on or off. If it is turned on, the camera will do its best to align the three shots automatically when it processes them internally. However, in doing so, it will crop them slightly in order to delete the outer edges of areas that are not in alignment. This setting is useful for handheld shots. If you are using a tripod, it is better to leave Auto Align turned off.

When the settings are all made, go back to the main HDR menu and set HDR to On. Then aim at the subject and press the shutter button. You will hear the shutter fire three times and a composite image will be saved to the memory card.

To test this feature, I took several shots of two watering cans partly in sun and partly in shadow. In Figure 4-87, I took a shot with HDR turned off. In Figure 4-88, I used the HDR setting at an interval of EV1, and in Figure 4-89 I used an interval of EV3. Then, for Figure 4-90, I took a series of images using Manual exposure mode at various exposure levels and combined them using Photomatix Pro HDR software.

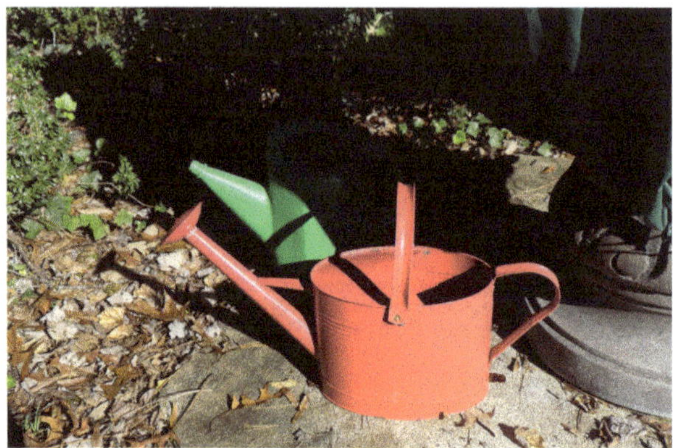
Figure 4-87. HDR Series: HDR Off

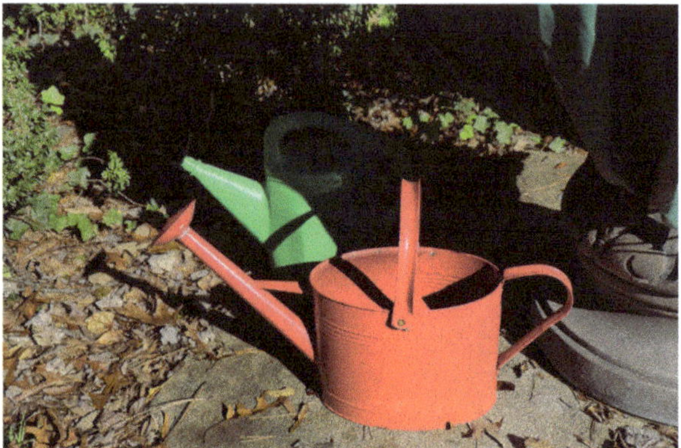
Figure 4-88. HDR Series: HDR EV1

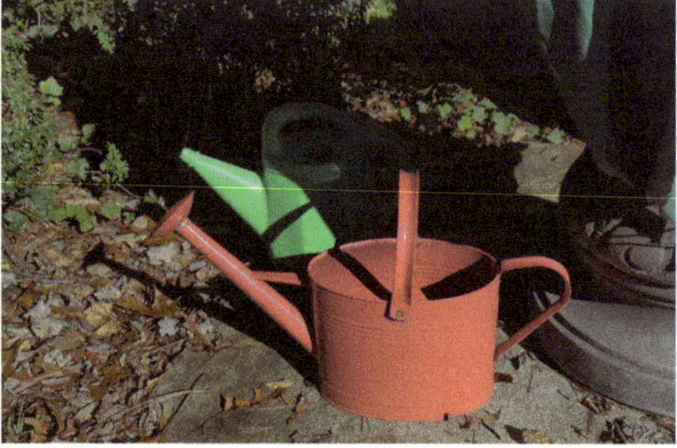
Figure 4-89. HDR Series: HDR EV3

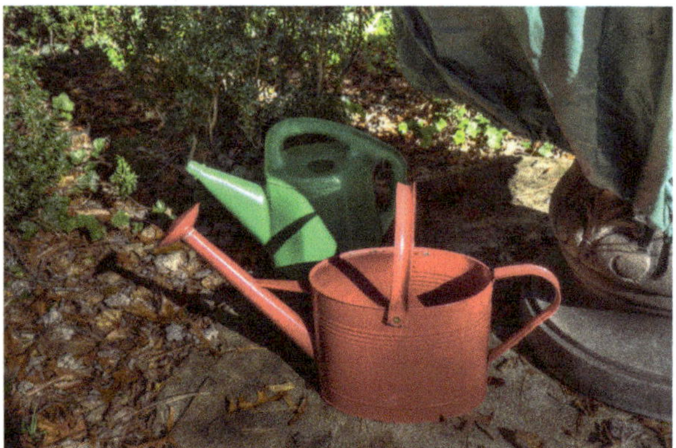
Figure 4-90. HDR Series: Photomatix Pro Composite Image

As you can see, the camera's HDR menu option did a fairly good job of reducing the heavy contrast, with more even exposure at the higher HDR setting. The composite image from the HDR software did a better job, but that is to be expected. The in-camera HDR option is a useful one when you are confronted with a scene with sharp contrast between light and dark areas.

The HDR menu option is not available when using flash, burst shooting, Raw for quality, Time Lapse Shot, 4K Photo, Post Focus, any form of bracketing, or Stop Motion Animation using the Auto Shooting setting. This option is available only in the four advanced (PASM) shooting modes.

Multiple Exposure

Multiple Exposure, the final option on the Recording menu, is more in the category of creative photography than control of normal image-making. It lets you create double, triple, or quadruple exposures in the camera. The steps to take are a bit unusual, because you actually carry out the picture-taking through the Recording menu system.

On the Recording menu, highlight Multiple Exposure, then press the Right button (or touch the menu option on the screen), which takes you to a screen with the word Start highlighted, as shown in Figure 4-91.

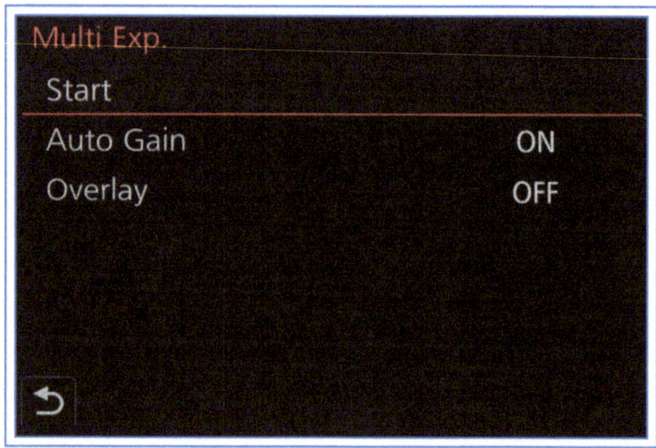

Figure 4-91. Multiple Exposure Menu Options Screen

Unless you want to overlay new images on an existing Raw image, as discussed below, make sure the Overlay option is set to Off. Then press the Menu/Set button to select Start. The screen will have the word End displayed; you can press the Fn3 button to end the process if you have had second thoughts.

If you are going to proceed, compose and take the first picture. At this point the screen will display the image you just took along with the choices Next, Retake, and Exit, as shown in Figure 4-92.

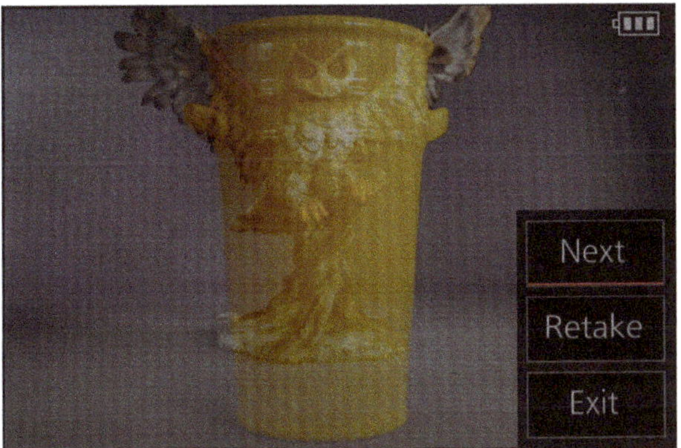

Figure 4-92. Multiple Exposure Screen After First Shot

If you're not satisfied with the first image, scroll to Retake and select that option with the Menu/Set button, then retake the first image. If you're ready to proceed to taking a superimposed image, leave Next highlighted and press the shutter button halfway down, or, if you prefer, press the Menu/Set button to select Next. Either action produces the interesting effect of leaving the first image on the screen and making the screen live at the same time to take a new image.

Compose the second shot while viewing the first one, and press the shutter button fully to record that image. You can repeat this process to add a third image, retake the second image, or exit the whole process. You can then add a fourth image if you want. When you are done, you will have a single image that combines the two, three, or four superimposed images you recorded.

Before you capture images using the Multiple Exposure procedure, the menu gives you the option of setting Auto Gain on or off. If you leave it on, the camera adjusts the exposure based on the number of pictures taken; if you turn it off, the camera adjusts the exposure for the final superimposed image. In my experience, the On setting produces results with clearer images of the multiple scenes; Off produces images that may have excessive exposure.

You also have the option of starting with a Raw image that was taken earlier by this camera. It has to be a Raw image, not a JPEG one, and it has to have been taken in a mode in which Multiple Exposure is available, which means one of the PASM modes.

To use this option, set the Overlay option of the Multiple Exposure menu item to On. Then, from the Multiple Exposure screen, highlight Start and press the Menu/Set button. The camera will display your images in playback mode. Scroll through them until you find the Raw image you want to use as the first image in the multiple exposure series. When it is displayed, press the Menu/Set button to select it as the first image of the series. Then line up the next image, with the Raw image displayed on the screen, and press the shutter button to take the next image; it will be overlaid over the existing Raw image. You can then proceed with the rest of the sequence, as before.

Figure 4-93 shows the final result of using the Multiple Exposure feature to include images of an owl figurine and a yellow vase in a single composite image. I adjusted this image somewhat in Photoshop to add contrast and darken it.

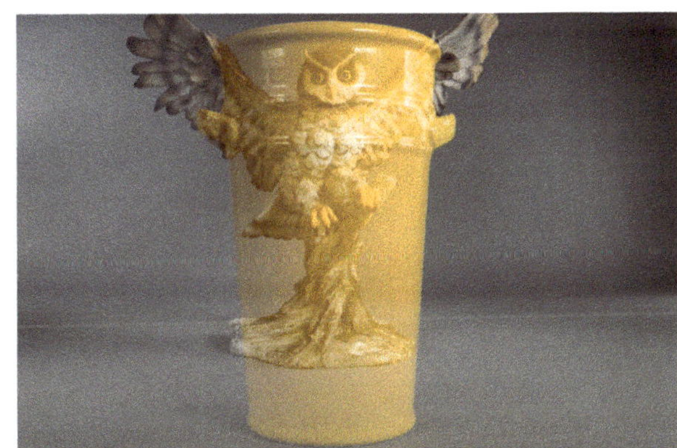

Figure 4-93. Multiple Exposure Final Image

Another kind of multiple exposure, involving a series of images of a subject in motion along a path, can be created using the Sequence Composition feature, which is discussed in Chapter 6.

Quick Menu

The C-Lux has another menu system with settings for recording images and videos. (I will discuss the menu for movie settings in Chapter 8.) This system is called the Quick Menu. It is not part of the regular menu system; instead, you get access to it by pressing the Fn3/Q.Menu button, located at the extreme lower left of the control area on the camera's back. (I am assuming the Fn3 button is assigned to the Quick Menu function, as it is by default; as discussed in Chapter 5, that button can be assigned to another function, and another button can be assigned to the Quick Menu function.)

When you press the Q.Menu button while the camera is in recording mode, a mini-version of the camera's menu system opens up, with several options in two lines, one at the top of the screen and one at the bottom, as shown in Figure 4-94.

Navigate through these menu options by pressing the Left and Right buttons, by turning the thumb dial, or by touching icons on the screen, until you find the category you want. The name of the setting that is currently active will appear near the top of the screen for items in the bottom row, and near the bottom of the screen for items in the top row. For example, in Figure 4-94, the Photo Style icon is highlighted at the top of the screen, and its name appears near the bottom of the screen. The highlight will wrap around between the bottom and top of the screen, so you can keep turning the thumb dial or pressing the Left and Right buttons to cycle through all of the items continuously.

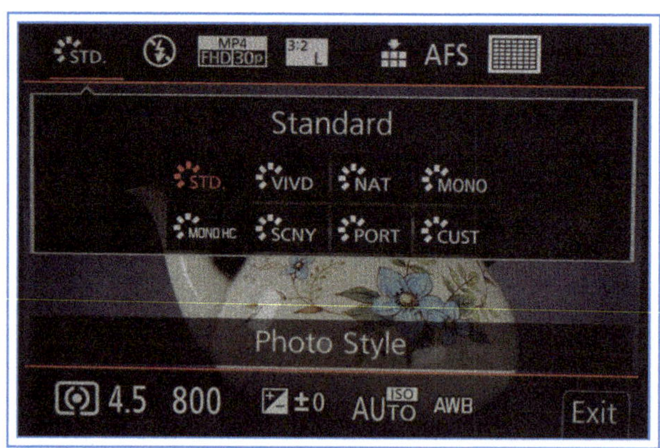

Figure 4-94. Quick Menu Screen with Photo Style Highlighted

If the item you highlighted is at the top of the screen, you can press the Down button to move down to the row or rows of icons with settings for that item. If the highlighted item is at the bottom of the screen, press the Up button to move to the row or rows of icons with settings. For example, Figure 4-95 shows the white balance item highlighted at the bottom of the screen. To move to the icons with settings for white balance, you would press the Up button to move the highlight into the area in the middle of the screen with those icons.

Once you have highlighted the icons with settings, move left and right through the sub-menu with the direction buttons, thumb dial, or touch screen. When you have highlighted the setting you want to make, you can then move to another item in the Quick Menu to make another setting. When you have finished making settings, press the Menu/Set button, the Q.Menu button, or the Exit icon in the lower right corner of the screen to exit from the Quick Menu to the recording screen. You also can press the shutter button halfway to return to that screen.

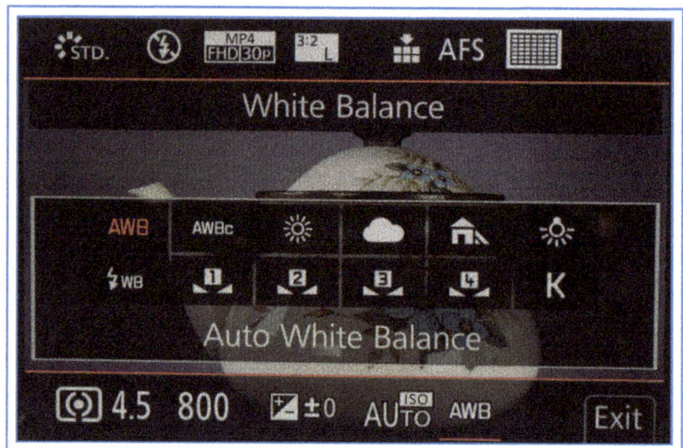

Figure 4-95. Quick Menu Screen with White Balance Highlighted

The menu options vary according to what mode the camera is in; not surprisingly, the Quick Menu offers the largest variety of choices when the camera is in Program, Aperture Priority, Shutter Priority, or Manual mode. It offers a smaller variety in Snapshot mode, though it still offers several choices.

The Quick Menu is a useful alternative to the Recording menu. This system lets you make certain settings very efficiently that otherwise would require a longer time, in part because you can see all available options at the same time on the screen as soon as you press the Q.Menu button.

For example, I find that the Quick Menu is an excellent way to select Raw or Fine quality for still images. Access to the feature is very fast this way, and, even better, when you later press the Q.Menu button again to go back to change the Quality setting again, the Quality option is still highlighted, and it takes just a couple of button presses or touches of icons on the screen to change from Raw to Fine or vice-versa.

You can customize the settings included on the Quick Menu using the Quick Menu item on screen 3 of the Custom menu. I will discuss that process in Chapter 7.

Chapter 5: Physical Controls

Not all settings that affect the recording of images and videos are on the Recording menu. Several important functions are controlled by physical buttons, switches, and dials on the C-Lux. In addition, the camera is equipped with a versatile touch screen, which is helpful for quick and efficient focusing as well as for controlling camera settings.

I have talked about many of these controls in previous chapters. But to make sure all information about physical controls is included in one place, I'll discuss each control, starting with the items on top of the camera as shown in Figure 5-1.

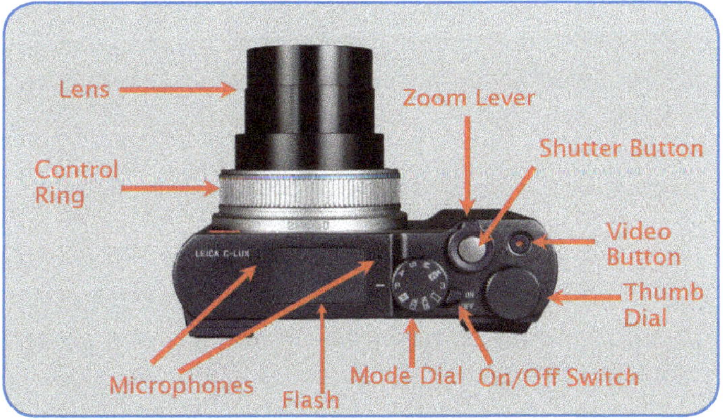

Figure 5-1. Controls on Top of Camera

Items on Top of Camera

Shutter Button

This control is the most important one on the camera. With the default settings, you press it halfway to check focus and exposure, and press it the rest of the way to record the image. You can press it halfway to wake the camera up from Sleep Mode, or to return to recording mode from a menu screen or from playback mode. You can press this button to take a still image while recording a video sequence, in most situations. When the camera is set for burst shooting or bracketing, you use this button to fire a burst of shots. When the shutter speed is set to T, for time exposure, in Manual exposure mode, you press this button once to open the shutter, and press it a second time to end the exposure. When you have turned on the 4K Photo option through the drive mode menu, pressing the shutter button starts and stops a 4K video recording. When that option is in use, you cannot use the shutter button to take still images. When the mode dial is at the Creative Video position, pressing this button starts or stops a video recording; you cannot take still pictures with the camera in that mode.

You can change the behavior of this button in a couple of ways using options on the Custom menu. With the Shutter AF item on screen 1 of that menu, you can disable the function of focusing when the button is pressed halfway. With the Half Press Release item on the same screen of that menu, you can set the camera so a half-press of the shutter button will release the shutter. I will discuss those options in Chapter 7.

Zoom Lever

The zoom lever is the ring with a small handle that encircles the shutter button. The lever's basic function is to change the lens's focal length to various values ranging between wide-angle, by pushing it to the left, and telephoto, by pushing it to the right. You can set the lever to zoom in specific increments (step zoom) using the Zoom Lever item on screen 4 of the Custom menu. When you are viewing pictures in playback mode, the lever enlarges the image on the LCD screen when pushed to the right, and selects different arrangements of thumbnail images to view when pushed to the left. Also, you can use this lever to speed through the menus a full page at a time, either forward or backward.

On/Off Switch

The on/off switch is at the rear of the camera's top, next to the mode dial. Slide it forward to turn the camera on and pull it back to turn it off. If you leave the camera unattended for a period of time, it automatically powers off, if the Sleep Mode option is turned on through the Economy option on screen 2 of the Setup menu. I'll discuss the Setup menu in Chapter 7, but this option can be set to be off altogether so the camera never turns off just to save power, or to turn the camera off after one, two, five, or ten minutes of inactivity. You can cancel the Sleep Mode shutdown by pressing the shutter button halfway. If you hold down the Playback button while turning on this switch, the camera will start up in playback mode.

Mode Dial

The mode dial is marked with icons or letters representing each of the camera's shooting modes, including Snapshot, Shutter Priority, Scene, and the others. Turn this dial to select a mode. That mode controls what features are available for shooting and how the camera's controls behave. You can shoot still images in any shooting mode other than Creative Video (M with movie camera icon). In that shooting mode, if you press the shutter button the camera will start (or stop) recording a movie. You can record a movie in any shooting mode except Panorama, by pressing the red video button on top of the camera. If the mode dial is at C, the mode is determined by the Custom Set Memory option on screen 1 of the Setup menu.

For the most automatic settings, turn the dial to the A icon, for Snapshot, and make sure the Snapshot item, the top icon on the list of menu icons, is set to the A selection, rather than A+.

Video Button

The red video button is located to the right of the shutter button. Press this button once to start recording a movie, and press it again to stop recording. As noted above, you can use this button to record a movie in any shooting mode except Panorama. In Chapter 8, I will provide details about how the various menu and control settings affect the recording of movies.

Thumb Dial

Although this dial is located on top of the camera, Leica calls it the thumb dial. This name makes sense, because you are likely to move this dial with your thumb at the rear of the dial while holding the camera. However, because it is located on top of the camera, I will discuss it in this section.

This dial has default functions similar to those of the control ring—the large, ridged ring around the lens. I will discuss that ring later in this chapter. (As I will discuss later, you can change the default functions of the control ring and the thumb dial through the Custom menu.)

The default function of the thumb dial varies according to the shooting mode that is currently set. Table 5-1 lists the default assignments of the dial for each shooting mode.

Table 5-1. **Default Assignments for Thumb dial in Various Shooting Modes**

Shooting Mode	Function of Thumb dial
Snapshot	No Function
Program	Program Shift
Aperture Priority	Adjusts Aperture
Shutter Priority	Adjusts Shutter Speed
Manual Exposure	Adjusts Shutter Speed
Panorama	Selects Picture Effects
Scene	No function, with two exceptions below
Scene–Appetizing Food Setting	Adjusts Aperture
Scene–Artistic Nightscape	Adjusts Shutter Speed
Creative Control	Selects Picture Effects
Creative Video	Adjusts Aperture or Shutter Speed if Exposure Mode Permits

The functions listed above for the thumb dial are the default functions programmed at the factory. You can change the function of the thumb dial through the Ring/Dial Set option on screen 3 of the Custom menu. If you use that menu option to select a setting other than the default, the dial will control a single setting, such as ISO, white balance, drive mode, or filter effects. The following list shows the possible assignments for the thumb dial.

- Default (see Table 5-1, above)
- Exposure Compensation
- ISO Sensitivity
- White Balance
- AF Mode
- Focus Mode
- Drive Mode

- Photo Style
- Filter Effect
- Aspect Ratio
- Highlight Shadow
- i.Dynamic
- i.Resolution
- Flash Mode
- Flash Adjustment

If you select an option other than Default, that setting will take effect for all recording modes in which the setting is available. If you select Highlight Shadow for the thumb dial, it will also be assigned to the control ring, and vice-versa, because one control adjusts highlights and the other adjusts shadows. (Highlight Shadow is the only setting for which that situation exists.)

Apart from its main functions, this dial has a few other uses. You can turn it to move through menu screens by one screen at a time. You can turn the dial to adjust the size of the focus frame when the focus mode permits that adjustment, or to adjust the size of the frame used for the Miniature setting of the filter effects. You can also use it to adjust the size of the light source for the Sunshine effect. This dial is also used to adjust the settings for the Highlight Shadow option on screen 2 of the Recording menu and to set the interval for white balance bracketing. In playback mode, turning this dial moves through your recorded images, and it is used to adjust the audio volume during a slide show or motion picture playback.

Built-in Flash Unit

The C-Lux's built-in flash is stored inside the top of the camera. In order to use it, you have to press the flash release lever, at the top center of the camera's back. In most shooting modes, you can control the operation of the flash using the Flash item on screen 2 of the Recording menu. You can bounce the light from the flash off of a wall or ceiling by gently pulling the unit back with a finger to direct its angle upward.

Microphone

The camera's built-in stereo microphone receives sounds through the small openings on either side of the built-in flash unit. Be sure not to cover up these openings when recording a movie, so as not to block the recording of sounds. This camera does not have any jack for plugging in an external microphone.

Controls on Back of Camera

Figure 5-2 shows the controls on the camera's back.

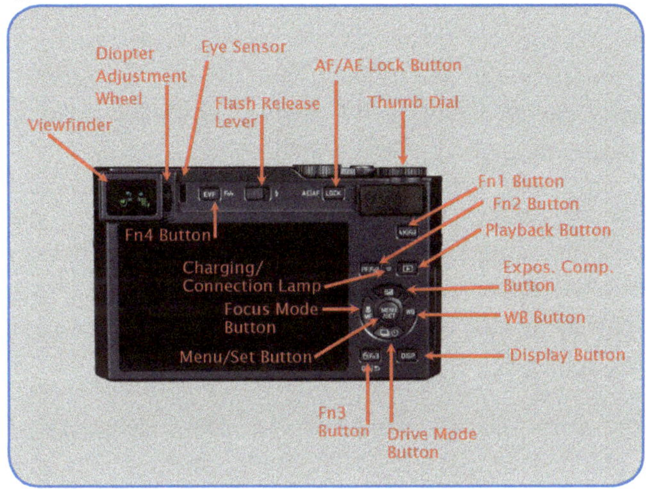

Figure 5-2. Controls on Back of Camera

Viewfinder, Eye Sensor, EVF Button, and Diopter Adjustment Wheel

The viewfinder window at the top left of the camera's back is where you can see the recording display and playback display when the viewfinder is in use. The vertical slot to the right of the window is the eye sensor. That device senses when your head is near the viewfinder window, and switches the display from the LCD screen to the viewfinder, if the camera is set for automatic switching of the view.

To change the way the view is switched between the viewfinder and the LCD screen, you can use the EVF button, labeled Fn4/EVF, to the right of the eye sensor. Each time you press that button, it selects a different setting. If you press it to select EVF/Monitor Auto, then the view switches between the viewfinder and the LCD screen automatically when your head (or something else) approaches the eye sensor. Otherwise, it can be set to EVF or Monitor, to keep the viewfinder or LCD screen permanently activated. These functions work only if the Fn4/EVF button remains set to its default function. If you don't need this switching function, you can reassign that button to carry out some other operation using the Function Button Set option on screen 3 of the Custom menu.

You also can control the switching between the viewfinder and monitor using the EVF/Monitor Switch menu option, a sub-option of the Eye Sensor item on screen 2 of the Setup menu. You can control the sensitivity of the eye sensor using the Sensitivity sub-option of the Eye Sensor menu item.

You also can set the camera so it will use its autofocus mechanism to focus on the scene when your eye approaches the eye sensor. That option is controlled using the Eye Sensor AF option on screen 2 of the Custom menu.

You can adjust the view in the viewfinder for your eyesight using the diopter adjustment wheel between the viewfinder and the eye sensor. If you wear glasses, you may be able to adjust this dial so you can see clearly through the viewfinder without your glasses.

The information displayed in the viewfinder is controlled by pressing the Display button. There are four different screens with various information; I will talk about those screens in the discussion of the Display button, later in this chapter.

Flash Release Lever

This button, at the top center of the camera's back, has just one purpose—to release the built-in flash unit so it will pop up. If you don't pop up the flash with this lever, the flash cannot be used. To release the flash, slide this lever to the right. When you are done with the flash, press it gently back into the camera until it clicks into place.

AF/AE Lock Button

The AF/AE Lock button is located at the upper right of the camera's back, just below the mode dial. Using the AF/AE Lock item on screen 1 of the Custom menu, you can set this button to lock both autofocus and autoexposure, or just one or the other. Then, you can press this button to lock whichever of those settings have been selected through the menu option. With the same menu option, you also can select AF-On. If you turn on that option, pressing this button operates the camera's autofocus system. That option gives the camera a capability for "back button focus," so named because you can press a button on the camera's back to focus the lens. If you want to turn off the shutter button's focusing function, you can do that by turning off the Shutter AF option on screen 1 of the Custom menu.

You cannot lock exposure with the AF/AE Lock button when the camera is set to Manual exposure mode, and the button does not function at all in either variety of Snapshot mode. When manual focus is in use, the button cannot lock focus. Zooming the lens cancels either type of lock. You can set the button to hold its setting without keeping it pressed, using the AF/AE Lock Hold item on screen 1 of the Custom menu.

Playback Button

This button, located to the upper right of the group of cursor buttons, is marked by a small triangle. You press this button to put the camera into playback mode. Press it again to switch back into recording mode. When the camera is placed into playback mode, the lens barrel will retract automatically after about 15 seconds, because the lens is not needed during playback operations. You can turn the retraction feature off using the Lens Retraction option on screen 6 of the Custom menu. If you hold this button down while turning on the camera, the camera will start up in playback mode.

Display Button

The Display button is at the bottom right of the camera's back, to the lower right of the group of cursor buttons. It has several functions, depending on the context. Its primary function is to switch among the several available display screens for the LCD screen or the viewfinder, in both recording mode and playback mode.

In recording mode, following are the screens you see on the LCD monitor from repeated presses of the Display button, when the Monitor Display Style option on screen 5 of the Custom menu (under the EVF/Monitor Display Settings item) is set to its bottom option, for the monitor style layout. The items displayed are slightly different if that menu option is set to the other setting, for live viewfinder style display layout. I will not include the touch screen icons in describing these screens, because the touch screen can be turned off, removing all such icons from the display.

- As shown in Figure 5-3, full display, including battery status, Picture Size, Quality, aspect ratio, Photo Style, flash status, ISO (if set to a specific value), white balance (if other than Auto White Balance), exposure compensation amount, movie quality and format, recording mode, metering mode, focus mode, AFS/AFF/AFC, AF mode, number of pictures or length of video that can be shot with the remaining storage, the histogram (discussed later), if it is turned on through screen 4 of the Custom menu, and the focus frame, if the current focus mode displays one. The aperture and shutter speed also will display briefly after exposure is evaluated, and one or both of those values will remain on the screen in some shooting modes.

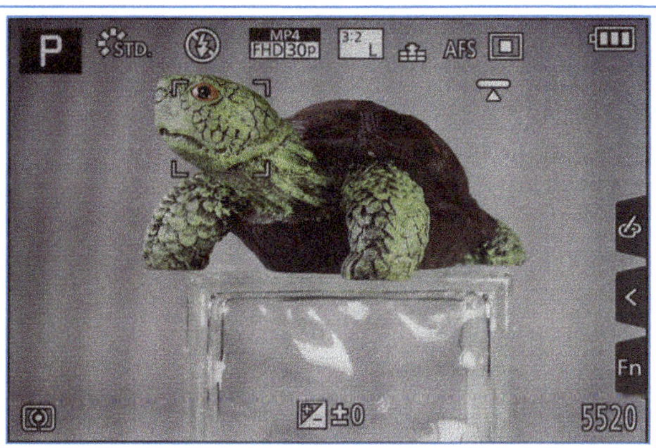

Figure 5-3. Shooting Screen with Full Information

- Blank display except for the focus area, if using a focus mode that displays a focus frame. The aperture, shutter speed, ISO value, and exposure compensation scale also will display briefly after exposure is evaluated (not shown here).

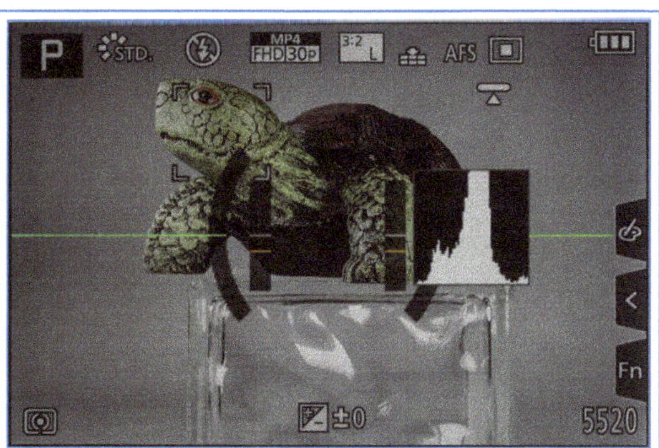

Figure 5-4. Shooting Screen with Level, Histogram, Focus Frame

- As shown in Figure 5-4, full information with level gauge, as well as histogram and focus frame if applicable.
- As shown in Figure 5-5, level gauge with focus frame if applicable.

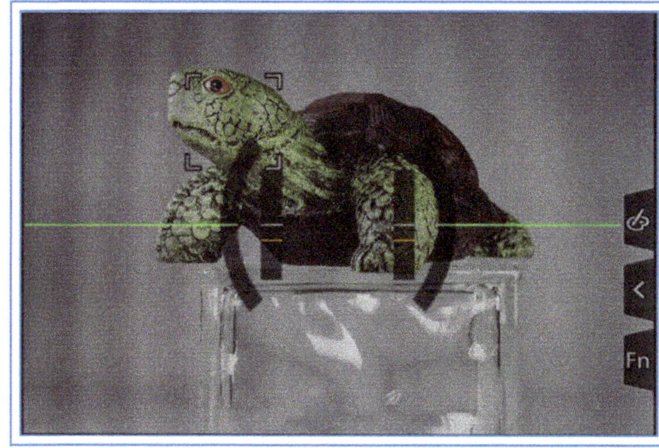

Figure 5-5. Shooting Screen with Level and Focus Frame

- Blank screen (black, with no information) (not shown).

In the basic Snapshot mode, the Display button produces the screens listed above, but the histogram does not appear even if it was turned on through the Custom menu. There also are other items that will appear on the information screens, such as the Guide Line grid if selected on screen 4 of the Custom menu, and icons for items such as the self-timer when they are activated.

The viewfinder uses the same display screens as those discussed above, except that it does not include the blank screen. The items displayed are affected by the EVF Display Settings option on screen 5 of the Custom menu (under the EVF/Monitor Display Settings item).

If the camera is set for playback, pressing the Display button produces the following screens.

- As shown in Figure 5-6, image with battery status, Picture Size, Aspect Ratio, Quality, flash status, recording mode, aperture, shutter speed, exposure compensation, ISO, white balance, and number of image out of total images,. (As with the recording mode displays, I am not including touch icons, because the touch screen may be turned off).

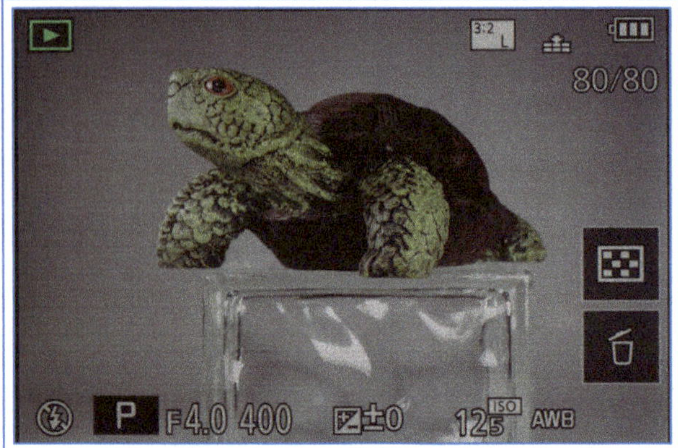

Figure 5-6. Playback Screen with Basic Information

As shown in Figure 5-7, a smaller image with the same information, plus date and time of image capture, image number, and some other settings, including metering mode and Photo Style. At the right side of that screen, the numbers in the upper right corner show which one of five available displays is currently shown. You can scroll through the five display screens using the Up and Down buttons or the touch screen. The first screen shows basic shooting information.

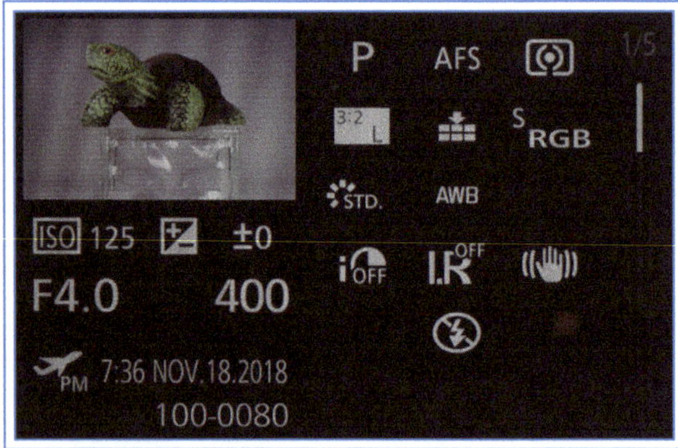

Figure 5-7. First Detailed Playback Screen

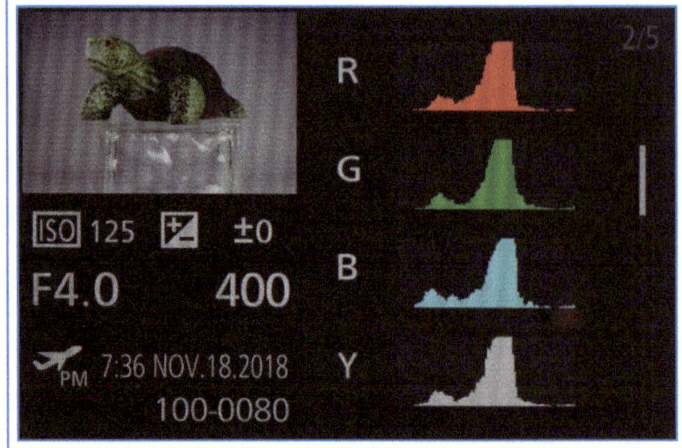

Figure 5-8. Second Detailed Playback Screen

The second screen seen by scrolling down, seen in Figure 5-8, shows the histogram, which is discussed further in Chapter 7. Basically, the histogram is a graphic display that shows the brightness of the image through peaks and dips. A normal histogram should have most peaks in the middle portion of the graph, for each color.

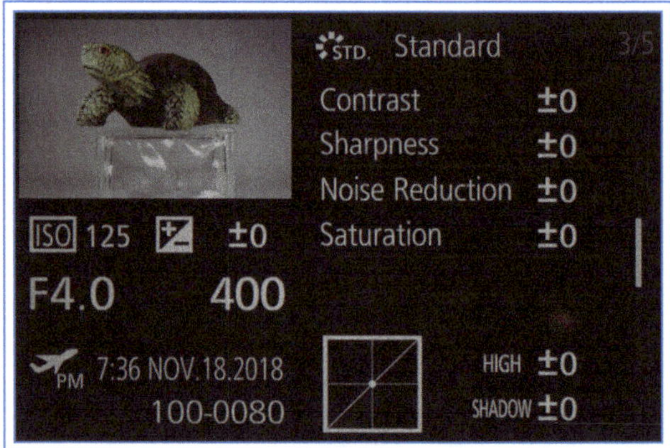

Figure 5-9. Third Detailed Playback Screen

The third screen seen by scrolling down, shown in Figure 5-9, displays the image's values for contrast, sharpness, noise reduction, and saturation, as well as its Highlight Shadows settings.

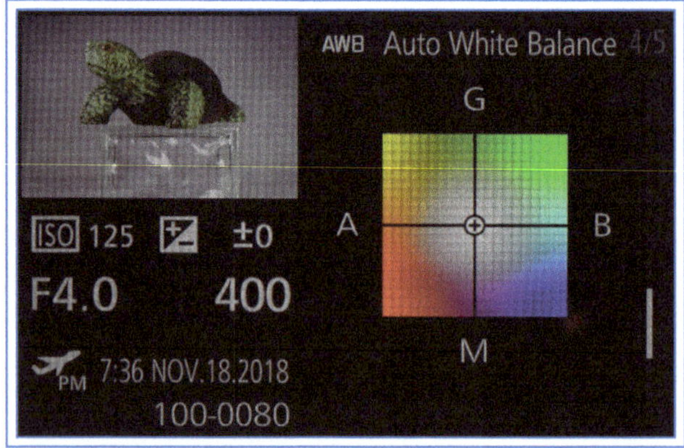

Figure 5-10. Fourth Detailed Playback Screen

The fourth screen seen by scrolling down, seen in Figure 5-10, shows the white balance adjustment screen, with any adjustment along the amber-blue or green-magenta color axis.

The fifth screen, seen in Figure 5-11, shows the actual and 35mm-equivalent focal length values for the image, as well as the setting for Long Shutter Noise Reduction.

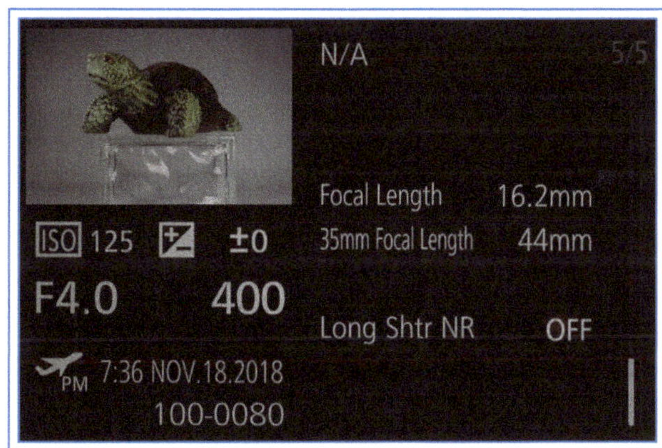

Figure 5-11. Fifth Detailed Playback Screen

- Another press of the Display button displays the recorded image with no other information, but flashing the highlights in areas that are overexposed. (This screen appears only if the Highlight option is turned on through screen 5 of the Custom menu. The highlights also will flash on the detailed information screens; this screen is added so you can see the overexposed areas without interference from information items.)
- Another press of the Display button shows the recorded image with no other information, and with no flashing highlights.

For motion pictures, the display is similar, except for some added information that applies to those files, including an icon showing that you can press the Up button to start the motion picture playing.

The Display button also has several other functions. You can press it to restore the focus frame to normal after you have moved it off center or resized it when using the 1-Area focus mode or one of the other modes that allows you to move or resize the focus point or points. If you need a reminder of the current date and time, with the camera in recording mode, press the Display button enough times to cycle back to the screen with the most recording information, and the date and time will appear on the lower left of the screen for about five seconds. Also, when you are viewing a menu screen, you can press the Display button when a menu option (or, in some cases, a sub-option or setting) is highlighted to see a brief explanation of that item.

Menu/Set Button and Direction Buttons

The C-Lux has a set of five buttons on its back in a circular pattern. Each button is marked with an icon for its primary function. In the center is a button labeled Menu/Set. I refer to the four outer buttons as direction buttons or cursor buttons (Left, Right, Up, and Down), and to the center button as the Menu/Set button.

Direction Buttons

The direction buttons act as cursor keys do on a computer keyboard, letting you navigate up and down and left and right through menus. Each of the buttons also has at least one other function, as indicated by the icon or label on the button. I will discuss those functions below.

Up Button: Exposure Compensation

The Up button is the exposure compensation button. It lets you adjust the brightness of images in all shooting modes except the basic Snapshot mode and Manual exposure mode.

In basic Snapshot mode, exposure compensation is not available, and the Up button has no function from the shooting screen. In Manual exposure mode, you cannot use the Up button for exposure compensation, because the button switches the functions of the thumb dial and control ring. In that mode, you have to use the Quick Menu, or set the control ring to control exposure compensation. Exposure compensation is available in Manual mode only when ISO is set to Auto ISO. When recording videos, exposure compensation is available only in Creative Video mode. The Up button can be used for that purpose only if Exposure Mode is set to P, A, or S. If it is set to M, you have to use the control ring or the Silent Operation touch icon to adjust exposure compensation, as discussed in Chapter 8.

In other modes, the Up button calls up the exposure compensation screen. From that screen, in modes other than Panorama and Creative Video, you can control exposure bracketing by pressing the Up button again. In Snapshot Plus and Creative Control modes, you can press the Fn1 button on the exposure compensation screen to get access to the defocus control option, as discussed in Chapter 3, which lets you select a different aperture setting to achieve a blurred background if possible.

Here is an example of how to control exposure to account for an unusual, or non-optimal, lighting situation. Suppose you have the C-Lux set to Program mode and you are photographing a fairly dark subject, such as a red model automobile in front of a white background, as shown in Figure 5-12.

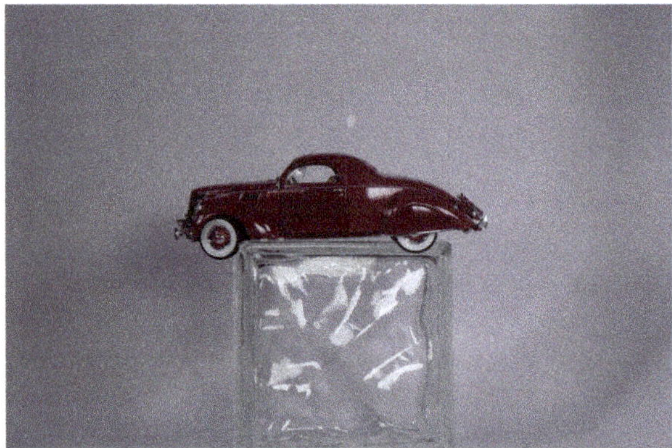

Figure 5-12. Scene in Need of Exposure Compensation

The camera will do a good job of averaging the amount of light coming into the lens, and will expose the picture accordingly. The problem is, the very light background will likely "fool" the camera into closing down the aperture, because the overall picture will seem quite bright. But the subject, which is not nearly as light as the background, will seem too dark in the picture. One solution to this problem is to use exposure compensation. (Another is to use spot metering.)

First, compose the image as you want. Then, press the Up button to place the exposure compensation scale on the display, as shown in Figure 5-13. Use the thumb dial, the Left and Right buttons, or slide your finger along the touch screen to select the desired setting. The values range from –5 to +5 EV, with one-third steps in between. EV stands for exposure value, a standard measure of brightness. If you move the value down to -5, the picture will be much darker than the automatic exposure would produce. If you move it to +5, the picture will be much brighter.

The camera's screen shows you how the exposure is changing, before you take the picture, as shown in Figure 5-14. In this case, after 1 1/3 EV of exposure compensation is added, the image becomes brighter and the automobile can be seen more clearly. The small EV scale at the bottom center of the display shows the amount of exposure compensation that has been applied after the exposure compensation screen has been dismissed, as shown in Figure 5-15.

Once you've taken the picture, you should reset the EV compensation back to zero so you don't unintentionally affect the pictures you take later.

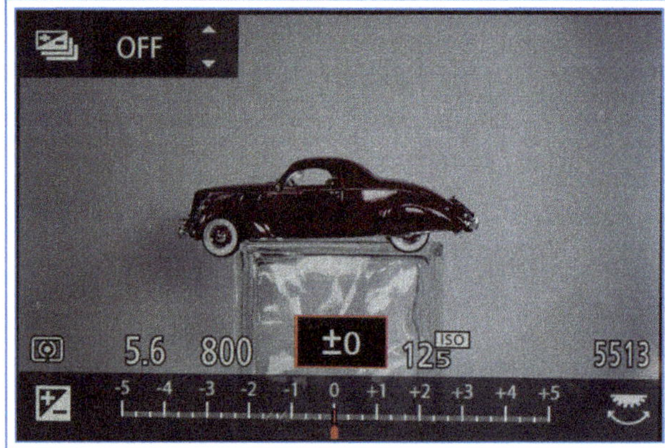

Figure 5-13. Exposure Compensation Scale

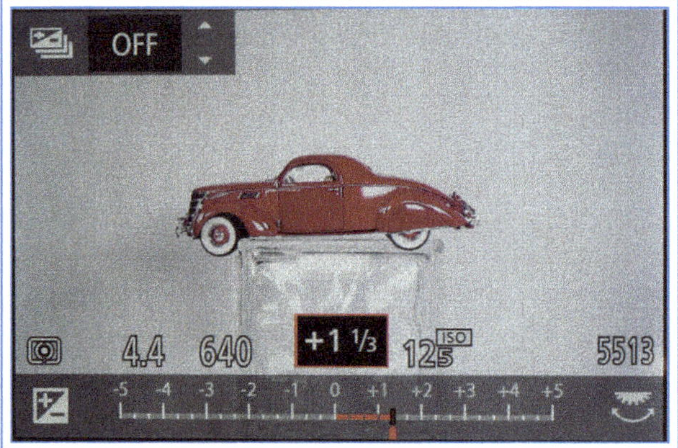

Figure 5-14. Exposure Compensation Adjustment on Scale

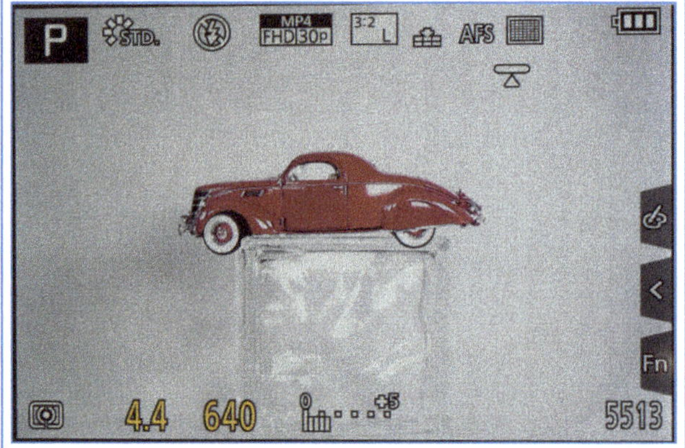

Figure 5-15. Exposure Compensation Amount on Shooting Screen

When the exposure compensation screen is displayed, in some shooting modes you can press the Up button again to turn on exposure bracketing and select options for the number of shots and the exposure interval. For example, Figure 5-16 shows the screen after I selected five shots with an EV interval of 1/3 stop. To make further adjustments to the bracketing settings, such as the order of exposures, you have to use the Bracket option on screen 4 of the Recording menu.

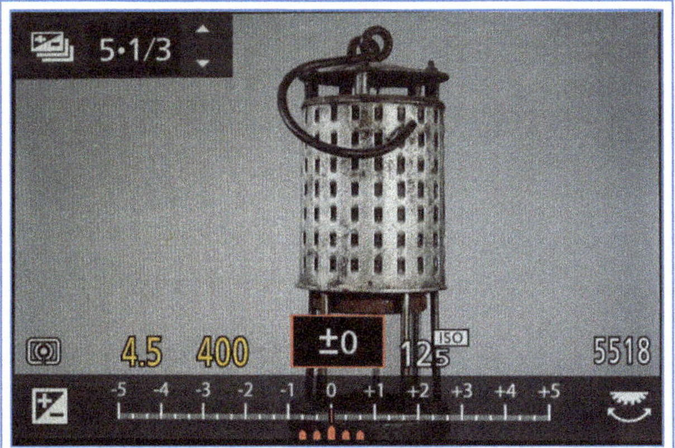

Figure 5-16. Exposure Bracket Setting on Screen

In playback mode, the Up button is used to start playing a motion picture or a panorama when the initial frame is displayed on the screen. The button also serves as a play/pause button once a movie has started playing, and it has various duties to move among settings on certain screens, such as the screen for saving Highlight Shadow values on the Recording menu, the screen for setting a custom white balance setting, and the screen for saving a Custom Multi frame for AF Mode.

Right Button: White Balance

The Right button calls up the menu for selecting the camera's setting for white balance. The white balance adjustment is needed because cameras record the colors of objects differently according to the color temperature of the light source that illuminates those objects.

Color temperature is a value expressed in Kelvin (K) units. A light source with a lower K rating produces a "warmer," or more reddish light. A source with a higher rating produces a "cooler," or more bluish light. Candlelight is rated about 1,800 K, indoor tungsten light (ordinary light bulb) is rated about 3,000 K, outdoor sunlight and electronic flash are rated about 5,500 K, and outdoor shade is rated about 7,000 K. If the camera is using a white balance setting that is not calibrated for the light source that illuminates the scene, the colors of the recorded image are likely to be inaccurate.

The C-Lux, like most digital cameras, has an Auto White Balance setting that attempts to set the proper color correction for any given light source. The Auto White Balance setting works well, and it will produce good results in many situations, especially if you are taking snapshots whose colors are not critical.

If you need more precision in the white balance of your shots, the C-Lux has settings for common light sources, as well as options for setting white balance by color temperature and for setting a custom white balance based on the existing light source.

You get access to this setting by pressing the Right button, which calls up the white balance menu screen at the bottom of the display, as shown in Figure 5-17.

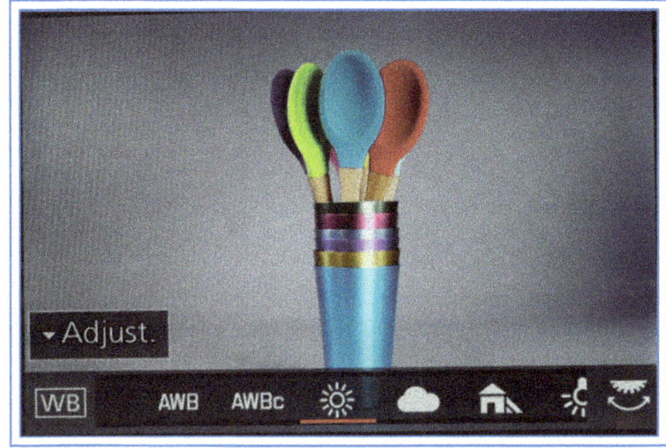

Figure 5-17. White Balance Menu

This menu includes the following choices for the white balance setting, most of them represented by icons: Auto White Balance (AWB); Auto White Balance with reduced reds (AWBc); Daylight (sun icon); Cloudy; Shade; Incandescent; Flash; White Set 1; White Set 2; White Set 3; White Set 4; and Color Temperature. (Only the first six options are shown in Figure 5-17; you need to scroll to the right to reach the others.)

Most of these settings are self-explanatory. You may want to experiment to see if the named settings (Daylight, Shade, Incandescent, etc.) produce the results you want. The AWBc setting is intended for use with incandescent lighting, to reduce the excessive red or orange hues that the normal AWB setting does not always compensate for properly.

If the preset options don't produce the results you need, you can set the white balance manually. To do that, you can use any one of the four White Set options, which let you measure the white balance based on the light that is actually illuminating your subject, and save a custom setting to that numbered slot in the camera's memory. Then, you can use that custom setting whenever you are faced with the same lighting situation in the future.

To set white balance manually, press the Right button to activate the white balance menu and scroll to highlight one of the four White Set icons, as shown in Figure 5-18. Press the Up button, and a yellow rectangle will appear in the middle of the display, as shown in Figure 5-19.

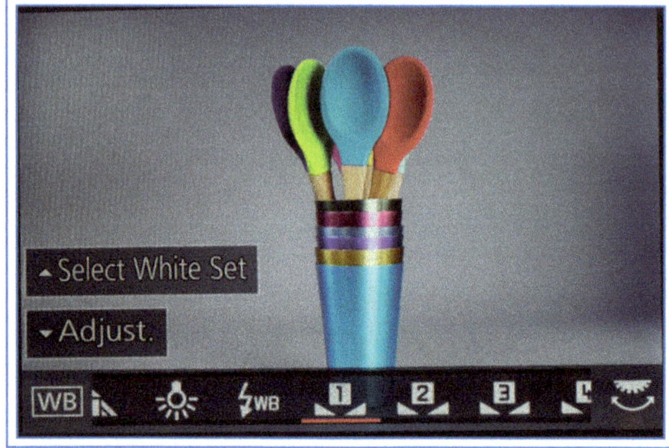

Figure 5-18. White Set Icon Highlighted on Menu

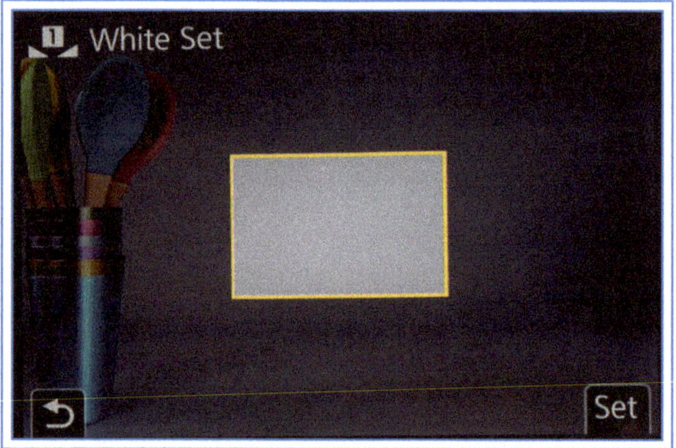

Figure 5-19. Screen to Set Custom White Balance

Aim the camera at a white or gray surface illuminated by the light source you will be using, and fill the rectangle with the image of that surface. Then press the Menu/Set button (or you can press the shutter button if you prefer) to lock in that white balance setting. The camera will display a Completed message if the setting was successful. Now, until you change that setting, whenever you select that preset value (White Set 1 or another slot, as the case may be), it will be set for the white balance you have just set. This system is useful if you often use a particular light source and want to have the camera set to the appropriate white balance for that source.

To set the color temperature directly by numerical value, choose the Color Temperature option from the white balance menu, as shown in Figure 5-20.

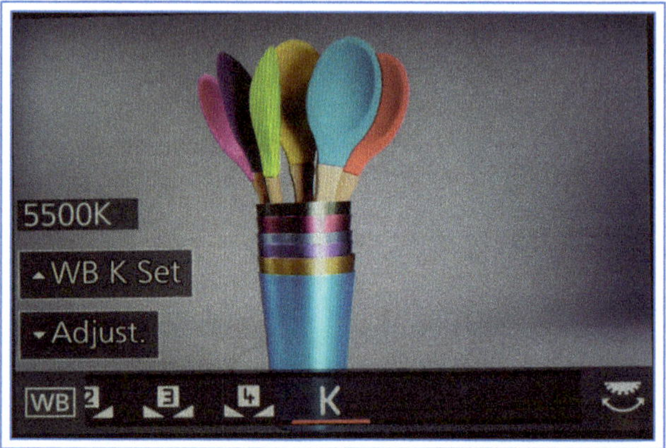

Figure 5-20. Color Temperature Icon Highlighted on Menu

Then press the Up button to pop up a screen with a value such as 2500K displayed. You then can press the Up and Down buttons, turn the thumb dial, or slide your finger on the touch screen to adjust that value anywhere from 2500K to 10000K in increments of 100K, as shown in Figure 5-21, where the value is set to 5500K.

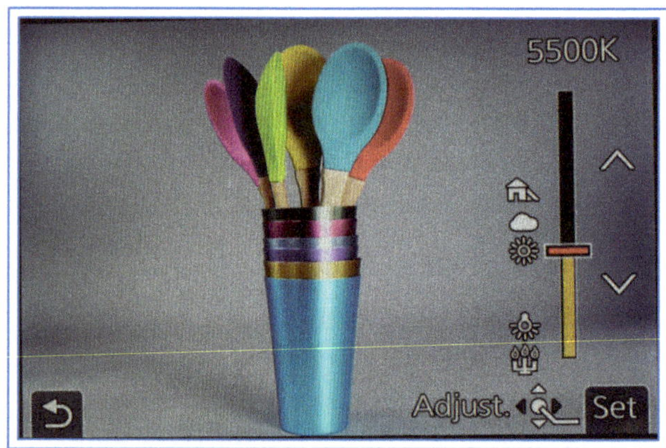

Figure 5-21. Color Temperature Set to 5500K

With this approach, you have to know the color temperature of your light source in order to make the setting. One way to find that value is to use a color temperature meter like the Sekonic C-700 color meter shown in Figure 5-22.

A meter like that is helpful when you need accuracy in your white balance settings, but it is fairly expensive, and you may not want to use that option. In that case, you can still use the Color Temperature option, but you will have to do some guesswork or use your own sense of color. For example, if you are shooting under lighting from incandescent bulbs, you can use 3,000 K as a starting point, because, as noted earlier, that is the approximate color temperature of that light source. Then you can try setting the color temperature figure higher or lower, and watch the camera's display to see how natural the colors look. As you lower the color temperature, the image will become more "cool" or bluish; as you raise it, the image will appear more "warm" or reddish. Once you have found the best setting, leave it in place and take your shots.

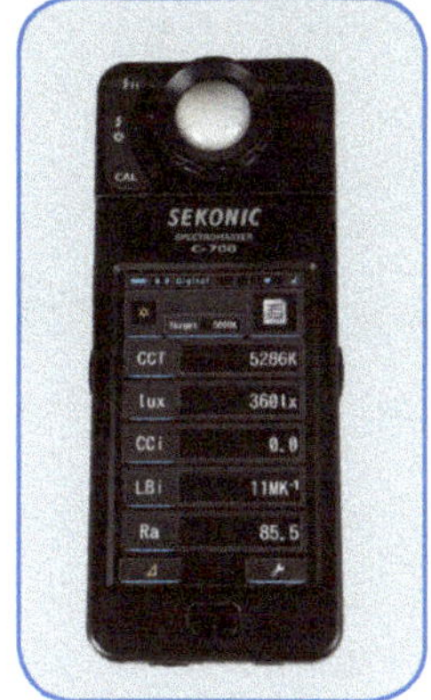

Figure 5-22. Sekonic C-700 Color Meter

Once you have made the white balance setting, either using one of the preset values such as Daylight, Incandescent, or Cloudy, or using a custom-measured setting or a color temperature, you can fine-tune the setting. To make this further adjustment, after you make your white balance setting, before pressing the Menu/Set button to return to the recording screen, press the Down button, and you will be presented with a screen for fine adjustments, as shown in Figure 5-23.

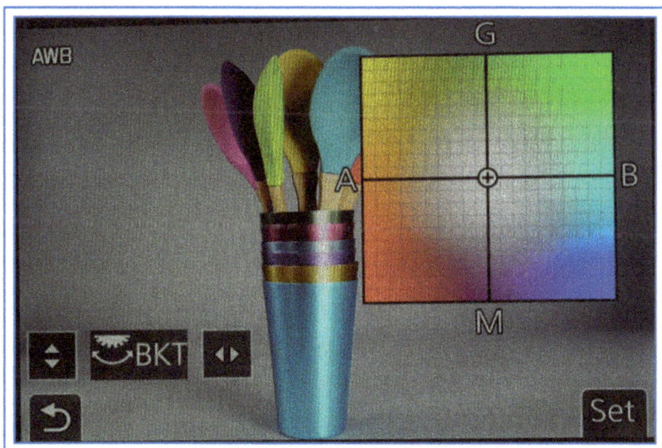

Figure 5-23. White Balance Adjustment Screen

You will see a box containing a pair of axes that intersect at a zero point, marked by a circle with a plus sign inside it. The four ends of the axes are labeled G, B, M, and A, for green, blue, magenta, and amber.

You can use all four direction buttons, or slide your finger over the colored square, to move the circle away from the center toward any of the axes, to adjust these four values until you have the color balance exactly how you want it. The camera will remember this value whenever you select the white balance setting that you fine-tuned. When you have fine-tuned the setting using this screen, the white balance icon on the camera's display changes color and/or adds an indicator to indicate what changes you have made along the color axes. If there was an adjustment to the amber or blue side, the icon changes color accordingly. If there was an adjustment to the green or magenta side, the icon will have a plus sign added for green or a minus sign added for magenta.

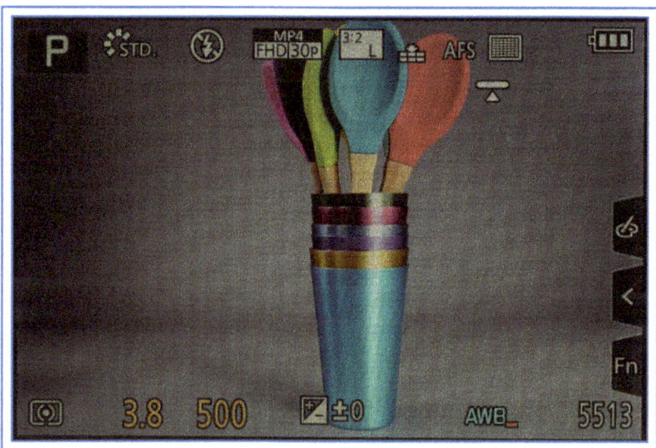

Figure 5-24. White Balance Adjustment Icon on Screen

For example, Figure 5-24 shows the icon, in the bottom right corner of the screen, after the white balance setting was adjusted toward the blue and magenta sides of the axes. If you want to reset the adjustment axes to the zero point, press the Display button (or touch the Reset icon) while the axes are displayed, and the circle will return to the center of the adjustment area.

When the color adjustment screen is displayed, you can also set up white balance bracketing, which I discussed in Chapter 4 in connection with the Bracket menu option. To do that, turn the thumb dial to the right or left to set up the bracketing interval along the amber-blue or green-magenta axis.

The chart in Figure 5-25 shows how different white balance settings affect images taken by the C-Lux. The images in this chart were taken under artificial light balanced for daylight, with the camera set for each available white balance setting, as indicated on the chart. In my opinion, the best results were obtained with the AWB, AWBc, Flash, and Custom settings. The Daylight and Color Temperature settings also appeared to match the actual color temperature quite closely, and the Cloudy and Shade settings did not do badly.

The Incandescent setting is the only one that yielded a result that clearly is incorrect.

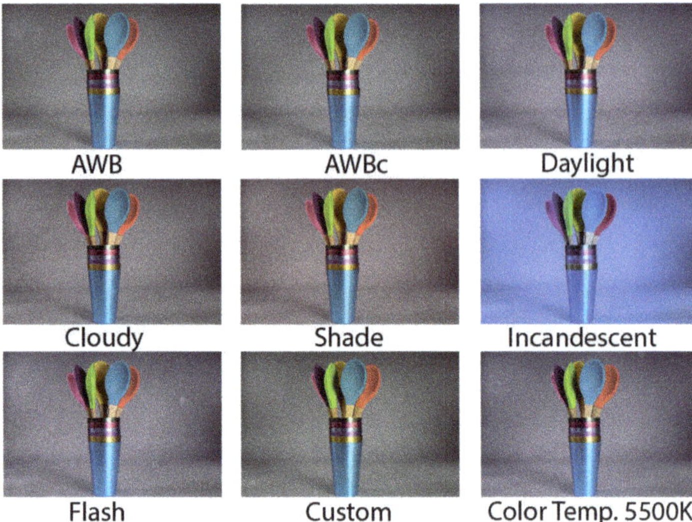

Figure 5-25. White Balance Comparison Chart

If you're shooting with Raw quality, you don't have to worry about white balance so much, because, once you load the Raw file into your software, you can change the white balance however you want. This is one of the advantages of using Raw. If you had the camera's white balance setting at Incandescent while shooting under a bright sun, you can change the setting to Daylight in the Raw software, and no one need ever know about the error of your shooting.

Besides giving access to white balance settings, the Right button has some miscellaneous functions. For example, when playing movies and slide shows, the Right button acts as a navigation control to move through the images, and it is used to navigate among the various portions of screens with settings, such as the Highlight Shadow and Photo Style screens. When you have selected a filter effect in Creative Control mode or with the Filter Settings menu option, you can press the Right button to get access to a screen for making an adjustment to that setting.

Left Button: Focus Mode

The Left button is marked with a flower icon and the letters MF, for manual focus. Pressing this button brings up the menu for selecting a basic focus mode, as shown in Figure 5-26. The four choices, from the left, are AF (autofocus), AF Macro, Macro Zoom, and manual focus.

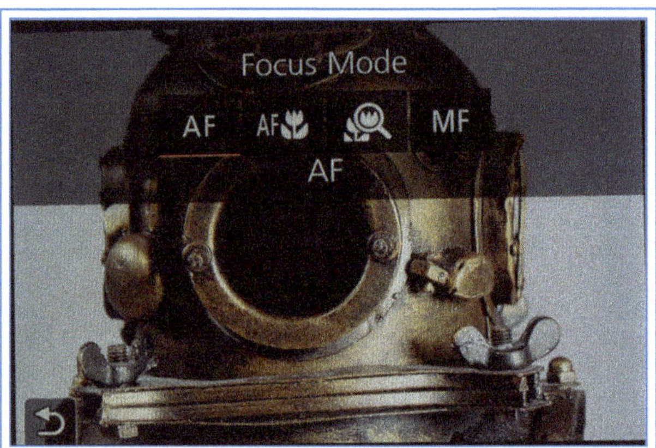

Figure 5-26. Focus Mode Menu

Autofocus

If you choose AF, the camera will use its autofocus mechanism, along with the settings you make for other focus-related options such as AF Mode, AFS/AFF/AFC, and others. The camera will use its normal autofocus distance range of 1.6 foot (50 cm) to infinity at the wide-angle setting, and 3.3 feet (1 m) to infinity at the telephoto setting.

AF Macro

If you choose AF macro, the camera can focus as close as about 1.2 inch or 3 cm, when the lens is zoomed back to its wide-angle setting. At the extreme telephoto setting, the lens can focus as close as 3.3 feet (1 m), the same as with normal autofocus mode.

Macro Zoom

If you choose Macro Zoom, you can focus at the same closeup distance as with AF Macro, but the camera will let you use digital zoom, at a magnification factor of up to three times normal, while still focusing at the minimum focus distance, with the optical zoom at its wide-angle setting. The Macro Zoom setting is not available with certain other settings, including Raw quality, Multiple Exposure, Handheld Night Shot, Panorama mode, high speed video recording, or with the HDR, Impressive Art, Toy Effect, Toy Pop, or Miniature Effect settings.

Manual Focus

If you choose manual focus, you will need to adjust the focus manually using the control ring. The process for using manual focus involves several possible steps, which depend on the settings for several Custom menu options. I will discuss the details of those options in Chapter 7. For now, to discuss the basics of using manual focus, I will assume that the MF Assist option on screen 3 of the Custom menu is turned on, and that the Touch Screen option is set to On under the Touch Settings item on that same screen of the Custom menu. I will also assume that the MF Assist Display item on screen 3 of the Custom menu is set to PIP (picture-in-picture), and that the Peaking and MF Guide items, on screens 4 and 5, respectively, are turned on.

With the above settings in place, press the Left button to bring up the focus mode menu. Select the MF option at the right by highlighting it and pressing the Menu/Set button or by half-pressing the shutter button to return to the shooting screen. Now, start turning the control ring (the large ring around the lens) to adjust the focus.

As soon as you start turning the ring, you should see a screen like that in Figure 5-27, with an enlarged block inset in the display, with white arrows at its sides.

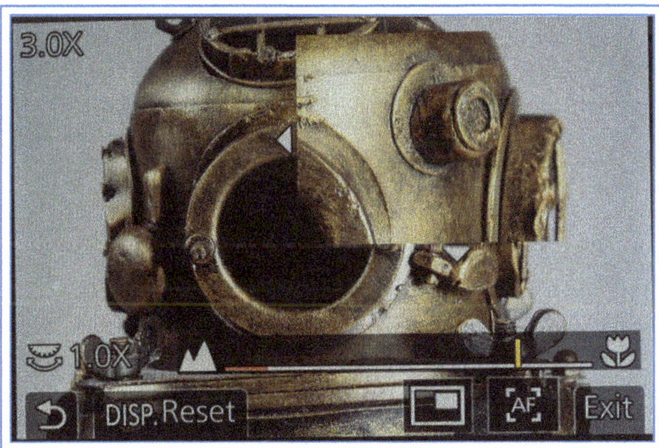

Figure 5-27. Enlarged Screen for Manual Focus

You can move that block around the screen with your fingers, and you can pinch or pull on the screen or turn the thumb dial to change the enlargement factor to anywhere between 3.0x and 6.0x normal. You also can use the direction buttons to move the block. When you have the enlarged block sized and located where you want it, turn the control ring to get the focus as sharp as you can. The peaking feature will place an increasing density of colored pixels at the areas that are in sharpest focus.

You can press on the touch icon that looks like a rectangle with a small, solid rectangle in its upper right corner to switch the view from the PIP setting to a full view, with the entire display enlarged. In that case, the enlargement factor can vary between 3.0x and 10.0x normal. You can press on the small AF icon to cause the camera to use its autofocus on the area in the center of the enlarged display. You can touch the DISP. RESET icon to make the focus point return to the center of the display. You can touch the EXIT icon to return to the normal-sized display. While you are adjusting focus, the MF Guide will appear near the bottom of the display, showing roughly where the focus point is located between the minimum focus distance and infinity.

I will discuss the options for assisting with manual focus further in Chapter 7.

Down Button: Drive Mode

The last of the cursor buttons to be discussed, the Down button, provides access to drive mode, which includes settings for the camera's burst shooting, 4K Photo, Post Focus, and self-timer options.

When you press the Down button, you will see a line of icons, as shown in Figure 5-28.

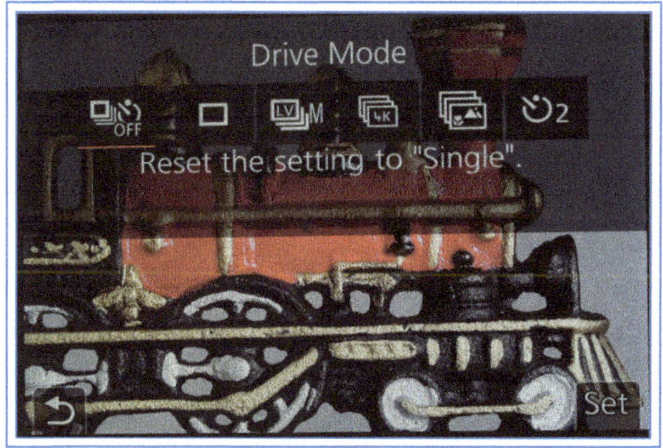

Figure 5-28. Drive Mode Menu

Scroll through them with the thumb dial, the Left and Right buttons, or by touching the icons on the touch screen. As you highlight each one, the camera places a label underneath it listing its function. From left to right, these icons have the following functions: burst shooting off; single shooting; burst shooting on; 4K Photo; Post Focus; and self-timer. I will discuss all of these functions below.

The first two icons on the drive mode menu have the same function—to turn off all burst shooting, including the self-timer. There is no functional difference between these icons; you can select either one when you want to make sure the camera is not set to use the burst, 4K Photo, Post Focus, or self-timer options. There are some camera settings, such as white balance bracketing and HDR, that do not function when one of the burst shooting options is selected. So, if you find a feature is not working, you may want to select the first or second drive mode icon to disable all burst features and see if that removes the conflict.

The third icon is used to activate burst shooting, which I will discuss now.

Burst Shooting

With burst shooting, sometimes called continuous shooting, the camera takes a continuous series of images while you hold down the shutter button. This capability is useful in many contexts, from shooting an action sequence at a sporting event to taking a series of shots of a portrait subject to capture changing facial expressions. I often use this setting for street photography to increase my chances of catching an interesting image.

To activate burst shooting, press the Down button, then scroll to the third icon from the left. It looks like a stack of frames with the letter H, M, or L beside it, for high, medium, or low speed bursts. Once this icon is highlighted, press the Up button (or touch the More Settings icon) to get access to more settings, and you will see icons with all three of those speed notations, as shown in Figure 5-29.

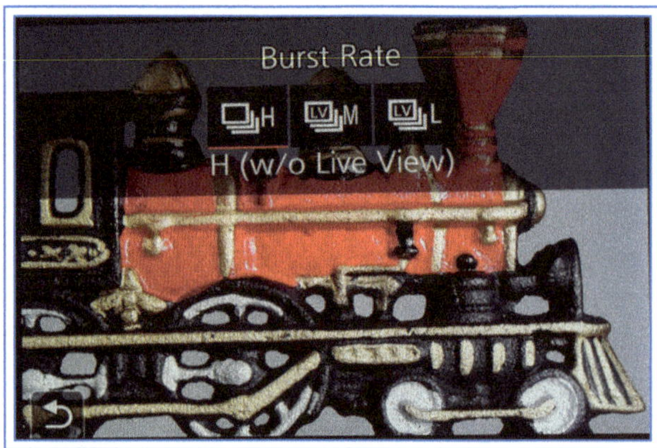

Figure 5-29. Burst Shooting More Settings Screen

Scroll through those icons to select the one you want to use, then press the Menu/Set button to activate it and return to the recording screen. I will discuss these three options in turn.

The first burst option is H, for high-speed shooting. With this setting, the maximum speed available is 10 frames per second (fps) with single autofocus or manual focus, and 6 fps with flexible or continuous autofocus. The camera provides an updated live view on its display during shooting with focus mode set to AFF or AFC, but not with AFS or MF. You can shoot with Raw quality. If the focus mode is set to AFS or MF, the exposure and white balance settings will be fixed with the first shot. However, if you set the focus mode to AFF or AFC, the camera will adjust focus, exposure and white balance for each shot, at the expense of a loss in speed of shooting. When it adjusts focus, the camera uses "predicted focusing," which means the camera tries to guess where the focus point should be located, which increases the speed of focusing but may sacrifice some accuracy.

With the next lower speed, M, for medium, the camera can shoot at up to 7 fps with AFS or MF and 6 fps with AFF or AFC. It provides an updated live view throughout the shooting, and performs almost the same as with the H setting with respect to focus and exposure. The one difference is that the focusing behavior varies according to the setting of the Focus/Release Priority option on screen 2 of the Custom menu. If that option is set to Focus when AFF or AFC is in use, the camera will focus normally, rather than using predicted focusing. If that option is set to Balance or Release, the camera will use predicted focusing, just as it does with the H setting for burst speed. (The Focus/Release Priority option, which is discussed in Chapter 7, lets you specify whether the camera should require an image to be in focus before releasing the shutter.)

Finally, with the lowest speed, L, for low, the speed drops to 2 fps with all focus modes. The live view is available and focus behavior is the same as with the M setting.

When the camera is set for burst shooting, if you press the shutter button halfway with one of the detailed information screens displayed, the camera displays the letter "r" followed by the number of images the camera can capture in a continuous burst. For example, in Figure 5-30, the display shows that the camera can capture 78 images, with Burst Rate set to H, Quality set to JPEG-Fine, and AFS selected for autofocus. When you press the shutter button down to capture the burst, that number will continuously decrease; it should reach zero at the point when the rate of shooting starts to slow down. However, in my tests, described below, I found that the number did not decrease by one unit for each shot. Instead, the camera often shot several shots before the number would decrease, so the total number of images captured in the burst often was greater than the "r" number indicated on the screen.

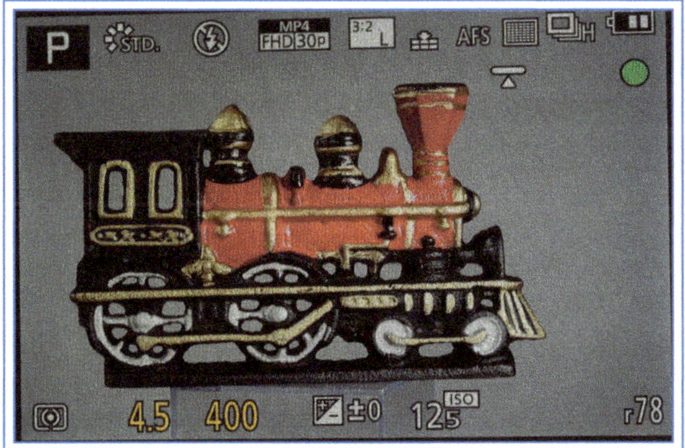

Figure 5-30. Shots Remaining in Burst Shown on Screen

With all burst shooting, the specifications for speed and numbers of images will vary according to conditions. When conditions are dark and the camera has to use a slower shutter speed, that factor alone will slow down the shooting. Other factors that affect shooting capacity and speed include image quality and the speed and capacity of the memory card in the camera. I carried out some indoor experiments with my C-Lux using a very fast card, the SanDisk Extreme PRO 512 GB SDXC card, rated in UHS Speed Class 3, the highest speed category currently available. I used Shutter Priority mode at 1/100 second in order to have consistent conditions and I set the Focus/Release Priority option on screen 2 of the Custom menu to Release. Table 5-2 shows the results of my tests.

Table 5-2. **Results of Burst Shooting Tests with Leica-C-Lux Camera**

Burst Mode	Image Quality	Image Size	Focus Mode	No. Images Before Slowdown
H	Raw & JPEG	L	AFS	29
H	Raw	-	AFS	33
H	Fine	L	AFS	105
H	Raw & JPEG	L	AFC	33
H	Fine	L	AFC	280+
M	Raw & JPEG	L	AFC	33
L	Raw & JPEG	L	AFC	45

The results did not always agree with the expected results according to the specifications, though Leica makes it clear that results will be affected by shooting conditions. Based on these results, my recommendation is to use the slower speeds when you don't need super-fast shooting. For example, if you are taking a portrait and would like to capture changing expressions but don't need to freeze an action as you might at a sporting event, try using the L or M setting to increase your chance of getting usable shots, especially if you are using continuous autofocus.

If you are shooting sports or other fast-moving events, you should get good results with the H setting, especially if the action is at a constant distance and you can use single autofocus. With continuous autofocus, I got more shots before slowdown than with single autofocus, but at a slower maximum burst speed.

The burst-shooting options are available in every shooting mode for still images, except for Panorama. However, there are several limitations on the use of burst shooting. You cannot use it with flash, or with the Rough Monochrome, Silky Monochrome, Miniature, Soft Focus, Star Filter, or Sunshine filter effect settings. You also cannot use it with some of the other special settings such as Multiple Exposure, White Balance Bracket, Time Lapse Shot, Handheld Night Shot, Glistening Water, Glittering Illuminations, or Soft Image of a Flower settings, during motion picture recording, or when using Stop Motion Animation with Auto Shooting turned on.

After shooting with any of the burst options, you are likely to see for at least a few seconds the red icon indicating that the camera is writing images to the memory card; while that icon is displayed, you should not try to take any more pictures, and you should not open the battery compartment cover or otherwise interfere with the camera's operation.

4K Photo

The fourth icon from the left for drive mode, labeled 4K, gives you access to the powerful 4K Photo features. The term 4K originated with 4K video recording, which is available with the C-Lux and other modern cameras. 4K is a video format that has about 4,000 (4K) pixels in the horizontal dimension, as opposed to the more standard HD (high-definition) formats that have about 1,920 (2K) pixels in that dimension. The 4K format is sometimes referred to as Ultra-HD.

With the C-Lux camera, a single frame of 4K video has 3840 horizontal pixels and 2160 vertical ones, for a total of about 8.3 megapixels. So, a single frame of 4K video has about the same resolution as a still image taken with aspect ratio set to 16:9 and picture size set to M. Because of the relatively high resolution of each frame of 4K video, you can use the 4K capability of the camera as another option for taking a high-speed burst of single images. The difference from normal burst shooting is that, with 4K Photo, the camera actually records a video sequence at its normal rate of 30 frames per second, and it can continuously record at that fast rate for up to 15 minutes, rather than the relatively short time the camera can record at a fast rate with normal burst shooting. As a result, you can record thousands of medium-resolution still images and then select the best ones from that group.

In order to use this option, as with 4K video recording, you need to use a memory card that is rated in UHS Speed Class 3.

The 4K Photo option has three sub-options with somewhat different functions, as discussed below. You select these settings in the same way as for the normal burst settings of drive mode. After you highlight 4K Photo on the drive mode menu, press the Up button to move to the screen shown in Figure 5-31, with three sub-options.

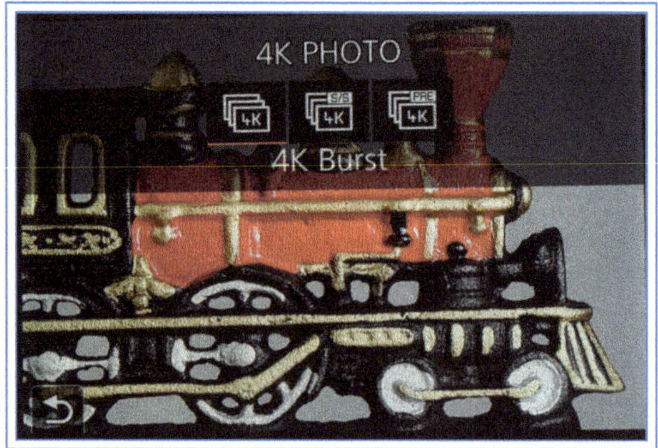

Figure 5-31. 4K Photo More Settings Screen

Highlight the one you want to select and press the Menu/Set button or select the icon on the touch screen.

You also can call up the 4K Photo Mode menu by pressing the FN1 button, assuming it remains assigned to its default setting as the 4K Photo button.

4K Burst

The basic option for the 4K Photo feature is called 4K Burst. With this option, the camera records a 4K video sequence while you press the shutter button and hold it down. This approach is useful when you are trying to capture a burst of shots of an activity with a fairly clear duration. For example, if a group of bicycle racers is approaching your position, when the cyclists get close, you can press the shutter button and hold it down until the racers have passed out of view. With this setting, the camera can record for up to 15 minutes at a time.

4K Burst S/S

The second selection is 4K Burst Start and Stop. With this option, the camera starts recording its 4K video sequence when you press and release the shutter button, and it records continuously until you press and release the button again. The idea with this approach is that you are letting the camera run so it can capture a burst of shots of an unpredictable activity. For example, if you are photographing a group of geese on a pond and you want to catch them in flight, you can start the camera recording and not stop it until they have actually taken off and flown away. While the recording is in progress, you can press the Fn1 button to insert a marker into the video file, to help locate points of interest during the editing process. You can insert up to 40 of these markers for a given recording. As with the other 4K Photo settings, the camera can record a sequence using this option for up to 15 minutes.

4K Pre-burst

With this final option, the camera actually records continuously, even before you press the shutter button. It retains only a short amount of action in its memory—about one second. When you press the shutter button fully down and release it, the camera records the scene for the one second that is already in its memory and for about one additional second, resulting in a sequence lasting about two seconds. You can use this option for a situation when you believe an action is about to happen, and you don't want to miss the beginning of it. For example, if you are watching a batter at a baseball game, you can press the shutter button as soon as the bat hits the ball, and you should catch the entire swing and impact.

With this option, because the camera records continuously even when you are not pressing the shutter button, the battery is run down more quickly than usual. So, you should not activate this setting until you are ready to use it.

All of the 4K Photo options are available for use in all still-image shooting modes except Panorama. Therefore, you can shoot these high-quality bursts in the more advanced modes, including Shutter Priority and Manual exposure. It often may be useful to select one of those modes, because you can then set the shutter speed to a fast setting, such as 1/1000 second, to increase the chance of capturing an image that is free from motion blur.

Of course, you can only use a shutter speed that fast when there is plenty of light, or the ISO setting is high. But, if you can do so, you should consider that possibility. If you use autofocus with any of these settings, focus will be adjusted continuously, regardless of the AFS/AFF/AFC setting on the menus. (This is because the camera is actually recording video, and in that mode, focus always is adjusted continuously when autofocus is in use.) You can use any aspect ratio you want.

With the 4K Burst and 4K Pre-burst options, no audio is recorded. However, with the 4K Burst (S/S) option, audio is recorded through the camera's built-in microphone. This audio is not played back when you play back the sequence in the camera. However, if you copy the sequence's .mp4 file to a computer and play it back, the audio track will be present. So, if you want to capture both still images and video with audio for a scene, this option can be a useful one.

Extracting a 4K Photo Still Image

Once you have recorded a 4K Photo sequence, you need to take further steps to extract a still image from it.

When you press the Playback button and find the sequence, press the Up button to enter 4K Photo playback mode, as indicated in Figure 5-32.

The camera will display a screen with a set of DVR-like controls at the bottom of the screen, as shown in Figure 5-33. You can touch those icons (or press the button associated with each icon, as indicated by the arrow next to each icon, to play or rewind, or to advance or go backward a frame at a time. (For example, to play through the frames at normal speed, press the Up button, or touch the play icon next to the upward-facing triangle.)

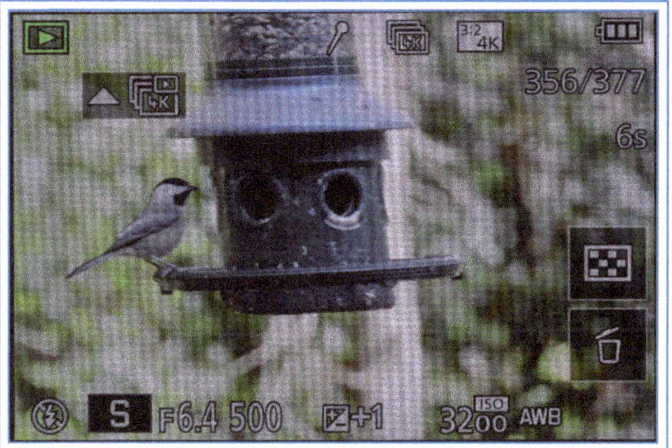

Figure 5-32. 4K Photo Sequence in Playback Mode

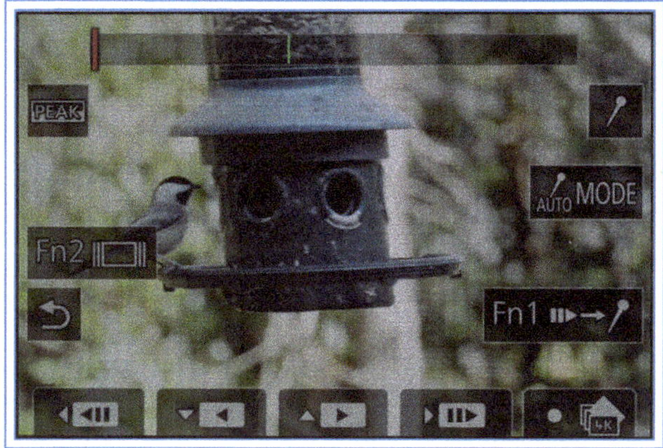

Figure 5-33. 4K Photo Playback Screen with DVR Controls

If you press the Fn2 button, as indicated by the icon on the screen, instead of the DVR-like controls, the camera will display a stack of frames outlined in red in the bottom left corner of the display, as shown in Figure 5-34. (The camera may initially display this screen instead of the DVR-controls screen. You can switch between these two screens by pressing the Fn2 button.)

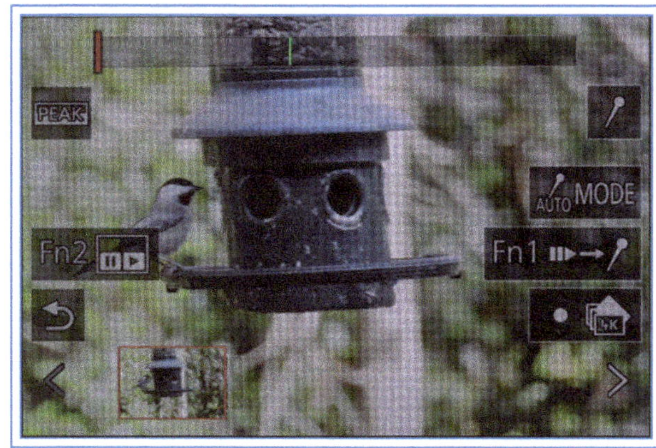

Figure 5-34. 4K Photo Playback Screen with Stack of Frames

With your finger, swipe along that stack to drag through the series of images, or turn the thumb dial or press the Left and Right buttons to move through the stack. A vertical red line will move through the progress bar at the top of the display to show how far through the group of images you have moved. If there are more than 60 images in the group, you can touch the right or left arrow icon on the screen, on either side of the stack of image icons, to move to the next or previous group.

You also can use markers to find single frames to extract from the file. You can use markers that you added during the recording process by pressing the Fn1 button. You also can add new markers during the playback and editing process. To do that, press the icon that looks like a pin with a round head, shown in the upper right corner of the display screen in Figures 5-33 and 5-34. Once you have inserted one or more markers, the camera will display the marker icon with a trash can icon when it displays the marked frame; you can press that icon to delete the markers.

In cases where the camera detects a face or significant motion, it will place an icon with the words Auto Mode below the pin icon. If you press the Auto Mode icon, the camera will display the screen shown in Figure 5-35, with choices of Auto, Face Priority, Motion Priority, or Off.

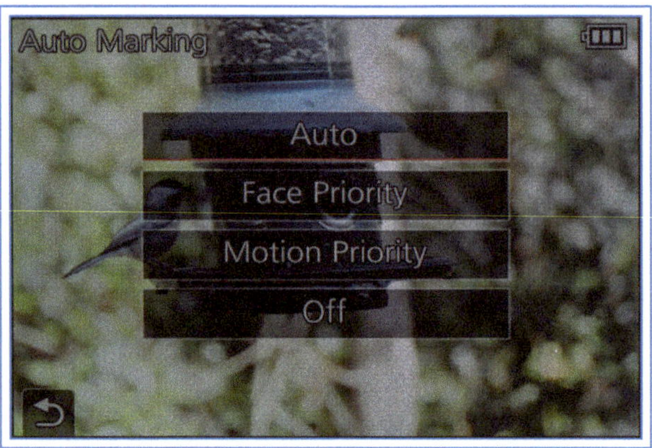

Figure 5-35. Auto Mode Options Screen

If you select Auto, the camera will automatically insert markers on frames where it detects the significant movement of a subject or the appearance of a person's face. If you select Face Priority, it will automatically insert markers on frames in which it detects the appearance of a face. If you select Motion Priority, it will automatically insert markers on frames in which it detects the significant motion of a subject. If you select Off, it will not automatically insert any markers; only markers that you inserted yourself will be available. The auto marking feature is not available for recordings made with the 4K Pre-burst setting.

Once the markers have been inserted, manually, automatically, or both, you can move from one marker to the next in the file in 4K Photo playback mode. To do that, press the icon on the right side the screen that shows the Fn1 label followed by a pause/playback icon and a right arrow pointing to a pin icon, or press the Fn1 button. When you do that, the screen will change to look like Figure 5-36. In this mode, you can move to the previous or next marker by pressing the Left or Right button. You can press the Fn1 button or the touch screen icon again to switch back to the normal navigation mode.

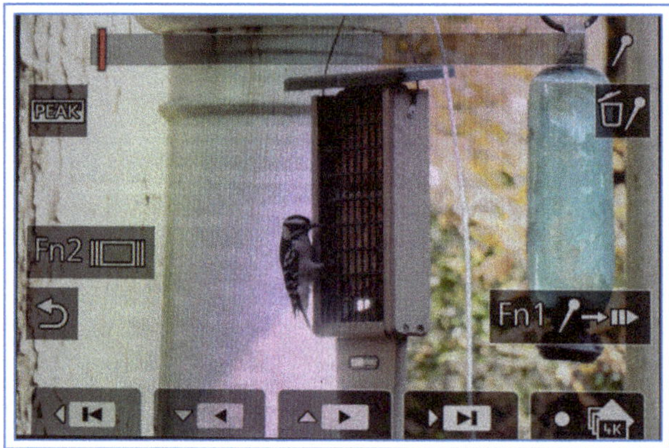

Figure 5-36. Screen to Move to Markers

Once you have moved through the file, using either markers or normal navigation or both, and found a frame you want to extract from the 4K Photo sequence as a still image, press the Menu/Set button, or touch the icon in the lower right corner of the screen that shows a white button next to the 4K label on a stack of frames. The camera will display the message shown in Figure 5-37, asking if you want to save the image. If you highlight and select Yes, the camera will save that frame.

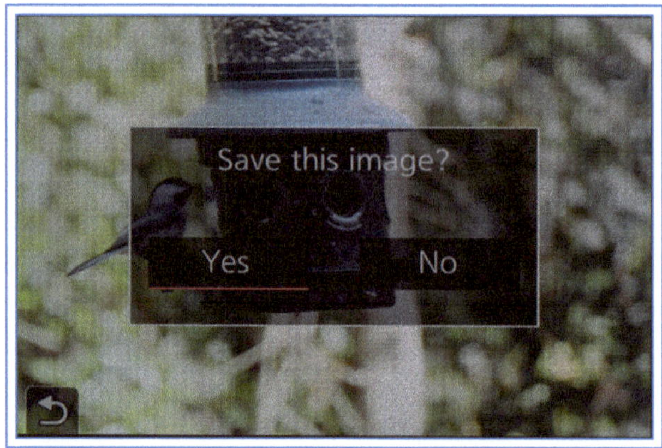

Figure 5-37. Confirmation Screen to Save 4K Photo Image

I have found the 4K Photo feature to be of great use, especially when I am trying to capture an image of a bird at a birdfeeder. The birds come and go rapidly and unpredictably. With this option, I can set up the camera on a tripod, activate 4K Photo (S/S), and leave the camera alone for 15 minutes. When I return, the chances are good that I will have captured an image like that in Figure 5-38, showing a bird in flight.

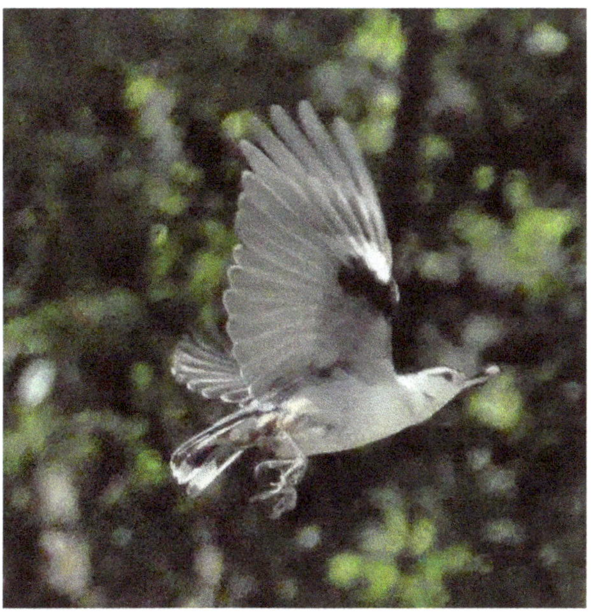

Figure 5-38. 4K Photo Example

There are two other ways to create still images from 4K Photo bursts, using options on the Playback menu: Light Composition and Sequence Composition. Those options let you extract multiple images from a 4K burst to create a still image from a combination of multiple shots, either shots with bright lights or shots from a motion sequence. Those options are discussed in Chapter 6.

Post Focus

This next option on the drive mode menu represents a powerful feature of the C-Lux. As its name indicates, this feature lets you choose the focus point of an image after it was captured. In order to accomplish this feat, the camera records a short 4K video sequence, continuously adjusting the focus for different parts of the scene. When the recording is finished, you can select one or more frames with the sharpest focus on the areas you are most interested in, and the camera will save JPEG images from those frames.

The only setting for Post Focus is to turn the feature on or off. You can do that by selecting it from the drive mode menu, or with the Fn2 button, if that button remains assigned to its default setting of Post Focus. (Of course, you could assign a different button to activate this feature, though it makes sense to leave the Fn2 button with this assignment, if you expect to use the feature.) You can use this option in any shooting mode except Creative Video and Panorama.

Once Post Focus is turned on, either through the drive mode menu or by pressing a function button, aim the camera at the subject and press the shutter button halfway. Because the camera is using 4K video mode, which crops the frame somewhat, you will see that the camera has zoomed in slightly. You may have to adjust the framing of the image to account for the increased focal length.

If the camera finds a focus point, it will display a steady green circle in the upper right corner. If it cannot find a focus point, the green circle will blink. When you are ready, hold the camera as still as possible and press the shutter button all the way down and release it. The camera will record a video sequence for several seconds, during which it will change the focus to every focus point it can find throughout the scene.

When the recording has finished, press the Play button to enter playback mode. You will see a screen like that in Figure 5-39, with a Post Focus icon in the upper left corner.

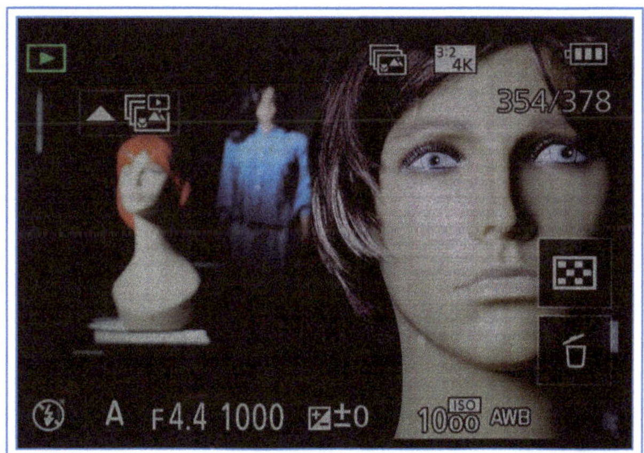

Figure 5-39. Post Focus Sequence in Playback Mode

Press the Up button or touch that icon, and you will see a screen like that in Figure 5-40, with various icons including a plus sign, a return arrow, Fn1, Fn2, and an icon in the lower right corner for saving an image from the sequence. On this screen, move your finger to any point where you would like focus to be fixed. If the camera is able to show an image with that focus point, it will briefly display a green frame at that point and change the focus to that location. For example, in Figure 5-41, after I touched the mannequin head in the foreground of the scene, the camera displayed an image with sharp focus at that point.

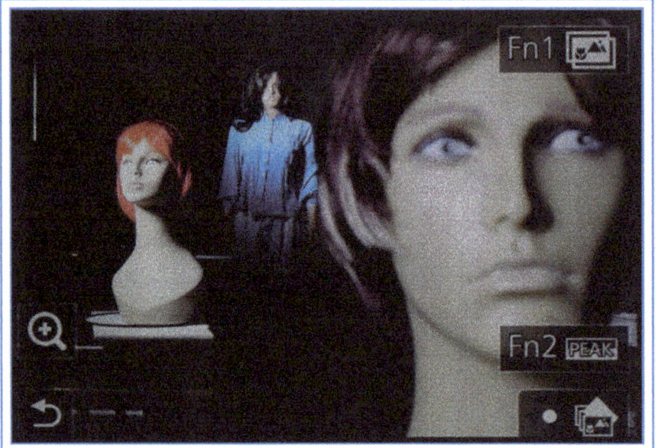

Figure 5-40. Post Focus Sequence Ready to Select Focus Point

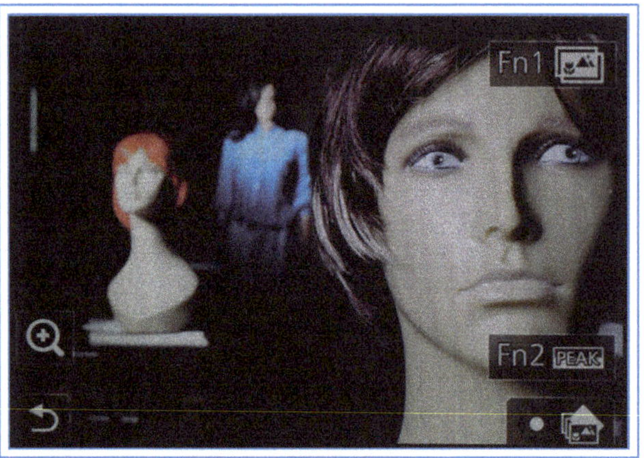

Figure 5-41. Focus Point in Foreground Selected

In Figure 5-42, after I touched the mannequin in the background of the scene, the camera displayed a frame with focus fixed on that area.

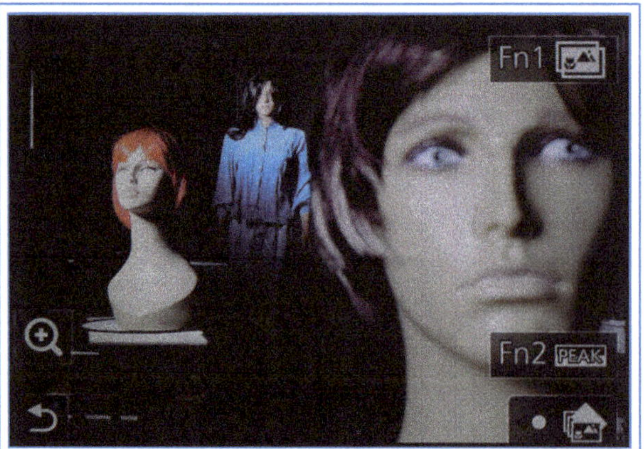

Figure 5-42. Focus Point in Background Selected

To adjust a chosen focus point in more detail, press the magnifying glass icon with the plus sign, or move the zoom lever to the right, to enlarge the image. The camera will then display a sliding scale at the bottom of the screen, as seen in Figure 5-43. Slide your finger along that scale, or use the Left and Right buttons or the thumb dial, to adjust the focus point in small increments until you have adjusted the focus location as precisely as possible. Then touch the return arrow in the lower left corner of the screen, or move the zoom lever to the left, to return the image to normal size.

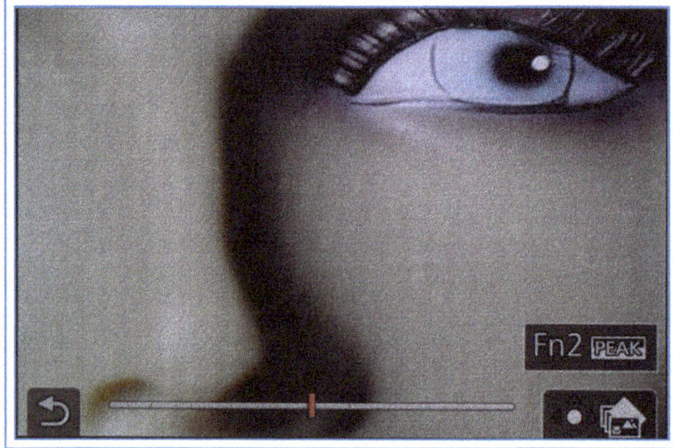

Figure 5-43. Post Focus Playback Magnification Screen

You also can press the Fn2 button or its on-screen icon, which causes the camera to turn on its peaking display, placing colored pixels at the areas of sharpest focus to help you determine where focus is sharp. Successive presses of that button or icon cycle through various levels of peaking.

When you have focus adjusted as you want it, touch the icon in the lower right corner of the screen, or press the Menu/Set button, and the camera will display the message shown in Figure 5-44, asking if you want to save this image. If so, highlight and select Yes, and the camera will save a JPEG image with the focus point set as you have selected. You can then repeat this process with other points, and save other images if you want.

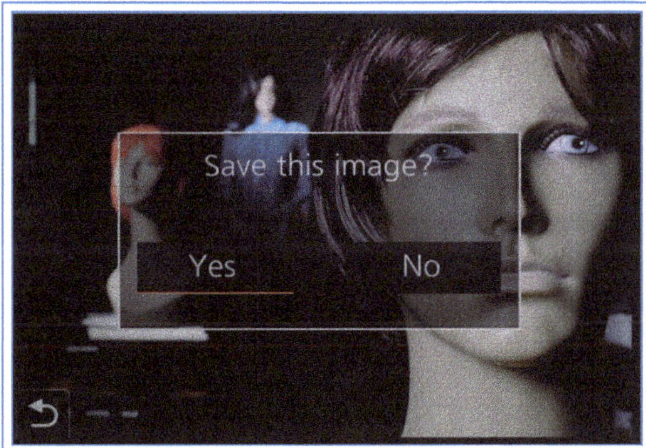

Figure 5-44. Confirmation Screen to Save Post Focus Image

Focus Stacking

Once you have recorded a set of images with the Post Focus option, you also can use those images to create a composite image using shots with different focus points, which has sharp focus throughout much or all of the area in the scene. To do this, when you are viewing a Post Focus series in playback mode, as in Figure 5-39, press the Up button to call up the Post Focus editing screen, which is shown in Figures 5-40, 5-41, and 5-42. On that screen, press the Fn1 button or touch its icon in the upper right corner of the display. The camera will display the screen shown in Figure 5-45, with choices of Auto Merging or Range Merging.

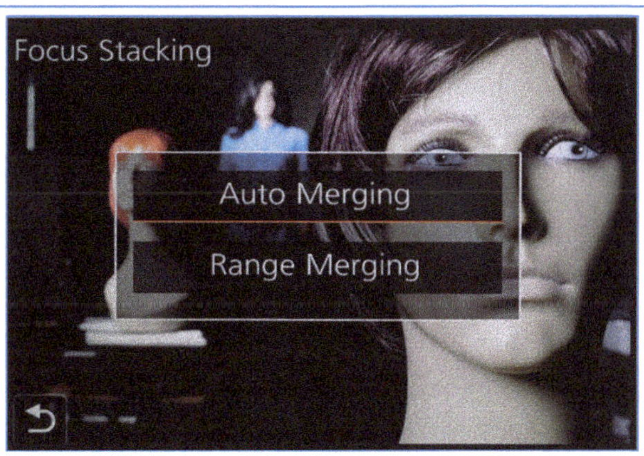

Figure 5-45. Focus Stacking Options Screen

If you choose Auto Merging, the camera will automatically select the shots that it deems to be the best for merging into a final image, giving preference to shots with focus points closer to the lens. The camera will create and save a final image that should have sharp focus in many or all areas, as shown in Figure 5-46.

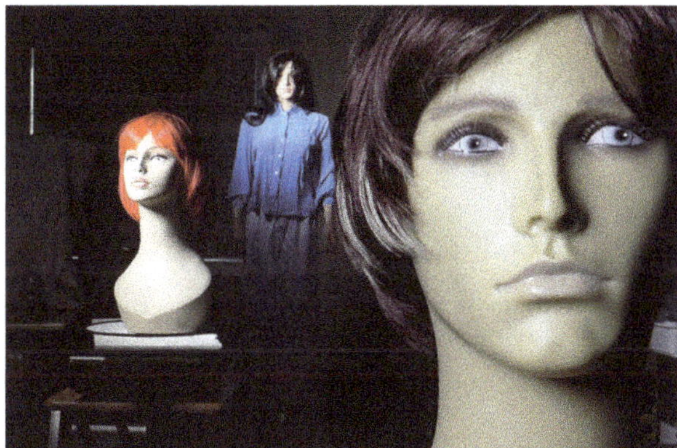

Figure 5-46. Focus Stacking Final Image

If you choose Range Merging, the camera displays the screen shown in Figure 5-47.

On that screen, touch a point to select it for inclusion in the range of focus points to be used for the final image. Touch it again to deselect it. You can keep touching more points or drag on the screen to include an area of the scene. You also can use the direction buttons to move a green selection frame around the screen and press the Fn2 button to select or deselect the point where the frame is placed.

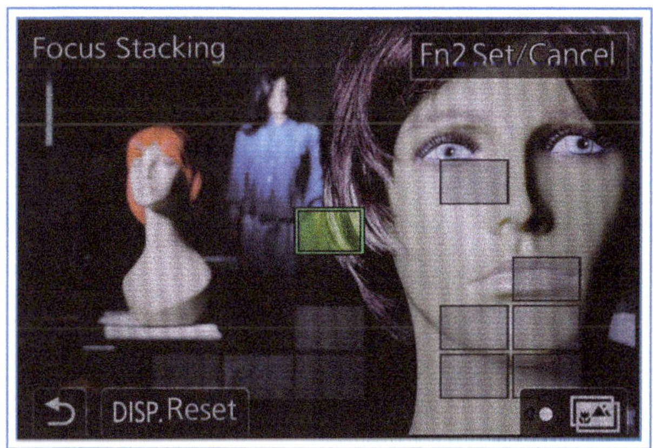

Figure 5-47. Range Merging Screen to Select Points

When you have selected two or more focus points, the camera will display those points and all other points between those focus points in a green shade, to show that they will be included in the final image, as shown in Figure 5-48. The camera will display gray frames for points that are not included in the focus area. You can press the Display button to select or deselect all points in the image at any time, to start over with a completely full or empty set of focus points.

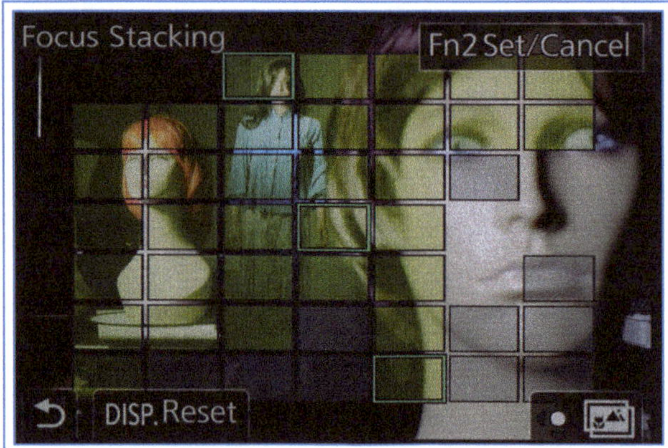

Figure 5-48. Screen with Range Merging Points Selected

When you have finished selecting the focus points to be included in the final image, press the focus stacking icon in the lower right of the image, or press the Menu/Set button, and the camera will display the message shown in Figure 5-49, asking you to confirm the merging of the focus points. Choose Yes if you want to proceed.

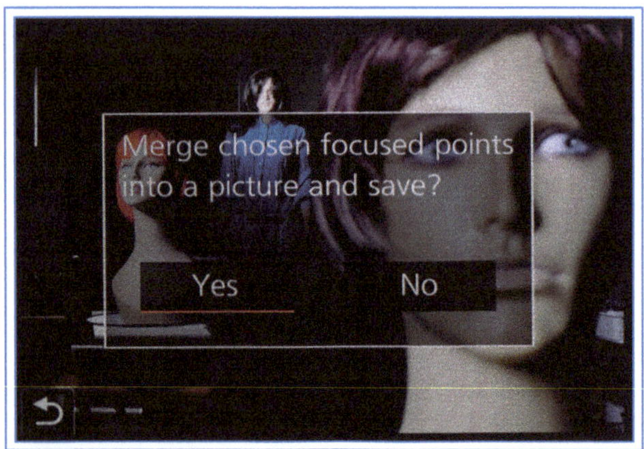

Figure 5-49. Confirmation Screen for Range Merging

Post Focus and Focus Stacking cannot be used with several settings of Scene mode and Creative Control mode, or when the Multiple Exposure option is being used. The camera cannot use the Raw setting for Quality, and the image will be limited to a size of eight megapixels. The camera will use the electronic shutter with a limited range of shutter speeds. However, you still can adjust many settings, and these features are very useful in situations where focus is critical or uncertain, such as macro photography. In a sense, Post Focus acts for focus as the Raw format does for white balance and exposure, which can be adjusted after the fact in a Raw image.

Self-timer

The last icon in the line of drive mode options represents the self-timer. When you activate the self-timer, the camera delays for the specified number of seconds (ten or two) after you press the shutter button before taking a picture. The ten-second setting is useful when you need to place the camera on a tripod and press the shutter button, and then run around to join a group of people the camera is aimed at. The two-second setting is helpful when you need to avoid jiggling the camera by pressing the shutter button as the exposure is taken. This is the case when taking extreme closeups or other shots for which focus is sensitive.

To activate the self-timer, scroll to the last drive mode icon and press the Up button (or touch the More Settings icon) to select further settings. You will see the display shown in Figure 5-50, with three options.

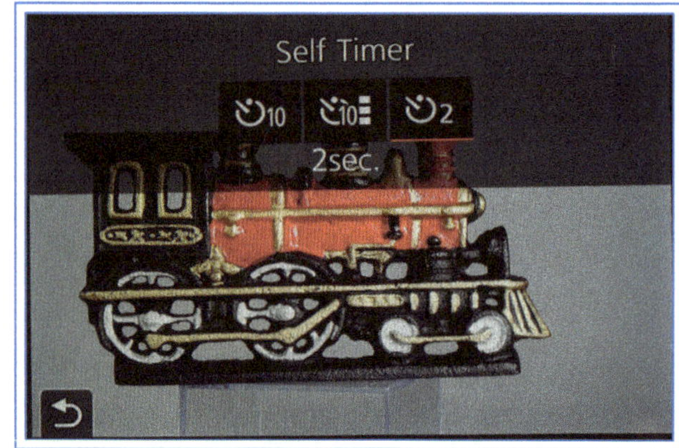

Figure 5-50. Self-timer More Settings Screen

From left to right, these selections are ten-second self-timer; ten-second self-timer with three images taken; and two-second self-timer. Select the setting you want with the Left and Right buttons, by turning the thumb dial, or by touching an icon on the screen. (You also can press the Up button repeatedly to cycle through the choices.) You can then press Menu/Set or half-press the shutter button to return to the recording screen.

An icon in the upper right corner of the display will show the current self-timer setting, as seen in Figure 5-51.

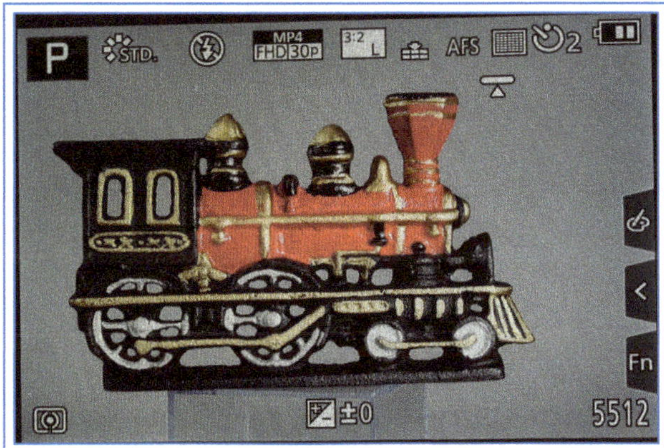

Figure 5-51. Self-timer Icon on Shooting Screen

Now you can wait as long as you want before actually taking the picture (unless the camera times out by entering Sleep Mode or you take certain other actions, such as turning on the 4K Photo option). Compose the picture and press the shutter button. The AF assist lamp, which also serves as the self-timer lamp, will blink and the camera will beep until the shutter is automatically tripped at the end of the specified time. The beeps and blinks speed up for the last second as a warning, when the timer is set to ten seconds. For the two-second option, the camera beeps four times and blinks five times as it counts down. You can cancel the shot while the self-timer is running by pressing the Menu/Set button.

If you choose the option with which the camera takes three pictures after the ten-second timer runs, the three shots will be spaced about two seconds apart, so tell your subject(s) to maintain their pose until all three images have been captured.

You can choose the self-timer option from the Self Timer item on screen 4 of the Recording menu. However, to activate the self-timer, you still have to select its icon from the drive mode menu. The self-timer can be set to remain active even after the camera has been powered off and back on. To make that setting, go to screen 6 of the Custom menu and set the Self Timer Auto Off option to Off. If, instead, you set that option to On, the self-timer will be deactivated when the camera is powered off. I use the two-second self-timer often, because I do a lot of shooting from a tripod and I like to avoid camera shake whenever possible. Therefore, I usually leave that menu option turned off, so the self-timer will be active when I turn the camera on for a new shooting session.

You cannot use the self-timer option for multiple shots when the camera is set for bracketing or Multiple Exposure, or when Simultaneous Record Without Filter is turned on. You cannot use the self-timer at all when recording motion pictures or using the 4K Photo, Post Focus, or Time Lapse Shot options.

Besides activating drive mode, the Down button has various other duties. For example, pressing this button takes you to the screen for fine-tuning a white balance setting, and it provides access to the screen with options for setting the location of focus areas from the AF Mode screen. When the camera is in playback mode, pressing the Down button selects an option for displaying grouped images, such as those taken with Focus Bracket. When you are playing a slide show or a movie, the Down button acts like a Stop button on a DVR to stop the playback completely. When you use the Video Divide function from the Playback menu, the Down button is used to "cut" a movie at your chosen dividing point. When you are viewing a group of images that were taken with the Time Lapse Shot, Stop Motion Animation, or Focus Bracket option, you can press the Down button to view the images individually rather than as a group.

Center Button: Menu/Set

The last button to discuss in the cursor buttons group is the button in the center of the pattern, labeled Menu/Set. You use this button to enter and exit the menu system, and to make or confirm selections of menu items or other settings. In addition, when you are playing a motion picture and have paused it, you can press the Menu/Set button to select a still image to be saved from the motion picture recording. You also can use this button to save a still frame from a 4K Photo sequence.

Function Buttons

The C-Lux has four physical function buttons, labeled Fn1, Fn2, Fn3, and Fn4. (There also are five virtual buttons called Fn5 through Fn9 that can appear on the touch screen; I will discuss them in connection with the touch screen, later in this chapter.)

Each of the four physical buttons has an assigned function by default, and each button also can be programmed to handle any one of a large number of possible operations when the camera is in recording mode. Three of the buttons also can be assigned a function for use in playback mode.

To program a button for a new assignment, you use the Function Button Set option on screen 3 of the Custom menu, which is discussed in Chapter 7. You also can press and hold the button for a few seconds to pop up the menu for changing the button's assignment.

Some of the items that can be assigned to these buttons are not available through any menu or other control, while some of them are options that can also be selected through the menu system or through another control. I will discuss all of those possible assignments later in this chapter. First, I will discuss the pre-assigned duties of the buttons.

Fn1/4K Photo Button

The Fn1 button, located at the far upper right of the camera's back, is assigned by default as the 4K Photo button. With that assignment, when you press the button the camera displays a menu for selecting one of the 4K Photo burst modes or turning 4K Photo off. You can reach a similar menu by pressing the Down button to bring up the drive mode menu, and then pressing the Up button when 4K is highlighted on the Drive menu.

The Fn1 button also has some other miscellaneous duties. For example, when you are using the Multiple Exposure or Time Lapse Shot option on screen 4 of the Recording menu, you can press this button to end the operation. When you are recording a 4K Photo sequence using the 4K (S/S) option, you can press the Fn1 button to add a marker to the sequence at any point. When you are viewing a sequence captured using the Post Focus feature, you can press this button to switch to the Focus Stacking option. The button also is used to change the size or position of the crop frame in the 4K live cropping operation. In any of these cases, the Fn1 button will not be available for any other assigned function.

Fn2/Post Focus Button

The Fn2 button is located to the left of the Playback button and to the upper left of the arrangement of cursor buttons. With its default assignment, pressing this button brings up the brief menu shown in Figure 5-52, allowing you to turn the Post Focus feature on or off. The other way to get access to this feature is through the Post Focus item on the drive mode menu, as discussed earlier in this chapter.

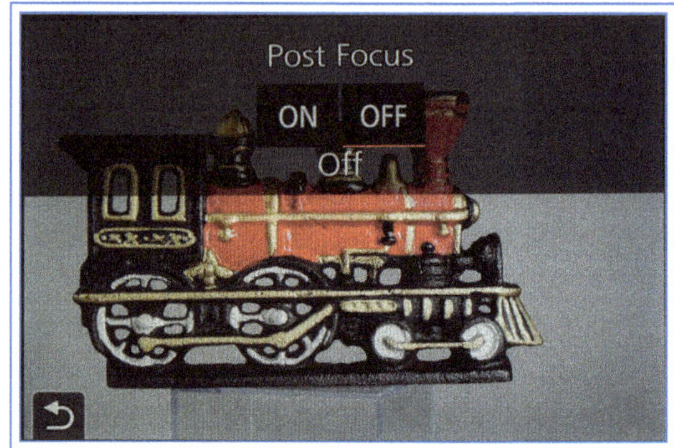

Figure 5-52. Post Focus Menu from Fn2 Button

The Fn2 button also has some miscellaneous functions permanently assigned to it. When you are setting up the autofocus area using the Custom Multi option of AF Mode, in which you select one or more of 49 possible focus zones, you press this button to lock in your selections after highlighting the desired zones. When you are using the 4K burst playback screen to select a still image from a 4K Photo burst sequence, you can press the Fn2 button to switch between the slide view screen and the playback screen with DVR controls. When you are using the Post Focus playback screen, you can press this button to highlight the in-focus areas of the image with focus peaking.

Fn3/Delete/Q.Menu/Cancel Button

The Fn3 button, located to the lower left of the cursor buttons, has several functions. First, as indicated by the trash can icon on the button, it serves as the Delete button. When the camera is set to playback mode, press this button while an image is displayed, and you are presented with several options: Delete Single, Delete Multi, and Delete All, as shown in Figure 5-53.

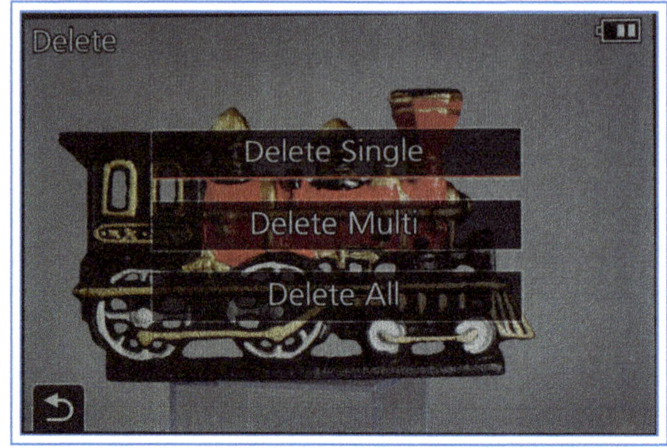

Figure 5-53. Delete Options Screen from Fn3 Button

Use the direction buttons, the thumb dial, or the touch screen to navigate to your choice. If you select Delete Single, the camera will display a confirmation screen; if you confirm the action, the camera will delete the currently displayed image (unless it is protected, as discussed in Chapter 6).

If you select Delete Multi, the camera presents you with a display of recent pictures, up to nine at a time per screen, as shown in Figure 5-54.

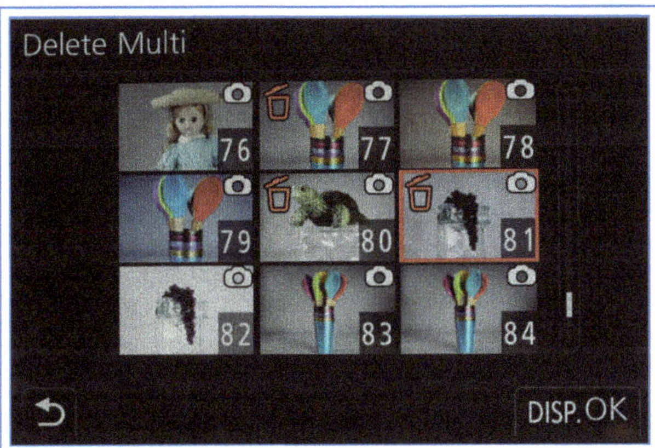

Figure 5-54. Delete Multi Image Selection Screen

You can scroll through these thumbnail images and press the Menu/Set button to mark any picture you want to be included in the group for deletion, up to 100 in total. You can press Menu/Set a second time to unmark a picture for deletion. When you have finished marking pictures for deletion, press the Display button or press the DISP. OK icon on the touch screen to start the deletion process; the camera will ask you to confirm, and you can highlight Yes and press Menu/Set to delete the marked images.

The Delete All option deletes all images on the memory card, unless you have rated some images with stars (as discussed in Chapter 6) and choose to delete all except those with ratings, as prompted by the camera after you select Delete All. You can interrupt a deletion process with the Menu/Set button, though some images may have been deleted before you press the button.

The Fn3 button also serves as a Cancel button, as indicated by the backward-curving arrow below the button. When you are viewing menu screens, you can press this button to cancel out of a selection or other event, such as the use of the Format command on the Setup menu to erase and re-format a memory card. When the Fn3 button can be used to cancel an action and return to a previous screen, the camera displays the curving arrow, as shown in Figure 5-54, for example.

In addition, the Fn3 button acts as the Quick Menu or Q.Menu button, as indicated by the label below the button. In this capacity, the button has only one function—to activate the Quick Menu. I discussed that menu system in Chapter 4. When you press this button while the shooting screen is displayed, you have instant access to several of the more important settings on the camera. You can customize the available choices using the Quick Menu option on screen 3 of the Custom menu, as described in Chapter 7. If you assign the Fn3 button to a new function through the Function Button Set option on screen 3 of the Custom menu, the button will no longer call up the Quick Menu.

Fn4/EVF Button

The Fn4 button is located just to the right of the electronic viewfinder's eye sensor window. As indicated by its label, this button is assigned by default to control the operation of the electronic viewfinder (EVF). Pressing the button repeatedly calls up the three possible settings for the EVF/Monitor Switch setting, which is an option found under the Eye Sensor item on screen 2 of the Setup menu. The three settings for that item are EVF/Monitor Auto, EVF, and Monitor. With the first option, the camera automatically switches the view from the monitor to the viewfinder when your head (or another object) comes close to the eye sensor, located to the right of the viewfinder. With the EVF setting, the view stays in the viewfinder. With the Monitor setting, the view stays on the LCD monitor. It is convenient to be able to switch this setting just by pressing this button, rather than digging through the menu system to find it.

Assigning Functions to Function Buttons

As I noted above, you can assign any one of numerous functions to any of the four physical function buttons, Fn1, Fn2, Fn3, and Fn4, using the Function Button Set option on screen 3 of the Custom menu. You also can bring up that menu option by pressing and holding any of the four physical function buttons for about two seconds.

The function you assign to a button will be carried out whenever you press the assigned button. Of course, the function will be carried out only if the present context permits. For example, if you assign the Fn1 button to activate the HDR option, and then press the Fn1 button while the camera is in Snapshot mode, nothing will happen, because the HDR option is not available in that recording mode.

Similarly, if you assign the Fn1 button to activate the level gauge option, and then press that button while using the Time Lapse Shot option from screen 4 of the Recording menu, the level gauge will not appear, because the Fn1 button is permanently assigned to interrupt the Time Lapse Shot operation.

Each of these four buttons can be assigned an option for use when the camera is in recording mode. Three of the buttons—Fn1, Fn2, and Fn4—also can be assigned one of a few functions for use in playback mode. A button can have both assignments at the same time, though, of course, only one of the options can be used at a time because the camera has to be in recording or playback mode for the given function to operate. Table 5-3, below, lists the functions that can be assigned to each button for use in recording mode. The buttons listed in parentheses are the default assignments for the listed functions.

Table 5-3. Possible Function Button Assignments for Recording Mode

Menu & Screen No./Normal Control Used for Function	Function
Down Button	4K Photo Mode (Fn1)
Down Button	Post Focus (Fn2)
Setup 1	Wi-Fi (Fn5)
---	Q.Menu (Fn3)
Red Video button	Video Record
Setup 2 (Eye Sensor option)	EVF/Monitor Switch (Fn4)
Custom 5	EVF Monitor Display Style
AF/AE Lock Button	AF/AE Lock
AF/AE Lock Button	AF-On
---	Preview
---	One Push AE
Touch Screen	Touch AE
Display Button	Level Gauge (Fn6)
---	Focus Area Set
---	Operation Lock
Recording 1	Photo Style
Recording 1	Filter Effect
Recording 1	Aspect Ratio
Recording 1	Picture Size
Recording 1	Quality
Recording 1	Sensitivity
Recording 1	AF Mode
Recording 1	AFS/AFF/AFC
Recording 2	Metering Mode
Recording 4	Bracket
Recording 2	Highlight Shadow
Recording 2	i.Dynamic
Recording 2	i.Resolution
Recording 3	Minimum Shutter Speed
Recording 4	HDR
Recording 4	Shutter Type
Recording 2	Flash Mode
Recording 2	Flash Adjustment
Recording 3	i.Zoom
Recording 3	Digital Zoom
Recording 3	Stabilizer
Creative Video 1	4K Live Cropping
Motion Picture 1	Snap Movie (Fn8)
Motion Picture 1	Motion Picture Rec. Quality
Recording 4	Silent Mode
Custom 4	Peaking
Custom 4	Histogram (Fn7)
Custom 4	Guide Line
Custom 5	Zebra Pattern
Custom 4	Monochrome Live View
Custom 4	Constant Preview
Custom 5	Recording Area
Custom 4	Zoom Lever
Up Button	Exposure Compensation
Right Button	White Balance
Left Button	Focus Mode
Down Button	Drive Mode
Playback Button	Record/Playback Switch
---	Off
---	Restore to Default

There are four functions that cannot be assigned to the virtual function buttons, Fn5 through Fn9: EVF Monitor Switch, AF/AE Lock, AF-On, and Operation Lock. Also, the virtual buttons cannot be used when the viewfinder is in use. The Fn9 button does not have a default assignment, unlike the other eight buttons.

Most of the settings in Table 5-3 are self-explanatory; they are options that also can be activated from one of the menus or with a dedicated control. For example, if a button is assigned to the Photo Style option, pressing the button calls up a menu or settings screen for that option from screen 1 of the Recording menu. The screen that is called up by pressing the function button may look different from the screen that is called up from the menu, but it will let you make the basic selection of the menu option. The level gauge is normally activated by pressing the Display button until a screen with that item appears. I will not discuss those assignments here; you can find details about those settings in the chapters that discuss the menu systems and physical controls.

However, there are several possible button assignments that are not found on the regular menus and are not normally activated by any control button. I will discuss those functions below.

Preview

The first non-menu setting, Preview, lets you see the effects of the current aperture and shutter speed settings on the final image before you take a picture. Ordinarily, when you aim the camera at a subject, the live view on the camera's display is set to provide a clear view of the scene, without giving effect to the current settings.

For example, suppose you are using Manual exposure mode for an indoor shot of two objects at different distances. Suppose you have set the aperture to f/8.0 to keep both items in focus with a broad depth of field and you have set the shutter speed to 1/250 second. If you aim the camera at the subjects, you will see a view like that in Figure 5-55, which does not show the effects of these settings.

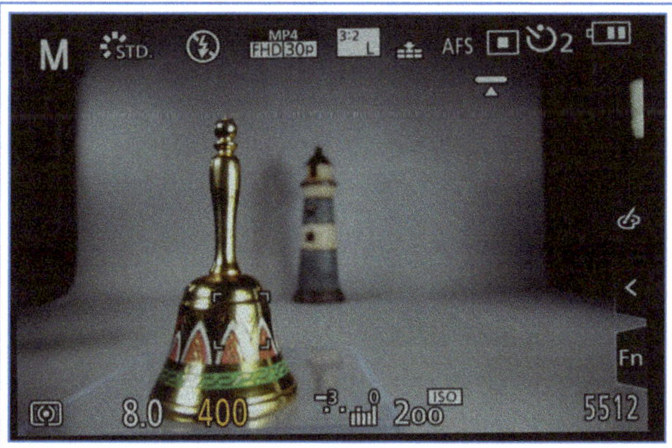

Figure 5-55. Shooting Screen Before Pressing Preview Button

Now, if Preview is assigned to the Fn1 button, press that button once and you will see a screen like that in Figure 5-56. For this view, the Preview feature has caused the camera to close the aperture down to the actual setting of f/8.0, which shows the effect of the broad depth of field, bringing the background into sharper focus. The message on the screen, Fn1 Shtr Speed Effect Added, means that the camera is currently displaying the effect of the aperture setting; if you press Fn1 again, the camera will also display the effect of the shutter speed setting.

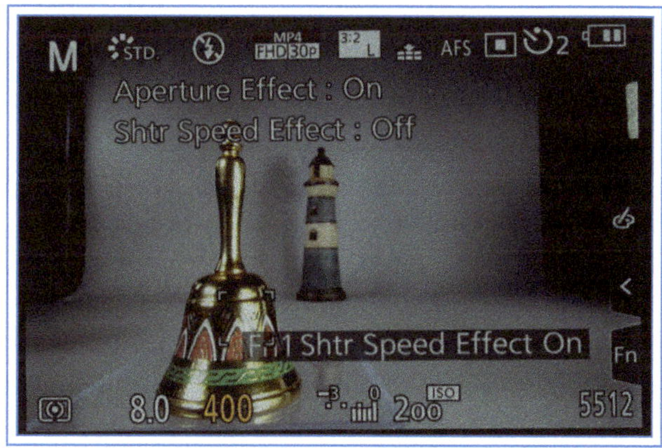

Figure 5-56. Shooting Screen After First Press of Preview Button

After you press Fn1 the second time, the recording screen will look like Figure 5-57. In this case, the camera is displaying the effects of both the aperture and shutter speed settings. The recording screen is quite dark, which shows that using the current shutter speed and aperture would result in a dark image. In addition, the message on the screen indicates that you can press Fn1 to end the preview.

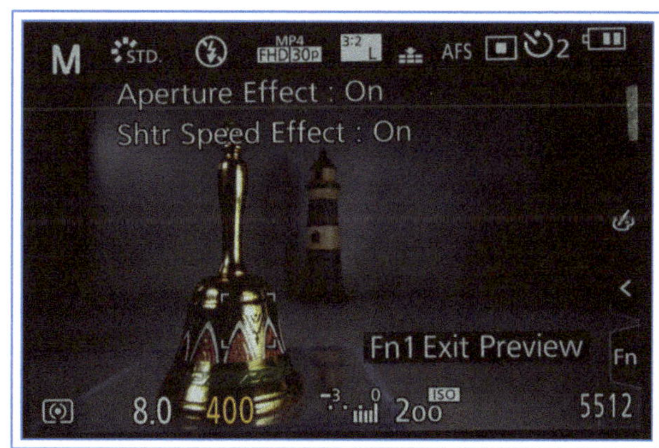

Figure 5-57. Shooting Screen After Second Press of Preview Button

If you have turned on Constant Preview through screen 4 of the Custom menu, the Preview function will not work in Manual exposure mode, because the preview will already be in effect. (The Constant Preview option works only in Manual exposure mode.) You can change the settings while the preview screen is displayed, to see how the changes will affect the image.

One Push AE

This next setting gives you a quick way to set the camera to achieve a normal exposure. It is of use only when the camera has been unable to expose the image properly given the settings you have made, including the aperture and shutter speed. For example, if you are using Shutter Priority mode and have set the shutter speed to 1/640 second with ISO set to 80, if conditions are fairly dark the camera may not be able to expose the image within a normal range. In that case, the aperture and shutter speed values will blink red on the display. At that point, press the function button assigned to One Push AE and the camera will change its settings to correct the exposure problem. When I tried these settings in a fairly dark room, the camera changed the shutter speed to 1/13 second, which produced a normal exposure.

I find this setting to be somewhat odd, because it is difficult to think when it would be useful. If you want the camera to make the settings, you can always use a mode such as Snapshot or even Program, and it very likely will be able to find settings that will expose the image properly. But, if you are just learning how to use the camera and feel it would be helpful to have this extra safety valve to rescue an image in a difficult lighting scenario, you might want to give it a try. It is available only in the PASM modes and Creative Video mode.

Touch AE

This option can also be activated by touching the Touch AE icon on the touch screen tabs, as I will discuss later in this chapter. If you assign Touch AE to a function button, you can turn on this option with one button push. Then, just touch the LCD display on the subject you want the camera to optimize exposure for. The camera will move a small blue cross over the area you touched, as shown in Figure 5-58.

Then press the Set icon or press the Menu/Set button to accept the new exposure setting. You can press the Display button or touch the DISP. Reset icon to reset the exposure point to the center of the display.

Focus Area Set

If you assign this option to a function button, when you press the button, the camera will immediately display a screen for adjusting the current focus setting. The actual result of pressing the button will depend on the current setting. For example, if you are using autofocus with the 1-Area AF Mode setting, pressing the assigned button will place the focus frame on the display with arrows, ready to be moved using the direction buttons. If the current AF Mode setting is Custom Multi, pressing the assigned button will call up the screen for selecting the pattern of focus zones. If you are currently using manual focus, pressing the button will call up a screen for adjusting the MF Assist area.

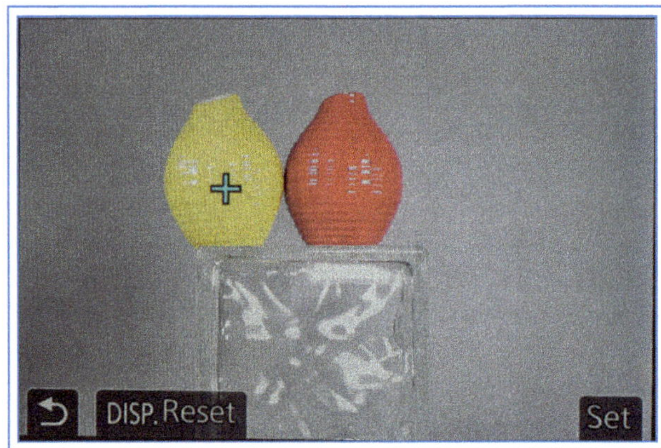

Figure 5-58. Blue Cross for Touch AE on Shooting Screen

This option can be useful if you often adjust the area where the camera focuses, so you don't have to go through extra steps to reach the screen to adjust that area.

Operation Lock

When this function is assigned to a button, pressing that button locks out the operation of the four direction buttons and the Menu/Set button, or the touch screen, or all of the above, while the camera is in recording mode. In order to specify whether the assigned button locks the operation of the cursor buttons, the touch screen, or both categories, you use the Operation Lock Setting option on screen 3 of the Custom menu.

You might want to use this feature if you don't want the current settings to be disturbed by the accidental press of a button or a touch of the screen. Once you have pressed this button, you will not be able to use the controls that were locked until you press the assigned function button again to cancel the lock. The camera will display an Operation Lock message at the top of the screen if you press a locked button.

The lock remains in place even when the camera is powered off and then on, so, if you find you cannot use the Menu/Set button when the camera is first turned on, try pressing the function buttons to see if the direction buttons and Menu/Set button have been locked with this feature. The lock applies only when the camera is in recording mode, so you can still use the cursor buttons and/or touch screen in playback mode, even while the lock is in effect.

Record/Playback Switch

If a button has this assignment for recording mode, pressing it will switch the camera into playback mode. However, pressing the assigned button in playback mode will not switch back to recording mode, unless the button has also been assigned to the Record/Playback Switch function for playback mode, as discussed below.

Restore to Default

If you choose this option for a given function button, that button will be restored to its default setting. Those defaults were shown earlier in Table 5-3.

Assigning Options to Function Buttons for Playback Mode

As I noted earlier, the camera also lets you assign a function to each of three function buttons—Fn1, Fn2, and Fn4—for use when the camera is in playback mode. The functions that can be assigned are the following:

- Wi-Fi
- EVF/Monitor Switch
- Record/Playback Switch
- 4K Photo Play
- Delete Single
- Protect
- Rating★1
- Rating★2
- Rating★3
- Rating★4
- Rating★5
- Raw Processing
- 4K Photo Bulk Saving
- Off
- Restore to Default

By default, the Fn1 button is assigned to Wi-Fi, the Fn2 button is assigned to Rating★3, and the Fn4 button is assigned to EVF/Monitor Switch.

The functions listed above are self-explanatory, except for Record/Playback Switch and the Rating entries. Record/Playback Switch was discussed earlier, for assignments in recording mode.

Rating entries let you quickly assign a rating to an image for video with a number of stars, from 1 to 5, though you can assign only three buttons to have functions in playback mode at any one time. The Rating function also is available on screen 1 of the Playback menu. When you have rated some images, you will have the option to delete all images except rated ones, by selecting Delete All after pressing the Fn3 button in playback mode, and then selecting Delete All Non-rating. You also can view rating information in software such as Adobe Bridge, where the rating shows up as stars in the thumbnail display.

LCD Monitor

The C-Lux's LCD monitor has a diagonal dimension of three inches or 76mm, with a resolution of about 1.2 million dots. It cannot tilt or swivel, but it has excellent features as a touch screen, which I will discuss below, as well as in discussions of menu options and other camera functions that use the touch screen.

Using the Touch Screen

A few basic pointers are helpful in understanding the use of the touch screen. First, the Touch Settings option, on screen 3 of the Custom menu, controls several important settings. I will discuss the details in Chapter 7. If the Touch Screen sub-option of Touch Settings is turned off, no touch screen functions are available. If the Touch Tab sub-option is turned off, there will be basic touch options, but none of the special tabs that appear at the right edge of the shooting screen. The Touch AF and Touch Pad AF sub-options control other aspects of the camera's touch screen functions.

Second, watch for icons that appear to be touchable, and try them out. It can't hurt to experiment, and you will eventually come to realize which icons on the screen are responsive to your touch and which ones are there only to provide information.

Third, don't forget that the touch screen operates in playback mode and with menu screens, not just with recording functions. In this discussion, though, I will concentrate on using the touch screen in recording mode.

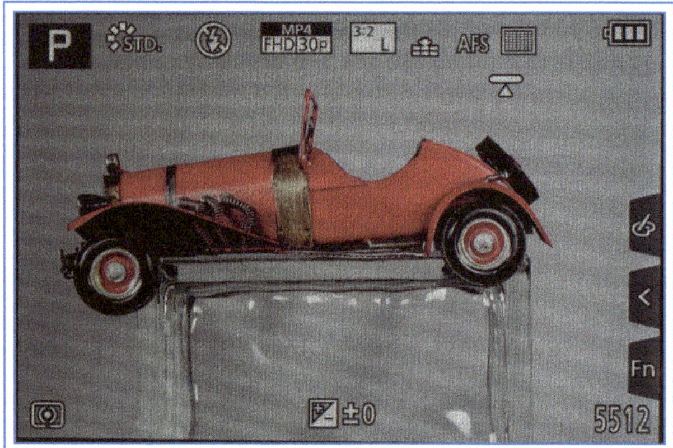

Figure 5-59. Touch Icons on Shooting Screen

Figure 5-59 shows the shooting screen in Program mode, with the touch screen settings turned on. At the right edge of the screen are three icons. From the top, these are the touch icons for controlling filter effects, for activating the touch tab, and for getting access to the virtual function buttons. In this image, all three of those icons are white.

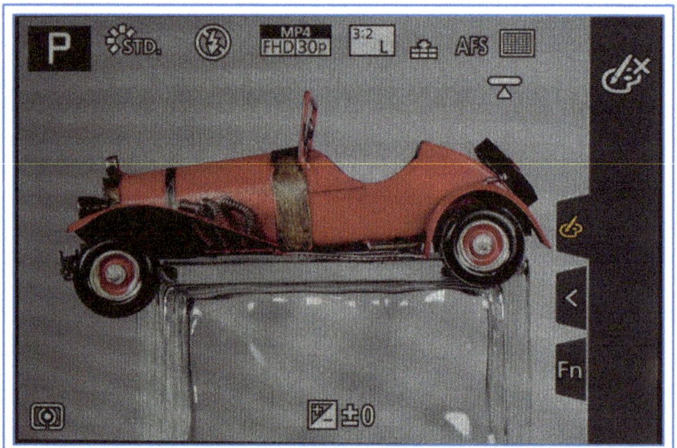

Figure 5-60. Touch Screen After Touching Top Icon

If you touch the top icon, the icons change, as shown in Figure 5-60. You will now see a larger filter effect icon with an X beside it. That icon means that filter effects are turned off. If you touch that icon, the currently selected filter effect, such as Impressive Art (IART), turns on, and the icons change again. To change the effect, touch the IART icon, and the camera will display a screen for selecting a different filter effect. When you are done with filter effects, touch the top icon again to turn off the effect. Then touch the small, yellow filter effect icon to collapse the touch tab area.

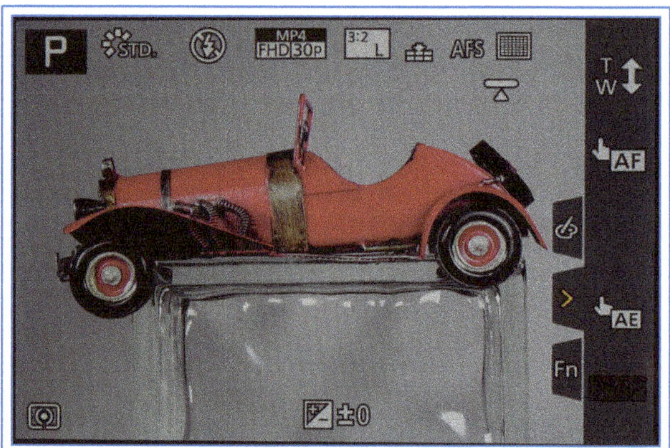

Figure 5-61. Touch Tab Icons Activated

The second of the three icons at the right of the screen is the left-facing arrow, which is the touch tab icon. When you touch that icon, the display changes as seen in Figure 5-61, to show various items in the touch tab area. From the top, these are the Touch Zoom icon, the Touch AF/Touch Shutter icon, the Touch AE icon, and the Peaking icon.

If you touch the Touch Zoom icon, it will turn yellow to show that it is active and the camera will display the Touch Zoom controls, as shown in Figure 5-62. You can then touch those controls to zoom the lens in or out.

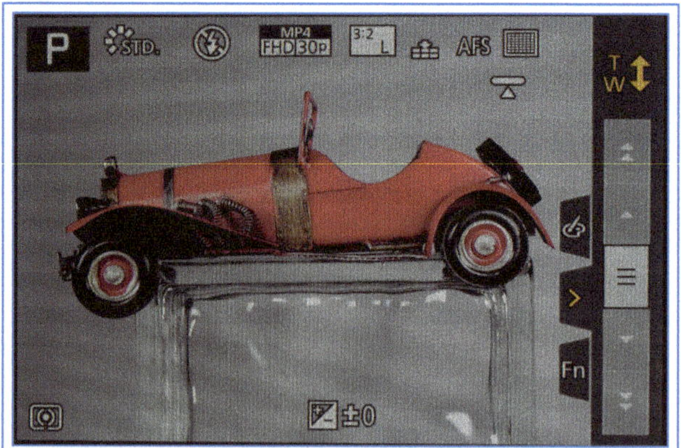

Figure 5-62. Touch Zoom Control Activated

Touch the yellow icon again to turn off touch zoom and get access to other items in the touch tab area.

The icon below the Touch Zoom icon is the Touch AF icon. If you touch it, it cycles through three settings: Touch AF, Touch Shutter, and Off. When it is set to Touch AF, as in Figure 5-61, you can touch the screen to set the focus point, using the current AF Mode setting. If you touch the icon, it switches to Touch Shutter, with a shutter icon next to the pointing finger. You can then touch the screen on any object you want the camera to direct its focus on, and the camera will take a picture without your having to press the shutter button. Touch the icon one more time to turn Touch Shutter and Touch AF off.

The next icon is the Touch AE icon. When you touch that icon, a small blue cross appears on the display, as shown earlier in Figure 5-58. Move that cross with your finger over the subject where you want the exposure to be evaluated, or just touch that area, then touch the Set icon. Touch the touch AE off icon at the left of the screen to cancel touch AE.

Finally, you can press the Fn icon at the bottom of the touch tab area to open up the area for the virtual function buttons, Fn5 through Fn9.

The display will then look like Figure 5-63, with the icons for those buttons visible. Touch any one of those icons to activate the function assigned to it. Earlier in this chapter I discussed how to assign a function to a function button. In this illustration, Fn5 is assigned to Wi-Fi, Fn6 to the level gauge, Fn7 to the histogram option, and Fn8 to snap movie. Fn9 is not assigned. When you have finished using the virtual function buttons, press the yellow Fn icon to collapse the Fn tab.

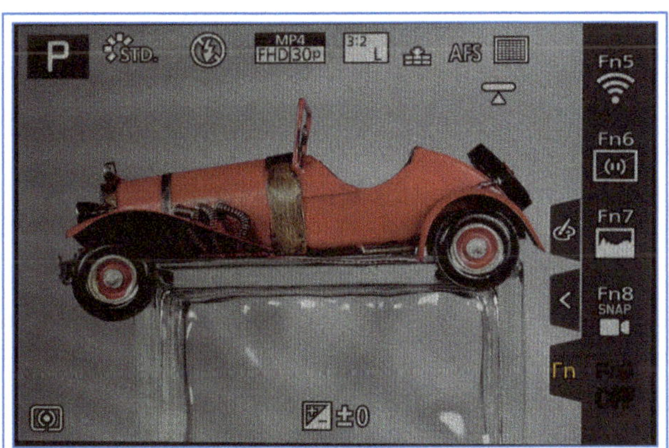

Figure 5-63. Virtual Function Buttons on Touch Screen

I will discuss the various other touch screen functions in connection with the appropriate menu items and camera operations as they come up in later chapters of this book.

Items on Front of Camera

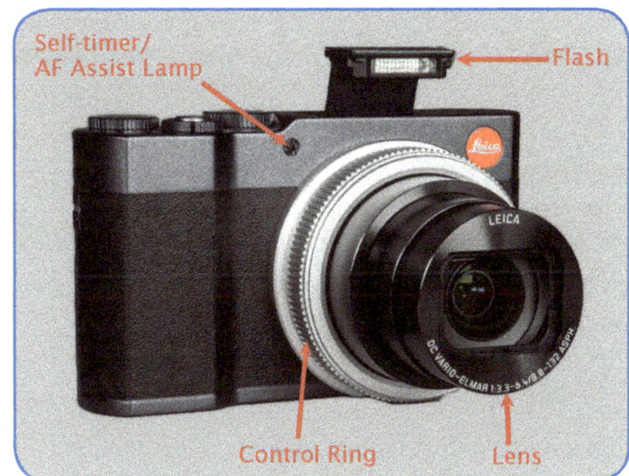

Figure 5-64. Items on Front of Camera

Control Ring

The control ring, shown in Figure 5-64 and also in Figure 5-1, earlier, is the unmarked ring around the lens. This control adds convenience to the operation of the C-Lux through its ability to be customized according to your preferences.

Whenever the camera is set to manual focus mode, turn this ring to adjust the distance at which the camera sets its focus. The display will vary according to settings you make for manual focus through the Custom menu.

When the camera is set to an autofocus mode, the control ring can control other options, according to how it is set through the Ring/Dial Set option on screen 3 of the Custom menu, as discussed in Chapter 7.

If you use the default setting, the ring controls various functions depending on the shooting mode. Table 5-4 lists the ring's default functions for each shooting mode.

Table 5-4. **Default Functions of Control Ring**

Shooting Mode	Default Function
Snapshot	Step Zoom
Program	Program Shift
Aperture Priority	Adjusts Aperture
Shutter Priority	Adjusts Shutter Speed
Manual Exposure	Adjusts Aperture
Panorama	Selects Filter Effects
Scene	No Function, with 2 exceptions below
Scene – Appetizing Food Setting	Adjusts Aperture
Scene – Artistic Nightscape Setting	Adjusts Shutter Speed

Creative Control	Selects Filter Effects
Creative Video	Adjusts Aperture or Shutter Speed if Exposure Mode Permits

If you use the Ring/Dial Set menu option to select a setting other than the default, the ring can control a single setting, such as ISO, zoom, white balance, or filter effects. The following list sets forth the possible assignments for the control ring.

- Default (see Table 5-4, above)
- Zoom
- Step Zoom
- Exposure Compensation
- ISO Sensitivity
- White Balance
- AF Mode
- Focus Mode
- Drive Mode
- Photo Style
- Filter Effect
- Aspect Ratio
- Highlight Shadow
- i.Dynamic
- i.Resolution
- Flash Mode
- Flash Adjustment
- Off (Not Set)

If you select an option other than Default, that setting will take effect for all recording modes for which that setting is available, except when manual focus is in effect. With manual focus, the control ring always controls focus. If you select Highlight Shadow for the control ring, it will also be assigned to the thumb dial, and vice-versa.

All of the settings that are available for the control ring are self-explanatory, except step zoom, which is discussed below.

Step Zoom

With this feature turned on, when you turn the control ring the lens zooms, but only to a series of specific focal lengths: 24mm, 28mm, 35mm, 50mm, 70mm, 90mm, 135mm, 160mm, 200mm, 250mm, 300mm, and 360mm. (Additional values are available if any of the extended zoom settings are turned on.) This feature allows you to select one of these specific settings easily. If you want to zoom the lens continuously instead, you can use the zoom lever, which will select any focal length, not just the designated steps. (You can set the zoom lever to use step zoom through the Zoom Lever option on screen 4 of the Custom menu, if you want.)

AF Assist/Self-timer Lamp

This small lamp gives off a bright reddish light when it carries out either of its two functions. First, when the camera is set to use autofocus, this light turns on when lighting is dim, in order to assist the autofocus mechanism in observing the scene and detecting focus points. You can control that behavior using the AF Assist Lamp item on screen 2 of the Custom menu. If you set that option to Off, the lamp will never turn on for autofocus assistance. You might want to make that setting in order to avoid disturbing a child or pet, or to avoid drawing attention to your camera. Even with that option set to turn the lamp off, the lamp will illuminate when the self-timer is used. The lamp will blink several times during the self-timer countdown.

Chapter 6: Playback

In this chapter I'll discuss the playback of images and videos on the C-Lux camera, including the features on the Playback menu.

Normal Playback

First, you should be aware of the settings for Auto Review on screen 4 of the Custom menu, which determine whether and for how long a newly recorded image stays on the screen for review. If your major concern is to check images right after they are taken, the Auto Review settings may be all you need to use. You can leave Auto Review turned off or set it to one, two, three, four, or five seconds, or to Hold. If you choose Hold, the image will stay on the display until you press the shutter button halfway to return to recording mode. You can set up different hold times for regular images, 4K Photo images, and Post Focus images, as discussed in Chapter 7.

To control how images are viewed later on, you need to use the options available in playback mode. For ordinary review of images, press the Playback button, marked by a small triangle, to the upper right of the cursor buttons. Once you press that button, the camera is in playback mode, and you will see the most recent image that was viewed in playback mode. To move back through older images, press the Left button or turn the thumb dial to the left. To see more recent images, use the Right button or turn the thumb dial to the right. To speed through the images, hold down the Left or Right button.

You also can use the touch screen to scroll through images and videos, if the Touch Settings item on screen 3 of the Custom menu has Touch Screen turned on. Drag across the screen with a finger in either direction to scroll backward or forward through the images.

Index View and Enlarging Images

When you are viewing an individual image in playback mode, press the zoom lever once to the left, and you will see a screen showing 12 images, one of which is outlined by a red frame, as shown in Figure 6-1. You also can touch the index screen icon, located above the trash can icon on the individual image.

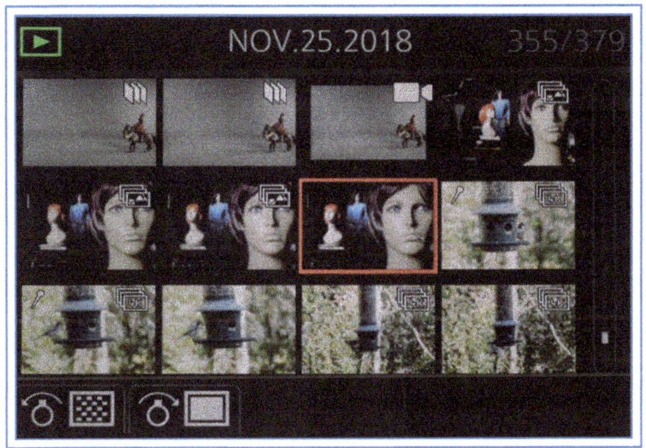

Figure 6-1. Index Screen with 12 Images

Press the zoom lever to the left once more or touch the index screen icon in the lower left of the index screen, to see an index screen with 30 images.

You can press the Menu/Set button to view the outlined image, or you can move through the images and videos on the index screen by pressing the four direction buttons or by turning the thumb dial. You can also drag on the touch screen to scroll the images.

From the 30-image index screen, one more press of the zoom lever to the left or a touch of the CAL icon brings up a calendar display, as seen in Figure 6-2.

On that screen, you can move the highlight to any date with a lighter gray background and press the Menu/Set button or touch the Set icon to bring up an index view with images from that date.

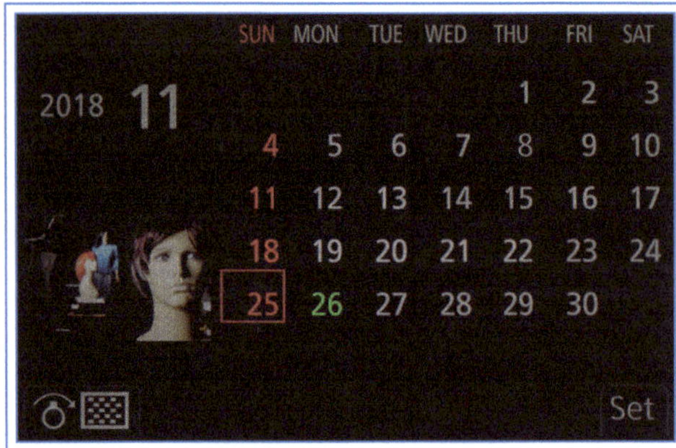

Figure 6-2. Calendar Index Screen

When you are viewing a single image or video, one press of the zoom lever to the right enlarges the image (or first video frame). You will briefly see a display in the upper right corner showing a green frame with an inset red frame that represents the area of the image that is filling the screen in enlarged view, as shown in Figure 6-3. When that inset frame disappears, you will just see the enlarged image with a few icons.

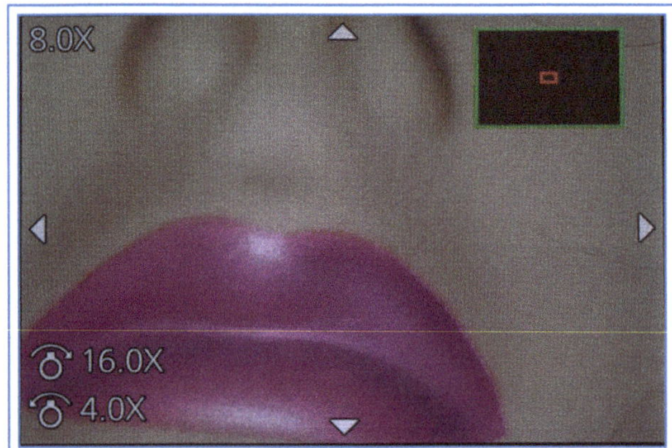

Figure 6-3. Enlarged Image in Playback Mode

If you press the zoom lever to the right repeatedly, the image will be enlarged to greater levels, up to 16 times normal. While it is magnified, you can scroll in it with the four direction buttons or by dragging on the touch screen. The red inset frame will reappear and will move around inside the green frame. To reduce the image size again, press the zoom lever to the left as many times as necessary or press the Menu/Set button to revert immediately to normal size. To move to other images while the display is magnified, turn the thumb dial.

You can enlarge an image to two times normal size by tapping on the touch screen twice. If you tap twice again, an enlarged image returns to normal size.

The Playback Menu

The Playback menu is represented by a triangle icon that turns red when highlighted. It is the last icon at the bottom of the line of menu icons at the left of the main menu screen, as seen in Figure 6-4.

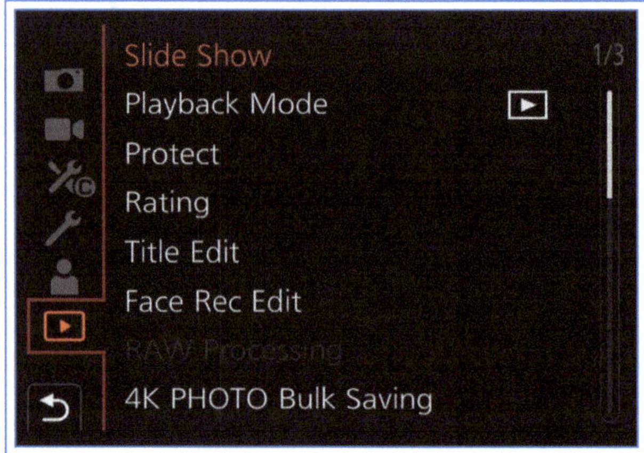

Figure 6-4. Icon for Playback Menu Highlighted at Left

This menu has three screens of options that control how playback operates and that give you access to special features. The first menu screen is shown in Figure 6-5.

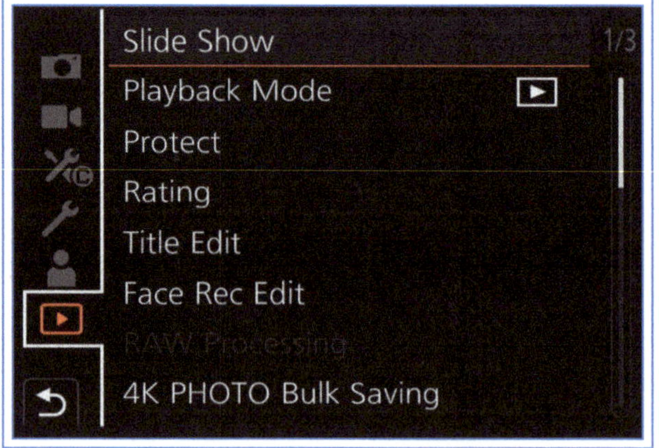

Figure 6-5. Screen 1 of Playback Menu

Slide Show

The first option on the Playback menu is Slide Show. Navigate to this option, then press Menu/Set or the Right button (or press the menu option on the touch screen), and you are presented with the choices All, Picture Only, and Video Only, as shown in Figure 6-6.

[Play] All

If you choose All from the Slide Show menu, you are taken to a menu with the choices Start, Effect, and Setup, shown in Figure 6-7.

Figure 6-6. Slide Show Menu Options Screen

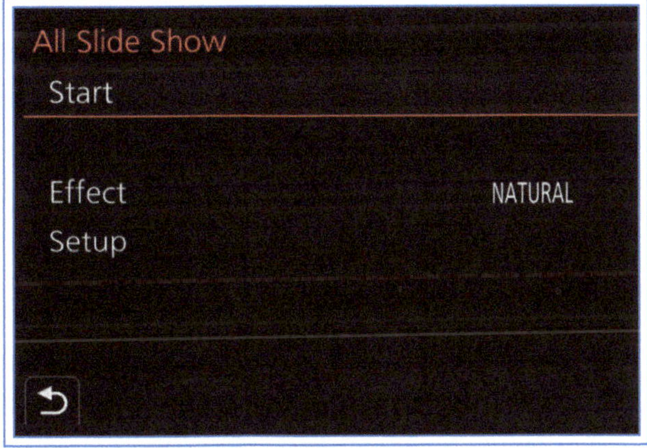

Figure 6-7. Slide Show Settings Screen

You can choose Start to begin the slide show, or you can select Effect or Setup first and make some selections. Setup lets you choose a duration of one, two, three, or five seconds for each still image, but you can only set the duration if Effect is set to Off. If you turn on any effect, the camera will automatically set the duration to two seconds per still image.

You can also choose to set Sound to Off, Audio, Music, or Auto, but only if some effect is selected. If no effect is selected, the Sound option can be set only to Audio or Off. With Off, no sound is played. With the Auto setting, the camera's music is played for still images, and motion pictures have their own audio played. The Music setting plays music as background for all images and movies, and the Audio setting plays only the movies' audio tracks.

Also, you can set Repeat On or Off. Note that you can set a duration even when there are videos included along with still images; the duration value will apply for the still pictures, but not for the videos, which will play at their normal, full length.

For effects, you have the following choice of styles: Natural, Slow, Swing, Urban, or turning effects off altogether.

Once the slide show has begun, you can control it using the direction buttons as a set of playback controls, the same as with playing motion pictures. The Up button controls play/pause; the Left and Right buttons move back or forward one slide; and the Down button is like a stop button; pressing it ends the slide show. The thumb dial adjusts audio volume. A small display showing these controls appears briefly on the screen at the start of the show. After it disappears, you can press the Display button to make it appear again. You also can use touch screen icons to control playback.

[Play] Picture Only/Video Only

These next two options for playing the slide show are self-explanatory; instead of playing all images and videos, you can play either just still images or just videos. If you select Picture Only, the camera will also include photos recorded in 4K burst mode or with the Post Focus feature. For Post Focus, though, the camera will only include one, well-focused image for each group of images.

The only difference between the options for these two choices is that, as you might expect, you cannot select an effect or a duration setting for a slide show of only videos; the slide show will just play all of the videos on the memory card, one after the other. You can use the Setup option to choose whether to play the videos with their audio tracks or with the sound turned off.

Playback Mode

The second option on the Playback menu, Playback Mode, is similar to the Slide Show option, in that it provides several choices for which images and videos are played. This option, though, controls which items are viewed when you are viewing them outside of a slide show. The C-Lux offers three choices for this option: Normal Play, Picture Only, and Video Only.

Normal Play is the mode for ordinary display of your images. This mode is automatically selected whenever the camera is first turned on or switched into playback mode. With this mode, you scroll through the images individually using the Left and Right buttons, by turning the thumb dial left and right, or by scrolling the touch screen with your fingers. Whenever an image is displayed on the screen, you can press the Fn3/Delete button to initiate the deletion process, and choose to delete a single image, multiple ones, or all images. You can press and hold the Left or Right button to speed through the images at a steady pace.

You can enlarge an image by pressing the zoom lever repeatedly to the right, with magnification ranging from two times up to 16 times, as discussed earlier. Reverse the process by moving the lever to the left. If you then keep pressing the lever to the left, you will reach screens that display 12 images, then 30 images, then the Calendar display, from which you can select images from any date on which images were taken. You also can double-tap the screen to enlarge an image to two times normal, or to return it to normal size when enlarged. You also can use touch screen icons to reach the index and calendar screens.

The Picture Only and Video Only options work for playback just as they do for the Slide Show option, as discussed earlier.

Protect

The next option on screen 1 of the Playback menu, Protect, is used to lock selected images or videos against deletion. To use this feature, choose Protect from the Playback menu, and then choose the images and videos to mark as protected, either a single item or multiple items (up to 999). The camera will display your images and videos, either singly or as thumbnails, and you can mark any image as protected by pressing the Menu/Set button or touching the Set/Cancel icon when the image or its thumbnail is displayed. A key icon will appear on each marked image.

Once the key icon appears, press the Fn3 button or the curved-arrow icon to exit from this screen. (Don't press Menu/Set on this screen; if you do, the protection will be removed.)

When you later display an image or video that was marked as protected, a key icon will appear in its upper left corner if you are viewing the playback screen that displays full information and the full-sized image. The Protect function works for all types of images, including Raw files and motion pictures. Note, however, that all images, including protected ones, will be deleted if the memory card is re-formatted.

Rating

This menu option lets you apply a rating system based on stars to images and videos on the memory card in the camera. You can rate any item with one to five stars, or leave it unrated. Once the ratings have been made, there are three ways you can use the system. First, if you press the Fn3/Delete button in playback mode, and then select the option to Delete All, you will see a screen like that in Figure 6-8, giving you the choices of Delete All or Delete All Non-rating. If you select the second option, the camera will delete all items that were not rated with at least one star.

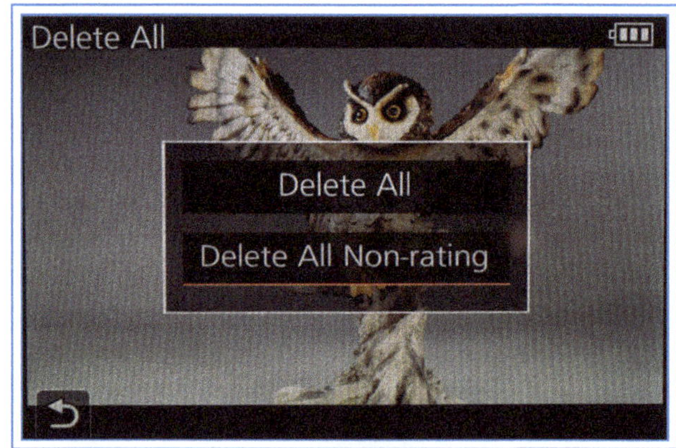

Figure 6-8. Option to Delete All Non-rating Images

Second, once the ratings have been entered, they will be visible and useful for sorting images in compatible software. For example, in Adobe Bridge, the stars show up below the image thumbnails, as shown in Figure 6-9.

Third, you can print all images with ratings when you are printing directly from the camera to a PictBridge-compatible printer.

You also can rate images and videos by assigning a star rating from one to five to a function button for playback mode, as discussed in Chapter 5.

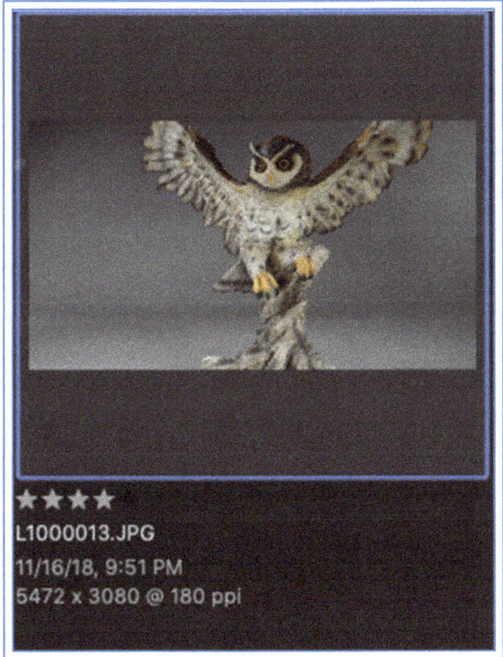

Figure 6-9. Rating Stars in Adobe Bridge Software

Title Edit

This next option on the Playback menu lets you enter a string of text, numerals, punctuation, and symbols for a given JPEG image or group of images through a system of selecting characters from several rows.

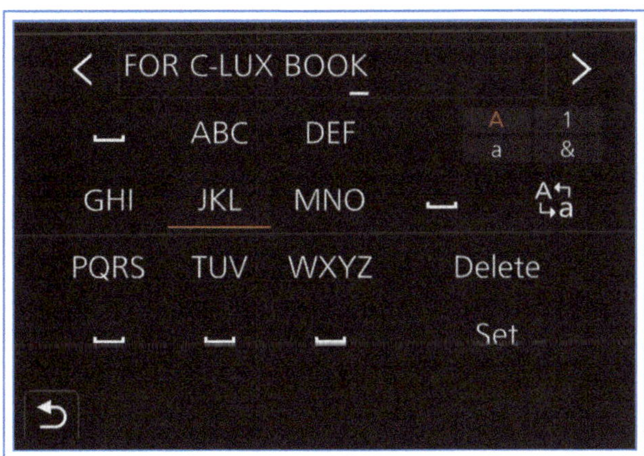

Figure 6-10. Title Edit Text-entry Screen

After you select this option from the Playback menu, choose one or more images to have text added and press Menu/Set or touch the Set icon to go to the screen with tools for entering text, shown in Figure 6-10. Navigate using the direction buttons to the block that contains the character to be entered. Then cycle through the choices in each block, such as ABC, using the Menu/Set button, and advance to the next space using the thumb dial. You can toggle between displays of capital letters, lower case letters, and numerals and symbols using the Display button. You also can touch the letters and icons using the touch screen to select them.

The maximum length for your caption or other information is 30 characters. You can use the Multi option to enter the same text for up to 100 images. You cannot enter titles for motion pictures, images from 4K Photo bursts, Post Focus images, protected images, or Raw images.

Once you have entered the title or caption for a particular image, it does not show up unless you use the Text Stamp function, discussed later in this chapter. The title is then attached to the image, and it will print out as part of the image. There is no way to delete the title other than going back into the Title Edit function and using the Delete key from the table of characters, then deleting each character until the title disappears.

Face Recognition Edit

This Playback menu option is of use only if you have previously registered one or more persons' faces in the camera for face recognition. If you have, use this option to select the picture in question, then follow the prompts to replace or delete the information for the person or persons you select. Once deleted, this information cannot be recovered.

Raw Processing

The Raw Processing option gives you tools for processing your Raw files in the camera. As I discussed in Chapter 4, the Raw format gives you great flexibility for adjusting settings such as exposure, white balance, sharpening, and contrast in post-processing software. But with the C-Lux you don't have to transfer your images to a computer to convert Raw files to JPEGs. You can adjust several settings in the camera and save the altered image as a JPEG, or just convert the Raw file to a JPEG with no alterations if all you need is a file that is easier to send by e-mail or view on another device.

If you're not certain whether a given image was shot with Raw image quality, press the Display button until one of the detailed information screens appears; the Raw label will appear next to the aspect ratio for all Raw shots, as shown in Figure 6-11.

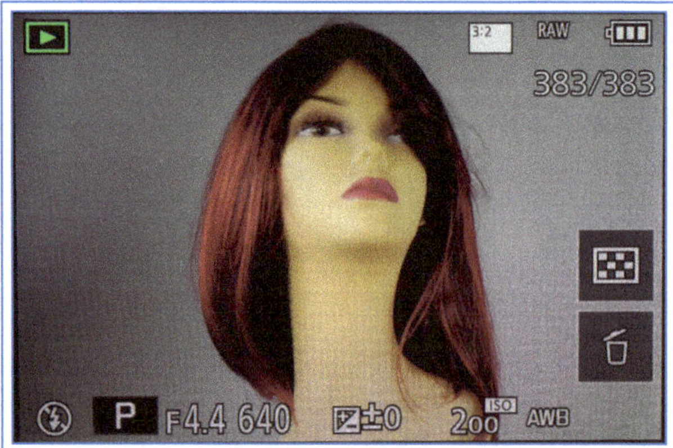

Figure 6-11. Raw Label on Image in Playback Mode

Once you have a single Raw image displayed on the screen in playback mode, highlight Raw Processing on the Playback menu, and press the Menu/Set button to select it. Then press the Menu/Set button again (or press the Set icon on the touch screen). The camera will display the Raw Processing screen, as shown in Figure 6-12, overlaid on the image you selected for processing.

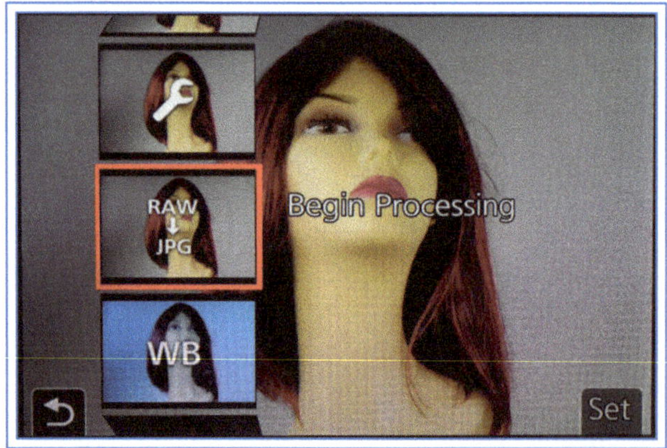

Figure 6-12. Screen to Select Image for Raw Processing

At the left of the display will be a series of thumbnail images, each with a label displayed to the right. Scroll through those thumbnail images using the thumb dial, the Up and Down buttons, or the touch screen, and press Menu/Set or the Set icon when the block for that thumbnail is highlighted with a red frame. Each of those thumbnail images represents an action you can take or a setting you can adjust.

For any setting other than Noise Reduction, Intelligent Resolution, and Sharpness, you can press the Display button to switch between the main setting screen, as shown in Figure 6-13, and a comparison screen, as shown in Figure 6-14, on which the camera displays several thumbnail images on the same screen so you can compare the effects of different settings as you scroll through them.

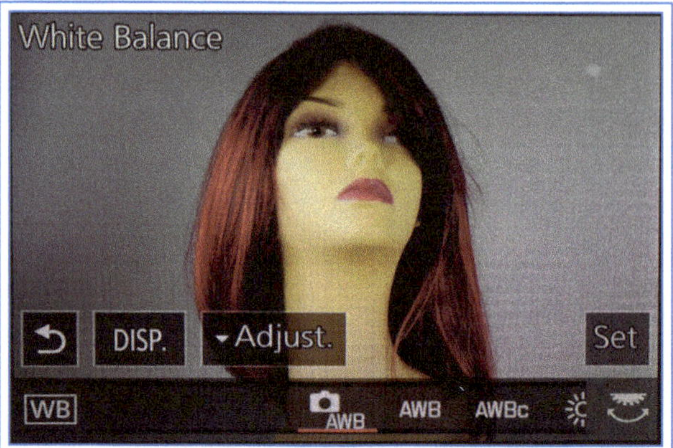

Figure 6-13. Raw Processing Main Screen for White Balance Setting

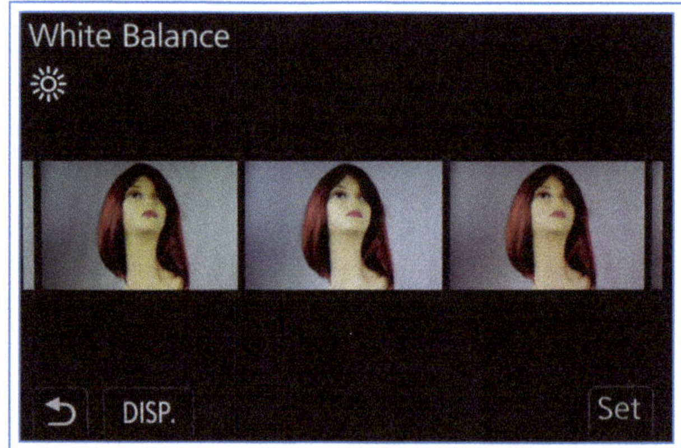

Figure 6-14. Raw Processing Comparison Screen for White Balance Setting

Also, for any setting, you can press the zoom lever to enlarge the image on the main setting screen so you can see the effects of the adjustment with a magnified view.

Following are descriptions of the individual items you can adjust.

Begin Processing. If you select this block, the camera will process all of the adjustments you have set using the other blocks. Before it proceeds to make those changes, it will show you a preview of how the processed image will look before you confirm the operation, as shown in Figure 6-15.

If you choose Yes, the camera will save a new JPEG image using all of the settings you have made. The new image will appear right after the existing Raw image on the camera's display, but it will have an image number at the end of the current sequence on the memory card.

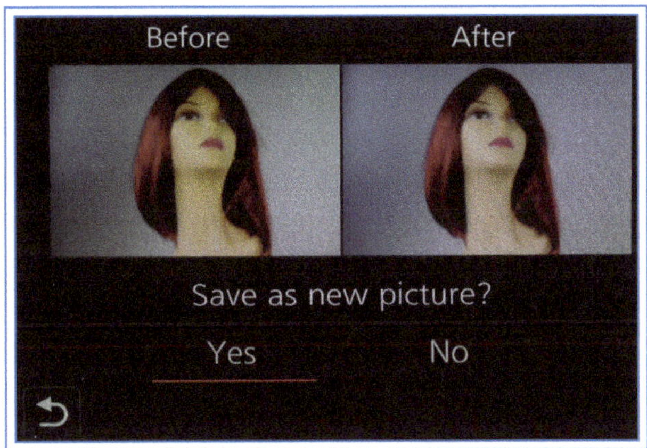

Figure 6-15. Begin Processing Preview Screen

White Balance. With this item, the camera will display the Raw image with the complete line of white balance adjustment icons at the bottom of the screen. (If you don't see that screen, press the Display button to make it appear.) As you scroll through those icons, the display will change to show how the image would look with the selected setting. If you select the color temperature option, you can press the Up button to select the numerical color temperature. For any setting, you can press the Down button to get to the screen with color axes for fine-tuning the white balance appearance.

Exposure Compensation. If you select this adjustment, you will be able to increase or decrease the exposure of the image, but only by up to plus or minus two EV levels, in 1/3 EV increments.

Photo Style. With this item, you can change the Photo Style setting to any option you want. If you choose Monochrome or Monochrome HC, you will also be able to set the Color Tone adjustment and the Filter Effect adjustment that simulates the use of a glass filter for black-and-white film. (Those two additional adjustments will appear later in the list of Raw Processing options.) If you select any other Photo Style setting, the Color Tone and Filter Effect adjustments will not be available. (The Saturation item will be available in place of the Color Tone adjustment.)

Intelligent Dynamic. The Intelligent Dynamic (or i.Dynamic) screen lets you set this adjustment at a level of Off, Low, Standard, or High, regardless of how it was set when the image was captured.

Contrast. This adjustment is somewhat unusual because, ordinarily, it is made as part of the Photo Style adjustment. With the Raw Processing option, it is separated out. With this item, you can adjust the contrast of your Raw image by as many as five units positive or negative.

Highlight. On the Recording menu, the Highlight item is included as one aspect of the Highlight Shadow item. With the Raw Processing option, Highlight and Shadow are provided as two separate adjustments. If you select this item, you can alter the brightness of the highlights in the image by up to five units in either direction.

Shadow. This item is similar to the previous one, but deals with shadow rather than highlight adjustments.

Saturation. As noted earlier, this item is available for adjustment if you have selected a Photo Style other than Monochrome or Monochrome HC. If you selected Monochrome or Monochrome HC, the Raw Processing menu option includes Color Tone as an adjustment in place of Saturation.

Color Tone. As noted above, if you choose Monochrome or Monochrome HC for Photo Style, the camera presents this item for adjustment in place of Saturation.

Filter Effect. As discussed earlier, if you choose Monochrome or Monochrome HC for Photo Style, the Filter Effect item is available to adjust; otherwise, it does not appear.

Noise Reduction. With this item, you can adjust Noise Reduction up to five units positive or negative.

Intelligent Resolution. With the Intelligent Resolution, or i.Resolution item, you can set this feature to Off, `Low, Standard, or High.

Sharpness. The last item in the line of boxes for adjustment is Sharpness, which, like Contrast and Resolution, is separated out from the Photo Style adjustment. You can change the level of this item up to five units in either direction.

More Settings. If you select this item, the camera will display a sub-menu with three items: Reinstate Adjustments, Color Space, and Picture Size. If you select Reinstate Adjustments, the camera will show you the image as it now stands with any adjustments you have made with the other settings. You can then proceed to cancel all of those adjustments if you want. The Color Space option lets you keep the color space setting the image was shot with, or change it to the other option, either Adobe RGB or sRGB. The Picture Size option lets you set the Picture Size to L, M, or S.

4K Photo Bulk Saving

This last option on screen 1 of the Playback menu gives you a way to save a portion of a 4K Photo burst as a group of individual pictures. As discussed in Chapter 5, the ordinary way to extract a single image from a 4K Photo burst is to scroll through the 4K Photo burst and select a single image to extract and save.

With 4K Photo Bulk Saving, instead of extracting a single image, you can extract a segment of images lasting up to five seconds, and save that group of 100 or more images as a burst, just as if it had been taken using the Focus Bracket, Time Lapse Shot, or Stop Motion Animation option. That is, the burst of images will be displayed as a single image in playback mode, until you press the Up button to view the individual images in the burst one by one. Here are the steps to use this feature:

1. Select the 4K Photo Bulk Saving menu option.
2. The camera will display all 4K Photo bursts that are available. Scroll through them to find the one you want to use, and press Menu/Set (or touch the Set icon) when it is displayed. If the sequence of shots is longer than five seconds in duration, the camera will display a message on a black screen saying it can produce a crop of five seconds' length, and telling you to select the start position. If the sequence is shorter than five seconds, the camera will display a message asking if you want to proceed with 4K Photo Bulk Saving; there is no need to select a start position in that case.
3. Use the on-screen controls to move through the burst of images and stop when the red cursor at the top of the screen is at the place where you want to start the five-second group of images. Press the Menu/Set button to select that position, and confirm it when the camera prompts you.
4. The camera will extract the five-second segment you identified, and save the individual frames from that 4K footage as images within a burst group. This process will take a fairly long time, probably several minutes.
5. When the process is complete, you will have a set of up to 150 images (125 for cameras using the PAL video system) with an icon in the upper left corner indicating that you can press the Up button for burst play and an icon in the lower left corner indicating that you can press the Down button to play the images individually.
6. If you press the Up button, the images will play back in a continuous stream, though you can pause and resume with the Up button. If you press the Down button, you will see a screen on which you can use normal playback controls to scroll through the images one by one, or press the Up button to play the sequence continuously, either from the current image or from the first one in the sequence.

The options on screen 2 of the Playback menu are shown in Figure 6-16.

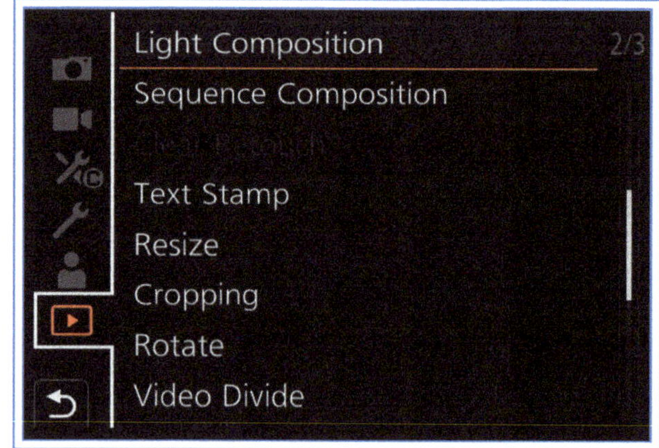

Figure 6-16. Screen 2 of Playback Menu

Light Composition

This next menu option gives you a way to select and combine multiple frames from a sequence that was shot using 4K Photo mode. This feature lets you build a composition with dramatic areas of light in different locations, such as from a series of fireworks bursts. Figures 6-17 through 6-19 illustrate this effect. Figures 6-17 and 6-18 are two images of a changing traffic light from a 4K Photo burst; Figure 6-19 is a composite that resulted from combining those two images along with one other, using the Light Composition option.

To use this option, select it from the menu, and the camera will display any 4K Photo bursts on the memory card in the camera. Scroll through those choices and press the Menu/Set button or the Set icon on the screen to select an image. On the next screen, select

Composite Merging or Range Merging. With Composite Merging, you can select any images from the 4K Photo burst. With Range Merging, you select the beginning and ending images of a range, and the camera includes all images within that range.

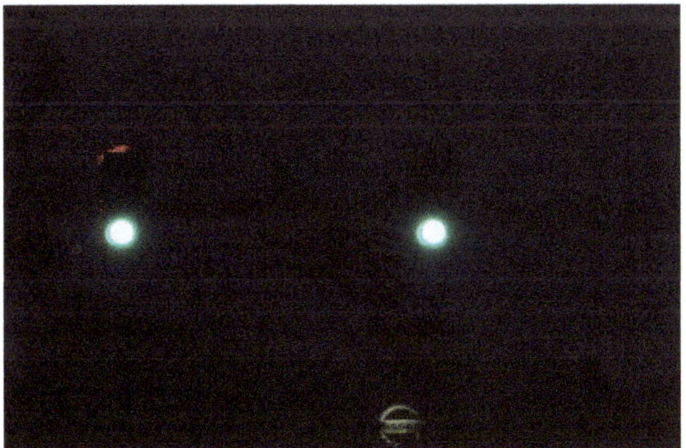

Figure 6-17. First Image for Light Composition

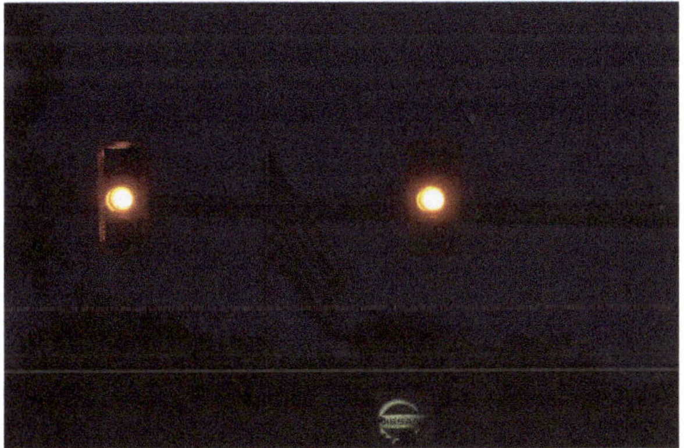

Figure 6-18. Second Image for Light Composition

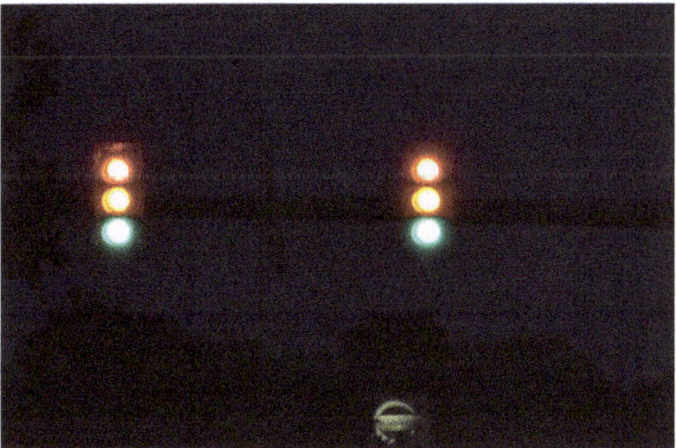

Figure 6-19. Final Light Composition

Then use the on-screen icons to select the images you want to include in the final composite. When you have finished, select Save, and the camera will display a message asking you to confirm, and telling how long it will take to produce the composite. If you confirm, the camera will create the composite image.

To achieve good results, you should have the camera on a tripod when capturing the 4K Photo sequence, so the backgrounds of the combined images will blend together seamlessly. Also, note that the camera will create the image using only the brightest parts of the component images, so, if the parts you want to combine are not the brightest parts, they will not be included in the composite image. Of course, if you are shooting a fireworks display, the fireworks bursts almost certainly will be the brightest parts of the image, but in other contexts this feature may not work as expected.

Sequence Composition

This option is similar to Light Composition in that it lets you create a composition using multiple frames from a 4K Photo burst, but this feature does not involve the use of bright lights. Instead, it involves the selection of multiple images of a moving person or object, to create a multiple-exposure effect that conveys a sense of motion by a single subject, such as a running or jumping person or a basketball in flight toward the basket.

To use this option, you first have to have captured a 4K Photo burst. For this feature to work well, the burst should be shot against a background that does not move, because the end result will combine three or more images against the background, and if the background has moved, the subject will not be seen clearly. So, if possible, shoot the 4K Photo burst using a tripod, with a relatively plain background.

Once the burst has been captured, select this menu option, and the camera will display all available 4K bursts on the memory card. Select the one you want to use, and press the Menu/Set button or the Set icon in the lower right corner of the screen. The camera will then display a screen like that in Figure 6-20, with controls for navigating through the file. Using those on-screen controls, navigate to the first frame you want to include in the final composition and press the Menu/Set button or the OK icon in the lower right corner.

The camera will display that frame and the choices of Next or Reselect. Choose Next, then navigate to the next frame to include and press Menu/Set or the Set icon again. (Or, if you want to discard the last frame chosen, choose Reselect.) The screen after selecting two frames will look like that in Figure 6-21.

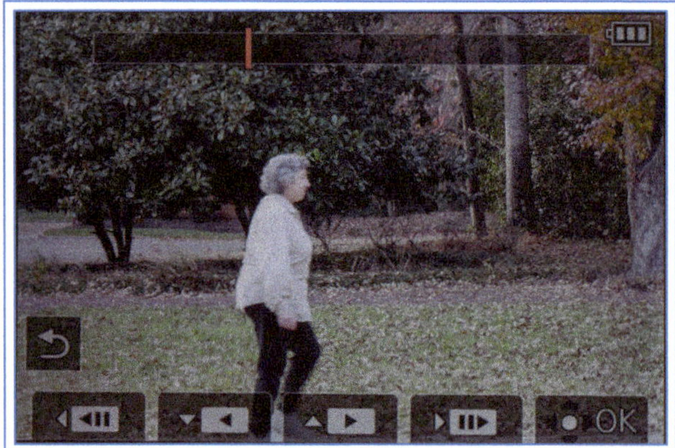

Figure 6-20. Sequence Composition Screen for Navigating File

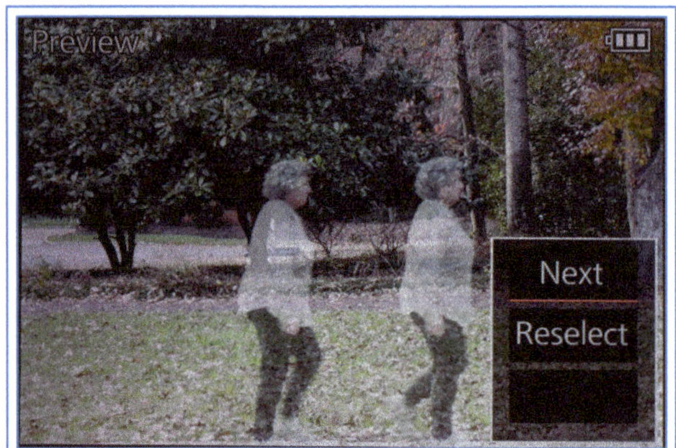

Figure 6-21. Sequence Composition Screen After Selecting Two Frames

When you have selected at least three frames, up to a maximum of 40, the choices on the screen will be Next, Reselect, or Save. At that point, you can continue selecting more frames or select Save to create the final product. An example is shown in Figure 6-22.

When you are selecting frames to include in the composition, try to select ones in which the subject does not overlap the subject from a previous frame. If they overlap, the subject will appear to "eat" away part of the adjacent frame, spoiling the overall effect.

Clear Retouch

This feature lets you erase parts of a recorded image by touching them with your finger on the camera's screen. It works only with normal JPEG images, not with Raw images, panoramas, movies, 4K burst shots, or shots taken with the Post focus option.

To use this option, select it from the Playback menu and scroll through your images until you find one to retouch. When that image is displayed, press the Menu/Set button or touch the Set icon on the screen. The camera will display a screen with Remove and Scaling icons at the right. Touch Remove and then drag or tap your finger on areas you want to erase from the image. The camera will color those areas, as shown in Figure 6-23.

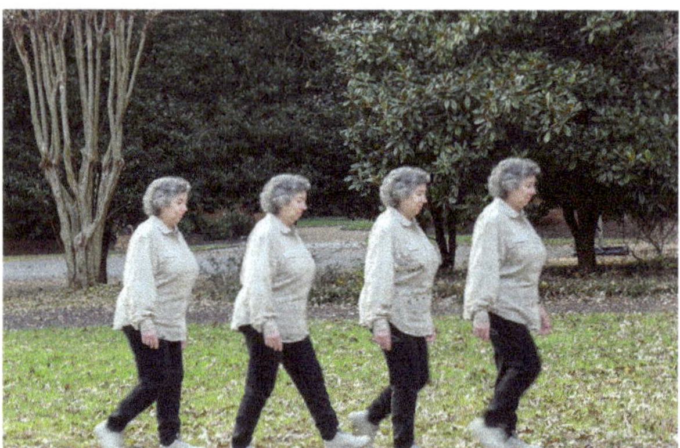

Figure 6-22. Sequence Composition Final Product

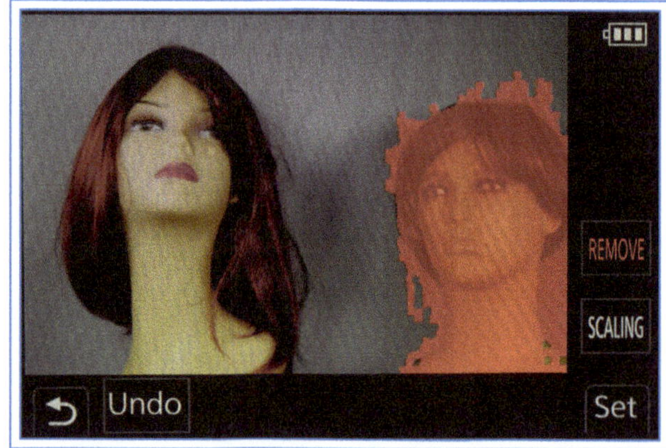

Figure 6-23. Clear Retouch Screen with Area Marked for Removal

Touch Scaling if you want to enlarge the screen before designating areas to remove. After you touch Scaling, you can pinch the screen apart with your fingers to enlarge it. Then press Remove to activate the removal process.

When you have finished touching areas to be removed, press the Set icon or press the Menu/Set button to finish the process. The camera will display a preview screen; touch the Save icon or press the Menu/Set button to save that version of the image. The camera will display a final confirmation screen for you to save the image as a new picture. Figures 6-24 and 6-25 represent the before and after versions of an image that I edited with this option to remove one of the figurines from the scene.

This feature could be useful if you are preparing some images for a quick presentation and need to remove an object from one or two shots, but it is no substitute for editing with a program such as Photoshop using a computer. It can work fairly well with a plain background like the one in the images here, but it can be difficult to get good results with a more complex background.

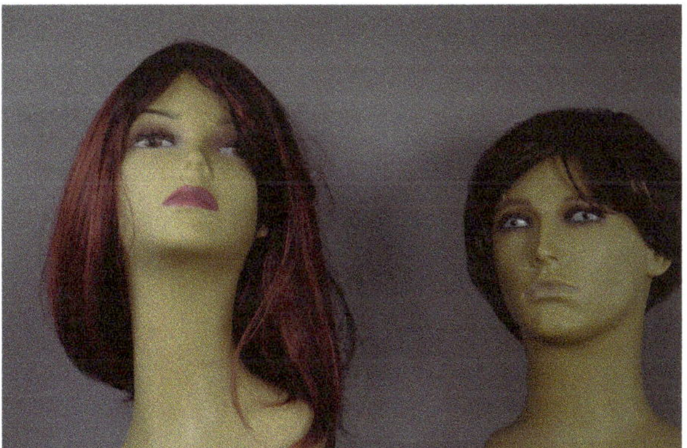

Figure 6-24. Clear Retouch Image Before Retouching

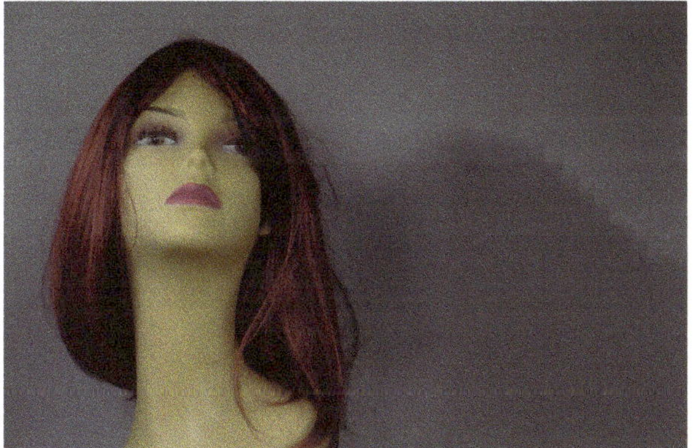

Figure 6-25. Clear Retouch Image After Retouching

Text Stamp

The Text Stamp function takes information associated with a given image and attaches it to the image in a visible form. For example, if you have entered a title or caption using the Title Edit function discussed above, it does not become visible until you use this Text Stamp function to "stamp" it onto the image.

Once you have done this, the text or other characters in the title will print out if you send the picture to a printer. Besides the information entered with the Title Edit function, the Text Stamp function lets you stamp the following other information: year, month, and day the shot was made, with or without the time of day; travel date (if set); location (if set). Also, you can apply this function to information from pictures taken with names for Baby 1 or 2 and Pet, if you have entered a name for your baby or pet, and to pictures that have names registered with the Face Recognition function.

To use this function, highlight Text Stamp on the menu screen and press Menu/Set. On the next screen, choose Single or Multi, and then select the image or images you want to add text to. When you have selected one or more images, press Menu/Set, highlight Set on the next screen, and press Menu/Set. You will then see a screen where you can select the items to be imprinted on the image or images.

When you have made the selections, press the Q.Menu button to return to the previous screen, select OK, and press Menu/Set. The camera will ask if you want to save the stamped image as a new picture; select Yes and press Menu/Set to carry out the operation. The text will be set in small, orange characters in the lower right corner of the image, as shown in Figure 6-26.

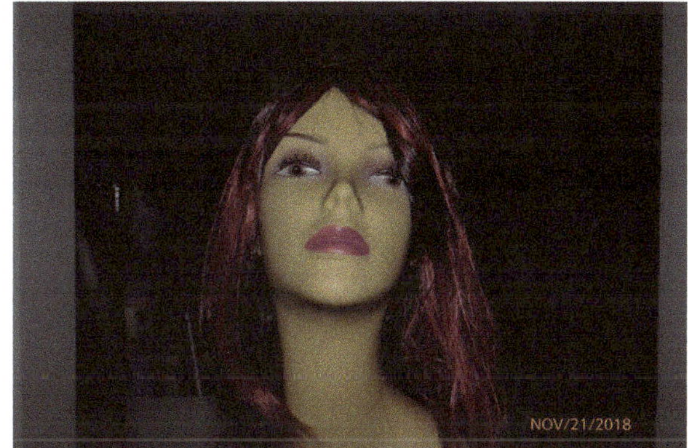

Figure 6-26. Text Stamp in Use on Image

This function cannot be used with Raw images, movies, 4K bursts, Post Focus images, or panoramas. The camera saves the text-stamped image to a new file, so you will still have the original. I have never found this function useful, but if you have an application that could benefit from it, it is available and ready to assist you.

Resize

This function from the Playback menu is useful if you don't have access to software that can resize an image, and you need to generate a smaller file that you can attach to an email message or upload to a website. After selecting this menu item, on the next screen you choose whether to resize a single image or multiple ones. Then navigate to the image you want to resize, if it's not already displayed on the screen.

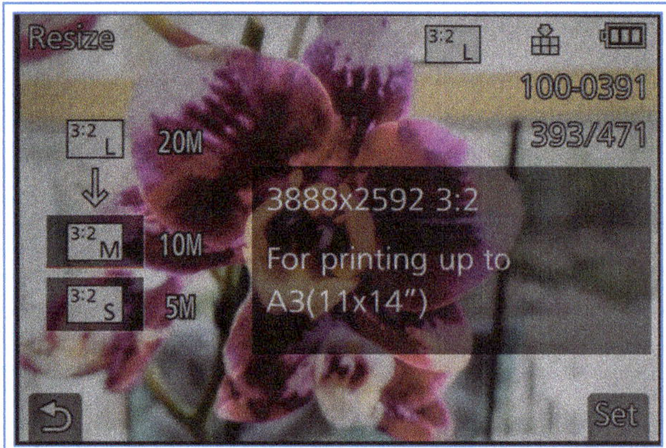

Figure 6-27. Resize Options on Screen

Once an image to be resized is on the screen, press the Menu/Set button or touch the Set icon to start the resizing process. Following the prompts on the screen as shown in Figure 6-27, highlight the size to reduce the image to. The choices may include M and S for Medium and Small, or just S for Small, depending on the size of the original image. When the option you want to use is highlighted, press Menu/Set to carry out the resizing process. The camera will ask you to confirm that you want to save a new picture at the new size.

As with the Text Stamp function, resizing does not overwrite the existing image; it saves a copy of it at a smaller size, so the original will still be available. The new image will be found at the end of the current set of recorded pictures. Raw images, 4K Photo or Post Focus images, panoramas, protected images, and motion pictures cannot be resized, nor can pictures stamped with Text Stamp. If you want to convert up to 100 images at the same time, select the Multi option and follow the same procedure.

Cropping

This function is similar to Resize, except that, instead of just resizing the image, the camera crops it to show just part of the original scene. To do this, select Cropping from the Playback menu and navigate to the image to be cropped, if it isn't already displayed, and press the Menu/Set button or touch the Set icon. Then use the zoom lever or touch the zoom icon to enlarge the image, and use the direction buttons or scroll with the touch screen to position the part of the image to be retained.

When the enlarged portion is displayed as you want, as shown in Figure 6-28, press Menu/Set or the Set icon to lock in the cropping, and select Yes when the camera asks if you want to save the new picture. Again, as with Resize, the new image will be saved at the end of the current set of recorded images, and it will have a smaller size than the original image, because it will be cropped to include less information (fewer pixels) than the original image. The Cropping function cannot be used with Raw images, motion pictures, 4K Photo or Post Focus images, panoramas, or pictures stamped with Text Stamp.

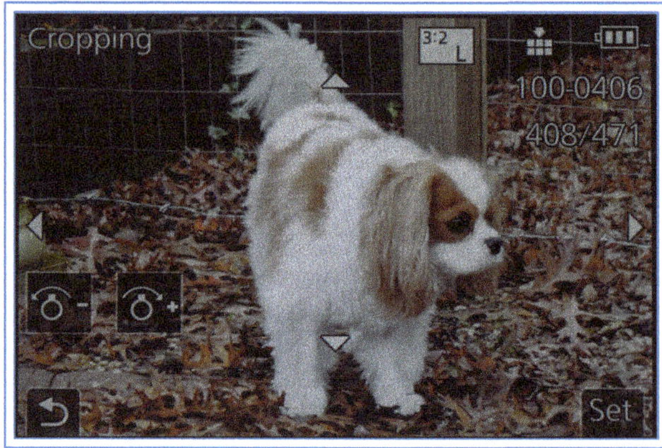

Figure 6-28. Image Ready to Crop in Camera

Rotate

When you take a picture in a vertical (portrait) orientation by holding the camera sideways, you can set the camera to display it so it appears upright on the horizontal screen, as in Figure 6-29.

The setting to make such images appear in this orientation is the Rotate Display option, which is discussed later in this chapter. If you have that option turned on, then the Rotate option becomes available, so you can manually rotate the image back to the way it was taken. If the Rotate Display option is not turned on, then the Rotate option is dimmed and unavailable for selection.

To use the Rotate menu option, select it and scroll to the image you want to rotate. Then press Menu/Set and the camera will display two arrows, as seen in Figure 6-30. Select the top arrow to rotate the image 90 degrees clockwise or the bottom one to rotate it 90 degrees counter-clockwise and press Menu/Set to do the rotation.

Video Divide

The Video Divide option gives you a basic ability to trim videos in the camera. Using this procedure, you can, within limits, pause a video at any point and then cut it at that point, resulting in two segments of video rather than one. You can then, if you want, delete an unwanted segment.

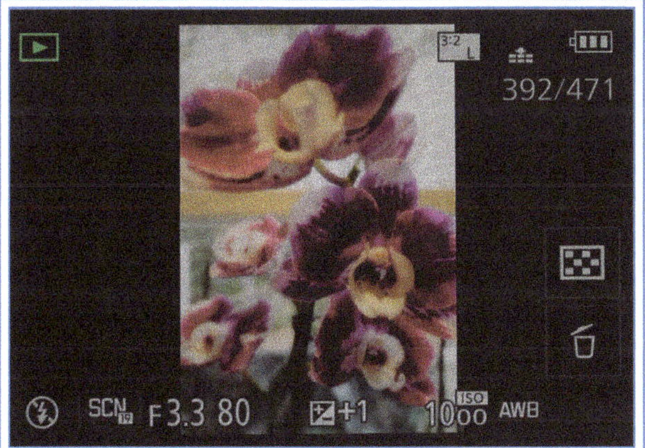

Figure 6-29. Image Captured Vertically and Displayed on Horizontal Screen

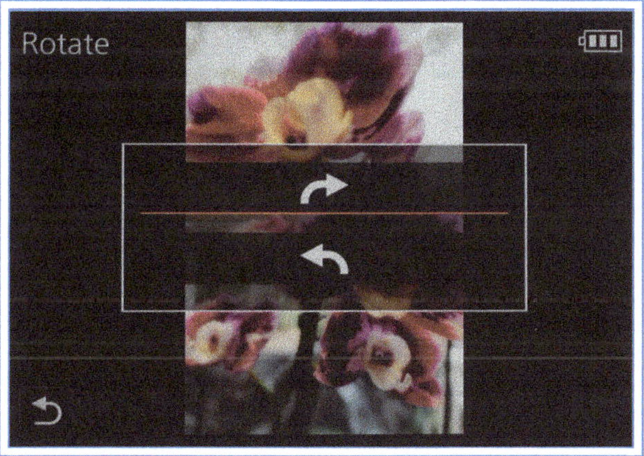

Figure 6-30. Rotate Option Ready to Apply to Image

To do this, highlight Video Divide on the Playback menu and press the Right button or Menu/Set to go to the playback screen. If the video you want to divide is not already displayed, scroll through your images using the Left and Right buttons or the thumb dial until you locate it.

You can recognize videos because they display the length of the video in the upper right quarter of the screen and a movie camera icon with an up arrow in the upper left, as shown in Figure 6-31.

The camera displays all your images here, including stills, so you may have to scroll through many non-videos until you reach the video you want. If you want to narrow the choices down to videos only, choose Video Only for Playback Mode on screen 1 of the Playback menu before selecting the Video Divide menu option.

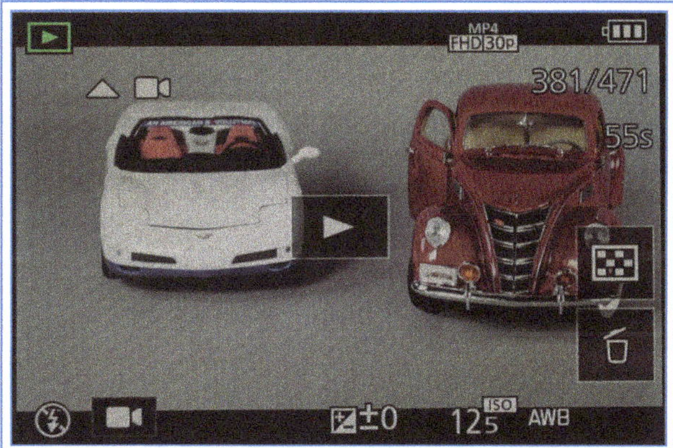

Figure 6-31. Video File Ready to Play in Camera

With the desired movie on the screen, press Menu/Set to start it playing. When it reaches the point where you want to divide it, press the Up button to pause the video. While it is paused, move through it a few frames at a time using the Left and Right buttons, until you find the exact point where you want to divide it.

Once you reach that point, press the Down button to make the cut. You will see an icon of a pair of scissors in the display of controls at the bottom of the screen. After you press the Down button, the camera will display the message shown in Figure 6-32, asking you to confirm the cut.

Highlight Yes and press Menu/Set to confirm. Now you will have two new videos, divided at the point you chose.

As I noted above, this is a basic form of editing. It can't be used to trim a movie too close to its beginning or end, or to trim a very short movie at all. But it's better than nothing, and it gives you some ability to delete unwanted footage without having to edit the video on your computer. Note, though, that this operation does not save a copy of the original video, so use it only if you are sure you want to divide the video file.

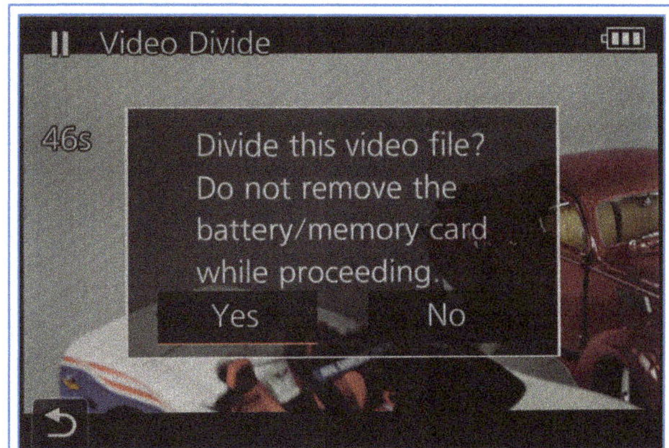

Figure 6-32. Screen to Confirm Video Divide Operation

The options on screen 3 of the Playback menu are shown in Figure 6-33.

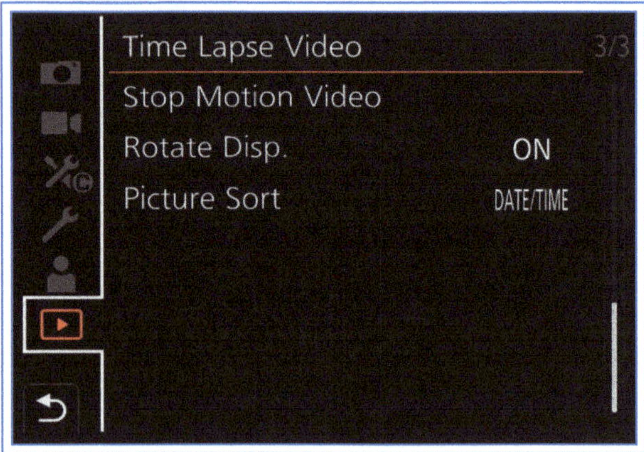

Figure 6-33. Screen 3 of Playback Menu

Time Lapse Video

This option lets you create a movie from a series of shots you took using the Time Lapse Shot feature on screen 4 of the Recording menu. As I discussed in Chapter 4, when you use that feature, the camera will ask at the end of the process if you want to create a movie from the group of time-lapse shots. If you say no, you can use this option on the Playback menu at a later time to create the movie.

When you select this option, the camera will display any groups of images that were taken with the Time Lapse Shot option. Scroll through those and select the one you want to make into a movie. Then press the Menu/Set button, and the camera will display the screen shown in Figure 6-34, where you can set the recording quality, frame rate, and whether to play the sequence normally or in reverse. Make your choices and press Menu/Set; the camera will then create the video.

Stop Motion Video

This option, similar to the previous one, is for creating a video from images you took using the Stop Motion Animation feature discussed in Chapter 4. As with the Time Lapse Video option, select this option, scroll to the group of shots you want to use to create the video, and select your desired options from the screen that appears, which has the same options as in Figure 6-34.

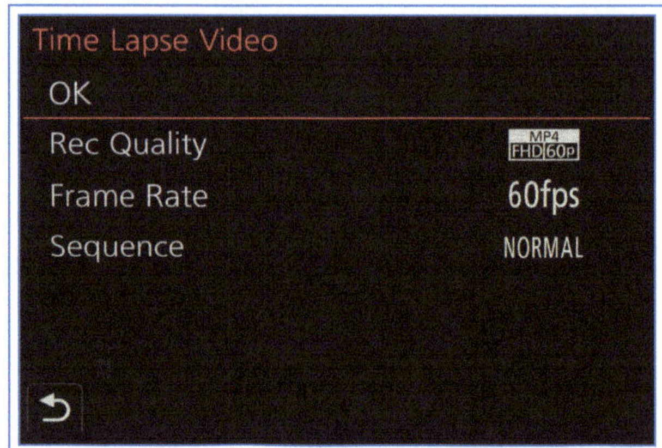

Figure 6-34. Time Lapse Video Menu Options Screen

Rotate Display

As I noted above in connection with the Rotate option, when the Rotate Display option is turned on, images taken with the camera turned sideways are automatically rotated so they appear upright on the horizontal display. If you want to rotate such an image so you can see it at a larger size, taking up the full display, use the Rotate menu option, discussed above.

Picture Sort

With this option, you can choose the order in which the camera displays images from the memory card. If you choose the default, File Name, the camera arranges them by folders, then by numbers within the folders. For example, the file names of your images might include entries such as L1000003, L1000010, L1020023, etc. If you have taken all of your images with the same camera, all of these images should appear in chronological order according to when they were taken. However, if you have taken images with several different cameras you may have multiple images with the same file names, or with file names that do not match the order in which the images were taken. In that case, you can choose the other option for this menu item, Date/Time, and the images will be displayed in order by the dates and times they were taken.

Chapter 7: Custom Menu, Setup Menu, and My Menu

In Chapters 4 and 6 I discussed the many options available to you in the Recording and Playback menu systems. The next menu systems to discuss are the Custom and Setup menus, which include options for controlling things such as focus, zoom, and the appearance of the display, as well as date, time, formatting, and audio options. I also will discuss the My Menu system, which lets you create a separate menu with your most-used options. As a reminder, you enter the menu system by pressing the Menu/Set button on the camera's back.

The Custom Menu

After pressing Menu/Set, press the Left button to move the highlight into the left column of menu choices, then use the Up and Down buttons to move to the tools icon with the letter C, as shown in Figure 7-1. (You also can use the camera's touch screen features to navigate through the menu system.)

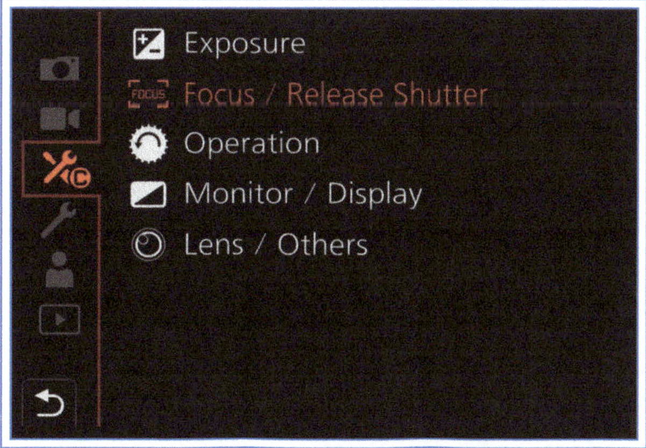

Figure 7-1. Icon for Custom Menu Highlighted at Left

Once that icon is highlighted, press the Right button to move to the next screen to the right, which reveals an intermediate set of categories: Exposure, Focus/Release Shutter, Operation, Monitor/Display, and Lens/Others. These five categories are subdivisions of the Custom menu. Leica presumably included these subdivisions to help you locate various Custom menu options quickly according to their functions, because there are so many menu options to keep track of. The other menu systems do not have this intermediate set of categories.

In any event, to get to the actual Custom menu screens, press the Right button one more time to navigate to the list of menu options, which occupy six menu screens, discussed below. (If the camera is set to the basic Snapshot mode, the Custom menu displays only one screen with three items.) If necessary, navigate to the top of the menu's first screen.

If you have to move forward or backward through several menu screens, you can press the zoom lever or turn the thumb dial to move through them a screen at a time in either direction.

I will discuss all of the Custom menu items below, starting with the first screen, shown in Figure 7-2.

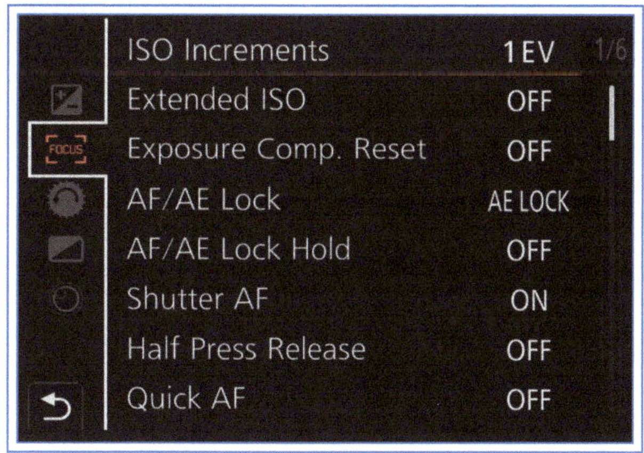

Figure 7-2. Screen 1 of Custom Menu

ISO Increments

Using this option, whose setting screen is shown in Figure 7-3, you can expand the range of values available for the setting of ISO.

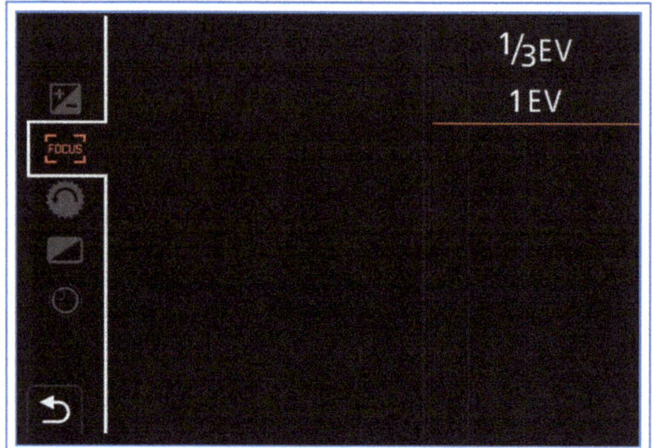

Figure 7-3. ISO Increments Menu Options Screen

Normally, when you set ISO to a numerical value, you can use only 125, 200, 400, 800, 1600, 3200, 6400, or 12500. However, if you select the increment of 1/3 EV instead of the normal 1 EV for this menu option, then several interpolated values for ISO are added, such as 250, 320, 500, 640, 1000, 8000, and others. You can then set these values from the Sensitivity item on screen 1 of the Recording menu.

Note that this menu option applies only to the settings you make yourself. Even if the ISO Increments option is set to 1 EV, the camera can still set intermediate ISO values when Auto ISO or Intelligent ISO is in effect and the camera is choosing the ISO value. I have never found a need to use the 1/3 EV option, so I leave this setting at its default value of 1 EV.

Extended ISO

The next option on the Custom menu, Extended ISO, can be turned either on or off. When it is turned on, you get access to the lowest ISO levels of 80 and 100, and to the highest value of 25000, which are not available otherwise. If you have set the ISO Increments option, discussed above, to 1/3 EV, then you will also get access to the ISO settings of 16000 and 20000.

The additional ISO values of 80, 100, and those above 12800 are considered "extended" because they are not values that are native to the sensor. Therefore, using one of them does not increase the dynamic range or improve the image quality; it just acts to change the light sensitivity of the sensor. Using a low value such as 80 ISO can be useful when you need to reduce the light sensitivity so you can use a slower shutter speed or wider aperture than you could otherwise. Using one of the very high values can be helpful when light is very low, as long as you don't mind the increased noise from using such a high value.

Exposure Compensation Reset

This option controls whether or not an exposure compensation value that has been set will be retained in memory when the camera is turned off or the recording mode is changed. By default, this option is turned off, and any positive or negative brightness value is not reset to zero. In other words, the value is retained in memory for the next time the camera is turned on, or the current recording mode is selected again.

If you set this option to On, then the exposure compensation value is reset to zero when the camera is powered off or the recording mode changes. I generally leave this option set to On, because I am unlikely to want to use the same amount of exposure compensation the next time I use the camera, and I might forget to reset it to zero on my own. However, if you have a practice of usually shooting with a certain amount of exposure compensation, you might want to leave this option off, so the value will be retained in memory from one shooting session to the next.

AF/AE Lock

This menu item lets you choose the function of the AF/AE Lock button, which is located beneath the mode dial on the back of the camera.

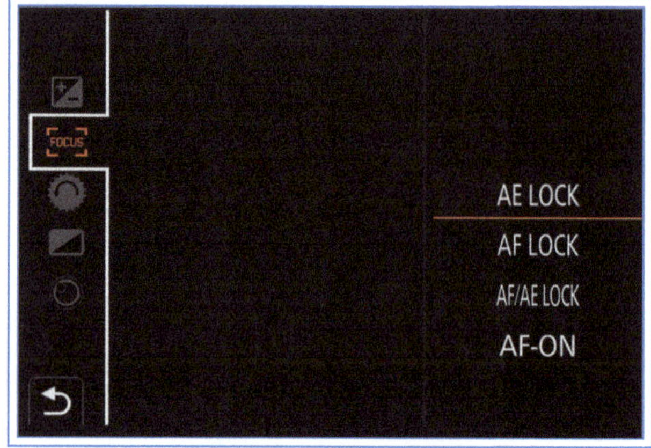

Figure 7-4. AF/AE Lock Menu Options Screen

You can use this option, shown in Figure 7-4, to control how that button locks autofocus (AF) and autoexposure (AE) settings.

If you select AE Lock or AF Lock, the camera locks only the one designated setting. If you choose AF/AE Lock, the camera locks both settings at the same time.

The camera will place icons on the recording display to indicate which of the values are locked, once you press the AF/AE Lock button and the values are locked in. The AF Lock icon will appear in the upper right corner and the AE Lock icon in the lower left corner. Figure 7-5 shows the display when both values are locked.

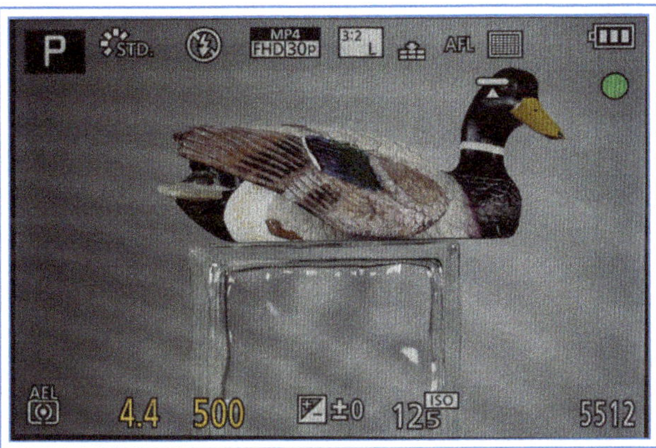

Figure 7-5. Shooting Screen with AFL and AEL Both in Use

It is not possible to lock exposure using the AF/AE Lock button in Manual exposure mode, or to lock focus when manual focus is in use. None of the button's settings function in either Snapshot mode.

If you select the final option, AF-On, pressing the AF/AE Lock button will cause the camera to use its autofocus system to focus on the subject, using whatever AF Mode setting is in effect to determine what area to focus on. If manual focus is in effect, the camera will still use the autofocus system when you press this button. This is a useful option as backup when you are using manual focus. You also can use it if you have set the Shutter AF option to Off, as discussed below, so pressing the shutter button halfway does not cause the camera to use its autofocus. You will then be able to press the AF/AE Lock button when you need to get the camera to focus again quickly. The ability to use a button on the back of the camera for focusing is sometimes called "back button focus."

AF/AE Lock Hold

This next menu option determines how the AF/AE Lock button operates. If you set AF/AE Lock Hold to On, then, when you press this button and release it, the camera retains the locked value(s). If you set this option to Off, you have to hold the button down to retain the value(s); when you release it, the locked value(s) will be released. This option is dimmed and unavailable for selection when AF/AE Lock is set to AF-On. With that setting, pressing the AF/AE Lock button causes the camera to use its autofocus, but not to lock focus, so it is not possible to "hold" the locked setting.

Shutter AF

This option lets you choose whether the camera will use its autofocus when you press the shutter button halfway, or not. With the default setup, with Shutter AF turned on, when the camera is set to an autofocus mode, it will evaluate the focus when you half-press the shutter button. With single autofocus (AFS), the focus will be locked as long as you hold the button in that position; with flexible autofocus (AFF), the camera will refocus if it detects movement, and with continuous autofocus (AFC), the camera will continue to adjust focus as movement occurs.

If you use this menu option to turn Shutter AF off, then the camera will not use its autofocus at all when you half-press the shutter button. There are several reasons why you might choose that setting. First, if you are taking a series of shots at the same distance, such as when you have the camera on a tripod and are taking shots of flat objects for auctions, you might focus once and then have no need to keep focusing. You can avoid using up the camera's battery for repeated uses of the autofocus system by turning Shutter AF off.

Another reason for using this option is if you prefer using the AF/AE Lock button to adjust autofocus. To do that, go to screen 1 of the Custom menu and set the AF/AE Lock menu option to AF-On. Then, when you press the AF/AE Lock button, the camera will adjust autofocus. With this setup (back button focus), you can adjust the focus whenever you want, and once you have it set as you want it, you can compose your shot and have the camera evaluate exposure without worrying that the camera will reset the focus to a different subject. You will be able to trigger the shutter to take another shot at any time.

Some photographers use this system with the autofocus mode set to AFC for continuous autofocus. Then, they can adjust focus at any time using the AF/AE Lock button, and press the shutter at any time without being concerned about focus. It's probably a good idea to give this setup a try and see if it works well for your type of shooting.

Half Press Release

This option lets you set the camera to capture an image when the shutter button is pressed halfway down, rather than requiring a full press, as is the normal situation. If you turn this setting on when Shutter AF is turned on, the camera will still adjust focus just before the image is captured, so the half-press of the button carries out both the autofocus operation and the image capture. If you have Shutter AF turned off, then you would have to use the AF/AE Lock button to adjust autofocus, with the AF-On option turned on for that button. (Or, of course, you could use manual focus.)

Using the Half Press Release option can speed up your shooting, because you don't have to go through the sequence of half-press followed by full press of the shutter button; you can just touch the button lightly to capture an image, or a burst of images if the camera is set for burst shooting. This system can work well if you won't be needing to make adjustments to focus or exposure after half-pressing the shutter button. When you are shooting in predictable, steady lighting at a constant distance and you need to shoot quickly, this option can be useful. Also, the ability to trigger the shutter with a light touch can help reduce the risk of motion blur from camera shake.

Quick AF

This next option on the Custom menu, Quick AF, can be turned either on or off. If you turn this setting on, the camera will focus on the subject whenever the camera has settled down and is still, with only minor movement or shake. You do not need to press the shutter button halfway down to achieve focus; the camera focuses on its own, as long as an autofocus mode is in use.

The advantage of turning Quick AF on is that you will have a slight improvement in focusing time, because the camera does not wait until you press the shutter button (or the AF/AE Lock button, if it is set for focusing) to start the focusing process. The disadvantage is that the battery will run down faster than usual. So, unless you believe a split second for focusing time is critical, I would stay away from this setting, and leave it turned off. The camera will still focus automatically when you press the shutter button halfway down; it just will take a little bit longer to bring the subject into focus.

The next items to be discussed are on screen 2 of the Custom menu, which is shown in Figure 7-6.

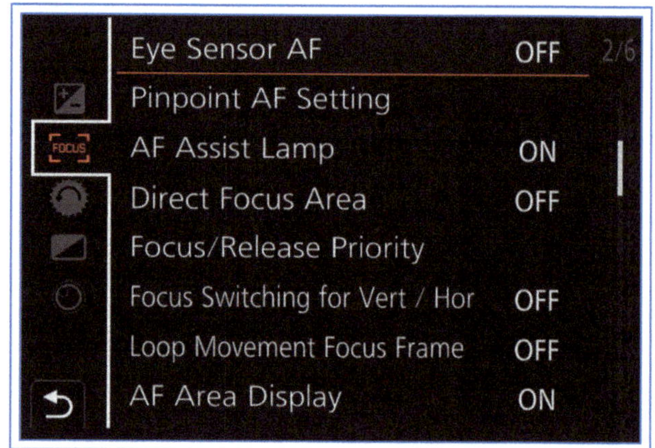

Figure 7-6. Screen 2 of Custom Menu

Eye Sensor AF

When this option is turned on and the camera is set to an autofocus mode, the camera will automatically use its autofocus mechanism to adjust focus as soon as your head approaches the eye sensor and turns on the electronic viewfinder. However, the autofocus system will work only once with this system, even if the camera is set for continuous autofocus. So, when you first put the camera up to your eye, the focus will be adjusted for whatever subject the camera is aimed at at that instant. The camera will not readjust the focus unless you then press the shutter button halfway or use the AF/AE Lock button, if that button is set up to adjust focus. The camera does not beep when focus is set with this feature.

This option can give the autofocus system a head start by bringing the scene into focus with an approximate setting, so it can quickly reach an exact focusing position when you press the shutter button halfway or use the AF/AE Lock button to make the final focus adjustments. I generally leave it turned off, but for snapshots it can be useful to have an approximate first cut at focusing take place as soon as you use the viewfinder.

This option works only when the viewfinder is turned on, either permanently or as your eye approaches it, through use of the EVF button or the Eye Sensor option on screen 2 of the Setup menu.

Pinpoint AF Setting

This menu option has two sub-options that control the operation of the Pinpoint setting for AF Mode. As I discussed in Chapter 4, with Pinpoint AF you can set a precise point for the focus area. Then, when you press the shutter button halfway to evaluate focus, the camera focuses at that point and enlarges the display briefly with that point centered, so you can judge the sharpness of the focus. The two sub-options of the Pinpoint AF Setting option, Pinpoint AF Time and Pinpoint AF Display, are discussed below.

Pinpoint AF Time

The Pinpoint AF Time option controls how long the Pinpoint AF display stays enlarged when you press the shutter button halfway. The choices are Short (0.5 second), Medium (1.0 second), or Long (1.5 second). If you release the shutter button before the specified time has passed, the display will revert to normal size. Because of that behavior, I prefer to set this option to Long. Then, the display will stay enlarged for a long enough time to let me judge the focus, but I can always release the shutter button early to revert the display to its normal size.

Pinpoint AF Display

This second sub-option lets you choose one of two options for the size of the enlarged display that appears when you use the Pinpoint option for AF Mode—Full or PIP (picture-in-picture). With Full, the entire display is enlarged by a factor of between three and ten times; with PIP, only the central part of the display is enlarged, by a factor of between three and six times. You can vary the enlargement factor by turning the thumb dial or pinching/pulling on the touch screen when the enlargement is active as you are setting the focus point using the AF Mode menu option. That enlargement factor will then take effect when you half-press the shutter button to focus using the Pinpoint AF option.

AF Assist Lamp

The autofocus (AF) assist lamp is the reddish light on the front of the camera, near the lens below the mode dial. The lamp illuminates when the ambient lighting is dim, to help the autofocus mechanism work by providing enough light to define the shape of the subject. Ordinarily, this option is left turned on for normal shooting, because the light only activates when it is needed in low-light conditions. However, you have the option of turning it off using the AF Assist Lamp menu option, so it will not turn on to help with autofocus. You might want to do this if you are trying to shoot your pictures without being detected, or without disturbing a subject such as a sleeping animal.

In Snapshot mode, you cannot turn off the AF assist lamp using this menu option, but you can use the Silent Mode option on screen 2 of the Recording menu to turn off the lamp, along with the flash and camera sounds. (Silent Mode is on screen 4 of the Recording menu in other shooting modes.) The lamp does not illuminate when you are using manual focus (unless you have set up the AF/AE Lock button to use the AF-On option and you press that button to cause the camera to use its autofocus).

The AF assist lamp also serves as the self-timer lamp. Even if you set the AF Assist Lamp menu option to Off, the lamp will light up when the self-timer is used; there is no way to disable the lamp for that function.

Direct Focus Area

This is another option that can be turned either on or off; it is off by default. If you turn it on, then, in recording mode, if you press any of the four direction buttons, the camera immediately displays a screen for adjusting the position of the autofocus area. For example, if AF Mode is set to 1-Area, Pinpoint AF, or Face/Eye Detection, then, when you press, say, the Left button, that button immediately activates the focus frame and starts moving it across the display. If you have AF Mode set to 49-Area or Custom Multi, then, when you press a direction button, the camera immediately displays the screen for selecting the focus zones to be included in the focus area. You can then keep pressing any of the direction buttons to adjust the area or use other controls to make other adjustments.

This option could be useful if you were in a situation when you need to adjust the focus area often, particularly with the 1-Area or Pinpoint AF options. I would not recommend using it with the 49-Area or Custom Multi options, because you need to do considerable adjusting with those options, and a split second of added speed will not be of that much use.

I do not use this option myself, because it is so easy to adjust the focus area without it. If you turn on Touch AF through the Touch Settings option on screen 3 of the Custom menu, you can just touch the screen to activate a movable focus area. Also, if you turn on Direct Focus Area, you lose the other functions of the direction buttons while this option is in effect. If you wanted to set white balance, exposure compensation, drive mode, or focus mode, you would have to use the Quick Menu, assign those functions to another button or to the control ring, or turn off this menu option before making that adjustment.

Focus/Release Priority

This option has two sub-settings to control whether or not the camera requires that sharp focus be achieved before the shutter can be released. The two sub-settings, AFS/AFF and AFC, provide options for the three choices for the AFS/AFF/AFC setting. You can set the camera's autofocus release behavior for the AFS/AFF settings separately from its behavior for the AFC setting.

For either AFS/AFF or AFC, you can set this option to Balance, the default option, Focus, or Release. If it is set to Focus, the camera will not take a picture until focus has been confirmed, when autofocus is in use. So, if you aim the camera at a subject that is difficult for the autofocus system to bring into sharp focus, such as an area with no sharp features in dim lighting, the camera may display a red focus frame and beep four times, indicating focus was not achieved. In that situation, if this menu option is set to Focus, the camera will not take the picture when you press the shutter button. If you set this option to Release, then the camera will take the picture even if it is not in focus. If you are using manual focus, then the camera will take the picture regardless of focus, even if you set the priority to Focus. If this option is set to Balance, the camera uses a compromise approach and tries to achieve focus, but will still release the shutter after some time has passed, even if it cannot get a focused shot.

The use of this option is a matter of personal preference and the situation you are faced with. If you are taking images of a one-time event, you may want to use the Release option so you don't miss a shot just because focus is slightly off. It's much better to get an image that is slightly out of focus than no image at all. But if you have time to make sure focus is sharp, you can use the Focus option to make sure you have focus properly adjusted before you capture an image. The Balance option is an appropriate compromise when focus is not absolutely critical.

This option also has an impact on the speed of burst shooting. As I discussed in Chapter 5, if this option is set to Focus, shooting may be slowed down as the camera attempts to adjust focus before recording each image, when you are using a burst setting with continuous focus adjustments.

Focus Switching for Vertical/Horizontal

When you have AF Mode on screen 1 of the Recording menu set to AF Tracking, 1-Area, or Pinpoint AF, the camera remembers where the focus frame was located for the last image you captured with that setting. So, if you turn the camera off and then back on, that frame will be located in the same place on the display as it was for the last shot. However, by default, the camera will only remember one location for the frame, and that location will not change if the camera is rotated 90 degrees from the horizontal to vertical position.

If you turn on the Focus Switching for Vertical/Horizontal menu option, the camera will remember the last position for the focus frame for the horizontal position as well as the last position for the vertical position. So, if you are rotating the camera to take different views of the same subject, moving the focus frame to the proper location for each orientation, the camera will remember those two locations and switch them as you rotate the camera.

This option works for the frame displayed for MF Assist enlargement when using manual focus, as well as for the autofocus frames mentioned above.

This option can be useful, and it does not cause any distraction when not needed, so I generally leave it turned on.

Loop Movement Focus Frame

This is another option which, like the previous one, controls the way the camera handles the positioning of movable focus frames and the MF Assist frame. Ordinarily, when you are using an AF Mode setting such as Face/Eye Detection, 49-Area, Custom Multi, 1-Area, or Pinpoint AF, when you move the focus frame or focus area around the screen, it stops at the edge of the screen. If you turn on the Loop Movement Focus Frame option, the frame or area will "loop" around from one edge of the screen to the opposite edge. For example, if you move the frame to the far right edge of the display, the frame will then appear at the far left edge and continue moving to the right. You may find that this feature gives you added flexibility in positioning the focus frame, focus area, or MF Assist enlargement frame exactly where you want it.

Note that this feature does not work when you are moving the frame or area with your finger on the touch screen, only when you are moving it with the cursor buttons. It does work with all four edges of the screen, not just the sides.

AF Area Display

This option lets you set the camera to display the area that is currently set for autofocus when AF Mode is set to 49-Area or Custom Multi and the focus zones have been changed from the default setting for that option.

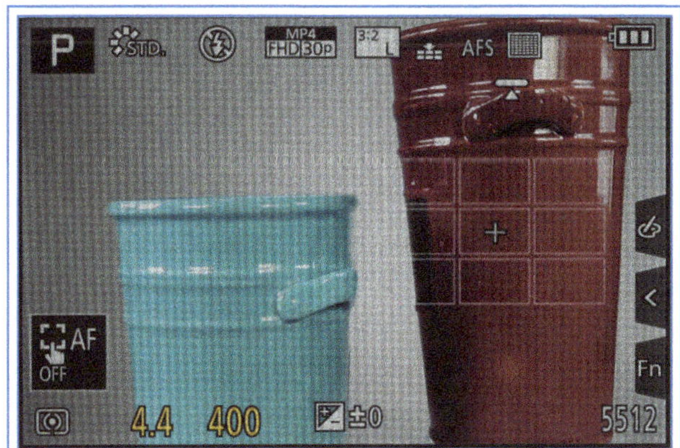

Figure 7-7. Focus Zones Displayed with AF Area Display Option

For example, if you have moved the focus zones for the 49-Area option to the right side of the screen, the camera will display the focus zones in white on the LCD screen, as shown in Figure 7-7. However, if you are using the 49-Area option with its default setting of focus zones in the center of the screen, the camera will not show any focus zones on the display.

This option is quite useful as a reminder of where the camera will direct its focus with these two AF Mode settings. It does not work when recording videos, when the camera is in Creative Video mode, or when recording 4K photos.

The options on screen 3 of the Custom menu are shown in Figure 7-8.

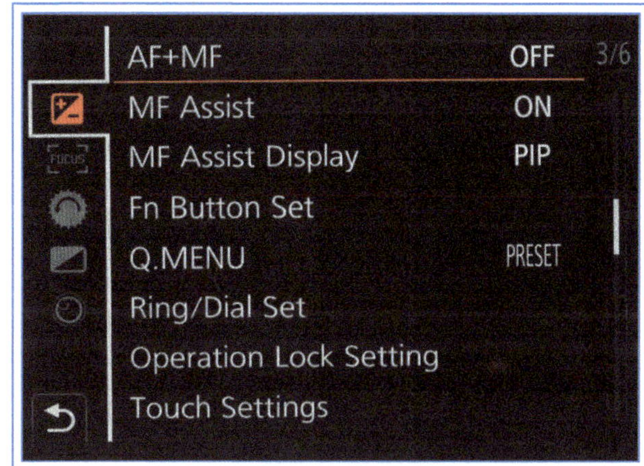

Figure 7-8. Screen 3 of Custom Menu

AF+MF

This is an on-or-off option that is turned off by default. If you turn it on, then, when the autofocus mode is set to AFS, for single autofocus, once you have pressed the shutter button halfway to lock focus, while holding the button in that position, you can turn the control ring to fine-tune the focus manually. Features such as MF Assist and peaking will operate if they are turned on through the Custom menu. This option also takes effect if you have locked focus with the AF/AE Lock button, when that button is set to lock autofocus or to the AF-On setting through screen 1 of the Custom menu.

This option is useful when, for example, you have locked focus on a group of small objects, and you want to make sure the focus is precisely set on one of those objects, such as on an object behind the others, or on a portion of one of them. Once the autofocus system has locked on the group, start turning the control ring while keeping the shutter button pressed halfway (or the AF/AE Lock button pressed, if applicable) to adjust the focus manually until you have it set exactly as you want.

Manual Focus (MF) Assist

The MF Assist option, together with the MF Assist Display option, discussed next, lets you set whether and how the recording screen display is magnified when you're using manual focus. This option can be turned either on or off.

If you leave MF Assist turned off, there is no magnification when you turn the control ring to adjust manual focus. If you turn MF Assist on, then, when you start turning the control ring to focus, the screen will immediately be magnified to help you adjust the focus. Also, before you start turning the control ring, you can tap on the screen twice to activate the MF Assist function. The display will be enlarged, and you can move the focus point by dragging the screen with your finger or by using the four cursor buttons. You can change the enlargement factor with the thumb dial or by pinching or pulling on the screen with your fingers. You can press the Display button or the DISP. Reset icon to return the focus point to the center.

The MF Assist option is not available for recording motion pictures, with the 4K Photo Pre-burst setting, or when Digital Zoom is activated.

MF Assist Display

The MF Assist Display option lets you set the area of magnification with MF Assist to Full or PIP (picture-in-picture), as seen in Figure 7-9. If you choose Full, the magnification uses up the whole display and varies between three and ten times normal. If you choose PIP, the magnification appears in a smaller window and the enlargement varies between three and six times normal.

As soon as you tap the touch screen twice or turn the control ring to start the magnification, the display will appear similar to Figure 7-10, which shows the MF Assist display when the Full setting is in effect.

You can use all four direction buttons or the touch screen to move the enlarged area around the display, and you can turn the thumb dial or pinch the touch screen to change the magnification factor. To reset the focus point to the center of the display, press the Display button. To dismiss the MF Assist display, press the shutter button halfway or press the Menu/Set button. Or, if you turned the control ring to start the magnification, the screen will return to normal size on its own after about ten seconds. You can then turn the control ring to bring the MF Assist display back on the screen if you want, or you can just press the shutter button to take the picture. You can switch between the full-screen and PIP views by touching the rectangular icon at the bottom of the display with a small inset white rectangle in its upper right corner.

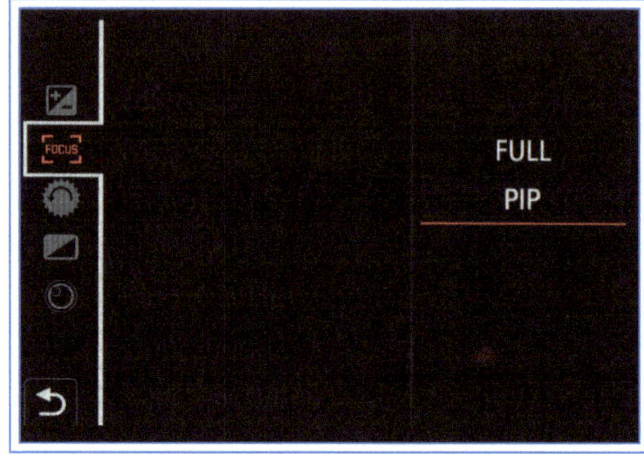

Figure 7-9. MF Assist Display Menu Options Screen

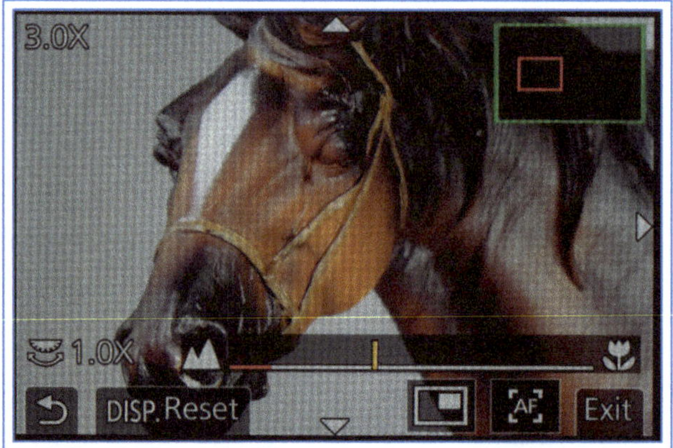

Figure 7-10. Shooting Screen with MF Assist in Use

Function Button Set

As I discussed in Chapter 5, the C-Lux has four physical function buttons labeled Fn1, Fn2, Fn3, and Fn4. It also has five virtual function buttons represented by icons on the touch screen, labeled Fn5 through Fn9. Each of those buttons, except for Fn9, has a particular function assigned to it by default. For all nine buttons, though, you can choose the function that is assigned when the camera is in recording mode. For the Fn1, Fn2, and Fn4 buttons, you also can choose a function to be assigned when the camera is in playback mode. To make those assignments, you use the Function Button Set menu option. (You also can change a button's assignment for recording mode by pressing and holding the button for a few seconds to call up a list of assignment options.)

When you highlight this option and press the Menu/Set button or the Right button, the camera will display the screen shown in Figure 7-11, letting you choose the settings in recording mode or playback mode.

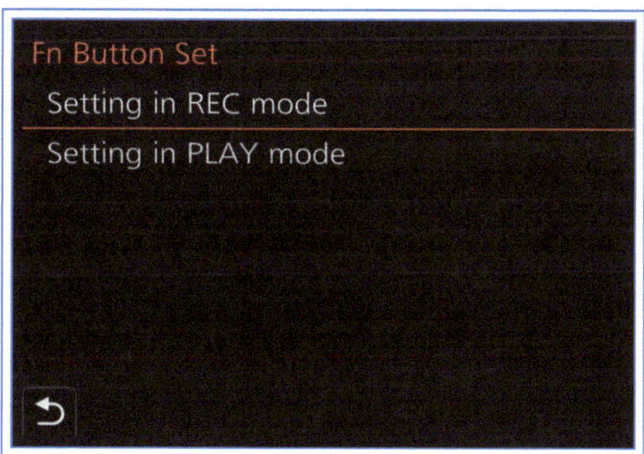

Figure 7-11. Function Button Set Main Options Screen

For now, select recording mode, and the camera will display the special screen shown in Figure 7-12, with a graphic display of the assignable buttons.

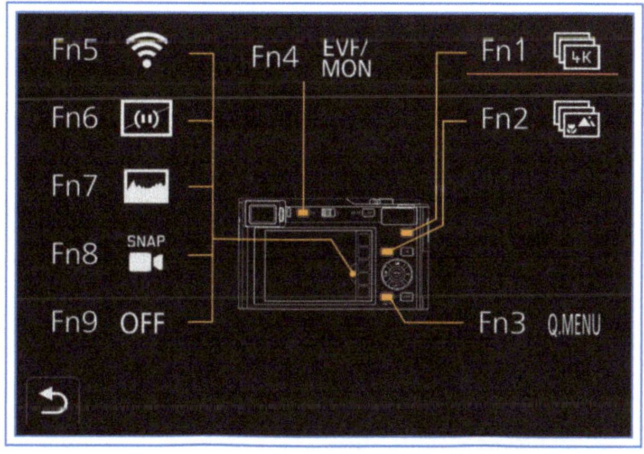

Figure 7-12. Screen to Select Function Button to Assign

On that screen, turn the thumb dial or press the Up and Down buttons to move the highlight to the button whose assignment you want to change, and press Menu/Set. (Or, just touch the button's icon on the touch screen.) You will then see a display like that in Figure 7-13, which highlights the current setting for that button on a sub-menu screen. Scroll through that series of nine or ten screens until you find the new setting you want to make, and press Menu/Set to confirm it. I discussed the possible settings in Chapter 5.

Don't forget that several of the items that can be assigned, including Photo Style, Flash Mode, Quality, AFS/AFF/AFC, and Metering Mode, also can be adjusted using the Quick Menu system by pressing the Q.Menu button and navigating through the easy-access menu that appears.

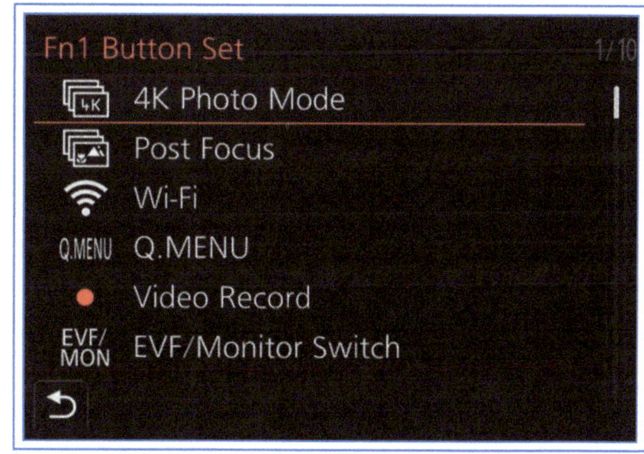

Figure 7-13. First Screen of Settings for a Given Function Button

Also, although most of the items that can be assigned to the function buttons also can be reached through the menu system or with a control button, there are some items that cannot readily be reached in those ways: Preview, One Push AE, Focus Area Set, and Operation Lock. I discussed those settings in Chapter 5.

You also can assign the Fn1, Fn2, and Fn4 buttons to carry out a function when the camera is in playback mode. To do that, go back to the main options screen for this menu item and select Setting in Play Mode, and the camera will display a screen similar to Figure 7-12, but showing only those three buttons. On that screen, select the button you want to assign a function for playback mode.

As discussed in Chapter 5, there are several settings available for assignment during playback mode: Wi-Fi, EVF/Monitor Switch, Record/Playback Switch, 4K Photo Play, Delete Single, Protect, Rating★1-Rating★5, Raw Processing, 4K Photo Bulk Saving, Off, and Restore to Default.

Quick Menu (Q.Menu)

This option gives you the ability to customize the settings that are available from the Quick Menu. As I discussed in Chapter 4, when you press the Q.Menu button, the camera displays an easy-access menu system that lets you select various settings quickly. By default, the Quick Menu includes 11 settings: Photo Style, Flash Mode, Motion Picture Setting, Picture Setting, Quality, AFS/AFF/AFC, AF Mode, Metering Mode, Exposure Compensation, Sensitivity, and White Balance. To keep those settings in place or restore them after custom settings have been used, select the Preset option for this menu item. If you want to set up the Quick Menu with your own selection of settings, select the Custom option for this menu item.

Once you have selected Custom for the Quick Menu item, exit this menu system and, from the shooting screen, press the Q.Menu button. On the screen that appears, use the Down button to move to and highlight the tool icon at the lower left of the display, as shown in Figure 7-14. (Or select that icon using the touch screen.)

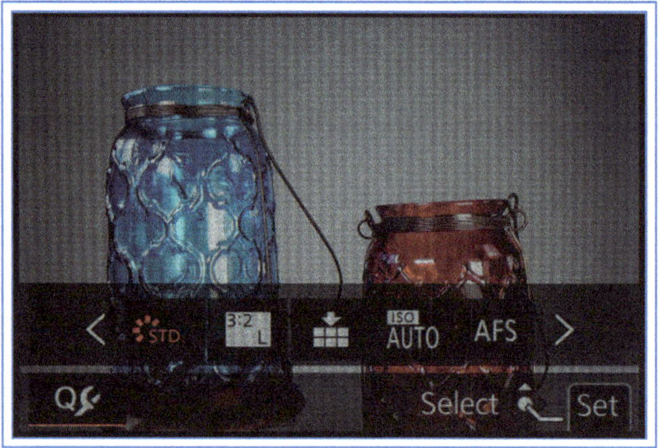

Figure 7-14. Tool Icon Highlighted on Quick Menu

When you highlight and select that icon, you will see the Q. Menu Customize screen, shown in Figure 7-15, after a screen with instructions appears briefly.

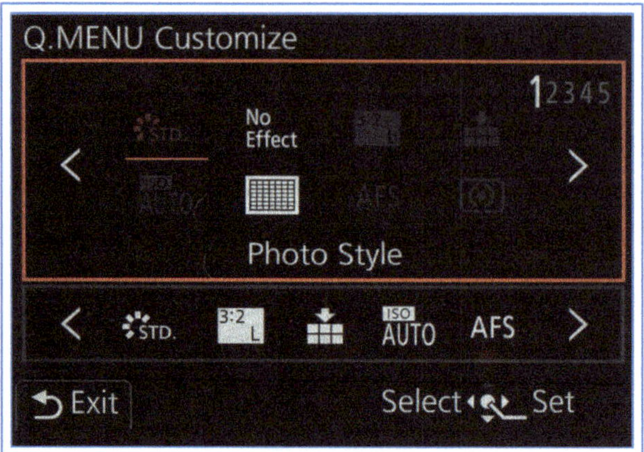

Figure 7-15. Quick Menu Customize Screen

On the Customize screen, navigate through the icons at the top of the display until you find the icon for a setting you want to install in the Quick Menu. With that icon highlighted in red, press Menu/Set and the camera will prompt you to move to the "desired position." At that point, one of the icons in the bottom row will be highlighted; use the thumb dial or the Left and Right buttons to move that highlight to the position where you want to locate the setting whose icon you selected from the top rows. If there is no blank space available in the bottom row, just highlight an occupied space and press Menu/Set; the new icon will replace the existing one.

An easier way to add icons to the bottom row is simply to touch an icon with your finger and drag it to the bottom row, onto an empty spot, or drag it onto an occupied slot to replace the icon that is already there. When you have finished adding icons to the Quick Menu, press the Q.Menu button to return to the shooting screen.

Ring/Dial Set

This next option on the Custom menu lets you set the function or functions of the thumb dial, at the top right of the camera, and the control ring, the large ring around the lens. When you select this menu option, the camera displays the screen shown in Figure 7-16. On that screen, highlight and select the icon for the control you want to customize, and the camera will display the available settings for that control.

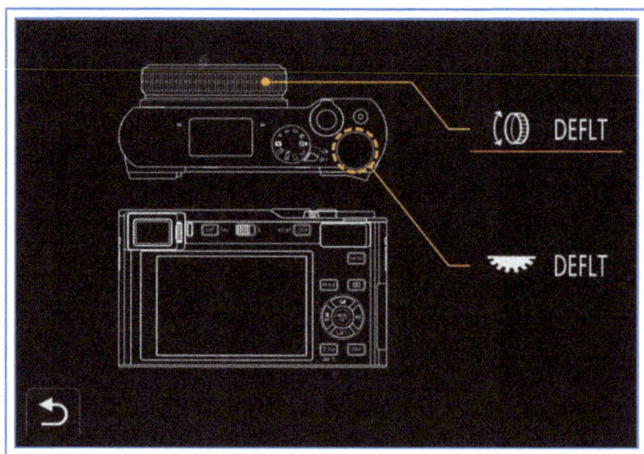

Figure 7-16. Ring/Dial Set Menu Options Screen

In Chapter 5, I discussed the settings that are assigned to each control by default, as well as the settings that can be assigned instead, using this menu option. I generally use the default settings, which are very useful, but, if you want to have the control ring or thumb dial control just one option, you can do that with this menu item.

Operation Lock Setting

This setting is related to the Operation Lock option for assignment to a function button through the Function Button Set item on screen 3 of the Custom menu. If you assign that option to a function button, when you press the assigned button, the effect will be to lock the operation of the cursor buttons, the touch screen, both, or neither, depending on the setting for the Operation Lock Setting menu item. As shown in Figure 7-17, you can set the locking of the cursor buttons or the touch screen to Off or On. (Off means the controls will not be locked; On means they will be locked.) The assigned settings will be effective when the camera is in recording mode, but not when it is in playback mode.

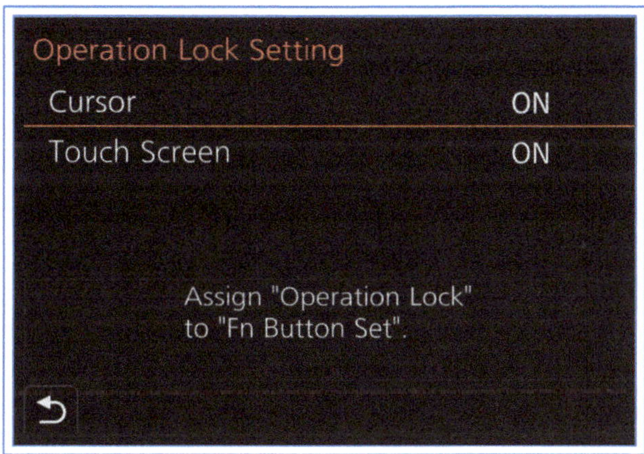

Figure 7-17. Operation Lock Setting Menu Options Screen

Touch Settings

With the four sub-options of this menu item, you can control several aspects of the operation of the C-Lux's touch screen capability. Those four sub-options are Touch Screen, Touch Tab, Touch AF, and Touch Pad AF, as shown in Figure 7-18.

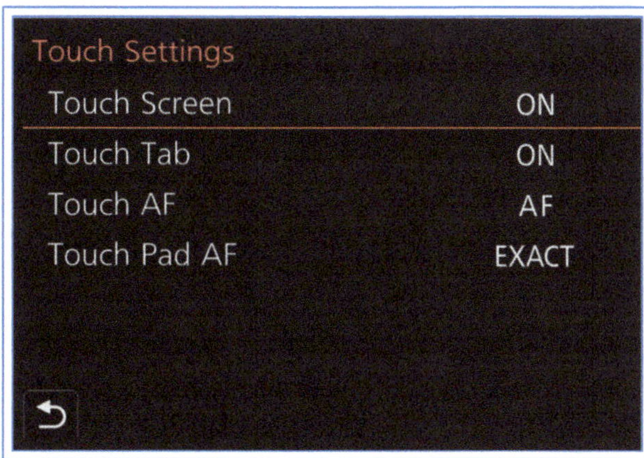

Figure 7-18. Touch Settings Menu Options Screen

Touch Screen

This first option can be turned either on or off. If it is on, the touch screen works as expected. If it is off, none of the touch screen operations are active, and the touch screen icons do not appear at all. The next three sub-options on this menu will be dimmed and unavailable in that case. However, even when the Touch Screen option is turned off, you can use the Clear Retouch option on screen 2 of the Playback menu, which requires that you touch the areas of an image that you want to remove.

If you prefer the classic operation of a camera that uses only traditional buttons and dials, you can leave this setting turned off and not have to worry about using the touch screen options. I find it useful to turn the touch screen off when I am using the viewfinder on a sunny day, because my nose may bump into the screen and activate a focus frame or otherwise cause distraction. However, the touch screen adds a great deal of convenience to using the camera, and in most situations I leave it turned on.

Touch Tab

In Chapter 5, I discussed the operation of the touch tab, a set of touch controls at the right edge of the shooting screen. When you touch the small left-facing arrow, the tab opens up to reveal controls for touch zoom, touch AF/touch shutter, touch autoexposure, and touch peaking (available when manual focus is in use). If you want to use the camera's other touch capabilities but not the particular functions available through the touch tab, you can turn this option off.

Touch AF

This sub-option enables or disables the use of the Touch AF and Touch AE functions.

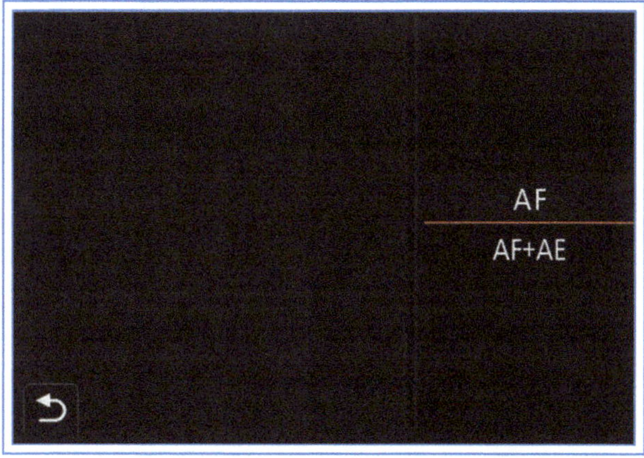

Figure 7-19. Touch AF Menu Options Screen

There are two possible settings for this item: AF or AF+AE, as shown in Figure 7-19. If you choose AF, you can change the location of the focusing area on the shooting screen just by touching the screen. If AF Mode on screen 1 of the Recording menu is set to Face/Eye Detection, 1-Area, or Pinpoint AF, touch the focus frame that is displayed on the screen, and you can then move that frame around the screen. You can change the size of the frame by pinching or pulling the area of the frame with your fingers. When you have the frame located as you want it, press the Set icon in the lower right corner of the screen, or press the Menu/Set button.

If the 49-Area option for AF Mode is in use, touching the screen brings up the screen for adjusting the area of the focus zones. If AF Mode is set to Tracking, touch a subject on the screen to start tracking that subject.

For Touch AF to operate properly, the Touch Shutter option must be turned off. Otherwise, the camera will take a picture when you touch the screen. To turn off the current AF operation, touch the AF Off icon on the left side of the screen.

The second choice of setting for Touch AF is AF+AE. If you choose this option, when you touch the screen, the camera uses the same focus frame at that location as with the 1-Area AF Mode setting, regardless of the AF Mode setting that is in effect. You can change the location and size of the focus frame by moving it with your finger and resize it by pinching and pulling the screen. In addition, the camera places a small, blue cross in the center of the frame and optimizes exposure for that area.

Touch Pad AF

The last sub-option for the Touch Settings menu item is Touch Pad AF. This option controls how the touch screen works when you are using the viewfinder and moving the autofocus frame around the display with your finger.

There are three sub-options: Exact, Offset, and Off. If you choose Off, this option is not activated at all. With Exact, you press on the screen in the position where you want the focus frame to be located on the viewfinder display. If you choose Offset, you can cause the focus frame to move just by moving your finger a certain distance in the desired direction, without pressing at the exact location of the frame in the viewfinder. I prefer the Exact option, because I can just press the screen where I want the focus frame to be located.

This option can be useful if you are taking pictures on a sunny day and need to move the focus frame around on the viewfinder display. However, if you don't need to move the focus frame often, it can be distracting, because your nose can touch the screen and put a confusing focus frame display in the viewfinder. If you find that problem arising, turn this option off.

The options on screen 4 of the Custom menu are shown in Figure 7-20.

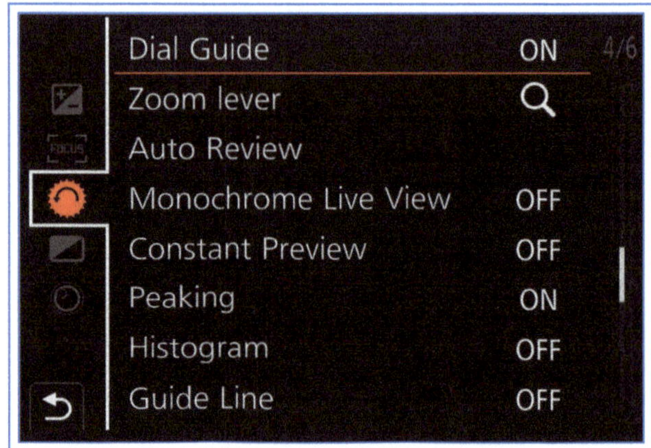

Figure 7-20. Screen 4 of Custom Menu

Dial Guide

When this option is turned on, the camera places a small diagram in the lower right corner of the display for a few seconds that shows the current functions of the control ring and thumb dial. The diagram appears when you switch the recording mode by turning the mode dial.

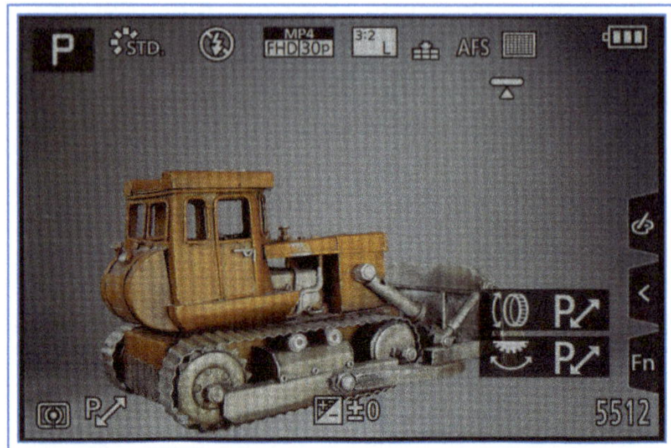

Figure 7-21. Dial Guide Display on Shooting Screen

For example, in Figure 7-21, the display shows that the control ring and the thumb dial both control Program

Shift, because the camera is in Program mode. If you move the mode dial to change the recording mode, the display will change accordingly and appear for another few seconds. I find this display helpful, and it disappears soon after appearing, so I generally leave it turned on.

Zoom Lever

This next option lets you control how the zoom lever operates. By default, this lever zooms the lens continuously through its full range of focal lengths, which is 24mm to 360mm if no enhanced zoom settings are in use. If you choose the second option here, the zoom lever uses step zoom, which allows the lever to zoom only to several preset zoom ranges: 24mm, 28mm, 35mm, 50mm, 70mm, 90mm, 135mm, 160mm, 200mm, 250mm, 300mm, and 360mm, when only the optical zoom is in use. It will not stop at any other focal length.

If you turn on other options for zooming, such as Digital Zoom, Intelligent Zoom, and Extended Optical Zoom, the step zoom function will take the focal length to further stages of 400mm, 500mm, 600mm, and others, depending on what settings are in effect.

As I discussed in Chapter 5, the control ring also can be assigned to operate step zoom, through the Ring/Dial Set option on screen 3 of the Custom menu (discussed earlier in this chapter). So, if you want to use step zoom, you can choose either the control ring or the zoom lever for that function.

My preference is to leave both the control ring and the zoom lever with their normal operation of zooming through the full range of focal lengths, rather than limiting them to the step zoom increments. However, if there are situations in which you want to have the zoom lens move in specific increments, you can use this option.

Auto Review

This option controls how long your still images are displayed immediately after they are recorded by the camera, and how the camera behaves during that display. The Auto Review menu option has four sub-options, as shown in Figure 7-22: Duration Time (Photo), Duration Time (4K Photo), Duration Time (Post Focus), and Playback Operation Priority.

When you select Duration Time (Photo), for images not taken using 4K Photo or Post Focus, the possible settings are Off, one second, two seconds, three seconds, four seconds, five seconds, or Hold. After the shutter button is pressed, the image appears on the screen (or not) according to how this option is set. If you choose Hold, the image stays on the screen until you press the shutter button halfway.

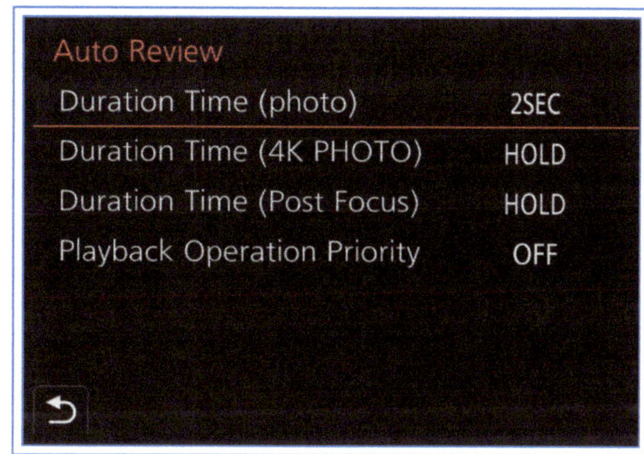

Figure 7-22. Auto Review Menu Options Screen

For the other two categories of images, 4K Photo and Post Focus, the only options are Off or Hold.

The second sub-option, Playback Operation Priority, controls whether you can perform playback operations on an image while it is displayed for a specific number of seconds under the Duration Time option. If Playback Operation Priority is turned on, then, when an image is displayed for one to five seconds under Auto Review, if you press a button such as Fn3 to delete an image, or a navigation button such as the Left or Right button, the camera will respond as if it were in playback mode, and carry out that operation. If Playback Operation Priority is turned off, pressing a button will have the effect it would have in recording mode. For example, if you press the Fn3 button, the camera will carry out whatever function is assigned to that button for recording mode, which, by default, is the Quick Menu function.

If Duration Time (Photo) is set to Hold, then Playback Operation Priority is automatically turned on, and the camera will act as if it were in playback mode at all times while a new image is displayed immediately after capture.

Auto Review does not work when recording motion pictures.

Monochrome Live View

When you turn this feature on, the camera converts the display to a black-and-white view of the scene it is aimed at. This feature might help you concentrate on composition and geometry in your image, without being distracted by colors. You also might find it easier to adjust manual focus with this view, because you can turn on peaking with a color that contrasts clearly with all parts of the display. The monochrome view does not affect the recorded image, which will be in color unless you have also selected a monochrome setting for the final image using the Photo Style menu option or one of the Scene mode or Creative Control mode settings that produce monochrome images.

Constant Preview

This option lets you see a preview of the effects of your exposure settings when the camera is in Manual exposure mode. When you turn this option on with the camera in that recording mode and then adjust shutter speed, aperture, or ISO, the display will grow darker or brighter to show how the settings would affect the final image. The display also will show how the aperture setting would affect the depth of field.

For example, if you set shutter speed to 1/125 second, aperture to f/8, and ISO to 1600 in a moderately lighted room with this option turned off, the camera's display will appear normal, showing the scene clearly. If you then press the shutter button halfway (assuming default settings for focus and shutter behavior), the display will grow dark and you will see more items in focus, reflecting the effects of the current settings. If you then turn this menu option on, you will see the same view you did when you pressed the shutter button halfway, even before pressing that button.

This setting can help if you need to see exactly what effect the current settings will have. However, in some situations it is better to leave this option turned off. For example, if you are shooting an image using an off-camera optical slave flash in Manual exposure mode, the camera will not realize that you are using the external flash, and the display screen may be quite dark with the settings you are using. In that situation, you might not be able to see the display to compose your image with this option activated, so you should leave Constant Preview turned off.

If you have a function button set to the Preview option and have the Constant Preview option turned on, pressing the function button in Manual exposure mode will not activate the Preview function, because it is already in effect through this menu option. The Constant Preview option has no effect when the camera's built-in flash is in use.

Peaking

This menu option controls another feature for assisting with manual focus. The peaking feature, when it is turned on, places colored pixels on the screen at areas that the camera determines are in sharp focus. As you turn the control ring to adjust focus, watch for the colored areas to reach their maximum intensity. When you see the largest areas of glowing pixels, focus will be sharp for the areas where those pixels appear.

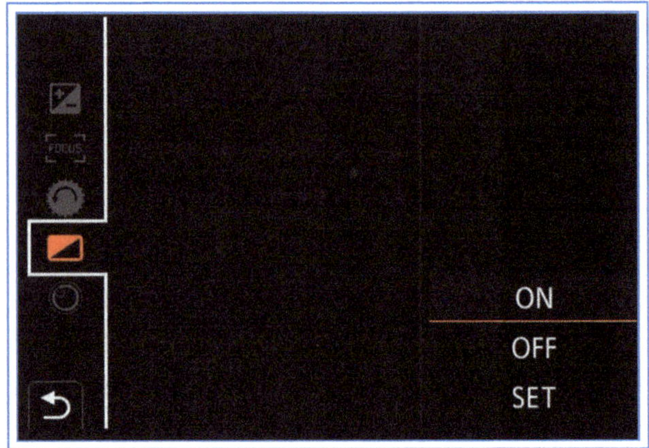

Figure 7-23. Peaking Menu Options Screen

The peaking menu item has three main options: On, Off, and Set, as shown in Figure 7-23. In most cases, I leave it turned on, because it operates only when manual focus is in effect and I find it helpful for most manual focusing situations. The Set option has two sub-options: Detect Level and Display Color, as shown in Figure 7-24.

The Detect Level can be set to High or Low. If you set it to High, the camera will require a higher degree of sharpness before it places pixels at a given focus area. With that setting, there will be fewer peaking pixels displayed than with the Low setting. You may find that it is easier to gauge the focus with fewer pixels, because you can adjust focus until those few pixels appear. However, in some situations, such as with objects that are lacking in straight lines or sharp features, you may find that it is preferable to set Detect Level to Low, so there will be more peaking pixels visible.

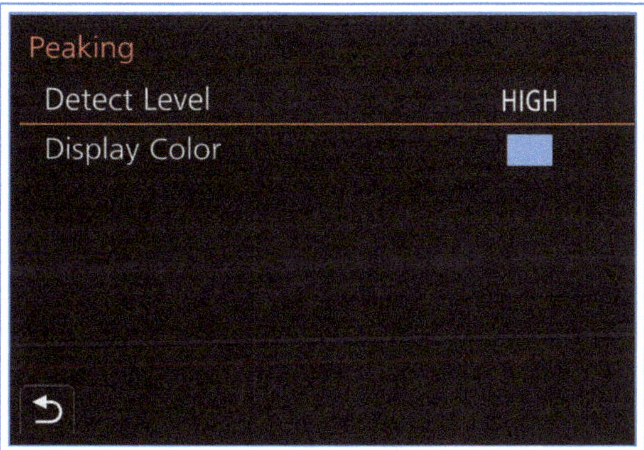

Figure 7-24. Peaking Set Options Screen

With the Display Color sub-option, you can choose light blue, yellow, yellow green, pink, or white for the peaking color if Detect Level is set to High, and you can choose dark blue, orange, green, red, or gray if the level is set to Low. It is a good idea to choose a color that contrasts with the scene you are photographing, so you can distinguish the peaking pixels from other parts of the image.

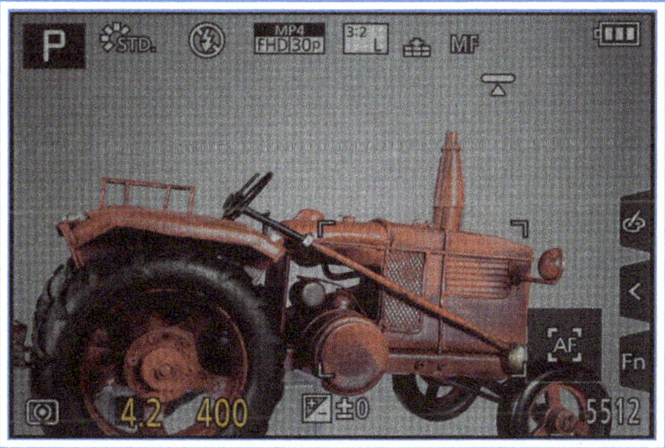

Figure 7-25. Peaking Turned Off

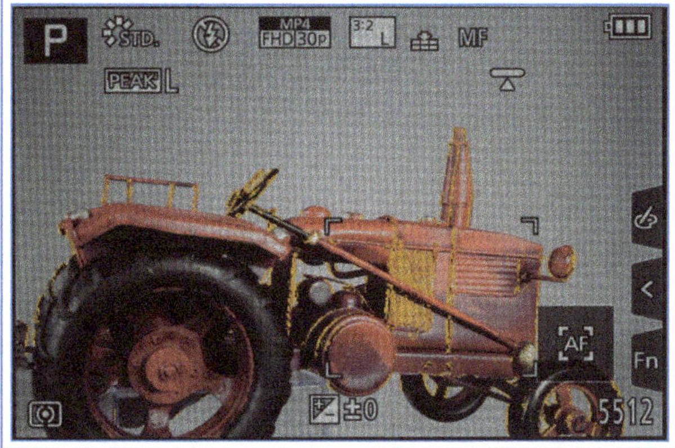

Figure 7-26. Peaking Set to Detect Level Low

Figure 7-25 and Figure 7-26 are two images that illustrate the use of this feature. Figure 7-25 shows the view with peaking turned off, and Figure 7-26 shows it with peaking turned on with Detect Level set to Low.

As noted above, peaking operates only when the camera is set to manual focus. If you set the AF/AE Lock button to the AF-On function on screen 1 of the Custom menu, peaking pixels will appear when you press that button to cause the camera to use autofocus, if manual focus is in effect. Peaking also operates if you adjust manual focus using the AF+MF option, discussed earlier in this chapter. Peaking does not operate when the Rough Monochrome filter effect setting is in use.

Histogram

The next menu option, Histogram, controls the display of the histogram in recording mode. A histogram is a graph showing the distribution of dark and bright areas in the image that is being viewed on the camera's screen. The darkest blacks are represented by vertical bars on the left, and the brightest whites by vertical bars on the right, with continuous gradations in between.

If an image has a histogram in which the pattern looks like a tall ski slope coming from the left of the screen down to ground level in the middle of the screen, that means there is an excessive amount of black and dark areas (tall bars on the left side of the histogram), and very few bright and white areas (no bars on the right). The histogram in Figure 7-27 illustrates this situation.

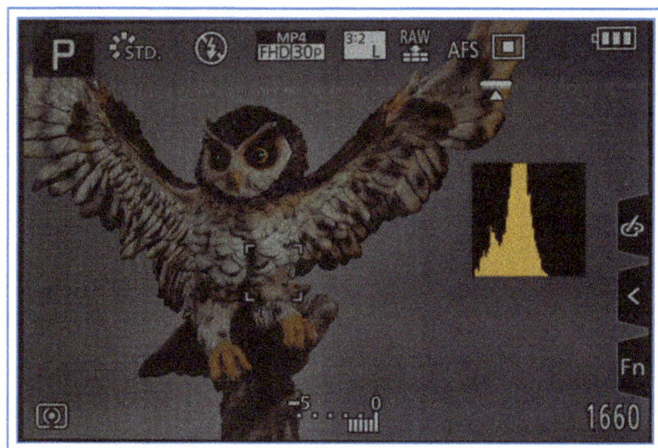

Figure 7-27. Histogram for Underexposed Image

A pattern moving from the middle of the graph up to peaks at the right side of the graph would mean just the opposite—too many bright and white areas, as in the histogram shown in Figure 7-28.

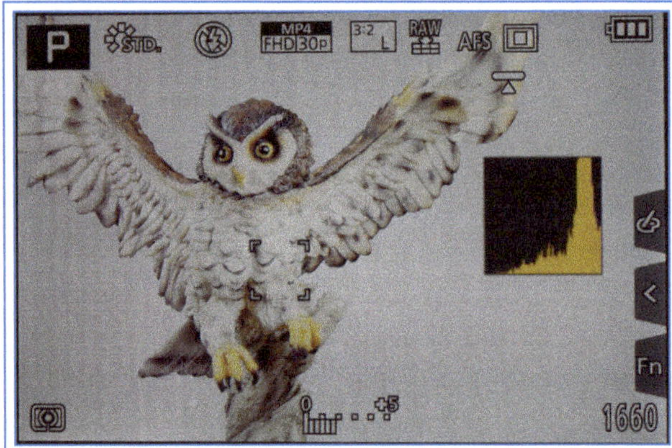
Figure 7-28. Histogram for Overexposed Image

A histogram that is "just right" would be one that starts low on the left, gradually rises to a medium peak in the middle of the graph, then moves gradually back down to the bottom at the right. That pattern indicates a good balance of whites, blacks, and medium tones. An example of this type of histogram is shown in Figure 7-29.

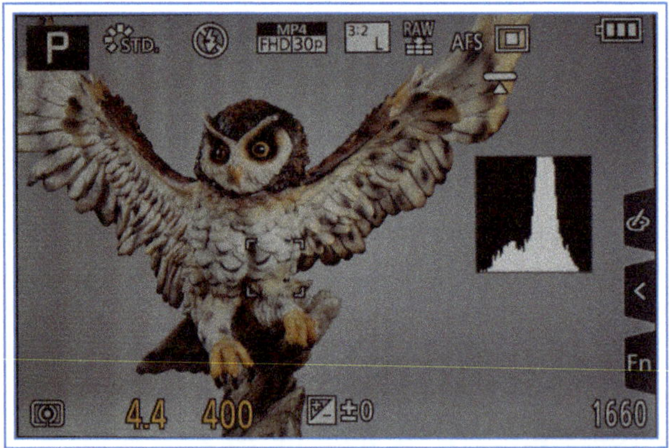
Figure 7-29. Histogram for Normally Exposed Image

In playback mode, the C-Lux includes one display screen with a histogram for the image being displayed. The camera does not, by default, display the histogram for the live view in recording mode. To turn on the histogram when you are shooting, you need to use this menu option.

The Histogram menu option has only two choices: On or Off. If you turn the histogram on, it will appear on the camera's display in recording mode, if a detailed display screen has been selected using the Display button, as shown in Figures 7-27 through 7-29.

The histogram does not display in the basic Snapshot mode. When the histogram is first activated, it appears in a red frame with arrows indicating that you can move it to any position on the display, as shown in Figure 7-30.

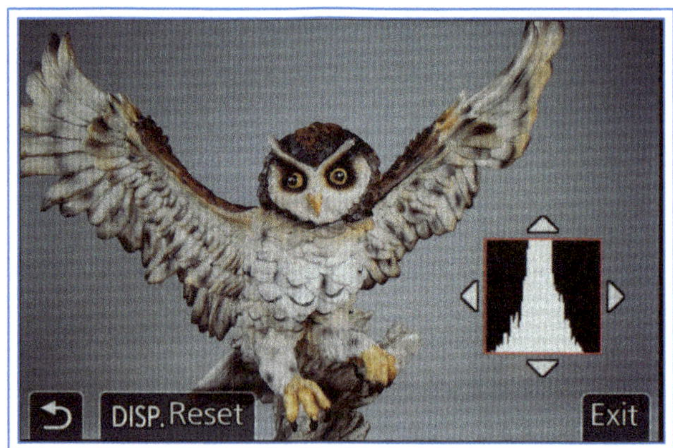

Figure 7-30. Histogram When Ready to Be Moved

You can move it with the cursor buttons or by dragging it on the touch screen. Once you have it located where you want it, press the shutter button halfway down to lock it in place. While it is movable, press the Display button to reset it to the center of the display. If you need to move it after it has been locked in place, you can touch it on the screen to reactivate it for moving. Or, you can go back to this menu option and select On for the Histogram item.

The histogram is an approximation, and you should not rely on it too heavily. It provides some information as to how evenly exposed your image is likely to be. (Or, for playback, how well exposed it was.) If the histogram is displayed in orange, that means the recording and playback versions of the histogram will not match for this image, because the flash was used, or in a few other situations.

Guide Line

This option lets you set grid lines to be displayed on the LCD screen (or in the electronic viewfinder) to assist you with the composition of your pictures. Once you select Guide Line from the Custom menu, you get to a screen with four options: Off, and three patterns of lines, as shown in Figure 7-31.

If you choose Off, no grid lines will be displayed. If you choose the top option, the camera will display a grid that forms nine equal rectangles on the screen. This choice can help you line up subjects, including the horizon, along straight lines. The second option is a pattern of 16 rectangles along with a pair of intersecting diagonal lines, which can help you locate your subject along diagonals as well as along horizontal or vertical lines. Finally, with the third option, the camera displays just two intersecting lines, one horizontal and one vertical, and lets you set their positions using the direction buttons or the touch screen. This option can be useful if you need to compose your shot with an off-center subject.

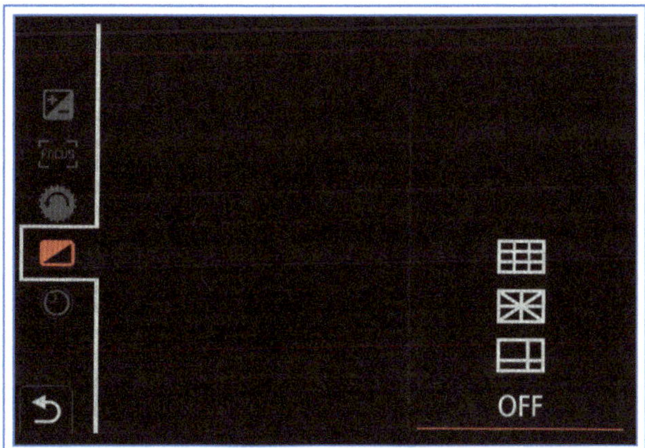

Figure 7-31. Guide Line Menu Options Screen

When any of the Guide Line options is turned on, the grid lines will display whenever the camera is in recording mode, regardless of the shooting mode. They will not display when you select the display screen that is blank. An example of the second option as displayed in shooting mode is shown in Figure 7-32.

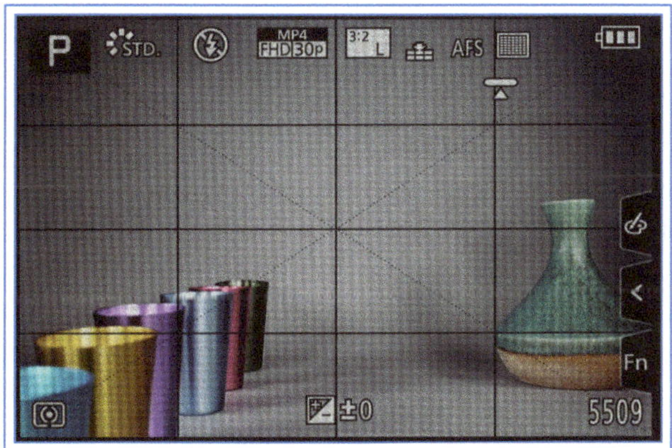

Figure 7-32. Second Option for Guide Line in Use

The next menu options are on screen 5 of the Custom menu, shown in Figure 7-33.

Center Marker

This option, when turned on, places a small cross in the center of the display, as shown in Figure 7-34, to help you keep the subject centered.

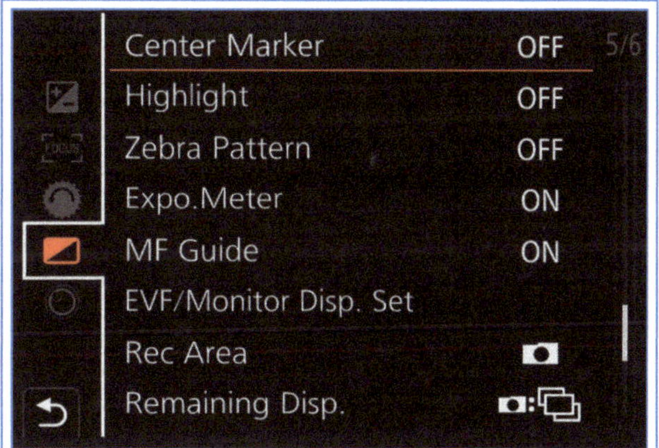

Figure 7-33. Screen 5 of Custom Menu

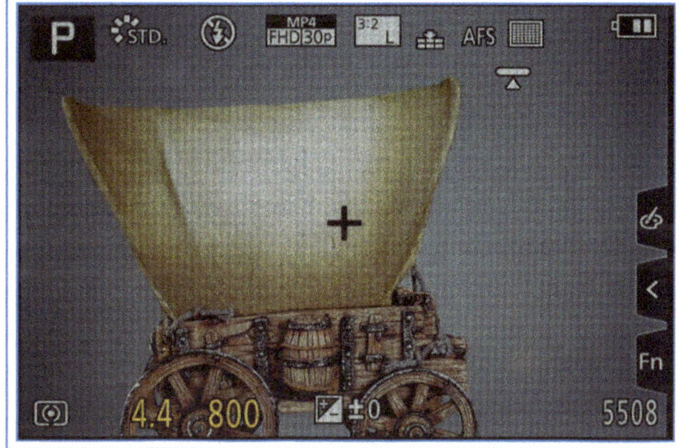

Figure 7-34. Center Marker in Use

This option can be particularly useful when recording video, because you may be distracted by the action and this marker may remind you to keep the most important part of the scene in a safe zone near the center of the display so it won't accidentally be cut off. This cross appears in all shooting modes and on all display screens that include the live view in recording mode.

Highlight

This feature produces a flashing area of black and white on areas of the image that are oversaturated with white, indicating they may be too bright. The flashing effect takes place only when you are viewing the pictures in Auto Review or Playback mode, on the LCD or in the viewfinder. That is, you will see the Highlight warning only when the image appears briefly on the screen after it has been recorded (Auto Review) or when you view the picture in Playback mode. This feature alerts you that the image may be washed out (overexposed) in some areas, so you may want to reduce the exposure for the next shot. If you find that sort of warning distracting, just turn this feature off. The flashing does not occur on one playback screen that shows the image only, with no information. So, even if this option is turned on, you can see your image without the flashing, by pressing the Display button to view that screen.

Zebra Pattern

This feature helps you gauge whether an image or video will be overexposed by setting the C-Lux to place a striped "zebra" pattern on the display in recording mode. You can select either left-slanting or right-slanting stripes to match the scene as well as possible, and you can set either type of stripes to a numerical value from 50% to 105% in 5% increments. For Zebra2, though, you can also choose Off for the value. I will discuss the reason for that setting later in this section.

The numbers from 50 to 105 are a measure of relative brightness or exposure on a scale where 0 represents black and 100 represents bright white. A value of 100 or 105 indicates overexposure. To make the settings, select the menu option and pop up the menu with sub-options of Zebra1, Zebra2, Off, and Set, as shown in Figure 7-35.

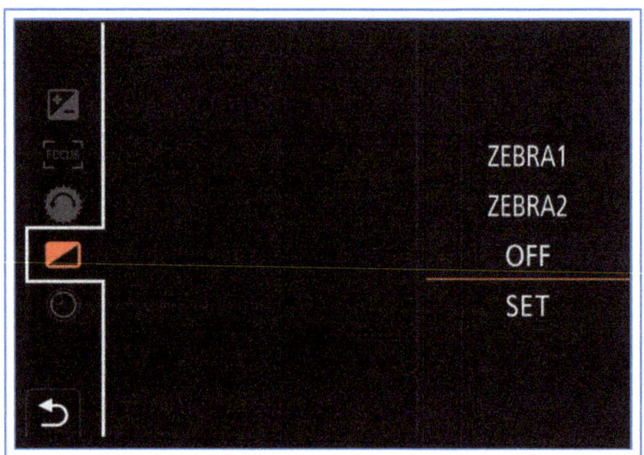

Figure 7-35. Zebra Pattern Menu Options Screen

Zebra1 generates stripes that slant from lower left to upper right and appear to move down to the right; Zebra2 generates stripes in the opposite direction. Use the Set option to set a numerical level for either Zebra1 or Zebra2, and then choose Zebra1 or Zebra2 from the menu to display that pattern on the screen.

When you turn this option on to any level less than about 90, you very likely will see, on some parts of the display, the "zebra" stripes that give this feature its name. When you see the stripes on part of the image, that means that area is at or above the brightness level that was set for the stripes. For example, if you select stripes set to the 65% level and aim the camera at the scene, the stripes will appear on any part of the display where the brightness level reaches 65% of bright white.

There are various approaches to using these stripes, which originated as a tool for professional videographers. Some photographers like to set the zebra function to 90% and adjust the camera's exposure so the stripes just barely start to appear in the brightest parts of the image. Another recommendation is to set the option to 75% for a scene with Caucasian skin, and expose so that the stripes appear in the area of the skin.

In Figure 7-36, I set the pattern to Zebra1 at 65% and exposed to have stripes appear on the subject's face.

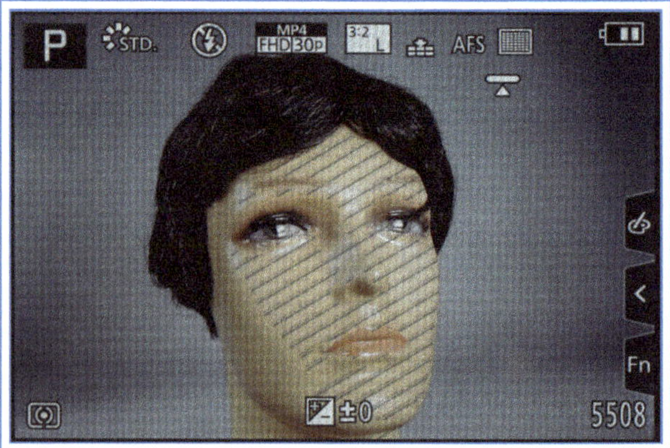

Figure 7-36. Zebra1 Pattern Set to 65%

As I noted earlier in this section, for Zebra2, you can set the brightness to any value from 50 to 105, and also to Off, which is not available for Zebra1. The reason for this setting is that, if you assign Zebra Pattern to a function button, when you press that button the camera cycles from Zebra1 to Zebra2 and then to Off. If you want to be able to turn Zebra on and off in the quickest way possible, you can set Zebra2 to a value of Off, so pressing the button will immediately switch from Zebra1 (at a numerical value) to Zebra2, which will be equivalent to Off.

Zebra Pattern is a feature to consider, especially for video recording, but the C-Lux has an excellent metering system, including both live and playback histograms, so you can manage without this option if you don't want to deal with its learning curve.

Exposure Meter

This feature gives you the option of having the camera display its Exposure Meter feature, which is a set of two graphical strips that appear when you are adjusting shutter speed, aperture, or Program Shift, as shown in Figure 7-37. The top strip shows the shutter speed value and the bottom one displays the aperture setting.

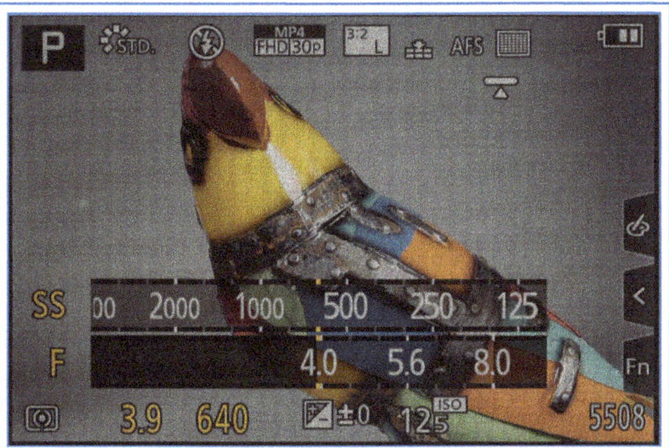

Figure 7-37. Exposure Meter Display for Program Shift

I find this display distracting and not all that helpful, so I leave it turned off, but you might find it useful in some situations.

MF Guide

If this option is turned on, then, when you are turning the control ring to adjust manual focus, the camera displays a scale at the bottom of the screen with an indicator that shows the approximate focus distance along the scale from far to near, with no numerical value for the distance. With this option turned off, the scale does not appear. An example of the scale is shown in Figure 7-38.

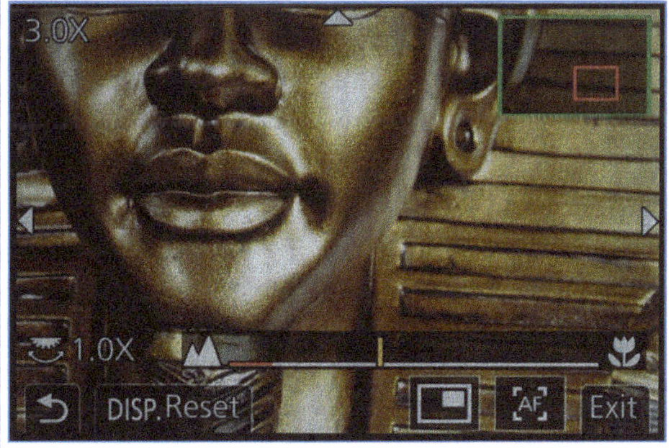

Figure 7-38. MF Guide Display on Shooting Screen

EVF/Monitor Display Settings

This menu item has two sub-options, EVF Display Setting and Monitor Display Setting, as shown in Figure 7-39, that let you adjust to some extent the display of information on the LCD screen and in the viewfinder.

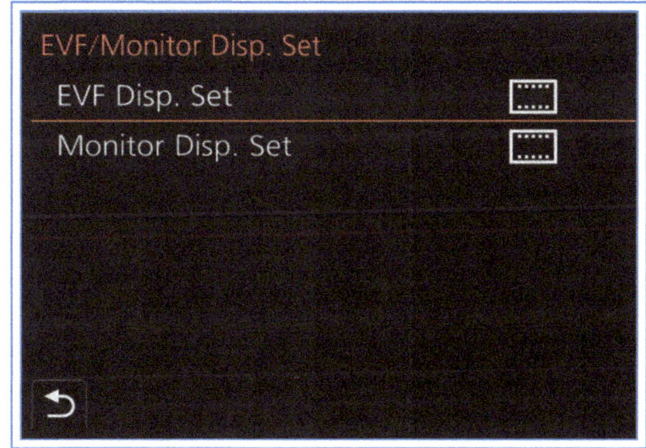

Figure 7-39. EVF/Monitor Display Settings Menu Options Screen

EVF Display Setting

This first sub-option controls how informational icons are displayed in the viewfinder. There are two choices, indicated by graphic icons, as shown in Figure 7-40.

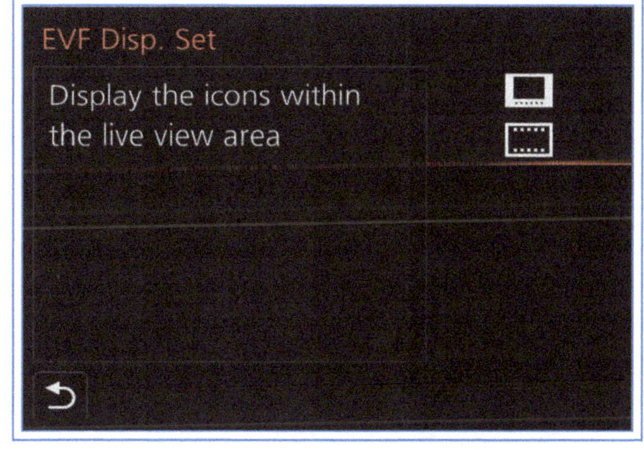

Figure 7-40. EVF Display Setting Menu Options Screen

With the top choice, known as live viewfinder style, several icons, including those for Metering Mode, ISO, exposure compensation, and number of images remaining, are displayed below the live view area, so you can see more of the live view with no icons blocking it. The view of the image is scaled down, letting you judge its composition more clearly. With the bottom choice, known as monitor style, all icons are placed within the live view area and that area extends farther down to accommodate them. The view of the image is slightly larger, letting you see details more clearly. I find the differences between these views to be minimal, but this is one way to tweak the viewfinder's operation.

Monitor Display Setting

This option is the same as the previous one, except that it applies to the LCD display, rather than the viewfinder. For this setting, I prefer the bottom option, which places all of the icons within the live view of the image, so you have a slightly larger view of the scene. I find that the icons do not significantly block the view.

Recording Area

This option lets you set the camera's recording screen to display either the recording area used for still photos or the area used for motion pictures. For still photos, that area is determined by the aspect ratio setting; for motion pictures, it is 16:9 for all settings.

The reason for having this menu option available is that the C-Lux does not ordinarily show the area available for motion picture recording until you press the red video button to start the recording. So, if the aspect ratio menu option is set for, say, 3:2, you will not see the actual shape of the motion picture recording screen until the recording starts, so you will not be able to compose the scene on the camera's monitor or in the viewfinder properly. But, if you set the Recording Area menu option to the Motion Picture option, then you will see the available recording area on the camera's screen before you start the recording.

The choice here depends on whether you are planning to capture still images or record motion picture sequences in your shooting session. To make the choice, just use this menu item to select the icon for the still camera or the icon for a movie camera.

Remaining Display

This feature lets you choose whether the camera's shooting screen shows how much video can be recorded with current settings in hours and minutes, or the number of still images that can be recorded, as shown in Figure 7-41, where the display in the lower right corner of the screen shows that number as 5508.

As shown in Figure 7-42, there are two options, illustrated graphically: the top option selects the display of still images remaining, while the bottom one selects the amount of video recording time available.

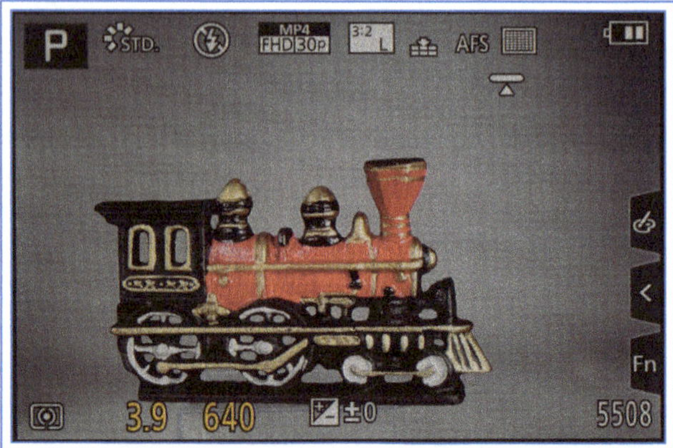

Figure 7-41. Remaining Display in Use on Shooting Screen

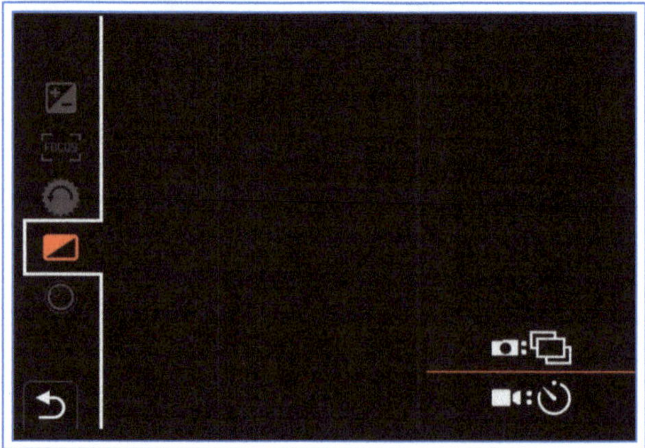

Figure 7-42. Remaining Display Menu Options Screen

As with the previous menu option, the choice depends on whether you are shooting mostly stills or videos.

Screen 6 of the Custom menu is shown in Figure 7-43.

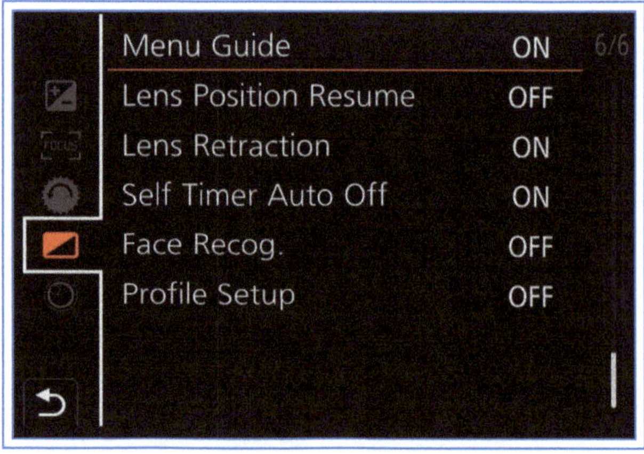

Figure 7-43. Screen 6 of Custom Menu

Menu Guide

This option determines what screen is displayed when you turn the mode dial to select Scene mode or Creative Control mode. If Menu Guide is turned on, then, when you turn the dial to the SCN or artist's palette position, the camera displays the selection screen for that mode. For example, if you turn the mode dial to the Creative Control position with this option turned on, the camera will display a screen like that shown in Figure 7-44, where you can immediately select a setting for this mode. For Scene mode, the camera displays the selection screen for choosing one of the numerous scene settings.

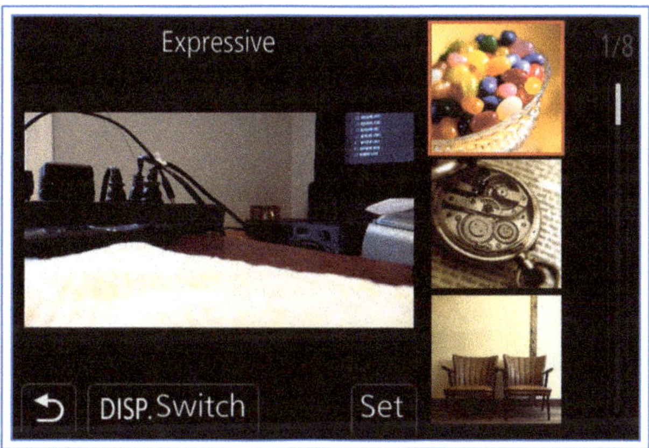

Figure 7-44. Menu Guide Display for Creative Control Mode

If this menu option is turned off, then, when the mode dial is turned to one of those two settings, the camera displays the recording screen, so you will be ready to start shooting an image or video without pausing to select a scene type or filter effect first.

What setting you choose for this option depends on whether you are likely to want to change the setting for either of these modes when you first select it. It is easy to change the setting from the recording screen; you can just touch the setting's icon in the upper left corner of the screen to bring up the selection screen, so I tend to leave Menu Guide turned off.

Lens Position Resume

If you turn on this option, then, after you turn the camera off and back on, the lens will return to its last zoom position and focus position. If this setting is turned off, the lens will zoom out to its 24mm setting when the power is turned on. This option is convenient if you need to use a particular focal length, such as 50mm, for a series of shots that will be interrupted by turning the camera off for periods of time. The focus position is restored for either autofocus or manual focus.

Lens Retraction

This menu option lets you control whether or not the lens automatically retracts about 15 seconds after the camera enters playback mode. If you turn this option off, then the lens does not retract in that situation; if it is turned on, the retraction takes place. I usually leave this option turned on, but if you want to alternate between reviewing your images in playback mode and taking more images, you might want to turn this option off so the lens does not have to extend repeatedly every time you return to recording mode.

Self Timer Auto Off

This next option controls whether the self-timer remains set after you turn the camera off and back on. If this option is turned on, then, when the camera turns off, the self-timer will be deactivated and will not be in effect when the camera is turned on the next time. If this option is turned off, then the self-timer will remain in effect even after the camera has been powered off.

How you use this feature depends on your particular needs. If you often use the self-timer, it can be convenient to leave it activated so it will be ready the next time you turn on the camera. Or, if you use it rarely, you can turn this option on so the self-timer will not be in effect when you don't want it.

Face Recognition

With the Face Recognition option, you can register the faces of up to six people so the camera will recognize them when Face Recognition is turned on. Here are the essential steps to follow.

Figure 7-45. Memory Option Highlighted for Face Recognition

First, go to the Face Recognition menu item and select the third option, Memory, as shown in Figure 7-45.

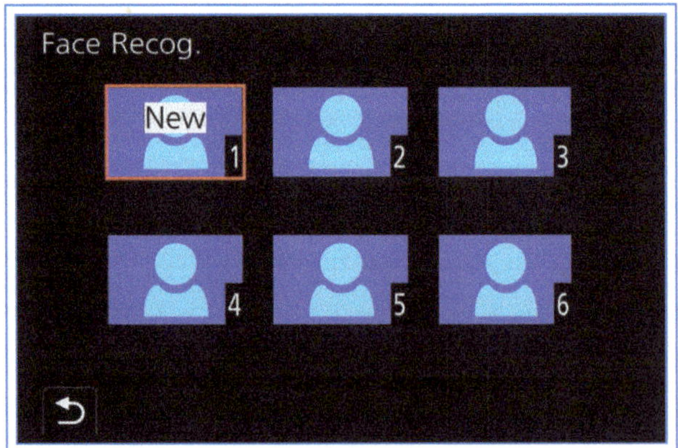

Figure 7-46. Screen to Select Block for New Face

Press Menu/Set (or use the touch screen) to go to the screen with six blue blocks, shown in Figure 7-46. Move the red highlight frame to the first available blue block that says New, and press Menu/Set; you will see the screen shown in Figure 7-47, which prompts you to position the face to be registered in the yellow frame.

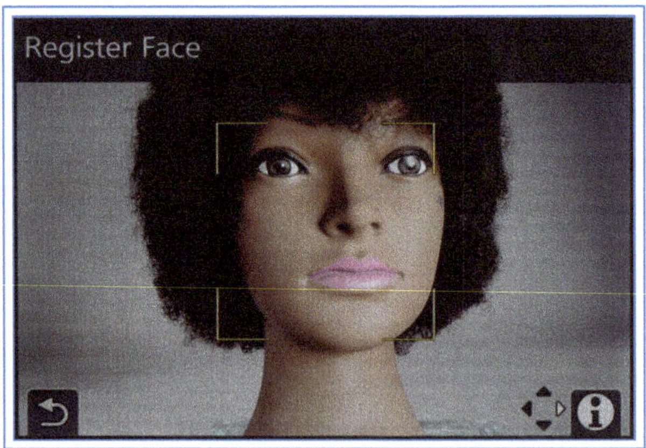

Figure 7-47. Screen to Photograph New Face to Register

When you have the face properly positioned, press the shutter button to take a picture. If the registration fails, you will see an error message. If it succeeds, you will see a screen like that in Figure 7-48. You can then proceed to enter data for the person, including name and birthdate.

Once you have one or more faces registered, you can turn Face Recognition on through this item on the Recording menu whenever you want the camera to try to recognize those faces. You also have to have AF Mode set to Face/Eye Detection on screen 1 of the Recording menu for the camera to use face recognition.

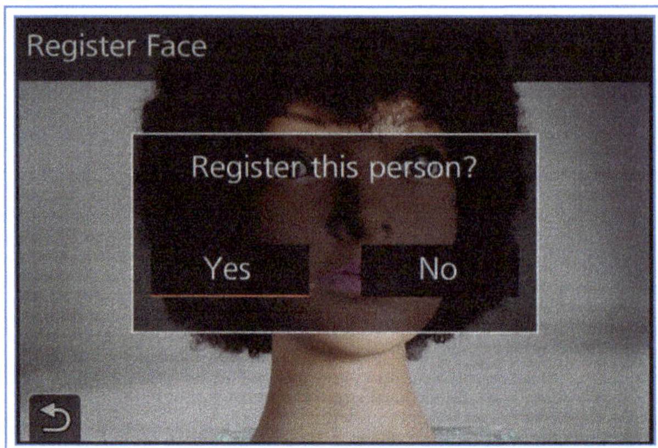

Figure 7-48. Screen When Face Successfully Registered

When the camera recognizes a face, it will place a frame over the face and display the name, if one was entered into the camera's memory, as shown in Figure 7-49.

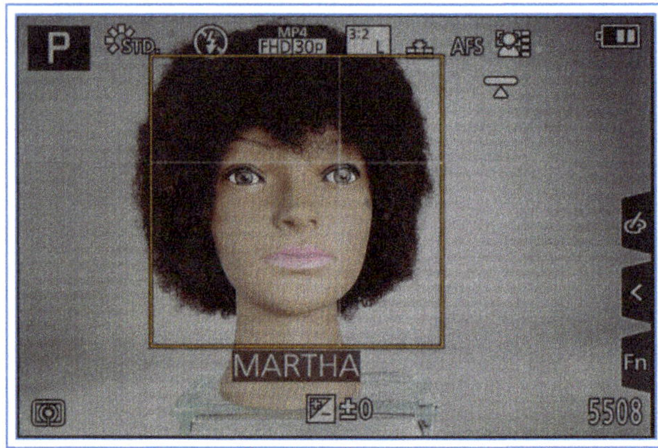

Figure 7-49. Screen When Camera Recognizes Face

The camera will adjust its focus and exposure for the recognized face or faces. It can recognize up to three faces at a time. When the image is played back, the camera will display the name and age of the person briefly, though that information does not become part of the image.

If you want, you can add additional images for any person, taken from different angles and in different lighting, to increase the camera's ability to recognize that person. To do that, choose the Memory option and then select the person for whom you want to add images. You also can edit the person's information, including name and birthdate.

I do not often use this feature, but I can appreciate how useful it could be if, for example, you are taking photos at a school event and you want to make sure the camera focuses on your child when you are aiming at a group of children.

If you don't want the camera to use face recognition, just turn this menu item off.

Profile Setup

This final option on the Custom menu lets you create profiles for two babies and one pet, so the camera will display the name and age of the baby or pet when you take a picture of him or her. For example, you can enter a profile for a baby named Charles, born December 16, 2018. When you take a picture of Charles, you can recall that profile and the camera will display his name and age as of the date the picture is taken. So, if you take his picture on June 20, 2020, with his profile activated, the camera will display: Charles 1 year 8 months. This information will be recorded with the image and it will display in playback mode with the detailed information screen, but it will not become a permanent part of the image unless you take further steps.

To imprint the information on the image, you can use the Text Stamp option on the Playback menu, as discussed in Chapter 6.

This menu option does not cause the camera to recognize a pet or baby; it just lets you call up the profile you have entered for Baby 1, Baby 2, or Pet. So, you actually could enter any name and birthdate in any of those three profiles. When you call up the profile and take a picture with the profile activated, the camera will record the name and age, regardless of the actual subject matter of the image.

The Setup Menu

The Setup menu, designated by the solitary wrench icon, has four screens of options for adjusting settings having to do with general camera functions. Its first screen is shown in Figure 7-50.

Custom Set Memory

This feature gives you a way to quickly change several shooting parameters without having to remember them or use menus or physical controls to set them. The camera lets you save three different groups of settings, each of which can be recalled instantly using the Custom (C) position on the mode dial, shown in Figure 7-51.

Here is how this works. First, you need to have the camera set to recording mode rather than playback mode, so if it's in playback mode, press the shutter button halfway or press the playback button to exit to recording mode. Then, set the camera to Program, Aperture Priority, Shutter Priority, Manual exposure, Scene, Panorama, Creative Control, or Creative Video mode. (You can't use the Custom Set Memory feature in Snapshot or Snapshot Plus mode.)

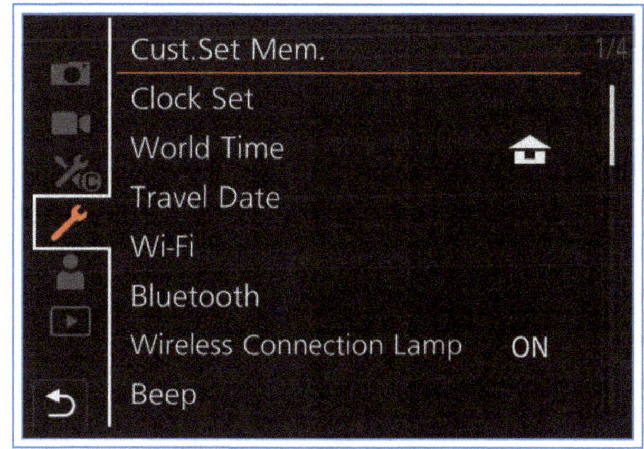

Figure 7-50. Screen 1 of Setup Menu

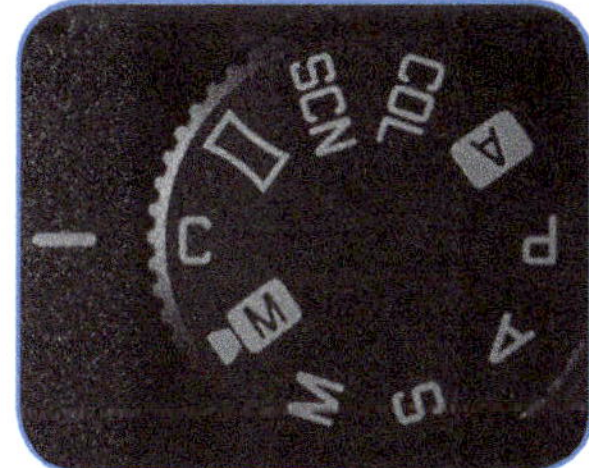

Figure 7-51. Mode Dial at C

Next, make all of the menu settings that you want to have stored for quick recall, such as Photo Style, ISO, focus mode, metering mode, i.Dynamic, and the like. Your custom set can include all of the items on the Recording Menu; all items on the Custom Menu except settings for Menu Guide, Face Recognition, and Profile Setup; and all items on the Motion Picture menu. You also can includes items from the special menus that are available in the Panorama, Scene, Creative Control, and Creative Video modes.

You cannot include settings for the Rotate Display and Picture Sort settings on the Playback menu, and you cannot include any items from the Setup menu. You can include white balance and drive mode, even though they are not set from the menu. Of course, you cannot add inconsistent settings. For example, you cannot adjust white balance if you have selected a filter effect. So, if you try to add both a white balance setting and a filter effect setting to a saved group, only the filter effect setting will be effective.

Once you have all of the settings as you want them, leave them that way and go to the Setup menu. Navigate to Custom Set Memory and select it, which gives you choices of C1, C2, and C3, as shown in Figure 7-52.

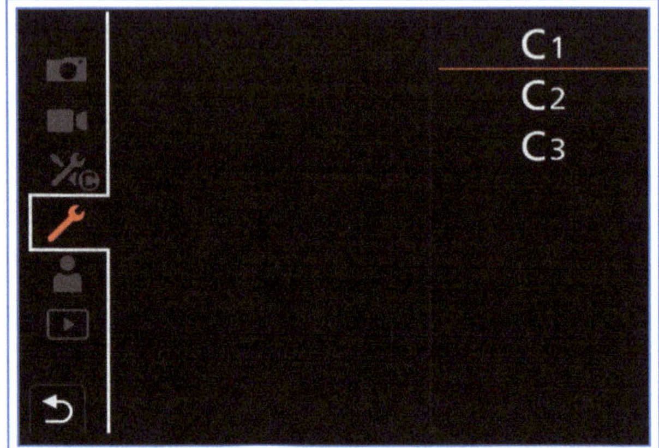

Figure 7-52. Screen to Save Slot for Custom Set Memory

Highlight the slot you want to save your settings in and press Menu/Set. The camera will display a message asking you to confirm this action; highlight Yes and select it to confirm.

When, at a later time, you want to use your set of saved settings, turn the mode dial to the C position and press the Menu/Set button. On the sub-menu that appears, shown in Figure 7-53, select C1, C2, or C3. You also can press the shooting mode icon in the upper left corner of the display and select a new C slot. Once you have selected the custom mode you want, you are still free to change the camera's settings, but those changes will not be saved into the Custom Set Memory unless you go back to the Setup menu and save the changes there with the Custom Set Memory option.

Although it has some limitations, Custom Set Memory is a powerful capability, and anyone who has or develops some favorite groups of settings would be well advised to experiment with this option and take advantage of its power.

Clock Set

When you use your C-Lux camera for the first time, it should prompt you to set the clock. If it does not do so, or if you later need to adjust the date and time, use this menu option. When you select it and press the Right button or Menu/Set, the camera will display a screen like that shown in Figure 7-54.

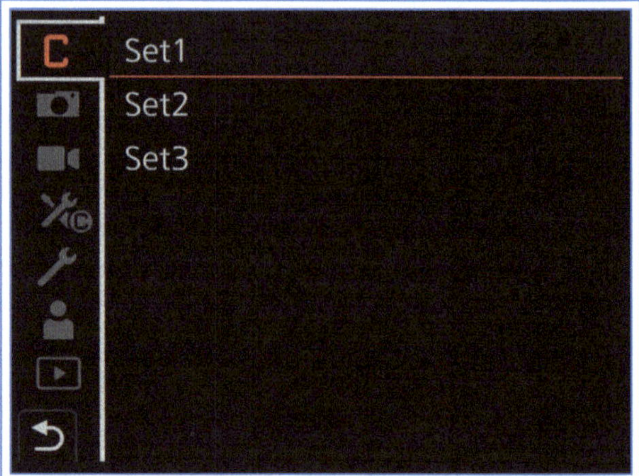

Figure 7-53. Screen to Recall Custom Set Memory Slot

On that screen, navigate through the blocks for time and date using the thumb dial, the Left and Right buttons, or the touch screen, and adjust the settings with the Up and Down buttons or icons. You can then highlight the Style block to select the order for month, day, and year and whether to use 24-hour format for the time. When everything is set properly, navigate to the Set block in the lower right corner of the display and select it to confirm the settings. (The Set block appears only if some change has been made.)

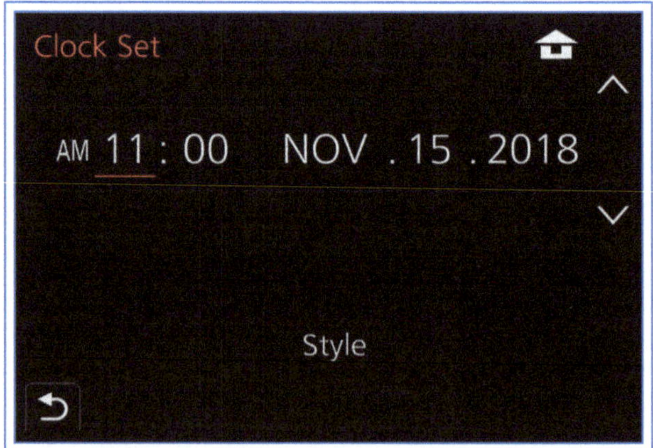

Figure 7-54. Date and Time Settings Screen

World Time

This is a handy function when you're traveling to another time zone. Highlight and select World Time to move to the next screen, which gives you the options of choosing Destination and Home. First, select Home and use the Left and Right buttons, the thumb dial, or the touch arrows to scroll through the world map as shown in Figure 7-55, and use the Menu/Set button or touch the Set icon to set your Home area.

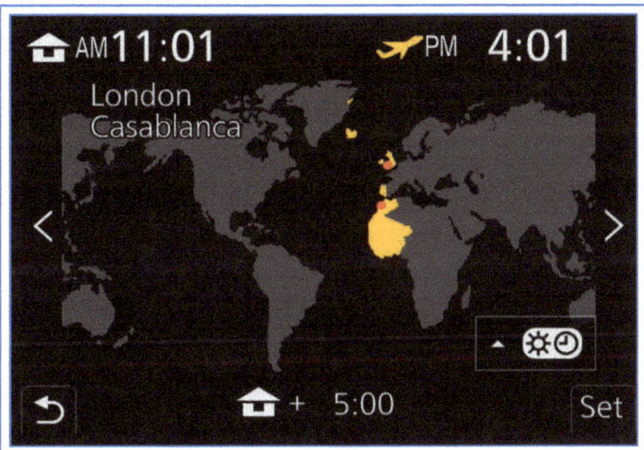

Figure 7-55. World Time Map Screen

Then, on the World Time screen, highlight Destination, and again scroll through the world map to select the time zone you will be traveling to. The map will show you the time in both locations. Press Menu/Set or touch the Set icon to select this zone for the camera's internal clock. Then, any images taken will reflect the correct time in the new time zone. When you return from your trip, go back to the World Time item and select Home to cancel the changed time zone setting.

On both the Home and Destination screens, you can press the Up button or touch the sun and clock icon in the lower right corner to turn Daylight Saving Time on or off for that time zone.

Travel Date

This menu item has two sub-options for entering information when you take a trip, so the camera can record that information with your images. First, Travel Setup lets you set a range of dates for the trip, so the camera can record which day of the trip each image was taken. When you return from the trip, if you use the Text Stamp function to "stamp" the recorded data on the images, the images will show they were taken on Day 1, Day 2, etc., of the trip. In addition, the camera will remind you of how many days remain before your trip, by displaying notations such as - 3 Days, etc., until the date of the trip arrives. The date entries for Travel Setup are self-explanatory; just follow the arrows and the camera's prompts.

After you set departure and return dates, you also can set the location, which will display along with the day number. To do that, after setting up the dates, select Location from the Travel Date menu item, enter the name of the location using the text-entry tools, and select Set from that screen, as shown in Figure 7-56.

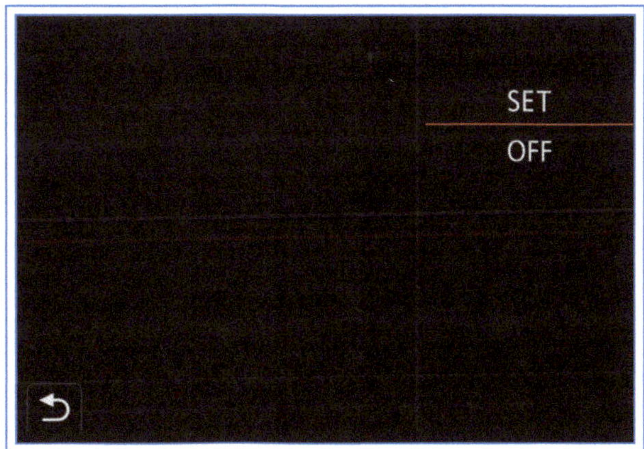

Figure 7-56. Screen to Set Travel Date Information

Wi-Fi

This option is used to set up a Wi-Fi connection with the C-Lux. I will discuss the Wi-Fi operations of the camera in Chapter 9.

Bluetooth

This option is used to set up a Bluetooth connection with the camera. As with the previous option, I will discuss this topic in Chapter 9.

Wireless Connection Lamp

This option lets you set whether the blue connection lamp located between the Fn2 and Playback buttons will light up when the camera is establishing or maintaining a Wi-Fi or Bluetooth connection. If this option is turned off, the lamp will not light for that purpose.

Beep

This last option on screen 1 of the Setup menu lets you adjust several sound items, as shown in Figure 7-57. First is the volume of the beeps the camera makes when you press a button, such as when half-pressing the shutter button to evaluate focus. You can set the beeps to off, normal, or loud. It's useful to be able to turn the beeps off if you're going to be in an environment where such noises are not welcome.

Second is the volume of the shutter operation sound. Again, it's good to be able to mute the shutter sound. Finally, you can choose from three shutter tones. If you want to silence all sounds quickly while also disabling the flash and the AF assist lamp, use the Silent Mode option on screen 4 of the Recording menu.

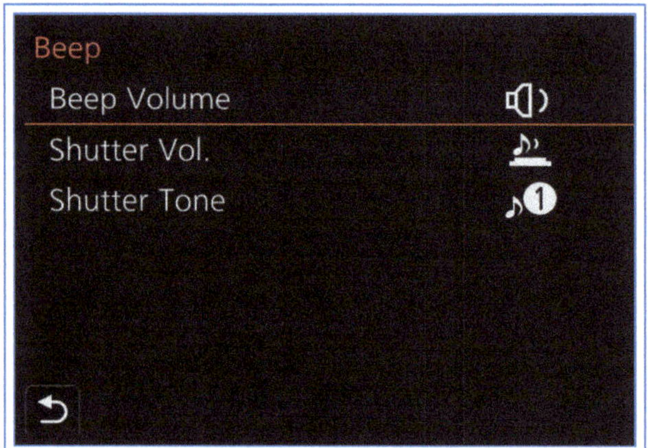

Figure 7-57. Beep Menu Options Screen

Screen 2 of the Setup menu is shown in Figure 7-58.

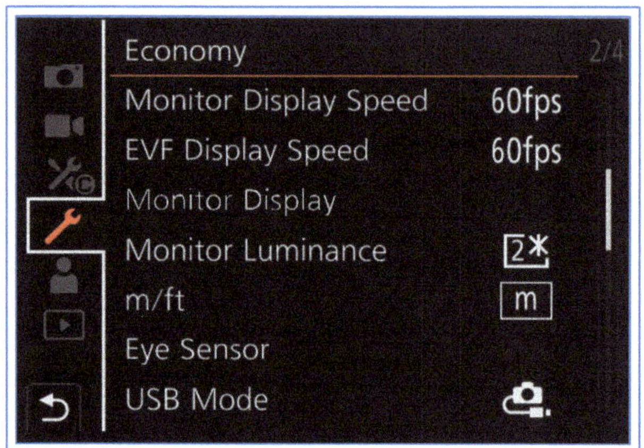

Figure 7-58. Screen 2 of Setup Menu

Economy

The next option on the Setup menu, Economy, has three sub-options: Sleep Mode, Sleep Mode (Wi-Fi), and Auto Monitor Off.

Sleep Mode

The Sleep Mode option puts the camera into a dormant state after a specified period when you have not used any of the camera's controls. The period can be set to one, two, five, or ten minutes, or the option can be turned off, in which case the camera never turns off automatically (unless it runs out of battery power). To cancel Sleep Mode, press the shutter button halfway and the camera will come back to life. Sleep Mode does not turn off the camera during a slide show or when an AC adapter is connected, or during the recording or playback of a motion picture, along with a few other situations.

Sleep Mode (Wi-Fi)

With this setting, the camera goes dormant after 15 minutes, but only if there is no Wi-Fi connection active. This setting is useful if you are using the camera for transferring images or another activity using a wireless network connection, which may require the camera to sit for fairly long periods without any controls being activated. If there is no Wi-Fi connection active, there is no need to let the camera stay active, so it can be powered down.

Auto EVF/Monitor Off

The Auto EVF/Monitor Off setting controls how soon the viewfinder or monitor turns off when no controls have been used for a time. The possible choices are five minutes, two minutes, or one minute. After the display goes blank, you can press any control button or touch the screen to restore the display. As with the Sleep Mode setting, this setting does not operate during slide shows, during a Time Lapse Shot session, and in a few other situations.

Monitor Display Speed

This option lets you choose either 60 fps (frames per second) or Eco30 fps for the operation of the camera's LCD display screen. The setting of Eco30 fps reduces battery use, but the display may not always refresh quickly enough to keep up with a fast-moving subject. In addition, with some settings, such as the Rough Monochrome or Silky Monochrome settings, the display slows down as the camera processes the effect. If you choose the 60 fps setting, the display will be better able to show any action smoothly, or to maintain a smooth appearance as you pan across the scene. The quality of the display may suffer slightly, but not badly. So, if you find the display stuttering or smearing, you may want to try the 60 fps option.

If you have this item set to Eco30fps, the Digital Zoom option is not available. The Eco30fps setting is not available when the camera is in Creative Video mode or when it is recording 4K photos or using Post Focus.

EVF Display Speed

This setting is similar to the above item, but it applies to the viewfinder rather than the LCD screen. Again, with the Eco30fps in effect for this setting, Digital

Zoom is not available for use, and the other restrictions on the use of the Eco30fps option apply as well.

Monitor Display/Viewfinder

This menu option is unusual because its name changes depending on whether you are viewing the menu on the LCD monitor or in the viewfinder. If you are viewing it on the monitor, it is called Monitor Display; if you are using the viewfinder, it is called Viewfinder. It operates the same way in either case. However, if you make adjustments to this item while using the monitor, those adjustments will affect only the monitor. You can make separate adjustments while using the viewfinder, and those adjustments will affect only the viewfinder.

As shown in Figure 7-59, which shows the version for adjusting the monitor, this option has five linear scales for making adjustments. Use the Up and Down buttons or the touch screen icons to select a scale, and then use the Left and Right buttons, the thumb dial, or the touch screen to adjust the settings on the scale for each item. The normal settings are in the middle of the scale; move the red blocks to the left of the scale to decrease a setting, or to the right to increase the value.

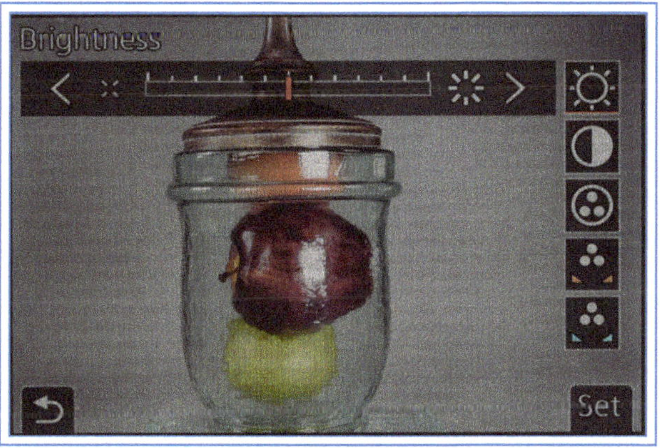

Figure 7-59. Monitor Display Adjustment Screen

Starting from the top, the scales control brightness, contrast, saturation, red tint, and blue tint. When you have made your adjustments on each scale, you have to press the Menu/Set button to make them take effect.

I have never found a need to adjust the settings for either the LCD display or the viewfinder, but if you find the color, contrast, or brightness of either display is not to your liking, you can use these adjustments as you wish.

Monitor Luminance

This setting affects the brightness of the LCD display, but not the viewfinder, though you can adjust it while using the viewfinder. This setting is different from the brightness setting of the previous menu option in that it provides overall, on-or-off adjustments, rather than a sliding scale. As shown in Figure 7-60, this menu item has four settings, each accompanied by an asterisk: A*, 1*, 2*, and 3*.

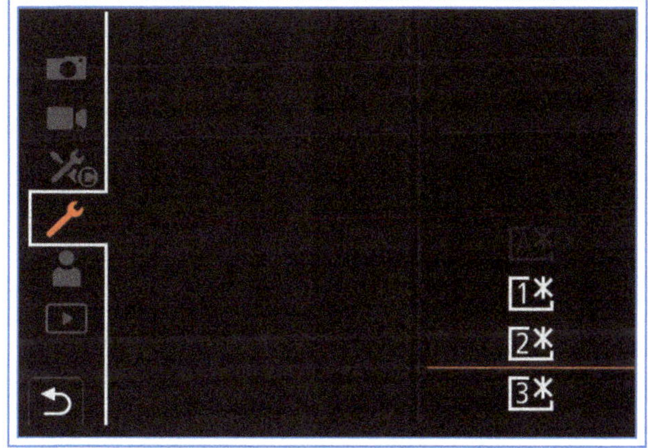

Figure 7-60. Monitor Luminance Menu Options Screen

With the A* (Auto) setting, the brightness will adjust according to ambient lighting conditions. With the 1* setting, the screen becomes extra-bright to compensate for sunlight or other conditions that make it hard to see the screen. It reverts to normal after 30 seconds, but you can press any control button to restore the brightness. The 2* setting provides standard illumination, and the 3* setting sets the display to a dimmer level than normal.

Using the A* or the 1* setting decreases battery life. If you find it hard to see the screen in bright sunlight and don't want to use the viewfinder, you might want to try the 1* setting to see if the added brightness gives you enough visibility to compose your shots or view your recorded images clearly.

I use the A* setting myself, and always keep an extra battery handy.

M/FT

This option lets you choose whether distance is displayed using meters or feet as the unit of measure on the zoom scale.

Eye Sensor

This next item on the Setup menu has two sub-options with controls for the operation of the eye sensor, the small slot at the right of the viewfinder that detects the presence of your eye (or another object). Those sub-options are Sensitivity and EVF/Monitor Switch, as shown in Figure 7-61.

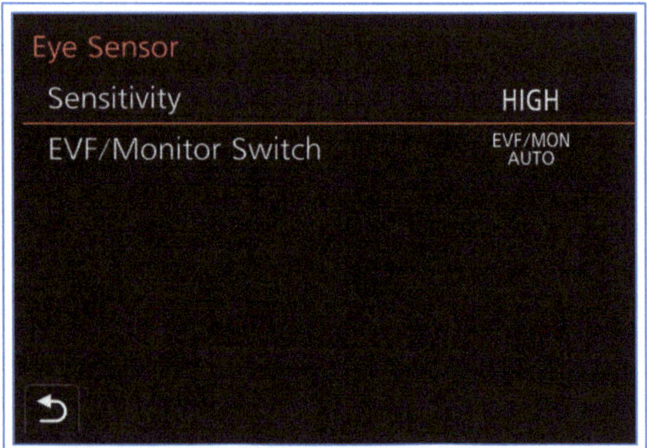

Figure 7-61. Eye Sensor Menu Options Screen

You can set Sensitivity to High or Low. I have not found much difference between these settings. If you find that the eye sensor is triggering the switch from LCD to viewfinder when you don't want it to, you can try setting this option to Low to see if that helps.

The other setting for Eye Sensor is EVF/Monitor Switch. There are three possible choices for this item: EVF/Monitor Auto, EVF, and Monitor. With the first choice, the camera will switch automatically between the LCD screen and the viewfinder as your eye approaches or moves away from the eye sensor. If you choose EVF, the viewfinder will always be in use; if you choose Monitor, the LCD display will always be in use.

I find it convenient to use the EVF/Monitor Auto option, so the camera will switch to using the viewfinder whenever my head comes near to the viewfinder. However, in some cases, such as if you are doing close-up shots from a tripod, you might want to leave the monitor always in use, even though your head may come near to the camera as you adjust a setting. Or, you might want to set the viewfinder to be in effect at all times when you don't want to have the LCD display illuminate to distract those around you.

You can also switch the behavior of the eye sensor by pressing the Fn4/EVF button, assuming it remains assigned to this option. (You can assign another button to this option if you want, but it makes sense to leave the Fn4 button with this duty, because it is located next to the eye sensor.)

USB Mode

If you are going to connect the camera directly to a computer or printer, you need to go to this menu item and select the appropriate setting from the choices shown in Figure 7-62: Select on Connection, PC (Storage), or PictBridge (PTP) (for connecting to a printer). PTP stands for Picture Transfer Protocol, a standard used for this type of connection.

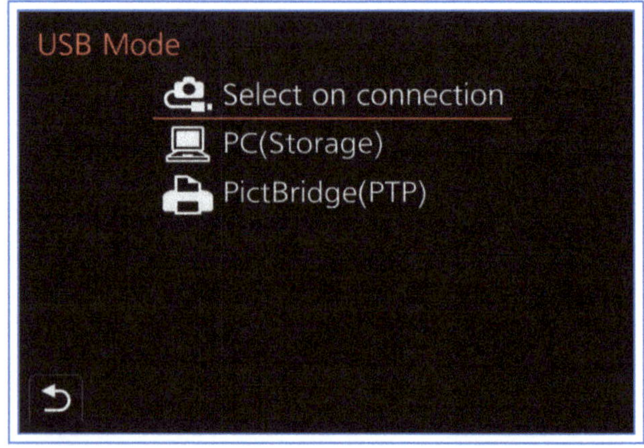

Figure 7-62. USB Connection Menu Options Screen

If you choose Select on Connection, you don't select the setting until after you have plugged the USB cable into the device to which you are connecting the camera. The C-Lux connects to a computer using the USB 2.0 connection standard, assuming your computer has a USB port of that speed. (If not, the camera will still connect at the slower speed of the computer's older USB port.)

Screen 3 of the Setup menu is shown in Figure 7-63.

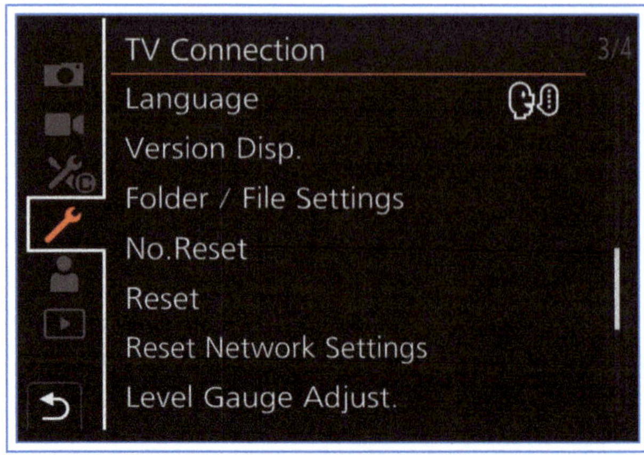

Figure 7-63. Screen 3 of Setup Menu

TV Connection

This menu item has three sub-options: HDMI Mode (Play), HDMI Info Display (Rec), and HDTV Link. The HDMI Mode option sets the output resolution for the images that are sent to an HDTV when the camera is connected to the TV with a micro-HDMI cable in playback mode. The available choices are Auto, 4K/30p, 1080p, 1080i, 720p, and 480p. Ordinarily, if you select Auto the images should appear properly on the HDTV. If they do not, you can try one of the other settings to see if the display improves.

The HDMI Info Display (Rec) option determines whether or not the camera outputs setting icons and other technical information when it is connected to an HDTV or other device, such as a video recorder or monitor, by a micro-HDMI cable in recording mode. If this option is set to On, then the signal that goes through the cable includes all of the information that appears on the camera's screen. If it is set to Off, then the signal going through the cable includes only the image or video (and audio, if applicable).

This option is of use when you are using the C-Lux to capture images while the camera is connected to a monitor. With this setting turned off, the signal sent to the monitor will include only the actual scenes viewed by the camera, rather than the setting icons, focus frames and other items that would not be wanted in the final images. However, this option's usefulness is limited because the C-Lux camera cannot output any signal through the HDMI port when it is recording video. So, although the camera can output a "clean" HDMI signal, that signal cannot originate with a video recording, only with recording of still images.

As a workaround for this issue, you can output a clean HDMI signal while the camera is in standby mode, when you have not pressed the video button to start video recording. In that mode, you can connect the camera to an external video recorder using a micro-HDMI cable, and the recorder can record the scene that is being viewed by the camera in standby mode.

I have done this successfully with an Atomos Shogun video recorder. With the HDMI Info Display option turned off, the recorder captured the scene viewed by the camera, with no icons or other extraneous information. The resulting video file was of excellent quality and could be readily imported into software for editing. However, it is expensive and cumbersome to use an external recorder, so this option is not one you necessarily would use often.

The HDTV Link option is for use when you are connecting the C-Lux to a compatible HDTV using a micro-HDMI cable. If you leave this option turned off, then the operations of the camera are controlled by the camera's own controls. If you turn it on, the HDTV's remote control can also control the operations of the camera, so you can play slide shows or review individual images and movies. This function may not work if the HDTV is not compatible with the HDTV Link protocol.

Language

This option gives you the choice of language for the display of commands and information on the LCD screen and in the viewfinder. Figure 7-64 shows the first of the five screens of the language selection option for my U.S. version of the camera.

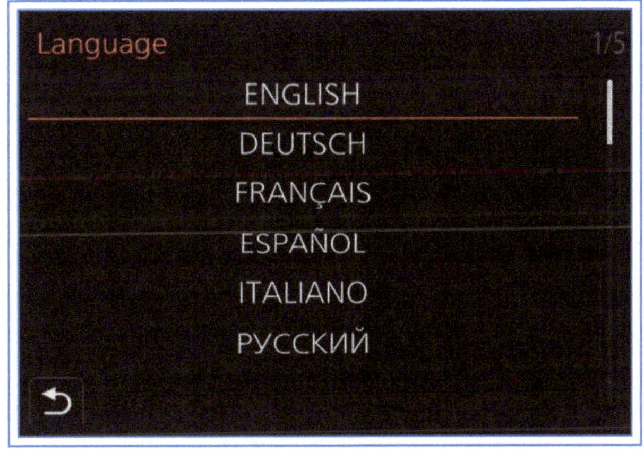

Figure 7-64. Language Selection Screen

Presumably, models sold elsewhere offer different choices. If your camera happens to be set to a language that you don't read, you can find the Language option by going into the Setup menu (look for the wrench icon), and then scrolling to this option, which is marked by an icon showing a person's head with a word balloon, as shown in Figure 7-63.

Version Display

This item has no settings; when you select it, it displays the version of the camera's firmware that is currently installed. As I write this, my C-Lux has version 1.0 of the firmware installed, as shown in Figure 7-65.

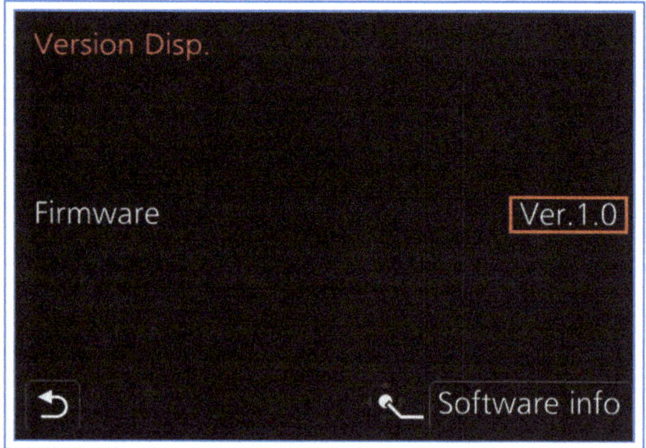

Figure 7-65. Firmware Version Display Screen

Figure 7-66. Select Folder Screen

Firmware is somewhat like both software and hardware; it is the programming electronically recorded into the camera, either at the factory or through your computer if you upgrade the firmware with an update provided by Leica. A new version of the firmware can fix bugs and can even provide new features, so it's well worthwhile checking the Leica website periodically for updates. Instructions for installing an update are provided on the website. The process usually involves downloading a file to your computer, saving that file to an SD card formatted for the camera, then placing that card in the camera so the firmware can be installed.

As of early December 2018, Leica had announced that it would be releasing a firmware update for the C-Lux in order to make it compatible with the company's new Fotos app for smartphones and tablets, but the firmware update was not available in time to obtain it and test it for this book. To check for this and other updates, go to the company's website at http://us.leica-camera.com/Photography/Compact-Cameras/Leica-C-Lux/Downloads.

Folder/File Settings

This menu item has three sub-options that let you control the camera's use of folders to store images and videos on the memory card in the camera.

Select Folder

When you select this option, the camera displays a screen like that in Figure 7-66 showing the names of folders that are currently available on the memory card in the camera.

On the right side of the display is the letter R for Remaining images, followed by a number indicating how many more items can be stored in that folder. (The maximum capacity of a folder is 1,000 files.) You can select the folder you want to use for storing any images you are about to create. This option can be useful if you need to separate business photos from personal ones, or travel ones from home ones, for example.

Create a New Folder

This option lets you create a new folder for storing images. This item has two sub-options: OK and Change. If you select OK, the camera will name the folder using the default label (which is LEICA for my camera). If you select Change, the camera will name the folder using a five-character label that you enter yourself. For example, the end result for the folder name can be in the form of 100LEICA, or, say, 100PARIS, to hold images from your trip to Paris. You enter the label using the same text-entry screen that was discussed earlier in connection with the Title Edit menu option on the Custom menu.

File Name Setting

This menu option has two sub-options for choosing how the camera names images: either Folder Number Link or User Setting, as shown in Figure 7-67. If you choose Folder Number Link (the default), a typical file name for an image stored in a folder named 102LEICA would be L1021430.jpg, with the number 102 in the file name taken from the folder number.

Figure 7-67. File Name Setting Menu Options Screen

If you choose User Setting, then you can specify any three characters (numbers, upper-case letters, or the underscore character) instead of the folder number. So, you could use your initials, or the date, or any other three-character string that would be useful to you. With the same example as above, if I chose my initials for the file name setting, the same image would be named LASW1430.jpg.

The first character of the file name will always be L or the underscore character, because those characters designate the color space setting for the image. L designates the sRGB color space, and the underscore character designates the Adobe RGB setting.

Number Reset

This function lets you reset the folder and image number for the next image to be recorded in the camera. If you don't use this option, the numbers of your images will keep increasing until they reach 999, even if you change to a different memory card. If you want each new card to start with images numbered from 1 up, use the Number Reset function each time you start a new card, or a new project for which you would like to have freshly numbered images. I prefer not to reset the numbers, because I find it easier to keep track of my images if the numbers keep getting larger; I would find it confusing to have images with duplicate numbers on my various SD cards.

Reset

This menu option resets all Recording menu and drive mode settings to their original states. It also resets all Setup and Custom menu settings to their original states, except for Face Recognition and Profile Setup settings, which can be reset separately using this option. This is a convenient way to get the camera back to its default mode, so you can start with fresh settings before you experiment with new ones. The camera prompts you several times, asking if you want to reset all Recording menu and drive mode settings; then all network settings; then all Face Recognition and Profile Setup settings; and then all other Setup/Custom menu parameters. Folder numbers and date and time settings are not reset by this option.

Reset Network Settings

This option resets all Wi-Fi and Bluetooth settings for the camera. You might want to use this option if you are selling your camera, to avoid giving away information about your wireless networks. You also might want to use this option if you are having trouble getting the Wi-Fi or Bluetooth settings configured and you want to make a fresh start.

Level Gauge Adjustment

This option gives you a way to make sure that the level gauge display is properly aligned. To use it, select the menu option, which will then display the screen shown in Figure 7-68, with choices for Adjustment and Level Gauge Value Reset. To make an adjustment, select the first option, and the camera will prompt you to place the camera on a surface that is known to be horizontal. When you press OK, the camera will display a screen with three horizontal lines and a Start icon. When the camera is set on a horizontal surface, press the Start icon on the screen or press the Menu/Set button, and the camera will carry out the adjustment.

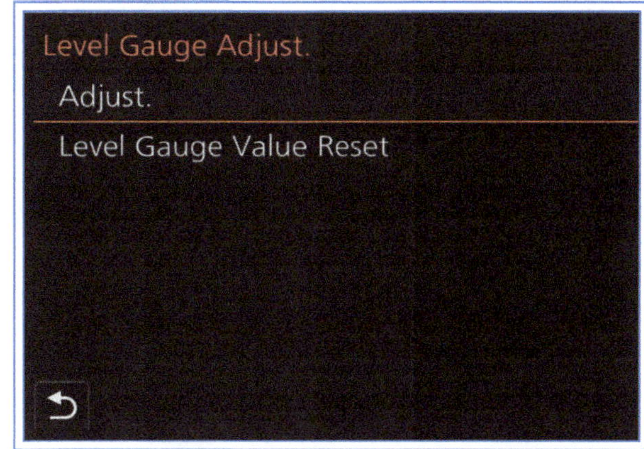

Figure 7-68. Level Gauge Adjustment Screen

If you later change your mind about using the adjusted calibration, select the second option, Level Gauge Value Reset, and the camera will restore its original default setting for the level gauge.

The fourth and final screen of the Setup menu is shown in Figure 7-69.

Figure 7-69. Screen 4 of Setup Menu

Format

This last item on the Setup menu is one of the more important menu options. Choose this process only when you want or need to completely wipe all of the data from a memory card. When you select the Format option, the camera will ask you if you want to delete all of the data on the card, as shown in Figure 7-70.

If you reply by selecting Yes, the camera will proceed to erase all images and videos, including any that have been locked using the Protect option on the Playback menu. It's a good idea to use this command with any new memory card you place in the camera for the first time so the card will be properly formatted to store new images and videos.

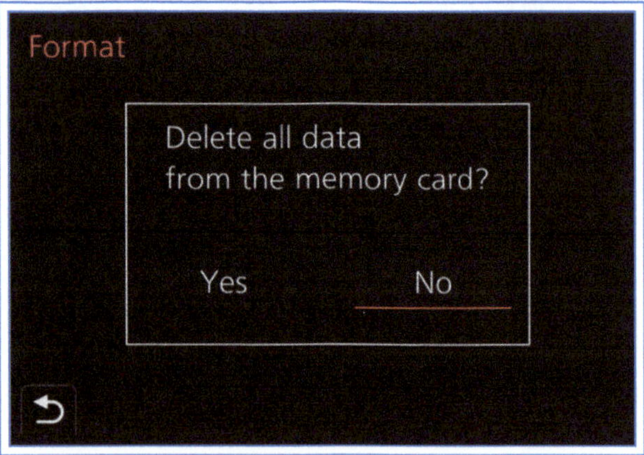

Figure 7-70. Format Confirmation Screen

My Menu

The My Menu system lets you create a customized menu system that holds up to 23 of your most-used options from the other menu systems. The My Menu option is represented by the figure of a human head and shoulders in the line of menu icons at the left of the menu screen, as shown in Figure 7-71.

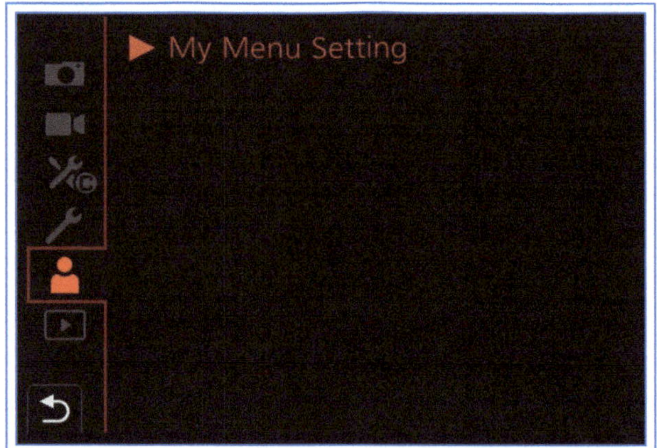

Figure 7-71. My Menu Icon Highlighted at Left

When you first use this system, select the My Menu Setting option, and you will be taken to a screen with the option to add items. Select Add, and you will see a screen like that in Figure 7-72, with the first items on a long list that spans 26 screens. Scroll through those options using the Up and Down buttons, the thumb dial, or the touch screen. You can speed through the screens using the zoom lever.

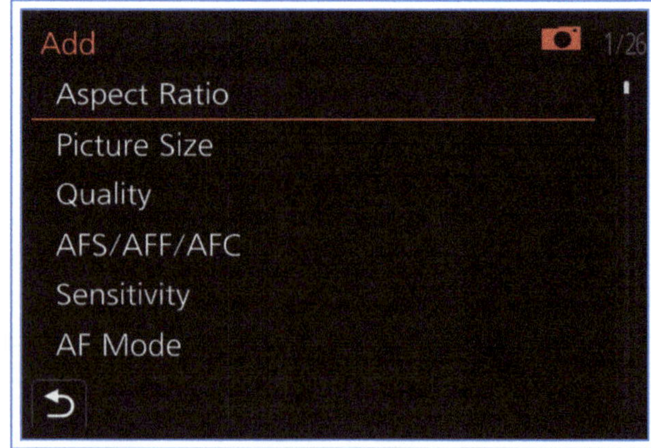

Figure 7-72. Screen to Select Items for My Menu

When you reach an item you want to add to My Menu, press Menu/Set (or touch the item on the screen) and the camera will display a confirmation box, asking if you want to save that item. If you select Yes to confirm, that item will appear on the My Menu list and it will be dimmed on the list of selections, so you don't accidentally select it a second time.

When you have selected up to 23 items, press the Fn3 button to go back to the main menu screen. You can now select the options on the My Menu screen without having to find them in their main locations on other menus. An example is shown in Figure 7-73, after I added several items to My Menu.

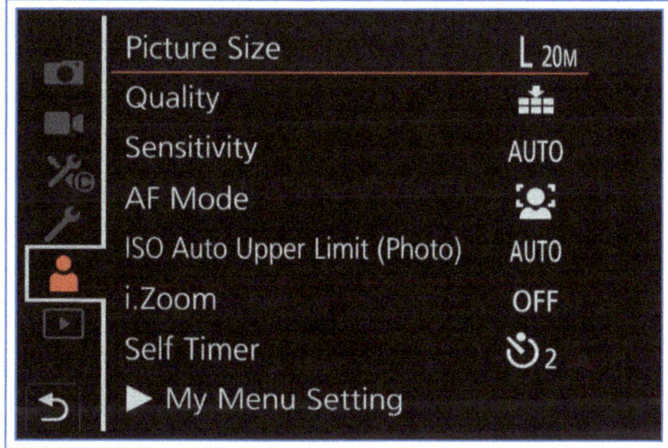

Figure 7-73. My Menu with Several Items Added

If you go back to the My Menu Setting option, you can now use the other options: Sorting, Delete, and Display from My Menu. The Sorting option lets you change the order of the options on the menu. The camera will prompt you to select an item and then select the new location for that item. The Delete item lets you delete items singly or all at once.

The Display from My Menu option lets you set what menu is displayed when you press the Menu/Set button to enter the camera's menu system. If you turn this option on, then the camera will display the options on My Menu, so you can go directly to your most-used options. If you turn this option off, then the camera will display whatever menu was last used.

Chapter 8: Motion Pictures

Until fairly recently, video recording features of compact cameras seemed to be included almost as afterthoughts, so the user would have some ability to record video clips but without many advanced features. Over the past few years, though, camera makers have increased the sophistication of the video functions of small cameras to a remarkable level. The C-Lux is not ready to take the place of a dedicated video camera for professional productions, because it lacks features such as jacks for external microphones and headphones while recording video. But in terms of pure video recording, it has very good abilities. I will discuss how to take advantage of those features in this chapter.

One general note to remember: With all recording formats other than the 4K formats, the C-Lux cannot record a single video sequence continuously for longer than 30 minutes. With the 4K formats, the continuous recording limit is 15 minutes.

Basics of C-Lux Videography

One aspect of motion picture recording with the C-Lux that can be somewhat confusing is how to select the shooting mode. For still photography with this camera, when you choose a shooting mode by turning the mode dial on top of the camera, that is the mode that you will shoot your pictures in. That is not quite how it works with movie recording. In the motion picture arena, where you set the mode dial has some effect on your shooting, but not as direct an effect as for still photos.

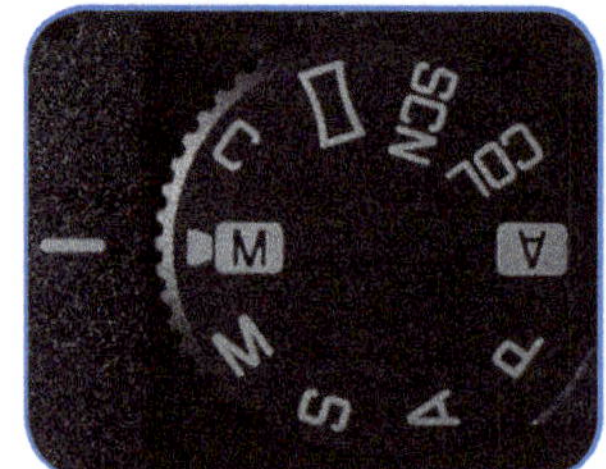

Figure 8-1. Mode Dial at Creative Video

If you look at the mode dial, as shown in Figure 8-1, you will see icons for the various shooting modes for still photography: Snapshot, Program, Aperture Priority, Shutter Priority, Manual, Custom, Panorama, Scene, and Creative Control. There is also one entry on the dial for movies, represented by the letter M with a movie camera icon: Creative Video mode, which is shown as selected in this illustration. However, because of the red video button, you do not have to set the mode dial to Creative Video mode to record a movie (though you certainly can, as I'll discuss shortly). In fact, you can set the mode dial to any of its settings except Panorama and still record a movie. (For the C setting, it depends on what shooting mode was saved to the Custom mode slot.) But the results may not be what you might expect based on the name of the shooting mode.

For example, when the mode dial is set to M for Manual mode, if you press the red button you will not be shooting video in Manual exposure mode. In fact, you'll be shooting video with the camera adjusting exposure automatically by setting the aperture and shutter speed. This is the same result you'll get with any of the four PASM shooting modes on the mode dial (Program, Aperture Priority, Shutter Priority, or Manual).

Here is where the situation gets slightly complicated. As I just noted, when you set the mode dial to some of the major still-shooting modes, such as A, S, or M, the camera does not follow that mode's behavior for setting exposure when you press the red video button. But the camera does use some (but not all) of the other settings that have been made in that shooting mode.

For example, if you have the camera set to Aperture Priority mode on the mode dial, when you press the red button to make a movie, the camera does not let you set the aperture; instead, it chooses both aperture and shutter speed. However, the camera does use some of the settings that have been chosen through the Recording menu and with the physical controls while the camera was in Aperture Priority mode, such as white balance, metering mode, and AF Mode. Of course, several options from the Recording menu make no sense when recording movies, and therefore have no effect when you press the red button, including Flash Mode, Bracket, and Burst Rate.

If you set the mode dial to Snapshot mode, the camera will take over even more of the settings for your movies. If you set it to Scene mode, it will use the basic settings for the type of scene you select, in many cases. For certain settings, though, the camera will use different scene types, as follows: For the Clear in Backlight scene type, the camera will use the Portrait type. For Clear Nightscape, Artistic Nightscape, Handheld Night Shot, and Clear Night Portrait, the camera will use what Leica calls the "Low Light mode." The camera cannot record movies at all using the Glistening Water, Glittering Illuminations, or Soft Image of a Flower scene setting.

If you set the mode dial to Creative Control, the camera will record a movie using the special effect that is selected for that mode, such as Expressive, Retro, or Impressive Art, with a few exceptions. The C-Lux cannot record movies using the Rough Monochrome, Silky Monochrome, Soft Focus, Star Filter, or Sunshine setting for that mode.

If you want more control over exposure settings while shooting a movie, that's the role of the movie-oriented setting on the mode dial, Creative Video.

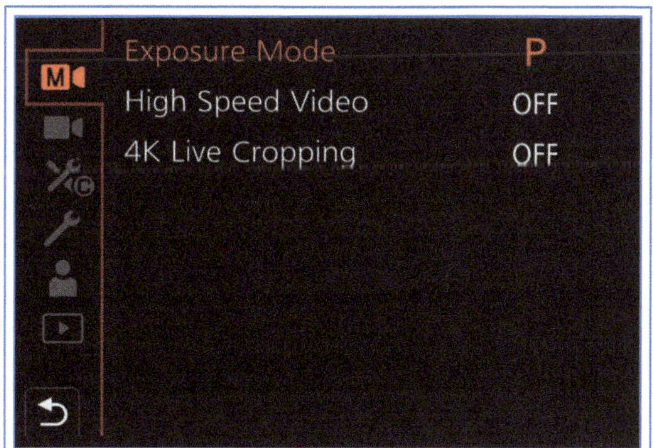

Figure 8-2. Icon for Special Creative Video Mode

After you turn the mode dial to that position, go into the menu system and select the top icon in the column at the left, which looks like a movie camera with the letter M and stands for Creative Video mode, as shown in Figure 8-2. This top menu icon represents a short menu called Creative Video; the icon below it, which looks like a movie camera without the letter M, represents the Motion Picture menu, which has many more options than the very short Creative Video menu.

Once you have selected the top menu icon, press the Right button to move to the menu screen and select the item at the top of the menu, Exposure Mode. The screen will display a menu of four choices: P, A, S, and M, for Program, Aperture Priority, Shutter Priority, and Manual Exposure, as seen in Figure 8-3. (You also can get to a screen for selecting an exposure mode by touching the icon in the upper left corner of the shooting screen that represents the currently selected mode.)

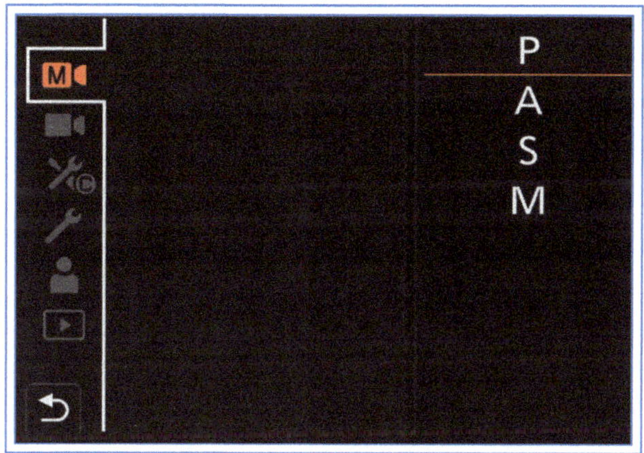

Figure 8-3. Exposure Mode Menu Options Screen

The choice you select for Exposure Mode will be in effect when you press the red button to record a movie in Creative Video mode. These modes work in ways similar to their still-photography counterparts, but they are distinctly separate, video-oriented shooting modes.

If you select Program, the camera chooses shutter speed and aperture, just as it does when recording movies with the camera set to one of the basic still-shooting modes on the mode dial (P, A, S, or M).

If you choose Aperture Priority, you use the thumb dial or control ring to select the aperture, and the camera will adjust its shutter speed for the correct exposure, if possible. The C-Lux has the same range of apertures available for setting in Creative Video mode as in the still-shooting modes: f/3.3 to f/8.0 when the lens is zoomed back to its full wide-angle position, and f/6.4 to f/8.0 when the lens is zoomed in fully.

If you choose Shutter Priority, you set the shutter speed and the camera sets the aperture. Because of the nature of video footage, which is normally recorded (in the United States) at 24 or 30 frames per second, the slowest shutter speed you can normally choose is 1/25 second (but see the note below under Manual Exposure mode, for an exception). You can choose from a wide range of faster shutter speeds, though. For motion pictures in Creative Video mode, the range of shutter speeds for video recording is from 1/25 second to 1/16000 second when recording with a 24 fps format, and from 1/30 second to 1/16000 second when recording with a 30 fps or 60 fps format.

If you choose Manual Exposure, you set both shutter speed and aperture, in the same way as for still photography. Of course, as with shooting stills, the camera will not make any changes until you change one or both of the values, so, if the lighting changes, the exposure may be incorrect.

There is one more benefit in terms of creative options if you shoot your video in this Manual mode: If you also have the focus mode set to manual focus, you can set the shutter speed as slow as 1/2 second. This shutter speed setting results in a video frame rate of two frames per second, considerably slower than the normal (U.S.) frame rate of 30 frames per second. It lets you record usable footage in conditions of very low light and can result in interesting effects, such as ghost-like streaks on the video frames if you move the camera. You would not want to use this slow shutter speed for taking video of a sporting event, but if you're making a science-fiction or horror movie, this feature could present some promising possibilities.

Note that you can change either shutter speed or aperture, or both, during your shot. So, for example, if you're shooting a movie in Creative Video mode using the Shutter Priority or Manual Exposure setting, you can gradually increase the shutter speed to a faster and faster value to make the picture fade gradually to black. One problem is that the motions of the thumb dial may be heard on the audio track. But you can correct that problem in post-production by replacing or editing the audio track using video editing software such as Adobe Premiere Elements, if you are so inclined.

With the Manual Exposure mode for video recording, you can adjust the ISO setting, as with the other advanced modes, and you can set ISO to Auto ISO or to a numerical value, though the highest value available for ISO is 6400 for motion picture recording. The lower limit is 125, unless Extended ISO is turned on, in which case the lower limit is 80. You can set the ISO upper limit for movie recording using the ISO Auto Upper Limit (Video) item on screen 2 of the Motion Picture menu.

With the Program, Aperture Priority, and Shutter Priority settings for Exposure Mode in Creative Video mode, you can adjust exposure compensation, just as with still photography, by pressing the Up button and then adjusting the on-screen scale. However, the scale permits adjustments only up to plus or minus 3 EV, rather than the plus or minus 5 EV range for still photography.

You also can adjust exposure compensation when Exposure Mode is set to Manual Exposure in Creative Video mode, but you cannot use the Up button for that purpose; you have to assign exposure compensation to the control ring using the Ring/Dial Set menu option, or use the Silent Operation touch icon for exposure compensation, as discussed later in this chapter. ISO must be set to Auto ISO in this situation.

When the camera is set to Creative Video mode, you can use the shutter button to start and stop video recording. In all other modes, pressing the shutter button will take a still picture, but in this one situation, you can use either the red video button or the shutter button to control movie-making. This means, of course, that you cannot take still pictures with the camera in this mode.

High Speed Video Recording

Another option for video recording in Creative Video mode is high speed video, which is selected from the single screen of the Creative Video menu, as shown in Figure 8-4. This is a specialized setting for shooting movies at a higher speed than normal, so the action will appear to be in slow motion when the footage is played at normal speed. To record using this option, you need to use a memory card rated in UHS Speed Class 3.

Once you have selected the High Speed Video option, there are very few other settings you can make for the motion pictures. They will be recorded at 120 frames per second, which is four times the normal speed for video recording (in the United States). Therefore, when the video is played back at the normal rate of 30 frames per second, the action will appear to be slowed down to one-fourth of the normal speed. You can use this option to analyze golf swings or other quick actions, or just to produce a dream-like aura for your scenes.

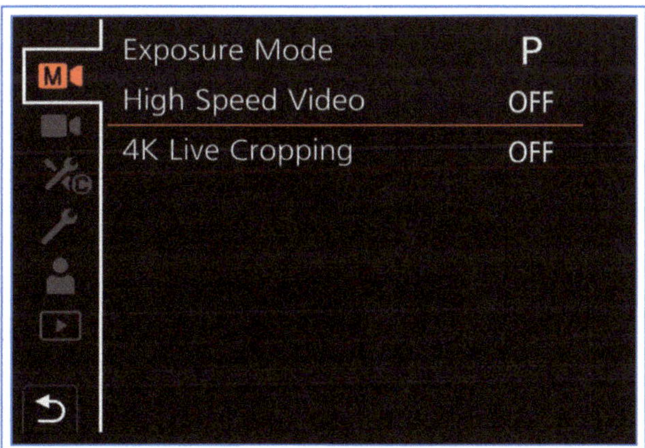

Figure 8-4. High Speed Video Highlighted on Menu

All high speed video is recorded using the MP4 format with full HD quality but with no sound. The AF Mode setting is fixed at 1-Area. You can choose from the complete range of options for the Photo Style setting, so you can, for example, record a slow-motion sequence in black and white. You cannot change the focus, zoom, exposure, or white balance settings once the recording has started. The maximum recording length is about 30 minutes, which will play back at normal speed for roughly 120 minutes.

Making Other Settings When Recording Movies

You likely will get excellent results if you use the camera's default settings and shoot your video using Snapshot mode and following the guidelines for exposure and focus discussed above. But there are numerous other settings you can make using the camera's physical controls and the menu system. I will discuss those settings next, so you can take advantage of the flexibility they provide for motion picture recording with the C-Lux.

The Motion Picture Menu

First, I will discuss a menu system I have not discussed in detail—the Motion Picture menu, designated by the movie camera icon. Later in this chapter, I will discuss the more specialized Creative Video menu, designated by the movie camera icon with the letter M. Before I discuss the individual items on these two menus, there are a few general points to mention.

As I noted earlier in connection with the Exposure Mode menu item, the Creative Video menu is very short, having only three items on it: Exposure Mode, High Speed Video, and 4K Live Cropping. Those three options are available only when the mode dial is at the Creative Video position, and that menu appears only when the mode dial is at that position. The Motion Picture menu, on the other hand, is available in all shooting modes except Panorama, because the camera can record video in any of those modes. (The Motion Picture menu does not appear in Creative Control or Scene mode if the current setting for that mode does not permit video recording, such as Star Filter or Glittering Illuminations.)

The Motion Picture menu has three screens in most recording modes, but only one screen with three items when the camera is in the basic Snapshot mode. In that mode, the only Motion Picture menu settings you can adjust are Recording Quality, Snap Movie, and AFS/AFF/AFC.

When the full Motion Picture menu is available, 13 of the items on that menu also appear as items on the Recording menu: AFS/AFF/AFC, Sensitivity, AF Mode, Photo Style, Filter Settings, Metering Mode, Highlight Shadow, i.Dynamic, i.Resolution, Diffraction Compensation, Stabilizer, i.Zoom, and Digital Zoom. These settings are included on the Motion Picture menu for convenience in setting them. You can adjust any of these 13 settings using either menu system, and the adjustment will take effect for both menus at the same time. For example, if you set Photo Style to Monochrome on the Recording menu, you will see that the Photo Style setting on the Motion Picture menu has also changed to Monochrome. Or, if you turn on Digital Zoom on the Motion Picture menu, you will see that Digital Zoom has been activated on the Recording menu as well.

Following is a discussion of all items that can appear on the Motion Picture menu, whose first screen is shown in Figure 8-5. I will not include detailed information here for the settings that also appear on the Recording menu; for more information about them, see Chapter 4. I will discuss the Creative Video menu items after the Motion Picture menu items.

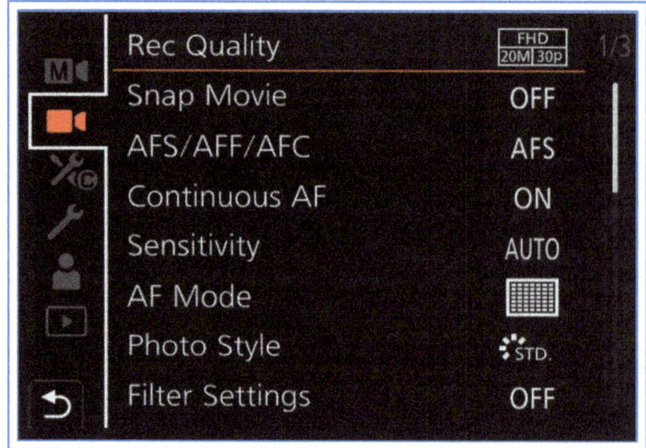

Figure 8-5. Screen 1 of Motion Picture Menu

Recording Quality

The only format available for recording video with the C-Lux camera is MP4, a standard format that is widely used for online video and computer editing. The Recording Quality menu option determines the level of image quality for your video footage.

The choices are the following, in descending order of quality: 4K/100M/30p; 4K/100M/24p; FHD/28M/60p; FHD/20M/30p; and HD/10M/30p, as seen in Figure 8-6. The 4K, FHD, or HD prefix indicates the level of resolution of the format: 4K (3840 x 2160 pixels), full HD (1920 x 1080 pixels), or normal HD (1280 x 720 pixels).

The 100M, 28M, 20M, and 10M figures state the maximum bit rate for each format, meaning the maximum number of megabits of information recorded per second. For example, the highest-quality format records up to about 100 million bits of information per second. The higher the bit rate, the more information is available to provide a clear image.

The last three characters of each format state the frames or fields per second that are recorded, along with the letter "p" standing for progressive. With progressive formats, the camera records full frames of information; with interlaced formats, not used on the C-Lux, a camera records fields, or half-frames, and then interlaces them to form full video frames.

In the United States the normal rate for recording and playing back video is 30 frames per second (fps). So, for example, the 4K/100M/30p format yields full HD video with the normal frame rate, recording 30 full frames each second. The 4K/100M/24p option is provided for those users who like to use a 24 fps video format. That frame rate is the one traditionally used by film-based movie cameras, and some people believe that using this standard provides a more "cinematic" appearance than the 30 fps option.

With the FHD/28M/60p setting, the C-Lux records 60 full frames per second, which are later translated into 30 frames for playback at the standard rate of 30 fps. However, if you want to, and your video editing software has this capability, you can play 60p footage in slow motion at one-half the normal speed and still maintain full HD quality. This possibility exists because the 60p footage is recorded with twice the number of full frames as 30p footage, so the quality of the video does not suffer if it is played back at one-half speed. (With other video formats, playback at half speed will appear choppy or jerky, because not enough frames were recorded to play smoothly at that speed.) So, if you think you may want to slow down your footage significantly with a computer for playback, you can choose the 60p setting.

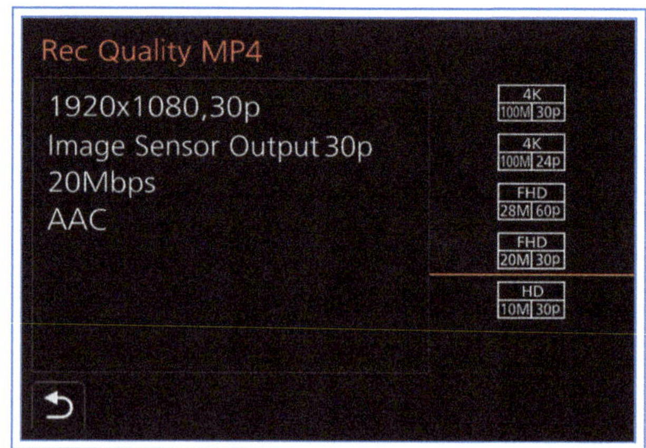

Figure 8-6. Recording Quality Options for MP4

The two available 4K options are special cases. The ability to shoot 4K video is one of the distinguishing features of the C-Lux camera. The standard known as 4K, sometimes known as UHD for ultra HD, is a relatively recent option for HDTVs. The 4K stands for 4,000, meaning each frame has a horizontal resolution of about 4,000 pixels. A standard HDTV has a horizontal resolution of 1920 pixels and a vertical resolution of 1080 pixels. The 4K format of the C-Lux has a horizontal resolution of 3840 and a vertical resolution of 2160. The overall resolution of this 4K image is about eight megapixels, while the resolution of full HDTV is about two megapixels, so a 4K picture has four times the resolution of full HDTV.

Of course, to get the full benefit of 4K video footage, you need to view it on a 4K-capable TV set or monitor. However, if your editing software permits, you can shoot using the 4K format and then convert it to the more standard 1080 format for ordinary HDTV sets. With that approach, your video footage will contain considerably more detail than if you just recorded it using one of the 1080 formats.

There is one caveat about recording with the 4K quality setting: As noted earlier in this chapter, to record with this format you have to use a memory card of the fastest speed class, which is UHS Speed Class 3.

If you are not planning to record using the 4K setting, the other MP4 formats give you excellent options. You can record in full HD with a 28 megabit-per-second bit rate, giving you excellent quality. You can choose 60p for highest quality and the ability to produce slow-motion footage at one-half speed, or the more standard 30p option. If you would like to work with smaller files that still produce excellent quality, you can choose to record with the HD/10M/30p option, which records using HD rather than FHD, meaning the image size is 1280 x 720 pixels, rather than 1920 x 1080.

Snap Movie

This feature lets you set up the camera to take a "snap movie," which is Leica's term for a video version of a snapshot. The resulting video is very short—just two, four, six, or eight seconds in duration, recorded using the FHD/20M/30p setting for Recording Quality. You can specify whether to add a pull-focus effect (sudden changing of focus from one object to another) or a fade-in and/or fade-out effect, to add extra visual interest. Here are the steps to follow.

1. Turn on the camera in any recording mode other than Panorama.
2. Select Snap Movie from the first screen of the Motion Picture menu.
3. Select Set from the sub-options, and set the recording time to two, four, six, or eight seconds, turn Pull Focus on or off, and leave Fade turned off, or select from white-in, white-out, black-in, black-out, color-in, or color-out. You have to scroll through two screens to see all of the Fade options. The white and black options fade to or from a white or black screen. The color Fade options involve transitions between color and monochrome.
4. Go back to the main options screen and select On for Snap Movie, then press the Q.Menu button to go to the shooting screen.
5. If you turned on Pull Focus, touch your finger on the screen over the object that should start out in focus, then drag your finger to the second object, which should have the focus "pulled" to it. (To use physical buttons for this setting, you have to assign AF Mode to a function button and press that button at each position for the pull focus frames.) This effect works best when the two objects are at two sharply different distances from the camera.
6. Press and release the video button and hold the camera as still as possible, keeping the pull focus objects in their proper locations on the display, if Pull Focus is turned on.

The result should be a brief video snapshot, optionally including a fade-in or fade-out effect, and possibly a pull focus action as well. The camera records sound, though it fades in or out if a fade option is selected. You might find it worthwhile to use this option with no effects as a way to record a brief view of a scenic vista or an historic site, for example.

AFS/AFF/AFC

This next menu option, as discussed earlier, mirrors the same setting on the Recording menu. It does not matter which one of these choices you select for purposes of autofocus for video recording, so you should select the option that you will want to use for recording still images. The camera's autofocus behavior for video recording is controlled by the Continuous AF menu option, discussed below. If you have Continuous AF turned off, the camera will not focus on its own during video recording; you have to press the shutter button halfway to cause the camera to use its autofocus mechanism. If you have Continuous AF turned on, the camera focuses continuously during video recording. (Of course, the focus mode has to be set to AF, AF Macro, or Macro Zoom for the camera to use autofocus at all.)

Continuous AF

As discussed above, this setting controls how the C-Lux uses its autofocus during video recording, assuming you have the focus mode set to an autofocus setting.

If the Continuous AF option is turned on, the camera will adjust its focus continuously as the distance to the subject changes. If it is turned off, the camera will use its autofocus only when you press the shutter button halfway.

Sensitivity

This menu option is available for selection only when the mode dial is set to the Creative Video position. Ordinarily, ISO sensitivity cannot be set to anything other than Auto ISO when recording motion pictures. However, in Creative Video mode, you can use this option to set ISO to Auto ISO, or to specific values of 125, 200, 400, 800, 1600, 3200, or 6400. It can be set to 80 if Extended ISO is turned on. If Auto ISO is in effect during movie recording, the upper limit for ISO is determined by the setting for ISO Auto Upper Limit (Video), discussed later in this section. Auto ISO is available for video recording at all times in Creative Video mode, including when Exposure Mode is set to Manual Exposure.

AF Mode

The AF Mode option operates as it does for still images. You can select a method of autofocus operation and place the frame or zones, as discussed in Chapter 4. However, the Pinpoint setting is not available for video. If you select it from the menu, the camera will use the 1-Area setting instead once the recording starts.

Photo Style

This setting lets you choose the "look" of your footage. It works the same as it does for still photos. The choices are Standard, Vivid, Natural, Monochrome, Monochrome HC, Scenery, Portrait, and Custom. For more details, see Chapter 4.

Filter Settings

This last item on screen 1 of the Motion Picture menu lets you select a filter effect for your video. Several of the settings are not available: Rough Monochrome, Silky Monochrome, Soft Focus, Star Filter, and Sunshine. None of the effects are available when High Speed Video or 4K Live Cropping is in use.

Screen 2 of the Motion Picture menu is in Figure 8-7.

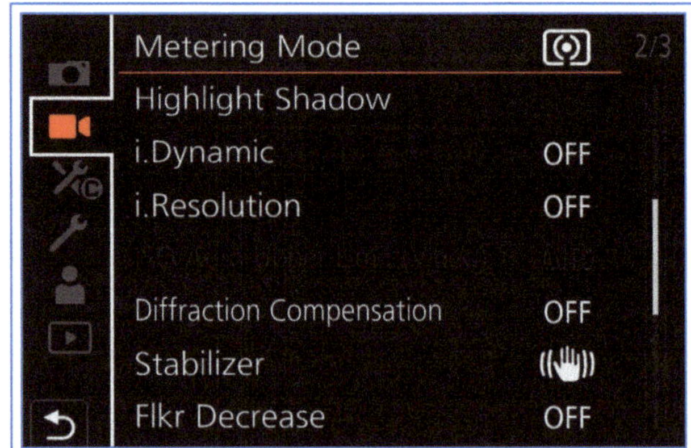

Figure 8-7. Screen 2 of Motion Picture Menu

Metering Mode

This menu option gives you access to the same three metering methods found on the Recording menu: Multiple, Center-weighted, and Spot. As with several other Motion Picture menu options, this one mirrors the item on the Recording menu; if either one is changed, the corresponding entry on the other menu is changed to the same setting. If AF Mode is set to an option with a movable focus frame, such as 1-Area, and Spot metering is also active, you can move the focus frame and Spot metering cross around the frame during video recording, just as with still shooting.

Highlight Shadow

This option, also, is identical to the corresponding one on the Recording menu.

Intelligent Dynamic

This setting works the same as the similar setting on the Recording menu and mirrors its setting.

Intelligent Resolution

This setting also works the same as its still-photo counterpart.

ISO Auto Upper Limit (Video)

This setting works in the same way as the ISO Auto Upper Limit (Photo), on screen 2 of the Recording menu works for still photos. This option sets the upper limit for ISO when ISO is set to ISO Auto on the Motion Picture menu. This value can be set to Auto, 200, 400, 800, 1600, 3200, or 6400. If it is set to Auto, the upper limit will be 3200. This menu option is available only when the camera is in Creative Video mode. In other modes, it is dimmed, as shown in Figure 8-7.

Diffraction Compensation

This setting operates the same way as the option on the Recording menu.

Stabilizer

This option works the same as the corresponding option on the Recording menu, except that, when recording motion pictures, the camera cannot use the Panning option, which corrects only for vertical motion of the camera.

Flicker Decrease

This last option on screen 2 of the Motion Picture menu is not available for selection when the mode dial is set to the Creative Video position; it is available only in the PASM shooting modes. It provides a way to set the shutter speed used for video recording to reduce the flickering effect that can occur in some cases. You can leave the option turned off, or select 1/50, 1/60, 1/100, or 1/120 second.

Screen 3 of the Motion Picture menu is in Figure 8-8.

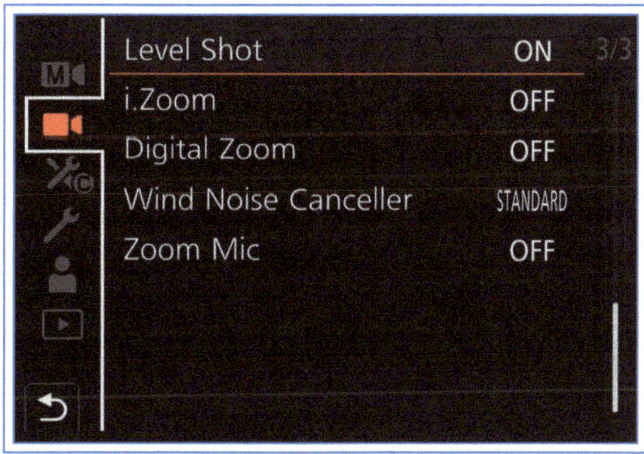

Figure 8-8. Screen 3 of Motion Picture Menu

Level Shot

This option is designed to correct a tilt away from the horizontal in a video sequence. When this function is turned on, if the camera detects that the camera is tilted to one side or the other, it will correct the tilt to make the video frame appear horizontal, to the extent possible. The camera uses electronic processing to crop the frame slightly to accomplish this leveling, so some pixels are lost at the edges of the frame.

I have found this function to be quite capable of straightening a video frame, within some limits. Figures 8-9 and 8-10 illustrate how well the camera leveled a scene shot with a considerable tilt.

For these images, I recorded two brief videos of the same scene with the camera on a tripod, in both cases with the camera tilted to one side, but with Level Shot turned on for one version.

Figure 8-9 is a still frame saved from the video with Level Shot turned off, showing the degree of tilt. Figure 8-10 is a frame from the video with Level Shot turned on, in which the camera electronically corrected the tilt so the scene looks level. Of course, there may be times when it is appropriate for the scene to be tilted. In that case, be sure to leave this option turned off. This feature does not affect still images, only video. It cannot be used with 4K video, high speed video, 4K Live Cropping, or in either of the Snapshot modes.

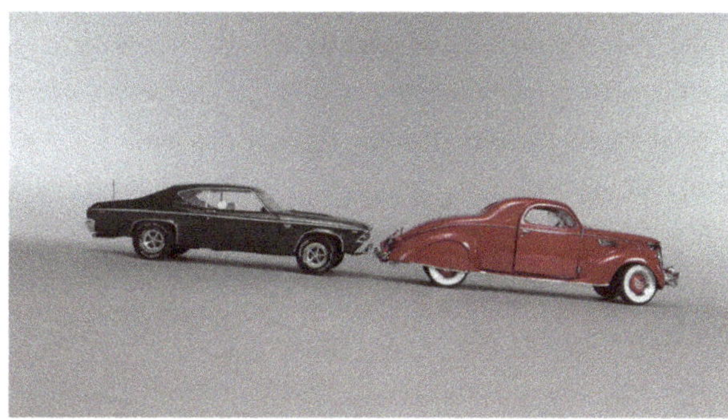

Figure 8-9. Level Shot Turned Off

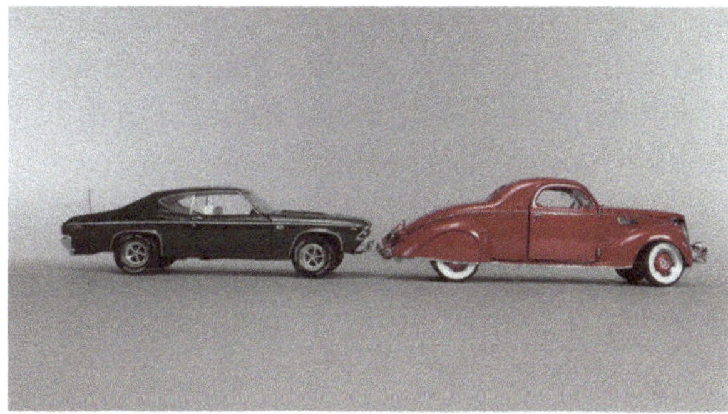

Figure 8-10. Level Shot Turned On

Intelligent Zoom

This setting is another one that is no different from the version on the Recording menu.

Digital Zoom

This is another setting that's the same as that on the Recording menu.

Wind Noise Canceller

This setting on the Motion Picture menu can be left turned off or set to Standard or High. If it is turned on at Standard, the camera attempts to reduce the noise from wind while recording a video sequence. With the High setting, the reduction of noise is stronger, and is more likely to remove some sounds other than wind noise. Either level of this processing may have an adverse effect on the quality of the audio. If you are recording casual scenes from a vacation, I recommend turning this option on when recording in a windy area. If you will be using video-editing software, though, you may want to turn this setting off, because, at either level, it can reduce some wanted sounds, and you can adjust the sound track later with your software to minimize the unwanted sounds.

Zoom Mic

This last option on the Motion Picture menu can be turned either on or off. If it is turned on, the camera's built-in microphone concentrates on recording more distant sounds as the lens zooms in. I have not found this option to make much difference, and I generally leave it turned off.

The Creative Video Menu

As I noted earlier, when the camera is in Creative Video mode, with the mode dial at the movie camera icon with the letter M, this second movie-related menu icon appears at the top of the list at the left of the menu screen, above the movie camera icon for the Motion Picture menu. The icon for the Creative Video menu has the letter M inside it, as shown in Figure 8-11. That illustration also shows the three items, discussed below, that appear on the single screen of this specialized menu.

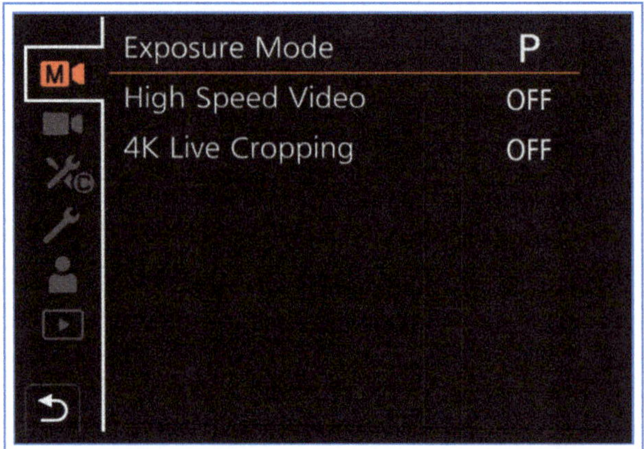

Figure 8-11. Single Screen of Creative Video Menu

Exposure Mode

I discussed this option earlier. It provides choices of Program, Aperture Priority, Shutter Priority, or Manual Exposure for the mode for recording motion pictures. With the Aperture Priority, Shutter Priority, and Manual Exposure modes, you can control aperture and/or shutter speed. With the Manual and Shutter Priority settings, you can select a shutter speed as fast as 1/16000 second and as slow as 1/25 second, depending on the recording format. With the Manual Exposure setting, you can select a shutter speed as slow as 1/2 second when manual focus is in effect.

High Speed Video

As discussed earlier in this chapter, this setting lets you record movies at 120 fps so they can be played back at one-fourth the normal speed for slow-motion footage.

4K Live Cropping

This feature takes advantage of the C-Lux's ability to shoot 4K video, to let you create full HD video footage that is more stable and quiet than might otherwise be possible. It is designed to address two problems with normal video shooting. First, if you pan the camera (move it from side to side) across a scene, unless you have a tripod with a fluid pan head or some sort of mechanical stabilizing system, the footage is likely to be somewhat jerky, moving unevenly from side to side and possibly jerking up and down as well. Second, if you zoom the lens in on a subject, there may be some jerkiness and some sound from the zoom mechanism.

With the 4K Live Cropping feature, you shoot such scenes in the ultra-HD 4K format, and, because of the extra resolution in 4K footage, the camera is able to crop the full video frames down to create an in-camera panning or zooming effect. For example, if you shoot a 4K scene showing a garden wall that is fairly distant, the camera can crop the video frames down to show the same wall closer up, in full HD instead of 4K, and artificially create a panning effect across that wall. Similarly, if you shoot a building in the distance, the camera can convert the 4K footage to a closer, HD view of the building and create a zooming effect in the camera.

Figure 8-12 shows how a view of items on shelves looked when shot in 4K, and Figure 8-13 shows how that scene looked after it was cropped using Live Cropping, so the camera could pan across it.

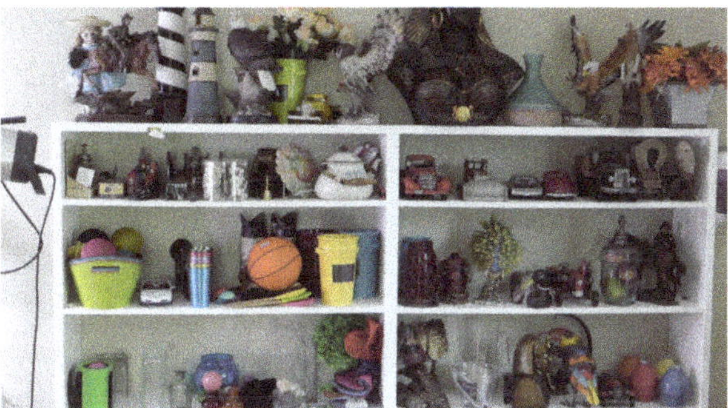
Figure 8-12. Frame from Scene Without Live Cropping

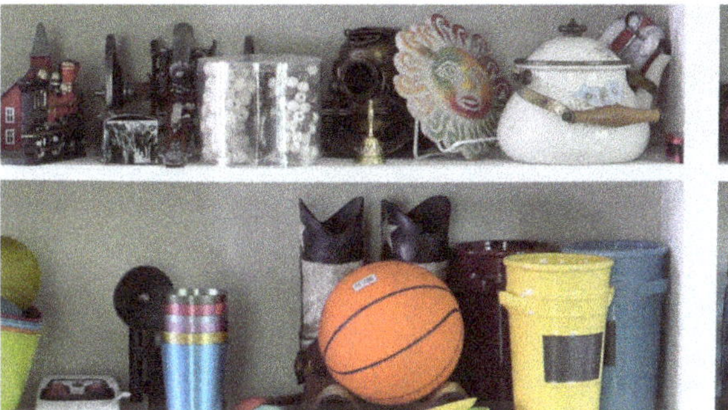
Figure 8-13. Frame from Scene With Live Cropping

These are the steps to take to use this feature.

1. Turn on the camera and set the mode dial to the Creative Video position.
2. Select 4K Live Cropping from the single screen of the Creative Video menu.
3. On the next menu screen, choose 20 seconds or 40 seconds. That is the duration the camera will use for the panning or zooming motion it creates.
4. The camera will display a screen like that in Figure 8-14, with a frame with arrows at the sides. (If you have used this feature previously, the camera will display both the start frame and the end frame from the last session, as is the case in this image.)

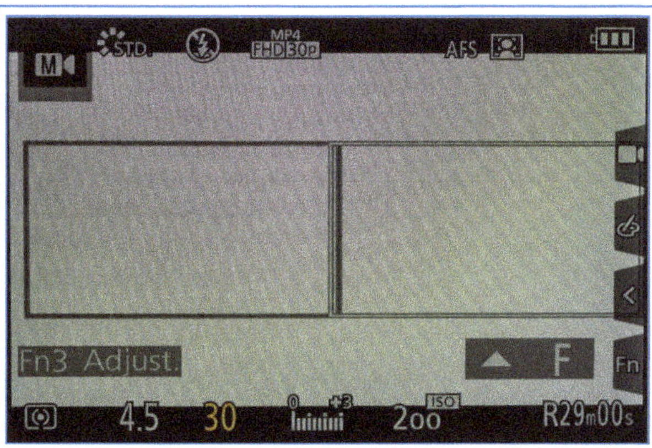

Figure 8-14. Live Cropping Setup Screen

5. Using the touch screen or the thumb dial and direction buttons, move the start frame where you want it to be placed and resize it as you wish. If there is a feature you want the camera to pan across, for example, set the frame over the starting area for the panning motion. Press the Menu/Set button or touch the Set icon to lock the frame in place.
6. The camera will then display the ending frame. (As noted above, this frame may already be displayed.) Use the same process to size and locate that frame over the ending area for the panning or zooming action. If you want the camera to create a panning action, keep both frames the same size. If you want a zooming-in effect, make the ending frame smaller than the starting frame; for a zooming-out effect, make the ending frame larger than the starting frame. Use the Menu/Set button or the Set icon to lock it in place.
7. If you need to go back and change the locations of the frames, press the Fn3 button to make the adjustment screen active again.
8. When the start and end frames are set as you want them, press the video button and release it, to start the recording. Hold the camera as steady as possible or have it on a tripod. After the set time period (20 or 40 seconds), the recording will end.

The result should be a smooth, professional-looking zoom or pan sequence, with no sounds from the zooming mechanism. This feature is worth experimenting with.

Recording Still Images During Video Recording

Whenever the C-Lux is recording a video sequence, you can press the shutter button to capture a still image. This function is available in all shooting modes in which movies can be recorded, except for Creative Video mode. In that mode, pressing the shutter button starts or stops a video recording. You can capture up to 40 still images during an HD video sequence, or up to 10 images during a 4K sequence. You can use the touch shutter function to take the pictures. All images will be JPEGs in the 16:9 aspect ratio, with a Picture Size that corresponds to the size of the video format in use (roughly 2 MP for HD and 8 MP for 4K). This function will not work when Snap Movie is turned on through screen 1 of the Motion Picture menu.

Using External Audio Recorder

Although the C-Lux has excellent features for recording video, Leica did not include a jack for accepting an external microphone, which makes it challenging to record high-quality audio with this camera. The stereo microphone built into the C-Lux records good-quality sound, but, with the superior video quality available with this camera, you may want to record audio using higher-quality microphones.

Fortunately, it is not difficult to do this with the C-Lux, using current technology and software. The best solution I have found is to use a separate digital audio recorder and then synchronize the sound from the recorder with the video from the camera.

If you use good equipment and software, it can be easy to use this type of system. I'll outline the steps I used; you may find equivalent techniques that work as well.

First, get a digital recorder like the Zoom H1, the Zoom H6, the Shure VP83F, the Tascam DR-40, or the Tascam DR-100mkII, which is discussed in Appendix A.

Set the external recorder to record high-quality audio in a .wav file and place it, or one or more microphones connected to it, in a location to receive the sound clearly.

Start the audio recorder, then start the camera recording video and audio.

When the recording is done, load the video file and its attached sound track, along with the separate audio file from the external recorder, into a video-editing program such as Adobe Premiere Pro CC, Final Cut Pro, or others. You also can use Plural Eyes, a program from redgiant.com that synchronizes audio and video. The software will compare the waveforms from the camera's sound track and the external audio track to move them into sync. With Premiere Pro CC, which I use, the procedure is to select the video track and the two audio tracks, right-click on them, and select Synchronize-Audio-Mix Down. The software will move the external audio track into sync with the video track.

Once the external audio track has been synchronized with the video track, you can delete the audio track recorded by the camera.

Of course, this system introduces more complexity and expense into your video-recording process. But, if you want the highest quality audio for your movies, it is worth exploring this method.

Using Physical Controls for Video Recording

Next, I will discuss options for using the camera's physical control buttons, switches, and dials in connection with video recording. The situation is complicated because each of the four physical function buttons can be assigned to any one of more than 50 options. Table 8-1 lists all of the physical controls and shows whether their settings will have an effect during video recording, as well as whether the control can be activated during video recording. For the function buttons, the table lists all of the possible assignments.

Table 8-1. **Use of Camera Controls Before and During Motion Picture Recording**

Control or Function	Effective if Used Before Video Recording	Effective if Used During Video Recording
	Physical Controls	
Control ring	Yes (depends on setting)	Yes (depends on setting)
Thumb dial	Yes (depends on setting	Yes (depends on setting)
Zoom lever	Yes	Yes
Exposure Compensation button	Yes	Yes (± 3 EV; Creative Video mode P, A, S only)
White Balance button	Yes	No
Drive Mode button	No	No
Focus Mode button	Yes	No
Display button	Yes	Yes

Control or Function	Effective if Used Before Video Recording	Effective if Used During Video Recording
Menu/Set button (access to menus)	Yes	No
AF/AE Lock button	Yes	Yes
Shutter button	Yes (start and stop video recording)	Yes (take still image or start/stop recording)
Playback button	No	Yes (stop recording and enter playback mode)
	Functions Assigned to Function Buttons	
4K Photo Mode	No	No
Post Focus	No	No
Wi-Fi	No	No
Quick Menu	Yes	No
Video Record	Yes	Yes
EVF/Monitor Switch	Yes	Yes
EVF/Monitor Display Style	Yes	Yes
AF/AE Lock	Yes	Yes
AF-On	Yes	Yes
Preview	No	No
One Push AE	Yes (in Creative Video mode)	No
Touch AE	Yes	Yes
Level Gauge	Yes	Yes
Focus Area Set	Yes	Yes
Operation Lock	Yes	Yes
Photo Style	Yes	No
Filter Effect	Yes	No
Aspect Ratio	No	No
Picture Size	No	No
Quality	No	No
Sensitivity (ISO)	Yes (Creative Video mode only)	Yes (Creative Video mode only)
AF Mode	Yes	Yes
AFS/AFF/AFC	Yes	Yes
Metering Mode	Yes	No
Bracket	No	No
Highlight Shadow	Yes	No
i.Dynamic	Yes	No
i.Resolution	Yes	No
Minimum Shutter Speed	No	No
HDR	No	No
Shutter Type	No	No
Flash Mode	No	No
Flash Adjustment	No	No
i.Zoom	Yes	No
Digital Zoom	Yes	No
Stabilizer	Yes	No
4K Live Cropping	Yes	No
Snap Movie	Yes	No
Motion Picture Setting	Yes	No
Silent Mode	Yes	No

Control or Function	Effective if Used Before Video Recording	Effective if Used During Video Recording
Peaking	Yes (if manual focus in effect)	Yes (if manual focus in effect)
Histogram	Yes	Yes
Guide Line	Yes	No
Zebra Pattern	Yes	Yes
Monochrome Live View	Yes	Yes
Constant Preview	No	No
Recording Area	No	No
Zoom Lever	No (can turn on step zoom, but no step zoom available during video recording)	No
Exposure Compensation	Yes	Yes (Up to ± 3 EV; Creative Video mode only)
White Balance	Yes	No
Focus Mode	Yes	No
Drive Mode	No	No
Recording/Playback Switch	No	Yes (stops recording and enters playback mode)

As you can see from the above table, there are many options for controlling the camera with the physical controls before and during video recording, though there are some limitations. For example, you can adjust Sensitivity (ISO) during recording using a function button assigned to that setting, but only in Creative Video mode. Also, you can only set it to Auto ISO or a value from 125 through 6400, unless Extended ISO is in effect. You can switch focus mode between autofocus and manual focus, but not during recording. However, you can move the autofocus area around the display during recording. You also can turn on or off the Zebra patterns, the histogram, or the peaking feature for manual focus while recording a video sequence.

You can control exposure compensation during video recording, but only ± 3EV and only in Creative Video mode. You can use the Up button for that adjustment when Exposure Mode is set to Program, Aperture Priority, or Shutter Priority. When Exposure Mode is set to Manual Exposure and Auto ISO is in effect, you can use the control ring, if it is assigned to control exposure compensation through the Ring/Dial Set option on screen 3 of the Custom menu. You also can use the touch icon for exposure compensation through the Silent Operation tab, discussed below.

You can select a Filter Settings effect that will work during recording, but you cannot select an effect during the recording. You cannot record a motion picture using the Rough Monochrome, Silky Monochrome, Soft Focus, Star Filter, or Sunshine effect. You cannot record a video at 4K quality using the Miniature setting.

When you use the Miniature effect for a motion picture, the camera does not record sound, and the footage is recorded at about one-tenth the normal speed, resulting in playback that is speeded up ten times faster than normal to help simulate the appearance of a tabletop model layout.

Using the Touch Screen During Video Recording

The touch screen is available for use during motion picture recording, provided the appropriate options are turned on through the Touch Settings option on screen 3 of the Custom menu. If Touch Screen, Touch Tab, Touch AF, and Touch Pad AF are turned on through that menu option, you can use all of those functions while the camera is recording a motion picture. However, these actions are limited by the same restrictions set out above in Table 8-1. For example, although you can use the Touch Tab to get access to various settings, you cannot turn on or off a filter effect during motion picture recording, because that function cannot be controlled during recording.

You can, however, use the touch screen to adjust zoom, autoexposure, and function button actions, provided the functions in question are available for use. If AF Mode is set to an option with a movable frame, such as 1-Area, you can use the Touch AF function to move the frame around the screen and resize it during a video recording. When the mode dial is set to a still-shooting mode, you can use the Touch Shutter function to take still pictures while recording a video.

Silent Operation

This option is available only when the mode dial is at the Creative Video position. In that mode, the camera gives you a special set of touch screen icons that you can use to control settings during motion picture recording, to avoid using physical controls that might make sounds that are recorded with the video.

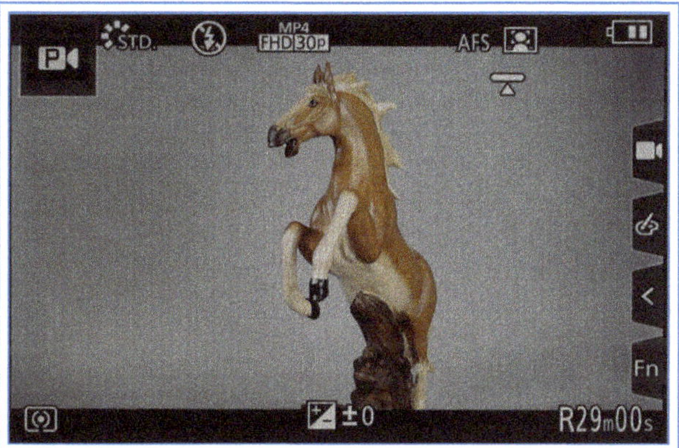

Figure 8-15. Touch Screen Icons in Creative Video Mode

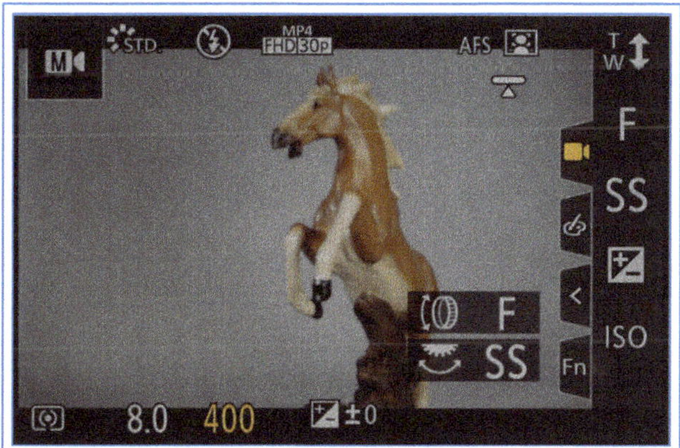

Figure 8-16. Silent Operation Icons Activated

To use this feature, once the mode dial is at the Creative Video position, before or after the recording is started, touch the movie camera icon at the top of the line of touch icons on the right side of the screen, as shown in Figure 8-15. The camera will open up a tab with a set of video-related icons, as shown in Figure 8-16.

Touch one of those icons to control the setting it represents. From the top, they stand for zoom, aperture, shutter speed, exposure compensation, and ISO. Of course, aperture and shutter speed are adjustable during video recording only if Exposure Mode is set to a mode that permits that adjustment—Aperture Priority, Shutter Priority, or Manual Exposure. To control the setting, use the touch slider control that appears beneath the active tab.

If you want to change to another setting, touch the top icon to open up the line of control icons again, and touch another one. When you are finished using the Silent Operation controls, press the movie camera icon on the screen to close this panel of controls.

Recommendations for Recording Video

Now that I have covered the essentials of how to record video footage with the C-Lux, here are some recommendations for how to approach that process. For everyday use, such as for video clips of a vacation trip or a birthday party, it's probably a good idea to stick with the Snapshot setting and, on the Motion Picture menu, set Recording Quality to FHD/20M/30p. The result should be excellent-quality video, well exposed, and ready to show on an HDTV or to edit in video-editing software.

If you aren't ready to deal with a whole host of manual settings, but would like to add some flashy coloring to your movie scenes, consider shooting in Program mode, and use the Filter Settings menu option to add an effect such as Impressive Art. If you would like to produce slow-motion footage, use the FHD/28M/60p setting for Recording Quality and slow the footage to one-half speed using your editing software. For even slower motion, use the High Speed Video setting on the single screen of the special Creative Video menu.

The possibilities for creativity with the C-Lux's movie-making apparatus are, if not unlimited, at least sufficient to provide a framework for a great array of experimentation. So consider the options, and don't hesitate to press the red video button when inspiration strikes.

Motion Picture Playback and Editing

To play a motion picture in the camera, display the file you want and press the Up button to start playback, as indicated by the movie camera icon and up arrow, shown in Figure 8-17. (If the icons have disappeared, press the Display button to bring them back on the display.)

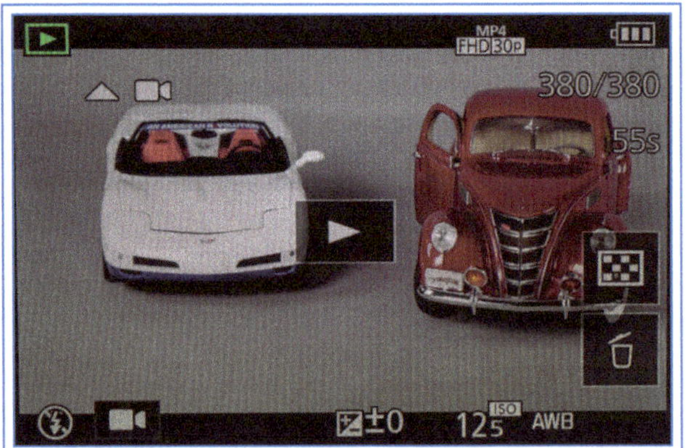

Figure 8-17. Movie Ready to Play in Camera

You also can touch the playback triangle icon in the center of the screen. The motion picture will start to play. The camera will briefly display at the bottom of the display a line of icons showing the playback controls, as shown in Figure 8-18: Up button for playback/pause; Right button for fast forward; Down button for stop; and Left button for fast backward.

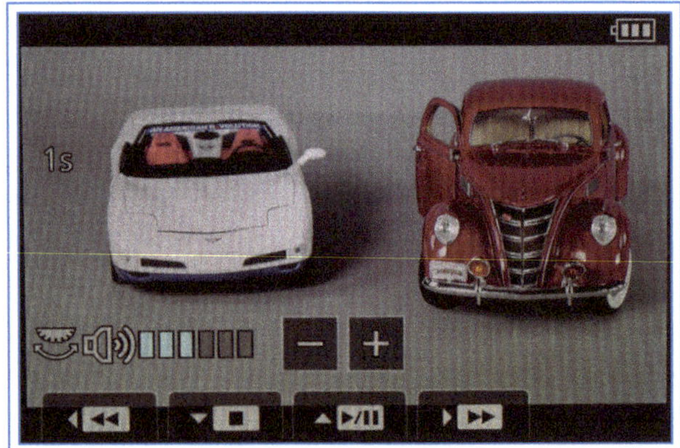

Figure 8-18. Initial Movie Playback Icons on Screen

Either during playback or when playback is paused, you can adjust the volume using the thumb dial. When playback is paused, the camera displays more icons, as shown in Figure 8-19: Left button for frame backward; Down button for stop; Up button for playback/pause; Right button for frame forward; and Menu/Set button to save a still frame from the video.

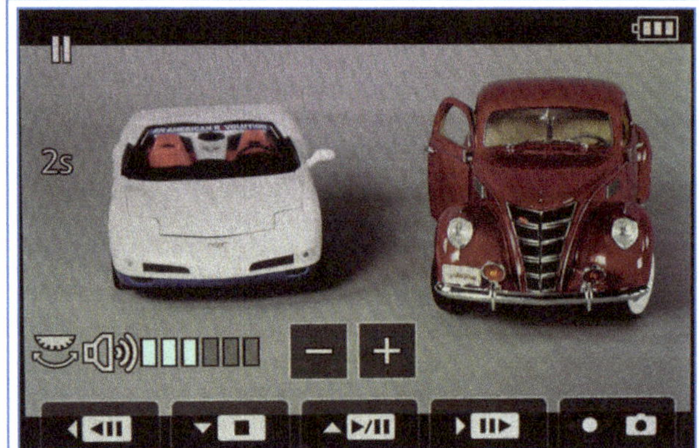

Figure 8-19. Movie Playback Icons when Paused

You cannot do much editing of a video in the camera, but you can trim its length or split it into two segments. To do that, follow the steps below.

1. Find the movie you want to divide and display it in playback mode. (You can use the Playback Mode menu option on the Playback menu to find all videos.)
2. Press the Menu/Set button and select Video Divide from screen 2 of the Playback menu.
3. Press the Menu/Set button or touch the Set icon to start playing the video in the camera.
4. Press the Up button to pause the video at the approximate place where you want to divide it.
5. Use the Right and Left buttons to locate the splitting point more precisely.
6. When you are satisfied with the position, press the Down button to divide the video into two sections, as indicated by the scissors icon in the group of icons at the bottom of the display, as shown in Figure 8-20.

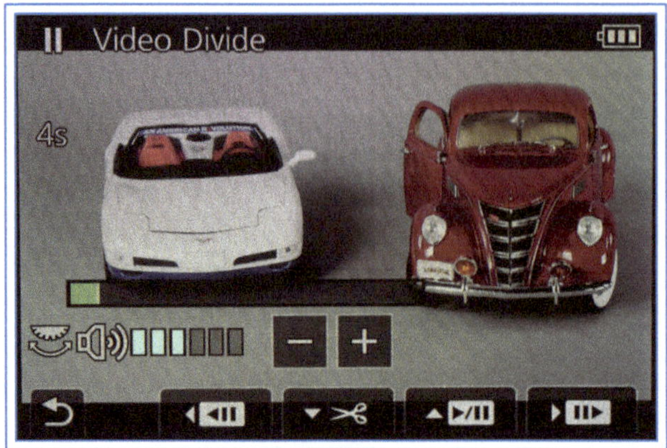

Figure 8-20. Screen with Scissors Icon for Video Divide

7. The camera will display a message asking you to confirm the operation. If you confirm it, the camera will divide the video into two parts. You will then have two separate video files; the original will no longer exist. You can delete either segment if you want, or keep them both.

You also can save a still image from a video file. To do that, follow the steps below.

1. Find the video that contains the image you want and start playing it in the camera.
2. At the approximate place where the image is located, press the Up button to pause the video.
3. Use the Right and Left buttons to find the location of the desired image.
4. Press the Menu/Set button or the corresponding touch screen icon, and the camera will display a message asking if you want to save this image, as shown in Figure 8-21.

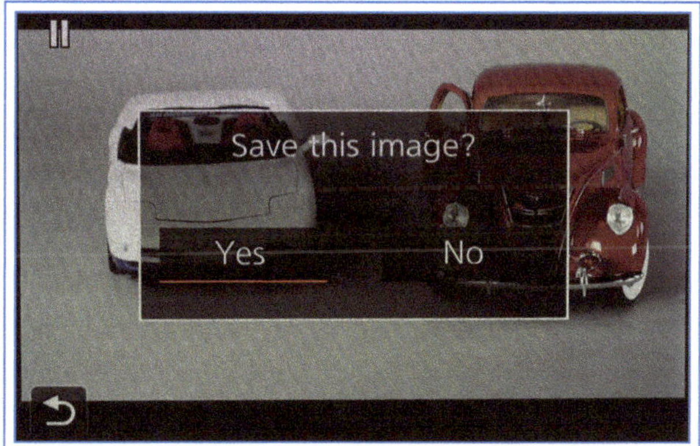

Figure 8-21. Confirmation Screen for Saving Frame from Video

5. If you confirm the operation, the camera will save the image in Fine quality with an aspect ratio of 16:9. The image's size will be 8 MP if the video was recorded with 4K quality, or 2 MP for other quality settings.

Editing with a Computer

You can edit video files from the C-Lux camera using most standard editing software that has been updated to handle recent video formats. For example, I have found it easy to import video from the C-Lux into the iMovie software on my Macintosh. One way to do that is to copy the video files from your camera's memory card to your computer. The MP4 files are easy to find on the card; they are in the same folders as the still images. For example, an SD card I am using now has .rwl (Raw), .jpg (JPEG), and .mp4 files in a folder whose path is LEICA:DCIM:100LEICA.

I also had no problems using the videos I recorded with the 4K quality setting. Because those files use the .mp4 format, they can be imported like ordinary MP4 files. Of course, they contain a great deal more data than ordinary files, so they may play in a slow and choppy manner in some software, but they can be imported and edited. Using Adobe Premiere Pro CC, I had no problem importing, playing, and editing the 4K video files on my Macintosh. I also was able to play a 4K video file on a computer using Windows 10, with the Movies and TV app.

Chapter 9: Wi-Fi, Bluetooth, and Other Topics

The Leica C-Lux camera can connect wirelessly to a smartphone or tablet using Wi-Fi and Bluetooth. Once those connections are established, you can accomplish several tasks using the smart device, such as controlling the camera remotely, transferring images from it, adding location information to images, and others. In the first part of this chapter, I will provide a general introduction to these features. In the later parts of the chapter, I will discuss some other topics that were not covered earlier in the book, including macro photography and street photography.

Note About Leica Fotos App

Before I discuss the use of Wi-Fi and Bluetooth features with the C-Lux camera, it's necessary to note that, as I write this section in December 2018, Leica has announced that it will update its new smartphone app, called Fotos, to work with the C-Lux, as well as other cameras. Leica also has said it will update the firmware of the C-Lux so it can work with that app. The app and the firmware update were not available in time for inclusion in this book. For details about this announcement, see https://www.reddotforum.com/content/2018/09/leica-releases-new-fotos-app-for-wi-fi-connectivity/. I do not know if Leica will continue to support the use of the C-Lux app, discussed below, after the Fotos app is available for this camera. However, the material in this chapter was accurate at the time it was written.

Using Wi-Fi and Bluetooth Features

The first step in using the various features made possible by Wi-Fi and Bluetooth is to establish the Wi-Fi and Bluetooth connections between the C-Lux camera and your smartphone or tablet. There are various approaches to making those connections. I will list below a series of steps I used to make the connections between my C-Lux camera and my iPhone SE, to illustrate one way that works.

1. Download the Leica C-Lux App from the App Store for Apple devices or the Google Play Store for Android devices. The icon for the app is shown on an iPhone in Figure 9-1.

2. On screen 1 of the camera's Setup menu, select Wi-Fi. Press the Right button or the Menu/Set button to go to the next screen and select Wi-Fi Setup. Under that option, go to the Wi-Fi Password option and make sure it is set to Off.

3. On screen 1 of the camera's Setup menu, select Bluetooth. Press the Right button or the Menu/Set button to go to the next screen and highlight another item also called Bluetooth, and choose Set. The camera will display a screen with the Pairing option highlighted. Select that option, and the camera will display a screen like that shown in Figure 9-2, displaying the Bluetooth ID of the camera and telling you to select that ID by pressing the Bluetooth button in the Leica C-Lux App.

4. Press the Bluetooth button in the upper left area of the app, as shown in Figure 9-3.

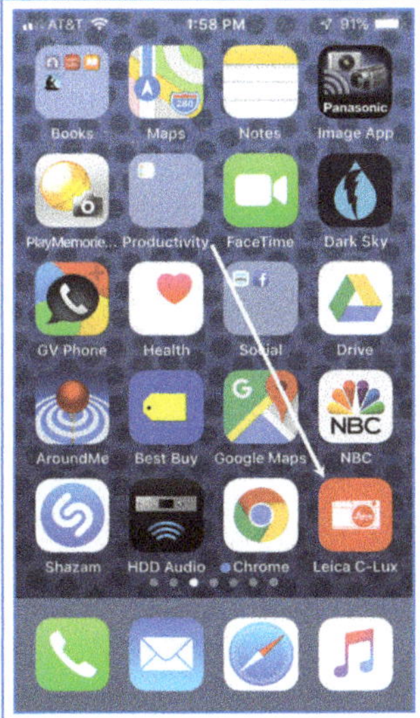

Figure 9-1. Leica C-Lux App Icon on iPhone Screen

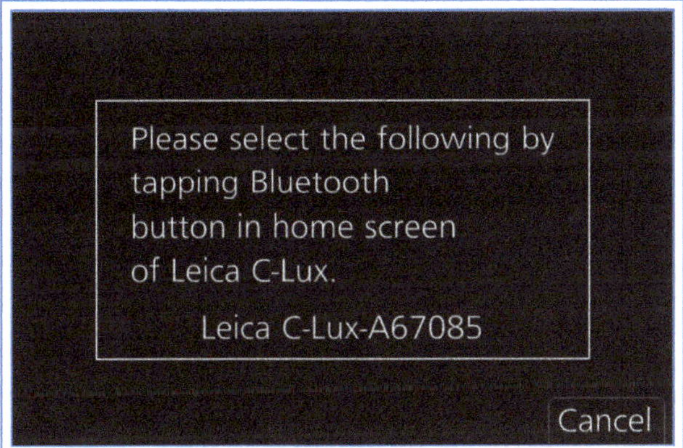

Figure 9-2. Camera's Screen for Bluetooth Connection

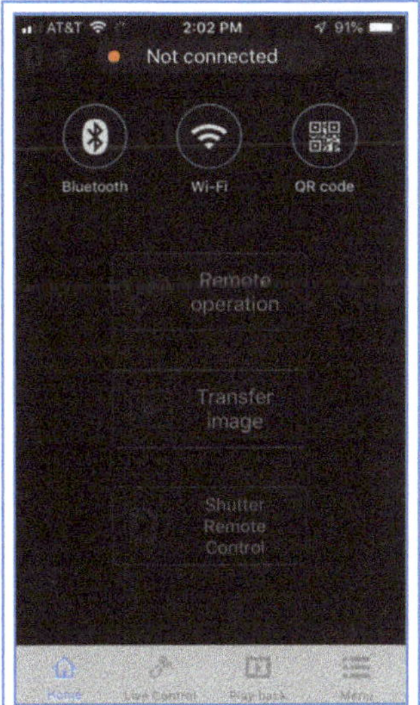

Figure 9-3. Bluetooth Button in C-Lux App

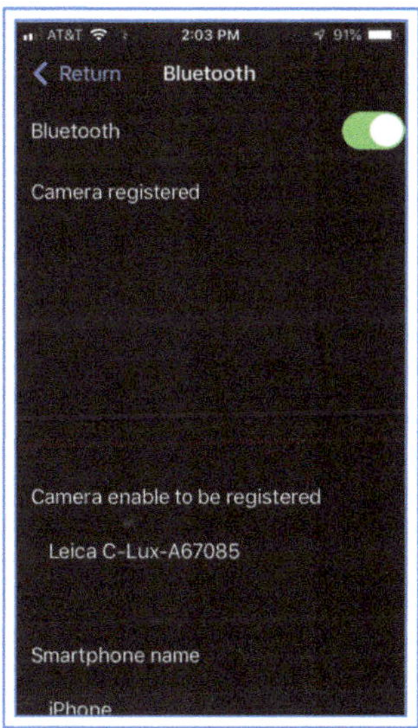

Figure 9-4. iPhone's Screen for Bluetooth Connection

5. You should see a screen on the phone like that in Figure 9-4, with the heading Camera Enable to Be Registered, with the network ID of the camera listed below. In this illustration, the ID is C-Lux-A67085. Tap that network ID to select it, and you should see a screen like that in Figure 9-5, advising you to go to the Settings/Wi-Fi screen on the phone to complete the setup.

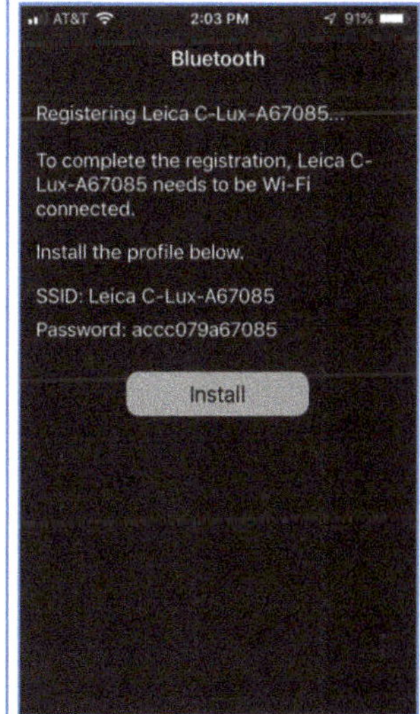

Figure 9-5. C-Lux App Message to Go to Settings App

6. On the phone's Settings/Wi-Fi screen, select the network ID of the camera to complete the connection of the camera to the phone. That screen should then look like Figure 9-6, with that ID selected by a blue check mark.

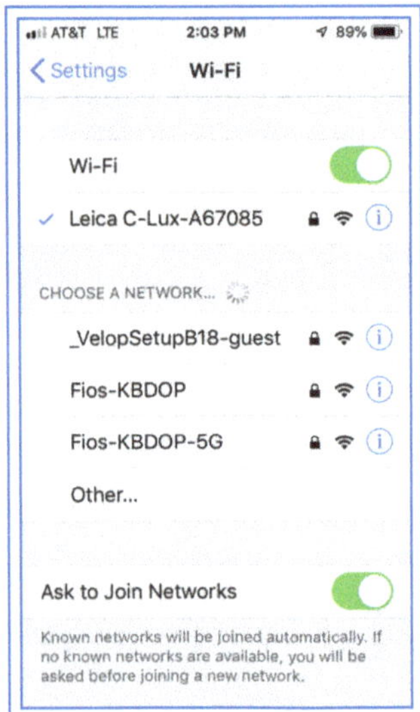

Figure 9-6. Settings/Wi-Fi Screen on iPhone

7. Return to the C-Lux App on the phone to carry out the activities that will now be available, as discussed below in this chapter. You should see a screen on the phone saying Registration is Complete, and then the home screen of the C-Lux App, as shown in Figure 9-7.

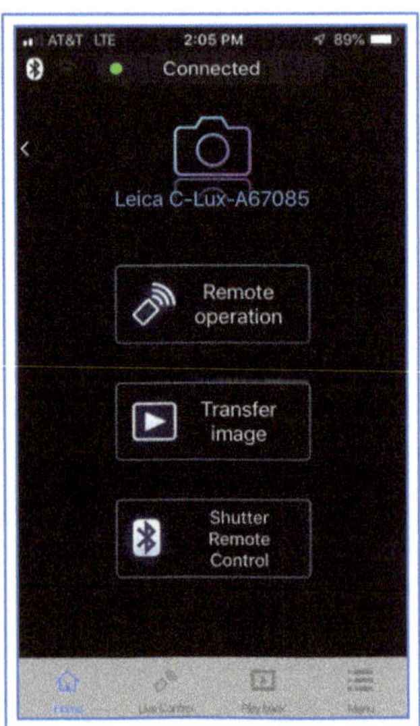

Figure 9-7. Home Screen of Leica C-Lux App

Controlling the Camera with a Smartphone or Tablet

Once you have established a connection between the camera and the phone using the steps above, you are ready to control the camera using the C-Lux App. Select the Remote Operation icon in the upper area of the phone's screen, as shown in Figure 9-7, and you will see a display on the phone like that in Figure 9-8.

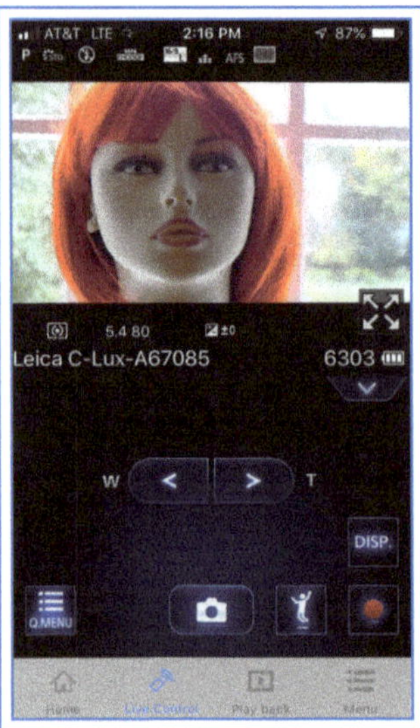

Figure 9-8. Remote Operation Screen in C-Lux App

You can touch the icons on this screen to zoom the lens in and out; change the mix of icons on the display with the DISP. icon; and get access to various other settings, including Photo Style, Filter Settings, Aspect Ratio, Picture Size, Quality, Focus Mode, Stop Motion Animation, Bracket, and others by pressing the Q. Menu icon, as shown in Figure 9-9.

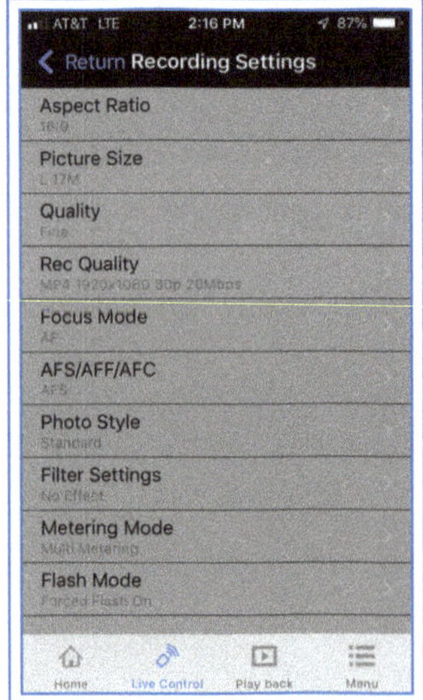

Figure 9-9. Quick Menu Items in C-Lux App

To take a picture, press the camera icon at the center bottom. To record a video, press the red button in the lower right corner. If you press the down-pointing arrow below the battery status icon, as seen in Figure 9-8, you will get access to additional settings, as shown in Figure 9-10.

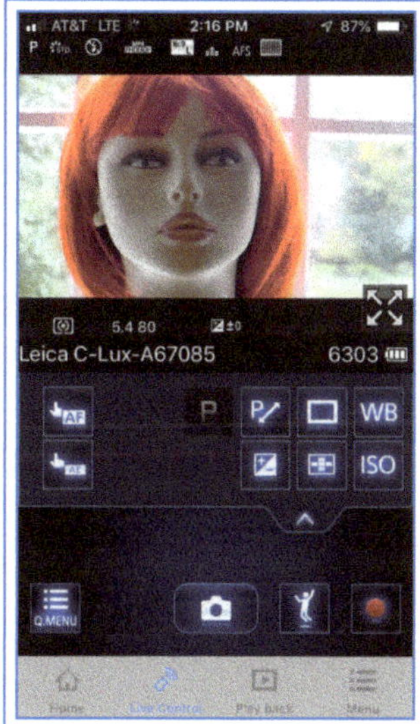

Figure 9-10. Screen with Additional Settings in C-Lux App

The touch focus icon causes the camera to focus where you touch the screen; the touch exposure icon does the same for exposure. The drive mode icon lets you select burst shooting, 4K Photo, Post Focus, or the self-timer, and the focus mode icon lets you choose Face/Eye Detection, Tracking, 49-Area, 1-Area, and other options.

The WB, ISO, and exposure compensation icons let you adjust those settings. If the camera is in a mode that lets you set aperture or shutter speed (or both), there will be an F icon (for f-stop or aperture) and/or an SS icon (for shutter speed), for making those settings. In Program mode, there will be a Program Shift icon. To change the recording mode, turn the mode dial on the camera.

You can touch the block with four arrows pointing in different directions, at the lower right corner of the live view area, to rotate the view to fill the screen, moving the controls to the edges of the screen, as shown in Figure 9-11.

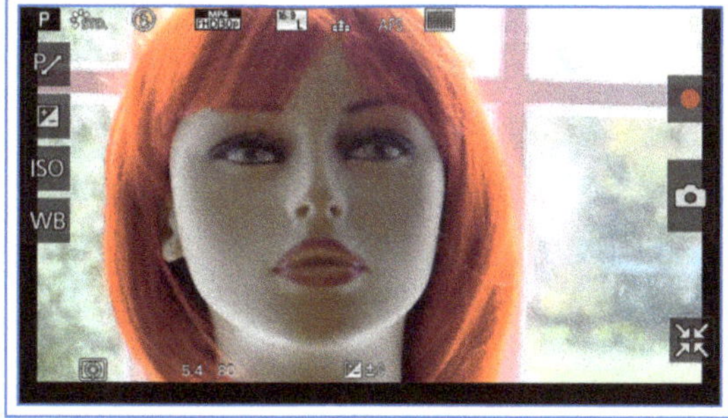

Figure 9-11. Rotated Live View in C-Lux App

You also can use a feature called Jump Snap, represented by the icon at the bottom of the app's screen that looks like a jumping person, as seen to the left of the red video recording icon in Figures 9-8 and 9-10. If you select that icon, you will see the screen in Figure 9-12, with settings for this option.

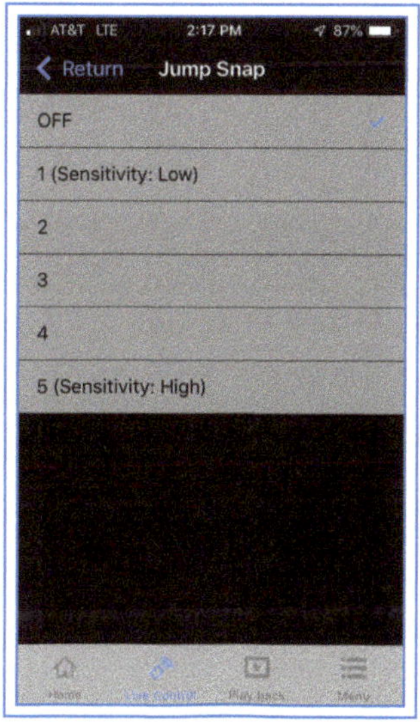

Figure 9-12. Jump Snap Settings Screen

You can leave it turned off or set the sensitivity to low or high. If it is turned on, you use it by aiming the camera at a person who is holding the phone while the app is active. The camera will sense when the person jumps, and will snap a still picture at the highest point of the jump. The result should be an image like that in Figure 9-13, showing the subject in a candid but awkward position.

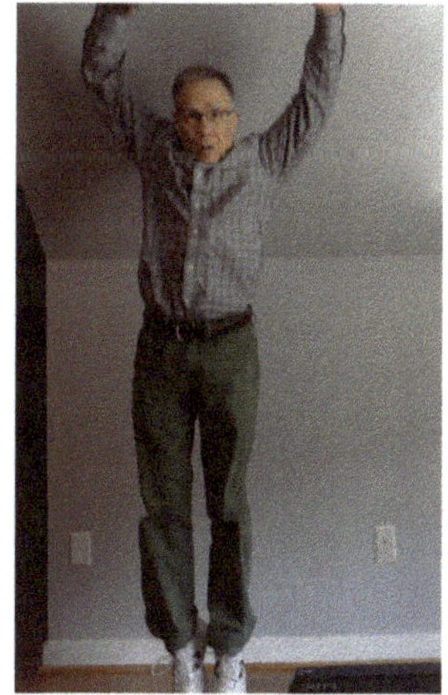

Figure 9-13. Jump Snap Example

Sending Images and Videos to a Smartphone or Tablet

Once the C-Lux is connected to your smartphone or tablet, instead of controlling the camera from your device, you can choose the option in the center of the home screen of the Leica C-Lux App, Transfer Image. When you select that icon, the phone will display a screen with choices of Transfer Selection or Batch Transfer, as shown in Figure 9-14.

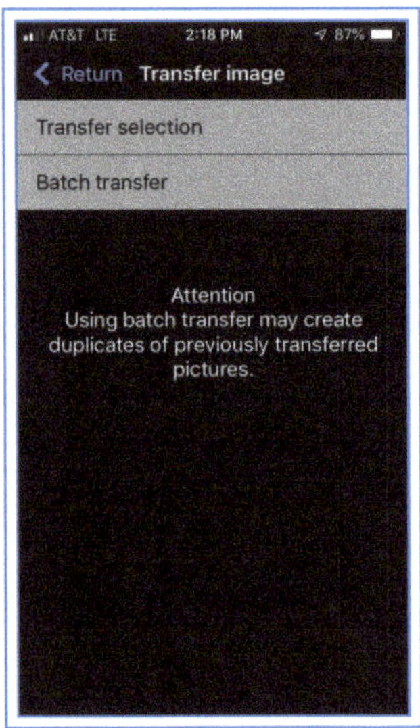

Figure 9-14. Transfer Image Options Screen

If you choose Transfer Selection, the phone app will display a screen like that in Figure 9-15, with thumbnail views for the images and videos on the camera's memory card.

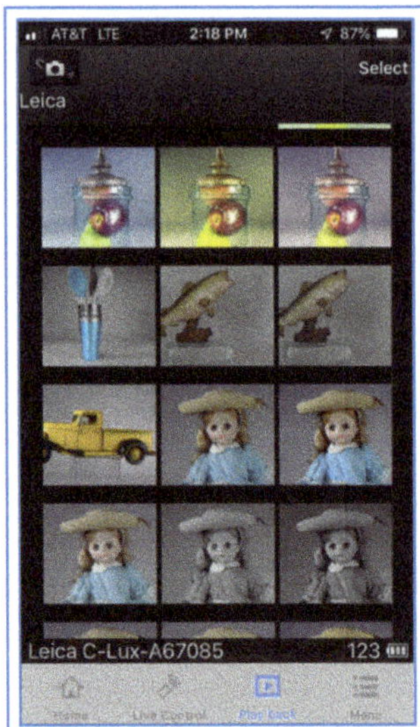

Figure 9-15. Transfer Selection Screen for Choosing Images

You can scroll through these images by flicking up and down the screen. It may take quite a while for all of the images and videos to load.

The thumbnails with a movie camera icon in the lower left corner represent motion picture files. Other thumbnails may have an icon showing a camera and a phone with a line through the circle around them. That icon means that item cannot be transferred to the phone because it is a 4K video, or a 4K Photo or Post Focus burst. Other images may have a label or icon indicating they are Raw files or burst shots. Raw images can be sent only to Android devices with fairly recent operating systems.

If you want to transfer one of the images or videos to your phone, first, tap on it to enlarge it on the display, as shown in Figure 9-16. If it is a video that can be played on the phone, you can press the Play icon on the phone's display to play it. If you select the icon at the lower left, showing an arrow going to a phone, the phone will display a message saying it is copying the file. You will then have a copy of that image or video in the standard area for photos or videos on the phone.

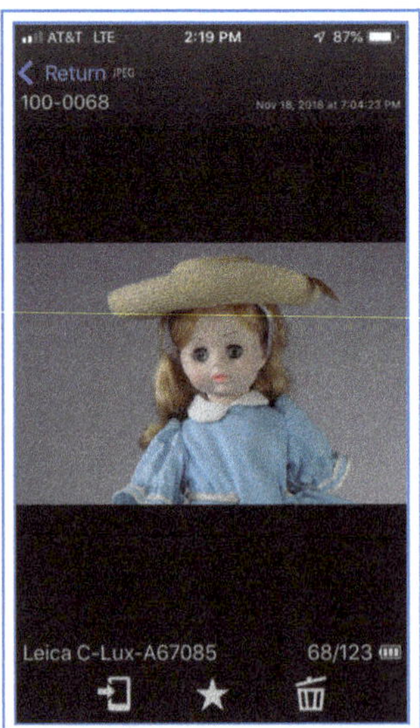

Figure 9-16. Individual Image Ready to Transfer or Share

On the main playback screen in the C-Lux App, shown in Figure 9-15, you can tap the camera icon in the upper left corner to switch between viewing the images and videos from the camera or those stored on the phone or tablet. Also on that screen, if you press the Select icon in the upper right corner, you can mark images and videos with green check marks by tapping them, as shown in Figure 9-17; once you have selected them, you can select the download icon (arrow going to phone) at the bottom of the screen to download them to the phone or tablet.

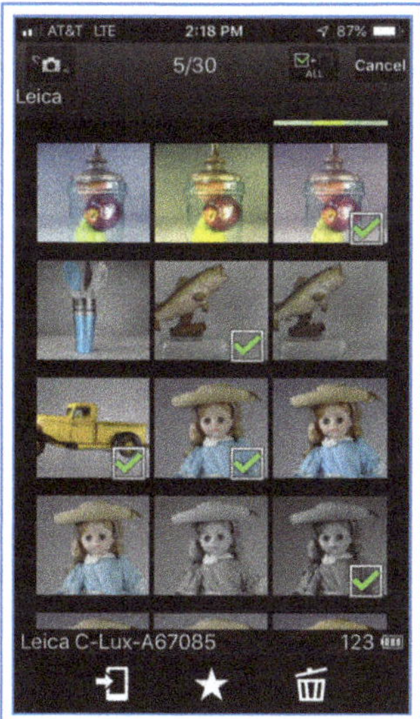

Figure 9-17. Green Check Marks on Images to Be Transferred

On an Android-based phone, from any screen that displays the sharing icon (two arrows going up out of a circle, as seen in Figure 9-18), you can tap that icon to bring up a menu that will let you upload an image or a group of selected images or videos to a social media site, including Facebook, Twitter, and others, as shown in Figure 9-18. This can be done only with an Android-based phone, at least as of this writing. With an iPhone, you can only transfer an image to the phone itself.

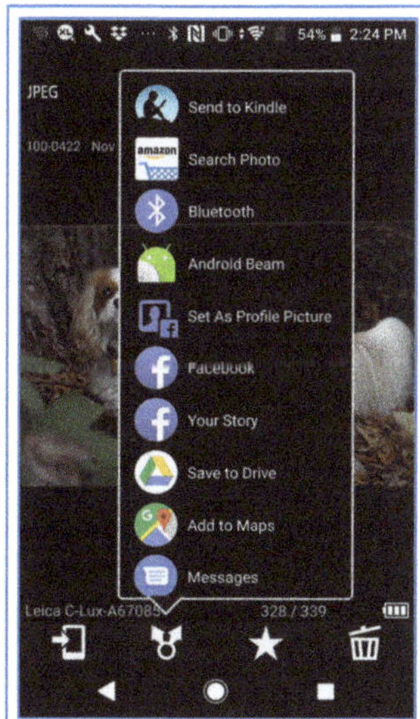

Figure 9-18. Menu of Social Media Sites to Upload to

You also can tap on the star icon at the bottom of the screen for an individual image to bring up a screen that lets you assign a rating of from one to five stars to the image, as shown in Figure 9-19. That rating will be available in software such as Adobe Bridge.

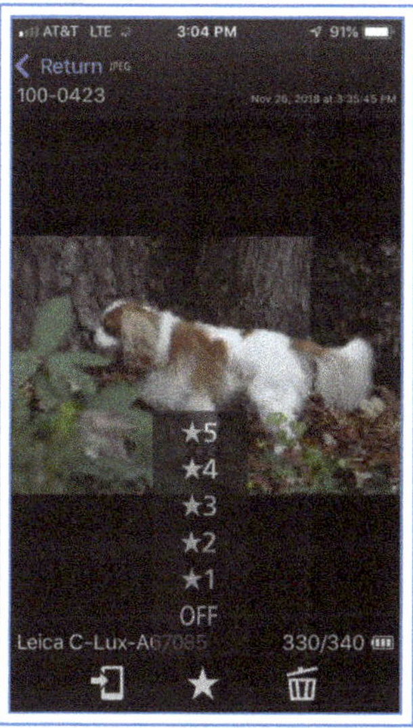

Figure 9-19. Menu to Apply Rating with Stars

Adding Location Data to Images

Using the wireless capabilities of the camera, you can add location information to images taken by the C-Lux, using GPS data transmitted to the camera from a connected smartphone. To carry out this function, follow the steps below.

1. Connect the camera to the phone using the steps set forth earlier in this chapter, or, if you have previously established a connection, go to the Bluetooth menu option on the camera, select Bluetooth, and turn it on, then start the C-Lux App on the phone, making sure Bluetooth is active on the phone.

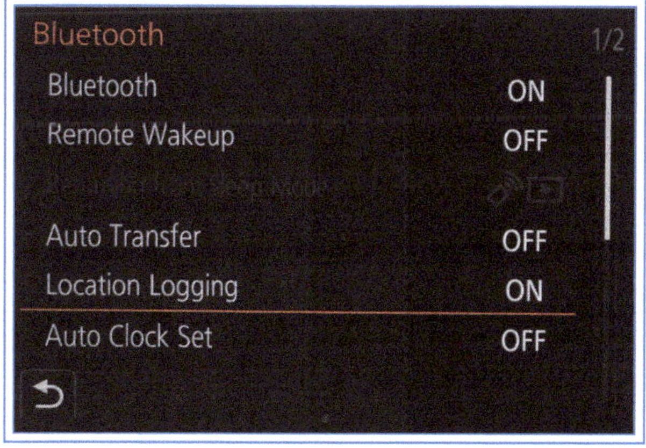

Figure 9-20. Location Logging Highlighted on Setup Menu

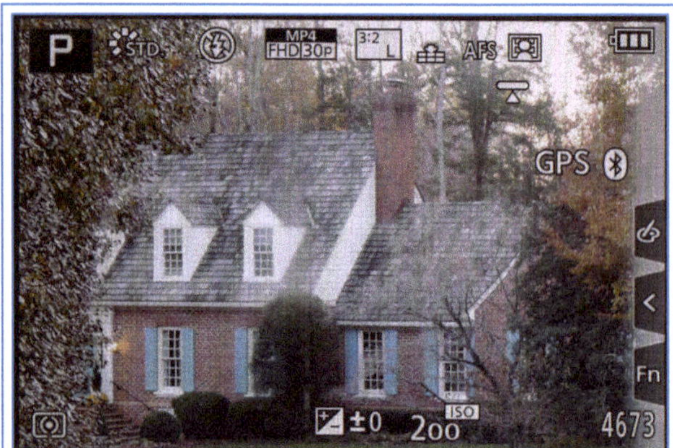

Figure 9-21. GPS Label on Camera's Recording Screen

2. On the camera, go to the Setup menu, select Bluetooth, then Location Logging, and turn it on, as shown in Figure 9-20. The letters GPS should appear, along with a Bluetooth symbol, in the upper right corner of the camera's recording screen, as shown in Figure 9-21. (If a Wi-Fi connection is still active also, a Wi-Fi symbol will appear instead of a Bluetooth symbol.)
3. Take pictures or record videos with the camera, and location information will be recorded in the metadata. That data can be read by many programs, such as Adobe Bridge, as seen in Figure 9-22. The GPS label will appear near the top center of the image when it is played back in the camera with the playback screen with basic shooting information.

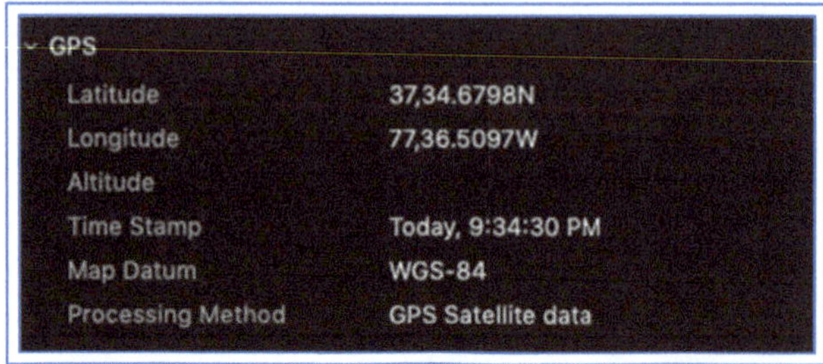

Figure 9-22. Location Data as Seen in Adobe Bridge Software

On the home screen of the C-Lux App, if you select Menu, the final icon at the lower right, you will see the screen shown in Figure 9-23, with options for the connection destination and other items. With the Playback Settings option, you can set the size for images copied from the camera or uploaded to websites.

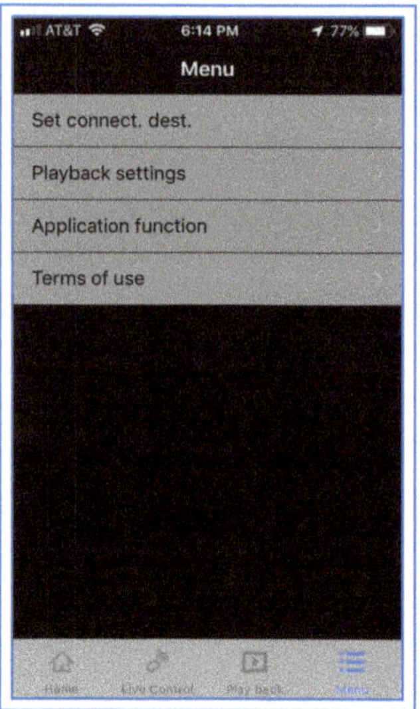

Figure 9-23. Items from Menu in C-Lux App

Turning the Camera On or Off Using Bluetooth

With the Bluetooth features of the C-Lux camera and the C-Lux App, you can turn the camera on or power it off using the app, without having to operate the camera's power switch. To do this, follow the steps below.

1. Establish a Bluetooth connection between the phone and the camera, using the steps described earlier.
2. On screen 1 of the camera's Setup menu, go to Bluetooth, select Remote Wakeup, and turn it on.
3. Turn the camera's on/off switch to the Off position.
4. Open the C-Lux App on the phone. On the home screen of the app, select Remote Operation. The app and the camera will both display messages reporting the status of the Bluetooth connection. The phone may prompt you to go to the Settings/Wi-Fi screen to connect to the camera's Wi-Fi network. Once that connection is made, you can use the C-Lux App to control the camera or transfer images, as discussed earlier.
5. To turn the camera off, tap the Off icon in the upper right corner of the C-Lux App's home screen, as shown in Figure 9-24.

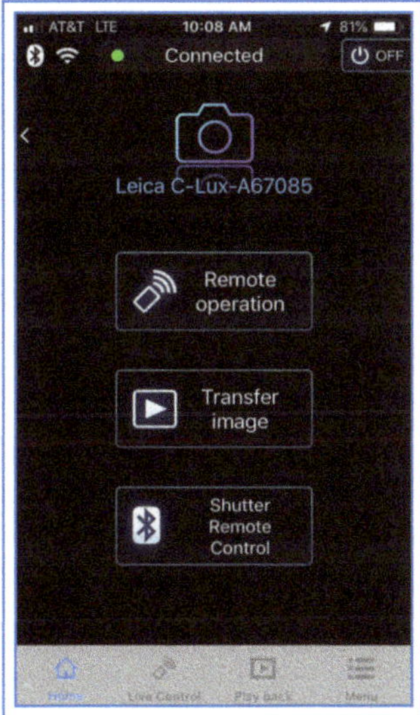

Figure 9-24. Off Icon on C-Lux App's Home Screen

Controlling the Camera's Shutter Button Using a Bluetooth Connection Only

When the camera is connected to the smartphone with the Bluetooth connection only, you can select the Shutter Remote Control icon in the lower part of the main C-Lux App screen, which brings up the screen shown in Figure 9-25. In order to initiate that connection once it has been set up previously, all you have to do is open the C-Lux App and tap on the Bluetooth icon, with the camera turned on. The Shutter Remote Control icon should then become active and available for selection.

With this feature, the C-Lux App does not display the live view seen by the camera; it displays only the remote control screen seen in Figure 9-25. The camera's On/Off switch must be in the On position for this feature to work. In addition, Auto Transfer must be turned off on the camera's Bluetooth menu. You can use the large button with the camera icon to take still images and the red movie button to start and stop video recordings. You can slide the camera icon button downward to lock it for burst shooting or time exposures.

Other Menu Options for Wi-Fi and Bluetooth

The C-Lux does not have a separate menu for Wi-Fi and Bluetooth options; those menu items are on the Setup menu, which was discussed in Chapter 7. However, in that chapter I did not discuss three items that are used only for wireless connections to the camera, so I will discuss them here. They are the last three items on screen 1 of the Setup menu, shown in Figure 9-26.

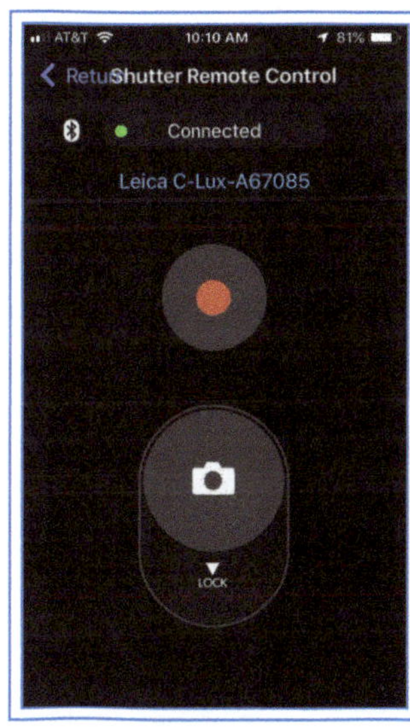

Figure 9-25. Shutter Remote Control Screen in C-Lux App

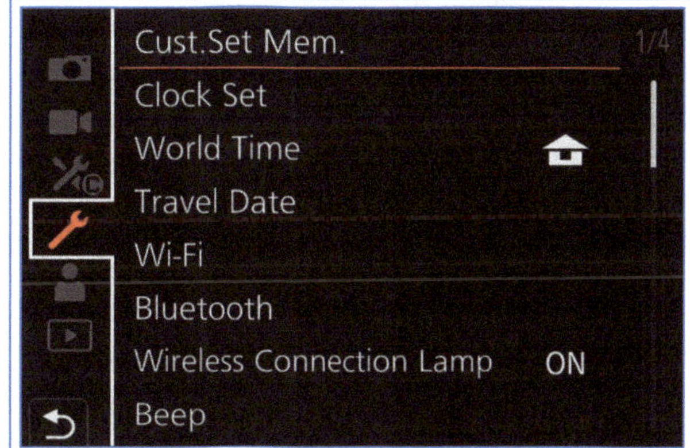

Figure 9-26. Screen 1 of Setup Menu

Wi-Fi

The Wi-Fi menu option has two sub-options, Wi-Fi Function and Wi-Fi Setup. If you select Wi-Fi Function, you will see the screen shown in Figure 9-27, with choices of New Connection, Select a Destination from History, and Select a Destination from Favorite. If you select New Connection, you will see the screen shown in Figure 9-28, with choices of Remote Shooting & View, Send Images While Recording, and Send Images Stored in the Camera. I discussed those options in the earlier parts of this chapter.

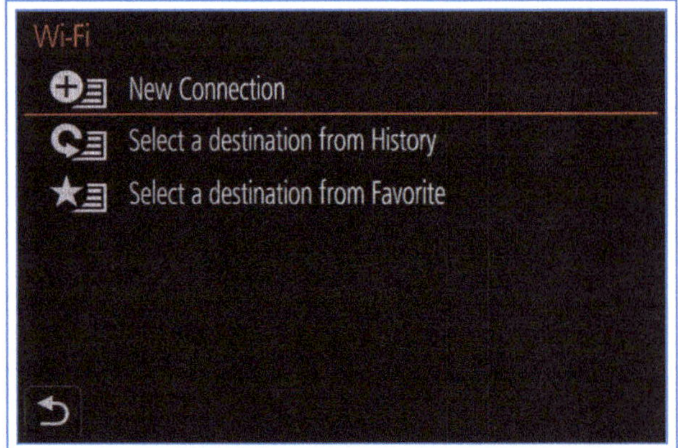

Figure 9-27. Wi-Fi Function Menu Options Screen

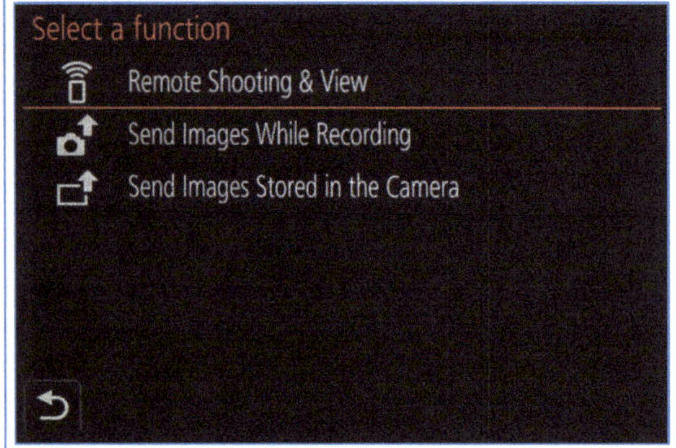

Figure 9-28. New Connection Menu Options Screen

If you return to the Wi-Fi menu item and select Wi-Fi Setup, you will see the screen in Figure 9-29, which is the first of two screens of options, discussed below.

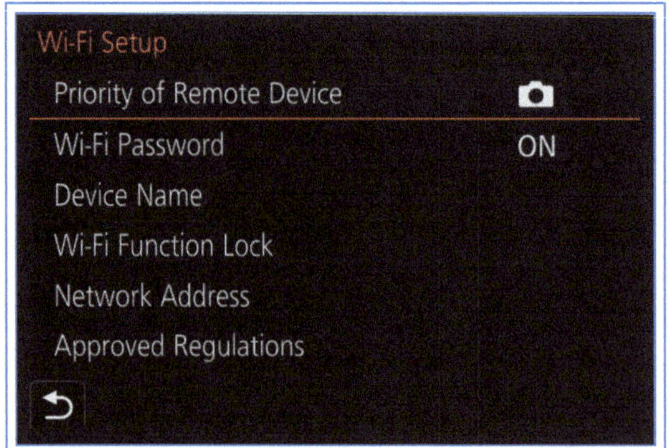

Figure 9-29. Wi-Fi Setup Menu Options Screen

Priority of Remote Device

With this option, you can give priority to either the camera or the remote device (smartphone or tablet) when they are connected wirelessly. If you select Camera, you will be able to control some settings using the camera's controls, such as the thumb dial, and you will not be able to control those settings using the smartphone. If you select Smartphone, you will be able to use only the smartphone to change settings; the camera's controls will not function for that purpose.

If you want to have maximum flexibility in making settings, choose Camera; if you want to make sure the camera's settings are not changed by accident or you will not have easy access to the camera during remote shooting, choose Smartphone.

Wi-Fi Password

This item can be turned either on or off. If it is turned on, you will need to enter a password to establish a Wi-Fi connection between the camera and a smartphone. You also can scan a QR code on the camera's display, instead of entering the password. I generally leave this option turned off in order to make it easier to connect the camera to my phone, but you might want to use a password for added security in some situations.

Device Name

You can use this option to change the SSID (network ID) of the camera, which is used to set up a Wi-Fi connection between the camera and a smartphone or tablet.

Wi-Fi Function Lock

This option lets you enter a four-digit number as a password for access to the camera's Wi-Fi functions. The password can be reset using the Reset Network Settings option on screen 3 of the Setup menu, so it does not provide much protection, and I have not used it.

Network Address

This item displays the MAC address and IP address of the camera. You may need this information in order to diagnose problems connecting the camera to a smart device or computer wirelessly.

Approved Regulations

This option displays data showing the approval of the camera by national regulatory authorities.

Bluetooth

The Bluetooth menu option includes two screens of sub-options. The first screen of those items is shown in Figure 9-30.

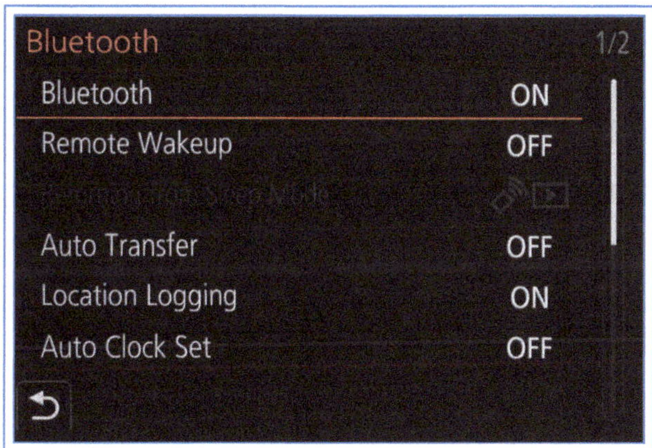

Figure 9-30. Bluetooth Menu Options Screen

Bluetooth

The first item on this menu, also called Bluetooth, is used to turn on or off the Bluetooth functions of the camera. When it is turned on, you can choose the Set option to pair the camera with a smartphone or tablet, as discussed earlier in this chapter. If this Bluetooth item is set to Off, then the rest of the items below it on the Bluetooth menu are dimmed and unavailable for selection. When it is turned on and the camera is paired with a smart device, the other items, discussed below, are available for use.

Remote Wakeup

The second item, Remote Wakeup, can be turned either on or off. If it is turned on, the camera can be activated remotely from a paired smartphone, when the camera's power is turned off.

Returning from Sleep Mode

The third item, Returning from Sleep Mode, is available for selection only when the Remote Wakeup item, discussed above, is turned on. In that case, you can select from the two options shown in Figure 9-31.

The top icon represents Remote/Transfer Priority. If you select that option, then, when you use Remote Wakeup to activate the camera, the camera will quickly be ready to use the Remote Operation and Transfer Image options. The bottom icon represents Shutter Remote Priority. If you select that option, then, upon remote wakeup, the camera will quickly be ready to use the Shutter Remote Control option.

Auto Transfer

The next item, Auto Transfer, can be turned either on or off. When it is turned on, the camera can be set to automatically send new images to a connected smartphone or tablet by Bluetooth. To use this feature, set the option to On, and the app will display the message shown in Figure 9-32, advising you to go to Wi-Fi settings on the phone and connect to the camera's Wi-Fi network. (If you are using an Android smartphone or tablet, the message will be slightly different; you should select Yes to proceed.)

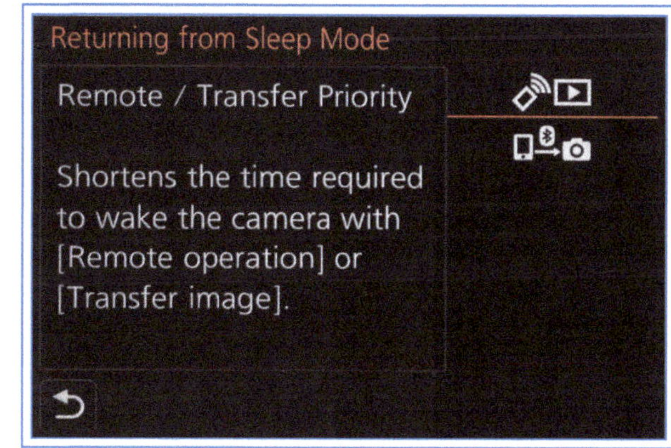

Figure 9-31. Returning from Sleep Mode Menu Options Screen

Once the Auto Transfer system has been set up, any new still pictures you take with the camera will automatically be copied to the normal area for photos on the phone or tablet. (This system will not transfer movies, 4K Photo images, or Post Focus images.)

Once the connection has been established, you can press the Display button to change the settings for the transfer process. You will see a screen like that in Figure 9-33, where you can select the size and file format of transferred Images.

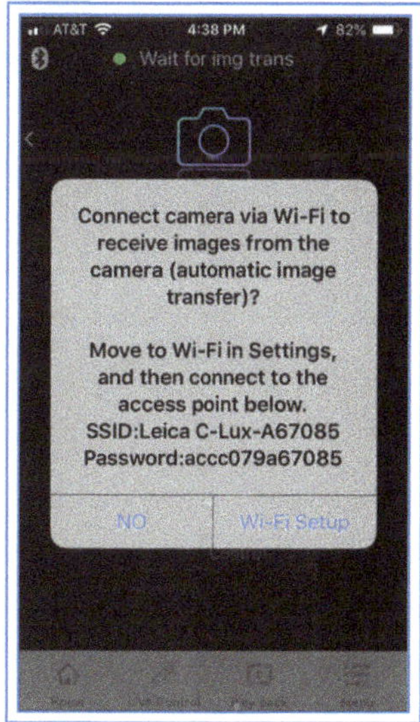

Figure 9-32. Message When Auto Transfer Turned On

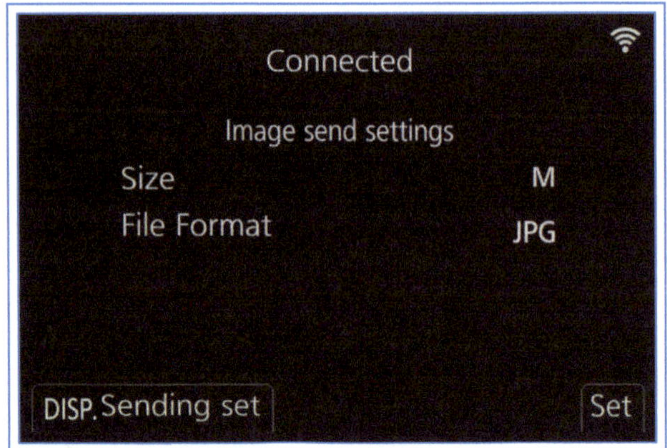

Figure 9-33. Screen to Change Settings for Auto Transfer Process

Location Logging

The next item, Location Logging, lets you set up the C-Lux App to record location data that can be transferred to images taken with the camera. I discussed the procedure for this operation earlier in this chapter.

Auto Clock Set

Next, the Auto Clock Set option lets you synchronize the time that was set for the camera using the Setup menu with the time on a connected smartphone or tablet. Once a Bluetooth connection between the camera and smart device is active, select this menu option and turn it on to synchronize the time settings.

Wi-Fi Network Settings

The final setting for the Bluetooth menu option, Wi-Fi Network Settings, is on the second screen of sub-options. It is available for selection when no Wi-Fi connection is active. You can use this menu option to register additional wireless access points for connecting to the camera. You can register up to 17 such devices. This option accomplishes the same thing as the New Connection option under the Wi-Fi Function item, which is found under Wi-Fi on the Setup menu.

Wireless Connection Lamp

This third and final wireless-related item on screen 1 of the Setup menu has the simple purpose of controlling whether or not the lamp on the back of the camera, located between the Fn2 button and the Playback button, lights up blue when a Wi-Fi or Bluetooth connection is active. If you find that light distracting, turn this menu option off.

Macro (Closeup) Shooting

Macro photography is the art or science of taking photographs when the subject is shown at actual size (1:1 ratio between size of subject and size of image) or slightly magnified (greater than 1:1 ratio). So if you photograph a flower using macro techniques, the image of the flower on the camera's sensor will be about the same size as the actual flower. You can get wonderful detail in your images using macro photography, and you may discover things about the subject that you had not noticed before taking the photograph. For example, I took a photograph of a detail from an ornate object in the art museum, using a focal length of 50mm with the AF Macro setting. The result, shown in Figure 9-34, provides a detailed view of the subject.

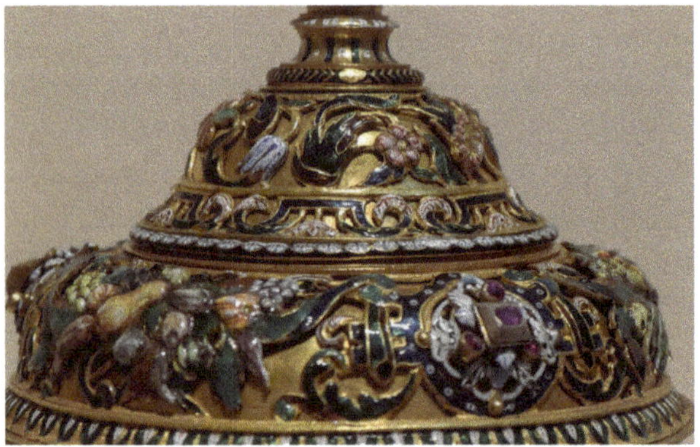

Figure 9-34. Macro Example

To shoot macro images with the C-Lux, you have only one basic setting to change: Press the Left button, marked with a flower and MF, to bring up the focus mode menu, and select AF Macro as shown in Figure 9-35.

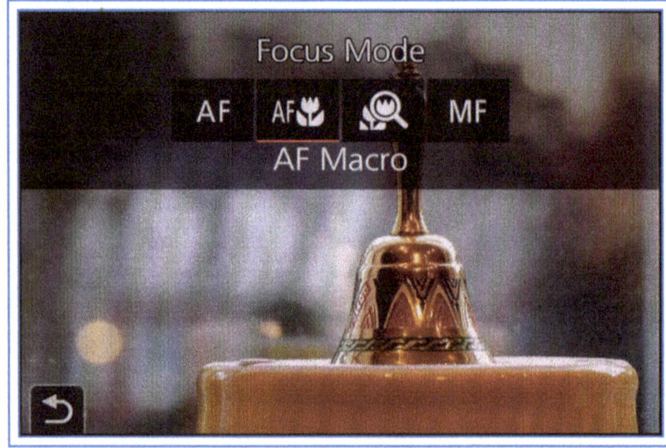

Figure 9-35. AF Macro Highlighted on Focus Mode Menu

Using AF Macro, the camera can focus as close as 1.2 inch (3 cm) from the subject, when the zoom lever is pushed all the way to the wide-angle setting. With the lens zoomed in for its full optical zoom, the camera can focus as close as 3.3 feet (one meter) in AF Macro mode. If the camera is not set to AF Macro mode, then the closest focusing point is about 1.6 foot (50 cm) when the lens is zoomed out to the wide-angle setting, or 3.3 feet (one meter) at the telephoto setting.

You don't have to use the AF Macro setting to take macro shots; if you use manual focus by selecting MF from the focus mode menu, you can also focus on objects very close to the lens. You do, however, lose the benefit of automatic focus, and it can be tricky finding the correct focus manually.

When using the AF Macro setting, you should use a tripod if possible, because the depth of field is very shallow at close distances and you need to keep the camera steady to take a usable photograph. It's also a good idea to use the self-timer. If you do so, you will not be touching the camera when the shutter is activated, so the chance of camera shake is minimized. If you want to use flash, you could consider using a special unit designed for closeup photography, such as a ring flash that is designed to provide even lighting surrounding the lens. You also could use the camera's built-in flash and place a small piece of translucent plastic or a light, neutral-colored cloth in front of the flash to diffuse it.

When doing macro photography with the C-Lux, you can take advantage of the Post Focus feature to increase the likelihood of getting a sharp image. See Chapter 5 for details about that feature, with which the camera records a 4K video sequence and extracts a sharp image with focus centered on an area you choose after the fact. You also can use Focus Bracket, discussed in Chapter 4.

One question you may have is: If the camera can focus down to 3 centimeters and out to infinity in AF Macro mode, why not just leave it set in AF Macro mode? The answer is that in AF Macro mode, the focusing system is set to favor short distances, and it is not as responsive in focusing on farther objects. So in AF Macro mode you may notice that it takes more time than usual to focus on subjects at greater distances. If you don't need the fastest possible focusing, you can just leave the camera set to AF Macro at all times, if you want the whole range of focusing distances to be available.

Street Photography

The C-Lux is well suited for street photography—that is, for shooting candid pictures in public settings, often without being noticed by the subjects. The camera has several good features for this type of work—it is lightweight and unobtrusive in appearance, so it can be held casually or hidden in the photographer's hand. Its 24mm wide-angle lens is excellent for taking in a broad field of view, for times when you shoot from the hip without framing the image carefully on the screen. You can make the camera completely silent by turning off the beeps and shutter sounds, and by using the electronic shutter. It has superior options for shooting bursts of images, so you can capture a large group of shots to choose from.

Here are some suggested settings you can start with and modify as you see fit. To get the gritty "street" look, set Photo Style to Monochrome, but dial in -2 Noise Reduction and -1 Sharpening. Set Quality to Raw & Fine to give you a good image straight out of the camera, but preserving your post-processing options. Set aspect ratio to 3:2. Set ISO to 800 for good image quality while boosting sensitivity enough to stop action with a fast shutter speed. Turn on burst mode at the High setting so you'll get several images to choose from for each shutter press.

When you're ready to start shooting, set the camera to Aperture Priority mode, with the aperture set to about f/4.5. When shooting in dimmer lighting conditions, you may want to open the aperture a bit wider, and possibly boost the ISO to 1600. You will probably want to leave the lens zoomed back to its full wide-angle position, both to increase the depth of field and to take in a wide angle of view.

In Figure 9-36, I took a different approach, using Program Mode with Photo Style set to Monochrome HC, and with burst shooting activated at its high speed to get a variety of shots.

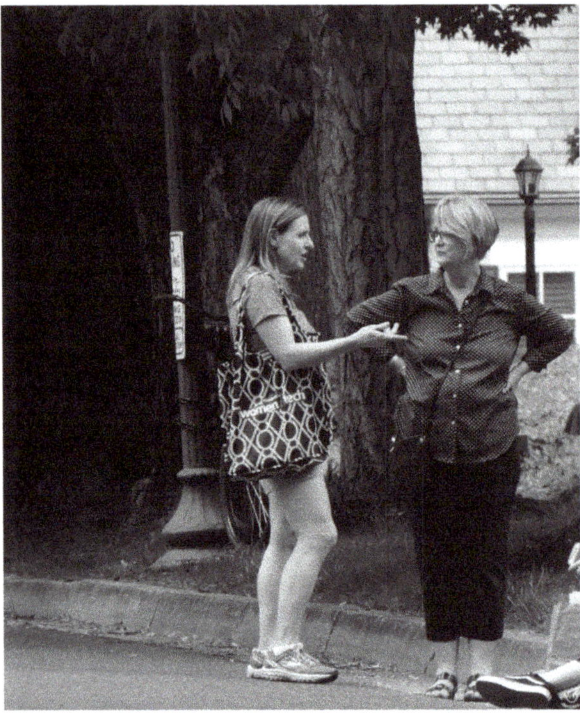

Figure 9-36. Street Photography Example

Connecting Camera to HDTV with Cable

Although you can send images wirelessly to a TV set or other device from the C-Lux, a simpler way to view images on a large screen is to connect the camera to an HDTV set using a micro-HDMI cable. You can find such cables readily online or at electronics stores. Just connect the small end of the cable to the HDMI port on the right side of the camera, as shown in Figure 9-37, and plug the larger end into one of the HDMI inputs on the HDTV. Then put the camera into playback mode by pressing the Playback button, and you can view your images and videos on the large screen.

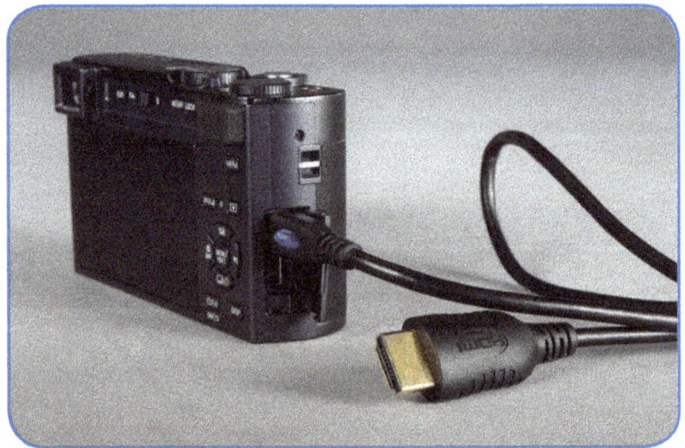

Figure 9-37. HDMI Cable Connected to Camera

With the C-Lux, you can also view the camera's output on an external HDTV set when the camera is in recording mode. If you do that, you can use the HDTV as a large monitor to check focus and composition for your images. However, you cannot view the camera's output on an external HDTV when the camera is recording a video; that capability is disabled. When the camera is recording a movie, it will display a message on the HDTV screen saying Now Recording Video, but not showing the live view, if an HDMI cable is connected.

To remove camera icons and other shooting information from the HDMI signal that is output, go to screen 3 of the Setup menu, select TV Connection, and set HDMI Info Display (Rec) to Off.

Appendix A: Accessories

The C-Lux does not need very many accessories, partly because of its compact size and built-in lens cover. It is possible to carry it in a pocket, and it does not need a lens cap. It does not have the ability to use threaded filters, although, if you feel a strong need to use filters, you may be able to construct a home-made adapter that lets you attach filters. For instructions for a similar camera model, see the YouTube video at https://youtu.be/yDWr4iWwD48. In addition, the camera has no accessory shoe, so you cannot readily attach an external flash unit or an optical viewfinder. However, there are several items that can be useful for getting the most out of your C-Lux.

Cases

As noted above, you do not really need to have a case for the C-Lux, because it is small enough to fit in a pocket and its lens is protected by the built-in lens cover. However, I usually like to keep my camera in a case or bag to protect it from bumps and external elements.

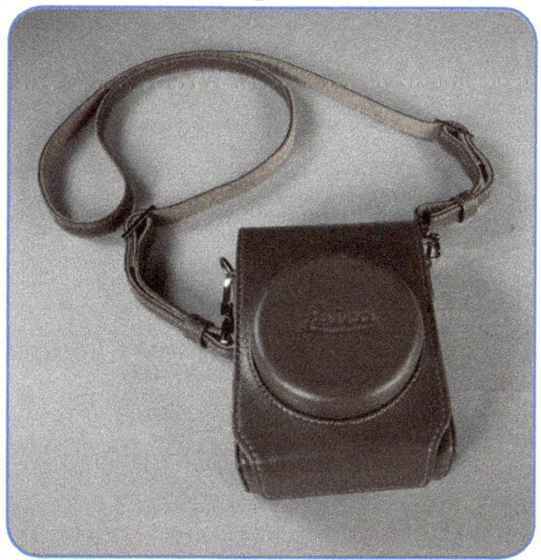

Figure A-1. Leica Leather Case Closed

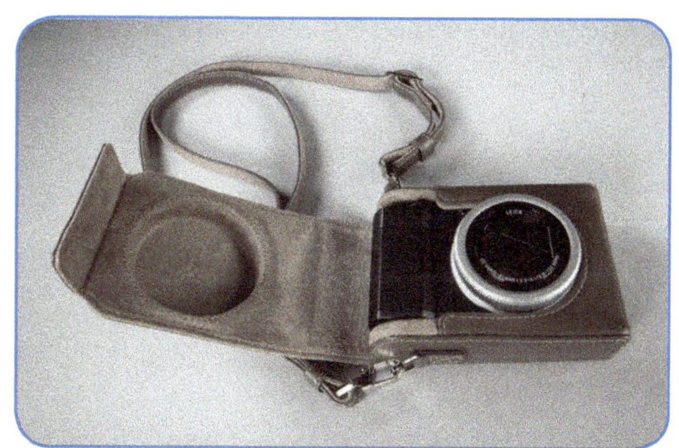

Figure A-2. Leica Leather Case Open

Leica offers a case specifically designed for the C-Lux camera, which is shown in Figures A-1 and A-2. This case is made of real leather, and comes with a matching strap that attaches to metal loops on the case. It looks nice and fits well, and has a convenient magnetic closure for its flap. However, you cannot get access to the controls while the camera is in the case; you have to take the camera out of the case to use it.

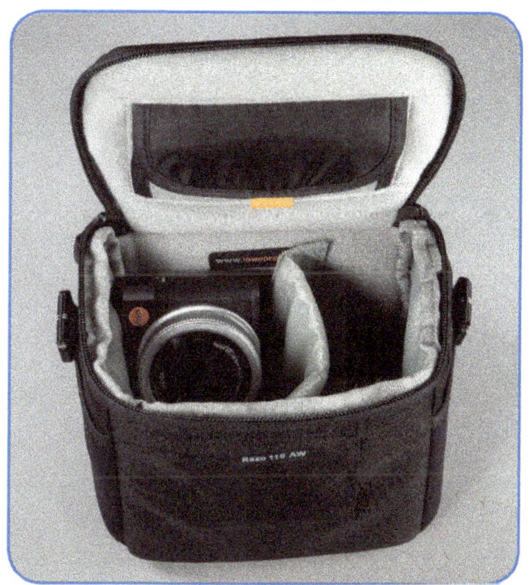

Figure A-3. Lowepro Rezo AW Case with C-Lux

With the C-Lux, I have sometimes used the Lowepro Rezo 110 AW, shown in Figure A-3. It is compact, but has plenty of room for the camera with an extra battery and charger. It has a loop to fit over a belt.

When I need to carry more equipment, I often use a pack like the Lowepro Inverse 100 AW, shown in Figure A-4 holding a different compact camera. This case has plenty of room for the camera and accessories. It also has expandable mesh pockets for holding two small water bottles, and, most important for me, it has straps for attaching a travel tripod under the bottom of the case.

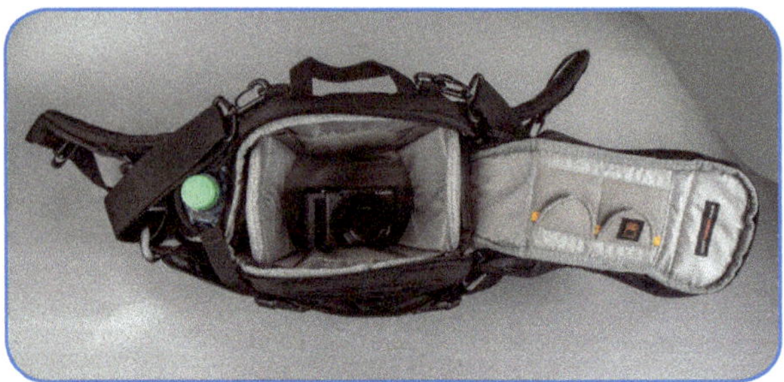

Figure A-4. Lowepro Inverse 100 AW Case

Another case I have used with the C-Lux is one that is not specifically designed for photography, but that has the features I need—the Eagle Creek waist pack, shown in Figure A-5. This item has plenty of room for the camera, batteries, and memory cards, and has two mesh pockets on the sides for water bottles.

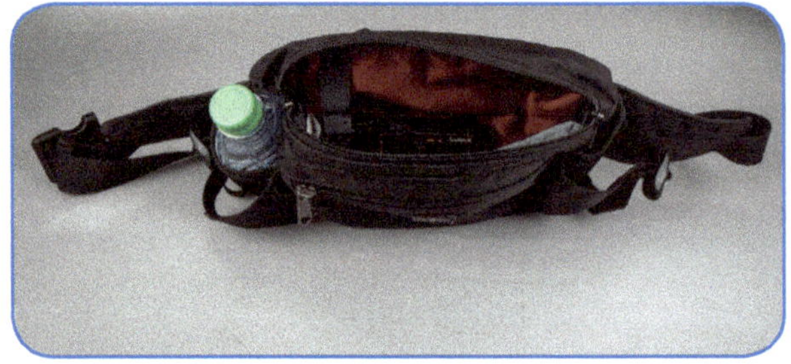

Figure A-5. Eagle Creek Waist Pack

Of course, there are many other possibilities; these are just four items that have worked well for me.

Batteries and Chargers

I use the camera pretty heavily, and I run through batteries quickly. You can't use disposable batteries, so if you're out taking pictures and the battery dies, you're out of luck unless you have a spare battery (or an AC adapter and a place to plug it in; see below). The Leica battery, model number BP-DC15-U (in the United States), is difficult to find and costs about $125.00 in the U.S. as I write this. You can find third-party replacement batteries from generic brands for considerably less.

If you cannot find a battery that is advertised as a replacement for the Leica battery, you can use batteries that are intended for use in the Panasonic DC-ZS200/TZ200 camera, which is very similar to the Leica C-Lux. For example, Figure A-6 shows a generic battery that I purchased for the ZS200. Look for Panasonic model number DMW-BG10, or a generic replacement for that battery.

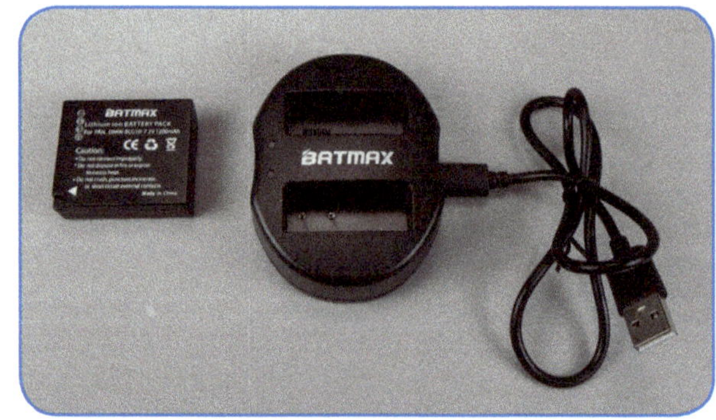

Figure A-6. Generic Battery and Charger for C-Lux

I have used generic replacement batteries extensively in my C-Lux with no problems. If you use a spare battery, it's useful to be able to charge it outside of the camera. To do that, you need an external charger, such as the Panasonic model no. DMW-BTC9, not shown here. You also can use a generic model, such as the charger shown in Figure A-6.

For everyday use, I often find it convenient to charge the battery inside the camera, especially if I am not using the camera too intensively. I can take a few shots, and then plug in a power source to recharge the battery before I take another group of shots. If you are working near an electrical outlet, you can just plug the camera's own USB cable and charger into the outlet and charge the battery that way. If you want a more versatile charger that can also charge your smartphone and tablet at the same time, you might try a device like the Anker 40-watt desktop USB charger, shown in Figure A-7. I often use this charger to charge my C-Lux, my iPhone, and my iPad at the same time, and it has no problems with that setup.

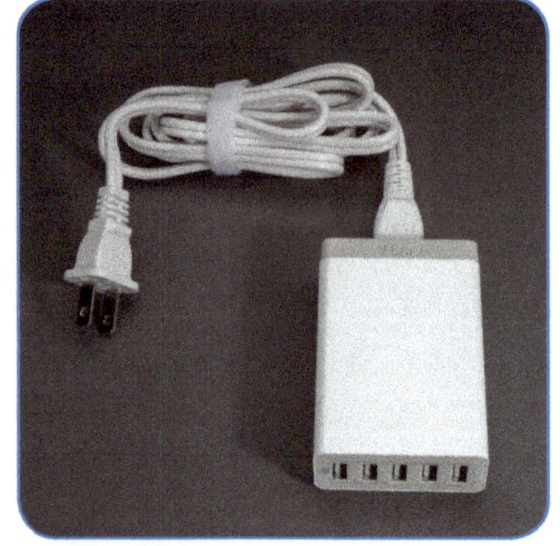

Figure A-7. Anker 40-watt Desktop USB Charger

For more portability, you might try a device like the Mophie PowerStation XL portable USB power supply, shown in Figure A-8, which will charge the camera's battery efficiently when the battery is in the camera.

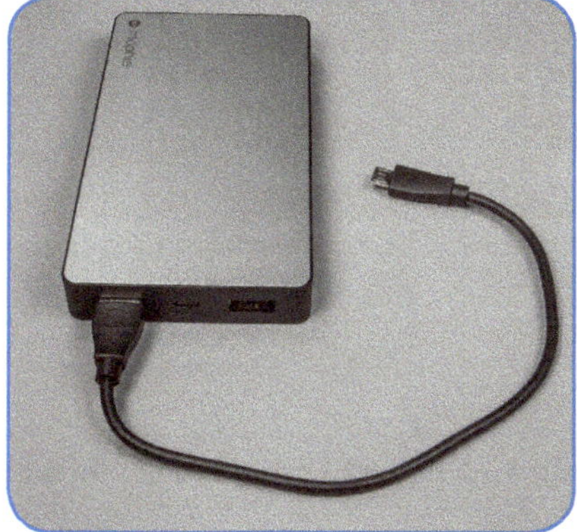

Figure A-8. Mophie PowerStation XL Portable USB Power Supply

AC Adapter

Another alternative for powering the C-Lux is the Panasonic AC adapter. (You cannot use the Anker USB charger, the Mophie USB battery, or similar devices to power the camera; such devices can only provide power for charging the battery inside the camera when the camera is turned off.) Leica evidently does not sell an AC adapter for this camera, but the Panasonic one works well with the C-Lux.

This accessory does a good job of providing a constant source of power to the camera. However, it is somewhat inconvenient to use. For use with the C-Lux, you need to obtain not only the AC adapter, Panasonic model no. DMW-AC10, but also another device called the DC Coupler, model number DMW-DCC11. That device looks like a battery, but it has a connecting port in its side. The adapter and the coupler are shown together ready to be connected to the camera in Figure A-9.

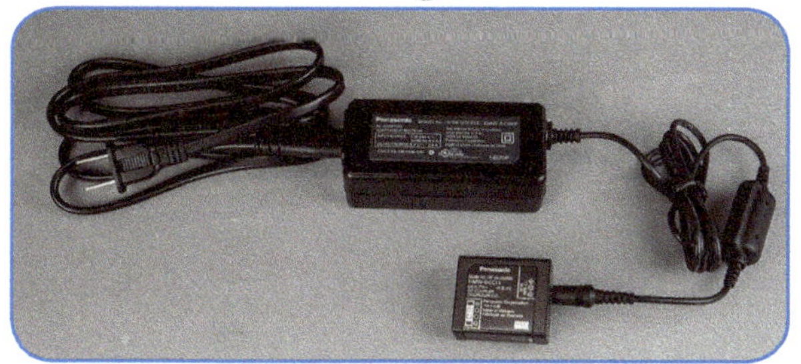

Figure A-9. Panasonic DMW-AC10 AC Adapter with DC Coupler

You have to insert the DC Coupler into the battery compartment of the camera, then close the battery door, open up a small flap in that door, and connect the cord from the AC adapter to the port in the DC Coupler, as shown in Figure A-10.

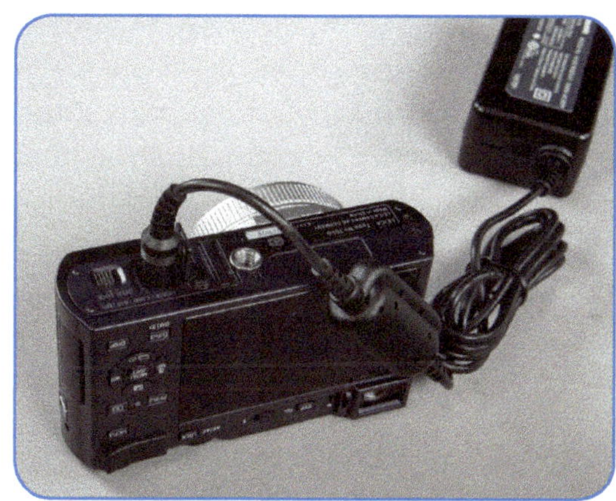

Figure A-10. AC Adapter Cord Going into Camera

This is not a very efficient (or economical) system, at least from the standpoint of the user. It is a clunky arrangement, and you can't get access to the memory card while the AC adapter is plugged in. But, if you need constant power for a long, uninterrupted period of time, this is the only way to get it.

Providing power to the camera is all this adapter does. It does not act as a battery charger, either for batteries outside of the camera or for batteries while they are installed in the camera. It is strictly a power source for the camera. It may be useful if you are doing extensive indoor work in a studio or laboratory setting, to eliminate the trouble of constantly charging batteries. It also could be useful for a lengthy series of time-lapse or stop-motion shots. For everyday applications and still shooting, though, the AC adapter should not be considered a high-priority purchase.

External Flash Units

Whether to buy an external flash unit depends on how you will use the C-Lux. For everyday snapshots not taken at long distances, the built-in flash unit should suffice. It works automatically with the camera's exposure controls to expose images well. It is limited by its low power, though.

If you need more flash power to take photos of groups of people in large spaces, or if you want to take advantage of the benefits of using off-camera flash, such as using multiple units and better angles for less harsh lighting, you can use optical slaves, which detect the light from the camera's small flash and fire their own flash when the camera's flash is fired.

One excellent unit with optical slave capability is the

LumoPro LP180, shown in Figure A-11. This unit has settings that let it ignore the pre-flash fired by the camera's built-in flash unit, which can confuse the optical slave and cause it to fire prematurely. When I used the LumoPro flash with the Leica C-Lux, I set the flash to its S2-1 mode, which caused it to fire at the proper time for a good exposure.

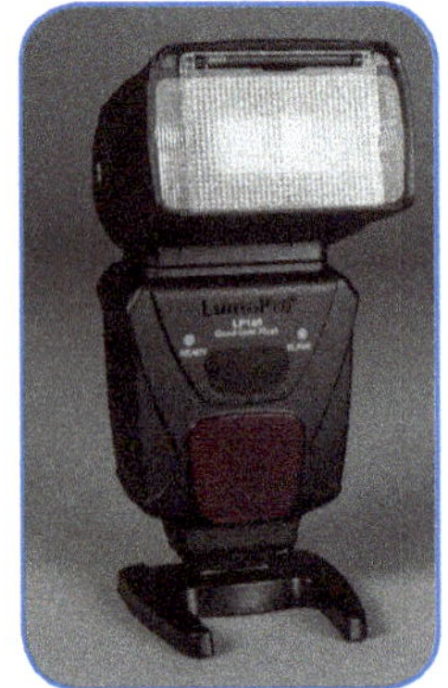

Figure A-11. LumoPro LP180 Flash

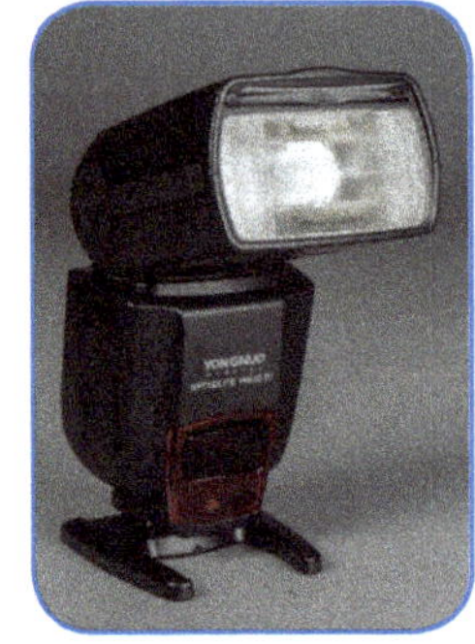

Figure A-12. Yongnuo YN560-IV Flash

When using a flash like this, you need to set the camera to Manual exposure mode. There are other flash units with similar capability, such as the Yongnuo YN560-IV, shown in Figure A-12. (It uses mode S2.) There also are separate optical slave units, to which you can attach any compatible flash unit.

External Audio Recorders

As I discussed in Chapter 8, the C-Lux camera has excellent video features but it has no provision for connecting an external microphone for high-quality audio. Although the built-in microphone records good-quality audio, you can get better results if you use an external audio recorder and synchronize the audio track from that recorder with the sound recorded by the camera.

One excellent piece of equipment for this purpose is the Tascam DR-100MkII recorder, shown in Figure A-13.

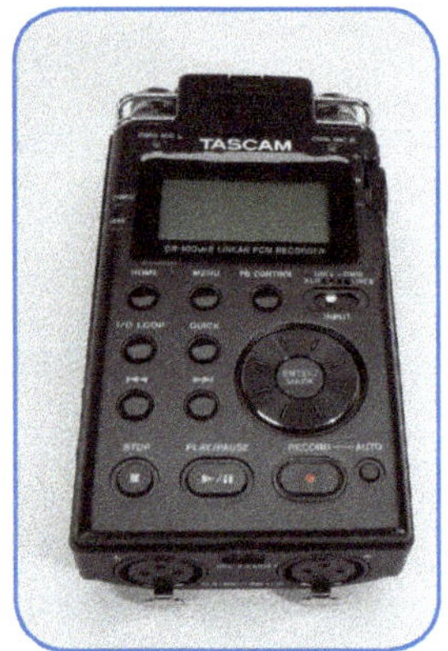

Figure A-13. Tascam DR-100MkII Audio Recorder

This recorder includes two sets of high-quality microphones, one set that is omnidirectional for recording lectures or classes, and another that is directional for recording concerts or other performances. The recorder also has two XLR inputs where you can connect high-quality microphones of your choice.

There are many other options that will work for this purpose, depending on your budget and needs, including the Shure VP83F, the Tascam DR-40, the Zoom H1, and the Zoom H6.

Gimbal

Because of the C-Lux's ability to record 4K video and its other excellent video features, including high speed video, Live Cropping, and others, the camera is well suited to cinematography. If you want to maximize its usefulness in this area, you may want to consider a gimbal, like the one shown in Figure A-14.

This device, the Zhiyun Crane-M, is one of many such stabilizing mechanisms now available for video production. The gimbal includes three small motors which constantly level the camera on three axes to counter movements made by the camera, even as you handhold the camera and walk with it. The result is smooth, stabilized video footage. This particular model is well suited for the size and features of the C-Lux.

Tripods

For time exposures, multiple exposures, HDR shots, and many other types of photography, it is virtually essential to use a tripod. In addition, for macro photography and any other shots for which focus is critical, it is desirable to have a solid support when using the camera. I have not attempted to survey multiple tripods; I will just mention two models that I have found to be especially useful because of their excellent features and light weight.

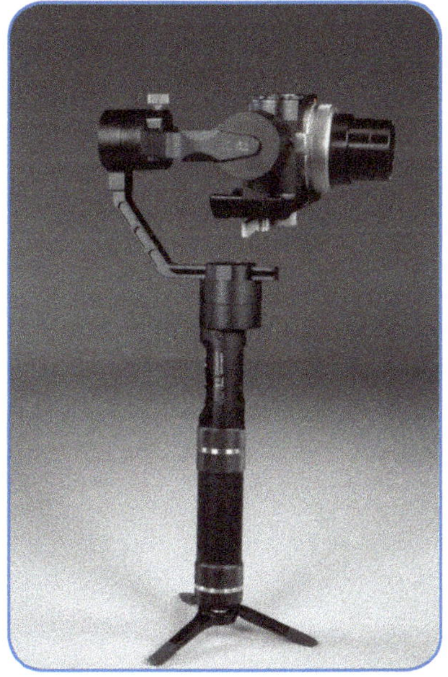

Figure A-14. Zhiyun Crane-M Gimbal with C-Lux

These models both are versions of the BeFree tripod by Manfrotto. The version shown in Figure A-15, model number MKBFRC4-BH, is especially light in weight because of its carbon fiber construction. Model number MKBFRA4-BH, shown in Figure A-16, is somewhat heavier because of its aluminum construction, but is considerably less expensive. Either one works very well with the C-Lux camera.

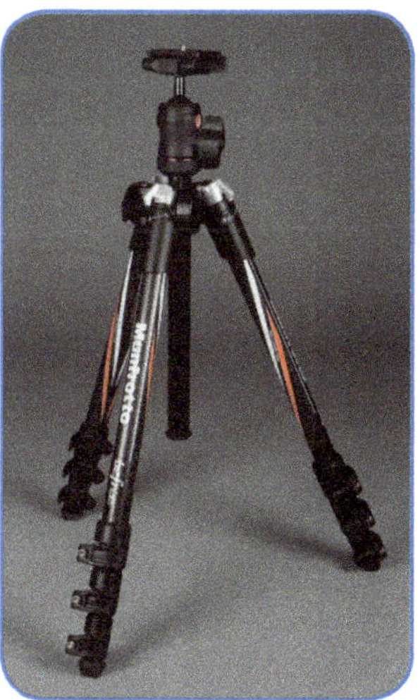

Figure A-15. Manfrotto Carbon-Fiber BeFree Tripod

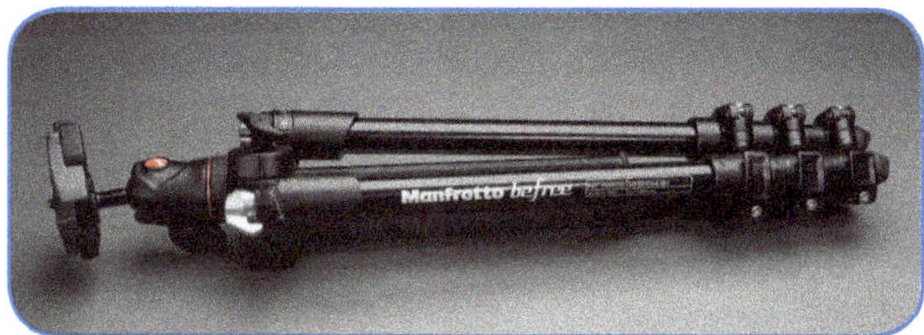

Figure A-16. Manfrotto Aluminum BeFree Tripod

Appendix B: Quick Tips

This appendix includes tips and hints for using the C-Lux that might be useful as reminders. These are small bits of information that might help you in certain situations, or that might not be obvious to everyone.

Use the movable autofocus area in conjunction with Spot metering. When you do this, using an AF Mode setting such as 1-Area or Pinpoint, you can move the focus and metering area together around the screen with the direction buttons or the touch screen, so you can focus and meter a small, specific area of your scene. This procedure can add precision to your metering and focusing, and give you more control over your results.

Use Manual exposure mode with Auto ISO. Not all cameras let you use Auto ISO with Manual mode. This feature lets you keep aperture and shutter speed at fixed values, while the camera adjusts ISO to obtain a normal exposure if possible. This is useful, for example, when you need to stop action with a fast shutter speed and also control depth of field with a narrow aperture. This feature also works when recording videos with the Creative Video version of Manual Exposure mode, but not when recording video in the still-shooting M mode.

Use exposure compensation in Manual exposure mode. This point is related to the previous one. When you are using Manual exposure mode with Auto ISO, you may also want to use exposure compensation so you can keep the shutter speed and aperture constant, and alter the exposure beyond what the ISO setting can accomplish. It's not immediately obvious how to use exposure compensation in this mode, because the Up button, which normally controls exposure compensation, has a different function in Manual mode (switching the functions of the thumb dial and control ring). To adjust exposure compensation in Manual mode, you need to use the Quick Menu, or you can assign it to the control ring using the Ring/Dial Set option on screen 3 of the Custom menu. You also can use exposure bracketing, through the Bracket option on screen 4 of the Recording menu. (You can't assign exposure compensation to a function button for use in Manual mode, because that button will then act just as the Up button does in that mode, switching the functions of the thumb dial and control ring.) When recording video in Creative Video mode with Exposure Mode set to Manual Exposure, you can adjust exposure compensation using the control ring option as noted above, or you can use the exposure compensation touch screen control, after touching the movie camera icon to activate the Silent Operation feature.

Diffuse your flash. If you find the built-in flash produces light that's too harsh for macro or other shots, try using a piece of translucent plastic as a flash diffuser. Hold the plastic up between the flash and the subject. An approach you can try when using fill-flash outdoors is to use the Flash Adjustment menu setting to reduce the intensity of the flash by -2/3 EV. Also, you can bounce the flash off of the ceiling if you pull the flash unit gently back with your finger.

Use the self-timer to avoid camera shake when the camera is on a tripod. Press the Down button, scroll to the self-timer item, and press the Up button to choose your setting. This feature is not just for group portraits; you can use it whenever you'll be using a slow shutter speed and you need to avoid camera shake. It can be useful when you're doing macro photography, also.

Use the 4K Photo option for burst shooting. With this option, activated from the drive mode menu (or assigned to a function button), you can set the camera to capture 4K-quality video that can generate a high-quality still image from each frame. This option gives you a burst shooting mode with Large-sized images and continuous focusing, at a rate of 30 frames per second (in the United States and other areas that use the NTSC video standard; 25 fps elsewhere). You have to use an SD card with a speed in UHS Class 3, but this is an excellent capability for action shots, shots of wildlife, and street photography. It also is useful when taking group photos, because you can choose a shot in which everyone is smiling or looking relaxed.

Create a custom autofocus zone that uses the entire focusing area. Although the C-Lux has an AF Mode setting called 49-Area, that setting actually uses no more than nine of the 49 possible focus zones. If you want to have a setting that uses the full extent of the display area, you have to create it yourself. To do that, use the Custom Multi option of AF Mode to create a focus setting with all 49 zones. Chapter 4 explains how to do this.

Use the zoom lever and the thumb dial to speed through menu screens. These options can save time when you need to scroll through menus with as many as six screens (or even more when using the Function Button Set option or adding items to My Menu). When a menu screen is displayed, press the zoom lever or turn the thumb dial in either direction to move forward or backward a full screen at a time.

Take advantage of the camera's built-in help system. Press the Display button when a menu option is highlighted, to see a brief description of that item. Press the Menu/Set button when the menu selection bar is on an item that is dimmed, to see why that item cannot currently be selected. (The camera will not always provide a reason, but in many cases it will.)

Be careful of using Raw for Quality when shooting with filter effects using the Filter Settings option or Creative Control mode. The C-Lux will let you set Quality to Raw when shooting with picture effects that are accessed through the Filter Settings menu option or Creative Control mode, such as Silky Monochrome, Impressive Art, Star Filter, and others. The recorded images will appear to have the effects added when viewed in the camera, but that is only because a small JPEG file is embedded in the Raw file. When you open the Raw file on a computer, the picture effect will not be there. You can try to recreate it using software settings, but I have not found any way to recover the full effect as recorded by the camera. (You may be able to retrieve the small JPEG preview file that is embedded with the Raw file, using a program such as Irfanview from Irfanview.com.) So, you might think you have taken some great shots using creative effects, but when you view them on your computer the effects will have disappeared. To avoid this problem, shoot using Fine, or, probably the best option, Raw & Fine for Quality.

Use the in-camera processing features before uploading images. The C-Lux has a good set of options for transferring images using Wi-Fi to a smartphone, tablet, or computer, and for uploading directly to social networks. Before you do that, you may want to use options on the Playback menu such as Raw Processing, Cropping, and Resize in order to send images at the optimal size and with the appearance you want. You also can use the Clear Retouch menu option to remove an unwanted person or object from an image.

Use the remote control capability of the Leica C-Lux App. With this app, you can take self-portraits and capture images and videos of birds and other subjects while controlling the camera from a distance through a wireless network. Set the camera on a steady tripod near a bird feeder to catch shots of birds, or set the camera in a good location to record video of a school play while you sit nearby and control the camera from your smartphone. You can change settings on the camera while it is under remote control, and use functions such as burst shooting and stop motion animation. In addition, you can look into using Leica's Fotos app, which was announced, but not yet available for the C-Lux camera, at the time this book was published.

Take advantage of the many shortcuts available with use of the touch screen. For example, when the camera is in Snapshot mode, touch the A icon in the upper left corner of the display to switch between Snapshot and Snapshot Plus modes. Or, in Scene Mode, touch the scene type icon in the upper left corner to select a different scene type.

Reassign a function button quickly. You can change the assignment of a function button to a menu option or other operation using the Function Button Set option on screen 3 of the Custom menu. To make that setting more rapidly, press and hold a physical function button for several seconds, and the camera will display a menu that lets you change the button's assignment.

Use the Post Focus feature in tricky focusing situations. When you are shooting extreme closeups or other shots where focus is critical, take advantage of the Post Focus capability, as discussed in Chapter 5. The camera will shoot a 4K video sequence using multiple focus points, and you can choose the most sharply focused shot after the fact. You also can use the Focus Bracket option under the Bracket item on screen 4 of the Recording menu to take shots with multiple focus points.

Set up the touch screen so it doesn't interfere with your shooting. When I use the viewfinder, I sometimes find that a movable focus frame or focus area appears unexpectedly in the viewfinder's display, interfering with my composition. This happens because my nose hits the LCD screen when the AF Mode option is set to 1-Area, 49-Area, or another setting that places a movable focus area on the display, with the Touch AF options turned on. To avoid this problem, go to Touch Settings on screen 3 of the Custom menu and set Touch AF and Touch Pad AF to Off. Another approach is to assign a function button to the Operation Lock option, and, on the Operation Lock Setting item on screen 3 of the Custom menu, set Touch Screen to On, meaning the touch screen will be deactivated when you press the button assigned to Operation Lock. Whenever you want to reactivate the touch screen, you can press the Function button again to remove the lock.

Start up the camera in playback mode when you just want to review images and don't want the lens to extend. To do this, hold down the Playback button while turning the On/Off switch to the On position. If you later want to record images, you can press the shutter button halfway down to switch the camera to recording mode.

Use the Auto Transfer capability. As discussed in Chapter 9, if you turn on Auto Transfer, the camera will automatically send new still images to a smartphone or tablet that is connected to the camera with Bluetooth.

Appendix C: Resources for Further Information

Photography Books

A visit to any large general bookstore or library, or a search on Amazon.com or other sites, will reveal the vast assortment of currently available books about digital photography. Rather than trying to compile a long bibliography, I will list a few books I have found especially helpful.

C. George, *Mastering Digital Flash Photography* (Lark Books, 2008)

C. Harnischmacher, *Closeup Shooting* (Rocky Nook, 2007)

H. Horenstein, *Digital Photography: A Basic Manual* (Little, Brown, 2011)

Websites

Following are several sites that are useful for finding further information about the C-Lux or about digital photography in general:

Digital Photography Review

http://forums.dpreview.com/forums/forum.asp?forum=1038

This is the web address for the "Leica Talk" forum within the dpreview.com site. Dpreview.com is one of the most established and authoritative sites for reviews, discussion forums, technical information, and other resources concerning digital cameras. If you have a question about a feature of the C-Lux, there is a good chance you can find an answer through this forum.

You also might want to look at the "Panasonic Compact Camera Talk" forum, which discusses cameras including the ZS200/TZ200, the Panasonic model that is very close in features and operation to the C-Lux. The address for that forum is:

http://forums.dpreview.com/forums/forum.asp?forum=1033

Official Leica Site

For technical information, downloads of firmware updates and manuals, and related information for the C-Lux camera, see the Leica site at:

http://us.leica-camera.com/Photography/Compact-Cameras/Leica-C-Lux

Official Panasonic and Related Sites

As noted above in connection with the Digital Photography Review discussion forums, it also can be useful to visit Panasonic websites for technical information, because of the similarity between the Leica C-Lux camera and the Panasonic ZS200/TZ200 camera. The following Panasonic sites have useful information about that model.

https://shop.panasonic.com/cameras-and-camcorders/cameras/lumix-point-and-shoot-cameras/DC-ZS200.html

The Panasonic company provides resources for the ZS200 at the above web address, including the downloadable version of the user's manual for the ZS200 and other technical information.

http://panasonic.jp/support/global/cs/dsc/

The link above is another address where Panasonic provides support information for the ZS200 camera.

http://www.cambridgeincolour.com

This site is an excellent resource for general information

about a wide range of photographic topics.

Videos

https://youtu.be/IN8VJQG1DaU

The link above leads to a video review of the C-Lux camera.

https://youtu.be/yDWr4iWwD48

The link above is to a video that gives detailed instructions for making a filter adapter for a compact Panasonic camera that has some similarities to the C-Lux.

https://youtu.be/xMNavx1PYOA

The link above leads to a detailed, hands-on review of the ZS200.

https://youtu.be/GEf-VXE5ZkY

The link above is to another good video summary of the ZS200.

https://youtu.be/5iJOiQ0PKz8

The link above is to a video I made showing how to control exposure compensation when the ZS200 camera is set to Manual exposure mode or to the Manual Exposure option within Creative Video mode.

Reviews of the C-Lux

Following are links to written reviews of the C-Lux:

https://www.photographyblog.com/reviews/leica_c_lux_review

https://www.shutterbug.com/content/leica-c-lux-compact-camera-review

http://www.slack.co.uk/leica-c-lux.html

https://www.pcmag.com/review/363503/leica-c-lux

https://www.news18.com/news/tech/leica-c-lux-review-a-premium-compact-camera-that-you-will-love-for-the-long-zoom-1871213.html

Reviews of the Panasonic ZS200/TZ200

The following reviews discuss the Panasonic ZS200, the Panasonic model that is very similar to the C-Lux:

https://www.dpreview.com/reviews/panasonic-lumix-dmc-zs200-tz200

https://www.imaging-resource.com/PRODS/panasonic-zs200/panasonic-zs200.HTM

https://www.techradar.com/reviews/panasonic-lumix-zs200-tz200

https://www.cameralabs.com/panasonic-lumix-tz200-zs200-review/

http://www.photographyblog.com/reviews/panasonic_lumix_dmc_tz200_review

https://www.ephotozine.com/article/panasonic-lumix-tz200--zs200--full-review-31930

http://www.photobyrichard.com/reviewbyrichard/panasonic-lumix-dc-tz220-tz200-zs22-tx2-review/

https://www.pcmag.com/review/359171/panasonic-lumix-dc-zs200

Index

Symbols

A

B

F

G

M

N

O

P

Q

R

T

U

V

W

Z

www.ingramcontent.com/pod-product-compliance
Lightning Source LLC
LaVergne TN
LVHW060638110826
845147LV00018B/1002
9781937986766